AMERICAN EDUCATION

CORRELATED TEXT-FILMS

DESIGN OF AMERICAN PUBLIC EDUCATION
This film explains the organization of the American democratic school system as opposed to an autocratic system; presents a philosophy of education which strives to develop responsible citizens in a democratic society. 16 minutes.

SCHOOL AND THE COMMUNITY
The problem of separation between the school and the community is discussed in this film. It indicates that teachers, parents, school officials, and the citizenry share responsibility for bringing them together. The benefits which the school and the community gain when they cooperate are shown. 14 minutes.

American education

FOURTH EDITION

CHRIS A. De YOUNG

*Professor of Education, Emeritus
and Former Dean of the University
Illinois State Normal University
Normal, Illinois*

WITH THE ASSISTANCE OF

RICHARD WYNN

*Professor of Education and
Associate Dean
School of Education, University of
Pittsburgh*

McGRAW-HILL BOOK COMPANY, INC.

*New York • Toronto • London
1960*

TO MY WIFE

Marion Edna De Young

Preface

This volume is primarily a textbook for education courses for prospective teachers. It is designed as an introduction to American education, which includes kindergartens, schools, colleges, universities, adult education, and all other forms of education supported in whole or in part by the public with time or money or both. Thus, private and parochial schools and colleges, also called "independent institutions," are included with the public schools as part of the American education system.

The book may also serve as a handy reference for teachers, principals, supervisors, superintendents, business managers, and other educational personnel. It is a direct aid in orienting members of boards of education, workers in parent-teacher organizations, and laymen in general to the scope of American education, its numerous problems, and its infinite possibilties. Graduate students will find it useful in providing an over-all view of American education as will students and teachers from other lands. For these reasons, it should be available for reference in high school, college, and public libraries.

As indicated, the primary function of the book is to serve as a basic text in undergraduate courses in education. The chapters are organized on the basis of the five major aspects of American education: (1) organization and administration, (2) areas of education, (3) personnel in education, (4) provisions for educational materials and environment, and (5) interpretation of education.

In this flexibly organized book the student may start with any of the five areas. If organization and administration is selected, the reader may wish to begin with the broad view of American public education provided in Chapter 1, National Program of Education. Or on the basis of his own experience in a local school system, he may want to progress from the smaller to the larger geographical areas: township, town, county, state, and nation. In that case, Chapter 4, Local School Districts, is used for the initial approach.

The future teacher may then study the internal structure and program of American education at all levels, despite the fact that he probably will teach in a specific area, such as the secondary school. Lifelong learning starts with birth, advances through the pre-elementary stages of home, nursery school, and kindergarten, and continues through elementary, secondary, and higher education. The capstone of adult education makes real the cherished goal of continual learning for modern Americans in a global, atomic, supersonic age.

People are very important in education; so the next group of chapters deals with the personnel involved in American education. The first chapter in this section concerns pupils, adding to the reader's growing knowledge of the typical and atypical learners. He sees then the evolution of teaching, analyzes some problems of the classroom teacher, and catches the challenge of a career in the teaching profession. He also discovers in Chapter 12 the diversity of educational work as he learns about school personnel other than classroom teachers, such as principals, superintendents, deans, school nurses, business managers, clerks, and bus drivers.

Materials, buildings, and finance are needed if the personnel is to function effectively; hence the next section is devoted to provisions for educational materials and environment. The broad curriculum of today is accented and reenforced by the cocurricular activities. While the success of both curricular and cocurricular activities is conditioned in part by educational supplies and equipment, such as school sites and buildings, these facilities are provided through educational leadership and financial support, discussed in the concluding chapter of this section.

The final portion of the book, which may be used as an initial problem approach or collaterally with each of the preceding sixteen chapters, deals with an interpretation of education. The concluding chapter, which also constitutes a brief review of the entire volume, gives the student the opportunity to analyze many educational issues, to evaluate the trends, and to synthesize his information and thinking into clearer concepts and a functioning philosophy of American education.

Chris A. De Young

Editor's introduction

National programs of education are so big in scope and so small in detail, so simple in purpose and so complex in procedure, so far from a single observer and so close to all observers that they are hard to evaluate by precise methods. Perhaps the conscious and systematic changing of a people's ways is a process so fraught with possibilities of tragic consequence that men shrink from the task of judging its worth. Certainly students of comparative education have not yet adopted a workable system of appraising culture changes in simple terms of the new needs, wants, problems, and goals which have produced these changes.

Because of a tendency in the United States to confuse the terms "national" and "federal," it should be emphasized that all the educational agencies of this country—federal, state, and local, public and private, school and nonschool—constitute the national system of education. The fact that even educators sometimes think of a national system of education in the United States as meaning a federal system indicates how hard it is to see the country's total pattern of education.

The educators are often more naive than the laymen in this regard. Professional as well as national pride holds them to an inadequate level of evaluation. They exclaim over the details of their professional machinery and then go on turning its cranks and greasing its cogwheels with unquestioning fidelity.

It is therefore particularly important that a broad view of the country's total system of education should be achieved by those whose daily work is with the details of the system. Prospective teachers need to acquire this over-all view early in their professional preparation. This is a technical necessity. A young teacher may enter the profession without knowing whether the additive method of subtraction is superior to the take-away method and still be able promptly to reach a high level of technical skill, but one who begins teaching with no adequate means of looking critically at all the methods, materials, personnel, and agencies of education can only imitate technical skills. The greatest technical fault in any profession is to use a method or device without knowing why it is used. It is an especially grievous and dangerous fault in that profession which calls for all the studied craft and inspired artistry, all the precise knowledge and controlled action, all the shrewd planning and glowing faith which a nation can devote to an activity that holds and foreshadows all its future.

The prospective teacher needs early to acquire this broad view; the experienced teacher must cultivate it both early and late. The present book is designed for both these teachers. In its first, second, and third editions it has demonstrated the soundness of its arrangement and approach. Its wide acceptance by the profession indicates its effectiveness in helping teachers and students of education to appraise their country's educational efforts on a high level.

This book was first published at the beginning of a new era in world education. It was an era in which the prestige and influence of the American school system were to be rapidly and colorfully extended.

In its earlier editions, this book played an important role in that extension of knowledge concerning American education. It was used from 1942 onward in universities and colleges to help prepare a new generation of American schoolteachers, young men and women whose destiny it was to live in a world very different in educational challenges and problems from the world of 1932, 1922, or 1912. It was employed on a large scale by the armed forces. It has served its country in occupied areas overseas. It has traveled as ambassador of American education to many lands.

Few authors of educational works have been so precisely and preeminently qualified for their tasks as has Dean De Young for the original writing and successive revisions of this book. He began the preparation of the volume with wide experience in and comprehensive knowledge of schools and teaching in the United States. He has used this experience and scholarship for many years in the education of American teachers. He has had a most distinguished record as consultant to national systems of education in Europe and Asia. His background fits him uniquely for presenting the total picture of American education both to Americans and to that growing number of persons in other countries who want to know about American education.

Harold Benjamin

Credits

District No. 1., Mamaroneck, N.Y., Sheldon Evans, business manager, Eleanor Donald, photographer.

291 Adapted from Archibald B. Shaw and John Lyon Reid, The Random Falls Idea: An Educational Program and Plant for Youth and Community Growth, *The School Executive*, March, 1956, 47–86.

292 Top to bottom: Catskill Area Project in Small School Design, Fynmore Photos; National Citizens Council for Better Schools; Radio and Television Education Department, Dade County Board of Public Instruction, Miami, Florida.

293 Top, Baldwin (N.Y.) Public Schools, Paul R. Hirni, photographer; center, Greensboro (N.C.) Public Schools; left, Keokuk (Iowa) Senior High School and Community College, Perkins & Will, Architects-Engineers, Reynolds Photography Inc.; right, Shoreline High School, Seattle, Wash., Mallis and DeHart, architects, Art Hupy, photographer.

306 Baldwin (N.Y.) Public Schools, Edith Miller, photographer.

307 Left, Dearborn (Mich.) Public Schools; right, Baldwin (N.Y.) Public Schools, Edith Miller, photographer.

308 Top to bottom; Baldwin (N.Y.) Public Schools, Herbert Breuer, photographer; Baldwin (N.Y.) Public Schools, Paul R. Hirni, photographer; Syosset (N.Y.) High School, Eggers and Higgins, architects, Don Morgan, photographer.

309 Top, Baldwin (N.Y.) Public Schools, Paul R. Hirni, photographer; bottom, Baldwin (N.Y.) Public Schools, Edith Miller, photographer.

340 Middleville Road High School, Northport, N.Y., Ketchum, Giná & Sharp, architects.

341 Top right, Baldwin (N.Y.) High School, Ketchum, Giná & Sharp, architects, Herbert Breuer, photographer; top left, Mattie L. Jones Elementary School, Tyler, Tex., E. Davis Wilcox, architect, Roland Chatham, photographer; bottom right,

Meadow Drive Elementary School, Mineola, N.Y., Ketchum, Giná & Sharp, architects, Marc Neuhof, photographer.

342 Top, Steel Lake Elementary School, Federal Way School District No. 210, John W. Maloney, architect, Educators Furniture and Supply Company, Hiram W. Dodd Building, Allentown, Pa., Wolf & Hahn, architects, Cortlandt V. D. Hubbard, photographer.

343 Top, Taylor Avenue Junior High School, Greenlawn, N.Y., Ketchum, Giná & Sharp, architects, Alexandre Georges, photographer; center, Baldwin (N.Y.) High School, Ketchum, Giná & Sharp, architects, Herbert Breuer, photographer.

351 Pacific Oaks Friends School, Pasadena, Calif., Todd Walker, photographer.

377 Right, Eastman Kodak Company, Jack Magers, photographer; left, Board of Education, City of New York; bottom, U.S. Department of Agriculture photograph by Forsythe.

378 Top, Philadelphia Public Schools, Edgar S. Brinker, photographer; bottom, National Citizens Council for Better Schools.

379 Top, Parkview High School, Springfield, Mo., Aetna Drivotrainer; bottom, New York State Department of Education.

380 Left, Baldwin (N.Y.) High School, Herbert Breuer, photographer; right, Academy of Our Lady of the Blessed Sacrament, Goshen, N. Y., Archdiocese of New York City.

407 Top left, Pearl River (N.Y.) Public Schools, Herbert Breuer, photographer; top right, U.S. Department of Agriculture; bottom right, New York State Citizens Committee for the Public Schools, Bob Wyer, photographer.

408 United Nations.

409 Bottom right, United Nations; bottom left, U.S. Department of State; top, U.S. Operations Mission to Cambodia.

411 Top left, University of Nebraska; top right, National Education Association.

Contents

AMERICAN EDUCATION

PART ONE

PROPOSED ORGANIZATION

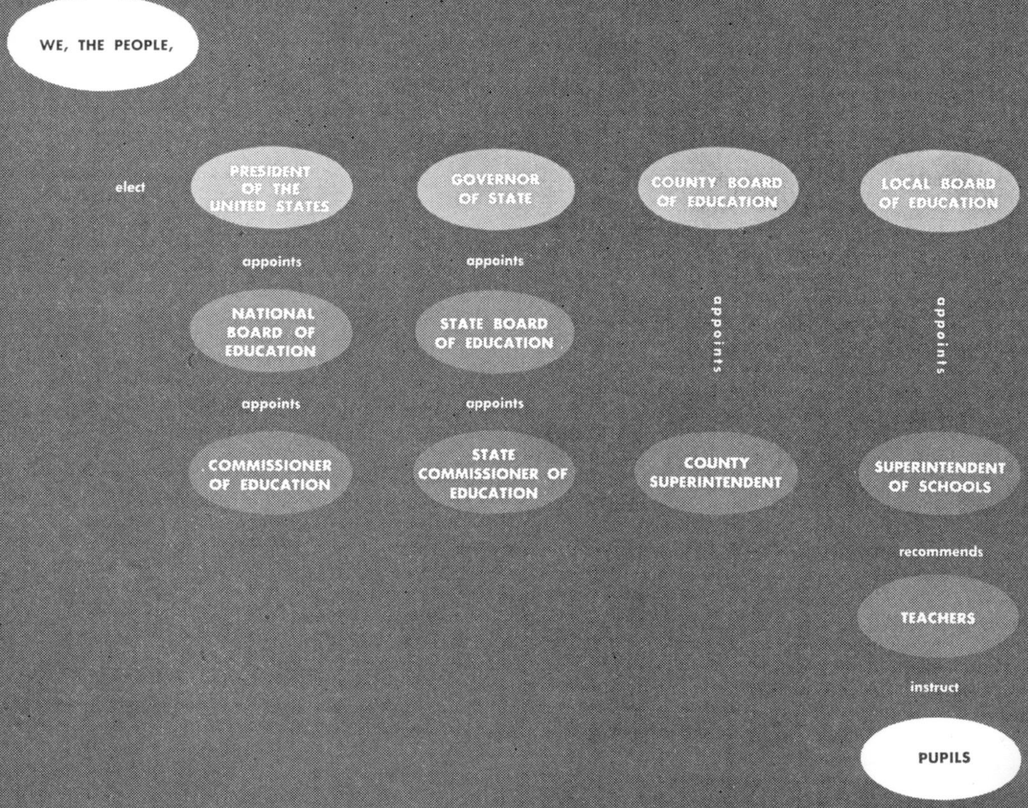

WE, THE PEOPLE,

elect

PRESIDENT OF THE UNITED STATES

GOVERNOR OF STATE

COUNTY BOARD OF EDUCATION

LOCAL BOARD OF EDUCATION

appoints

appoints

appoints

appoints

NATIONAL BOARD OF EDUCATION

STATE BOARD OF EDUCATION

appoints

appoints

COMMISSIONER OF EDUCATION

STATE COMMISSIONER OF EDUCATION

COUNTY SUPERINTENDENT

SUPERINTENDENT OF SCHOOLS

recommends

TEACHERS

instruct

PUPILS

Organization
and administration
of public education

American education is presented here in five major sections, the first of which is Organization and Administration. The first and highest unit in the hierarchy of organizations is the national, which is vitally related to the state, county, and local educational systems (see opposite page).

Although the Constitution does not mention education or schools, the federal government has a direct and indirect interest in public education. The chief educational agency of the United States is the Office of Education, with its Commissioner of Education, in the Department of Health, Education, and Welfare, a Cabinet post created in 1953. The U.S. Office of Education has expanded its staff greatly to meet new needs and demands. Many national activities are connected with those of other countries, especially in the United Nations Educational, Scientific, and Cultural Organization (Chapter 1).

The adoption of the Tenth Amendment to the Constitution of the United States made education primarily a state function. Although the state may delegate some of its authority to the local or intermediate districts, the state commissioner of education serves as the chief centralizing agent for public education within the state (Chapter 2).

The postwar period has witnessed a marked trend toward larger school units. Some school units are as large as a township or county. These may be intermediate units between the state and local districts (Chapter 3).

American public education has its local application in the public school district, which is usually administered by an elected board of education and an appointed superintendent of schools. The local school district is a striking example of grass-roots democracy. School administration in a dynamic democracy calls for a high order of educational statesmanship. Organization and administration should be the servants and not the masters of education (Chapter 4).

chapter 1

grow
better

National program
of education

In the United States, education has been regarded as fundamental to the preservation of our democracy and a preeminent force in our search for the good life. Jefferson believed that "if the condition of man is to be progressively ameliorated . . . education is the chief instrument for affecting it." The story of the advance of American civilization is, in large measure, the story of American education.

Although the Constitution of the United States makes no reference to education, the justification for federal support of education is found in the "general welfare" clause of the Constitution. From the very beginning of our history as a nation, starting with the Northwest Ordinance of 1785, the federal government has encouraged and extended education through grants of land and money. Educational programs are conducted by the federal government in special jurisdictions, such as in the District of Columbia, the armed forces, and many dependencies. The federal government is supporting an increasing number of international activities in education. The U.S. Office of Education in the Department of Health, Education, and Welfare is the centralizing agency for much of the federal government's activity in education.

A national system of education is slowly emerging. Many proposals have been advanced for its improvement.

Foundations

The development of education in America is one of the most interesting chronicles in American history. Our system of free, universal schools is one of the most unique and significant characteristics of our society. It is unique because free public education for all is a bold and visionary ideal without precedent in the history of mankind. It is significant because the story of our national strength and prosperity is, in large measure, the story of our schools. Truly the development of our educational system is one of the noblest and most distinguishing expressions of American civilization.

Americans have always had great faith in the power of education. Alexis de Tocqueville, the brilliant French scholar who visited the young Republic shortly after its founding, observed that "the universal and sincere faith that they profess here in the efficaciousness of education seems to me to be one of the most remarkable features of America." How well has this faith been justified?

Education and Democracy. The founders of our Republic regarded education as the key to liberty. They looked upon the spread of knowledge as the fundamental safeguard of the freedom, equality, and self-government which had been won through the struggle for independence. Jefferson warned that "if a nation expects to be free and ignorant, it expects that which never was and never will be." Universal suffrage cannot endure without universal education. Ignorant men will not long remain free. By providing free public education for all young Americans, the door to literacy, inquiry, and understanding has been opened to virtually all of our people.

The public schools, through their great contribution to public knowledge and understanding, have strengthened and perpetuated the ideals of American democracy. Our schools have helped our people to make democracy work. We have carved a nation across a continent. We have established justice and domestic tranquility and have secured the blessings of liberty. We have held our nation together through all manner of crises, including a civil war. We have met successfully the challenge of domestic and foreign tyrants. In time of war, our citizen-soldiers have outfought the finest professional armies. These achievements could be accomplished only by a people well-schooled in self-government, loyal to their ideals, and dedicated to the responsibilities of citizenship.

But the battle for freedom must be won anew with each generation. The false promises of communism and the threat of the cold war press new and unprecedented demands upon American democracy. Our people are confronted constantly with compelling domestic and international issues that summon deep understanding and wide knowledge. The need for more leaders of high quality in nearly all areas of human endeavor was never more acute. These and other circumstances place a heavy burden upon our schools. Schools must be strengthened so that education can continue to contribute to our search for a more perfect union.

Education and Society. America was settled by the greatest migration in the history of mankind—a migration of poor and oppressed people, discontented with the tyranny and inequality of opportunity abroad. Immigrants came to our shores with vastly different languages, religions, cultures, political faiths, racial and national backgrounds, social and economic status. To the public school fell the task of making 30 million new American citizens. No other nation ever assimilated such a heterogeneous population as rapidly and as completely. These people came to America in search of a classless society where there would be equal opportunity. Throughout our history, visitors from other lands have been struck by the general equality of conditions achieved by our people. In school classrooms and playgrounds of America, children of varied backgrounds have learned and lived equality. Despite the great diversity of our people, we have built a strong national unity—"one nation, under God, indivisible, with liberty and justice for all."

Free public education has unlocked the door of opportunity for millions. Great scientists, statesmen, athletes, artists, teachers, businessmen, physicians, lawyers, and others have risen in America despite diversity of race, religion, national origin, social or economic position of family. In perhaps no other country is it possible for people of modest origin to rise so far and so fast. In no other country have the com-

*Education is regarded as
the means for the preservation
of democracy . . .*

*New York
University Hall
of Fame
symbolizes
the great men
who have
arisen in
America
despite diverse
backgrounds.*

mon people achieved such a large measure of political power, social status, and economic prosperity. The success of America is the story of faith in the common man.

But the ultimate in social progress has not yet been achieved. Members of racial and religious minority groups are sometimes discriminated against in schooling, employment, and even in voting. Insidious forces still seek to marshal American against American and to fan bigotry and prejudice.

devoted behavior

Education and Economic Well-being. The march of American invention and production has been the envy of the world. According to a recent study of our economy, with only one-seventeenth of the world's population, the United States produces nearly half of the world's goods and consumes nearly a third of the world's goods and services. The real income of 170 million Americans exceeds the real income of the 600 million people in Europe and Russia and far surpasses the total income of more than one billion inhabitants of Asia. The average American worker has completed almost twelve years of schooling—an average higher than that attained in any other nation—and is the most productive worker in the world. Widespread vocational education has contributed substantially to this record. Engineering and technical schools have provided thousands of persons with the technical knowledge needed to lead in the advance of discovery and invention. Agricultural colleges have helped develop a farming industry that feeds not only our people but also millions of people around the world. Although many other factors have contributed to our miracle of production, universal public education has been a preeminent force. Chester Barnard, former president of the New Jersey Bell Telephone Company, observed that "the basic process by which the productive capacity of society is maintained or increased is by education."

Nevertheless, our economic position is not without blemish. Although America finds the

*Eighth graders from Bass High School
survey slum housing conditions
in their citizenship course,
"Building Atlanta's future."*

means for much of its material needs, financial support for certain nonmaterial needs, notably education, public health, and social services, often lags dangerously. Labor and management relations are often characterized by distrust and cleavage. If the intellectual level of advertising in America is any criterion, there is reason to believe that the American is not always a wise consumer. Many products, such as automobiles, are designed deliberately for early obsolescence rather than for long, efficient use. The tremendous variety of jobs in the world of work poses for youth an enormous problem of career selection for which our vocational guidance facilities are hardly adequate. These and other problems will continue to challenge the best of our economic and educational resources.

Education and Individual Excellence. American democracy has always cherished the dignity and worth of the individual. Respect for the individual has been proclaimed in the Declaration of Independence and in our Constitution. This doctrine has been invoked to resist special privilege and to sustain social, economic, political, and civil rights of our people. Both our democracy and our educational system are committed to the full development of the individual citizen. Perhaps no other nation guards the rights of the in-

dividual as zealously as the United States. No other educational system makes as diligent an effort to adapt learning experiences to the needs, interests, and capacities of the individual learner.

However, much progress remains to be made. American schools still fail to provide educational opportunity rich and extensive enough to enable each individual to reach his maximum level of self-realization. Precious talents of many of our people remain undiscovered and undeveloped, resulting in valuable loss of manpower.

Education and Morality. Both American democracy and American education are concerned with moral and spiritual values. These values include respect for law and government, acceptance of the dignity and worth of the individual, devotion to honesty and integrity, dedication to truth and rational inquiry, acknowledgment of the universal brotherhood of mankind, and recognition of the importance of human life. Our schools have contributed much to the ethical foundation of our government and society, have stimulated the spiritual growth of our people, and have enriched human relationships among our people. Home and church have shared these concerns with the school.

Again, formidable progress remains to be made. Invasions of civil and political liberties are still all too frequent. Anti-intellectualism is unfortunately evident in many aspects of our society. Truth and freedom of inquiry are frequently violated. Discrimination, especially by race and by religion, is still evident among many of our people. Moral decisions of unprecedented magnitude confront us both on

*the economic
well-being
of the people ...*

*Tucson, Arizona, mothers
show primary-grade children how
to brush their teeth properly.*

the domestic and the international scene. The school systems must continue to develop a moral and spiritual consciousness among our people that will endure through the dangerous era in which we live.

If De Tocqueville were to return today, he would find that early American faith in education well founded. Undoubtedly he would have agreed with the eminent American historian Henry Steele Commager, who concluded that "no other people ever demanded so much of education as have the American. None other was ever so well served by its schools and educators." As one group of distinguished Americans phrased it:

The public schools justified the faith of the American people. Like other institutions, they are not perfect; like any institution they have shortcomings. But their contributions have been significant and lasting. The United States would not be so democratic, so prosperous, so satisfying to the individual, and so strong in mind and spirit as it is today were it not for the nation's record in developing and supporting public schools.[1]

Thus the sober study of American education is a rewarding adventure in one of the truly great chronicles of American history.

[1] Educational Policies Commission, *Public Education and the Future of America*, National Education Association, Washington, D.C., 1955, p. 76.

Development of federal activities in education

In this chapter is a historical calendar containing significant events in the evolution of federal interest in education. The educational events listed are notable milestones on the highway leading toward a national plan of education. Although the column on the right does not chronicle all significant events, it does designate outstanding dates in the development of a national program of public education during more than one hundred seventy years. Parallel with these events are listed eras in the development of the United States.

The events listed in the calendar, and others, are described under (1) Basic Federal Legislation, (2) Education for National Defense, (3) Federal Grants—Nonvocational, (4) Grants for Vocational Education, (5) Other Federal Provisions for Education.

BASIC FEDERAL LEGISLATION

Northwest Ordinance and Education. Between the official ending of the Revolutionary War in 1783 and the establishment of the Union in 1789, the Congress of the Confederation was faced with many problems, one of which was the westward movement into the new territory

Farmers in Douglas County, Illinois, learn how to prevent wheat-crop damage by insects from extension entomologist of the U.S. Department of Agriculture.

Students work in chemical laboratory at New York University's College of Engineering.

Business practices teacher at Franklin Central School, New York, shows students how to operate mimeograph machine.

ceded by the states to the central government. Congress adopted in 1785 a system of rectangular surveys for its new territory, by which the land was divided into townships, 6 miles square, to be further subdivided into 36 sections, 1 mile square. This ordinance of 1785, reaffirmed two years later, ended with the significant words, "There shall be reserved the lot number sixteen of every township for the maintenance of public schools within the said township." Thus the economic foundation was laid for a future land and school policy in the Northwest.

In the year 1787 the famous Northwest Ordinance stated that the following important principle should be applied to states to be carved from the territory: "Religion, morality, and knowledge being necessary to good government and the happiness of mankind, schools and the means of education shall be forever encouraged." Although it is customary to consider this statement in the Northwest Ordinance as a philanthropic gesture on the part of Congress, the bald facts are that mercenary motives also actuated the proposal, for the Continental Congress, which needed money urgently, wanted to sell land. In addition to the two townships given in each state for university purposes, section 16 in every township or one thirty-sixth of the entire Northwest Territory was legally set aside for the maintenance of public schools. The first actual application of this land-grant policy for education was not made until the admission of the state of Ohio in 1803.

In the meantime, the members of the Constitutional Convention had drafted their document and the required nine states had ratified it, so that in 1789 the Constitution of the United States went into effect. This great document, which Gladstone said "was the most wonderful work ever struck off at a given time by the brain and purpose of man," is silent upon the subject of education. The Constitution contains neither the word "education" nor "schools."

Why was education omitted from this famous document? Several answers to the question might be proposed. The framers of the Constitution were undoubtedly afraid of a centralized control, for they had just fought a war for freedom from external domination. The prevailing view was that of state rights. Furthermore, education in those days was the function of the church, the home, and private agencies. The majority of the signers of the Constitution were themselves products of the old aristocratic doctrine that education was for

those who could afford to pay for it, and they probably had very little or no sympathy with the idea of schooling for all. Then, too, at the time, there were weightier problems than education. The wilderness had to be wrested from the Indians, and a new economic and political order had to be established.

Despite the fact that education is not mentioned in the United States Constitution, indirect justification for a national program of instruction may be found in several of its provisions, as indicated later. The "general welfare" clauses, in the Preamble and in the sec-

tion on taxation, are the closest approach to an authorization. The Preamble reads:

We the people of the United States, in order to form a more perfect Union, establish justice, insure domestic tranquility, provide for the common defence, promote the general welfare, and secure the blessings of liberty to ourselves and our posterity, do ordain and establish this Constitution for the United States of America.

Certainly the promotion of "the general welfare" entails the federal obligation to advance public education.

That the central government is not to control education is evident from the Tenth Amendment to the Constitution which by implication definitely left the subject of education to the individual states: "The powers not delegated to the United States by the Constitution, nor prohibited by it to the states, are reserved to the states respectively, or to the people." The implied prohibition against the establishment of a centralized system has markedly influenced the direction and scope of federal participation in education.

*the development
of individual excellence . . .*

EDUCATION FOR NATIONAL DEFENSE

From the days of the earliest settlements through the modern age of atomic energy and supersonic speeds, the people of the United States have been interested in defense. During and after World War II, the preparation for defense assumed a distinct educational emphasis. General Dwight D. Eisenhower, later President of the United States, said upon his inauguration as president of Columbia University:

If this were a land where the military profession is a weapon of tyranny or aggression—its members an elite caste dedicated to its own perpetuation—a lifelong soldier could hardly assume my present role. But in our nation the army is the servant of the people, designed and trained exclusively to protect our way of life. Duty in its ranks is an exercise of citizenship. Hence, among us, the soldier who becomes an educator or the teacher who becomes a soldier enters no foreign field but finds himself instead engaged in a new phase of his fundamental life purpose—the protection and perpetuation of basic human freedoms.

This educational accent has continued under the Reorganization Act of 1947, which unified the services under a Secretary of Defense, to whom the Secretaries of the Army, Navy, and Air Force are all responsible. Some of the various educational activities of these three departments are tersely mentioned here.

Army Training. The first educational institution authorized by the federal government was the United States Military Academy at West Point, New York. It was established by the congressional act signed by President Jefferson in 1802. Supported entirely by the federal government and conducted under the auspices of the Department of Defense, this collegiate institution provides theoretical and practical training for prospective officers in the regular army. The entrance requirements and standards are very high. Many graduates have won distinction in civil life as engineers. In addition to the United States Military Academy, two groups of army schools have developed: the general service schools, including the Command and General Staff School, the Army Industrial College, and the Army War College; and the special service schools, such as the Army Dental School and the School of Aviation Medicine.

The Army's education program extends from the first grade up through the university. Many thousands of soldiers have learned to read and write and have received the Army's fourth- and fifth-grade certificates. Others have earned the eighth-grade certificate. On the high school level thousands, by passing successfully the General Educational Development Tests, have acquired a high school diploma or equivalency certificate from their home states. In higher education, some American universities have gone overseas to provide courses for soldiers abroad.

Navy Training. Congress decided in 1845 that an institution was needed to accomplish for the Navy what West Point was doing for the Army, so a naval training school was established at Annapolis, Maryland, the site of the first Federal Constitutional Convention. In 1850 this school became known as the United States Naval Academy. Under the auspices of the Bureau of Navy Personnel, it is supported entirely by federal funds. As at West Point, the course is usually four years in length, and the graduates are commissioned as ensigns. Postgraduate work and special training fields also have been added.

The Reserve Officers' Training Corps (RO-TC) program is conducted in colleges and universities throughout the country.

Merchant Marine Academy. The Navy, Marine Corps, and the Merchant Marine have, from their earliest history, been joined by an inseparable relationship. The Merchant Marine or commercial marine, which consists of the vessels carrying on the water-borne trade of the nation, sprang up in wartime when the great need for transporting American goods all over the world developed a parallel need for officers. The Merchant Marine Academy, located at Kings Point, Long Island, New York, was authorized by Congress to confer a bachelor of science degree beginning with the class of 1950, and in 1956 was made the nation's fifth permanent service academy. The graduates are commissioned reserve ensigns, United States Naval Reserve, as well as ensigns in the United States Maritime Service. Like the students at the Naval Academy, their campus is the seven seas.

Air Force Training. In 1947, for the first time in the history of the United States, a separate department was created for the Air Force. The educational program of the Air Force, formerly a part of the Army and Navy, now is independent in a new age of rocket-fired, jet-propelled, push-button planes and satellites sailing into outer space. The Air University provides advanced professional work in constituent schools from the time of commissioning to retirement.

A government-financed Air Force Academy, along the lines of the United States Military and Naval Academies, opened its doors in temporary quarters in 1955, prior to settling at Colorado Springs.

Others. Many other phases of military education, including special   for women and technical instruction in guided missiles, satellites, and baby moons, have evolved under the aegis of the federal government. The government furnishes officers to serve at land-grant colleges; it cooperates with the ROTC; and it trains men for the Marine Reserve Corps and for numerous other military and semimilitary duties. These have valuable implications for civilian programs of today and for the participation of the federal government in various civilian and defense activities of tomorrow.

FEDERAL GRANTS—NONVOCATIONAL

Land Grants for Education. With the admission of the seventeenth state, Ohio, to the Union in 1803, the federal government actually inaugurated its epoch-making practice of giving the 1 mile square section of each township for general educational purposes. With certain exceptions and variations, this practice was continued with each new state admitted. With the admission of California in 1850, the gift con-

*the strengthening
of morality ...*

Syracuse, New York, high school student participating in driving-safety contest learns respect for law.

Elementary pupils in Pleasant Ridge, Michigan, learn respect for life.

sisted of two sections. Three states—Utah, Arizona, and New Mexico—received four sections. The total of these land grants is estimated at 90,000,000 acres, or almost 150,000 square miles. The extent of this area is larger than the combined territory of the three adjacent states of Ohio, Indiana, and Illinois. The funds derived from the sale and lease of these original school lands form the major part of the permanent school funds of several states. Although some of the funds were poorly managed, these gifts of the federal government to education have been extremely significant.

Besides these lands, many other federal land grants have been made, both conditional and unconditional, including the saline lands, the swamplands, and the internal improvement grants. There have been donations to seminaries of learning, normal schools, universities, and other types of educational institutions, including especially the land-grant colleges of agriculture and mechanic arts, as established by the first Morrill Act and expanded by subsequent enactments.

Money Grants for Education. The federal government has also aided the public schools by money grants at different times. The first of these subventions followed the admission of Ohio, when 5 per cent of the sales of all public lands in the states was turned back to them. Some of this money was spent for schools. About half the commonwealths receiving the small fund from the so-called surplus revenue act of 1836 used it for schools. Other money grants, which in part or whole have gone to schools, have included the Direct War Tax Refund of 1891, which was devoted to education in three states; the Forest Reserve Income Act of 1908, according to which 25 per cent of the money received from each forest reserve goes to the schools or the roads of the county containing the reserve; and the Mineral Royalty Act of 1920, by which the federal government returns to each state a proportion of the royalties on the production of nonmetallic mineral deposits on public lands. One reason why California has developed such a superior system of junior colleges is that all its proceeds from the Mineral Royalty Act go to institutions of that special type. A few states have benefited from the Taylor Grazing Act. All states have received other specialized funds, such as help in inventorying school buildings

and as an important instrument in advancing international understanding.

Children at Islamia High School, Sialkot, Pakistan, learn about the United States and their neighbors in other parts of the world.

*Representatives of three nations
study the globe in a geography course
at the United Nations International School,
Parkway Village, near New York City.*

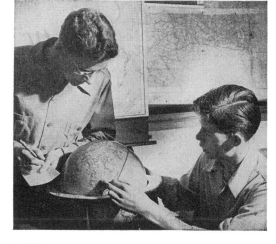

*In Madison, Wisconsin, high school students
chart distances in a rapidly shrinking universe.*

and in providing some construction and operating costs in federally affected areas.

Among the nonvocational money grants has been that for school lunches. This grant, which began in the depression era of the 1930s, was put on a permanent basis in 1947. The enactment in 1944 of the historic GI Bill of Rights was followed in 1951 and 1952 by laws for disabled and other veterans of recent military service. These laws have provided perhaps the largest expenditure of federal funds ever made for any educational purpose.

GRANTS FOR VOCATIONAL EDUCATION

Land-grant Colleges and Universities. The United States has always been very aggressive in promoting vocational education through both land and money grants. By the first Morrill Act in 1862, each state received 30,000 acres for each senator and representative then in Congress. All proceeds from the sale of these lands were to be invested at 5 per cent and the proceeds in each state to be used for "the endowment, maintenance, and support of at least one college where the leading object shall be, without excluding other scientific and classical studies and including military tactics, to teach such branches of learning as are related to agriculture and the mechanic arts."

These colleges, 69 in number, have been very influential in the fields of agriculture, engineering, and home economics. The original act has been supplemented by other grants in the second Morrill Act, the Nelson Amendment, and the Bankhead-Jones Act of 1935.

Agricultural Experiment Stations. Further federal impetus was given vocational education through the Hatch Act of 1887, which appropriated $15,000 annually to each state and territory having an agricultural college. The purpose expressed in the law was "to promote scientific investigation respecting the principles and applications of agriculture science." Thus the agricultural experiment stations were established. Later acts subsequently increased these appropriations.

Federal Extension Service. Although the United States government had already established agricultural colleges and experimental stations, it felt that the vocational work was still incom-

NATIONAL DEVELOPMENT		THE DEVELOPMENT OF FEDERAL RELATIONS TO EDUCATION
The struggle for independence and constitutional government	**1787**	Northwest Ordinance provided that "schools and the means of education shall be forever encouraged"
Launching the new nation	**1791**	Tenth Amendment to U.S. Constitution reserved education to the states
Maritime troubles and the War of 1812	**1803**	Public lands given for education in Ohio
Era of good feeling	**1818**	First money granted to the states for education by federal government
Jacksonian Democracy		
Westward migration and expansion		
	1862	Land-grant colleges established by first Morrill Act
Controversy and war between the states		
	1865	Freedman's Bureau created
Aftermath and reconstruction	**1867**	Department of Education created in national government
Immigration and industrial growth		
The progressive era		
World War I	**1917**	Smith-Hughes Act provided federal assistance for vocational education
Normalcy and prosperity		
Depression and recovery	**1933**	Emergency education grants started
	1939	U.S. Office of Education transferred from Department of the Interior to Federal Security Agency
World War II	**1944**	GI Bill for veterans' education passed by Congress
	1946	Membership of United States in UNESCO approved by Congress
	1948	Mundt law for global program in education approved by Congress
The Cold War struggle	**1953**	U.S. Office of Education made part of Department of Health, Education, and Welfare with Secretary in President's Cabinet
	1954	Segregation in public schools ruled unconstitutional by U.S. Supreme Court
	1955	White House Conference on problems of school housing, finance, personnel, and organization held
	1958	National Education Defense Act enacted
	1960	Golden Anniversary White House Conference on Children and Youth called by President

NATIONAL DEVELOPMENT   **THE DEVELOPMENT OF FEDERAL RELATIONS TO EDUCATION**

HISTORICAL CALENDAR

plete because the results were not reaching the consumers—the farmers and the housewives. So Congress passed in 1914 what is known as the Smith-Lever or Agricultural Extension Act. The proceeds from this annual grant are used for conferences, meetings, institutes, classes, traveling demonstrators, and county agents—a man to work among the farmers and a woman to help the housewives, especially in the rural communities. In the Smith-Lever Act was applied for the first time the practice, now under severe criticism, of matching federal and state aid. Additional grants for agricultural extension have been provided through succeeding acts and through direct appropriations.

Smith-Hughes Act for Vocational Education in Secondary Schools. The movement for federal aid to vocational education at the secondary school level did not develop until the twentieth century. Between 1900 and 1910 a number of organizations such as the National Association of Manufacturers, the National Metal Trades Association, the National Education Association, the American Federation of Labor, and others advocated facilities for vocational education in the public schools. In 1906 the National Society for the Promotion of Industrial Education was established. In 1914 Congress authorized the appointment of a Commission on National Aid to Vocational Education. In 1917 President Woodrow Wilson signed the Smith-Hughes Act, which provided annual federal funds for distribution to the states for vocational education in public schools of less than college grade. These appropriations, again on the matching basis, were for teachers and supervisors of agriculture, home economics, trade and industrial subjects; for teacher training in these subjects; and for studies in vocational education. Supplemental legislation extended the benefits to some of the dependencies of the United States.

George-Deen Act and Aid in Distributive Occupations. This act, which became effective in 1937, provided "for the further development of vocational education in the several states and territories," and more than doubled the amount of money previously available for vocational education. Prior to this, only four fields were given federal support: agriculture, trades and industries, home economics, and the training of teachers in these subjects. This act recognized as worthy of federal aid a new field of vocational training, the distributive occupations, such as selling; it gave a somewhat indirect recognition to another field, the public service occupations, including positions such as that of the school janitor. It broke the precedent in the financing of vocational education which required that federal funds be matched dollar for dollar by state and local funds.

Vocational Rehabilitation. After some experimentation, the federal government adopted in 1920 the Vocational Rehabilitation Act, which appropriated money to the states for the training of handicapped persons so that they may, whenever possible, be placed in self-supporting, remunerative employment. This service and that for vocational education have been extended to some of the dependencies through other acts.

Other legislation dealing with vocational rehabilitation is the Social Security Act of 1935. The U.S. Office of Education and the Social Security Board cooperate in occupational research and in the formulation of state plans for physically handicapped persons who have become permanently disabled through accident or disease or who have been born with serious physical defects. The program is carried out by the casework technique rather than by the public schools; nevertheless it is a public educational service. Most significant are the provisions of the federal rehabilitation acts for war veterans, popularly known as Public Law 16. Thousands of veterans, including paraplegics, have been rehabilitated. Through vocational rehabilitation, millions of handicapped persons have been helped to a life of usefulness and independence.

Vocational Guidance and Placement. In its general evaluation of the federally aided programs of vocational education, the advisory committee stated that the services of guidance and placement had not received adequate emphasis. The George-Barden amendment has helped to remedy the situation. Under this act, federal funds were made available for the first time for counseling youth, training vocational counselors, and conducting allied activities, including research in guidance and placement. The Veterans Administration has rendered vocational services "beyond the call of duty."

Vocational Education and National Defense. Prior to the official entry of the United States into World War II, the federal government launched its defense training, which developed into a huge war program. Congress in 1938 established the Civil Aeronautics Authority, which in the following year inaugurated a pilot training program. In 1940 the first appropriations were made by the federal government for summer training programs in schools and colleges for workers essential in national defense. In the same year the U.S. Office of Education was allotted several million dollars for a program under which state boards of vocational education and local school officials offered vocational training facilities through the National Youth Administration (NYA), now defunct. World War II—and the Korean conflict, in a lesser degree—caused the nation as a whole to overaccent vocational education. The launching of the Russian satellites in 1957 caused many Americans to advocate a "cash and crash" program for science.

OTHER FEDERAL PROVISIONS FOR EDUCATION

Numerous other significant and interesting subventions and activities have become a part of federal legislation on behalf of education. Some of the agencies created thereby are no longer in existence, as in the case of the Freedman's Bureau, through which the government undertook some work independently of the states. The Freedman's Bureau aided schools in the South for Negro children, and helped to establish in Virginia the Hampton Normal Institute, a pattern for Negro education.

Annual Appropriations to Privately Controlled Institutions. The federal government has given financial support to some institutions not under its control. It donated land to Tuskegee Institute and now makes annual appropriations to the following three institutions, which are privately controlled but supervised by the federal Department of Health, Education, and Welfare:

1. American Printing House for the Blind, located in Louisville, which was incorporated by the Legislature of Kentucky in 1858.
2. Columbia Institution for the Deaf, located in the District of Columbia, which was incorporated by Congress in 1857.
3. Howard University, located in the District of Columbia, which was incorporated by Congress in 1867.

Making annual appropriations to privately controlled institutions, however, is not routine with Congress.

The GI Bill of Rights. As previously indicated, the greatest single venture of federal government in education has been the schooling of veterans of World War II and of other veterans. The United States is spending billions of dollars on education for GI Joes and Jills who interrupted or postponed their studies to help win World War II or to defend democracy against communism.

Concerning the first bill, former Chancellor Robert M. Hutchins of the University of Chicago wrote, "The GI Bill of Rights is a historic enactment because it makes it possible for the veteran to go to college even if his parents have no money. It thus removes, for a large class of our citizens, the greatest, the most unjust, and the most unwise limitation on higher education." The GI bills have enabled millions of young men and women to attend high schools, colleges, universities, specialized schools, and adult education classes throughout the land. Several hundred also have studied abroad under their provisions. The quantitative and qualitative impact upon American education of the federal GI scholarships cannot be estimated. These scholarships enabled a whole generation of young men and women to extend their education substantially.

The National Defense Education Act. The entry of Russian and United States satellites into outer space generated national concern that American intellectual excellence, particularly in the physical sciences, be assured in the interests of national defense. In 1958 the Congress enacted legislation providing money for loans to college students; fellowships for graduate students, particularly those interested in college teaching; equipment for science, mathematics, and foreign language teaching; improved training of personnel engaged in guidance and counseling; improvement and expansion of instruction in foreign languages; and the development of audio-visual aids for educational purposes. The national budget for 1960 provided approximately one hundred fifty million dollars for the administration of the National Defense Education Act.

Additional Federal Activities in Education. Several temporary subventions were granted during the depression era of the 1930's. These included the Civilian Conservation Corps, National Youth Administration, Works Progress Administration, Public Works Administration, and other agencies.

Although most federal activities in education are conducted by regular agencies of the national government, several special committees and conferences are created periodically to consider problems in education and related areas. For example, White House conferences are held at intervals of approximately ten years to study the welfare of children. Several advisory committees have been authorized by Congress to study the relationship of the federal government to education.

The main channel through which have flowed by various appropriations made by Congress for the development of a national program of education is the U.S. Office of Education in the Department of Health, Education, and Welfare.

U.S. Office of Education

EVOLUTION OF OFFICE

The "common-school revival," championed by Horace Mann in the 1840s in Massachusetts, caused people all through the then settled portions of the United States to think in terms of schools. Other educational statesmen came forward, notably Henry Barnard, who led the movement for a national agency for education. The dire effects of the Civil War in the sixties and the reunion of the states gave rise to a new interest in national education. In 1866 a proposal for a federal bureau of education was presented to Congress by James A. Garfield. The "Department of Education" bill was finally approved March 2, 1867.

The Basic Law. The original act as adopted during the presidency of Andrew Johnson is as follows:

BE IT ENACTED *by the Senate and the House of Representatives of the United States of America, in Congress Assembled,* That there shall be established at the city of Washington, a department of education, for the purpose of collecting such statistics and facts as shall show the condition and progress of education in the several states and territories, and of diffusing such information respecting the organization and management of schools and school systems and methods of teaching as shall aid the people of the United States in the establishment and maintenance of efficient school systems, and otherwise PROMOTE THE CAUSE OF EDUCATION throughout the country.

39th Congress, 2nd Session
Approved by President Andrew Johnson
March 2, 1867

Thus was the legal foundation laid.

Subsequent Changes. Two years later, owing primarily to opposition by some of the states, the department was made an "Office of Education" in the Department of Interior. The title, changed in 1870 to "Bureau of Education," was restored in 1929, and is now officially the "Office of Education." The duties and activities of the Office have accumulated until now it is a huge national clearinghouse for education.

On July 1, 1939, in connection with the general governmental reorganization plans, the U.S. Office of Education was transferred from the Department of the Interior to the Federal Security Agency. In 1953 the Office became a part of the newly created Department of Health, Education, and Welfare, with a secretary in the President's Cabinet. This marked an important milestone in the history of federal education.

APPROPRIATIONS FOR FEDERAL OFFICE

A significant change in the federal Office has been the growth in appropriations. The funds are of two general types: (1) regular expenditures for administration of the Office itself, and (2) grants-in-aid for distribution to the states through the Office.

Appropriations for Administration. The administration of the national headquarters at Washington requires an outlay for personnel, equipment, necessary travel, printing, and other items. From a meager appropriation in 1867 of about fifty thousand dollars, the annual expenditures have gradually increased to several million dollars.

Grants-in-aid to the States. The Office is a channel through which flow the annual grants-in-aid to be distributed to the states, territories, and outlying possessions for educational purposes. These funds are more than a hundred times larger than those for the direct use of the U.S. Office of Education. The money is primarily for land-grant colleges, vocational education, vocational rehabilitation, and defense education.

FUNCTIONS OF THE OFFICE OF EDUCATION

Commissioner Lawrence G. Derthick describes the role of the U.S. Office of Education:

Down through the years, the Office has concerned itself with providing leadership without domination and assistance without interference. Following the American tradition of the local control and support of education, born and nurtured on the frontier, the Office has helped the states and communities shape a national pattern and policy of education. This pattern is diametrically opposed to that found in many foreign nations, where the central ministry of education exercises overall control of schools.[2]

The three main functions of the Office are (1) research, (2) administration of federal educational grants, and (3) educational services to local, state, national, and international agencies.

Research. The Office conducts a variety of research projects in such areas as school enrollment predictions, costs of college education, studies of school building needs, financial and property accounting, studies of education in other lands, and a variety of others. In its *Biennial Survey of Education in the United States,* the Office serves as chief bookkeeper for the nation's schools, reporting a mass of statistical data relative to state and local school systems.

The Office also administers an extensive cooperative research program with colleges, universities, and state departments of education, as authorized by legislation in 1956 and by the National Defense Education Act in 1958. These research projects deal with such problems as education for the mentally retarded, juvenile delinquency, selection of school administrators, the educational implications of our expanding technology and economy, population mobility, educational television and other audio-visual aids, and school plant planning.

[2] Lawrence G. Derthick, "The New Commissioner Looks at the U.S. Office of Education," *The School Executive,* vol. 76 (July, 1957), pp. 19–21.

Administration of Federal Educational Grants. The U.S. Office of Education administers many but not all of the federal funds appropriated for education, such as the aid to school districts affected by federal installations, grants for vocational education, land-grant funds, aid for library services in rural areas, and many others.

Educational Services. The U.S. Office of Education renders a variety of services to local, state, national, and international agencies. It conducts surveys and renders consultative help to local and state school systems. It conducts an extensive publications service through the Superintendent of Documents, Government Printing Office, Washington, D.C. These publications include research monographs, periodicals, newsletters, pamphlets, articles, and speeches. The best known of its periodicals is *School Life*, which is published monthly. The Office calls conferences on various educational problems, presents exhibits and radio and television broadcasts. It cooperates with the State Department in international teacher exchanges and with the International Cooperation Administration for the technical training of foreign educators in America and for the recruitment of American education specialists for service abroad. It serves as a clearinghouse for the assistance of foreign students entering American colleges and universities. The Office also provides an information center and library on all phases of American education.

ORGANIZATION OF FEDERAL OFFICE

Naturally, activities so numerous, for an audience so varied, demand a large staff of workers. These are organized in various groups under the general leadership of the United States Commissioner of Education. Committees also cut across divisional lines, as the Inter-divisional Committee on the Educational Implications of Atomic Energy.

The regular full-time staff of the Office has increased from five workers in 1867 to several hundred. Many additional helpers are needed,

since some important fields are undeveloped or placed on a temporary basis. The United States Commissioner of Education has been seriously handicapped by lack of an adequate permanent staff.

UNITED STATES COMMISSIONER OF EDUCATION

History of Commissionership. In 1838 Henry Barnard came to Washington, D.C., in search of reliable facts on the schools of the nation; he found none. For thirty years he led the movement for a federal fact-finding agency, which culminated in the congressional act, already quoted, creating the federal Department of Education in 1867. It was indeed fitting that Henry Barnard was selected as the first United States Commissioner of Education. The first principal of the New Britain Normal School, the first state superintendent of schools for Rhode Island, and a former state superintendent for Connecticut, he brought to this new national office a rich experience in public education.

List of Commissioners. Fourteen men have held the office of United States Commissioner of Education, a title that has not changed. Their names and the years in office are indicated below:

Commissioner	Years in office
Henry Barnard	1867–1870
John Eaton	1870–1886
N. H. R. Dawson	1886–1889
William T. Harris	1889–1906
Elmer E. Brown	1906–1911
Philander P. Claxton	1911–1921
John J. Tigert	1921–1928
William J. Cooper	1929–1933
George F. Zook	1933–1934
John W. Studebaker	1934–1949
Earl J. McGrath	1949–1953
Lee M. Thurston	1953–1953
Samuel M. Brownell	1953–1956
Lawrence G. Derthick	1956–

*What are some of the ways
in which the federal government and
its agencies support education?*

*Educators from other lands examine the
resources of the materials laboratory in the
U.S. Office of Education.*

*School children, like these in Vidalia, Georgia,
enjoy hearty lunches at reduced cost
through the auspices of the national school lunch
program, administered by
the Agricultural Marketing Service
of the U.S. Department of Agriculture.*

Terms of Office. The commissioner, appointed with the consent of the Senate by the President of the United States, upon the recommendation of the Secretary of Health, Education, and Welfare, serves an indefinite term. Sometimes a change in Presidents is followed by the appointment of a new commissioner. The terms have ranged from seventeen years for W. T. Harris to less than three months, Commissioner Thurston having died in office shortly after his appointment.

DUTIES OF COMMISSIONER

Main Duties. The duties of the commissioner, as originally prescribed by law, are "to collect such statistics and facts as shall show the condition and progress of education in the several states and territories"; to diffuse such "information respecting the organization and management of schools and school systems and methods of teaching as shall aid the people in the maintenance of efficient school systems and otherwise promote the cause of education"; and also "to present annually to Congress a re-

port embodying the result of his investigation and labors, together with a statement of such facts and recommendations, as will, in his judgment, subserve the purpose for which the department is established." A significant duty of the commissioner is the last one listed, viz., that of taking soundings to determine the progress of the educational ship of state. The annual reports and biennial surveys are replete with information and, as standard works of educational reference, are distributed in large numbers to libraries and professional workers. These reports contain many interesting side lights on educational history.

Other Activities. In addition to the original duties already mentioned as belonging to the commissioner and the U.S. Office of Education, many others have accumulated over the years. Among these may be listed voluntary cooperation with numerous educational agencies, as in the promotion of American Education Week; special tasks assigned by the President of the United States, as the request for the Office to

Many of the Michigan State University students here registering for courses are veterans whose education is subsidized through the GI Bill of Rights, administered by the Veterans Administration.

The U.S. Department of Defense is responsible for the training of future military officers at military schools such as the Air Force Academy near Colorado Springs, Colorado.

Government experts help Weld County, Colorado, farm families plan their crops for the year ahead.

Other federal activities in education

EDUCATION IN SPECIAL FEDERAL JURISDICTIONS

The national government assists in promoting education in the special school district of Washington, D.C., the territories, the outlying possessions, the Trust Territory, the federal reservations, and other countries through the United States Point Four program, United States Operations Mission, and United Nations Technical Assistance Program. The importance of education in such widespread and strategic areas is obvious. Because of the unique needs of these disparate groups, their educational problems are difficult but challenging.

Among the interesting educational systems in these overseas areas are those in the ex-Japanese Mandated Islands, now called the Trust Territory, transferred in 1947 to the United States by the United Nations Security Council. They comprise the Marshall, Caroline, Palau,

act in an advisory educational capacity; duties imposed by congressional enactments, as by the George-Barden Act; and the surveillance of film service and radio, assigned to the Office by one of the presidential reorganization plans. The Office has also been called upon to extend and expand its services in the territories and dependencies of the United States and in many countries overseas.

and Marianas Islands (with the exception of Guam). The United States has done more than conduct experiments in atomic energy on its atolls of Bikini and Eniwetok; it has unleashed in the whole Trust Territory the power of educational energy that transforms rather than destroys. The chain reaction from this significant educational experiment may spread from atolls to islands and mainlands.

EDUCATION OF SPECIAL GROUPS

Education of the Indians. In a social science class in a Michigan high school, students were asked to write an essay entitled, "Who Is a True American?" A member of the class, a young full-blooded Ottawa Indian, wrote just two words, "I am." The Indians were the first Americans. In an early report of a United States Commissioner of Education, the whites are referred to as Anglo-Americans. For a long time the issue was Indian education versus Indian destruction. In 1870 the commissioner stated that up to that time 8 million dollars had been spent for educating Indians and at least 500 million dollars for killing them.

The early missions are credited with starting schools for Indians. The first federal appropriation for this purpose was made in the early 1800s. Private funds also went to Indian education. The origin of Dartmouth College can be traced to Moore's Indian School for the education of the Indians.

By the act of June 2, 1924, every American Indian now born in the United States is a citizen of this country. Approximately one-third of a million Indians live in the United States. It is significant that the Indians, although less than one-half of 1 per cent of the total population, are increasing—they are not a dying race. They usually live in concentrated areas and exhibit strong ethnic characteristics. The largest tribal groups are the Navaho, Sioux, and Chippewa. The largest Indian settlements are located in Oklahoma, Arizona, New Mexico, and South Dakota. Some Indian reservations cannot support all their inhabitants. The problems

of Indian welfare and education, as in the case of Negroes, are more acute in some states than in others.

The administration of Indian education in the United States is under the Office of Indian Affairs. The children attend different types of schools: government-reservation and nonreservation boarding schools, government day schools, state public schools, and mission and private schools. The majority go to the public schools; the federal government pays their tuition if they are not residents of the school district. In addition to federal appropriations for Indian service, large sums are expended from Indian tribal funds for education. Many schools are community centers for adults as well as children. Certainly the Indian—the first American and the first of America's forgotten men—is entitled to the best in education, but he generally does not get the best. He often lives in "that cultural void between two civilizations."

Negro Education. Negroes constitute almost one-tenth of the population of the United States. The education of this large group is of major concern to the nation, as well as to the Southern states where the majority of Negroes reside.

An important feature of the second Morrill Act in 1890 was the recognition by Congress of separate land-grant colleges for "white and colored students." A year earlier the federal government voted its first grant to Howard University, a privately controlled institution for Negroes, which today enrolls several thousand students in its many graduate and undergraduate schools. Founded immediately after the Civil War, this institution was named after its first president, General Howard of the Freedman's Bureau.

The U.S. Office of Education has conducted several surveys of Negro education, including colleges and universities, secondary education, and vocational education and guidance. Although their schooling is primarily a responsibility of the states, the federal government can, through equalization funds and other means, supplement these efforts on behalf of one-tenth of the nation's population.

The United States Supreme Court, in its historic decision of 1954, held that racial segregation in the public schools violates the United States Constitution. At that time 17 states and the District of Columbia maintained public school segregation by specific law, and 4 more states permitted it. For many years these states had justified their policy as giving "equal but separate" facilities to Negro and white children. The Court ruled that, even if facilities are equal, intangible factors prevent separate from being equal.

To separate [Negro children] from others of similar age and qualifications solely because of their race generates a feeling of inferiority as to their status in the community that may affect their hearts and minds in a way unlikely ever to be undone. . . . We conclude that in the field of public education the doctrine of "separate but equal" has no place. Separate educational facilities are inherently unequal.

In this unanimous decision of the highest tribunal of the land are involved many complex problems: *When* should public schools be ordered to abolish segregation, *who* should enforce the terms, *how* can educational integration be applied, and *what* can be done to help house and finance programs for nonsegregated pupils? Obviously no uniform pattern for educational integration can or should be applied. Furthermore, evolutionary processes will be employed in implementing a concept that is revolutionary to many people. As indicated by *Time* magazine, "The Supreme Court's decision was another vital chapter in one of the greatest success stories the world has ever known: the American Negro's 90-year rise from slavery."

Other Ethnic Groups. Mexicans comprise about 1 per cent of the population of the United States. Some communities in the southwestern part of the United States are predominantly Mexican.

Large numbers of white people in the United States are foreign born, but, aside from Americanization classes, not much has been done on a national scale for their education. Numerous racial groups of children and adults, including displaced persons, many of whom have difficulty with the English language and the American way of life, have not been given the special care and education necessary for their role as citizens in a democracy.

Other Special Groups. The education of children of federal employees residing on government reservations, in dependencies, and at foreign stations is a unique problem facing the national government. Children in these areas are assured of free public schooling only if the federal government makes special provision therefor. During World War II, Congress provided financial aid to schools overburdened with war-caused enrollments. Since then the Lanham Act also provided school district assistance where it was needed because of reactivation or establishment of defense activities. Partial support is given to some schools at naval stations. Government buildings and cars sometimes lend indirect assistance to schools on reservations. The Tennessee Valley Authority maintains public schools and other educational facilities for children and adults. Where there is a concentration of children of federal employees abroad, as in the countries of Germany and Japan, special schools have been established under federal auspices. Federal personnel in foreign lands, however, often face the necessity of enrolling their children in private or foreign schools, or of sending them back to the United States for their education. It has been recommended that Congress establish a permanent policy by which all children of federal employees residing on a federal reservation or at a foreign station will be assured the right of free education.

Equality of educational opportunity means that each child should be educated in terms of his needs, interests, abilities, and limitations. Special attention is needed by several million children—blind and partially blind, deaf and hard-of-hearing, crippled, defective in speech, delicate, mentally gifted, mentally retarded, socially maladjusted, and otherwise handicapped (described in Chapter 10). The federal government aids atypical children and adults through general grants such as that for vocational rehabilitation and by specific projects such as the American Printing House for the Blind in Louisville, Kentucky, and the Columbia Institute for the Deaf in Washington, D.C.

DEPARTMENTAL PROGRAMS OF EDUCATION

Federal programs of education are conducted also by (1) the executive departments, each under a secretary in the President's Cabinet, and (2) other agencies, such as the Veterans Administration.

Executive Departments and Their Programs of Education. Several educational and semieducational agencies and services are sponsored by the major executive departments of the United States. Chief of these, of course, is the Department of Health, Education, and Welfare with its U.S. Office of Education, previously mentioned. Illustrative of other educational programs sponsored by executive departments are the military academies in the Department of Defense, the national school lunch program in the Department of Agriculture, prison education in the Department of Justice, and the school for postal inspectors in the Post Office Department. Directly under the President of the United States are several agencies that have direct educational significance, as, for example, the Bureau of the Budget, which prepares estimates for educational expenditures.

Other Federal Enterprises and Their Programs of Education. Every branch of the federal government conducts several educational activities either directly or indirectly, either in cooperation with the U.S. Office of Education or independently. Only a few of these agencies and their activities can be catalogued here. Congress has its committees on education in

both the House and Senate. The United States Supreme Court renders its interpretations in the form of decisions affecting education, as in the Dartmouth College case, the McCollum and Zorach decisions on public schools and religious instruction, the opinions on segregation in schools and colleges, and the interpretations on loyalty legislation affecting educators. Independent federal establishments that furnish educational services include the Library of Congress and its Copyright Office, the Government Printing Office, the Pan-American Union, the Smithsonian Institution, the National Museum, the National Gallery of Art, the National Academy of Sciences, the Commission of Fine Arts, the Atomic Energy Commission, and the National Science Foundation. Much educational research is conducted in the nation's capital and sponsored by the Congress of the United States.

Fig. 1-1, showing federal funds expended for education by the various agencies of the federal government, gives some idea of the scope, purposes, and variety of educational programs administered by the federal government.

The number of federal activities is ample evidence that the government of the United States is seeking "to promote the general welfare" of its citizens through public education.

ROLE OF UNITED STATES
IN INTERNATIONAL EDUCATION

The general welfare of citizens in the United States and other countries includes the well-being and education of all peoples in a global, atomic, supersonic space age. The United States government, as a member of the United Na-

Fig. 1-1. The federal government spends a substantial sum of money through many governmental agencies to help in the support of various kinds of education. (This figure is based upon data derived by the authors from various sources in the public domain. Such is also the case in other figures in this book when the source of data is not indicated.)

KIND OF EDUCATION	Expenditure, 1956-57
Higher education	$ 1,032,374,000
Elementary and secondary education	$ 656,632,000
Research in educational institutions	$ 133,478,000
Adult education	$ 87,220,000
International education	$ 50,139,000
Education of Merchant Marine and military for defense	$ 34,497,000
Inservice training of civilian personnel	$ 3,485,000
TOTAL	**$ 1,997,825,000**

AGENCY		Expenditure, 1956-57
Department of	Health, Education, and Welfare	$ 490,736,000
	Agriculture	$ 399,381,000
	Interior	$ 90,425,000
	Defense	$ 69,332,000
	State	$ 47,115,000
	Labor	$ 5,899,000
	Treasury	$ 3,375,000
	Commerce	$ 3,346,000
	Justice	$ 530,000
Veterans Administration		$ 813,955,000
National Science Foundation		$ 33,181,000
Atomic Energy Commission		$ 30,717,000
District of Columbia		$ 4,310,000
Canal Zone		$ 3,647,000
Federal Civil Defense Administration		$ 707,000
Tennessee Valley Authority		$ 582,000
National Advisory Committee for Aeronautics		$ 580,000
Federal Deposit Insurance Corporation		$ 7,000
TOTAL		**$ 1,997,825,000**

tions, and especially the American teachers, are intensely interested in education throughout the world. The teacher of today and tomorrow needs to be a cosmopolite—a world citizen who is at home both in his own country and abroad—in an age of interdependence. This interest of American educators in international education is two fold: (1) in sharing with other countries the democratic way of life as taught and lived in these United States, and (2) in learning from the democratic countries, most of which are much older than the United States, how to prolong and enrich education. Educational reciprocity is the goal.

being mutual

Efforts at International Cooperation in Education. The Office of Education in the United States—a human melting pot—has long maintained a special department for comparative education, which later became the Division of International Educational Relations. Through the Pan-American Union, the United States has for years cooperated in educational and cultural activities with the American republics. In 1941 the Office of Inter-American Affairs was created by the United States to stimulate and coordinate certain inter-American activities, including education. In 1944 a joint Canada–United States Committee on Education was appointed. At Endicott, New York, in 1946, the United States was host to the First World Conference on Education attended by delegates from 30 nations. Illustrative of the many world-minded commissions and committees in the United States are the Committee on International Education of the American Association of Colleges for Teacher Education, and the Commission on International Education of Phi Delta Kappa International. The teachers of the United States are active in the World Confederation of Organizations of the Teaching Profession. Many American educators have served as consultants in Germany, Austria, Japan, Korea, and other lands. Thousands have participated in teacher-exchange programs. Among the postwar federal laws for educational exchange have been the Fulbright Act of 1946, the more permanent Smith-Mundt Act of 1948, the Point Four program enabling legislation of 1950, and the joint resolution providing for participation in UNESCO.

UNESCO. Official and striking evidence that educational isolationism is dying both here and abroad is found in the organization and program of UNESCO—the United Nations Educational, Scientific, and Cultural Organization—founded in 1945. UNESCO is one of the specialized agencies provided in the Charter of the United Nations and affiliated with the Economic and Social Council. Its broad purpose is "to contribute to peace and security by promoting collaboration among the nations through education, science, and culture."

As indicated in the Preamble to the UNESCO Constitution, "Since wars begin in the minds of men, it is in the minds of men that the defenses of peace must be constructed." Alexander Meiklejohn said of the organization: "Its aim is the development of that international intelligence upon which the success of any United Nations activity depends." The historical roots of UNESCO lie deep in history; its genesis is in the medieval community of scholars. According to *International Conciliation,* the "menace of psychopathic nationalism and advanced military technology" are the immediate factors which brought it into existence. The beginnings of this international organization are sketched briefly here.

The definite origin of UNESCO can be traced to the Conference of Allied Ministers of Education in 1942. The United States was not present but sent observers for the meeting the next year. In 1944 the United States government sent to London a delegation for educational and cultural reconstruction. An American delegate, the late Grayson Kefauver, remained in London to maintain liaison with the Conference of Allied Ministers of Education.

In the meantime, the San Francisco Conference, which adopted the Constitution of the United Nations, passed a resolution favoring the idea of an international organization for education, science, and culture. The Conference of Allied Ministers of Education modified their plans, which served as the basis for discussion at a United Nations meeting in London in November, 1945. Forty-four governments were represented at this Conference and seven international organizations sent observers. The United States delegation cooperated with the other nations in preparing a new draft constitution and establishing a preparatory commission. The first meeting of the General Conference of UNESCO was held in Paris in November, 1946.

Official approval by the United States came in July, 1946, when both houses of Congress passed a joint resolution providing for membership and participation by the United States in UNESCO, and authorizing an appropriation therefor. In signing the joint resolution President Harry S. Truman said:

The government of the United States will work with and through UNESCO to the end that the minds of all people may be freed from ignorance, prejudice, suspicion, and fear and that men may be educated for justice, liberty, and peace.

United States National Commission for UNESCO. The United States Congress, in officially approving its active membership, established a national commission for UNESCO in 1946. This commission of 100 educational leaders is entrusted with the responsibility of formulating policies for the United States as a member of the group. Thus government and citizenry are cooperating on an international scale to help education win the race with disaster.

Archibald MacLeish, an American delegate to the first session of UNESCO in Paris, said, "History may be about to teach us that the Parliament of Mankind can only be attained through the Republic of Letters."

UNESCO aims to help end educational isolationism and promote intellectual interdependence. In a highly scientific age which splits atoms, it helps unite peoples of the world. In an outer space age that sends satellites around the world, it helps bring peace to the inner man in all parts of the earth. An ancient Chinese proverb says, "The journey of a thousand miles begins with but a single step." The organization of UNESCO may prove to be the single step in education's long journey to lasting peace.

An evolving national system

A democracy is not static; it either advances or dies. Certainly education in a democracy strives to advance; thus a national system of education is slowly evolving in America.

Henry W. Holmes, former dean of the Harvard Graduate School, wrote in answer to his own question, "What do you mean by a *national* system of education?": "I do not mean a system run from Washington. . . . It means a system that can do a national job. A national job in education is compatible with immense variation in local patterns; such variation is, indeed, a necessary element in making American education national."

From the highest educational official in the land down to the youngest member of a student council in an elementary school, there is the desire to perfect American education. This striving toward perfection is furthered collectively by many nongovernmental groups. These organizations, through their nationwide membership and numerous activities, assist especially in formulating policies, in implementing goals, and evaluating programs.

PRINCIPLES AND PROPOSALS
FOR IMPROVEMENT OF NATIONAL SYSTEM

Basic Policies and Proposals. Four basic policies and principles are suggested to guide the future developments of the federal program in education as a service of primary importance:

1. The federal government should continue to exercise, within properly defined limits, without federal control, educational functions demanded by changing national needs.
2. The federal government should limit its action in the states to two broad functions: fi-

nancial assistance, when and where needed; and leadership of a stimulating but non-coercive character.

3. The decentralized pattern of public educational organization developed in the United States, involving basic control and administration of education by the states and localities, is sound democratic policy and should be continued and improved.

4. The heterogeneous pattern of administration needs to be better coordinated so that education receives from each political unit —federal, state, county, intermediate unit, and local district—the maximum contribution that organization can and should make in a dynamic democracy.

mixed

Specific Proposals. Suggestions by various groups and individuals for improving the national system of education in the United States include:

1. Creating a national commission or board, composed of 12 to 15 outstanding citizens, to provide a catalytic agent for education

2. Establishing an adequate federal educational agency as an independent office of the federal government, since the existing U.S. Office of Education is inadequate

3. Establishing a separate department of education, with a secretary of education in the President's Cabinet

4. Coordinating federal activities in education through a federal council on education, consisting of one representative from each of the several executive departments

5. Coordinating many federal-state programs through a national council on public education, composed of the several state superintendents, under the chairmanship of a secretary or commissioner of education

6. Coordinating governmental and nongovernmental educational agencies through a national conference on education

7. Creating a federal fund for aiding general education and equalizing educational opportunity and burden through the United States

8. Providing federal funds or loans for specific purposes, such as school buildings

9. Increasing the grant to the U.S. Office of Education

10. Providing federal scholarships and fellowships.

11. Granting subsidies for a national theater

12. Founding a national university at Washington, D.C., similar to the Australian National University at Canberra

13. Developing a national curriculum comprising a common set of values and contributing a common fund of knowledge, by a nongovernmental national association of scholars

Dozens of other recommendations affecting national education have been proposed by various groups and commissions, such as the Hoover Commission on Organization of the Executive Branch of Government. In its quest for the best, the nation will ever seek improvement in education. The role of the federal government in education is the subject of much controversy. Such controversy primarily centers around the issue of federal aid for education. This and other related issues are discussed in Chapter 17.

CONCLUSION

The present decentralized system of American public education does not and should not exclude the possibility of an improved, coordinated federal program of leadership and cooperation.

The individual's sense of national citizenship has developed rapidly in recent years. It is evident that all citizens face a common responsibility and that they share a common destiny which depends heavily upon the scope and quality of their education. From this common destiny, a national educational system is slowly evolving. It is not a new concept. Certainly it was in the minds of the statesmen who wrote the Declaration of Independence. It is today in the minds and hearts of educational statesmen who are perfecting an unwritten declaration of educational interdependence. This growing knowledge and feeling of educational interdependence, between state systems of education and between them and the national government, are the bases for helping boys and girls and men and women to live a fuller life, as envisioned in the great American dream.

Summary

The advance of American civilization is largely the story of the improvement of American education. Education is regarded as the vehicle for the preservation of democracy, the improvement of society, the economic well-being of people, and the strengthening of morality.

The federal government has encouraged education through grants of money and land for such purposes as national defense, vocational education, education of veterans, Indian and Negro education, international education, and the education of federal employees.

The U.S. Office of Education, a part of the Department of Health, Education, and Welfare, conducts and stimulates research, administers some of the federal grants for education, and provides certain direct services for local, state, national, and international educational agencies. The Office is administered by the United States Commissioner of Education.

The national government maintains schools in the District of Columbia, the territories and outlying possessions of the United States, and on federal reservations. Through the United Nations, UNESCO, and the Foreign Operations Administration, the United States government contributes to the improvement of education in other lands. The Departments of Defense, Justice, and the Interior, as well as the governmental agencies, operate certain special-purpose schools.

The United States Supreme Court, as the guardian of the Constitution, influences educational practice by reviewing the constitutionality of educational provisions. Legislative and executive committees and commissions study and advise with regard to educational policies and programs throughout the country.

It is widely believed that the federal government should continue to exercise certain educational functions without controlling state or local systems of education; that these functions should include primarily financial support, leadership, and stimulation. Several proposals have been advanced for improving national provisions for education. A national system of education is slowly evolving in the United States.

Suggested activities

1. Turn to the historical calendar in this chapter and study the sequence of significant educational events in the column captioned The Development of Federal Relations to Education.
2. Investigate the requirements for obtaining an overseas assignment in education—Fulbright, Smith-Mundt, etc.
3. Outline the report of a recent meeting of UNESCO. Evaluate the work of the organization.
4. Outline the ways in which the federal government encouraged schools in the early days.
5. Explain why the words "schools" and "education" were omitted from the Constitution.
6. Discuss the implications for education in the Tenth Amendment to the Constitution.
7. Prepare a brief history of the U.S. Office of Education.
8. Investigate the differences between the U.S. Office of Education and the national offices of education in other countries, particularly England, France, and Russia. (See I. L. Kandel, *The New Era in Education*, Houghton Mifflin Company, 1955, Chapter 6.)
9. List the duties of the United States Commissioner of Education.

10. Examine an *Annual Report of the United States Commissioner of Education.*
11. List those characteristics of the national program for education in the United States which you consider most noteworthy.
12. Discuss the types of aid granted to school districts by the federal government during and since World War II.
13. List the geographical areas, other than the 50 states, where the U.S. Office of Education assists in promoting education.
14. Describe the major features of the educational system in one of the United States dependencies.
15. Report on how the public schools in the District of Columbia are conducted.
16. Describe briefly six or eight United States Supreme Court decisions which have had major impact upon education in the United States.
17. Outline the activities of the federal government in vocational education.
18. Describe one of the newer federal activities in education of special interest to you.

Bibliography

Books

American Association of School Administrators: *Educational Administration in a Changing Community*, 37th Yearbook, National Education Association, Washington, D.C., 1959, chap. 5. Reviews the historical roots of our educational system and relates it to present-day needs.

Bereday, George Z. F., and Luigi Valicelli (eds.): *Public Education in America*, Harper & Brothers, New York, 1958, pp. 154–160. A study of the influence of the federal government upon education.

Butts, Freeman, and Lawrence A. Cremin: *A History of Education in American Culture*, Henry Holt and Company, Inc., New York, 1958, pp. 425–427, 580–584. History of the U.S. Office of Education and proposals for its future are presented along with discussion of the relation of the three branches of government to education.

Campbell, Roald F., John E. Corbally, and John A. Ramseyer: *Introduction to Educational Administration*, Allyn and Bacon, Inc., Boston, 1958, chap. 2. Presents the historical setting of education in the United States, the evolution of schools and their basic characteristics.

Counts, George S.: *Education and American Civilization*, Bureau of Publications, Teachers College, Columbia University, New York, 1952. An excellent treatment of our educational heritage, the forces that have shaped it, and the challenges that lie ahead.

Educational Policies Commission: *Public Education and the Future of America*, National Education Association, Washington, D.C., 1938, part IV. This venerable statement on the proper role and function of the federal government in education is still a classic.

Federal Legislative Policies, National Education Association, Washington, D.C., 1960. Annual summary of federal legislation affecting education.

Handbook—Office of Education, U.S. Office of Education, Washington, D.C., 1957. This handbook presents a good, concise description of the organization and operation of the U.S. Office of Education with a directory.

Hunt, Herold C., and Paul R. Pierce: *The Practice of School Administration*, Houghton Mifflin Company, Boston, 1958, chap. 17. Reviews the history of federal influence and participation in education—the U.S. Office of Education, federal grants, and federal programs in education.

It's Older than the Constitution, National Education Association, Washington, D.C., 1957. A good historical digest of federal grants for education.

Morphet, Edgar L., Roe L. Johns, and Theodore L. Reller: *Educational Administration: Concepts, Practices, and Issues*, Prentice-Hall, Inc., Englewood Cliffs, N.J., 1959, chap. 8.

Deals with federal relationships to education with special attention to the issues involved.

Wahlquist, John T., and Patrick J. Ryan: *An Introduction to American Education,* The Ronald Press Company, New York, 1958, chap. 7. Discusses the relationship of the federal government to education and the history of this development.

Periodicals

Anderson, H. R.: "Status for the U.S. Commissioner," *School Life,* vol. 64 (December, 1956), p. 390. Editorial approving career status for United States Commissioner and removal of the position from political influence.

Derthick, Lawrence G.: "The New Commissioner Looks at the Office of Education," *The School Executive,* vol. 76 (July, 1957), pp. 19–21. The Commissioner reviews the major services of the Office: research, administration of federal grants, and educational services.

Edwards, Newton: "Authority over Education Is Shifting toward the Federal Government," *The Nation's Schools,* vol. 58 (October, 1956), pp. 61–64. Argues that the welfare clause and Bill of Rights give the federal government extensive power over education which it is using increasingly.

"Farflung Educational Programs: I.C.A. Programs," *School Life,* vol. 38 (June, 1956), pp. 8–9. Map and article reveal extensive program of ICA through education and technical assistance throughout the world.

Land, William G.: "Federal Educational Policy," *Phi Delta Kappan,* vol. 40 (November, 1958), pp. 106–108. Warns that federal educational policy must be clarified for the general welfare or run the risk of "grab bag," special interest legislation.

Stoke, Harold W.: "National Necessity and Educational Policy," *Phi Delta Kappan,* vol. 40, (April, 1959), pp. 266–269. Argues that the nation is entering a period in which national necessity may work the most profound transformation in the relationship of the federal government to education.

chapter 2

State systems of education

The Tenth Amendment to the federal Constitution delegates to the states those powers, including education, which are neither reserved to the federal government nor denied to the states. Thus education has become a legal function of the states and 50 different state school systems have emerged. Although states delegate much of the operational responsibility for schools to local school districts, all states make constitutional and statutory provision for the organization and coordination of educational effort within the state.

The Constitution of Hawaii, for example, provides that:

The State shall provide for the establishment, support and control of a statewide system of public schools free from sectarian control, a state university, public libraries and such other educational institutions as may be deemed desirable, including physical facilities therefor. There shall be no segregation in public educational institutions because of race, religion or ancestry; nor shall public funds be appropriated for the support or benefit of any sectarian or private educational institution.

Consequently, the real locus of legal power over schools resides at the state level of government. The state legislature, which represents the people of the state, enacts broad policy through statutes. More specific policy and planning are developed by the state board of education, which serves the state school system in much the same way that the local board serves the local school district. In many states, additional state boards have been created to guide various phases of education.

The chief state school officer, usually known as the commissioner or superintendent of education, serves as the executive officer of the state board and as the leader of the state department of education. The state department serves as the staff of the chief state school officer, providing leadership for the state and rendering a wide variety of services to education.

Thus, through the legislature, the governor, the state board of education, the chief state school officer, and the state department of education, in cooperation with local lay people and professional educators, the state system of education is strengthened and developed.

Foundations

Education Primarily a State Function. Several states laid school foundations prior to the official beginning of the nation. Some states had permissive legislation authorizing free instruction only for children of the poor. The weak and crumbling foundations of schools free to paupers only were gradually replaced by a strong state system free to all. As indicated, the Tenth Amendment to the Constitution was ratified in 1791. The national legal cornerstone for state public education is firmly cemented in this amendment, which reads, "The powers not delegated to the United States by the constitution, nor prohibited by it to the states, are reserved to the states respectively, or to the people." By implication, therefore, education, one of the unmentioned powers thus reserved, is a state function. Judicial edicts in the form of numerous court decisions bear out this inference. It must be recalled that many states existed before the national government came into being and that, when the states formed a federated union, they surrendered but a portion of their sovereign rights to the central government.

More evidence that education is a function of the individual states is found in the provisions of the so-called GI bills, in which Congress specified that only the individual states can decide what schools, colleges, or employers are qualified to train veterans receiving money from the federal government.

Early and recent history, psychological slogans such as "state's rights," physical and human geography, political structure and practical prudence postulate that the states must serve as the solid, undergirding, nationwide foundation for American public education. Of course, the federal government may "promote the general welfare" and may contract with the states. It may, indeed, establish and support schools or offer contributions in aid of education; but its legal status [government] seems to be that of an outside party contracting with the state, for it may not levy on state property for the support of such schools, nor may it attempt to guide the state-approved administrative machinery. The federal government has, however, enforced certain stipulations regarding the use of the land which it gave to the states and has exercised control over vocational agriculture and home economics instruction through the granting of land and funds. These functions it has acquired gradually with the cooperation of the states. Collectively, the state systems form the firm foundation for free education in America.

Since education is a responsibility of the various commonwealths, its control is said to be decentralized. Obviously, the absence of a strong centralizing agency does not promote uniformity among the states, and certainly not within the states. Although the power to enact laws may be centered in the state government, the administration of such laws may be decentralized in that they are enforced by scores of county and local superintendents and boards of education. Dissimilarity, a striking characteristic of the state school systems, naturally produces marked inequalities.

Most states have general constitutional provisions for the establishing of schools. Some state constitutions contain very specific sections on education; usually, however, under a general mandate, the legislature, reinforced by the courts, determines the organization and administration of the schools.

Relation of Education to State Government. As indicated in Fig. 2-1, the legislature, which represents the people, enacts broad educational policy through statutes. The legislature is the most important and influential agency for educational policy making in the state. It establishes the general organization for educa-

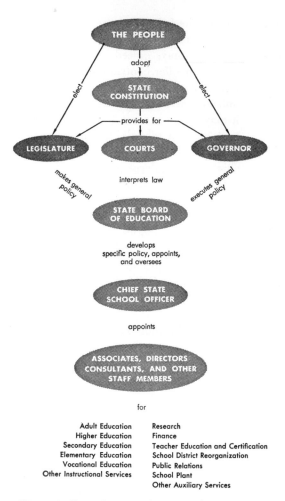

Fig. 2-1. *Organization of a typical state system of education.*

ing power to determine whether the authority shall be exercised by a state board of education, or distributed to county, township, or city organizations throughout the state." Thus the legislature is regarded as the ultimate source of authority over public education within the state.

The governor, who is elected by the people, has important powers over education. He has authority over the administration of the state budget, which finances the work of the department of education as well as the other agencies of government. He exercises influence over legislation. Many governors serve as ex officio members of state boards and commissions which develop educational policies and programs. In a few states the governor appoints the chief state school officer, and in the majority of states he appoints the members of the state board of education. Aside from his formal powers, the governor exercises considerable influence through his leadership of the body politic.

The state judiciary also exercises considerable influence over educational practice and policy. Courts are frequently called upon to protect the legal rights of individuals and organizations, to clarify the legal prerogatives of schools, and to interpret the law. Courts are not interested in the wisdom of educational practice. The proper safeguard against unwise educational policy is at the polls. However, relief from illegal or unconstitutional educational practice is properly sought through the courts. It is commonly accepted in America that the law is what the courts say it is. Thus judicial decisions have the effect of law until the law in controversy is changed by the legislature. Many important decisions by courts have altered the course of public education. Some of these decisions include affirmation of the right to establish high schools at public expense; the right of teachers to act in the place of parents in their relations with pupils; the protection of the teacher against dismissal without cause; and many others.

tion; determines the scope of education; establishes the means for the financial support for schools; appropriates money for state aid to education; charters institutions of higher learning; approves or denies plans to extend or alter the educational system in any major way. In a number of states, the legislature also appoints the members of the state board of education. As the Supreme Court of Indiana observed, "The authority over schools and school affairs . . . is a central power, residing in the legislature of the state. It is for the law-mak-

Role of State Education. From his long experience F. P. Graves, former New York Commissioner of Education, concluded that the state administrative agency should render the educational opportunities of the state more effective by holding the local communities up to a high standard of attainment and by encouraging them to rise above this level through new achievements. The better method for implementing these goals is stimulation rather than compulsion. The accent is on function rather than structure. As to the function of the state in education, the National Council of Chief State School Officers recommends that the state:

Coordinate all education within its borders

Determine the extent and quality of the foundation program

Establish minimum standards

Prepare a plan of financial support

Develop, evaluate, and adapt plans

Cooperate in a system of uniform records and reports

Provide consultative services

Administer programs made available by the federal government

Promote equality of educational opportunity for all

Utilize local, state, and national resources

Help plan, produce, and approve educational materials

In order that the state program may function, the work must be structured properly.

State Organization and Administration. No state has undertaken to administer and supervise public education directly through constitutional provisions or legislative action; instead, each one has delegated at least some of these responsibilities to state or institutional boards. Although a state board of education is general, the powers and duties of these boards differ markedly. One central agency or several boards may be in charge of public schools and other educational institutions, as explained later.

The usual pattern consists of (1) the state board of education, which is the policy-making body, (2) the state superintendent of public instruction, who is the chief executive of the board, and (3) the state department of education with its staff members, who carry out the policies of the board of education under the immediate direction of the superintendent. Together, these three forces are responsible for developing a state program of education. The relationships of these bodies are illustrated in Fig. 2-1.

State boards

In order to develop a broad program of education, the state had to create an agency through which it could act. Just as a local community has a board of education to determine policies to be carried out by its chief executive officer, as discussed in Chapter 4, so too the state has a central body to plan for education.

EVOLUTION OF STATE BOARDS OF EDUCATION

Of the beginnings of state boards of education, F. P. Graves wrote:

Looking first to the state school board, we find that the earliest foundation was that of the Board of Regents for New York in 1784. To this body was granted supervision over collegiate and academic education throughout the state, and the institutions incorporated under its control have ever since been jointly known as the University of the State of New York. There was no other state board organized until 1825, when North Carolina created a body known as the President and Directors of the Literary (or permanent school) Fund. Other boards were then started in various states for special purposes, but not until Massachusetts established its State Board of Education in 1837 were many powers and duties assigned to any of them.[1]

The bill for establishing this important board in Massachusetts was written by James G. Carter, a staunch friend of better schools, and

[1] F. P. Graves, *The Administration of American Education*, The Macmillan Company, New York, 1932, pp. 535–536.

was officially signed by Horace Mann, who was then president of the senate. The act called for a board of ten members, consisting of the governor and the lieutenant governor as ex officio members, and eight additional persons to be appointed by the governor with the consent of the council. Upon the official announcement of the membership of the board, Horace Mann, one of the appointees, who sensed its importance in Massachusetts and its potential influence throughout the land, wrote in his diary under the date of May 27, 1837:

This I believe to be like a spring, almost imperceptible, flowing from the highest table land, between oceans, which is destined to deepen and widen as it descends, diffusing fertility and beauty in its course; and nations shall dwell upon its banks. It is the first great movement toward an organized system of common education, which shall at once be thorough and universal. Every civilized state is as imperfectly organized, without a minister or secretary of instruction, as it would be without ministers or secretaries of State, Finance, War or the Navy.[2]

This board was empowered to appoint a secretary and to fix a reasonable salary, not to exceed $1000 a year. Although he did not

[2] Mary Peabody Mann, *Life of Horace Mann*, centennial edition, National Education Association, Washington, D.C., 1937, p. 72.

seek the office, Horace Mann was appointed the first secretary. On the day he communicated his acceptance, he wrote in his journal, "Henceforth so long as I hold this office I devote myself to the supremest welfare of mankind upon earth. An inconceivably great labor is undertaken. With the highest degree of prosperity, results will manifest themselves but slowly. The harvest is far from the seedtime."[3] From the perspective of a hundred and more years, it is easy to see that the pioneering efforts of the inspired and indefatigable Horace Mann as secretary of the state board in Massachusetts rightfully earned him the title "father of public school education." Other leaders, such as Henry Barnard, DeWitt Clinton, Thaddeus Stevens, Caleb Mills, and John Swett, also helped to develop American public education through their harmonious and productive relationships with state agencies.

Every commonwealth in the United States has one or more state boards, dealing with special aspects of education. For example, the federal government required some type of state board before it would grant aid for vocational education. Some states have special boards which deal with a limited area of education, such as a selected phase of higher education, the state teachers colleges.

[3] *Ibid.*, pp. 80–81.

School law is enacted by the legislature, often upon recommendation of the governor. Here the Governor of New York addresses a joint session of the state legislature.

The real power over education resides at the state level of government.

The state board of education, such as the New York Board of Regents, is the educational policy-making body at the state level.

The state board with some control and supervision of elementary and secondary school systems is organized in all the commonwealths except Illinois. Some of these states have had such a board for years, whereas a few are of very recent origin.

Just as the county and local school systems need a board of education, the state as a whole should maintain such a group. This board, as the chief educational authority, helps to develop policies and programs for the state department of education. The type of board determines in a measure the nature of its long-term and short-term planning.

SELECTION OF BOARDS OF EDUCATION

The major modes of determining membership on the state boards of education are by ex officio status, election, and appointment. The trend over the past fifty years has been away from ex officio boards. In a few states, board members are elected by the people. In most states, the governor appoints members to the state board of education. The Problems and Policies Committee and the Educational Policies Commission recommend "the appointment by the governor or election by popular vote of a state board of education of outstanding citizens of broad vision to replace the in-

State department of education personnel work with local teachers, school boards, and citizens throughout the state.

effective ex officio state boards which exist in some states." Election is recommended by the National Council of Chief State School Officers.

QUALIFICATIONS OF STATE BOARD MEMBERS

The question of professional qualifications of board members is a controversial one. There are those who insist that the board be com-

The New York State Supervisor of Citizenship Education plans curriculum materials for the schools.

A local board of education meets with a specialist in the Kansas Department of Education to discuss the problems of accreditation.

The finance division of the Kansas department disburses state school aid to local districts.

posed entirely of laymen. A few states require that some of the members be educators. Most states omit any specific reference to professional qualifications as a prerequisite to board membership.

A qualifying clause in a few states where members are appointed is that "different parts of the state shall be represented." In Wyoming "not more than four members of such board shall be from one political party." That state adds the important general qualifications, which should be applied everywhere, that the members "shall be appointed solely because of their character and fitness. All members of the board shall be persons of mature years, known for integrity, culture, public spirit, business ability, and interest in public education." The National Council of Chief State School Officers recommends that "the non-partisan lay state board be composed of 7 to 12 able citizens, broadly representative of the general public and unselfishly interested in public education." The legal qualifications for members of the state board of education take on significance only as public-spirited citizens demand the best.

DUTIES OF STATE BOARDS

A state may have many boards for specific purposes. In most instances, however, the major educational responsibilities are assigned to one central agency, which is usually the general state board of education. Originally its chief task was the distribution of state "literary" funds and kindred duties. Today this board is invested with greatly enlarged powers. including the general oversight of the entire state public school system. Like the school board in the local district, it is usually the policy-forming body, "determining state educational policies within the statutory framework provided by the legislature." Its major task in some states is the appointment of a state superintendent who serves as the chief executive officer of the board. Like city boards, it also makes appointments recommended by the superintendent and approves budgets prepared by him.

OTHER STATE EDUCATIONAL BOARDS

Many commonwealths assign to bodies other than the state board of education the various aspects of the educational program. Among the several hundred state educational boards are:

The textbook commission, which selects textbooks to be used in schools throughout the state

The board of trustees or regents, which manages the state university

The teachers college board, which presides over the affairs of the state teachers colleges

The board or boards of control, which have charge of one or more institutions of higher learning

The board for vocational rehabilitation, which collaborates with the federal board in reestablishing in industry persons injured or otherwise handicapped

The board for vocational education, which works with the federal government especially in promoting Smith-Hughes activities

The board of examiners, which prepares and conducts examinations for teachers seeking to be certified

The retirement or pension board, which collects the receipts and controls the distributions for teachers' pensions

The board of charities and corrections, which takes charge of and provides for the proper training of feeble-minded, deaf, blind, crippled, and other handicapped persons

In recent years one notes a tendency toward reducing the number of ancillary state boards and centralizing the control of educational affairs in the hands of a single state board of education, which has general supervision of all the schools. This may be supplemented by another board, which has charge of the institutions of higher learning in the state. One also detects a trend toward making the state superintendent the coordinator of all educational activities in the commonwealth.

State superintendents and commissioners

In several instances the president or secretary of the state board of education is the chief educational executive of the state. The evolution of this central office often antedated that of the state board of education.

EVOLUTION OF STATE SUPERINTENDENTS

Historically and professionally, instruction preceded administration. In the earliest schools there were only pupils and teachers—no administrators. Then slowly evolved the procession and profession of educational administration. The establishment of city superintendencies was preceded by the creation of a chief state official for education. New York in 1812 was the first to have a state school officer. The first commonwealth continuous office was established in Michigan in 1829. The Massachusetts State Board of Education, in engaging Horace Mann as its energetic secretary in 1837, exerted much favorable influence. Even before the Civil War, each employed a chief school officer, designated by various titles. In 1913 Delaware reestablished the office after abandoning it for a quarter of a century. Since then all states have had the office continuously.

The most common designation is "state superintendent of public instruction." The term "commissioner of education" is also widely used, especially in the Eastern States. A title in harmony with the concept of public *education* rather than mere *schooling* is that used by Louisiana, viz., "state superintendent of public education." In line with the trend toward cooperation among educational agencies—public, private, and parochial—the term "state superintendent (commissioner) of education" seems the best. The name, however, is not so significant as the manner in which the official is selected and his qualifications for the

all-important task of providing strong educational leadership in the state.

SELECTION OF CHIEF EDUCATIONAL OFFICER

Three practices in the selection of the chief state school official are popular election, appointment by the governor, and appointment by the state board of education.

It is unfortunate that in the majority of states the chief school officer is elected by popular vote. In a recent caucus, one political party selected its candidate for state superintendent on the basis of geography, since the political leaders wanted their candidates for the various offices to be distributed throughout the state. Many state superintendents have had to spend much time in office, particularly during the latter part of the term, building political fences for reelection. These superintendents are likely to have to think more about the next election than about the next generation. Fortunately, there is a sharp trend away from the election of chief state school officers. In a few states the chief state school officer is appointed by the governor. The preponderance of opinion is against this practice also.

In more than a third of the states the chief state school officer is appointed by the state board of education. The number of states employing this practice is increasing rapidly. This is the method recommended by the White House Conference on Education and generally favored by experts in education. It is considered desirable that the candidate for this important office be chosen by the small group of competent people most directly concerned with the position and directly related to the work of the state superintendent, namely the state board of education.

QUALIFICATIONS AND TERM OF OFFICE

The qualifications and term of office of the chief educational official, like those of other officeholders, are usually stipulated specifically in the laws, although in a few cases, where the board of education appoints the state superintendent, the board is given some latitude.

Qualifications. An example from the school laws of Maryland indicates the general tenor of the requirements for the state superintendent: "He shall be an experienced and competent educator; a graduate of a standard college, have not less than two years of specific academic and professional graduate preparation in a standard university, and not less than seven years' experience in teaching and administration." Most legal definitions of qualifications are general, and rightly so; however, they should be specific enough to provide a pattern by which the electors, or the group or person selecting the superintendent, may be guided in the quest for the most competent person. Usually a master's degree is the minimum academic preparation.

Term of Office, Tenure, and Salary. The median legal term of office for the superintendent or commissioner is between three and four years. The specified term may be as short as one year, and as long as six years, and in a few states tenure is indefinite in the sense that the incumbent serves as long as his work is satisfactory to the appointing agency. The length of time in office averages about five or six years, with a resultant high degree of turnover. This is due partly to the political manner in which the superintendent is elected or selected in some states and occasionally to the legal stipulation that an incumbent is ineligible to reelection after serving a few years. Tenure is longer when the superintendent is appointed by the state board than when he is elected or appointed gubernatorially. Sound educational administration suggests that the term of office be many years, subject to the best judgment of the state board, in order to ensure continuity in policy and staff personnel. Furthermore, the salary must be commensurate with the importance and labors of the office. Many cities pay their local superintendents more than the state gives its chief educational official.

Naturally this does not draw the best talent into the state office.

DUTIES OF STATE SUPERINTENDENTS

Most duties of the state superintendents fall into a few main categories: statistical—compiling data on the schools of the state; advisory and judicial—giving advice to school boards and county superintendents, and interpreting the laws; supervisory—promoting means for improving the schools and instruction; administrative—distributing state monies and certificating teachers; integrative—attending meetings of various state boards and coalescing the various educational elements in the state; and special—such as filling vacancies in county superintendencies.

SUPERINTENDENT'S RELATIONSHIPS
WITH OTHERS

A state superintendent may be talented, well educated, and industrious and yet not be a success in office because of his inability to work and get along with others. He needs to be able and willing to confer with officials from other states, to integrate the disparate efforts of the numerous educational workers within the state, and to cooperate with his subordinates.

Nationwide Relationships. No state can exist by itself economically, nor can it do so educationally. The state superintendent therefore seeks to learn from other departments of education and to pool his interests and achievements with others. To this end he affiliates himself with other state superintendents and commissioners in their national organization, the National Council of Chief State School Officers. Occasionally he and other officials may be called by the United States Commissioner of Education into conference on nationwide problems. The state superintendent's work is connected with the U.S. Office of Education, to which he sends statistics and other data and from which he receives federal grants for vocational education and other assistance.

State-wide Relationships. The state superintendent also has important working relationships within the state he serves. First of all comes his relationship to the state board of education. Usually the superintendent serves as secretary or president, or at least as an ex officio member. He may also belong to other state boards which have numerous educational and semieducational duties. Here, serving as a coordinator, he tries to integrate the work of all the boards. He comes into close contact with many other state officials in the health, highway, safety, buildings, legal, and other departments, and with the officers of the state education association.

County and Local Relationships. Naturally the state superintendent, in the hierarchic form of organization, can demand that certain duties be fulfilled by subordinates. In a sense the county superintendent of schools is a member of the state department, representing it in dealing with the local boards of his county. Many a state commissioner calls an annual conference of all county superintendents and local school directors to promote better relationships and to improve the schools. Naturally the state superintendent will have to depend largely on his headquarters staff to represent him in many of these vital relationships.

State departments

EVOLUTION OF STATE DEPARTMENTS

In the days when Gideon Hawley was the state superintendent of schools in New York, and Horace Mann the secretary of the state board of education in Massachusetts, each was the state department of education. But, as the concept of the state's function in education broadened, no single official, even in a small commonwealth, could handle all the work; gradually there was an increase in staff personnel. As late as 1890, however, the median number of staff members was only two. After 1917 came a rapid growth in department personnel owing to three major causes: the new duties devolving upon the department as a result of the passage of the Smith-Hughes vocational education law; the startling revelations from physical, mental, and literacy tests administered during World War I; and the growing appreciation of the need for a strong state program of education to meet present-day needs. Today every state provides its chief school officer with an organization and staff, usually known as the state department of education. This department is not to be confused with the state board of education. For example, Illinois has no state board of education, but has a department of education under the direction of the superintendent of public instruction. A state department can operate without a state board, but not vice versa.

ORGANIZATION OF STATE DEPARTMENTS

At the head of this department is the state superintendent or commissioner of education. Next in line are the assistant or associate superintendents or commissioners, other assistants, supervisors, and staff members.

Figure 2-1 portrays all the organization of a typical state system of education, showing the divisions of the state department and the relationships among the state department, superintendent, state board, governor, legislature, and courts.

The department of education is usually located in the state capital and housed in the capitol building. With the increasing complexity of their work and the numerous additions to their staff, most departments are cramped in small quarters designed many years ago. In large states a separate building houses the state superintendent, his assistants, and other members of the staff. New York State was the first to have a state superintendent of schools—Gideon Hawley—and was also the first to erect a building for education. "Central schoolhouses," such as those in Sacramento, Harrisburg, and Albany, are needed in other states.

Function of the State Staff. The staff members of the department of education are not mere machine operators; they are educational servants. Their functions may be classified under three major headings: regulatory, operational, and leadership. In order to perform these duties, state departments have generalists and specialists.

Personnel and Activities. The staff of the state department may be divided into two main types according to professional training: professional, such as school visitors; and nonprofessional, such as clerks and stenographers. These groups are usually assigned specific tasks in terms of qualifications and experience.

The personnel of the department should be employed by the state board of education upon nomination by the chief state school officer. All appointments should be made on the basis of merit and fitness for the work. The state department should be adequately staffed to provide all needed services.

Each year the U.S. Office of Education, through the Superintendent of Documents, publishes a list of all the principal state school officers. More than one hundred different services are reflected in their official designation.

In all areas of service the three main functions of state departments are implemented with appropriate activities:

Regulatory. This broad function involves three types of activities: development of standards, rules, and regulation; examination and inspection to determine compliance; and instigation, where necessary, of compliance procedures.

Operational. Among the direct operational activities of these departments in some states are the supervision of teachers colleges, trade schools, schools for the handicapped, adult education classes, and other miscellaneous programs.

Leadership. Creative leadership, the key to the door of the state department, stimulates long-range planning and professional leadership, highly competent consultative and advisory services, leadership in research, coordination of the educational programs of the state, and maintenance of vigorous public relations for the state educational program.[4]

Many groups, including the Hoover Commission on Organization of the Executive Branch of the Government, have favored special grants for the administration of state departments of education. Unless the state departments are given more financial assistance than they have received in the past, they cannot do their part in developing broad programs.

State programs

Chapters 3 and 4 emphasize the important role played by the educational subdivisions within the state. However, in a hierarchic form of organization, authority flows from the head or source. Upon the individual state, therefore, rests the grave responsibility of developing a program of instruction for all its people. Supreme Court decisions reinforce constitutional and legislative provisions for establishing state programs of education.

Each commonwealth is faced with the direct responsibility of organizing and promoting a functional state-wide system of public education which should extend from kindergarten through college and adult life. In the development of this program, certain principles or procedures ought to be adopted as a tentative guide. In line with these principles, under the direction of the state department, all the people and agencies of the state participate in developing the plans.

ELEMENTS IN STATE-WIDE PROGRAMS

Many basic ingredients make up a state program of education. A few of these are presented here with illustrative material.

[4] American Association of School Administrators, *The American School Superintendency*, National Education Association, Washington, D.C., 1952, pp. 341–342.

Development of Educational Goals. Many leaders have relied too heavily upon educational machinery and have not given sufficient thought to educational policies. These policies or philosophies should underlie all education. Several states have worked out basic goals.

Construction of a Foundation Program. The translation of the educational goals into daily practice necessitates a state foundation program. Such a plan, often known as the state's minimum program, consists of a careful formulation of minimal essentials for local communities, and a raising of such requirements from time to time as resources and conditions permit.

The Council of State Governments listed the following six essentials for the sound administration and operation of state school systems:

1. Provision for systematically obtaining and studying the facts as a basis for policy decisions.

2. A state policy-making agency for education through which the will of the people may be voiced and the interests of the state protected.

3. Local administrative units of sufficient size to promote effective local control and to provide appropriate educational opportunities at a reasonable cost.

4. Provisions calculated to assure high-quality professional leadership for both state and local agencies.

5. Conditions conducive to maintaining well-qualified staffs of teachers for all phases of elementary and secondary education.

6. A system of financing that will provide sufficient funds and distribute them in such a way as to assure adequate educational opportunities for all and to encourage both sound administration and a high degree of local initiative.[5]

Several states have fallen short in nearly all

[5] *The Forty-eight State School Systems*, Council of State Governments, Washington, D.C., 1947, pp. 7 and 8.

these essentials, and all states are weak in at least one. Items 3 and 5 are often Achilles' heels.

Reorganization of Local Administration. The effective working of a foundation program often calls for the reorganization of administrative areas, as indicated in Chapter 3. Helpful principles and procedures are found in the report of the National Commission on School District Reorganization.

State Financial Support. A problem basic to both the realignment of administrative units and the development of a stable, state-wide program of education is that of financial support, considered in detail in Chapter 16. An appraisal of state-aid systems reveals that not a single state had attained a desirable status with respect to the financing of public education. Nowhere, however, is the entire burden of school support left to the local school districts; the relative amount of the total cost borne by the state treasury varies from less than 6 to over 90 per cent. Delaware adopted in 1921 the policy of paying for the entire state-approved cost of all public schools. The general plan of paying for the foundation program with funds derived from state-wide sources was followed by North Carolina (1931), West Virginia (1933), and numerous other states.

A marked trend in the financing of education in recent years has been the establishment of a fund for equalizing the educational opportunities and burden within the state. These funds, discussed in Chapter 16, are based on the important principle of collecting the school money where it is and distributing it where the pupils are. The establishing of an equalization fund which is scientifically sound and administratively feasible demands a searching survey of the educational needs, a careful estimate of the costs, and an accurate analysis of the ability of the state to support education and other activities.

Many revised educational programs have originated in a state survey which calls specific attention to the basic need for complete reorganization of the archaic district systems as the initial step toward developing better schools. Helpful check lists and handbooks for a self-survey plan for school systems have been prepared. All phases of state-wide education should be subjected to close analysis in order to determine both the *status in quo* and the distance to be traveled in order to reach minimum standards. The state department of education may well help schoolmen and laymen to conduct resurveys and develop continuous self-surveys. The governors of the various commonwealths, assembled in the Council of State Governments, agreed that "education of the youth of the land is one of the fundamental duties of government, and . . . the provision of adequate and efficient machinery for that purpose is one of the principal costs of government." It therefore launched a series of studies of education—the first ever to be conducted by an agency of all the states in the Union. Utilization of the survey data and recommendations is important. Most reports, prepared by dint of much effort and expense, collect annual layers of dust upon obscure shelves. Occasionally the results are interpreted in public meetings and discussions throughout the state. The acid test of a satisfactory survey is its implementation through an improved program of education for all.

COOPERATIVE, STATE-WIDE, LONG-TERM PLANNING

In developing these programs, many agencies other than the state school officials exercise a tremendous power. The educational associations through their committees, the presidents of institutions of higher learning, the county superintendents, the association of school board members, the parent-teacher association, the women's and businessmen's groups—these

and many others help to prepare the way. For example, many agencies interested in public education are represented in the Florida Citizens Committee on Education and the Mississippi Citizens Council on Education.

Unfortunately, there is a large amount of duplication and lost motion in an eccentric program. More scientific and concentric methods are needed if state systems are to be rescued from the doldrums of short-lived planning. All states must have a long-term planning commission to plot the course for education and other social services for years to come. Several states, beginning with Kansas in 1933, have established a legislative commission that drafts model laws and recommends changes to the legislatures. Education laws in the various states should have a greater degree of uniformity.

A state program for the continuous development of education, like any worth-while reform, calls for four basic steps: education, agitation, legislation, and dedication. Education of school people and laymen as to the need for progress requires months and years devoted to local, state-wide, and national programs of study and analysis. Agitation for change should not precede educating the public and the legislature but should either follow or accompany it. Legislation is not the final goal, for it does not guarantee successful educational results. Dedication to the perennial problems of school improvement will pave the way for state-wide and national progress in education. The extent to which the state should assume control over education, at the expense of federal and local government, is still subject to disagreement and to wide variation in practice. This issue and others relative to the role of the state are discussed in Chapter 17.

Summary

The Tenth Amendment to the federal Constitution delegates the function of education to the states. Although local districts assume much of the operational responsibility for schools, education is a legal function of the 50 states.

In general, the state constitution sets the general legal framework for education; state courts maintain the constitutionality and legality of educational practice; the legislature enacts broad educational policy; the state board of education establishes specific policy and regulations; the state department, under the leadership of the state superintendent or commissioner, administers the state program of education.

In a few states the state board members hold ex officio status, in some they are elected by the people, but in most states they are appointed by the governor. The chief state school officer serves as executive officer of the board and as the leader of the department of education. In most states the chief state school officer is elected by the people. In some states he is appointed by the board of education, which is regarded as preferred practice. The major functions of the department of education are classified as regulatory, operational, and leadership. These departments vary widely in their size, scope, function, and influence.

Suggested activities

1. Review the historical development of education in your state.
2. Discuss the implications for education in the Tenth Amendment to the United States Constitution.
3. Prepare an interesting biography of Horace Mann, the first secretary of the Massachusetts State Board of Education. Similar reports may be made about Henry Barnard, Thaddeus Stevens, Caleb Mills, John Swett, and John D. Pierce.
4. Report on the lives and works of persons who helped develop education in your state.
5. Investigate and report on some important court cases that have affected educational practice in your state.
6. Draw an organization diagram of your state, showing the educational boards and the relationships that exist between them.
7. Find out the following in regard to your state superintendent of education: term of office, qualifications, salary, and duties.
8. Examine the last annual report of your state superintendent of public instruction.
9. Discuss the desirability of state adoption of textbooks for all schools.
10. Define what is meant by a foundation or minimum program for a state.

Bibliography

Books

Beach, Fred F., and Robert F. Will: *The State and Education*, U.S. Office of Education, Government Printing Office, Washington, D.C., 1955. Exhaustive description of the organization and operation of state systems of education with basic data about each state.

Cremin, Lawrence A. (ed.): *The Republic and the School: Horace Mann and the Education of Free Men*, Bureau of Publications, Teachers College, Columbia University, New York, 1957. Excerpts from Horace Mann's *Annual Reports* with emphasis upon their relevance to today's educational problems.

Eastmond, Jefferson N.: *The Teacher and School Administration*, Houghton Mifflin Company, Boston, 1959, chap. 5. Describes organization for education at the state level of government.

Educational Policies Commission: *The Structure and Administration of Education in Ameri-*

can Democracy, National Education Association, Washington, D.C., 1938, part 3. This classic statement presents generally accepted principles concerning the proper role, organization, and operation of the state and its educational agencies.

Edwards, Newton: *The Courts and the Public Schools*, University of Chicago Press, Chicago, 1955, chap. 1. Describes the legal relationship of the state and education, citing important judicial decisions.

Hunt, Herold C., and Paul R. Pierce: *The Practice of School Administration*, Houghton Mifflin Company, Boston, 1958, chap. 16. Describes the functions of state boards, chief state school officers, and state departments in the general control of education.

Thurston, Lee M., and William H. Roe: *State School Administration*, Harper & Brothers, New York, 1957. An exhaustive treatment of the organization, functions, and trends of state educational agencies and the relationship of the state to education.

Periodicals

Crewson, Walter: "State Department Assumes Its New Leadership Role," *The School Executive*, vol. 78 (November, 1958), pp. 23–25. A description of the expanding responsibilities and activities of the New York State Department of Education.

Frederick, W. L.: "Education As a Responsibility of the State," *Educational Record*, vol. 39 (July, 1958), pp. 261–268. An analysis of the state's responsibility for education and the challenges that lie ahead.

Fuller, Edgar: "You and Your State Department of Education," *NEA Journal*, vol. 45 (March, 1956), pp. 165–166. Urges the importance of understanding and support of the work of state departments by members of the profession.

"Hawaii—Education in Our 50th State," *The School Executive*, vol. 78 (July, 1959), p. 33. Describes briefly the organization and administration of education in Hawaii.

Holden, A. John, and Edgar Fuller: "Your State Backs Your School," *NEA Journal*, vol. 47 (December, 1958), pp. 645–646. Describes the problems of state departments: turnover of personnel, low salaries, heavy load, expanding duties, and the importance of retaining local initiative.

Morphet, Edgar I.: "Improving State Programs of School Support," *Phi Delta Kappan*, vol. 40 (March, 1959), pp. 243–246. Suggests procedures for appraising state educational programs and describes characteristics of a satisfactory minimum undertaking.

National Education Association: "State and Education: Ability, Burden, Effort, and Achievement," *Research Bulletin*, vol. 36 (February, 1958), pp. 24–29. Statistics showing the differences among the states in their ability and efforts to support education financially.

Planck, Carolyn H.: "Schools in Our 49th State," *NEA Journal*, vol. 47 (December, 1958), pp. 600–602. An interesting description of education in Alaska—its special problems and unique characteristics.

chapter 3

County
and intermediate
school units

Orientation

A commission of the American Association of School Administrators studying school organization in 1958 concluded that "the real trouble is outmoded school district organization—school district organization that is now called upon to provide services, to perform functions, and to operate programs that were scarcely dreamed of when it was established." The same study pointed out that—

More than three out of four districts employ 10 teachers or less.

More than half of the districts in the country operate elementary schools only.

There are thousands of districts that operate no schools at all.

Thus one of the pressing problems of American education is in the reorganization of small, inadequate school units into larger units capable of providing adequate educational opportunity for all children and youth. Considerable progress has been made in the reorganization of districts but much remains to be done.

In most states, local school units are organized around districts, towns or townships, cities, or counties. In many states, the county serves as an intermediate unit between the local district and the state. The organization and operation of the county unit varies widely among the states.

Foundations

As towns and villages in early America grew, the one-room school gave way to multiroom buildings. In larger communities, multibuilding school systems became common. In rural areas, however, the one-room school continued in isolated communities. But as automobiles and paved highways reduced the isolation of rural areas, the inefficiency of the one-teacher school district became increasingly evident. To provide better education for rural youth, township and county units of government organized educational programs for the children within their boundaries. As the frontier was pushed back, most of the states west of the Mississippi organized into districts for school purposes. In most states, county school units were organized to serve as an intermediate unit between the local and state units. Thus many different kinds of school units emerged among the states.

Types of districts

Figure 3-1 portrays the different types of school district organization among the 50 states.

State Districts. Delaware typifies the state-centered type of educational organization where, except for the cities of Wilmington and Dover, operational responsibility for schools is centered largely in the state. In all other states, a large measure of responsibility for the operation of schools is delegated to many operating units within the state.

County Units. Utah, Nevada, New Mexico, and the Southeastern states, except Mississippi and South Carolina, are organized on the county unit plan. Although the county is the unit for some of the school administrative functions in most states, it is the actual operating unit in the above states. In these states, schools are under the control of elected county boards of

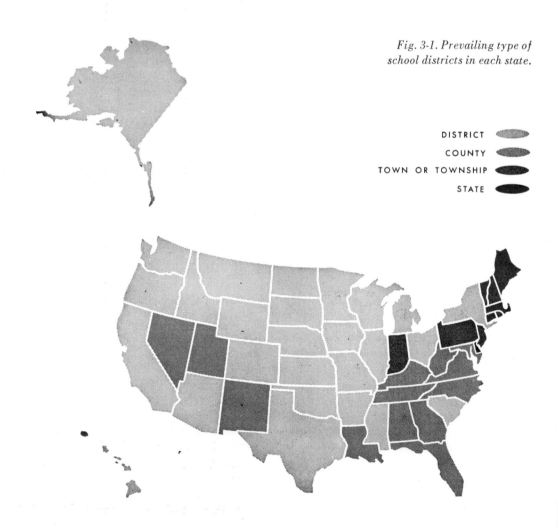

Fig. 3-1. Prevailing type of school districts in each state.

DISTRICT

COUNTY

TOWN OR TOWNSHIP

STATE

education. School revenue is gathered largely through county taxes. Schools are administered by the county superintendent of schools, who is appointed by the county board in some states and elected by popular vote in others. In county units of organization, the county superintendent's functions are similar to those of a local superintendent. Where a city is included in the county, a separate district including the city is often organized apart from the county which may surround it.

Town and Township Units. The New England states, Pennsylvania, New Jersey, and Indiana are organized for education on a town and township basis.

In most states, the original survey divided the county into towns and townships which became the basis for school organization. Under the township system, many cities, incorporated villages, and towns, and some consolidated schools are set apart as independent school districts. In some states, such as Illinois, high schools are organized on a township basis but with smaller districts within the township operating their own elementary schools.

The New England town, which usually comprises a cohesive combination of urban and rural territory, is a natural geographic center and a much more logical school unit than the townships of most states, which took their form from early surveys, Indian trails, or cow paths, in many instances. In New Jersey, Pennsylvania, and Indiana, town or borough school districts exist within township units. Town and township units are controlled by popularly elected local boards of education and administered by superintendents or supervising principals appointed by the board. In town and township districts, much of the school revenue is derived from local taxes. Many town and township districts are too small to operate efficient school programs.

District Unit. In most Western states and in Michigan, Ohio, Mississippi, South Carolina,

and New York, the district is the local school unit. The majority of these districts are smaller than the other types of units described previously. Many districts, particularly in the Midwest and West, operate one-teacher schools. Many operate no schools at all, sending their students to other school systems. In most instances, these districts were established by early surveys and have little relationship to natural community boundaries or to logical school organization.

This type of organization is therefore considered least efficient. Districts are controlled by elected boards of education. Larger districts are administered by superintendents or supervising principals appointed by the board. However, many districts are too small to justify the employment of an administrator.

District and State. Alaska presents an unusual combination of district and state organization for education. Because of the absence of intermediate taxing units such as counties and townships, all schools, except for the organized districts, are administered directly by the state. The organized districts, which are found in the more populous areas, operate under local control very much the same as districts in other states.

City Unit. In all states, large cities operate their own school systems independently of the county, township, or district in which they lie. In cities it is not uncommon for school board members to be appointed by the mayor or city council rather than elected by the people.

Regional Districts. In New Jersey, New York, Illinois, and California particularly, a number of local units combine to form a regional high school unit, while operating their elementary school units independently. A common disadvantage of the regional high school district is the lack of articulation between elementary and secondary schools.

County and intermediate units

School organization in America developed first at the local level. But as state systems of education began to emerge, the need for an intermediate unit between the state and local level became apparent. In most states the county superintendent's office fulfills this function. The previous discussion of the county unit was with reference to those states where the county unit was also the local operating unit. This discussion relates to the county office in states having local school units.

The county office had its beginnings as an arm of the state. At first, this office fulfilled largely clerical and statistical functions. At present, the character of the county office is in process of change. In most states the county unit is controlled by a county board of education, elected by the people or by the local boards of education within the county. The unit is administered by a county superintendent who is elected by the people in most states and appointed by the board in others. This position is now regarded as a professional position. However, short terms of office, low salaries, and the rigors of campaigning for the job—conditions that prevail in many states—detract from the attractiveness of the position. The county superintendent serves as the executive officer for small towns, townships, or districts within the county too small to employ a full-time administrator. The superintendent renders service also to the larger school units in the county. This service is typically of an advisory nature. Most county superintendents lack sufficient clerical help and professional assistance.

There is a growing tendency toward regarding the intermediate unit as an entity not necessarily coterminous with the county. Highly populated counties, for example, might include several intermediate units. Sparsely populated counties might be combined to form one intermediate unit. A study of the intermediate unit in Pennsylvania, for example, recommended that the 67 county school units in the state be reorganized to form about half as many intermediate units. Consequently, the terms "county unit" and "intermediate unit" are not exactly synonymous. But in reality, the county unit is the intermediate unit in most states and will probably remain so for many years because of the long tradition.

The National Commission on School District Reorganization has defined the intermediate unit as "an area comprising the territory of two or more basic administrative units and having a board, or officer, or both responsible for performing stipulated services for the basic administrative units or for supervising their fiscal, administrative, or educational functions. . . . The distinguishing feature of the intermediate unit is that its officer or board exercises only supervisory or service functions in relationship to the basic units."[1]

A study of the intermediate unit in New York State concluded that it should serve five major functions: adaptation, general supervision, coordination, special cooperative services, and administrative procedures. The adaptation function is aimed toward helping school districts grow and improve through such activities as conferences and workshops. General supervision includes advisement and consultation with local boards, administrators, teachers, and lay citizens. This consultation may deal with the interpretation of school law or state regulations, advice on school financing or school building, sharing of new educational practices, or a host of other ideas. The coordination function has to do with strengthening interrelationships among the local units. It may mean the development of standard testing programs or student records; the development of common policy for interscholastic sports and other activities that involve many local units within the county. In many states the intermediate unit coordinates plans for the reorganization or consolidation of local school units. The provision of special cooperative

[1] National Commission on School District Reorganization, *Your School District*, National Education Association, Washington, D.C., 1948, p. 52.

services is an effort to provide cooperatively certain special services that could not be provided by individual local units working alone. Many counties provide county film libraries, bookmobiles, curriculum materials centers, and other services that could not be provided by small local units individually. Many intermediate units employ psychologists, nurses, dental hygienists, special education teachers, circuit teachers, and other specialized personnel shared by small local districts that could not support these services otherwise. Finally, certain administrative procedures lend themselves well to the intermediate unit, particularly in rural areas. The purchase of school supplies, the operation of school transportation systems, and the provision of special education for handicapped students are examples of procedures sometimes administered directly by the intermediate unit.

In general, then, the intermediate unit finds its best role in *coordination and service* rather than *control over* local districts. Thus the intermediate unit makes it possible for students in rural areas to enjoy certain advantages that would ordinarily be denied to students in small school systems. Despite the trend toward urbanization and the increased efficiency of transportation and communication, it is inevitable that a sizable proportion of school children will continue to live in sparsely settled areas where small schools predominate. The County and Rural Area Superintendents Association, a department of the National Education Association, offers leadership and stimulation to intermediate units in their service to rural school systems.

Reorganization of Districts

At the close of World War II there were about 103,000 school districts in the United States. Through the reorganization of local units, this number has been reduced through the past decade and a half to about 45,000. This progress has been almost phenomenal. Nevertheless, there is room for much additional progress. About one district in five is too small to operate any schools of its own. Over half of the districts in the nation operate no high school program. A great many school districts are still much too small to provide even the most basic educational opportunity for their children.

The Advantages of Reorganization. The reorganization—or consolidation or "redistricting," as it is sometimes termed—of school districts into larger administrative units usually results in a number of advantages. The larger enrollment included in the reorganized district makes possible the extension and enrichment of the educational program through advanced courses, accelerated programs, remedial work, and in many other ways. New courses of study and richer educational experiences can be provided. More specialized personnel, such as librarians, guidance personnel, vocational teachers, administrators, and others, become feasible. More specialized school facilities, such as laboratories, shops, health rooms, and libraries, can be provided. Large districts are better able to provide their own high schools, junior colleges, and adult education programs. Thus, the reorganization of local school units results usually in a richer program of education and in greater equalization of educational opportunity and financial burden.

Thus far, reorganization has been considered in terms of the consolidation of small rural school districts. However, a new problem in school district reorganization—the suburb—has exploded upon the educational scene since the war. Over the past half century there has been a strong trend from rural to urban living. More recently this trend has been from rural and urban to suburban centers. School enrollments in some suburbs have increased fantastically. Levittown, New York, grew from 47 pupils to over 20,000 in a decade. One Long Island school district titled one of its annual reports, *The Year We Opened Six Schools.*

This suburban development results in the

*One of the urgent problems of
American education is the
reorganization of small, inadequate
school units into larger
school systems capable of providing
adequate educational opportunity
for all youth.*

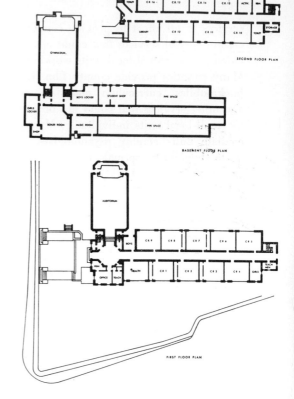

*Several years ago, the voters of Bedford Hills,
New Castle, North Castle, and Pound Ridge
in New York's Westchester County decided
to merge their school districts into one.
What has consolidation meant to school and
community in Bedford Central School District No.
2, as the new school system is now known?
Comparison of floor and site plans between the old
and new illustrates clearly
the improved educational program made possible
by the new facilities.*

urbanization of areas that were formerly rural
or semirural. Frequently this happens with
explosive speed and force. This growth pays
little attention to school district lines. New
population centers swallow up old villages and
towns and merge into a large amorphous mass
overreaching many little school districts that
now have no natural cohesion. Large housing
developments often deluge suburban districts
with big new enrollments without comparable
increases in taxable wealth. Thus the children
may be located in one district and the industrial sources of wealth in another. In many
suburbs, schools just cannot be built fast
enough. Church basements, fire halls, and
other makeshift quarters are pressed into service as schools. Frequently schools must be
operated on double and even triple sessions.

Thus reorganization of suburban school districts is badly needed but often most difficult.
Reorganization legislation has usually been
designed for sparsely populated, stable rural
areas rather than for heavily populated, rapidly changing suburban districts. With their
rapidly growing populations and lack of social

*Previously this two-story building housed
kindergarten through high school in Bedford
Hills. Increased enrollments forced the use
of the basement as a classroom. Since the transfer
of the high school to the new building,
this and other local schools in the four towns
have been remodeled into modern elementary
schools relieving crowded conditions
while keeping elementary schools close
to the people in each town.*

and economic cohesion, suburban school districts find concerted action toward consolidation difficult. The rural structure of municipal
government and school organization and operation often exists long after it has become
obsolete. Thus the special problems of suburban schools in district reorganization have
not yet been solved satisfactorily in many
metropolitan areas.

The Disadvantages of Reorganization. However, the reorganization of local school units
may create new problems. If the close relation-

The new Fox Lane High School now provides
expanded and better facilities for
a real junior-senior high school program.

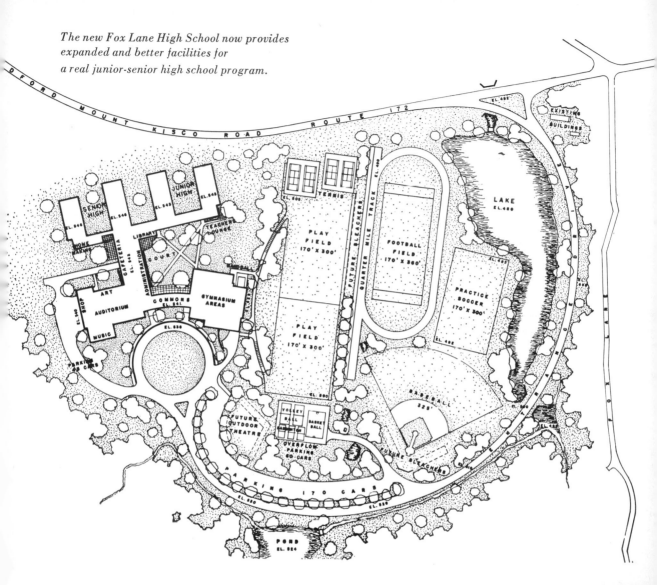

Many special spaces, like this commons room,
have been provided in the new high school to satisfy
educational, recreational, and cultural needs.
Other units include a large library,
dining facilities, well-equipped science, music,
and special service areas.

However, it is now necessary to transport many
youngsters to this new building, which
is widely used by the communities as well.

53

ship of the schools to the natural community and to the people is sacrificed in the name of efficiency, then something that money cannot buy will be destroyed. Structural remodeling will not perform miracles. Educators and laymen sometimes cherish false hopes as to what it will accomplish. Although the immediate danger is remote, the creation of larger school units may be carried so far that centralization produces more evils than does decentralization.

The Criteria of an Adequate School District. In general, it can be said that an adequate school district should satisfy three basic criteria. First, it should be large enough to be able to provide adequate basic educational opportunity at reasonable cost. Estimates of adequate size vary, but it is clear that, except in very sparsely populated areas, an enrollment of 1,600 pupils in grades 1 to 12 should be regarded as minimum. One recent study stressed that a school district ought to be large enough to have 100 students in its senior class. Second, a school district should be large enough to include sufficient wealth. Although small districts are not necessarily poor, nor large districts wealthy, the per-pupil wealth tends to increase as the size of the district increases. Again, there is no universal agreement on what level of wealth is adequate. One common rule of thumb suggests that there should be about $25,000 of true valuation per child of school age. A reasonable tax would yield from this base sufficient money for a fairly adequate program. Obviously, the amount of state aid would influence this consideration. Third, a school district should include a natural geographic area. Ideally, a school district boundary should include those people who are held together by common ties and interests—economically, socially, culturally. School districts should encompass rather than bisect natural communities.

Methods of Reorganization. Reorganization of school districts is usually accomplished through one of three patterns: through legis-lative decree, through local initiative, or permissively through planned programs. Some states, such as Nevada, have abolished all local school districts and reorganized them into county units by legislative decree. Some state legislatures have decreed that all districts beneath a certain size must be reorganized into larger units. Most states have attempted to accomplish reorganization through laws prescribing the procedures by which local citizens or officials might reorganize local districts through their own initiative. This may be done through consolidation, annexation, or transfer of territory. In this procedure, proposals for reorganization are initiated locally, sometimes presented to the voters on referendum.

Many state legislatures are reluctant to compel reorganization but disinclined to endure the slow progress that is made under local initiative. Thus an increasing number of state legislatures are enacting laws that will stimulate reorganization where needed but also retain some permissive features. Such plans often provide for the development of a state-wide plan for reorganization based upon studies of local needs and conditions. Counties or other subdivisions conduct studies of redistricting needs and develop proposals that are submitted to local electorates or to local boards of education for approval. The state department of education usually provides policy and procedures and provides stimulation and leadership. In many states, encouragement is generated through state-aid programs that provide financial advantages to reorganized districts. The third procedure is a more recent development than the other two and is increasing in frequency.

Transportation of Pupils. In a consideration of consolidation and the state minimum program of education for all children, one cannot ignore the important factor of the availability of education. The democratic principle of equal educational opportunity demands the daily transportation of pupils to school. Some states have dormitories for secondary school students. At present many rural youths are denied high school education because they cannot reach the school.

The transporting of children is not a new educational undertaking. Beginning in a Massachusetts district in 1840, it continued without legal authorization until 1869 when Massachusetts passed the nation's first permissive transportation law for the conveyance of pupils to and from public schools. By 1920 pupils were being carried to and from school in all the states, with or without specific legal sanction. Today the provision of transportation facilities for school children is generally mandatory under certain conditions. It is estimated that one-third of all public school pupils ride to and from school each day. Although school buses are the usual means of conveyance, the "old gray mare" and the railroads still serve in some communities, especially during the winter months. The problem of transportation is not of equal importance in all the states, and within states wide variations exist in the proportion of pupils carried by bus. Great differences also exist in safety measures. The National Conference on School Transportation has prepared a code of standards for the selection and training of school bus drivers.

The transportation of pupils is more than a local problem. Many state treasuries provide financial assistance in defraying the cost of pupil travel as a means toward equalizing educational opportunity and burden. Several state departments lend technical assistance in the mapping of school bus routes. Because of the close relationship between the transportation of pupils and the consolidation of districts, each state should make continuous analyses of both matters.

Coordination of Administrative Units. "Coordination" is a general term that covers the integrating activities of legal or extralegal groups, such as a state department or accrediting association, in bringing together small components. These efforts require not only voluntary cooperation and legal consolidation of schools but also a higher authority to appraise existing practices, recommend minimal standards, and integrate the disparate units. Despite practical obstacles, the work of coordinating the various school administrative units within and between states must progress. Upon this task the well-wishers of education everywhere, and especially the state and national authorities, must focus their attention. The maintenance of the individuality of a local school district is important, but even more vital is uniformity in the minimal essentials of sound school organization and administration. This topic is also considered in Chapter 2.

A program for the reorganization of school units should contain immediate and long-term plans involving three basic elements: (1) the educational plan, which contains a general statement of the philosophy involved and also definite educational specifications for the reorganized units; (2) the spending plan, which involves translating the educational criteria into proposed expenditures; and (3) the financing plan, which proposes means for meeting the cost of the educational program. The last two aspects are treated in Chapter 16. The emphasis here is on the educational program.

Educational Emphasis in Reorganization. The educational plan should form the basis for the whole program of realignment. A monetary definition has the advantage of objectiveness, but it fails to define the component elements of the educational program sufficiently for the purposes of constructing an administrative unit. In other words, the content as well as the cost of the educational program must be accurately ascertained. For example, larger districts attract better-educated teachers and have more kindergartens. The locality in which the child receives his education cannot be ignored in the reforms in school organization and administration.

Future

As the population of the nation increases and becomes still more urbanized, the number and size of city school districts will increase. The wide variety of other types of districts will continue. However, continued reorganization of school units will further reduce the number of small, marginal local units. More and more states will accelerate reorganization permissively through planned programs that offer financial incentives to reorganized districts.

However, it is apparent also that a large part of the nation will remain rural in character for the foreseeable future. If rural people are to enjoy educational opportunity of quality and scope equivalent to that in urban areas, the intermediate school unit will have to be developed more fully and more widely. It is in the intermediate unit that the greatest change may take place in the years ahead. Prototypes of effective intermediate units are already discernible, particularly in New York and California.

Considerable variations will continue to exist in the relationship among federal, state, intermediate, and local units. The federation concept, by which educational functions are assigned to federal, state, intermediate, or local levels, according to where they are performed best, appears to be emerging. In any event, it is clear that a large measure of responsibility for the operation of schools will continue to reside in the local school district described in Chapter 4.

Summary

Since education is a function of the state, organization of educational units varies widely among the states. With some exceptions, most New England school units are organized by towns and townships, most Southeastern states by counties, and most Western states by districts. Cities usually maintain their own school systems apart from the county, township, or district in which they lie. School units are controlled by elected boards of education except in those cities in which boards are appointed.

In most states, an intermediate unit serves a liaison role between the state and local level. This intermediate unit is the county in most states. Ideally, however, it might include several counties or only a part of a county. The function of the intermediate unit should be one of coordination and service rather than control. The intermediate unit is currently undergoing considerable change.

In the decades since the war, the number of local school districts has been reduced by half through reorganization of districts. Since many present districts are too small to provide a basic educational program at reasonable cost, considerable reorganization remains to be accomplished.

Reorganization tends to enrich and extend the educational program, but may reduce the close relationship between school and community. Ideally, school districts should be sufficiently large to contain enough students and wealth to provide a basic educational program at reasonable cost. School districts should also be congruent with natural communities. The most promising procedure in redistricting results from local adoption of reorganization patterns developed on a state-wide basis. The reorganization of school districts has increased greatly the number of school children transported to school. The school bus has become an important vehicle in providing the rural child with more adequate public schooling.

Suggested activities

1. Review the historical evolution of county education.
2. What is meant by an intermediate unit in school administration?

3. Examine in the school laws of your state the legal relationship between the local and county school officials and between the latter and the state school officials.

4. Draw a map of the school district in which you live. Analyze it with respect to the three criteria of an adequate district described in this chapter.
5. List the advantages and disadvantages of each of the methods of reorganization described in this chapter.
6. Procure or prepare a school map of a county. Study its geography and locate the school districts.

Bibliography

Books

American Association of School Administrators: *School District Organization*, National Education Association, Washington, D.C., 1958, chap. 1, 4, 8–10, 13. Establishes the urgent need of reorganization of districts, desired characteristics of well-organized districts, legislation for reorganization, and a look into the future of this problem.

Cooper, Shirley, and Charles O. Fitzwater: *County School Administration*, Harper & Brothers, New York, 1954. Discusses the development and present status of the county unit with recommendations for its modification and further development.

Department of Rural Education: *Community School and the Intermediate Unit*, National Education Association, Washington, D.C., 1954. Deals with the role of the intermediate unit in helping to build schools that are better related to community needs and resources.

————: *Effective Intermediate Units, A Guide for Their Development*, National Education Association, Washington, D.C., 1955. Establishes the criteria for an adequate intermediate unit and provides guide lines for their development.

————: *Rural Education—A Look Forward*, National Education Association, Washington, D.C., 1955. Examines the unique problems of rural education and suggests how these needs can be better met.

Fitzwater, C. O.: *School District Reorganization, Policies and Procedures*, U.S. Office of Education, Government Printing Office, Washington, D.C., 1957. A status study of the progress in school district reorganization and current policies and procedures in effect in the various states.

Hunt, Herold C., and Paul R. Pierce: *The Practice of School Administration*, Houghton Mifflin Company, Boston, 1958, chap. 15. Discusses the origin and development of different types of school units, the problems of reorganization, and principles to be observed in the consolidation of districts.

Morphet, Edgar L., Roe L. Johns, and Theodore Reller: *Educational Administration: Concepts, Practices, and Issues*, Prentice-Hall, Inc., Englewood Cliffs, N.J., 1959, chap. 10. Deals with the changing character of the intermediate unit and the problems and issues of school district reorganization.

Periodicals

Campbell, Roald F.: "Feelings Are Facts in School District Reorganization," *The Nation's Schools*, vol. 57 (March, 1956), pp. 58–60. Shows how the feelings of people and their loyalties to old school districts impede reorganization and how this can be approached.

Crawford, E. R.: "Problem: The Administration of the Reorganized School District," *Teachers College Journal*, vol. 29 (May, 1958), pp. 96–98. Discusses the administrative problems that are unique to the reorganized school district.

Dawson, Howard A., and Robert M. Isenberg: "Status Report on District Reorganization," *NEA Journal*, vol. 48 (February, 1959), pp. 75–76. A review of progress in school district organization showing how reorganization has reduced the number of small schools.

Fitzwater, Charles O.: "Trends in School District Reorganization," *School Life*, vol. 39 (April, 1957), pp. 5–7. Shows how the pattern of school district reorganization is changing and the effects of this upon education.

Hay, Roy M., Frank P. Leathers, and Charles T. Roberts: "Organization of Schools and Administrative Units," *Review of Educational Research*, vol. 25 (October, 1955), pp. 334–350. A review of research on the organization of schools, reorganization of districts, the intermediate unit, and the internal organization of schools.

Isenberg, Robert, and others: "Every School Can Have Specialized Services thru the Intermediate Unit," *NEA Journal*, vol. 45 (March, 1956), pp. 174–179. Describes the variety of special services that can be made available to all schools through an effective intermediate unit.

Polley, John W.: "More Public Responsibility for City and Suburban Schools," *The Nation's Schools*, vol. 61 (June, 1958), pp. 47–49. Discusses the unique problems of the large school systems and rapidly growing suburban districts with emphasis upon keeping control close to the people.

Strolle, R. S.: "Educating Citizens for Reorganization," *The Nation's Schools*, vol. 58 (December, 1956), pp. 48–49. Stresses the importance of helping the public understand the problems and advantages of reorganization and how to approach the task.

Strong, Manuel: "Marie R.," *NEA Journal*, vol. 48 (October, 1959), pp. 30–32. Tells in a fascinating way how a county superintendent with a dedicated heart and pioneering spirit transformed a primitive county school system into an effective modern operation.

Warringer, C.: "County Wide Plan for Shared Program," *The School Executive*, vol. 76 (June, 1957), pp. 64–66. Illustrates how a county unit provides cooperative services to districts that could not undertake them alone.

Although education is a legal function of the state, much of the operational responsibility for schools is delegated to local school districts. Thus the history of public education in America is largely the story of the local school system. This tradition of strong local control of education is one of the most distinctive traditions of American democracy. It has served to keep the schools responsive to the people and the people interested in their schools.

Decentralization of educational control has resulted in a wide variety of school districts, differing greatly in size, organization, and program.

The administration of local schools is vested in a board of education elected by the people and in professional school administrators appointed by the board. These positions are of large consequence and beckon the most highly competent persons. The organization of local school systems is being modified in the direction of greater democratization so that the knowledge and experience of more people, both lay and professional, can be capitalized more fully.

As the Educational Policies Commission has emphasized, "Faith in the local administration of schools is a part of democratic tradition. It is important that all the people should feel responsible for their government. In no area is it more necessary than in the provision of public education that the thinking, desires, and ambitions of the people be made effective."

chapter 4

*Local
school districts*

Foundations

The little villages of the colonies were the first school unit prototypes in America, preceding by many years county, state, or national units of school organization. The local school district had its beginning in a quaint law, known as "the Old Deluder Satan Law," enacted by the Massachusetts Bay Colony in 1647, nearly 150 years prior to the founding of the Republic. This statute required every town of 50 families

The tradition of strong local control of education is one of the most distinctive characteristics of American democracy.

In this typical suburban community, the people themselves had to decide whether or not a new high school would be built. Before the buildings were designed, committees of citizens, school board members, administrators, and teachers met to study educational philosophy and needs. Then, working with an architect and educational consultant, they planned a school building designed to meet their requirements. They brought the results of their study to the public who would vote on the bond issue for the new building.

At a community meeting to acquaint the citizens with the need for a new plant, students study charts showing estimated costs.

or more to appoint one of their people to teach reading and writing since "one chief point of that old deluder, Satan, [is] to keep men from knowledge of the Scriptures."

Colonial America was largely rural. Wide-open spaces separated the little villages that dotted the land. Transportation and communication were difficult. It was quite natural for schools to be organized around local communities, since state and national government had not yet emerged. The founders of America who had struggled for independence from oppressive centralized government were not disposed to let the important function of education rest with the central government after it was established. These and other circumstances established firmly the tradition of strong local control of education in America. Because of America's great faith in education, the schools have been kept close to the people. This has also helped to keep the people close to the schools.

Local School Districts. The United States has more than 100,000 independent units of government, each with the power to spend money and to perform services for the citizenry. These units range in size from the federal government with millions of employees down to the smallest type of school district with one teacher. About forty-five thousand of these legal units are school districts of various types and sizes. About seven thousand operate no schools of their own, sending their pupils to other districts.

In the broad sense, the local school district is the smallest administrative unit. Local school districts are administered by a superintendent of schools under the direction of the board of education which is commonly elected by the people. Districts too small to employ an administrator are administered by the board of education.

Relationship of Local, Intermediate, and State Units. This is a good point for reviewing the relationship of the local, intermediate, and state units. The chart at the beginning of Part 1 illustrates these. The local district is the unit which really operates the schools. The county or intermediate unit, as described in Chapter 3, serves as a liaison agency between the local and state units. This intermediate office should stimulate, assist, and lead the local unit, serving as an intermediary for both the local district and the state.

Using model floor plans, the principal explains how the unusual form offers the same space but more special advantages than the conventional form.

One citizen asks, "Why the zigzag instead of rectangular shape for some of the buildings?"

The state department oversees and assists both the local and the intermediate units under policy set by the state board of education and administered through the chief state school officer and his staff. The state board derives its authority from the legislature and the governor, as described in Chapter 2.

The most significant aspect of this organization pattern is that the ultimate source of authority for education at the local, intermediate, and state level is with the people who, through their franchise, have control over the entire administrative machinery. In no other society is the control of the people over education so complete at all levels of government. This is one of the most unique and significant aspects of American government. It has had a profound effect upon the development of American education.

Legal Status of Districts. The Tenth Amendment to the Constitution definitely implies that education is a function of the state and not of the federal government. Usually the states delegate the major responsibilities for school operation to the local educational subdivision, which in area may be as small as a rural school district of 5 square miles in Illinois or as large as a county unit of 17,000 square miles in Nevada. Legally, then, subject to the laws passed by the state legislature, the control of the school system resides in the board of education elected by the people in the district, as indicated on the chart opening Part 1. The board is both a local and a state instrument.

According to school laws, the board of education is the legal authority representing the state. It is an artificial body created by a general or specific law to maintain a system of public education in a certain territory. A state attorney general says, "A school board is a body politic and corporate. It is purely a creature of the state. Its power may be enlarged, diminished, modified, or revoked by the legislature." Although there are limitations, the board has broad legal powers, such as the right to buy and sell property, erect buildings, and enter into contracts. It is a quasi corporation, subject to numerous laws.

In this overview of American public education, it is pertinent to emphasize the extreme importance of school law. Many students and teachers do not realize that their daily acts within the school are markedly affected by school laws, many of which have been extant for a long time. Even teachers in service, administrators, and board members reveal an appalling dearth of knowledge as to school laws. This information is readily found in federal and state constitutions, state statutes, and case law or judicial opinion. Copies of the state laws, as revised periodically, can be obtained from the state superintendent of public instruction or from the state capitol. The National Education Association makes periodic studies of legislation throughout the United States. The National Organization on Legal Problems of Education issues periodic reports. The *Annual Yearbook of School Law* contains a topical summary of decisions of the higher courts in cases involving school law. Through such decisions the higher courts of the various states and the Supreme Court of the United States have established many common-law principles of exceeding importance. In the exercise of its duty the court cannot do otherwise than revert to first principles: the consideration of the purpose for which the schools were established as indicated in the law or in antecedent custom.

Teachers in the audience study the list of facilities they helped to plan in earlier committee meetings.

Types of local schools

ATTENDANCE AND ADMINISTRATIVE UNITS

The legislature creates or makes possible the establishment of school districts of various types. It is desirable to distinguish between units for attendance and those for the administration of education. An attendance unit, usually established by the local board, is defined as the area served by a single school building, such as a Horace Mann School in a city system. An ad-

A citizen contemplates a photograph of the present overcrowded library . . .

ministrative unit, usually the legal school district, embraces all the area under a single system of control and may include one, two, or over a hundred attendance areas.

LOCAL DISTRICTS OF VARIOUS SIZES

Local administrative units are of many sizes. According to the federal census tabulations, all areas under 2,500 population are rural. County and intermediate school districts are considered in Chapter 3. Divisions are here classified roughly as (1) rural, (2) village, (3) city, and (4) suburban.

Rural Districts. The smallest district, the one-teacher school, is sometimes one-pupil as well. The one-teacher schools of America, usually one-room also, are disappearing rapidly in favor of the more modern and consolidated schools. Some of the rural elementary schools have two or more teachers, and most rural high schools have at least three teachers. Not all rural schools are small.

Village Districts. A village school usually has more than one teacher and may have one or more buildings. The organization and administration of village, community, and small city schools often include an administrator, who is usually known as the superintendent or supervising principal. He may be assisted by a principal or head teacher in each building.

while others watch and listen.

City School Districts. The population varies from cities of several thousand to the New York City school district with a population of 8 million people. (Only eight states enroll more pupils than does the New York City system.) An illustration of a medium-sized school system is that of Santa Monica, California, a city of approximately 100,000 people. The people, as the electorate, choose the members of the board of education, who in turn select the superintendent of schools, their chief executive officer. Under his direction the schools of that city are administered through a three-department organization: business, including such activities as the preparation of budgets and contracts; professional, with such duties as supervision and research; and instructional, embracing teaching and learning on all levels from elementary schools through the junior college, plus the special services of adult and technical education.

After the meeting, the custodian sizes up the building plans from his point of view . . .

Suburban Districts. A rapidly growing type of school district which may combine some of the characteristics of a rural, village, and/or city system, is that found in the outskirts of crowded cities. Suburban or near-urban schools have increased markedly in the past decade.

Probably the most severe inequalities to children because of outmoded school districts are to be found in the areas near urban centers where the districts that were designed to meet the needs of an agricultural society still prevail, and cannot cope with the suburban problem—the growing edge of the nearby city in rural school districts. The problem springs from such developments as large trailer camps or low-cost housing subdivisions mushrooming in an otherwise rural area.

Other factors stimulating the growth of these districts are: improved roads, increase in autos, high cost of city living and taxes, inadequate play and garden space in overcrowded cities, and the developing of business establishments away from the limited-car-parking areas and high-tax centers. Since 1945, the dawn of the atomic age, and since 1956, the inauguration of the modern space age, the psychology of fear has augmented the hegira of people and business from cities.

Some established suburban schools are the most outstanding in the nation, while others, newfledged, are afflicted with special problems including population pressures, penurious public purses, and lagging legislation.

OTHER TYPES OF DISTRICTS AND SCHOOLS

Special Charter School Districts. Some schools, usually city schools, have a special charter granted directly to the local district by the state. Although the majority of these districts were established in the early history of the state's educational development, some of them operate under a special charter of special laws because of the size of the district. The multiplication of especially chartered districts is likely to complicate school administration within the state; hence there is a trend toward bringing all existing school districts under the general school laws.

Other Classifications of School Systems. According to the educational level of the offerings, the two basic classifications are elementary and high school districts, to which have been added the junior college and municipal university areas. In addition, there are many districts classified on a geographical or civil basis, some of which are described in Chapter 3. Among the special types are town, township, county, parish, consolidated, community, and non-high school. Some states designate districts by sizes, as first or second class. A wide variation in nomenclature of districts is found between states and within states.

The general impression that every square foot of soil in the United States is a part of an organized school district is not valid. Several states have portions unorganized for educational purposes. The school laws usually guarantee free schooling to all pupils residing in such areas.

Laboratory Schools. Many laboratory or experimental schools, on the elementary and secondary levels, are in reality public in that they are practice or training schools for state institutions that prepare teachers. Generally no tuition is required and the pupils are admitted as to a public school, although the limitation of facilities and the experimental nature of the work may restrict the enrollment. The American Association of Colleges for Teacher Education has been active in improving the laboratory schools. Numerous laboratory schools are affiliated with or are part of nonstate or independent institutions. Experimental schools have stimulated profound changes in educational practice throughout the United States and abroad.

Parochial and Private Interest in Public Education. The earliest schools and colleges in America were parochial and private. Educa-

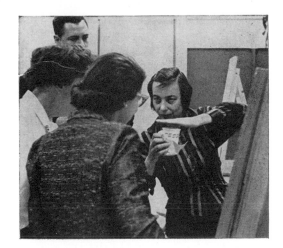

the chairman of a citizens committee explains that "our schools are full up to here . . ."

tional advance in the early years of the United States was due primarily to the interest and support of the church, just as today in foreign countries such as India much financial and educational impetus is given to schools from missionary funds and zeal. Today many children do not go to a public school, since it is not compulsory to attend a public institution. The Oregon anti-private school law, which sought to compel all pupils to attend public schools, was held unconstitutional by the Supreme Court in 1925. In the parochial field, the Roman Catholic Church maintains the largest number of elementary and secondary schools. The parochial schools have been, are, and will be educational and spiritual bulwarks in a nation that practices freedom of religion—one of the basic four freedoms. The private school affects public education because it is often a trail-blazer due to its greater freedom.

In addition to billions of dollars given to private schools by individuals, many millions have been donated to public schools and colleges. Furthermore, numerous educational foundations and boards have given millions indirectly to public education by furnishing funds for research, experiments, and stimulation of education within the nation, states, and local communities.

Private and parochial interest in education calls for close coordination with the public

while other members of the audience join the superintendent of schools in refreshments . . .

and the meeting breaks up into informal conversation.

schools. Only by the cooperation of parochial, private, and public schools can education present a united front against the common foes, ignorance and superstition.

Boards of education

Nearly every school district in the United States is governed by a group of laymen designated the selectmen, the board of education, the school board, the board of trustees, the school committee, the township board of education, or the county board of education. These board members are the direct representatives of the people in the school district.

Evolution of School Boards. Historically the board of education developed in the following manner. At first the planning was done by all the interested persons in the community. Then developed the practice of appointing temporary committees. Then these temporary committees were replaced by permanent committees. There gradually developed the pattern of selecting boards of education, accountable to the people, who were given the responsibility for organizing and administering free schools. The autonomous school district, organized separately under an elected board of education, is essentially an American institution.

Electorate and School Boards. Basically the genesis of control of public education resides in the people. "We, the people," elect representatives who, as a board of education, take the place of the unwieldy larger group, the electorate. The board of education is indeed a personalized mechanism of democratic government, yet the electorate has manifested in the past a gross ignorance and a careless neglect of its duties in the conduct of American public education. This attitude of *laissez faire* is sometimes revealed in the small number of voters who cast their ballots in the election of a school board. Citizens should maintain active interest in their schools. This interest should be manifest in voting at school elections, visiting schools, attending board meetings, and participating in parent-teachers associations. Good schools tend to be found in those communities where there is a high level of public understanding and interest in education.

In recent years, there has been evidence of a substantial renaissance of public interest and concern for education. This interest has been intensified by international competition in the exploration of outer space. The importance of education in the struggle for national security and the responsibility of citizens in educational planning are being more fully recognized. Newspapers, magazines, radio, and television are focusing attention upon educational issues and problems to an extraordinary degree. Citizens advisory committees on education at local, state, and national levels have multiplied from a handful at the close of World War II to nearly fifteen thousand. Membership in parent-teachers associations has grown to over ten million members, making it the largest organization in American society. William Carr, executive secretary of the National Education Association, recently reported that never before in the nation's history has American education enjoyed such "unprecedented public interest and support." Wise boards of education are seeking to capitalize on this surge of public interest for the improvement of education.

Size, Tenure, and Selection of Boards of Education. There has been no uniformity in the number of persons on a board of education or in their term of office. The trend in recent years has been toward boards composed of not more than nine elected members. There should be enough members to represent the different points of view in the community. The three-member board found so often in rural and small-town districts does not meet all these criteria.

Methods of nominating board members vary greatly. They may be nominated by petition, primary election, individual announcements, citizens' committees, mass meetings, or school district meetings. The members are usually elected, although they may be appointed by the mayor and council, by county commissioners, by city managers, or by self-perpetuating boards.

Terms of office for school board members vary from one year to several. Authorities in educational administration recommend the election of board members at large rather than by wards, and on a nonpartisan basis.

Early studies of the social composition of city boards of education revealed a heavy preponderance of business and professional men to the exclusion of men and women from the middle and lower socioeconomic levels of society. In recent years, the composition of boards appears to be shifting to include more housewives and more skilled and semiskilled workers. A larger number of union members are now found on boards of education. Collectively, the members of the board of education should reflect a variety of vocational experiences, educational interests, and leadership abilities so as to represent the community broadly. School board members should be chosen from the best men and women obtainable in the community.

Qualifications of Board Members. The magnitude of education, as expressed by its annual expenditure of several billion dollars, emphasizes the need for a very careful selection of board members. Among the qualifications usually specified by law are that the candidate shall be over twenty-one years of age, a legal voter, and a resident in the school district. Besides these legal stipulations, however, a member of a board of education should possess many other desirable qualities: interest in schools, willingness to subordinate self-interest, open-minded and creative outlook, courage in facing criticism, willingness to give time to the office, skill in working with people, respect of the community, forward-looking attitude, reasonably good education, friendliness and cooperativeness, understanding of the community, ability to discuss school affairs. Of

greatest benefit is intelligent cooperation among the members of the board and between the board and the community.

Unfortunately board members do not always promote the best welfare of the school. Hardened politicians, not content with the devastation inflicted on city governments, realize that the schools, employing many people and handling millions of dollars, are tempting objects for despoliation. The school system should be made an uninteresting and unattractive field to political spoilsmen. It is "bad politics for even a corrupt spoils administration to use the schools, and good politics to stay out." By and large, however, the schools are governed honestly, largely because the majority of board members take seriously their responsibilities and duties.

Distinguished service awards, honorary degrees, and other forms of recognition are given annually by state educational associations, colleges, and other groups to members of boards of education who have rendered notable service to education in the local community, state, and nation. These tributes are challenges to men and women everywhere to serve their community as members of boards of education.

Functions and Powers of Boards of Education. The board of education is primarily a policy-forming and appraisal-making group. The board is generally granted broad powers by the state and is invested with much discretionary power in the details of its work. The chief responsibilities of the board of education include:

1. The development and improvement of the educational program
2. The selection of the chief administrative officer and the provision of the professional and nonprofessional staff
3. The provision of funds and facilities
4. The maintenance of good relations between the school and the community

Too many boards of education limit their attention to school buildings to be used during school hours by school children on school days during the school months. The modern board of public education places all its facilities at the disposal of all members of the community for education at all hours of the day during the entire year. It is a board of *public education* rather than a *school* board.

Board Organization and Procedure. Most boards of education are organized with a president who presides at the meetings, and a secretary or clerk who may serve as the treasurer. Business is conducted usually in open meetings held in the school once a month, except in large city systems where the board may convene more frequently.

Much planning is transacted through committees. Among the typical standing committees are finance, building and grounds, school management, teachers, and public relations. In recent years, however, the tendency is away from standing committees. If the board meets as a committee of the whole, each member will be more thoroughly informed on all school affairs and able to render more intelligent service. As a general rule there should be no standing committees, since too frequently committee action predetermines board action. If there are committees, certainly the superintendent of schools should serve on all of them as an ex officio member in order to integrate the policies and actions of the board.

RELATIONSHIPS OF BOARDS OF EDUCATION

The board of education plays a unique role in American life. Its work impinges on so many areas of public interest that it becomes interdependent with many groups. As the elected representatives of the people, the board members must be able to keep in contact with their constituents or at least to gauge their pulse. The importance of such connections is manifested in the increasing prevalence of committees on public relations. Many boards encourage laymen, teachers, and students to attend their sessions, except when personnel matters make a closed session desirable. Some broadcast or televise part of their meetings. Public relations in American public education are further detailed in Chapter 16.

Among the vital relationships maintained by the local school board with other organizations and officials are those with the city government, with other school boards, in area, state, and national affiliations, and with the superintendent of schools, whose work is treated in the last part of this unit. Many boards work closely with citizens' committees.

Fiscal Independence and Dependence. The tendency has been to divide school districts into two categories on the basis of their fiscal relationship to the city government:

1. *Fiscal independence.* Those school districts, in which the board of education generally has authority to raise and expend funds without the consent of the municipal government, are financially independent.
2. *Fiscal dependence.* Conversely, those school districts which are a department of some civil agency, such as a city, and hence must depend on it for budget approval and revision, are said to be fiscally dependent.

It is impossible to draw a clear line of demarcation between these two groups, since there is a gradual shading off from one extreme of positive independence to the other of irrevocable dependence. Authorities in political science usually favor the dependent boards, whereas educational writers in the main agree that the school district should be fiscally independent.

School Board Organizations. A significant development is the banding together of school boards in the common cause of education. In many states the board members have joined formal organizations, by counties, by groups of counties, or by the entire state. The state associations are linked in the National School Boards Association—a group that is emerging as a potent force in American public education. Many board members have profited by attending the annual conventions of county, state, and national school boards associations. These associations render many other valuable services to local boards.

Administration

The Evolution of School Administration. As the one-room school was displaced by multi-room schools, it became necessary to have someone in charge. Frequently, one of the teachers was designated head teacher with certain authority over other teachers. However, as the school grew still larger and its operation more complicated, a full-time building administrator, or principal, had to be appointed. Thus the principalship emerged in America long before the superintendency.

As villages grew into cities, several school buildings were established within a school district and the need arose for system-wide administration and supervision of schools. At first this task was undertaken by a school committee of laymen. But the supervision of schools by committees proved quite unfeasible and the committees were supplanted in time by a single school superintendent. In early times, he was a layman, usually paid less than the principals, and responsible only for the business affairs of the district. The first school superintendents were appointed in Buffalo and Louisville in 1837. The importance of the superintendency became increasingly apparent, and the responsibilities of the office were gradually expanded. As the office became more responsible, the qualifications of the position became more professional.

As school systems grew larger and administration more complicated, administrative staffs were increased by the addition of assistant superintendents, instructional supervisors, and other specialists. Positions such as business manager, curriculum director, personnel manager, director of buildings and grounds, and others became quite common in city districts. After the beginning of the twentieth century the study of educational administration and supervision was introduced into the curricu-

lums of graduate schools of education. Certification requirements for administrative positions were established by the states. School administration was well on its way toward professionalization.

The Legal Status of Administration. The superintendent of schools is regarded as the chief executive officer of the board of education and as the educational leader of the school system. The principal is considered the educational leader of his school, accountable for the total educational program of his building. The duties and responsibilities of superintendents and principals are defined in the school law codes of the states and supplemented by rules, regulations, and job descriptions adopted by the local board of education.

The legal status of the superintendent's position is not too well defined in some states. In most states he has no legal tenure, serving short terms of office at the pleasure of the board of education that appoints him. Unfortunately the average superintendent of schools remains in one position for only about six years. One study referred to him as "the itinerant schoolmaster" and lamented his inability to remain in one position long enough to make his maximum contribution.

The principal, unlike the superintendent, enjoys legal tenure in most states. This means that he cannot be dismissed from his office except for good and sufficient cause. Thus principals are usually employed on indefinite, rather than short-term appointments, and in general enjoy longer tenure in office than superintendents.

Functions of School Administration. The functions of administration can be classified in four general areas: administration of the educational program, administration of finance and facilities, personnel administration, and administration of school-community relations. The following outline illustrates some of the responsibilities included in these major functions:

Administration of the educational program
Scheduling of the school program
Planning and supervising school activities
Supervising the work of teachers
Evaluating the school program
Supervising the processes of curriculum revision

Administration of finance and facilities
Budgeting, expending, and accounting for school funds
Requisitioning and controlling the use of school supplies
Supervising the use of school buildings and facilities
Planning new school buildings
Supervising the maintenance and repair of school facilities

Personnel administration
Recruiting, selecting, and assigning teachers
Helping teachers to grow professionally
Administering salaries, sick leaves, teacher records, etc.
Promoting, dismissing, and retiring of teachers
Enumerating, admitting, and placing students
Supervising behavior of students
Supervising the guidance, records, and attendance of students

Administration of school-community relations
Reporting educational progress and needs to the public
Meeting with community groups interested in education
Planning parent workshops, open houses, study groups, etc.
Participating in community life

The administration of the educational program is regarded as the central and most important function of administration. School buildings, records, faculties, budgets, and all the rest of the school environment have meaning and importance only to the extent that they contribute to the quality of instruction and learning.

Qualifications of School Administrators. School administration has become a complex and exacting profession that demands a high order of competence and statesmanship. In general, the competencies or skills required for school administration can be classified into three categories: conceptual skills, human relations skills, and technical skills.

Conceptual skills revolve about ability to deal effectively with *ideas*. School administrators must understand the broad relationships between education and social, economic, and political forces. For example, the relationships between the national economy, taxation, and school finance must be perceived. The administrator must be perceptive of forces which create new educational needs—forces such as automation, space travel, increased life span, the cold war, and many others. He must be able to perceive the probable effects of changes in school policies and school law. The school administrator should be able to discern quality in the school program and conceive means of strengthening weak aspects of the program. Conceptual skill demands a high level of intelligence in dealing with abstractions and an open, inquiring, and creative mind. Conceptual skill is greatly enhanced through broad general education.

Human relations skills relate to the ability to work effectively with *people*. Much of what the administrator accomplishes he undertakes through people. Several studies have shown that administrators (also teachers) succeed or fail largely on the basis of their ability to get along with people. This means that administrators should have interest, understanding, and respect for people. Human relations skills are largely a function of the administrator's personality and character, although these skills can be improved through experience and through study of the social sciences, particularly social psychology.

Technical skills relate to the ability to work with *things*. The school administrator must be able to judge the quality of school buses, school furniture, and equipment. He should know how to prepare and administer a budget. He must have knowledge of technical aspects of school buildings and grounds. He must be able to develop good schedules, records, and reports. Thus the administrator must be able to work with details and to master the inanimate aspects of the school environment. Technical skills are gained largely through education and experience.

The school administrator should have broad background in general education and wide understanding of the society which education serves. He must also have rich professional education from which he derives his understanding of teaching, curriculum, guidance, supervision, finance, public relations, research, and many other fields of specialized knowledge in education. Most states now require at least a year of graduate study for certification in school administration. A few states have increased certification requirements for administrators to include two years of graduate study. The American Association of School Administrators recommends two years of graduate study for certification for the superintendency. The number of school administrators with doctorates is gradually increasing.

The school administrator gains much of his competency through experience—experience both as a teacher and as an administrator. Most states require a minimum of three years of teaching experience for certification in administration. In addition, the school administrator gains valuable experience in his professional associations. Most superintendents belong to the American Association of School Administrators and to other national and state organizations which offer rich opportunities for growth in service through their publications, conventions, workshops, and other activities. National and state associations for elementary and secondary principals provide these administrators with similar opportunities for professional growth.

The distinguished school administrator is a person of broad vision who sees the full potential of education in its march toward the improvement of mankind throughout the world. His concept of the job must not be limited by the walls of his school or the boundaries of his school district. He should visualize himself as the energizer of all of the educative forces in the community. Indeed, there is some disposition to title him the superintendent *of education* rather than the superintendent of schools. Moreover, the ablest school administrator sees his community ultimately in national and international dimensions rather than in neighborhood or city limits.

The school administrator must be a person of high character. He should possess a rich philosophy of education and of life, anchored in the enduring values of Judeo-Christian morality. His conduct should be attuned to the golden rule if he is to set an exemplary moral tone for the school system. His behavior should demonstrate high professional ethics and he should be fair and honest in his relations with people. He should be able to subordinate personal interests and self-aggrandizement to the best interests of public education. The school administrator should be aware of the great social consequences of his position.

The able school administrator is a person of sound personality, well balanced emotionally and socially. He should be friendly and personable, self-confident and modest, adaptable and creative. He should have deep understanding and acceptance of self.

Finally, because of the physical rigors of his job, particularly the superintendency, the administrator should be a person of sound physical health with abundant vigor and stamina.

The qualifications of school administration have been discussed at some length because of the crucial importance of educational leadership in our society. The quality of the school system, like any other organization, is to a large extent measured by the shadow of the man who leads it. Educational administration represents a high order of social responsibility, surpassed in importance by few, if any, other professional callings. As Ellwood Cubberley, one of the earliest and most distinguished students of school administration, has aptly observed:

The opportunities offered in this new profession to men of strong character, broad sympathies, high purposes, fine culture, courage, exact training, and executive skill, who are willing to take the time and spend the energy necessary to prepare themselves for large service, are today not excelled in any of the professions, learned or otherwise. No profession offers such large personal rewards, for the opportunity of living one's life in moulding other lives, and in helping to improve materially the intellectual tone and moral character of a community, offers a personal reward that makes a peculiarly strong appeal to certain types of men and women.[1]

Organization

School organization may be described as a means of clarifying and distributing tasks, responsibilities, and authority among individuals and groups in an orderly manner consistent with the purposes of the enterprise. The internal structure of school systems varies widely according to the size and nature of the enterprise. Small school systems have small, simple organizations. Larger districts have much larger and more complex structures. Moreover, there are substantial differences of opinion regarding the form of effective organization. Studies reveal an appalling lack, in most districts, of sufficient administrative and supervisory personnel to discharge the ever-increasing responsibilities of school administration and supervision for expanding school populations.

Figure 4-1 illustrates the organization proposed for a New Jersey city system by a survey team. The school system has an enrollment of 21,000 students. This chart illustrates several

[1] Ellwood P. Cubberley, *Public School Administration*, Houghton. Mifflin Company, Boston, 1929, pp. 220–221.

important principles and promising trends in school organization and administration.

Unit Control. The organization provides for unit control, which means that there should be one responsible head, namely the superintendent, who reports directly to the board of education. Opposed to this are a number of school systems that operate under dual or multiple control, in which a business manager, and perhaps others, are coordinate with the superintendent. Unit control also implies that each subordinate will be responsible directly to only one superior rather than to a number of bosses. However, it is quite desirable for a subordinate to have "lines of cooperation," but not "lines of authority," with a number of experts in the organization.

Democratic Organization and Administration. Good organization provides for wide participation in educational planning and decision making. The circles on the chart in Fig. 4-1 indicate the machinery for democratic school administration—lay advisory committees, teacher councils, curriculum committees, PTA councils, and student councils. If schools are to prepare young persons for intelligent and effective citizenship in a democracy, opportunity must be provided for the observation and practice of democracy at work within the school. Moreover, it is increasingly apparent that wiser decisions are usually reached when many minds tackle the problem. Perhaps no aspect of school administration has received as much attention in recent years as the importance of democratizing the administration of schools. Administration is no longer thought of as synonymous with a *position* but rather as a cooperative *process*, engaging at times the best talents of all of the people in the organization.

New Role for Administrators. The role of the administrator and supervisor is increasingly regarded as one of stimulation, assistance, coordination, appraisal, and help, rather than one of inspection and command. In former years when teachers were poorly trained and when the administrator or supervisor was expected to be more expert than all others in all aspects of school work, administrators and supervisors operated largely through inspection and command. They exercised power *over* people rather than power *through and with* people. Classrooms were inspected and teachers were instructed or commanded with respect to their duties. However, as teachers acquired better education and higher professional stature, and as newer and better concepts of the leadership role emerged, the processes of administration and supervision also have changed.

Today the educational leader is regarded as the stimulator, coordinator, or helper of teachers. Titles such as "director" and "supervisor" are giving way to "coordinator," "consultant," and "helping teacher." Note in Fig. 4-1 that many specialists work as staff officers (helpers) rather than as line officers (commanders). The central administrative office in the Ridgewood, New Jersey, school system is now known as the Education Service Center rather than as the central office. This trend, while not yet universal, promises better and more effective working relationships between supervisors and teachers. The older, more monolithic organizations had top-heavy staffs of experts in line positions who tried to influence change through their status rather than through solid help and service. More and more ideas and changes are being initiated at the bottom rather than at the top of the organizational hierarchy. This newer trend is consistent with learnings yielded by the study of group dynamics.

Greater Freedom for Schools and Teachers. Good organization provides a maximum of freedom and initiative to teachers and schools, which is consistent with efficient operation and prudential control. In simpler words, school organization is being decentralized. Organization charts are becoming flatter rather than taller. The number of levels of administrative hierarchy between the teacher and the superintendent are being reduced, with the result that greater autonomy is being given to individual teachers and buildings within the system. Teachers are being given more room to be different, experimental, creative, and adaptive. It is reasoned that if decentralization is good for the nation, then further decentralization of authority and responsibility within schools is also desirable. Several large city school districts, notably Atlanta and Chicago, have modified their organization in the direction of decentralization.

Homogeneous Assignments. Homogeneous assignments are becoming more common. Note in Fig. 4-1 that administrative positions are assigned to particular *functions*, such as program, plant and business, research, adult education, and others, rather than to educational *levels*, such as elementary and high school. Effort is made to center ultimate responsibility for discrete functions in one person so that accountability is not divided and so that the same function is not administered piecemeal by a number of persons with narrow and conflicting responsibilities.

Written Policy Statements. Although it is not apparent from the chart, there is a distinct and desirable trend in school organization toward written policy statements and job descriptions. These are commonly made available through handbooks and local school codes so that they may be known to all. When the ground rules are established in writing and when they are determined before, rather than during, controversy, there is less opportunity for misunderstanding, conflict, and arbitrary action among the people involved.

Leaders of High Ability. Although good organization is important, the quality of the persons in the organization, particularly those in leadership positions, remains fundamental. As Alexander Pope put it, "For forms of government, let fools contest; what e'er is best administered is best." Administration and organization should be the servant, not the master, of education. Schools are not organized and conducted in order to provide a board member, superintendent, teacher or any other particular person with a job; schools are dedicated, in all their functions, to the supreme and worthy purpose of education for a democratic society.

Obviously many issues with respect to the organization, role, and function of the local school district still remain. These issues are discussed at length in Chapter 17. In its early, restricted scope, schooling was for children. But modern American education is now so broad and extensive that it embraces learning for all.

To be genuinely democratic, American education should include the five major levels described in Part 2: pre-elementary, elementary, secondary, higher education, and adult education.

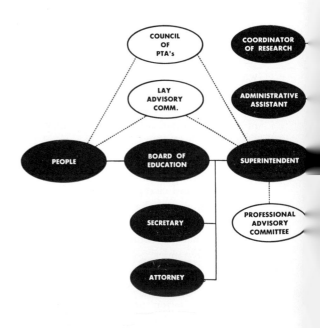

LEGEND: LINE OF AUTHORITY ————
LINE OF COOPERATION ············

Summary

Most of the responsibility for the operation of schools resides with the local school district. However, school districts are regarded legally as creations of the state. This decentralization of operational control has resulted in a wide variety of educational quality and practice. The local school district took form before intermediate, state, and federal levels of organization. This has strengthened the tradition of local control of education, one of the most unique characteristics of American education.

The 45,000 districts in the United States range in size from large city school systems to small districts that operate no schools at all. More than half of the school systems are in communities that have populations of less than two thousand.

Except in some city districts, local boards of education are elected by the people. The major functions of the board of education include the development and improvement of the educational program, the selection of the chief administrator and the professional and nonprofessional staff, the provision of funds

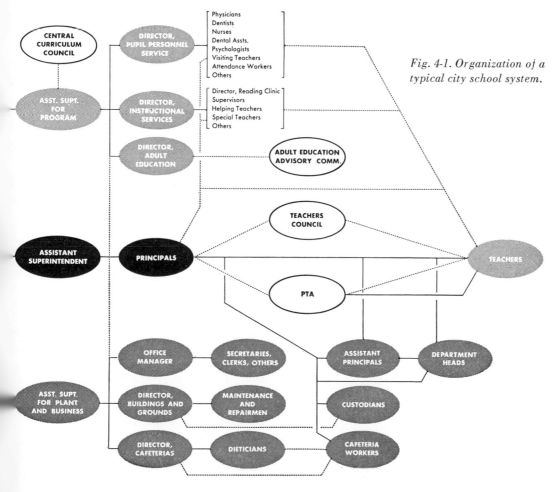

Fig. 4-1. Organization of a typical city school system.

CENTRAL CURRICULUM COUNCIL

DIRECTOR, PUPIL PERSONNEL SERVICE

Physicians
Dentists
Nurses
Dental Assts.
Psychologists
Visiting Teachers
Attendance Workers
Others

ASST. SUPT. FOR PROGRAM

DIRECTOR, INSTRUCTIONAL SERVICES

Director, Reading Clinic
Supervisors
Helping Teachers
Special Teachers
Others

DIRECTOR, ADULT EDUCATION

ADULT EDUCATION ADVISORY COMM.

TEACHERS COUNCIL

ASSISTANT SUPERINTENDENT

PRINCIPALS

TEACHERS

PTA

OFFICE MANAGER

SECRETARIES, CLERKS, OTHERS

ASSISTANT PRINCIPALS

DEPARTMENT HEADS

ASST. SUPT. FOR PLANT AND BUSINESS

DIRECTOR, BUILDINGS AND GROUNDS

MAINTENANCE AND REPAIRMEN

CUSTODIANS

DIRECTOR, CAFETERIAS

DIETICIANS

CAFETERIA WORKERS

and facilities, and the maintenance of good relations between the school and the community. School board members should be chosen from among the most able, interested, and forward-looking citizens in the community. These boards of education should be fiscally independent from municipal government and free from political influence and control.

The superintendent of schools is the executive officer of the board and is appointed by the board. The superintendent, principals, and other administrative officers are responsible for the administration of the educational program, personnel, funds and facilities, and school-community relations. These administrative positions call for persons with vision and ability. Many states are strengthening the requirements for these positions.

The internal organization of school systems is undergoing several significant changes in the direction of larger, better-prepared central staffs; more democratization through the use of lay committees, teachers' councils, and other cooperative efforts; and more orderly assignment of functions through written rules and regulations.

Suggested activities

1. Study the important historical milestones in the evolution of local school administration.
2. Draw a diagram showing how a local public school system is organized.
3. Draw a map of a city. Locate on it all the school buildings—public, private, and parochial.
4. Study and report on the relationship between the local school officials and the municipal officials.
5. Find out when school board elections are held in your district and what the election procedures are.
6. Attend an annual school district meeting or election.
7. Interview a board member to ascertain his personal interest in board membership and his qualifications for it.
8. Prepare an exhibit of educational materials from a local school system.
9. Examine annual reports of school boards and superintendents.
10. Give examples of democratic and undemocratic procedures in schools.
11. Discuss the main functions of educational organization in a democracy.
12. Discuss practical ways in which school systems can encourage and capitalize upon public interest in education.

Bibliography

Books

American Association of School Administrators: *Educational Administration in a Changing Community*, 37th Yearbook, National Education Association, Washington, D.C., 1959, chaps. 2, 3. Description of how the community setting affects schools, particularly the development of educational policy.

———: *Professional Administrators for America's Schools*, 38th Yearbook, National Education Association, Washington, D.C., 1960. Reports on a comprehensive study of the experience, preparation, selection, and in-service development of the nation's school administrators.

———: *School Board-Superintendent Relations*, 34th Yearbook, National Education Association, Washington, D.C., 1956, chaps. 2–4. Describes the organization, operation, and function of boards of education and their relationship to the school superintendent.

Gross, Neal: *Who Runs Our Schools?* John Wiley & Sons, Inc., New York, 1958. A very interesting study of the realities of local school operation—how superintendents, boards of education, pressure groups, and the rest of the community interact.

Hamilton, Robert H., and E. Edmund Reutter, Jr.: *Legal Aspects of School Board Operation*, Bureau of Publications, Teachers College, Columbia University, New York, 1958, chaps. 1, 4. The legal structure and authority of the board of education and its relation to employed personnel are discussed.

Hunt, Herold C., and Paul R. Pierce: *The Practice of School Administration*, Houghton Mifflin Company, Boston, 1958, chaps. 8, 11. Discusses the relationship between schools, the home and community; also good discussion of the job of school administration.

Melby, Ernest O.: *Administering Community Education*, Prentice-Hall, Englewood Cliffs, N.J., 1955, chaps. 6, 13, 15, 16. Discusses the shortcomings of present school administration, the importance of community leadership for education, and the proper roles and working relationships among administrators, teachers, and lay persons.

Miller, Van, and Willard B. Spaulding: *The Public Administration of American Schools*, World Book Company, Yonkers, N.Y., 1958, chaps. 4, 19, 22. Deals with the effects of the community upon education, and the work of the school administrator with emphasis upon putting democratic principles into practice.

Morphet, Edgar L., Roe L. Johns, and Theodore L. Reller: *Educational Administration: Concepts, Practices, and Issues*, Prentice-Hall, Inc., Englewood Cliffs, N.J., 1959, chap. 11. Discusses the board of education, school administrators, and the issues involved in their joint operation.

National Society for the Study of Education: *Community Education*, University of Chicago Press, Chicago, 1959. Scholarly discussion of the interrelationship between the school and the community and how each can be utilized to strengthen the other.

Reeder, Ward G.: *The Fundamentals of Public School Administration*, The Macmillan Company, New York, 1958, chaps. 1–4. School administration as a profession and its importance to American democracy are discussed along with work of boards of education.

Periodicals

Bruce, Imon E.: "When the Citizens Are on Your Side," *The School Executive*, vol. 77 (July, 1958), pp. 40–41. Tells the story of how local citizens' committees helped solve the school problems in Hot Springs, Ark.

Edwards, Violet, and Bernard Joslin: "When Citizens See the Schools in Action," *The School Executive*, vol. 76 (February, 1957), pp. 78–81. A case study of how a citizens group in Buffalo got a firsthand look at their schools and underwent a rich learning experience of their own.

Foskett, John M.: "How a Community Makes up its Mind," *NEA Journal*, vol. 48 (February, 1959), pp. 53–54. Describes the dynamics of decision making regarding education in school communities.

Fowlkes, John G.: "Epic Document on Training, Selecting Administrators," *The Nation's Schools*, vol. 61 (May, 1958), pp. 52–53. A discussion of a proposal that will strengthen the professional preparation, selection, and in-service education of school administrators.

Hunter, Madeline: "Dear Mr. Superintendent," *NEA Journal*, vol. 44 (September, 1955), p. 349. A letter from a teacher to a superintendent setting forth the qualities that teachers like in administrators.

McGhehey, Marion A.: "So You Want a Good School Board!" *The School Executive*, vol. 77 (August, 1958), pp. 42–44. Presents the qualities needed by good board members and suggests means of retaining members.

Swanson, J. Chester: "Community, Schoolboard, Superintendent, Staff," *NEA Journal*, vol. 45 (February, 1956), pp. 76–77. A former superintendent discusses the proper relationships between the community, board of education, school administrators, and teaching staff.

Werthimer, Jerrold L.: "Tying Strings Together," *The Nation's Schools*, vol. 60 (November, 1957), pp. 57–59. The writer interviewed the superintendent of schools of San Francisco to present an interesting firsthand account of his philosophy of school administration.

Wynn, Richard: "What's New in Administrative Organization?" *The School Executive*, vol. 76 (October, 1956), pp. 71–73. New trends and desirable principles of school organization are discussed.

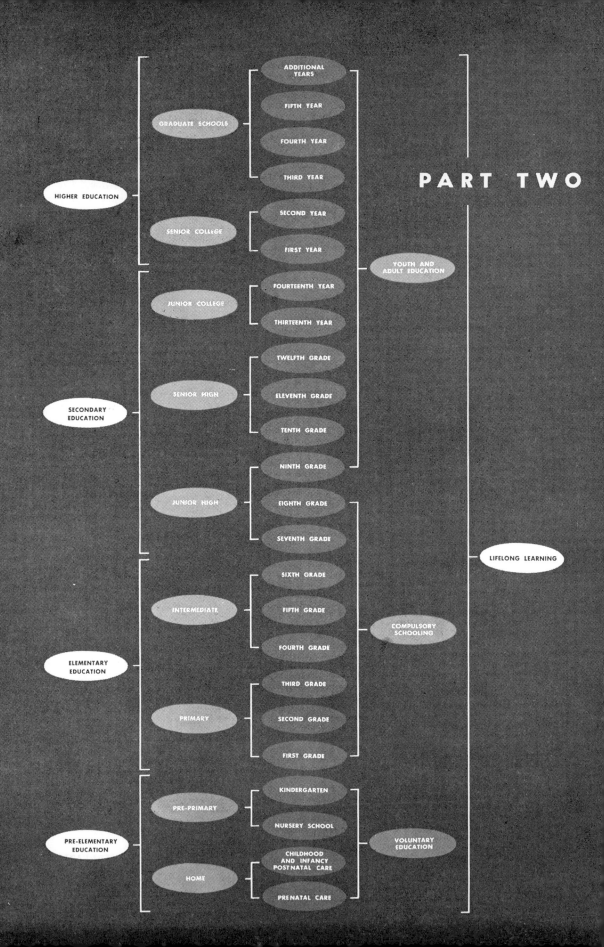

PART TWO

HIGHER EDUCATION

GRADUATE SCHOOLS
- ADDITIONAL YEARS
- FIFTH YEAR
- FOURTH YEAR
- THIRD YEAR

SENIOR COLLEGE
- SECOND YEAR
- FIRST YEAR

JUNIOR COLLEGE
- FOURTEENTH YEAR
- THIRTEENTH YEAR

YOUTH AND ADULT EDUCATION

SECONDARY EDUCATION

SENIOR HIGH
- TWELFTH GRADE
- ELEVENTH GRADE
- TENTH GRADE

JUNIOR HIGH
- NINTH GRADE
- EIGHTH GRADE
- SEVENTH GRADE

ELEMENTARY EDUCATION

INTERMEDIATE
- SIXTH GRADE
- FIFTH GRADE
- FOURTH GRADE

COMPULSORY SCHOOLING

LIFELONG LEARNING

PRIMARY
- THIRD GRADE
- SECOND GRADE
- FIRST GRADE

PRE-ELEMENTARY EDUCATION

PRE-PRIMARY
- KINDERGARTEN
- NURSERY SCHOOL

VOLUNTARY EDUCATION

HOME
- CHILDHOOD AND INFANCY POSTNATAL CARE
- PRENATAL CARE

Areas of
public education

American education spans the whole lifetime of the individual: it enrolls him at birth and graduates him at death. As indicated in the educational ladder on the opposite page, the four major sequential levels of lifelong learning are (1) pre-elementary, (2) elementary, (3) secondary, and (4) higher education; related to these is (5) education for adults.

The first, the pre-elementary period, includes prenatal and postnatal care as well as the early nurture and education of the child. The principal agencies for providing care and education at this early level are the home, the nursery school, and the kindergarten. This period reaches up to the elementary school age of approximately six years (Chapter 5).

Elementary education lays the firm foundation for all-round growth of the child through developing in him basic skills, habits, attitudes, and knowledges. The elementary schools in the United States enroll almost one-sixth of all Americans on the mainland, and are the main instruments for equipping persons with a common general education (Chapter 6).

Secondary education is broadened and lengthened to include all the curricular and cocurricular activities of the preadolescent, adolescent, and postadolescent youth. Theoretically it spans the period covering the junior high school, the senior school, and the junior college. It adds to the general education of youth and often provides some degree of specialization. Eighty-five per cent of youth of high school age are in school (Chapter 7).

Higher education includes both undergraduate and postgraduate study. College and university undergraduate life with its crowded activities may be a prelude to intensive postgraduate work, but more often it is the terminus of formal schooling. However, college enrollments are increasing (Chapter 8).

Education for out-of-school youth affords to an ever-increasing number of young Americans the opportunity for intellectual and social growth. Adult education, the final stage in lifelong learning, can yield satisfying fruits through a rich and varied program of activities (Chapter 9).

chapter 5

Pre-elementary education

After one of his lectures, Francis Wayland Parker, the pioneering educator, was asked by one of the women in the audience:

"How early can I begin the education of my child?"

"When will your child be born?" Parker asked.

"Born?" she gasped. "Why he is already five years old!"

"My goodness, woman," he cried, "Don't stand there talking to me—hurry home. You have lost the best five years!"

Pre-elementary education seeks to capitalize upon these "best years." It provides planning, organization, and guidance for this important early phase of child growth and development. It provides an easy and gradual transition from the simple, small-group, family-life setting to the larger, more complex and rigorous setting of elementary education. Although academic learning is not stressed during this period, readiness for learning is nourished. Important social, emotional, and physical development takes place during this formative period.

Pre-elementary education is concerned with parental and family-life education, early childhood education in the home, nursery school, and kindergarten. It is one of the most important, yet least well-established phases of the entire educational realm.

Foundations

Importance of Early Childhood. Authorities on early childhood education stress the extreme importance of the earliest years in the development of the individual, since it is during this formative period that the foundation is built for future growth. But a child's life really begins at fertilization. The nine months from conception to birth markedly affect the well-being of a child. Furthermore, the findings of children's laboratories and nursery schools suggest that the first half-dozen years of a child's life may be more important for educational purposes than all the other years, since many habits that underlie successful living are formed then. The basic philosophy toward life itself often has its roots in infancy and early childhood. Therefore, continuous close cooperation between the home and schools is necessary, especially during what may be called the preschool or pre-elementary period of a child's life.

Pre-elementary education covers the whole period from the child's birth until his entrance into elementary school at the age of six or seven years. The term "pre-elementary" seems more appropriate than "preschool," since the nursery school and the kindergarten are part of the school system in many cities. Furthermore, pre-elementary concerns the child not only from two to six years of age but from birth to entrance into the elementary school.

PIONEER WORK IN PRE-ELEMENTARY EDUCATION

During the early nineteenth century, many efforts were made to protect small children from neglect and overwork. In France Rousseau emphasized nature as a guide in the early education of young children, as pictured in *Émile*. The Reverend Jean F. Oberlin instituted schools for very young children, which later developed into the *écoles maternelles* (mother schools). Among the English philanthropists and leaders were Robert Owen, who started the infant school movement, Samuel Wilderspin, James P. Greaves, and The Reverend Charles Mayo. In Germany the leader in pre-elementary education was Froebel.

Pioneer Work of Froebel. The year 1837 was rich in important events in education. In America, Horace Mann was beginning his work as secretary of the state board of Massachusetts and Mary Lyon was opening her school for women which was to develop into Mount Holyoke College; in Blankenburg, Germany, Friedrich Froebel was starting the first kindergarten called a *Kleinkinderbeschäftigungsanstalt*.

Not until 1840 was the school solely for pre-elementary children called by its significant name *Kindergarten* (children's garden). The kindergarten was Froebel's crowning contribution to educational thought and practice. He did not plan kindergartens just for the children of the poor, but for all classes. Froebel had a diversity of educational experience as a teacher in a preparatory school, as a tutor of three boys upon whom he practiced some of Rousseau's ideas, and as a friend living with a group of students at Pestalozzi's unique school at Yverdon, where he was a devoted follower but intellectual critic of Pestalozzi.

His book *The Education of Man* is the account of his school for boys at Keilhau. This publication was followed by his *Autobiography* and *Mother Play and Nursery Songs*. His heart was broken when in 1851 the arbitrary Prussian Edict closed his kindergartens. He said quietly, "Such opposition throws us back on our principles." He then commenced to plan for the transference of his kindergarten work to America, where, he said, "A new life is freely unfolding itself and a new education of man will find a footing."

Early Kindergartens in America. The history of kindergartens in America is summarized in the Pre-elementary Education column in the historical calendar in this chapter. The first kindergarten in America was established by Mrs. Carl Schurz in her home in Watertown, Wisconsin, in 1855. Four years later, Elizabeth Peabody and her sister, Mrs. Horace Mann, established a kindergarten in a house in Boston.

The growth of the kindergarten may be divided roughly into five periods. (1) The pioneer stage, which had Boston as its center, stressed a few of the most important of Froebel's teachings. (2) The philanthropic era, which began in Florence, Massachusetts, valued the kindergarten largely as a reformatory or redemptive influence. (3) The strictly educational stage, which started in St. Louis, Missouri, accented scientific study of the principles underlying kindergarten education. (4) The fourth period, which started in Chicago and spread over the nation, is the maternal or pa-

NATIONAL DEVELOPMENT		THE DEVELOPMENT OF PRE-ELEMENTARY EDUCATION
Controversy and war between the states	**1855**	First kindergarten in America founded in Watertown, Wisconsin
	1868	First training school for kindergarten teachers started in Boston
Aftermath and reconstruction	**1873**	First permanent kindergarten established as part of the St. Louis public school system
	1877	First church that included kindergarten established in Toledo
	1892	International Kindergarten Union (now Association for Childhood Education) formed
Immigration and industrial growth	**1893**	First settlement house that included kindergartens organized at Northwestern University
	1897	National Congress of Mothers (now the National Congress of Parents and Teachers) organized
		Association of Day Nurseries of New York City organized
	1908	Child Study Association of America organized
The progressive era	**1912**	Federal Children's Bureau established
	1913	Division of Kindergarten Education created in U.S. Office of Education
World War I	**1919**	First nursery schools established in America
	1923	American Child Health Association formed
Normalcy and prosperity	**1925**	National Council of Parental Education formed
	1933	Nursery kindergartens started by Federal Emergency Relief Act
Depression and recovery	**1936**	Legislation implemented by Congress for maternal, child health and child welfare services
World War II	**1948**	Funds voted by Congress for United Nations International Children's Emergency Fund
The Cold War struggle		
	1960	Virtually all states have provided legislation authorizing public education below grade 1

HISTORICAL CALENDAR

rental era. Like the third stage, it is still extant. It aims at making the kindergarten a link between the home and the school, and at strengthening the foundations of family life. The kindergarten took on an international family aspect when the United Nations kindergarten was organized at Lake Success, New York, in 1947. (5) The current period is one of professional growth and experimentation.

In connection with the second or philanthropic period, the first church to include the kindergarten in its parish work was the Trinity Church of Toledo, and the first social settlement in slum areas to establish a kindergarten was that of Northwestern University in Chicago. The third stage is an important one, and the credit for its launching goes to Susan E. Blow. Interested in Froebel's philosophy, she had attended training schools for kindergarten teachers in Germany and in New York City, where a young woman taught by Froebel's widow in Germany had started what became a training school for kindergartners. With the cooperation of her superintendent of schools, William T. Harris, Miss Blow opened in St. Louis in 1873 the first public school kindergarten. About ten years later the school kindergarten movement had won so many adherents that the National Education Association added a kindergarten department. By 1900 many large city schools and several universities and normal schools had set up kindergarten departments. About 1910 the methods of the late Maria Montessori of Italy gained many adherents in this country. This able teacher placed great emphasis upon sense training through special teaching materials and upon the freedom of the child. Others who have greatly influenced the American kindergarten through experimental schools are G. Stanley Hall, John Kraus, Maria Kraus-Bolte, Samuel Chester Parker, John Dewey, William H. Kilpatrick, Anne Moore, Alice Temple, Nina Vandewalker, Laura Zirbes, Patty Smith Hill, Elizabeth Harrison, and Edna Dean Baker.

The federal government, through its Children's Bureau, established in the Department of Labor under Grace Abbott in 1912, and its *1913* Kindergarten Division organized a year later in the U.S. Office of Education, has given impetus to the kindergarten movement. It gave substantial aid through the establishment of nursery schools as part of the federal emergency education program.

Beginnings of Parental Education. With the evolution of the kindergarten, there gradually developed an interest on the part of parents, particularly mothers, in a study of early childhood. Meetings were started for this purpose. In 1894 a mothers' conference was called by a kindergarten teacher in Chicago. Three years *1897* later the National Congress of Mothers was organized in Washington, D.C., by a group interested in little children, the home, the school, and the community. In 1900 a formal charter was granted to this organization, which is now called the National Congress of Parents and Teachers. The parent-teacher associations are local, county, state, national, and international in scope. Their major objective is child welfare.

A powerful agent in the development of child health, parental education, and maternal care has been the federal Children's Bureau, already mentioned, which administered what was officially known as the Maternity and Infancy Act of 1921. This law for several years provided federal grants of money to each state accepting the terms of the act and making financial and administrative arrangements for it. It has been supplanted by the Social Security Act of 1936 which, in addition to care for crippled children, provides for maternal care, child health, and child welfare services.

Origin and Development of Nursery Education. The genesis of nursery education goes back to the beginning of families, and in some countries parents are still solely responsible for teaching their young children. Gradually, however, this responsibility is being delegated to established schools. In the United States the nursery school is of rather recent origin. Although this delegated task of nursery education is rather new in the educational system of the United States, it has long received attention in other countries.

The founding of nursery schools in the United States illustrates the fact that sometimes the first is last. Although in the chronology of the child's life the nursery school precedes the kindergarten, historically the development of the nursery school came last. The major growth of the nursery movement in this country has taken place in the last few decades.

The kindergarten and the nursery school have a common origin in the early infant school, which appears to have been philanthropic in purpose. As early as 1897 the Association of Day Nurseries of New York City was organized. Although the first public nursery school was started in 1919, the United States had less than three hundred nursery schools up to the advent of the federal nursery school program in 1933, and most of these schools were under private or semiprivate control. The family-life education program of the now defunct WPA, which included nursery schools, parent education, and homemaking, greatly stimulated the development of pre-elementary education during the depression era of the early 1930s.

Many institutions of higher learning have also been active in the education of the pre-elementary school child. The kindergarten-primary department of Teachers College, Columbia University, opened a nursery school in 1921. The Merrill-Palmer School of Homemaking in Detroit established the first nursery school to be used as a laboratory for the education of young girls. The first land-grant college to inaugurate a nursery school in connection with its home economics department was Iowa State College in 1924. The next year Cornell and Ohio State Universities started similar schools. Probably the first nursery school for the use of high school students in homemaking was in Highland Park, Michigan. The accumulated influence of all these efforts has markedly affected pre-elementary education in (1) the home, (2) the nursery school, and (3) the kindergarten.

Home care and training

The modern home has been referred to ironically as a place for boys and girls to park when they have no other place to go or as a place to watch TV. Although this may be partly true, nevertheless, most homes are more than mere houses.

The home is the child's first school. It is there that he learns to talk, to walk, to play, to work, and forms basic habits. No teacher can afford to underestimate the power of the home, for it is a physical, mental, social, emotional, and spiritual center for the child.

PARENTAL AND FAMILY LIFE EDUCATION

The child's first teachers are his parents; hence they should have definite knowledge of and guidance in their responsibilities and duties. Parental education is child- and parent-centered. With this dual and immediate objective of better and happier children and also parents is coupled the ultimate aim of a better civilization. Parental information may be offered to young people long before they marry and have children, while they are still in high school, college, or continuation school. Usually, however, it is given to adults who are already parents, and it may embrace prenatal and postnatal care as well as child study.

The story is told of a visiting nurse who called on an expectant mother in a slum district to help her. "So you're tryin' to tell me how to raise my children," the mother shouted, "me what's buried seven of 'em!" Efforts are being bent toward changing such an attitude. Some parent-teacher associations sponsor the project of enrolling expectant mothers in classes that meet with the school nurse or doctor. Many city, county, and state health departments distribute free literature on the care of mothers and babies. Uncle Sam's best seller is a publication of the Government Printing Office entitled *Infant Care*.

The home is the base for most preschool learning activities.

Here the child develops primary relationships with . . .

his peers . . .

and adults.

Among the organizations which today promote the study of children and family life are the National Council of Parent Education, the National Congress of Parents and Teachers, the Child Study Association of America, the American Association of University Women, and the American Home Economics Association. Parent education has also become a part of the regular work of departments in some states. As early as 1926 California created its Bureau of Child Study and Parent Education, using a special grant of money from the Laura Spelman Rockefeller Foundation. Many universities, as well as state departments of education, have received financial aid for child study from similar foundations.

Colleges and Family Life Education. Many colleges are performing significant services in the fields of preparental and postparental guidance. Vassar College, for example, in 1926 inaugurated an Institute of Euthenics—the improvement of the race through environment. Its initial objective was to offer to Vassar alumnae who were mothers the results of scientific research in learning, human behavior, child development, and the techniques of homemaking. The study of pre-elementary children has been advanced by numerous child institutes, such as the one established at Teachers College, Columbia University, in 1924 under the name Institute for Child Welfare Research. At the Iowa Child Welfare Research Station the plans definitely made for school-parent activities and parental education include conferences during registration, teacher and school contacts, contacts with other staff members, and provisions for the study of child development. Beginning with the enrollment of mothers during pregnancy, the Harvard Center for Research in Child Health and Development has followed for several years the growth and development of several hundred boys and girls from birth. The Yale Clinic of Child Development and numerous others have been instrumental in stimulating and organizing a number of important studies and experiments particularly relating to the problems of infants and young children. Monographs published by the Society for Research in Child Development of the National Research Council contain many interesting and helpful scientific studies of child development.

Local Schools and Parental and Family Life Education. Of the various formal agencies promoting parental education, the local school—public or independent—offers the greatest possibilities for development. These established institutions give instruction to future parents —both boys and girls—in home economics; conduct classes for adults who are expectant parents; hold baby clinics; provide guided observation in play groups; and organize family centers for consultation. They may become the nucleus of the parental education program in the community, with the cooperation of all agencies interested in child welfare, especially the home.

EARLY CHILDHOOD EDUCATION IN THE HOME

Modern society treasures children as its greatest resource. Prenatal and postnatal care give children a good start in life, thereby increasing their worth to society. The foundations for a child's future are laid in the home, which is the citadel of early childhood.

Pestalozzi was intensely interested in education in the home. His last formal speech, given when he was more than eighty years old, was entitled, "The Simplest Methods Whereby to Educate a Child at Home from the Cradle to the Sixth Year." The chief objectives of the training and education of the child, up to the time he enters upon the period of group living away from parents, are those found in a good home. The Children's Charter pledges for every child a home and that love and security which a home provides; and for that child who must receive foster care, the nearest substitute for his own home.

Robert J. Havighurst, chairman of the Committee on Human Development at the University of Chicago, lists for infancy and early childhood several vital developmental tasks, most of which are "home work" for the child and parents. Some of these developmental tasks are listed in Chapter 9.

In the early family life of the child, the home is preeminently the educational and social center: it is both a school, with the parents as teachers, and a social laboratory of human relationships. Consequently, the home should be a well-designed and appropriately furnished place for living and learning. In a world of change, the child should find the home a haven of hope, a place made increasingly secure by local, state, and national efforts in child and maternal welfare.

Nursery education

SCOPE OF NURSERY EDUCATION

The educational system in the United States was not planned from the bottom up. It is like a long and strong ladder which lacks several rungs at the bottom. To supply these missing rungs, the nursery school and kindergarten are being established. Most adults have never attended either nursery school or kindergarten, since the development of these institutions is of relatively recent date.

The day nursery and the nursery school are the most common forms of organized education for very early childhood. The day nursery is a social welfare institution designed to give day care to the child of the working mother. With approximately one-third of the married women employed, the day nursery is an important educational agency. The nursery school, which has characteristics of both a nursery and a school, in a sense is a downward extension of the kindergarten so that children at an earlier age may benefit from supervised educational and social experiences.

General Types. There are five basic types of nursery schools. Some city school systems operate nursery schools that are organized within the elementary school unit. This arrangement, similar to that of most kindergartens, is considered quite acceptable. [2] A few school systems have organized nursery schools within an administrative unit of early childhood education that includes nursery, kindergarten, and primary levels. [3] A few secondary schools have affiliated nursery schools, thereby providing high school homemaking and social studies classes with direct experiences with young children. [4] A number of colleges and universities have established nursery schools to serve as laboratories for the training of nursery school teachers, or for education in child care or family life. [5] But more than half of the nursery schools in America are separate from other educational units. Most of these independent nursery schools are sponsored by welfare agencies, foundations, churches, or other private organizations.

Nursery schools, as well as kindergartens, may be classified according to their main source of financial support, as: public (local, state, and federal), parochial, and private. The number of nursery schools that are a part of the local public school system and supported entirely by the local board of education is very small. When there seemingly is not enough public school money available to educate the primary pupils properly, obviously the preprimary children will not be given much consideration. Fiscal facts—the dearth of public funds and the increase in personal wealth—enhance the role of the independent nursery school, both private and parochial.

Some private nursery schools are of very fine quality. Some specialize in meeting the needs of exceptional children. Some are mere day-care centers rather than real schools. Some operate for only half days. But most private nursery schools offer full-day programs. Unfortunately, some are irresponsibly managed, here today and gone tomorrow.

AIMS OF NURSERY EDUCATION

Clark Moustakas and Minnie Berson of the famed Merrill-Palmer School have provided an excellent statement of the aims of the nursery school:

We see the nursery school as an educational center that furthers the full development of the young child and the successful functioning of a group of young children. Its goal is to maintain a balance between spontaneous behavior and conformity to society's standards. It is concerned with the feelings and attitudes of young children and their developmental skills. It seeks to help children realize their potential and at the same time aids them to accept the limits of life in a democratic society.

The nursery school recognizes how important it is for young children to learn routine health habits. Activities are planned to strengthen and facilitate the use of their large and small muscles, build coordination, and develop sound, strong bodies.

The nursery school guides the child in experiencing the stimulation and enjoyment that come from the association with persons both younger and older than himself, as well as with those of the same age. It offers many opportunities for sharing and cooperating and helps children learn when and how to share.

The encouragement of rational thinking, fair play, self-reliance, and individual freedom and responsibility are all part of the nursery school's value. . . .

The nursery school must be concerned with the enhancement of the child's individuality, and the development of attitudes, interests, understandings, and beliefs which will enable the child to be a happy, secure, contributing member of society. To reach these goals the nursery school must have an emotionally warm, friendly, relaxed atmosphere.[1]

PROGRAM AND PROCEDURES

The Curriculum. The curriculum of the nursery school, if one can technically call it such, is broad in scope, for it is planned to meet all the needs of growing youngsters from two to four years of age.

Authorities agree that it is necessary to look upon the pupil as a learner from birth and to realize that the habits of learning are more important than the actual material learned. The learning activities are of two general kinds: those that are routine in nature, that is, occur at a specific time every day; and those in which the child is given a choice of activity, which vary from day to day. These activities are usually organized into a flexible schedule.

Program of Activities. The planning of a nursery school program depends a great deal upon the length of the daily session. Some schedules cover only two to four hours, whereas some all-day nurseries are planned on a ten-hour day basis. The activities usually cover the hours from 8:30 A.M. to 3 or 3:30 P.M., or longer, if necessary, for children of working mothers. The following is an illustrative list of everyday activities that provide the requisite learning experiences:

9:00	Arrival and health inspection
9:00–10:00	Free play
10:00–10:15	Toilet
10:15–10:30	Stories and discussion
10:30–10:45	Singing and dancing
10:45–11:00	Snack
11:00–11:30	Free play and toilet
11:30	Departure

[1] Clark E. Moustakas and Minnie P. Berson, *The Nursery School and Child Care Center*, Whiteside, Inc., New York, 1955, pp. 17–18.

In some schools, the age groups are separated. Most groups have full-day sessions. The schedules are adjusted by the teacher to meet the needs of each age level. For younger children, rest periods are provided and free play periods are usually shorter. Singing, dancing, and storytelling are handled more informally with younger children.

Naturally, a good nursery school takes into account the home conditions under which the child lives. It does not exist as an isolated unit but is an integral part of the community, supplementing other agencies supported by the people.

What are the activities in a typical nursery school day?

There is time for . . .

self-expression . . .

play . . .

Nursery School Staff. The superior nursery school has a balanced, competent staff of teachers and other specialists to assist in the areas of parent education, health, and food preparation. Small nursery schools often pool their resources in order to obtain all the needed talent for working with young children. It is essential that all staff workers understand and like little children and their parents. Teachers and other personnel workers are discussed in Chapters 11 and 12.

CURRENT PRACTICES
IN NURSERY SCHOOL EDUCATION

By way of recapitulation, some of the many interesting and significant practices current in nursery schools are mentioned briefly. The *status in quo,* however, may not necessarily represent the best ideas and highest ideals.

The terminology employed in early childhood education is being revised. For example, "child-and-mother school" or "family-life school" may replace "nursery school." "Preschool" or "prekindergarten" as applied to nursery school is being discarded, since the terms suggest modification of a program designed for older children. The entire period of growth from two to eight years of age is being considered as a unit for guidance and instruction.

The scope of the nursery school is being broadened. Now it is not merely a safe place to leave a child; rather, it is an educational center for all-round growth. Emphasis is placed upon emotional as well as mental, physical, and social adjustments.

discovery . . .

The clientele is changing and enlarging. The nursery school is no longer either a luxury for a few favored children of well-to-do families or a pauper's home. The middle economic group is beginning to reap the benefit of preschool service. Children in new housing projects and in rural areas are being included. A marked trend is the provision of nursery school education for exceptional children. Many handicapped boys and girls profit even more from early training than do normal youngsters.

More attention is being devoted to nursery school readiness. Among the main factors considered in determining a child's readiness for group experiences are his age and general maturity; his ability to give and take, to form attachments to other adults besides his mother, and to exchange affection and interests with his peers; and his desire to come to nursery school. Pre-nursery school parties are often used as an orientation device.

rest . . .

and refreshments.

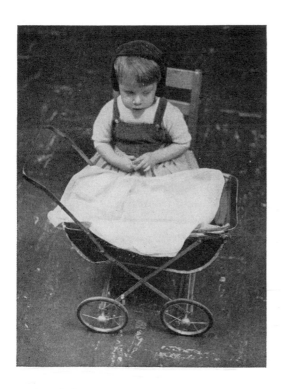

contemplation . . .

Physical facilities of the modern nursery school include an exposure with plenty of light; ground-floor quarters that are attractive, clean, and safe; space for playing, working, eating, sleeping, bathing, and cooking; radiant heat to warm the cold floors; equipment suited to the child's size and maturity; and direct exits to a covered veranda and enclosed shaded playground. The buildings are being made as attractive as homes.

Research and observation play an important part in the program. Nursery school is thus becoming a clearinghouse for improved homemaking policies and practices. College and high school home economics departments are establishing nursery schools as observation and practice centers, for example, at Vassar College and in the high school in Highland Park, Michigan. Thus the unit trains preschool children, adolescents, and adults for participation in wholesome family living. The staffs are producers, consumers, and interpreters of research in child growth and other areas of early childhood education.

Modern programs of early childhood education include guidance for both parents and prospective fathers and mothers, so that they are playing a greater role in assisting the nursery staff. Thus the gains effected by the children in both school and home are consolidated.

Parent and family-life education has become a part of the regular work of many state departments of education. Some states have established a Council of Parental Education to assist the state departments in developing programs of parent education and nursery schools. A position, Consultant in Family-life Education, was established in the U.S. Office of Education. This consultant assists the states in developing programs of education for home and family life to reach both sexes and all age groups.

The increase in the number of babies and parents and the high employment rate for married women have increased the need for baby sitters. Some high schools and public health units give courses or lessons for girls who take baby-sitting seriously.

The nursery schools are reexamining their function in the community. Demonstration centers for community programs in home and family-life education have been established in several centers in the United States.

Child accounting systems, which take into consideration the whole child, are being improved. This includes a continuing census of the number of potential nursery school children. Cumulative recording and evaluating are increasing.

More and more states are providing some form of financial aid for nursery schools, or are authorizing permissive taxation at the local level. Various other laws are being enacted to aid the nursery school and the young child.

State departments of education are providing more guidance for and supervision of nursery schools, including higher standards of cer-

tification for teachers. Nursery school personnel is being enlarged and improved. Some nurseries have specialized workers such as recreation directors, dietitians, parent-education specialists, home counselors, and other social caseworkers. Welfare services, such as those performed by visiting housekeepers, are helping to improve conditions in the home. These traveling mothers render many services for children. The health program includes the regular services of a physician and daily inspection by a qualified person.

FUTURE OF NURSERY SCHOOLS

Quantitatively, the future for nursery schools is bright. According to *Time,* in 1975 the United States will need to set a "fifth plate" for every four now on the table. The large increase in the number of children—over four million a year—has stimulated the demand for more nursery schools.

The nursery school today occupies a marginal position just outside the public school system, somewhat similar to that held for many years by the kindergarten. When kindergarten education becomes a universal or compulsory part of the school system, the nursery school may then enter on a mandatory-on-petition basis and eventually take its place as the beginning unit in the American public school system. As the Educational Policies Commission states, "The nursery school now is the new child in the family of public education." The future of the work lies in coordinating the nursery schools with the next higher educational units, especially the kindergarten.

Kindergarten

SCOPE OF KINDERGARTEN EDUCATION

Kindergarten education usually covers the period of schooling just before the child enters the first grade, whether he has had nursery school experience or not. The entrance age is generally set at four or five years, although some junior kindergartens admit younger children. Several recent studies of eye growth and reading readiness reveal that a child six years old chronologically may not always be ready for reading experience and that he can more profitably spend some time in the preprimary or kindergarten group.

Nursery School and Kindergarten. The nursery school may be compared, rather than contrasted, with the kindergarten. Compared with kindergarten, the nursery school admits younger children, generally from two to four years of age; operates usually on a full-day schedule; keeps a closer touch with the home because the child is younger; provides more opportunities for parental education; stresses more the physical care and development of the child; gives more attention to eating, sleeping, and kindred habits; gives more guidance to children in learning independence in self-control, personal care, respect for property rights, etc.; shows the child how to do a thing with a minimum of telling or explaining; utilizes less appeal to group opinion; has equipment and supplies on a smaller scale; has fewer children per teacher; and does not enroll so many children. The differences, however, are primarily those of degree. As the child goes from the nursery school to the kindergarten, the scope of his learning experiences widens.

The separate problems of the nursery school and the kindergarten are joined in the common responsibility of providing continuous, broadening, and deepening experiences for the children. Among the numerous means of correlation between the nursery school and the kindergarten are: accurate record-keeping of the child's progress, the planning of teacher-education programs so that prospective nursery and kindergarten teachers see their work as related, the elimination of excess emphasis upon organization units, and the development of a comprehensive philosophy of education that carries through from nursery school to adult education.

Kindergarten and Home. Since for many children the first contact with an actual school situation comes in the kindergarten, a constant, vital relationship should exist between the kindergarten and the home. This relationship may be promoted by various means. Some kindergarten teachers send reports to the parents on items such as food difficulties, the amount of sleep or play, or emotional disturbances. The mothers may also inform the teachers about the daily home life and antecedents of the children. In many communities, a home visitation plan releases each kindergarten teacher one afternoon a week to call upon parents. A home visit by the teacher and a school visit by the mother provide direct means of solving jointly many perplexing problems.

Types of Kindergarten. Kindergartens may also be classified by type according to general categories, viz., research, teacher education, home economics, social service, behavior problems, cooperative, summer school, nursery and kindergarten combined, private, federally supported, and public school kindergarten. The two most common forms of affiliation are with private organizations and the public school. According to methodology of teaching, kindergartens are sometimes Froebelian, Montessorian, conservative, middle-of-the-road, or progressive. Whatever the label, the prevailing type of kindergarten is that which seeks to educate the whole child from four to six years through supplementing the home, the nursery school, and other educational agencies.

Enrollments. Although most kindergartens are found in systems of 2,500 population and over, the increase in consolidated elementary schools is bringing the advantages of the kindergarten to many rural communities. Although kindergartens are theoretically for children from four to six, the ages actually range from two to seven years. Owing to the increased birth rate, the kindergarten enrolls many more pupils than formerly. Still, only about 50 per cent of the five-year-olds and 70 per cent of the six-year-olds are in school. Millions of children miss the advantages of kindergarten because many communities do not provide this opportunity. Much pioneering still remains to be done if the purposes and program of the kindergarten are to be widely accepted.

AIMS OF KINDERGARTEN

For those who have not attended a nursery school, the kindergarten is an extension of home life; for others, it is a continuation of the work begun in the home and the nursery school. The general aim of the kindergarten, which is unhampered by requirements in subject matter and skills, is to give the child abundant opportunity for enriched experiences.

The National Education Association has summarized the main goals of the kindergarten as those of promoting: (1) children's health, (2) children's safety, (3) the ability to work alone despite the presence of others, (4) the techniques of working with others in groups, (5) broad opportunities for contacts with other children and adults, (6) a wide variety of experiences that will reveal their interests and aptitudes, and (7) readiness in reading, writing, and number work they will do in the first grade.[2] The general principle is that of assisting children from the age of four to six years in their developmental tasks—present and future. These aims take shape and substance through a full program of carefully planned activities, based upon sound physiological and psychological principles.

PROGRAM AND PROCEDURES

Principles Underlying the Modern Kindergarten Program. The kindergarten program is extremely flexible—it has no required subjects. The key principle is learning by doing. In planning the curriculum, attention is given prima-

2 Adapted from Research Division, *The Value of the Kindergarten*, National Education Association, Washington, D.C., 1952.

Kindergarten helps young children to . .

care for themselves . . .

learn good health habits . . .

develop readiness for reading . . .

progress physically . . .

rily to promoting physical, mental, social, and emotional growth.

The psychological and physiological principle that colors most of the activities in the kindergarten is that of readiness. As early as 1915 John Dewey said, "Maturity is the result of slow growth of powers. Ripening takes time: it cannot be hurried without harm." The kindergarten therefore withholds certain formal training, such as instruction in actual reading, but it provides rich experiences that will help prepare the child for the elementary grades. These experiences include bringing the child into a school learning environment; enlarging his circle of friends through the addition of another adult—the teacher—and many peers; enriching the child's speaking vocabulary; training in speech through careful enunciation and pronunciation; creating interest in books through storytelling and looking at books; developing left-to-right eye movement through reading a story told in pictures; stimulating arithmetic readiness through counting objects and seeing numbers; and facilitating development in writing through drawing, cutting, and other forms of eye and hand coordination, including creative painting. The readiness goal and others are implemented through a flexible schedule of activities.

Perhaps the most valuable experiences gained through kindergarten activity are those

and explore the outside world.

which strengthen social relationships, such as: learning to care for possessions, developing respect for the property of others, gaining a concept of group property, taking turns and sharing, listening to the group, talking before the group, group planning, evaluating experiences, using conventional greetings and requests.[3]

Schedule of Activities. Most kindergartens have a morning and an afternoon group. The following is an illustrative morning program from the Bakersfield, California, kindergarten:

Morning session

9:00– 9:20	Opening. Flag salute
	Greeting song. Roll call
	Conversation
9:20– 9:45	Work period
9:45– 9:55	Evaluation
9:55–10:00	Clean up
10:00–10:20	Play period
10:20–10:25	Rest
10:25–10:40	Rhythms
10:40–10:55	Story time
10:55–11:05	Songs
11:05–11:10	Dismissal

As this schedule indicates, the kindergarten provides a carefully selected educative environment replete with sensory impressions and with materials stimulating to the self-activity of the young child.

With due respect to Froebel as a great pioneer, the tendency for many years was to cling too tenaciously to his principles. Today in many kindergartens little of the traditional is left, owing to discoveries of oculists and nerve specialists. For example, these scientists have urged less use of minute materials which call into play the small undeveloped muscles of the eye and hand, and greater use of large materials to exercise the muscles of the arms, back, and abdomen. Swings, sleds, carts, large

[3] Jerome E. Leavitt (ed.), *Nursery-Kindergarten Education*, McGraw-Hill Book Company, Inc., New York, 1958, pp. 99–101.

blocks, ropes, and similar equipment are symbols of the new kindergarten.

CURRENT PRACTICES

Current kindergarten practices supplementing those reported previously for nursery schools include the following:

Unfortunately, the size of the typical kindergarten is increasing as a result of shortage of funds and superabundance of children. The traditional provision of two or four semesters is supplemented by three-semester programs in several schools.

A public-relations program for the kindergarten, including a brochure for parents, has been developed in many schools.

A trend is to integrate the kindergarten as part of a continuous program in early childhood education. The kindergarten is losing its status as an isolated part of the school system and is being incorporated as part of a primary unit embracing the nursery school and kindergarten, plus the lower two or three grades. There is more intervisitation between nursery school, kindergarten, and first-grade teachers.

Better provision is being made for the introduction of children to kindergarten. Sometimes they attend for a few days prior to their first year of attendance. In some cases, a few children start each day, rather than all at once. Similar efforts are being made to smooth the transition from kindergarten to elementary education.

The transition from kindergarten to first grade is facilitated through the emphasis upon readiness in all forms, especially upon reading readiness. The modern kindergarten, while not teaching reading, provides indirect preparation for reading. It is copiously stocked with books suitable for children of the kindergarten age. But all six-year-olds are no longer assumed to be *ipso facto* ready to read.

More attention is being given to developmental tasks which are set by the maturing of the child, his creative self-motivation, and the demands of society.

Many subjects, such as fine arts and science, are filtering down into the kindergarten. Almost every topic under the sun is discussed. Much emphasis is centered upon creative self-expression.

Many multisensory aids, such as phonograph records and films, help the child to understand the wondrous world of material things. They also assist the teacher in interpreting to parents and public the role of the kindergarten. Radio and television are being used increasingly, especially in parental education. A kindergarten of the air was first established in Perth, Australia, and later another in Toronto, Canada. The latter, designed especially for rural areas, includes in its program health talks, songs, stories, suggestions for handwork, and radio-side games.

As with the nursery school, more kindergartens are being established for exceptional children. Greater attention is now given to psychiatric and psychological treatment of emotionally disturbed children.

Early childhood evaluation is more comprehensive and functional than in yesteryears. Parents help supplement the anecdotal records of developmental processes; these are collected and interpreted by teachers and other members of the kindergarten staff. Mental and achievement tests form ancillary aids in guidance.

Parochial and private school kindergartens continue to play an important role in early childhood education and research.

Most teachers colleges and universities offer courses in teacher education for kindergartners. Contrary to traditional practice, the modern kindergarten teacher is often one of the most highly educated instructors in the system. The teaching is often the best in the school. No body of teachers more closely reconciles theory and practice than do the kindergarten teachers.

The majority of the state legislatures have considered early childhood education of sufficient importance to enact legislation providing specifically for the establishment and maintenance of kindergartens as a part of the public school system.

FUTURE OF KINDERGARTENS

Much research is helping to improve practices. Yale Clinic Institute of Child Development is one of several devoted to clinical and guidance services and research in early childhood education.

The future presages a steady growth in the number of kindergartens and in their enrollments. The increase of pupils in the elementary schools diminishes the rooms and finances available to house and support more kindergartens. More state departments will add to their staffs specialists in the supervision and guidance of local programs for early childhood education. All states in time will permit the local school board to establish kindergartens by special election, petition, or decision of the board, and will grant aid for their support. Permissive legislation will be replaced by the compulsory establishment of kindergartens on a voluntary attendance basis. In view of the fact that waves of retrenchment often cause public school authorities to abandon kindergartens, the interest of the young children must be safeguarded against such reverses through adequate legislation. The gradual acceptance of the kindergarten as a legitimate and permanent part of the public school system is inevitable. It will continue its vestibule function and open doors to wider horizons. Qualitatively, the work of the kindergarten will rise with the uplift in standards for the physical facilities, for the educational program, and for the education of teachers.

Summary

Pre-elementary education relates to the very important early years of child growth and development, covering the period from birth to entry into elementary education.

The pioneering work in pre-elementary education dates back to Froebel. Although there were a few prototypes of pre-elementary schools in early America, the movement did not really gain momentum until after World War I. It is still not widely established.

Pre-elementary education begins with the care and training of the young child in the home. In many ways, these are the most important years in life because they include the period of most rapid growth. Children are very formative in these years and are influenced greatly by the quality of their home life.

Day nurseries and nursery schools exist in many forms—sometimes operated privately, sometimes integrated with the public school program, sometimes associated with high schools or colleges as laboratories. However, most nursery schools are separate from other educational units and are operated by private agencies.

Nursery schools were originated to care for children of working mothers. But today nursery education seeks to bring organization, planning, and guidance to the growth and development of children through their formative years. These programs are very informal, providing for supervised play, storytelling and discussion, singing, dancing, and other similar activities. Nursery schools aim to smooth the young child's difficult transition from the family setting to the school environment. They provide opportunity for children to adjust to larger groups before the more formidable tasks of kindergarten and first grade are encountered.

The kindergarten also exists in both the public and private domain. However, a larger proportion of kindergartens than nursery schools is affiliated with public school systems. Nevertheless, large numbers of young children, particularly those attending small school systems, are still denied kindergarten experience. The kindergarten seeks to develop readiness for learning and to guide the mental, social, emotional, and physical development of children. Thus children's experience with people and with the world is broadened so that more effective learning can take place in later years.

In the future, further expansion of pre-elementary education is most probable. The gradual acceptance of this type of education as a legitimate and permanent part of the public school program seems inevitable.

Suggested activities

1. Review the historical foundations of pre-elementary education found in the second column of the historical calendar in this chapter.
2. Discuss the statement: "The home is the child's first school."
3. What can one learn about children from baby-sitting?
4. Study the program of a national organization especially interested in the pre-elementary child, such as the Child Study Association of America or the Association for Childhood Education International.
5. Attend a child study meeting and observe the type of program.
6. Write up a case study of some child under six years of age.
7. Discuss the relationships between home economics education and the pre-elementary child.
8. Study photographs or take pictures of children in action.
9. Prepare a detailed program for parental education.
10. Discuss the selection and use of toys in the home.
11. Outline the progress of nursery schools.
12. Study the history of the kindergarten in the United States.
13. Prepare a brief biography of Froebel, "the father of the kindergarten," G. Stanley Hall, Susan Blow, or any other pioneer in pre-elementary education.
14. Discuss the necessary qualifications for teachers in pre-elementary schools.

Bibliography

Books

Early Education, National Education Association, Washington, D.C., 1956. This pamphlet presents a compilation of 16 of the best statements on early childhood education.

Heffernan, Helen (ed.): *Guiding the Young Child*, D. C. Heath and Company, Boston, 1959. Discusses the young child—his needs, interests, and growth patterns—and how he can be guided in his development.

Leavitt, Jerome E. (ed.): *Nursery-Kindergarten Education*, McGraw-Hill Book Company, Inc., New York, 1958. An excellent discussion of nursery and kindergarten education with illustrations of programs and activities.

Let's Look at Kindergartens, National Education Association, Washington, D.C., 1955. This illustrated pamphlet gives an interpretation of the need for and advantages of kindergarten experiences for children.

Moustakas, Clark E., and Minnie P. Berson: *The Nursery and Child Care Center*, Whiteside, Inc., New York, 1955. An authoritative treatment of the nursery school drawn from experience with the famed Merrill-Palmer School.

Portfolio on More and Better Schools for Children under Six, Association for Childhood Education International, Washington, D.C., 1958. Discusses the need for pre-elementary education and shows how this need is met in several communities.

Read, Katherine H.: *The Nursery School: A Hu-*

man *Relations Laboratory,* W. B. Saunders Company, Philadelphia, 1955. Stresses the importance of the nursery school in helping young people learn to live happily with each other and with adults.

Sheehy, Emma D.: *The Fives and Sixes Go to School,* Henry Holt and Company, Inc., New York, 1954. Describes this level of early childhood education with attention to its purposes and programs.

Wills, Clarice, and William H. Stegeman: *Living in the Kindergarten,* Follett Publishing Co., Chicago, 1956. Describes the kindergarten in terms of the life and growth of children and their preparation for later school life.

Periodicals

Association for Childhood Education International, Committee on Teacher Preparation: "Standards for Teachers in Early Childhood Education," *Childhood Education,* vol. 35 (October, 1958), pp. 65–66. Considers the academic background and professional experience of teachers in nursery schools, kindergartens, and primary grades.

Chamberlain, Orlo R., and Robert R. Chamberlain: "Do Children Need Pre-school Experiences?" *Childhood Education,* vol. 32 (April, 1956), pp. 371–373. Shows the importance of pre-elementary education in developing interpersonal relationships important for later adjustment.

Foster, Luella M.: "Using an Infant Study Center," *Journal of Home Economics,* vol. 49 (October, 1957), pp. 646–648. Describes a center for the observation by students and parents of infants under two years of age.

Gabbard, Hazel F.: "A Nation's Concern for Kindergartens," *School Life,* vol. 41 (May, 1959), pp. 10–11. Describes the growing awareness of the values of pre-elementary education and the rise of forces compelling demand for this level of education.

Gilpatrick, Naomi: "We Coped with the First Satellite," *The Instructor,* vol. 67 (May, 1958), pp. 32f. An account of the fascinating way in which a kindergarten teacher helped children grasp the basic concepts of space satellites, an interesting example of kindergarten work.

"How Are the Fives Faring in Your Town?" *Childhood Education,* vol. 35 (September, 1958), pp. 25–26. Outlines the reasons why kindergartens must be made available to all children and means of improving existing ones.

Lloyd, Elizabeth C.: "Nursery Education, Our Responsibility," *Journal of Education,* vol. 137 (May, 1955), pp. 2–4. Makes a plea for wider understanding and acceptance of the role of nursery schools.

Mullen, Frances A.: "Pre-school Area of Special Education," *Education,* vol. 77 (April, 1957), pp. 468–474. Shows the role of pre-elementary education for blind, physically handicapped, mentally retarded, and emotionally disturbed children.

"Shall We Send Him to Nursery School?" *National Parent Teacher,* vol. 51 (March, 1957), pp. 14–16. Viewpoints of five experts—educator, psychiatrist, pediatrician, parent, and childhood education specialist—on the values of nursery schools.

Smith, Hyrum M.: "Studying the Child in the Kindergarten," *NEA Journal,* vol. 45 (February, 1956), pp. 80–82. Stresses the importance of the kindergarten as a means of getting to know children and anticipating their problems in later school years.

chapter **6**

*Elementary
education*

In an earlier period of history, the public elementary school of America was known as "the common school." As Henry Barnard was careful to point out, "The common school should not longer be regarded as common, because it is cheap, inferior, and attended only by the poor and those who are indifferent to the education of their children, but common as the light and the air because its blessings are open to all and enjoyed by all." Although elementary schools have changed substantially and although we no longer refer to them as common schools, they have indeed retained their common clientele. The children of many cultures, nationalities, races, economic levels, and religions have learned to respect each other through their associations during their most formative years in elementary education.

Although the common school was influenced by European traditions, it is fundamentally an American institution. Its basic purpose is the all-around development of the child from six to twelve years of age, with particular emphasis on equipping him with basic skills, attitudes, and appreciations. General education for all is its main function.

Elementary schools throughout the country represent diversified patterns and variegated programs. The traditional divisions are primary, intermediate, and upper grades or junior high school.

The programs of the various elementary schools are determined in a measure by their objectives and organization. The teaching and learning procedures are as diversified as their curriculums, varying from ultraconservative to ultraprogressive. The elementary school has an assured future in American democracy.

The importance of elementary education can hardly be overestimated. Children of elementary school age are in a highly formative period of life and the content of the elementary school curriculum is most fundamental to sound growth and development. Therefore it is most imperative that strong programs of education be established.

NATIONAL DEVELOPMENT		THE DEVELOPMENT OF ELEMENTARY EDUCATION
	1633	Elementary school established by the Dutch in New York
	1642	Earliest colonial educational law passed in Massachusetts
The Colonial period	**1651**	Existence of dame school recorded in New Haven
The struggle for independence and constitutional government		
Launching the new nation	**1789**	Massachusetts school law required a school in every community
Maritime troubles and the War of 1812		
Era of good feeling	**1834**	Free elementary education first adopted by Pennsylvania
Jacksonian Democracy	**1837**	"Common school revival" started by Horace Mann
Westward migration and expansion	**1852**	First compulsory law for part-time school attendance passed by Massachusetts
Controversy and war between the states	**1890**	First full-time compulsory school attendance law passed in Connecticut
Aftermath and reconstruction		
	1893	Six-six plan of school organization recommended by Committee of Ten
Immigration and industrial growth	**1895**	Report of NEA Committee of Fifteen on Elementary Education presented
	1896	Experimental school established at University of Chicago by John Dewey
The progressive era		
World War I	**1918**	Compulsory education made effective in all states
Normalcy and prosperity		
Depression and recovery	**1948**	Basic policy for elementary education presented in *Education for All American Children*
World War II		
The Cold War struggle	**1953**	Report of Mid-century Committee on Outcomes in Elementary Education published by Russell Sage Foundation
	1958	NEA Department of Elementary School Principals published comprehensive research study, *The Elementary School Principalship*

HISTORICAL CALENDAR

Foundations

Early Beginnings of Elementary Education. In colonial America elementary schools were organized much later than the universities. An exception occurred in New York State where, under Dutch rule, a free, tax-supported elementary school was established in Fort Amsterdam in 1633. When New Netherlands became New York, the resultant change in policy retarded the development of public elementary education in New York State.

Colonial New England and especially Massachusetts took the first steps toward the permanent establishment of schools for the common people. Some time after the settling of Massachusetts, the law of 1642 was passed. It gave to town officials the "power to take account from time to time of their parents and masters and of their children, especially of their ability to read and understand the principles of religion and the capital laws of the country, and to impose fines on all those who refuse to render such accounts to them when required." This was followed by the "Old Deluder" law of 1647 which required the various towns to establish and maintain schools and even imposed a fine of £5 for failure to do so. Numerous laws were passed in the colonies in regard to free education. But permissive rather than mandatory legislation was the usual type of school regulation. Thus the colonists permitted free public education in theory but in practice supported few free schools.

Dame Schools. Elementary education in the eighteenth century was entrusted to reading and writing schools. These were followed by "dame schools," the first record of which is found in New Haven, Connecticut, in 1651. Usually a dame taught her own children and others from the neighborhood in her home between household tasks. These dame schools

were primarily for little children; when older pupils came to school in the winter, a man teacher was usually employed. The dame schools, were followed by primary schools that became nonsectarian forerunners of the modern elementary system.

Nonsectarian Schools. Public education struggled to become nonsectarian. Throughout the colonial period elementary education had a strong religious tone. Moral and religious truths were emphasized constantly. The school was often made the servant of the church, and numerous religious denominations established their own schools. The pupils were usually taught reading, writing, arithmetic, singing of hymns, prayers, and catechism. Often parochial schools were granted aid from state funds. Gradually the pendulum swung from one extreme to the other—from sectarianism to secularism. The first state to adopt a constitutional provision prohibiting sectarian instruction was New Hampshire in 1792. Today it is illegal in most states to teach the Bible or to give sectarian instruction in publicly supported schools. *why?*

Elementary Schools Free and Open to All. Elementary education in America encountered many obstacles, including the social beliefs and prejudices that the colonists carried with them from the old country. Prevailing ideas in England, Germany, France, and other countries influenced the New World. The concept of social classes or castes extant in England during the colonial period made education a matter of private rather than state support. Persons of wealth sent their children to privately supported schools or engaged tutors to teach them at home. For those unable to do this, pauper schools were established. But because of the stigma attached to being a pauper, the very schools set up for poor children were often not patronized by them. Many influences and many persons working over a long period of years brought about gradually the establishment of free public schools for all children. Pennsylvania in 1834 adopted a state program of free schools. Other states followed this example until today elementary education is free and available to all.

Elementary Education Compulsory. Another struggle was to make elementary education compulsory. One hundred years ago attendance was generally optional. The histories of the colonies reveal the gradual adoption of the principle of compulsory elementary education, but records are strangely silent as to the degree of its enforcement. One may look to Massachusetts for the contribution of the law and to Connecticut for its administration and methods of enforcement. The first state compulsory school attendance law was adopted in Massachusetts as late as 1852; this legislation for part-time compulsory attendance was followed in 1890 by Connecticut's full-time requirement. Compulsory schooling was bitterly opposed by many people who argued that it deprived the parents of their inalienable rights, it was not necessary in order to secure attendance, it was an uncalled-for assumption of powers by state governments, it was inimical to the spirit of free democratic institutions, and it was an obstacle in the employment of child labor.

The majority of states now demand that every normal child attend the elementary school for at least eight months annually between the ages of seven and sixteen, or until he has completed the eighth grade. Several states have enacted laws raising the compulsory school age to eighteen years.

Many Foreign Influences on Elementary Education. Compulsory education was one of several ideas that were undoubtedly borrowed from other lands, particularly Prussia. For several years elementary education abroad was studied intensively for suggestions that could be adopted by or adapted to the American primary school. Victor Cousin's *Report on the State of Public Instruction in Prussia,* which appeared first in French and in about 1835 in English, was widely read in America. Calvin E. Stowe, the husband of Harriet Beecher Stowe who aroused America with her picture of slavery in *Uncle Tom's Cabin,* exercised a tremendous influence upon American education through the publication of his *Report on Elementary Education in Europe* (1837). This was studied by many state legislators. That same year Horace Mann as secretary of the state board of Massachusetts launched what became known as the common school revival. Mann, who in 1843 had visited schools in England, Ireland, Scotland, Germany, Holland, and France, published his carefully prepared observations in his famous *Seventh Annual Report,* which lauded the Prussian educational system and produced his celebrated controversy with the Boston schoolmasters, whom he defeated singlehanded. Henry Barnard in 1854 wrote his *National Education in Europe,* which also left its imprint. Although American education has been influenced from abroad, the American elementary school, indeed, our entire educational system, is distinctly American. It had no precedent anywhere in the world. Its singular character has been shaped largely by ideas, visions, aspirations, and values unique to America.

PIONEERS IN ELEMENTARY EDUCATION

Elementary education in the United States has been affected by various educational leaders, both here and abroad, who struggled valiantly for those reforms that today make the elementary school the most progressive unit of American public education. Among these foundation builders who helped lay the bases for American education are Comenius, Rousseau, Pestalozzi, Herbart, Mann, Barnard, Parker, Dewey, and Kilpatrick.

John Amos Comenius (1592–1670). One of the earliest concepts of general universal education originated in the mind of a Moravian churchman of the seventeenth century, viz., Comenius (or Komensky, if the Bohemian name is used).

His program advocated "the teaching to all men of all the subjects of human concern." He severely criticized the schools as "the slaughterhouses of the mind where ten or more years are spent in learning what might be acquired in one." This he said was due to the fact that the mind was fed mostly on words. He, the father of realism in modern education, fought against verbalism and for concreteness. In order to make teaching more concrete he prepared a pictured encyclopedia, *Orbis Pictus*, in which each word is defined and illustrated. This was the first picture book successfully adapted to the teaching of young children. He helped make education less remote, less austere, more sympathetic, and more interesting to children. Because of his early formulation and practical application of sound educational principles, Comenius, though still submerged in obscurity, is one of the leading figures in the history of education abroad and also in America. He died in the Netherlands— a land very susceptible to his influence; and it was in Dutch New Amsterdam in the New World that the public school idea thrived early.

Jean Jacques Rousseau (*1712–1778*). One who helped to explode traditional ideas on the training of young children was the Frenchman Jean Jacques Rousseau. Education, according to Rousseau, should be "according to nature." The learner would then develop the capacity with which he is endowed. Rousseau led the revolt against the extreme insistence upon facts and subject matter and the subordination of the child. He was the progenitor of the child-centered elementary school.

Johann Pestalozzi (*1746–1827*). Pestalozzi, likewise a true pioneer, was born in Switzerland. In his masterpiece, *Leonard and Gertrude*, he stated that the aim of education was the natural and systematic development of all the powers of the individual. He believed that a child developed in accordance with definite laws and that the aim of education was to assist nature in the observance of these laws. Pestalozzi was unique in that he practiced his theories. His school in Switzerland attracted attention throughout the Western world. Americans who had visited this school with its homelike atmosphere suggested for American education many improvements based upon their observations and his work. Pestalozzi himself considered that his recognition of observation as the basis of all knowledge was his real contribution to the methodology of elementary education. He emphasized sense perception and object lessons. Especially through his disciple, Fellenberg, he promoted the idea of associating manual activities and industry with education. Though many of his theories have been proved erroneous and many of his methods became frozen formality, nevertheless his basic ideas, his demonstration teaching, and his experimentation have exerted a tremendous influence upon elementary education both abroad and in America.

Johann Herbart (*1776–1841*). Among other influential foreign teachers were Froebel, who, as indicated in Chapter 5, started the kindergarten, and Herbart, who was a German philosopher. The latter studied at Jena and became a pupil of Fichte but later rejected most of Fichte's system and developed his own. His ideas affected both philosophy and education. He taught that character is the main aim of education, which has its real beginning in knowledge and its final end in action. His numerous principles such as those of the "many-sided interests," correlation of subjects, and apperception were introduced into the United States under the leadership of his disciples, notably Charles De Garmo and Charles and Frank McMurray, at Illinois State Normal University, Normal, Illinois. What is now the National Society for the Study of Education was founded at Normal in 1895 as the National Herbart Society. Herbart was one of the first educators to give a scientific approach to the study of education. In his methodology, he developed the five formal steps as follows: preparation, presentation, comparison, generalization, and application. This formula is found in detail in older texts on general methods of teaching. These pedagogical steps have had a marked influence on elementary as well as on secondary education. Some of Herbart's ideas are reflected today in the Morrisonian method of unit teaching.

Horace Mann (1796–1859). Known as "the father of the common schools," Horace Mann, during his 12 years as the secretary of the state board of education in Massachusetts, started the common school revival. Armed with no legal authority, but by dint of persuasion, Mann helped to improve the housing of pupils and the professional preparation of teachers. He lengthened the elementary school term and won an increased measure of popular and financial support for the schools and teachers. In his 12 annual reports, published at the end of each year of his secretaryship, and in his *Common School Journal*, which he started in 1838, Mann covered almost every phase of education. Much of this material is up to date even today. Through his efforts the first normal school was established at Lexington, Massachusetts, in 1839. His indefatigability extended his influence beyond Massachusetts to the nation and, through his friend Sarmiento, to the public schools in Chile and Argentina.

Henry Barnard (1811–1900). Henry Barnard occupied a place similar to that of Horace Mann in Massachusetts by serving as state commissioner of education in Connecticut from 1838 to 1842 and in Rhode Island from 1843 to 1849. After having absorbed Pestalozzi's ideas in Europe, Barnard promoted these ideas in America. His book *Pestalozzi and Pestalozzianism* is one of the outstanding books in English on the subject. Barnard edited the *American Journal of Education*, which treated almost every phase of education here and abroad. He established the first teachers institute in 1839 and improved the training of elementary teachers. As the first United States Commissioner of Education, Barnard helped to raise the status of education, particularly in elementary schools.

Colonel Francis Parker (1837–1902). Among the American educational pioneers who enriched the elementary curriculum was Francis Parker, who became the leader of the progressive movement. After varied experiences, such as teaching in rural and city schools, fighting in the Civil War, and experimenting with new methods in a normal school in Ohio, he was elected superintendent of schools at Quincy, Massachusetts. There he became famous as a leader of the Quincy movement, which embodied some of Froebel's principles in making the school less artificial and conventional. Children were taken outdoors for lessons in science and geography, and teachers were given much freedom and expert supervision. His greatest work was that as principal of the Cook County Normal School at Chicago and later as principal of the Chicago Institute, afterward the School of Education of the University of Chicago. Parker was a lover of children, and he had the rare insight to see teaching problems from the standpoint of the child. His enthusiasm and earnestness brought to the Cook County Normal School students from all parts of the country. These teachers whom he trained have gone far in improving the elementary schools of America. Among his writings, which have also had a marked influence, are *Talks to Teachers*, *Talks to Pedagogues*, *How to Study Geography*, and *Course in Arithmetic*. His writings, lectures, and teaching prepared the way for John Dewey.

John Dewey (1859–1952). The leading American educational philosopher and molder of the policies of the elementary school was John Dewey. In 1896 Dewey established an experimental school at the University of Chicago where he tried out some of his educational plans. In 1904 he joined the faculty of Teachers College, Columbia University, where he taught and influenced thousands of teachers.

His book *School and Society*, published in 1899, affected markedly the function of the school in society. Among his other publications, some of which have been translated into a dozen languages, were: *Interest and Effort, Democracy and Education, How We Think, Quest for Certainty, Experience and Education,* and *Logic: The Theory of Inquiry*. It is said that contributions made by most of his books are in inverse proportion to their size; the small ones, such as *School and Society*, had a greater influence than his huge volume, *Quest for Certainty*. He was widely known and honored in both the Orient and the Occident.

The Gary public school system, which modified its program in 1941, and other innovations in elementary school organization, such as the Winnetka system, were inspired by John Dewey. His emphasis upon doing and living was basic in the elementary school program. The following quotation is a brief sample of his philosophy:

If one attempts to formulate the philosophy of education implicit in the practices of the newer education, we may, I think, discover certain common principles amid the variety of progressive schools now existing. To imposition from above is opposed expression and cultivation of individuality; to external discipline is opposed free activity; to learning from texts and teachers, learning through experience; to acquisition of isolated skills and techniques by drill, is opposed acquisition of them as means of attaining ends which make direct vital appeal; to preparation for a more or less remote future is opposed making the most of the opportunities of present life; to static aims and materials is opposed acquaintance with a changing world.[1]

Dewey's philosophy was not so simple that it can be expressed adequately by one quotation or chapter. In America, the John Dewey Society publishes a yearbook on various phases of his pragmatic philosophy and of progressive education. Some of Dewey's ideas have been misinterpreted and misapplied. Nevertheless,

the progressive idealism of John Dewey and his followers has had a very significant and constructive influence upon all levels of learning, but especially upon the elementary school.

William Heard Kilpatrick (1871—). As a professor of education for many years at Teachers College, Columbia University, and since his retirement in 1937, Dr. Kilpatrick has indoctrinated thousands of elementary and secondary school teachers who have flocked into his classes, attended his lectures, or read his books. Among his publications are *The Project Method, Foundations of Method,* and *Source Book of Philosophy*. Kilpatrick has stimulated the emphasis upon life activities for school children and has defined learning as living. As an interpreter, he has given impetus to progressive education. Of course, the philosophy of Kilpatrick, like that of any thinker, does not stand alone. Each pioneer is the recipient of thought processes leading down to his day; he is, in a sense, the interpreter for his own time and a prophet for the days yet to come.

Other Leaders. Numerous leaders, including traditionalists like William Chandler Bagley and psychologists like Edward L. Thorndike, have made substantial contributions to elementary education. School reforms have been brought about through committee reports, such as that of the Committee of Ten, of which Dr. Charles W. Eliot of Harvard was chairman. This famous group recommended in 1893 that a six-six plan of organization replace the traditional eight-four plan. Among the superintendents of schools who have instituted drastic reforms in elementary education are: W. T. Harris of St. Louis, who led the revolt not only against Pestalozzian formalism by substituting natural science for precise object lessons, but also against rigid gradations of pupils and inflexible promotions; Edward A. Sheldon, who started the Oswego movement for improving elementary curriculums and methods in Oswego, New York; and Carleton Washburne, formerly of Winnetka, Illinois, who, as a dis-

---

[1] John Dewey, "Experience and Education," *The New York Times*, March 6, 1938, p. 10.

ciple of Frederick Burk, introduced the so-called Winnetka plan for meeting individual differences in the elementary school. *What is plan?*

Articulation with Pre-elementary Education. The modern elementary school is closely joined to pre-elementary work, particularly for children who enter the first grade with some school experience either in the nursery school or kindergarten or both. Although an increasing number of pupils have this orientation, the first school contact for most children comes in the first grade. Those beginners who have not had the benefit of preschooling ought to visit the first grade several times before they are actually enrolled. Going from a home with a few members into a classroom with 25 or more pupils is a difficult adjustment for many children. Every effort should therefore be expended to make possible an easy entrance into the elementary school.

The experiences in the nursery school and kindergarten should be vitally related to the first year of the primary school. The so-called primary unit, an organization embracing kindergarten through grade 2 or 3, has provided a setting in which beginning elementary school experiences are adjusted so as to remove or to reduce failure.

Whatever the organization, a child's first school experience ought to be preceded by a physical examination. In 1925 the National Congress of Parents and Teachers inaugurated the summer roundup for physical examinations of all children entering school in the fall. This clinic, held in the summer, gives particular attention to the preschool child in order that physical defects may be discovered and corrected if possible before he enters the first grade. Many schools follow the summer examinations with a recheck in the fall. These clinics should be continuous. Periodic health examinations are necessary safeguards in all grades and at all ages, for it obviously is better to prevent illness than to seek to restore lost health. The ultimate objective of the summer roundups is an annual health inventory from childhood through adulthood.

Scope of Elementary Education. Elementary education is difficult to define because of the extreme variety of practices in its organization, administration, and curriculums. In terms of children's ages, it is the educational institution for pupils from approximately six to twelve or fourteen years of age. In terms of grades, elementary education includes theoretically grades 1 through 6; in practice, however, it generally embraces grades 1 through 8, as indicated in Fig. 6-1.

The common subdivisions of the elementary school are usually grouped as: primary, grades 1 through 3; intermediate, grades 4 through 6; and upper, grades 7 and 8. Naturally there is overlapping between divisions and organization units. The kindergarten may be included in the primary level, whereas the junior high school is usually considered a part of secondary education.

These three major areas should not be construed as disparate units, but rather as components of an organized whole since child growth and development is continuous rather than periodic. A child's growth is not measured in annual rings like a tree. In order to eliminate some of the numerous artificial divisions, several grades may be combined. This is a frequent practice in rural schools where the teachers thus reduce the number of classes. In many school systems, the traditional emphasis on eight disparate grades is being modified. For example, some schools neither promote not detain pupils at the end of the first grade. The first two or three years of elementary education are considered a primary unit, and not until the end of the third year is the child promoted to the next area. Modern theory suggests "year" for "grade." Some schools obliterate grade lines and organize the six or seven years as a unit, the latter embracing the kindergarten, as indicated in the last column of Fig. 6-1.

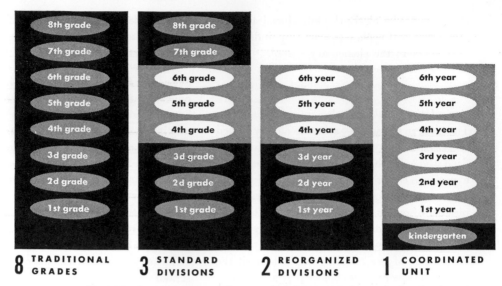

| 8 TRADITIONAL GRADES | 3 STANDARD DIVISIONS | 2 REORGANIZED DIVISIONS | 1 COORDINATED UNIT |

Fig. 6-1. Scope and organization of elementary education. In the first pattern on the left, elementary education consists of eight compartments called grades, with rigid promotion policies and practices. In the next pattern, the number of divisions is reduced to three, primary, intermediate, and upper grades, with greater articulation and flexibility. In the second column from the right, the seventh and eighth grades are assigned to secondary education, and the two remaining components become the upper and lower elementary school. In the pattern on the right, there is one continuous six-year unit, with the possible addition of the kindergarten, which replaces the traditional grade organization.

Elementary School Enrollments. A striking phenomenon of American public education is that the number of pupils enrolled in both public and private elementary schools is increasing markedly, as shown in Fig. 6-2. It is estimated that public and private elementary school enrollments will reach 37 million before 1970. At present, over 95 per cent of the children of elementary school age are attending school. About 15 per cent of these are enrolled in private schools.

Purposes

Elementary education generally is concentrated upon developing in the child a command of the fundamental processes or tools of learning. Although elementary education accents the intellectual, it is broader than this. It involves the education of the whole child—mentally, physically, socially, esthetically, and ethically.

IMMEDIATE OBJECTIVES OF
ELEMENTARY SCHOOL

Although the various parts of the entire American school system contribute markedly to the general objectives of education, each has its unique role to play in the drama of education. These special functions are the immediate objectives or directives of that particular school unit.

As examples of elementary school objectives, two sets of purposes are presented.

Education for All American Children. The Educational Policies Commission states that the first requirement for a school is that it

Enduring values of democracy

1. The democratic ideal calls upon citizens to face their problems with self-reliance and initiative, and to conduct their lives without unnecessary demands upon their fellow members of society. This ideal requires that our young citizens master thoroughly many different kinds of learning.

2. Citizens in a democracy exhibit a concern for the general welfare, a feeling of kinship with others, a respect for the laws and social institutions which protect our rights and the rights of others.

3. Each member in a democratic society should participate, freely and intelligently, in the process of arriving at important decisions which affect the group of which he is a part.

Ways of promoting these values

1. A good elementary school, therefore, will help to develop those basic skills and that sturdy independence and initiative which will enable our citizens to attack the problems that face them and to press forward toward ever-improving solutions.

2. A good elementary school, therefore, strives for the discovery and full development of all the humane and constructive talents of each individual.

3. A good elementary school, therefore, emphasizes social responsibility and the cooperative skills necessary to the progressive improvement of social institutions.[2]

rest upon values that are good. The second requirement is that it be efficient in promoting these values.

The controlling values in the United States may best be summed up in the one word "democracy." Three of the enduring values that guide and direct the education of all children in American democracy, and respective ways by which they may be implemented in the elementary school, are shown in the table above. The broad values of American society thus seek to determine the general goals of the elementary school.

Report of Mid-century Committee on Outcomes in Elementary Education. This study, sponsored by Russell Sage Foundation, Educational Testing Service, the U.S. Office of Education, and the Department of Elementary School Principals, produced the following outline of goals abridged by the author of this book:

1. *Physical development, health, and body care.* This is a broad category that involves

[2] Educational Policies Commission, *Education for All American Youth*, National Education Association, Washington, D.C., 1953, pp. 2–4.

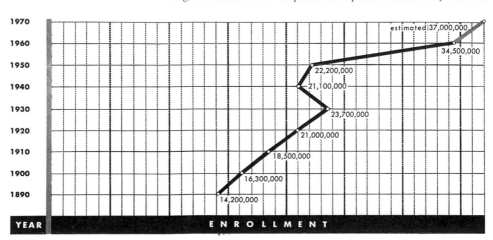

Fig. 6-2. Enrollment in public and private elementary schools.

health, safety, sportsmanship, and an understanding of growth and maturation.

2. *Individual social and emotional development*. This includes mental health, emotional stability, and growth of personality. Emphasis is on such goals as understanding and improving oneself.

3. *Ethical behavior, standards, values*. This area includes respect for law and for the customs and mores of the culture. It involves sportsmanship, kindliness, helpfulness, integrity, and honesty.

4. *Social relations*. This goal is devoted to the individual as a person in his personal-social relations with others, and consideration for the needs, interests, motives, convictions, and ideals of others.

5. *Social world*. This considers the child in terms of the structure and the institutions of our culture in relation to community, state, and nation.

6. *Physical world* (the natural environment). This goal is centered on an enlarged concept of science, both biological and physical, and the use of methods of science in solving problems in science and in everyday living.

7. *Esthetic development*. Emphasis is placed on appreciation and expression in art, music, and the crafts. The moral, the intellectual, and the emotional aspects of esthetic development are all included.

8. *Communication*. This covers the wide variety of means by which man communicates with man: reading, writing, composition, correct usage, spelling, punctuation, speaking, and listening.

9. *Quantitative relationships*. This includes arithmetic and the elementary aspects of algebra and geometry. Emphasis is placed on an understanding of how our number system works and greater competence in using numbers.[3]

This excellent study details further for each of the nine objectives: knowledge and under-

[3] Nolan C. Kearney, *Elementary School Objectives*, Russell Sage Foundation, New York, 1953, pp. 52–120.

standing, skill and competence, attitude and interest, action pattern, and determining conditions. Obviously, the accepted ultimate and immediate goals of elementary education affect the type of school.

Types

It is impossible to group all elementary schools into mutually exclusive categories, for there is overlapping even within major types. Some schools defy classifications or labels. Among the major types are those classified according to (1) size, as one or two teachers, and location, as rural or village; (2) sources of financial support, as public or private; (3) methodology of instruction, as traditional, middle of the road, or progressive; (4) internal organization, as the platoon type; and (5) special schools, as those for atypical children, such as the crippled. A terse description of these illustrative types follows.

SIZE AND LOCATION OF SCHOOLS

The simplest form of elementary organization is the small school—the one-teacher or one-room school. Here all six, seven, or eight grades are seated in one room, and a teacher may have as many as thirty classes a day, depending upon the number of pupils, their placement in grades, the curriculum, and the flexibility of administration.

The medium-sized elementary schools are found in the villages and the small cities. Usually one teacher is assigned to each grade or class, and a principal serves as the head of the building or system.

The large schools are located in the larger population centers. Two or more teachers may be assigned to a grade, or a departmental organization may be utilized. The largest elementary school system is in New York City, which has several hundred elementary schools.

SOURCES OF SUPPORT AND CONTROL

The elementary schools may also be grouped according to the main sources of their financial support or control, viz., public, or nonpublic, the latter embracing both parochial and other private schools.

Public Elementary Schools. The elementary schools supported by public taxation are by far in the majority and enroll approximately 85 per cent of all the pupils who attend the elementary grades. These form the backbone of American public education.

Nonpublic Elementary Schools. Nearly five million (about 15 per cent of all American elementary pupils) attend private elementary schools—both parochial and nonparochial. The word "parochial" originally meant parish or the district committed to one pastor. Parochial schools are those established and supported by religious sect or denomination. Their curriculums usually include moral and religious instruction and courses in the Bible, church traditions, and church history. Of the children attending private elementary schools, by far the largest number is enrolled in Catholic parochial schools, the next in Lutheran. Torah Umesorah (Hebrew for "religious law and tradition") is an active organization devoted to the promotion of Jewish all-day schools. The National Council of Torah Education reported in 1959 that enrollment in Jewish day school systems had increased from 2,000 to 40,000 pupils in the last decade.

The nonparochial private schools may be differentiated from the parochial in that they are supported primarily by nonchurch funds and that they do not give instruction in religion, particularly in the tenets of any specific denomination. The private schools often carry a very high tuition rate, which may or may not include board and room. Frequently they are endowed, but most of the financial support comes from fees and donations. The most progressive methods are often developed in private schools that are unhampered by the constant criticism of a tax-conscious public.

Of all elementary school pupils in each state, that proportion which attends private elemen-

The basic purpose of the elementary school is the all-around development of the child from six to twelve years, with particular emphasis on equipping him with basic skills, attitudes, and appreciations.

Young scholars learn . . .

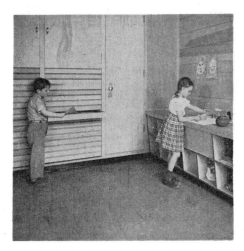

1

to take care of possessions . . .

and their health . . .

2

tary schools varies. The greatest number of private elementary schools is found in the Northeastern and Middle states. The United States Supreme Court, by declaring the Oregon Act of 1922 unconstitutional because it violated the Fourteenth Amendment, established the

3

to deal with numbers . . .

measure . . .

principle that a state may not, through its police power, prohibit private education.

PHILOSOPHY AND METHODOLOGY

The classification of elementary schools according to ideology and methodology of the teachers and administrators is difficult, for most schools vary in the degree to which they support different philosophies. It is also extremely difficult to classify many philosophies of education because there are many variations. However, most current controversy hinges over two conflicting schools of thought: the progressive and the essentialist.

X *The Progressives*. The concept of progressive education has been developed by John Dewey and William Kilpatrick, already mentioned as pioneers in the development of elementary education. The progressives believe that the curriculum should be built upon practical problems and experiences of contemporary life with less organization by subject matter. They stress the development of the total child through activity-centered teaching with emphasis upon informal learning, flexible promotions and groupings, and greater freedom for the teacher and the learner.

4

5

*and observe
physical phenomena.*

The Essentialists. This philosophy has been enunciated by Professor Boyd Bode in his book *Progressive Education at the Crossroads* and by Professor William Bagley, who helped to organize a group called the essentialists. More recently Albert Lynd, in his book *Quackery in the Public Schools*, and Arthur Bestor, author of *Educational Wastelands*, have joined the attack against the progressives. Their complaints against progressive education allege that chaos results from too much attention to children's interests, that the three R's and other fundamentals have been neglected, that intellectual discipline has been undermined, that much time and effort have been wasted, and that watered-down curriculums have resulted in insignificant content. They urge a return to traditional methods of teaching with emphasis upon systematic training in subject matter, more rigorous academic standards for all learners, exclusive attention to mental development rather than social or emotional develop-

They learn to express themselves through . . .

reading . . .

7

drama . . .

8

foreign language . . .

6

9

and music.

ment of the learner, and more attention to discipline. This issue is discussed further in Chapter 17.

Between these two extremes are scattered the majority of the elementary teachers. Many take the middle of the road, recognizing the importance of basic knowledge and necessary skills and yet giving constant heed to the needs, interests, and abilities of the child as well as those of the adult. Even within the same building one may find teachers whose procedures are traditional, middle of the way, or progressive. A teacher, in the span of several years or even a single year, month, or day, may reflect varying degrees of conservative or progressive ideology.

INTERNAL ORGANIZATION OF SCHOOLS

The number of classifications under this heading is endless. Grade, division, and unitary organization are illustrated in Fig. 6-1. Mention is made here of selected policies or practices that have important bearing upon the organization of schools:

Neighborhood Lower Elementary School. This unit, planned for kindergarten through the third or fourth grade, enables small children to attend school within a few blocks of home. Every child goes home for lunch. The teachers have released noon-hour periods. Home contacts are more frequent. Less space is necessary for school sites. These community schools are found in many new suburban developments.

Typical Classroom Organization. In a typical situation in a public or parochial or private school, a teacher is in direct charge of a group of pupils in a fixed location—a classroom—which may commonly be known as Miss Smith's room or the third grade. The teacher may be assisted in the teaching of such specialized subjects as art or music.

Self-contained Classroom Units. This has the single teacher as the base unit for the organiza-

tion within the school. Often the room has all the facilities so that a child need not leave it during the morning or afternoon session. The teacher is often responsible for handling all subjects.

Departmentalization. This type of organization is not as popular as in past years, especially for the lower grades. It is usually employed in the upper grades. The subjects are taught by special teachers, the pupils passing from one subject teacher to another. Varying degrees of departmentalization are found.

Ability Grouping. The much-debated practice of grouping pupils according to ability is followed in one or more schools in a large number of cities. There is currently much interest in ability grouping of gifted children.

Platoon Organization. This type of organization, with its nomenclature borrowed from the military, is not widely used. It permits a high degree of room utilization and enables a homeroom teacher to be with her group of pupils for one-half of each day. During the remainder of the time the pupils go to special subject rooms, such as art, music, speech, physical education, and library science. Some schools use modified platoon systems.

Elimination of Grade Lines. Classification of pupils into broader school units or divisions, rather than into the traditional grades, is increasing in city school systems. Wherever grade lines are being eliminated, for the most part in the lower portion of the elementary school, the tendency to extend the plan farther into the pattern of school organization seems quite definite and pronounced. Some cities have ungraded primary units for all pupils.

Ungraded Classes. A device in school organization, particularly helpful in providing special opportunities for exceptional children, is the ungraded room. The great majority of such classes have been maintained for slow-learning pupils, and often they have been known as opportunity rooms. In rare instances gifted children also have been classified in ungraded classrooms for enriched programs of study adapted to their special interests and abilities.

Remedial Classes. Groups classified separately for remedial instruction, particularly in such foundation subjects as reading and arithmetic, are widely but not universally used.

Individualized Instruction. Many plans of individualized instruction have been developed and used in America, especially in elementary schools. Some have attracted nationwide attention, such as the Dalton and Winnetka plans. Other schools have incorporated the essential elements of individualized instruction in which each pupil more or less independently pursues his own project or works on his own contract for at least part of the day.

Class Periods of Indefinite Length. Several schools have abandoned their traditional fixed periods of so many minutes each, substituting for this fixed schedule a flexible arrangement which, subject to the teacher's control, has periods indefinite in length and variable from day to day.

Schools for Atypical Children. In the larger cities a marked trend is that of separating by buildings particular types of pupils for special instruction. More frequently special rooms and teachers are set aside for the care of the non-typical pupils. One type of school is for the gifted pupils; another is for the slow learners; others are for those physically handicapped, as the Spalding School for crippled children in Chicago; or for those socially atypical, as the Montefiore School in the same city.

Then, too, there is the part-time or continuation school for employed boys and girls. Special instruction in the elementary subjects is also provided through night school classes attended by older pupils and adults.

Experimental Schools. Although all schools are in a sense experimental, some are especially designated as experimental or demonstration. These include the large number of elementary schools affiliated with universities and teachers colleges as the training ground for student or cadet teachers. Where practice teaching is done entirely off the campus in affiliated schools, the campus elementary school may become a purely laboratory or experimental school for research, exploration, and demonstration.

The elementary school is noted for its experimental procedures. Sometimes these follow a special plan of teaching or curriculum, such as the Gary plan, the Dalton plan, the McDade plan (Chicago), the Winnetka plan, the Community School (Glencoe), and the San Angelo plan.

Many variations are found in the length of the school year. One is the all-year school, which offers the complete program throughout the entire calendar year. Some schools follow a modified form by offering a summer term after the regular year. As indicated later, the elementary school is the testing ground for many reforms that later creep up into the secondary schools and colleges.

Program and procedures

EDUCATIONAL PROGRAM

In the typical elementary school of the past, with its program broken into eight divisions or grades, the pupil had to master the subjects in one grade before he could progress to the next. In many schools today the organizational pattern has been reduced to six years, plus the kindergarten. This stretch of years is considered, at least in theory, as one continuous period of growth for the child. Generally, however, for purposes of classification and promotion, certain grades or years are grouped into areas of development.

The programs of the elementary grades, as mentioned earlier, are usually grouped into three levels: (1) the primary, (2) the intermediate, and (3) the advanced or presecondary.

Primary Grades. The first three grades are usually called primary. Where the kindergarten is a basic part of the early schooling, the grouping may be kindergarten-primary. Some also add the nursery school. Although in the primary grades the central activity is reading, the child develops other essential abilities, such as writing, spelling, and working with numbers. The child develops not only mentally but also physically, socially, and emotionally. The primary area is the most interesting and significant division of public education.

Intermediate Grades. These are usually the fourth, fifth, and sixth grades. The most important curricular activity is still that of reading, but the emphasis is on extensive and enriched reading rather than its mechanics and on the skillful use of the basic tools acquired in the primary grades. Subjects other than those taught in the primary grades are usually added in the fourth grade. This heavy load of new subjects results in an abrupt transition into the fourth grade and a high percentage of failure. The pupil must be prepared for the transition from grade to grade and from primary unit to the intermediate grades; hence in the lower grades learning materials and activities are by degrees introducing him to such areas as social science and natural science. In the more progressive schools no one subject or field of interest is the particular domain of any grade or year. A pupil, whatever his grade or age, is not withheld from learning materials useful to him at his particular stage of development. As in the primary grades, emphasis in the intermediate years is given to the intellectual development of desirable individual and social skills, habits, and attitudes. A quiet but observable trend in elementary education is the gradual but effective merging of the primary and intermediate grades into a unified elementary school.

Advanced Level. This area usually includes grades 7 and 8, which in the modern interpretation belong to the period of secondary education. In numerous schools this transfer of the upper grades from elementary to secondary education has been effected only in theory. Many a so-called junior high school consists merely of glorified seventh and eighth grades which continue with the traditional curriculum and the old philosophy of the upper grades. Unfortunately, the pupils, particularly in the traditional seventh and eighth grades, are subjected to a recapitulation of material supposedly learned earlier. The place and function of the junior high school are considered in Chapter 7.

CURRENT PRACTICES
IN ELEMENTARY EDUCATION

A few current practices in elementary education are here presented in abbreviated form.

Organization and Administration. The primary purpose of the pattern of an elementary school is to foster the maximum development of every child. Hence, the trend in organization is toward simplicity and flexibility. A reduction in arbitrary divisions is effected through a reorganization of administrative units, as, for example, a unified six-year program in place of eight disparate grades. Grade classifications are made more flexible or are eliminated, especially in the primary area. In some cities the primary grades have been withdrawn from platoon organization. A reduction has been made in the number of grades, classes, and subjects. One-teacher schools are being reduced in number.

More schooling is being provided. The school day has been lengthened in communities like Long Beach, New York, where forty minutes were added to provide time for enrichment activities. The school week has been lengthened in some cities, as Madison, Wisconsin, to include informal activities on Saturdays. Many systems provide summertime supervision for recreational and educational programs in an elongated educational year. Rochester, Minnesota, has offered a full-time summer program for more than a decade. Southern states have lengthened their seven-year school system by adding a year.

Buildings and Other Facilities. With the great influx of young children, many boards of education cannot provide permanent elementary school buildings, so hundreds of temporary or semipermanent structures have been erected. Many are portable schoolhouses.

More and more buildings for elementary schools are of the one-story type. They blend more harmoniously with surrounding residential buildings and are more homelike to the young children. Many are small neighborhood schools.

School buildings and equipment are made more flexible and functional and are more creative in design. In many elementary schools a workroom is placed between two classrooms or is a part of the room so that small groups can work on construction activities at any time during the day. Equipment with a high degree of flexibility is installed. Running water and toilet facilities are within or adjacent to classrooms, especially for small children. In many new schools, each classroom is provided with its own outside exit. Libraries are used extensively for enrichment.

Curriculum and Teaching-Learning Procedures. The pupil in the elementary school is introduced gradually to the curriculum. A well-graduated program of preprimary experiences is provided in order to facilitate the work of the first year. Reading readiness is emphasized.

The curriculum is becoming more flexible. In connection with time allotments for major fields of learning, some schools set up weekly percentage ranges of time with minimum and maximum ranges of time to be spent each week on each major division.

Curricular materials are being reorganized in different relationships and with different purposes. The correlation, or fusion, of related materials and activities helps to integrate learning. Many teachers organize materials as teaching-learning units.

Many curricular materials are being shifted in the light of studies on maturation. Formal instruction in arithmetic is often withheld until the second or third year, but incidental and planned situations for building number concepts are introduced early. There is a downward extension of several fields, such as social science and science, into the lower grades.

New and neglected areas are now emphasized. Instruction in science is being extended and enriched. Foreign languages, particularly French and Spanish, are being undertaken in some elementary curriculums. Much more use is made of handicrafts, including pottery, metal, and woodwork. Language and the fine arts are used increasingly as means of unleashing the creative efforts of pupils. Print-script writing instead of cursive is used in the lower grades because of its similarity to the printed words. United States history and government are accented. More emphasis is placed on helping children to learn about other peoples of the world and to develop sympathetic attitudes and understandings toward them.

Learning in the elementary school is cooperative enterprise. The classroom work is actively and realistically coordinated with other service departments of the school. The home is taken into partnership in many school experiences of the learner. Class mothers are often used to assist the teacher in routine tasks. The elementary schools have extended their learning experiences into the community especially through the go-and-see plan of educational trips.

Television (both closed-circuit and commercial channels) is being used much more widely in elementary school instruction. Sometimes the educational television program is received in the classroom as part of the formal school program. Sometimes the student is asked to view certain programs of educational importance at home. In metropolitan New York, seven or eight hours of educational programs are telecast daily into 60 per cent of the school children's homes over a radius of 100 miles. These programs range from English lessons for children of Puerto Rican descent to science lessons for teachers.

Outdoor education, including school camping, soil conservation, reforestation and wildlife study, instruction in farming, historical research, recreation, and therapy for handicapped children, has been introduced in various areas of the country, particularly in Illinois and Michigan.

Pupils and Teachers. Pupils receive much individual attention. But this is being jeopardized by increased enrollments and larger classes. Pupil progress is being evaluated more carefully, especially in view of the current criticism of elementary education. Teachers, especially in the primary unit, are assigned for a period of two or three years to the same group of pupils. Special attention is being given to enriched programs of instruction for gifted students. Provisions for handicapped pupils are being improved and expanded. The mobility of the population causes many changes in class rolls.

The modern elementary school stresses intellectual development first, but does not neglect personality development and guidance. It seeks to exalt genuine personality. Several elementary schools have established child-guidance clinics. Cumulative records, including anecdotal reports, contribute to evaluation and functional guidance purposes. Sociometric devices are more widely used.

In connection with the modern accent on democracy, there is increased opportunity for pupils to do socially useful work. Student councils are used increasingly as means of promoting democracy in the administration of elementary schools. A cooperative attack upon elementary school problems is made by pupils,

teachers, school administrators, parents, and community leaders. Several schools are using the cooperative group plan which is an adaptation of departmentalization but calls for a small number of teachers working as a unit, with almost daily conferences among themselves.

The staff is being enlarged and improved. Many schools have added specialists. More elementary schools have trained librarians and are improving school libraries. The teachers of elementary pupils are becoming better educated, but there still exists a great shortage of well-qualified personnel. These are but a few of the numerous significant changes that are being effected in the modern elementary school.

A Few Contrasts. Some past and present elementary school procedures are paralleled in columnar arrangement on page 119.

Certainly this transition from the past to the present is not complete in all schools. Many schools are still more typical of the past than the present. Educational change is a slow process. However, rapid technological development and recent intensive criticism of education have accelerated educational change. It is evident that these is a real thirst for new ideas and a greater readiness for change. Elementary education, eager to improve on the past, will undoubtedly continue to be a fruitful field for experimentation and, accordingly, the most progressive area in American education.

Future

Bulging enrollments have brought elementary education many growing pains. To match quantitative increase there must come a qualitative growth in which attention will be shifted from mass education to improved personal learning and living. This calls for more time from pupils, parents, and teachers.

Thus emerging, elementary education is not a destination but a journey, with learners and teachers always en route to better teaching, learning, and living. In this process the key person is the teacher, but her Achilles' heel is

Past	Present
Child plunged into first grade	Pupil prepared through preprimary experiences
Traditional subject matter used	Curriculum enriched and broadened
Oral reading emphasized	Oral and silent reading, especially the latter, stressed
Words called in reading	Thought-getting and comprehension sought
One basic reading text used	Several books utilized
Library facilities restricted	Library made the heart of the school
Alphabet used in beginning reading	Sentence or story method employed
Reading largely restricted to copyrighted books	Experience reading from pupil-made stories also used
Impractical arithmetic problems assigned	Practical arithmetic based on experience and needs
Short penmanship periods used	Legibility sought in all written work
Geography and history taught in isolation	Social studies and interrelationships stressed continuously
Facts memorized for sake of disciplining the mind	Memorization used as a means of acquiring useful information
Factual materials stressed as the end products	Facts used as a means toward the end of understanding and interpretation
Isolated words spelled orally in spelling period	Spelling made a part of all written sentences
Structural physiology memorized	Functional health education made to contribute to healthy living
Fine and applied arts permitted	These arts encouraged as emotional and creative outlets
Mass imitation employed	Creative expression cultivated
Teacher hired as schoolmaster	Teacher made a director of learning and guidance
Discipline imposed by teacher	Growth in pupil responsibility and citizenship cultivated
Formal report card issued with numerical notation	Written descriptive progress reports and teacher-parent conferences utilized
Mental development of child made chief objective of elementary school	All-round development of pupil made the supplemental goal of education
Lock-step progress through the grades	Flexible grouping of children in different areas of learning
Same educational experiences for entire class	Varied experiences provided with special attention to the gifted and the handicapped
Instruction confined to formal classroom procedures	Informal, out-of-school learning experiences capitalized
Institutional buildings and equipment	Homelike buildings and furniture with more effective use of space, light, and color

her limited preparation for enlarged tasks. Upon teacher improvement, in the last analysis, depends the betterment of elementary education. Higher standards for both preservice and in-service education are necessary. Then, too, the elementary teaching staff may well include more young men who understand boys and work with them in their out-of-class activities.

Elementary education forms the backbone of American public education, and it must shape the sinews of democracy. An unfulfilled objective is that of providing every person, no matter what his age or condition, with the equivalent of an elementary education. This will mean more rigid enforcement of compulsory attendance, more attention to handicapped children, and more evening schools for those youth and adults who lack elementary courses. Furthermore, as educational opportunities increase for youth and adults, the elementary school will cease to be a terminal institution, and will be a vital link in the chain of lifelong learning.

Summary

The modern elementary school, although distinctly American in character, has been influenced by European traditions. Comenius, Rousseau, Pestalozzi, Herbart, Mann, Barnard, Parker, Dewey, and Kilpatrick have made particularly important contributions to the development of elementary education. Enrollments have nearly doubled in the past half century, making elementary schooling virtually universal in America.

Elementary schools provide basic learning for all children. They seek to stimulate mental, physical, social, emotional, esthetic, and moral development, as well as understanding of the world and its people, communication skills, and quantitative relationships. The general goals of elementary schooling emerge from the broad values of American democracy.

Elementary schools exist in wide variety—of programs, organization, philosophy, size, and control. There are public and private schools; large, medium, and small schools; traditional and progressive schools; and schools organized by grades, subjects, student activities, and otherwise.

Considerable contention exists relative to whether elementary education ought to be based upon the philosophy and methodology of the progressives or the essentialists. Elementary education in general is more progressive and experimental than other levels of education.

The elementary school is presently adopting a variety of new procedures largely in the direction of increased flexibility and democracy. Curriculums are being reorganized and extended to provide better integration of subject matter and enriched learning. Increased emphasis is being given to science and languages. Greater effort is being made to adapt learning experiences to the individual abilities and needs of students. Grouping of children according to their ability and the elimination of grade classifications are growing trends in this direction. Increased attention is being given also to the needs of the gifted and handicapped children.

Elementary school buildings have become more flexible and functional, as well as more creative, in design. Instructional materials are more plentiful, attractive, and effective. Television is being used more widely and effectively as an instructional tool. Standards of preparation and in-service development of teachers have been strengthened.

The future of elementary education poses the familiar dilemma that applies to all levels of educational enterprise: "How can elementary schooling be provided for all of the children of a rapidly increasing population without any sacrifice of quality?"

Suggested activities

1. Review the historical evolution of elementary education found in the second column, labeled Elementary, in the historical calendar in this chapter.
2. Prepare a brief history of elementary education in your own state.
3. Trace the historical development of a subject such as reading.
4. Prepare a biography of a pioneer in elementary education.
5. Contrast the methods of teaching and discipline in a typical elementary school of fifty years ago and of today.
6. Draw a picture illustrating the difference between old-time and modern classroom pro-

cedure followed in the typical elementary school.

7. Observe how holidays, such as Thanksgiving and Christmas, and seasonal activities are employed in teaching in the elementary school.

8. Investigate the place of student councils in the elementary school.

9. Examine the laws of your state as to the legal ages for compulsory education, preparation of elementary teachers, etc.

Bibliography

Books

Ambrose, Edna, and Alice Miel: *Children's Social Learning*, NEA, Association for Supervision and Curriculum Development, Washington, D.C., 1960. Presents suggestions, derived from research, concerning the kind of school and home environments that support effective social learnings and democratic interaction.

Brogan, Peggy, and Lorene Fox: *Helping Children Learn*, World Book Company, Yonkers, N.Y., 1955, chap. 1. An explanation of how learning takes place in young children and the implications for the school program.

Caswell, Hollis L., and Arthur W. Foshay: *Education in the Elementary School*, American Book Company, New York, 1957, chaps. 2, 3, 14. Presents a history of the elementary school, its characteristics, a check list for evaluating an elementary school, and a look at the future needs of elementary education.

Elsbree, Willard S., and Harold J. McNally: *Elementary School Administration and Supervision*, American Book Company, New York, 1959, chaps. 12–14. Discusses admission policies and practices, classification and grouping, and pupil progress in the elementary school.

Herrick, Virgil E., and others: *The Elementary School*, Prentice-Hall, Inc., Englewood Cliffs, N.J., 1956, part 3. Outlines and describes curriculum areas—language arts, social studies, science, arithmetic, health, recreation, and the arts.

Hunnicutt, C. W., and William J. Iverson (eds.): *Research in the Three R's*, Harper & Brothers, New York, 1958, pref., pp. 261–264, 347–351. Reveals the wealth of knowledge from research illuminating the work of the teacher in the skill subjects.

Klausmeier, Herbert J., and others: *Teaching in the Elementary School*, Harper & Brothers, New York, 1956, chap. 4, part 3. Describes the content, planning, and application of the elementary school curriculum; guidance and the reporting of pupil progress.

Primary School Portfolio, Association for Childhood Education International, Washington, D.C., 1956. This attractive collection of leaflets focuses upon the behavior, personality, and physical and mental traits of six- to eight-year-olds and their primary school day.

Saucier, W. A.: *Theory and Practice in the Elementary School*, The Macmillan Company, New York, 1956, chap. 15. An analysis of methods of classifying pupils and promotion policies and practices.

Shane, Harold G., and E. T. McSwain: *The Elementary Curriculum*, Henry Holt and Company, Inc., New York, 1958, chaps. 3, 4. Explains the function of evaluation in improving the elementary curriculum and the conflicting values in American culture which cause problems in planning the instructional program.

Periodicals

Abraham, Willard: "The Bright Child in the Elementary Classroom," *NEA Journal*, vol. 48 (March, 1959), pp. 57–58. Examines the practical problems of dealing with the intellectually gifted child in elementary education, with suggestions for handling the problem.

Ahrens, Maurice R.: "Tomorrow's Elementary Teacher," *NEA Journal*, vol. 47 (January, 1958), pp. 21–22. Discusses the kind of preservice preparation and in-service development needed by elementary teachers in the future.

Balcom, Lois: "San Angelo Builds Three Rails for the Three R's," *The Reporter*, vol. 19 (October 30, 1958), pp. 28–31. Describes a new trend toward flexible grouping for instruction in elementary schools.

Frazier, Alexander: "New Expectations and the Elementary School," *NEA Journal*, vol. 47 (November, 1958), pp. 546–548. Argues for careful examination of new proposals that are being advanced, the importance of open minds and experimentation.

Goodlad, John I.: "More about the Ungraded Unit Plan," *NEA Journal*, vol. 44 (May, 1955), pp. 295–296. Describes the purposes and nature of ungraded school units, a new kind of class organization that departs from lock-step grade organization.

Harap, Henry: "Today's Elementary School," *NEA Journal*, vol. 46 (February, 1957), pp. 78–80. Describes the typical instructional program and teaching methods of today's elementary schools.

Hoppoack, Anne S.: "No Time for Panic," *National Elementary School Principal*, vol. 37 (May, 1958), pp. 38–44. The author pleads for the primacy of human values in the age of science and the importance of protecting individuality.

Shane, Harold G.: "Children's Interests," *NEA Journal*, vol. 46 (April, 1957), pp. 237–239. Reports research material showing the nature of children's interests and how they can be utilized in the school curriculum.

Thompson, Ethel: "The Ungraded Plan Helps Provide for Continuity of Learning," *NEA Journal*, vol. 47 (January, 1958), pp. 16–18. Urges the elimination of separate grades in primary education, allowing children to advance as their ability and readiness permit.

Tyler, Ralph W.: "Clarifying the Role of the Elementary School," *Elementary School Journal*, vol. 57 (November, 1956), pp. 74–82. Argues that the task of the elementary school is to arouse and maintain interest and skill in the understanding and solution of new problems.

chapter 7

*Secondary
education*

The classic landmark in the development of secondary education in America is the famous Kalamazoo case, tried by the Supreme Court of Michigan in 1874. A taxpayer sought to restrain the Kalamazoo school board from levying a tax to support a new public high school. But Chief Justice Cooley, in a historic decision that was to affect profoundly the course of educational development, ruled: "Neither in our state policy, in our constitution, or in our laws, do we find the primary school districts restricted in the branches of knowledge which their officers may cause to be taught, or to the grade of instruction that may be given."

After that, high schools multiplied so rapidly across the land that secondary school enrollments doubled in every decade for the next half century. Thus secondary education for all American youth became a reality, an accomplishment still unapproached by any other nation.

Secondary education includes the education of youth between the ages of approximately twelve through twenty, including the junior high school and the junior college. It embraces every phase of the process by which society seeks to develop socially significant abilities and characteristics in preadolescent, adolescent, and postadolescent individuals. It is broader and longer than what was traditionally encompassed by the four-year high school. Today secondary education has doubled in length; it covers the seventh through the fourteenth year of schooling, extending downward to include the junior high school and upward to embrace the junior college.

Modern secondary education is presently undergoing a critical reexamination. It is teeming with changes. Undoubtedly the future will witness many more. However, change in American education is not a new phenomenon. Indeed, one of the most salient features of this nation's schools has been their remarkable ability to change.

NATIONAL DEVELOPMENT		THE DEVELOPMENT OF SECONDARY EDUCATION
Discovery and early settlements	**1635**	First Latin grammar school founded in Boston
The Colonial period	**1751**	Franklin Academy organized in Philadelphia
Maritime troubles and the War of 1812		
	1821	First English high school for boys organized in Boston
Era of good feeling	**1826**	First high school for girls initiated in Boston
Jacksonian Democracy		
	1856	First coeducational high school established in Chicago
Controversy and war between the states		
	1872	Taxation for secondary schools upheld in Kalamazoo case
Aftermath and reconstruction		
	1884	Manual training high school started in Baltimore
Immigration and industrial growth		
	1893	Recommendations of Committee of Ten published
	1902	First public junior college established in Joliet, Illinois
The progressive era		
	1907	G. Stanley Hall's classic *Adolescence* published
	1910	First public junior high schools opened
World War I		
	1918	Report of Commission on Reorganization of Secondary Education published
Normalcy and prosperity		
	1933	Reports of National Survey of Secondary Education presented
Depression and recovery		
	1941	Eight-Year Study by Progressive Education Association published
World War II		
	1950	Cooperative Study of Secondary School Standards revised
The Cold War struggle		
	1952	Educational Policies Commission published report, *Education for All American Youth*
	1953	Council for Advancement of Secondary Education formed
	1956	First high school seniors received National Merit Scholarships
	1959	Conant's study, *The American High School Today,* published

HISTORICAL CALENDAR

Foundations

The history of secondary education is usually chronicled in three rather distinct periods named after the institution characteristic of each era: (1) the Latin grammar school, (2) the tuition academy, and (3) the free public high school. Leonard V. Koos, director of the National Survey of Secondary Education, states that the present century has brought to the American educational scene another period (4) distinguished by the vertically extended or reorganized secondary school. The significant events are listed in the historical calendar.

Latin Grammar School. The Boston Latin School—the first secondary school in America —had for its British forerunners the Winchester (1394) and the Westminster (1561) schools. The first step toward organizing the Latin grammar school in America was taken by Bostonians on April 23, 1635, in a town meeting, where it was voted "that our brother, Philemon Pormont, shal be intreated to become scholemaster for the teaching and nourtering of children with us." In August of the following year 45 inhabitants of Boston subscribed a sum of money to maintain a "free schoolmaster for the youth with us, Mr. Daniel Maud being now also chosen thereunto." Such efforts as these mark the beginnings of secondary education in the colonies, and by 1700 approximately forty grammar schools had been founded in New England. The schools of secondary education were not so common everywhere.

In the Middle and Southern colonies private tutors were engaged and many young boys and girls were sent back to Europe for schooling. The academy in the South as in other parts of the United States was called a product of the frontier period and the laissez faire theory of government. It was usually private or denominational.

The main purpose of the Latin grammar school was to prepare pupils for college. This major objective was clearly stated in the Massachusetts law of 1647, which decreed that "when any town shall increase to the number of 100 families or householders, they shall set up a grammar school, the master thereof being able to instruct youth so far as they shall be fitted for the university. . . ." The Latin grammar schools, especially the earlier ones, offered a limited curriculum. As indicated by its name, the school was primarily restricted to the study of classical languages and literatures. It was very selective in character and sought to establish an aristocracy of educated intellectuals.

Admission to the Latin grammar schools was usually conditioned by the social and economic rank of the applicant. A sort of dual system, patterned on a European plan, prevailed in early American education. In this system an elementary education open to all was distinct from a secondary education closed to all but a chosen few.

Financial support for the Latin grammar school was provided in one or more of the following ways: tuition, donations, taxation, leases, legacies, lotteries, and land grants by civil authorities or private persons. Its control was at first considered the right and duty of the clergy since most of the pupils pursued studies that fitted them for the ministry or professions. Gradually the Latin grammar schools with their emphasis on theology began to lose their popularity. Leadership in the community was no longer with the clergy but rather with the town and commercial executives. Out of the new economic and social conditions in America arose the next period of secondary education, viz., that of the tuition academy.

The Tuition Academy. Benjamin Franklin, who has never been accorded his just place in American education, was primarily responsible for the establishment of the first academy. Franklin in his *Autobiography* thus describes the genesis of the academy:

The first step I took was to associate in the design a number of active friends, of whom the Junto furnished a good part; the next was to write and publish a pamphlet, entitled *Proposals Relating to the Education of Youth in Pennsylvania*.[1]

These proposals contained many practical and progressive suggestions. According to Carl Van Doren, "In a day of rigid classical schools, Franklin took his stand with reformers like Milton and Locke and the most advanced contemporary Americans."[2] A board of 24 trustees was formed, of which Franklin was president from 1749 to 1756. This academy, which absorbed a charitable school erected in 1740 and later became the University of Pennsylvania, opened in a hired house in Philadelphia in 1751. The curriculum was broader than that of the Latin grammar school, although not so extensive as Franklin planned it should be. Since it aimed to prepare for life as well as for the ministry, its students included those not intending to go to college as well as the college bound.

Although a large number of academies were founded between 1750 and 1800, the movement reached its greatest height in the decade from 1840 to 1850, flourishing best in Massachusetts and New York.

best in N.Y. and Mass.

[1] Benjamin Franklin, *Autobiography*, Century Company, New York, 1901, p. 203.
[2] Carl Van Doren, *Benjamin Franklin*, The Viking Press, Inc., New York, 1938, p. 192.

The academies differed from the Latin grammar schools in several aspects. Besides expanding the curriculum to include such fields as commerce and science, the academy permitted young women to enter. From the days of Mary Chilton, the first woman to step off the *Mayflower*, to the present, women have played a conspicuous role in American life, yet their education was grossly neglected for many decades.

The academy, supported in the main by tuition and donations, was semipublic in control. In its organization, administration, and program it was more democratic than the Latin grammar school. The person in charge was usually called the headmaster or principal. Several private academies still exist in the United States as military academies or special schools, but most of the older ones have either disappeared or been transformed into public high schools.

The Free Public High School. The third period in the history of the American secondary school covers the rise and growth of the free public high school, inaugurated with the establishment of the English Classical School in Boston in 1821. This school for boys, later called the English High School, was followed by a high school for girls in the same city in 1826. During the next half-century various types of high

Fig. 7-1. Enrollment in public high schools.

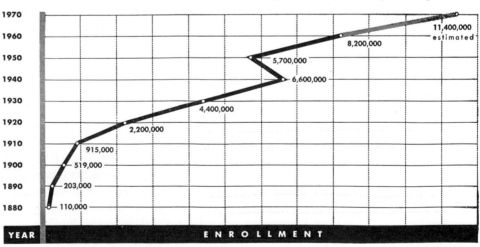

schools were organized. Among these were the first coeducational high school, started in Chicago in 1856, and the first manual training school, founded in Baltimore in 1884. Many factors contributed to the steady development of these schools, particularly in the democratic West.

The Kalamazoo case decision of the Supreme Court of Michigan in 1874 became famed in school law because it lent legal sanction to the movement for the establishment of publicly supported high schools. Similar decisions followed in several other states, thus removing any question as to the legality of having communities tax themselves for the support of public high schools. The Kalamazoo decision thus paved the way for a phenomenal growth in this new institution of democracy. High school enrollments doubled each decade for the next sixty years, as shown in Fig. 7-1. High school enrollments declined slightly during the late 1940s and early 1950s because of the low birth rate that prevailed during the depression. However, with the phenomenal increase in births in the postwar years, secondary school enrollments are rising sharply again and are certain to continue to rise during the coming decade, reaching a total of more than eleven million by 1970.

Nowhere in the world is so large a percentage of youth attending high school as in America. In most European countries, less than one-fifth of the population of high school age are in school. Nearly 90 per cent of secondary school age youth are attending high school in the United States. The attainment of high school education by virtually all American youth is one of the truly great phenomena of American democracy and one of the greatest sources of our strength. Unfortunately, some young people are still unable to attend high school, largely because of economic reasons.

The Extended Secondary School. As previously mentioned, the history of the American secondary school is usually divided into three stages. A fourth period is here in which a new type of institution is slowly evolving, viz., the vertically extended secondary school or the reorganized high school.

Of this new period in the evolution of secondary education, Leonard V. Koos says:

I refer to the extensions of the high school downward to effect junior-high school reorganization and upward to include junior college years. Many communities, to be sure, have made the extension in one direction only, either downward or upward. However, many other communities have introduced the extensions in both directions and have thereby achieved an 8-year period of secondary education. In the light of the fact that all the earlier types in our succession of secondary schools have been dominantly 4-year institutions, the emergence of an institution covering a period twice as long is change notable enough to mark a new type.[3]

That the twentieth century marks the beginning of the fourth period is substantiated by the reports of the National Survey of Secondary Education. Two new public institutions have arisen, viz., the *junior college,* which was first established in 1902 in Joliet, Illinois, and the *junior high school,* which was first organized in 1910 in Berkeley, California, and Columbus, Ohio. Reorganization is modifying the last two years of the elementary school, the four years of high school, and the two years that follow. A steady movement is evident toward the reorganization of existing high schools and the establishment of such secondary schools as junior, junior-senior, and senior high schools, and junior colleges.

The downward extension of secondary education, which commenced with the establishment of the first junior high schools in 1910, was preceded by the upward extension, which began with the organization of the first junior college. Although the earliest public junior college was that at Joliet, Illinois, founded in 1902, the Decatur Baptist College, which was founded

[3] Leonard V. Koos, "The Rise of the American High School," address presented at the Sixty-ninth Convocation of the University of New York celebrating the 150th anniversary of the establishment of the University, October 13, 1933.

in Texas in 1891 and reorganized as a private junior college in 1898, claims the distinction of being the oldest junior college. Some of the privately controlled junior colleges began as academies or seminaries over a hundred years ago, as is the case of Colby Junior College, which started as the New London Seminary in New Hampshire in 1837. The organization of junior colleges is described later in this chapter.

LEADERS IN SECONDARY EDUCATION

Three hundred years and more of secondary education in America have produced some three hundred leaders in this field. Only a few can be mentioned here. One of the earliest was the versatile Benjamin Franklin (1706–1790), who replaced the narrow curricular offerings of the Latin grammar school with an enriched program in the Franklin Academy. His uncommon common sense helped to make secondary education more practical. Another leader, G. Stanley Hall (1846–1924), through his monumental work *Adolescence*, published in 1907, helped to make secondary education more aware of the psychological needs of youth.

Another pioneer thinker in this field was Charles W. Eliot (1834–1926). Although he is best known for his long and effective service as president of Harvard University, his imprint upon secondary education is indelible. His efforts to raise the entrance requirements for Harvard were reflected in the improved standards in the high schools. His provisions for choice in entrance units allowed greater freedom in secondary curriculums. His work as chairman of the national Committee of Ten (1890) led eventually to the junior high school movement. His oral and written emphasis on seeing, hearing, and feeling stimulated the development of vocational education in the secondary schools.

Another university president who directly influenced the secondary schools was William Rainey Harper (1856–1906), who received his Ph.D. degree at the age of nineteen and became president of the University of Chicago at thirty-five. As chairman of a national committee, he recommended that the period of elementary education be reduced. His argument that the small, ineffective college should drop senior work and become a junior college earned for him the title "father of the junior college."

The University of Chicago added another leader in secondary education in the person of Leonard V. Koos, already mentioned in connection with the extended secondary school and the National Survey of Secondary Education. He has emphasized the role of the reorganized secondary school.

Another personality in secondary education is Thomas H. Briggs, professor emeritus of secondary school administration at Teachers College, Columbia University. Through his contact with hundreds of secondary school principals and teachers in his college classes, through his numerous publications, and through his chairmanship of the Committee on Orientation of Secondary Education, he has had tremendous influence on secondary education in America and abroad.

James Bryant Conant, another former president of Harvard University, in 1959 completed a significant contribution with a thorough study of American secondary education. This study, reported in *The American High School Today* and financed by a grant from the Carnegie Corporation, emphasized the importance of identifying the most able high school students and challenging them with advanced work, but without segregating them into special schools. He concluded that high school guidance programs should be strengthened to encourage wise selection of courses and vocations. It was Conant's finding that the most compelling problem confronting secondary education is the elimination through district reorganization of small high schools with their sharply limited programs.

To this group of statesmen, college presidents, and university instructors could be added an endless list of secondary school principals, classroom teachers, and board members who daily display courage, vision, and common sense in striving to make the objectives of secondary education function in a given locale. These collectively have helped to change America—educationally, socially, and economically.

Purposes

CHANGING CONCEPTS OF SECONDARY EDUCATION

Objectives [handwritten]

The objectives or directives of secondary education have been numerous and varied. In the days of the Latin grammar school, the main aim was to prepare a select group of boys and a few girls for both college and life activities. Within the last fifty years, however, have come changed concepts of what should be the objectives and who should be the recipients of secondary education. Contrast with modern objectives the statement from the report of the Committee of Ten in 1894 that the high school should be planned for "that small proportion of all the children in the country—a proportion small in number, but very important to the welfare of the nation—who show themselves able to profit by an education prolonged to the eighteenth year, and whose parents are able to support them while they remain so long at school."

Seven Cardinal Principles of Secondary Education. A well-known set of objectives of historical significance is that prepared in 1918 by the Commission on the Reorganization of Secondary Education, which advocated "such reorganization that secondary education may be defined as applying to all pupils of approximately twelve to eighteen years of age." Briefly stated, these seven objectives, usually called the Cardinal Principles of Education and applied to elementary as well as secondary education, are: (1) health, (2) command of fundamental processes, (3) worthy home membership, (4) vocational efficiency, (5) civic participation, (6) worthy use of leisure time, (7) ethical character. These objectives stress life out of

school as well as in school. They resemble somewhat the activities listed in 1859 by Herbert Spencer in his essay "What Knowledge Is of Most Worth?" and those presented by Bobbitt in 1924 in his *How to Make a Curriculum*.

Issues and Functions of Secondary Education. A vital force in formulating the objectives and program of secondary education has been the National Association of Secondary-school Principals, a department of the National Education Association. Under the dynamic and intelligent chairmanship of Professor Thomas H. Briggs of Teachers College, Columbia University, the Committee on Orientation in 1933 published statements of "Issues and Functions of Secondary Education." These have been studied in a large number of discussion groups throughout the United States, each state being organized under a coordinator. Issues, as defined by Briggs and the committee, are the questions of fundamental policy that have grown out of conflicting opinions, policies, and practices. They are to be decided primarily by reference to philosophies rather than by fact-finding and by experimentation, although the latter are needed to direct judgments.

The Committee on Orientation also prepared a statement of special functions for secondary education in the United States. These particular tasks, which may in varying degree begin in the later elementary school and continue at least till the end of the junior college, are briefly: (1) integration, (2) satisfaction of needs, (3) revelation of racial heritage, (4) exploration of interests, aptitudes, and capacities, (5) systematization and application of knowledge, (6) establishment and direction of interests, (7) guidance, (8) differentiation and general education, (9) methods of teaching and learning, (10) retention and direction of pupils. These functions, to be modified in the light of developments, represent a perennial challenge to all laymen and educators.

Education for All American Youth. Prior to developing a basic set of principles for elementary

*The American high school,
once restricted to a college
preparatory institution
serving a small percentage of youth,
has expanded its enrollment
enormously to include
nearly all youth of high school age.
The modern secondary school
attempts to meet these needs
of all youth . . .*

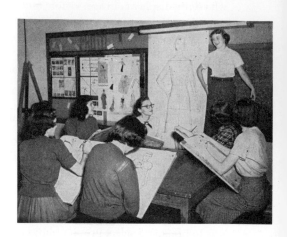

to acquire salable skills . . .

*Detroit high school students
study dress design.*

education in its volume *Education for All American Children*, the Educational Policies Commission published *Education for All American Youth*, in which it formulated policies for secondary education. This was supplemented by *A Further Look*. Schools should be dedicated, said the commission, to the proposition that every youth in these United States—regardless of sex, economic status, geographic location, or race—should experience a broad and balanced education which will:

1. Equip him to enter an occupation suited to his abilities and offering reasonable opportunity for personal growth and social usefulness.
2. Prepare him to assume the full responsibilities of American citizenship.
3. Give him a fair chance to exercise his right to the pursuit of happiness.
4. Stimulate intellectual curiosity, engender satisfaction in intellectual achievement, and cultivate the ability to think rationally.
5. Help him to develop an appreciation of the ethical values which should undergird all life in a democratic society.

The commission further adds that it is the duty of a democratic society to provide opportunities for such education through its numerous schools. It is the obligation of every youth, as a citizen, to make full use of these opportunities; and it is the responsibility of parents to give encouragement and support to both youth and schools.

Life Adjustment Education for Youth. In 1947 the Commission on Life Adjustment Education for Youth was created. This commission, which consists of representatives from several national organizations, including the U.S. Office of Education and the National Association of Secondary-school Principals, has stimulated programs that more adequately meet the imperative needs of students now in school. Even more, it has encouraged the types of education required for adolescent youth who drop out of school because their needs are not satisfied. The goals, "Imperative Needs of Youth," are summarized in the photographs and also are described in detail in various publications, including *Education for All American Youth— A Further Look*. The commission has implemented its goals through a persistent and continued attack on the problems of secondary education. In recent years the life adjustment concept itself has been subjected to attack, as indicated in Chapter 17.

*to develop
good
health
and physical
fitness . . .*

to perform the duties of citizenship.

Pearl River, New York, students
donate their weekend to a town cleanup project.

The maximum development of the ability and desire in each individual to make the greatest possible contribution to all humanity through responsible participation in, and benefit from, the great
privileges of American citizenship.

*American Association of School Administra-
tors Yearbook Commission.* In 1958, the AASA
Yearbook Commission, in its study of *The
High School in a Changing World,* reappraised
the goals of secondary education:

This Commission is concerned that this nation
might fail to realize its greatest destiny because of
inadequate provision for the education of our
youth. Its members believe that American youth
represent our greatest national resource and that
if such a resource is to be a firm foundation for
the future greatness of this nation, a program devoted to the development of American youth must
have great goals, the achievement of which will
tax our clearest thinking and demand our maximum efforts.

This Yearbook Commission acknowledges and
supports, as the legitimate and critically important goals of our secondary schools:
The maximum development of all the mental,
moral, emotional, and physical powers of the individual, to the end that he may enjoy a rich life
through the realization of worthy and desirable
personal goals . . .

Types

To meet the varied purposes of secondary education and the diverse needs of secondary pupils many types of schools have developed. As
indicated in Fig. 7-2, when secondary education is restricted to four years it is traditionally the function of one institution, viz., the
high school. In some communities secondary
education is extended downward two years to
embrace the last two years of what was elementary education, plus the traditional four
years of the high school period, thus creating
the undivided or six-year secondary school. In
communities where there is rigid separation of
the elementary and secondary schools, the secondary period of learning may reach not downward but upward to include the junior college
in connection with the regular high school.
Many cities are now reorganizing secondary
education into a unified eight-year program or
into two divisions—the lower secondary school,

covering grades 7, 8, 9, and 10, and the upper secondary school, embracing grades 11, 12, 13, and 14. These seem to be two of the future patterns for secondary education. Currently there is much emphasis upon the eight-year model, divided into three sections, the junior high school (7, 8, and 9), the senior high school (10, 11, and 12), and the junior college (13 and 14). To this classification may be added other groupings by years or special curricular schools, such as vocational.

JUNIOR HIGH SCHOOLS

Seventh- and Eighth-grade Schools. In its shortened form the junior high school may consist of two grades, the seventh and eighth. Many so-called junior high schools, however, are merely glorified seventh and eighth grades minus the philosophy, program, and procedures of the genuine junior high school. The latter is more than a grouping or regrouping of grades, and new names. School board members and administrators do not produce a junior high school by erecting a new building with the words "Junior High School" carved in stone over the entrance. Teachers do not create a junior high school curriculum by using pupil textbooks labeled *Junior High School Mathematics*, *Junior High School English*, etc. Even where

the seventh and eighth grades are grouped with the ninth, a real junior high school may not exist. Adding the ninth grade may be as incongruous as sewing a new piece of cloth onto an old garment. What is needed is a new pattern and a new institution—a junior high school in name, function, and curriculum—dominated by the philosophy and purposes of secondary rather than elementary education.

Junior High School. This school, first called intermediate, was later christened the junior high school. Arising out of dissatisfaction with the established order of things, the junior high school has advanced until it now forms the lowest rung on the ladder of secondary education. Although its progress was retarded during World Wars I and II, this institution has taken Herculean strides, particularly in the larger cities. Its usual range embraces the seventh, eighth, and ninth grades, although the last is often omitted. As just indicated, however, the junior high school is more than a regrouping of grades. It is a program to meet the needs of immature, maturing, and mature pupils.

The National Survey of Secondary Education listed nine major features of the organization of junior high schools: (1) flexibility in admission and promotion, (2) arrangement of instruction, (3) program of studies, (4) extra-

Fig. 7-2. *Organizational patterns of secondary education.*

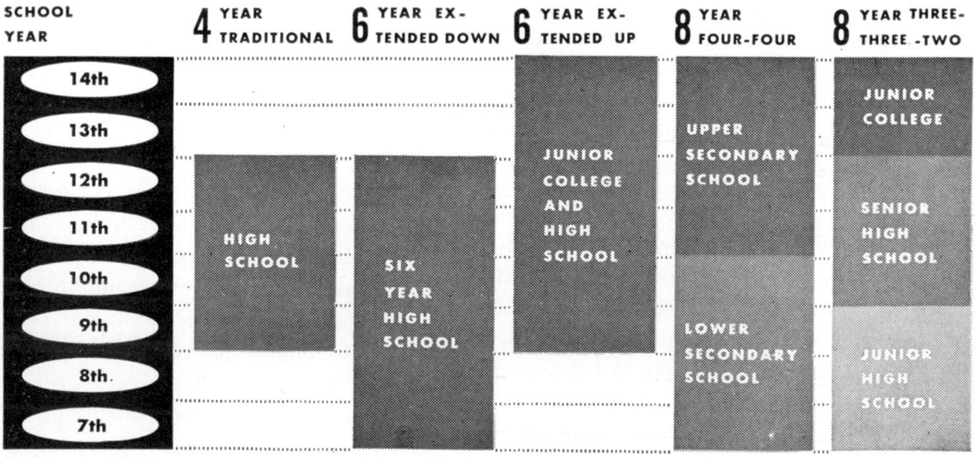

curriculum program, (5) educational-vocational guidance, (6) special features for articulation, (7) specially trained teaching staff, (8) supervision of instruction, (9) special housing and equipment. According to nation-wide surveys of actual practices in junior high schools, there is much room for improvement. Junior high school administrators appear to be more influenced by past practice and by financial expediency than by advanced theory.

INTERMEDIATE SECONDARY SCHOOLS

The middle area of secondary education usually embraces the senior high school, or the typical four-year high school, or variations thereof.

Senior High School. This is usually a three-year high school with grades 10, 11, and 12 linked with a junior high system for grades 7, 8, and 9. Often the existing buildings determine what the organization of the high school shall be. In cities with a fluctuating population and changing building facilities, the first-semester students of the tenth grade may be housed in the senior high school one year and in the junior high building the next.

Although the graduation requirements from the four-year schools are 16 units, those for the senior high are reduced to 12. Since colleges and accrediting agencies are not vitally concerned with the content of the last year of junior high schools (the ninth grade), wider experimentation and more orientation are possible in a six-three-three organization than in an eight-four plan. The six-three-three system, however, has the disadvantage of an extra hyphen (indicating a transition) not found in the eight-four plan. With an increase in attendance units, the need for articulation is also increased. On the other hand, once the students are in the senior high, its holding power is stronger than that of the four-year school since the usual ninth-grade drop-outs have come during or at the close of the junior high period. With the

Teen-agers learn to appreciate good family life and become successful homemakers . . .

Teen-agers learn to care for infants.

*to
use
goods
and
services
wisely . . .*

increasing growth of the junior high is linked the future of the senior high school.

Four-year High School. The secondary school that includes grades 9, 10, 11, and 12 is the prevailing type of high school organization in the United States. Under present conditions it will continue to lead in states like California, New Jersey, and Illinois, where many high schools under a separate board of education are divorced from the elementary school district. This practically prohibits the combination of seventh, eighth, and ninth grades. The high school commencing with the ninth grade is also

to learn the methods of science . . .

popular in small rural areas and may be only a two- or three-year institution. Although several states still recognize these two- and three-year schools, the regional accrediting associations do not put their stamp of approval upon them because of their limitations in equipment, staff, enrollment, curriculums, and social living.

The traditional four-year school is undergoing significant changes. Especially since the beginning of the present century, marked internal improvement has been effected. Where it is neither desirable nor possible to reorganize the four-year high school into a new type of secondary school, much is being done to rejuvenate the existing institution. Even though the four-year unit does not reorganize externally, it can improve internally through curricular modifications and other changes. The comprehensive high school, offering a common core plus a wide variety of experiences for all adolescents, is a unique national contribution.

JUNIOR COLLEGES, COMMUNITY COLLEGES, AND OTHER POSTSECONDARY INSTITUTIONS

Position of the Junior College. Traditionally, a junior college has been defined as an institution of higher education that gives two years of work equivalent in prerequisites, scope, and thoroughness to the work done in the first two years of college. On the other hand, the conviction is growing that the junior college, as well as the freshman and sophomore years of colleges and universities, belongs to the secondary school level. California, which ranks first in the number of junior colleges, has made the independent junior college a definite part of its common school system, and rightly so, since the junior college should not be a separate entity. Whether it belongs to secondary or to higher education may be a debatable issue, but the junior or community college should be integrated with the high schools on one hand and with the higher institutions on the other.

Its Growth. The junior college, a product of the twentieth century, has spread gradually from West to East. Originating in Illinois and Texas, it has had the greatest growth in the western and southwestern parts of the United States. Junior colleges now exist in almost every state. The growth in the number of colleges and their enrollments is revealed quite strikingly in Fig. 7-3. Data on junior colleges and their enrollments are published in the annual directory of the *Junior College Journal.*

Types of Junior Colleges. The legal control of junior colleges is vested in (1) public bodies, viz., city, township, county, state, and district officials; (2) the church, with Roman Catholic, Methodist, and Baptist in the lead, and other religious organizations such as the YMCA; and (3) private corporations independent of church or state, such as Penn Hall Junior Col-

to appreciate beauty in art, music, and nature . . .

Erie, Pennsylvania, high school students sketch a view of Lake Erie.

lege for women located in Chambersburg, Pennsylvania. Approximately one-half are public, but their enrollments far outnumber those in the other two types. The typical junior college is coeducational.

The President's Committee on Education Beyond the High School recommended the creation of two-year colleges as "the next logical step in filling in and rounding out our educational system." To accommodate fully our rapidly expanding college-age population in present four-year colleges appears to be a staggering financial burden. Community colleges offer an opportunity for large numbers of American youth to extend their education at minimum cost since many students can remain at home while attending. It is apparent that the community college is as widely needed today as the four-year high school was a few decades ago. Such a college would fit into the local educational structure in much the same way that the high school has done. Community colleges are clearly destined to increase in number and influence.

Another type of junior college is the specialized one—the technical institute or institute of applied arts and sciences. For example, New York State, after an extensive survey of postwar educational needs, launched a number of postsecondary technical institutes whose regular program provides two years of education and training for post-high school youth or others whose maturity, needs, interests, and abilities justify admission. Some of these schools are designed primarily for general regional service, but a few postsecondary institutes are for highly specialized occupations, to serve either the upstate area or the whole state.

Origin of Junior Colleges. Originally the junior college was considered a two-year institution, but today its program may extend over one, two, three, or even four years. As to method of establishment, these colleges may be classified on the following bases: (1) adding two years to the high school, (2) subtracting two years from the college, (3) affiliating with existing colleges and universities, and (4) organizing a separate new institution. Authorizing legislation usually falls into two categories: *general,* such as a state-wide law for

to live and work cooperatively with others.

the establishment of junior or community colleges, and *specific*, such as a separate charter for an institution. Some states, like New York, have both types of legislation.

Their Functions. The four well-known functions of the junior college suggested by W. S. Greenleaf are: *(1) popularization of higher education,* or offering college opportunities to local high school graduates and adults who would otherwise be deprived of a college education; *(2) preparatory,* or providing two years of standard college work or professional work for entrance to the senior college or professional school; *(3) terminal,* or preparing students in two years for a career and for social citizenship; and *(4) guidance,* or aiding in shaping the lives of young students and directing them educationally and vocationally. These functions demand an extensive curriculum for youths and adults.

Their Curriculums. Most curriculums of the various junior colleges may be grouped into (1) basic courses, stressing general education and culture; (2) preparatory courses for advanced study, leading toward the bachelor's degree or beyond; (3) semiprofessional courses, preparing for professional schools such as journalism; and (4) occupational courses, usually terminal in nature and leading directly to employment. These types are described in the next chapter, but reference is made briefly here to general and terminal education in secondary and postsecondary institutions.

General Education in Secondary and Postsecondary Education. The basic purpose of secondary education must be accented, especially in a highly specialized and scientific age. This fundamental function is general education, the common denominator that develops a basic and wide range of competencies which one needs as a person and a citizen in a democratic society. The general education one acquires in the elementary school must be supplemented by further common learnings in secondary and postsecondary education. The President's Commission on Higher Education in its recommendations for community colleges states, "If the semiprofessional curriculum is to accomplish its purpose it must not be crowded with vocational and technical courses to the exclusion of general education." The Regents' plan for technical institutes in New York provided for the multiple task of combining technical training with general education. In the earlier years of secondary education the highest priority should be given to general education, while in

Fig. 7-3. Enrollment in junior colleges.

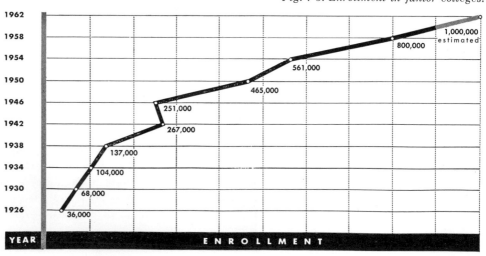

*They also learn
to use leisure time well . . .*

*to think and speak clearly,
to listen and
read with understanding.*

postsecondary institutions an adequate balance must be maintained between general education and activities leading to occupational competence.

Terminal Education. The Commission on Junior College Terminal Education, working under the auspices of the American Association of Junior Colleges through a grant from the General Education Board, found that most junior college students do not continue their education beyond this limit, yet only about a third of the young men and women enrolled are taking courses that are terminal in character. Obviously, junior colleges should devote more attention to the development of terminal education, including not only vocational and semiprofessional training but also general cultural education for social and civic intelligence.

In this connection, the query is raised: "Should completion of junior college work be officially recognized?" Some type of formal benediction seems desirable. In India, for example, the intermediate degree is given to those who successfully complete two years of work beyond the high school. Associate in Arts or Associate in Science is the degree usually granted in America. In a program shorter than two years a certificate is generally awarded. Since the junior college is at present in a sort of no man's land between secondary and higher education, practices in granting degrees and building curriculums are in a state of flux.

Role of Junior Colleges and Postsecondary Institutions. The junior college is likely to produce the most important readjustment in our whole educational system. The depression, postdepression, war, and postwar periods have consolidated and strengthened the position of the junior colleges in America. In California they are banded together in sectional associations as well as in a state federation. In many states they form independent associations, as in Oklahoma, or constitute a part of the state teachers association, as in Iowa. The American Association of Junior Colleges, chartered in 1920, has its national headquarters at Washington, D.C. *The Junior College Journal* is its official publication. This association's comprehensive study of the role of the junior colleges, with particular emphasis on terminal education, states: "If junior colleges, instead of trying to imitate the 4-year program, would offer courses close to the interest of the student and suited to his abilities, they would begin to occupy one of the most important places in American education."

For many years the junior colleges, community colleges, and technical institutes, as the youngest members of the educational family, were on the defensive. Their arrival tended to jeopardize the traditional solidarity of the college; furthermore, the question was raised as to whether these colleges were regular members of the public education group. The legality of taxation for their support was debated as in the earlier case of the high school. In 1930 the Supreme Court of North Carolina held that the city of Asheville had the right to tax itself to maintain a junior college out of funds set aside for the conduct of a public school. The parallel between the Kalamazoo High School case and the Asheville case is obvious. In most states the maintenance of public junior colleges has been legalized by specific statute. Recurring unemployment for youth of the post-secondary age, the complexity of modern living, and the inability of present four-year colleges to provide for the avalanche of college-age students have promoted the demand for vertical and horizontal extension of educational opportunities. As the concept spreads that secondary education does not end with the high school, there will be a marked increase in junior colleges, community colleges, and technical institutes, which probably will become the people's colleges.

OTHER SECONDARY SCHOOLS

This general classification includes schools that may extend over all levels of secondary and postsecondary education.

Vocational Schools. The main group is that of the vocational or technical schools so prevalent in large cities and in certain states, notably Wisconsin. In several foreign countries the vocational choices of young people are decidedly restricted by a rigid selective examination in the elementary school, by the requirement of prolonged compulsory military or national service, by the social limitations such as a caste system, or by the handicap of extreme poverty. In the United States, although the vocational choices of young people may be modified somewhat by factors outside themselves, there is no predestined career that a boy or girl must follow. This situation has tremendous implications for vocational guidance in secondary schools. The National Defense Education Act has stimulated the improvement of guidance services. The years to come will undoubtedly see much more emphasis upon prevocational and vocational guidance in all secondary schools. Many parents, however, are demanding that their children take fewer vocational courses and more academic subjects.

Other Types. Many other types of special secondary schools might be listed in the following categories: size—small, medium, or large; pupils—those gifted in art or music; sex—girls, boys, or coeducation; age—adolescent or adult; organization—platoon or six-year school; legal control—public, private, or parochial; methodology or philosophy—liberal, middle-of-the-road, or conservative; school time—part-time, continuation, correspondence, night school, or summer, camp, or year-round school; and numerous others.

Practices

A few of the more salient characteristics of modern secondary education are presented here through brief descriptions of some current practices in (1) organization and administration, (2) curriculum and teaching-learning procedures, and (3) personnel.

Organization and Administration. Modern secondary education postulates its organization and administration upon the concept of an extended educational period of approximately eight years. Both the junior high schools and the junior colleges are dynamic components within the complete program of secondary school organization. The traditional organization of secondary education as a short-span high school institution is giving way to various patterns of structural reorganization, embracing such variations as the three-three and the four-four plans.

Private and parochial high schools are increasing in number. Enrollments in parochial high schools doubled in the past decade. One of every ten secondary students attends a nonpublic high school.

Although secondary education is the period usually designated as general education, specialized schools are increasing in number and effectiveness. We find, for example, the Apprenticeship and Journeyman School in San Francisco, the High School of Music and Art and the Maritime High School in New York City, the Brooklyn High School of Automotive Trades, and the Miami, Florida, Technical High School. The latter offers a boat-building course which attracts students from several states. New York State has established a number of regional and state-wide technical institutes. Despite the appropriate existence of private and specialized high schools, the comprehensive high school, as Conant points out, should continue without radical alteration to serve the great majority of youth of secondary school age.

any types schools

State programs of secondary education are being promoted and coordinated through state educational agencies, such as the state departments. The establishment of junior colleges and community colleges as "community-wide centers of social and civic education for both adults and youth" calls for more state aid for junior colleges.

Regional associations that accredit secondary schools are stressing qualitative standards as well as revising quantitative measures. An example is the Cooperative Study of Secondary School Standards.

The relationship between secondary schools and institutions of higher learning have been markedly improved. Releasing secondary schools from the usual course and unit require-

ments for college entrance has stimulated more effective programs in these schools. The domination of high schools by colleges and universities is decreasing. Effective cooperation is increasing. Dartmouth College, for example, conducts a series of lecture-demonstrations in physics to supplement the courses given to students in nearby high schools. Thus the expensive laboratories and skilled faculty of a college are made available to extend and enrich the high school curriculum.

Curriculum and Teaching-Learning Procedures. The objectives of secondary education, embracing all areas, are being adjusted to the functional needs of students and society, rather than being too heavily oriented to college preparation. The emphasis today is upon giving students opportunities to become and to be intelligent, happy, self-sustaining members of a democracy. These objectives are being implemented through a strong program of amalgamated curricular and cocurricular activities. Consideration of developmental tasks is producing curriculum changes.

Schools have introduced many new instructional areas, such as automobile driving, aviation, atomic energy, radioisotopes, home economics for boys, income-tax calculations, democratic living, semantics, Hebrew, international relations, radio and television, work experience, labor relations, electronics, mental hygiene, world literature, economics, social institutions, public education, personal typing, general shop, etc. In several high schools that have revised their curriculums, separate courses in the same general field have been fused. For example, history, economics, civics, geography, sociology, and related subjects are coalesced in the broad survey of social science. Instruction in mathematics, science, and foreign languages is being extended and strengthened. A striking example is the increased offering of Russian. At the time of the launching of the first Sputnik, only 16 American high schools offered courses in Russian, but by 1960 the number exceeded 400.

youths attend secondary schools because complexity of society necessitates it, and there is too much unemployment.

Advanced placement programs are becoming more common. These programs may either provide college-level courses to brilliant high school seniors or permit able high school students to enter college early, following an accelerated high school program. These and other modifications have been developed to accelerate and enrich the education of very gifted young people. Ability grouping by subjects is being practiced more widely with special attention given to both the academically talented and the slow learners. Summer schools are becoming more common, providing bright and ambitious students opportunity to take more electives and slow students a chance to repeat subjects.

The technological aspects of agriculture, industry, defense, commerce, and allied fields are demanding more and more prevocational, semioccupational, and vocational work in the secondary schools. Smith-Hughes aid, which restricted the use of federal funds to courses of "less than college grade," has delayed the development of vocational education in junior colleges and technical institutes.

The Smith-Hughes and George-Barden Acts have promoted much more emphasis upon the work-study plan of education. This type of realistic community education is exemplified in the home experience project, where housewives cooperate with local school authorities in opening their homes to senior and junior homemaking students.

The methodology of extrinsic teaching is giving way to an emphasis upon motivation, which produces intrinsic learning. The development of teaching-learning units has led to the reorganization of traditional courses around personal problems and realistic experiences. Newer instruments are being devised to measure growth and outcomes in junior and senior high schools and junior colleges. They are designed as a part of a broad program of evaluation, which is replacing mere pencil-and-paper tests. State-wide evaluation programs are increasing.

Personnel. The complexity of modern civilization, which necessitates more education, and the recurrent unemployment situation, which postpones the entrance of youth into regular gainful employment, are two of the many forces bringing more youth to the secondary schools of America. The democratic provisions of supplying state aid for transporting rural students and paying all or part of the tuition charges are giving more rural youth the benefits of secondary education. In some cases, dormitories have been provided for youth attending public high schools. Residential boarding schools are increasing. School cafeterias are important adjuncts of modern high schools, especially in consolidated school districts.

14 yrs. of schooling A minimum of fourteen years of schooling for everyone is in consonance with the need for a higher level of education for all persons in the American democracy. The recipients of secondary education include both youth and adults. Many secondary school plants are being kept open day and night in the interests of preparing youth and adults "to function efficiently —vocationally, avocationally, and civically."

Large crowds of students graduating from the elementary schools are knocking on the doors of the high school for admittance. Quantitatively there is a huge reservoir of students. Secondary students are urged and motivated to remain in school longer.

Manpower shortages have demanded increased emphasis upon the guidance of youth. Greater effort is being made to identify early those students of high ability so that their high school programs of study can be planned to encourage fuller development of their talents. Much attention is devoted to keeping student personnel records, including test scores, anecdotal records, parent or student interviews, photographs, etc.

Special attention to veterans has been given by secondary schools through high schools for veterans, credit for military service and General Educational Development Tests, trade schools, apprenticeship programs, and correspondence courses, especially those furnished by the United States Armed Forces Institute (USAFI). The GI bills, through federal grants or scholarships, have enabled many veterans to complete their secondary education.

There is a definite trend toward employing only teachers who possess a master's degree or its equivalent. Secondary school teachers, as the best-educated members of the public school family, are called upon increasingly to participate in and to share democratically in the preparation of policies and programs for the education of youth. Self-evaluation of teachers themselves and of their schools, as promoted through the Cooperative Study of Secondary School Standards, is helping to raise the standards of secondary schools.

Future

During the past decade particularly, American public education has been the subject of widespread study and criticism. The high school, more than any level of education, has been the center of the most vigorous scrutiny and criticism. For example, it is argued that Russian and other European secondary programs are better; that too many soft courses of little intellectual value have been introduced; that separate high schools with rigorous curriculums should be established for the intellectually gifted students; that students unable to meet tough academic standards ought to be eliminated; that vocational education ought to give way to more general education; and that extracurricular activities should be de-emphasized. These issues are discussed in Chapter 17.

Regardless of the eventual outcome of these controversies, it is apparent that American secondary education is undergoing substantial modification. However, it is clear that the American concept of the comprehensive high school is sound. The ideal of extending the common school to include high school education for all American youth has been achieved. Indeed, this is one of the most significant accomplishments of American education. However, much remains to be done before it is possible to provide mass education for all and, at the same time, to challenge the highly intellectual to the full measure of their ability. It is clear that both quantity and quality can be provided in American high schools, although patterns of curriculum and instruction must be modified to accomplish this end.

The AASA Yearbook Commission concludes its appraisal of the high school in the American scene in these terms:

This relatively young institution has now come of age and is ready to assume the grave responsibilities and obligations of maturity. This new and demanding role of secondary education is intertwined with America's future. As the early school contributed to the development of democracy, the secondary school of tomorrow will be a dynamic force in the perpetuating and refinement of our free society. America's destiny is in the minds and hearts of its youth.[4]

After this period of secondary education, with its emphasis on general education for all and on special preparation for practical life for those who will not go beyond secondary education, the schools of higher learning then offer a wide variety of opportunities for continuing institutionalized education. In the next chapter, these opportunities for higher education are presented, and in the chapter following, the education of adults is treated.

Summary

The American high school has emerged from four periods of development: the Latin grammar school, the tuition academy, the free public high school, and the vertically extended or reorganized secondary school. Since 1880, the high school has grown phenomenally, both in numbers and enrollment, and will continue to

[4] American Association of School Administrators, *The High School in a Changing World*, National Education Association, Washington, D.C., 1958, p. 368.

grow in the foreseeable future. Nearly 90 per cent of American youth of high school age are in attendance, a far greater proportion than in any other country. This has been one of the most unique and significant accomplishments of American education.

Several classic statements have been made of the purposes of secondary education: <u>the Seven Cardinal Principles, the Ten Imperative Needs of Youth.</u> More recently, an AASA yearbook enunciated two fundamental purposes: the maximum development of the mental, moral, emotional, and physical powers of the individual to enjoy a rich personal life and the maximum development of the ability and desire of each individual to make the greatest possible contribution to all humanity. The high school has been the focus of intensive study and criticism. Secondary education is presently undergoing substantial change.

Several types of secondary education have been developed, including the four-year high school, the six-year high school, the junior high school, the senior high school, the junior college and others. The nature of the junior college is still somewhat confused, since it is regarded by some as an upward extension of secondary education and by others as a modification of higher education. In any event, it appears that the junior college is on the threshold of even more rapid development in the future.

Secondary education has been established to prepare gifted students for college, to provide general education for all, and to provide practical preparation for the problems of life for those who will not attend college. Many new areas of opportunity have been introduced into the high school curriculum. Greater care is being given to the guidance of high school students.

The high school is undergoing a transition from a four-year institution to a broader unit encompassing the junior high school, the senior high school, and the junior college.

Suggested activities

1. Review the development of secondary education in the historical calendar.
2. Prepare a special report on the Kalamazoo High School case or the Asheville case, showing the effects of the court decision.
3. Compare secondary education in America with that in England, France, Germany, or an oriental country.
4. Prepare a survey of your own high school graduating class, including such data as how many went to college, how many are out of school, how many are gainfully employed. Draw conclusions.
5. Make a list of subjects you studied in high school. What changes would you recommend if you were to take the work again?
6. Study the college entrance requirements of your state university. How do these influence the high school curriculum?
7. Prepare a spot map of your state or county indicating the location and size of the secondary schools.
8. Study the work of agencies that accredit the high schools in your state. List their standards for accrediting high schools.
9. Describe vocational education as found in a secondary school today.
10. Describe the locus, purpose, procedures, and results of a significant experiment in junior college education, for example, at Blackburn or Stephens College.
11. Report on the topic "Private and Parochial Secondary Schools in the United States."
12. Examine the certification requirements for teachers of secondary schools in your state.
13. List the special qualities and preparation that you think a secondary school teacher should possess.

Bibliography

Books

American Association of School Administrators: *The High School in a Changing World*, National Education Association, Washington, D.C., 1958, chaps. 1–4. Discusses the pressures of society, the needs of youth, the secondary program, and the relation of the high school to the community.

Chase, Francis S., and Harold A. Anderson: *The High School in a New Era*, University of Chicago Press, Chicago, 1958, pp. 3–19, 263–272. Traces the historical development of the high school and shows how laymen help in planning secondary education.

Conant, James B.: *The American High School Today*, McGraw-Hill Book Company, Inc., New York, 1959. Widely acclaimed book presenting the characteristics of present secondary education and establishing recommendations for its improvement.

Developments in the Secondary School Program, National Education Association, Washington, D.C., 1956. Traces new trends in secondary education with particular attention to the curriculum.

French, William M.: *American Secondary Education*, The Odyssey Press, Inc., New York, 1957, chaps. 11, 12. Describes the role and nature of parochial and other private secondary schools in American society.

French, Will, J. Dan Hull, and B. L. Dodds: *American High School Administration*, Rinehart & Company, Inc., New York, 1957, chaps. 3, 4. Presents the background of secondary education in American society and shows how secondary schools are organized.

Crambs, Jean D., William J. Iverson, and Franklin K. Patterson: *Modern Methods in Secondary Education*, The Dryden Press, Inc., New York, 1958, chaps. 1, 4, 23. Discusses the nature of effective high school curriculums and teaching.

Gruhn, William T., and Harl R. Douglass: *The Modern Junior High School*, The Ronald Press Company, New York, 1956, chaps. 1–4. Presents the background, philosophy, strengths, and weaknesses of the junior high school and looks at curriculum trends.

Hand, Harold C.: *Principles of Public Secondary Education*, Harcourt, Brace and Company, Inc., New York, 1958, chaps. 1, 4, 13. Outlines the problems of secondary school teachers, describes the principles of secondary education—its accomplishments and prospects for the future.

High School Discipline in American Society, National Education Association, Washington, D.C., 1956. Tackles the problem of discipline, shows its basic causes, and suggests means whereby the causes can be removed and the victims helped.

Roberts, Roy W.: *Vocational and Practical Arts Education*, Harper & Brothers, New York, 1957, chap. 20. Outlines the basic principles of vocational education and its proper role and function in secondary education.

Periodicals

Anderson, Vernon E.: "Things Are Happening in Secondary Education," *NEA Journal*, vol. 44 (March, 1955), pp. 167–169. Describes new trends in high school education: the rise of the core curriculum, greater attention to general education, life adjustment education, and the relation of learning to life.

Barnes, Melvin W.: "The Nature and Nurture of Early Adolescents," *Teachers College Record*, vol. 57 (May, 1956), pp. 513–521. A description of the growth and development of youth through junior high school age.

Baron, George: "Secondary Education in England: Some Present Day Trends," *Teachers College Record*, vol. 57 (January, 1956), pp. 211–221. An interesting account of high schools in England which are facing many of the same dilemmas as their American counterparts.

Brink, William G.: "What Is a Good Secondary School?" *High School Journal*, vol. 41 (April, 1958), pp. 308–314. Establishes some of the characteristics of quality in high schools.

"Crisis in Education," *Life*, vol. 44 (March 24,

1958), pp. 25–37. A picture story comparing a Russian high schoolboy and his U.S. counterpart, concluding that the latter is inferior.

Elicker, Paul E.: "The Next Twenty-five Years in Secondary Education," *Education Digest*, vol. 23 (March, 1958), pp. 9–11. A penetrating look at the future of secondary education including the prediction that high school teachers will be more greatly respected.

French, Will: "The Changed Role of the American High School," *Teachers College Record*, vol. 56 (April, 1955), pp. 355–370. Explores the European roots of the American secondary school and its transition to its present status.

Kvaraceus, William C.: "What about High School Hoodlumism?" *National Parent Teacher*, vol. 53 (January, 1959), pp. 4–7. Analyzes the disturbing spread of violence and brutality among youth, cites the causes, and suggests a bold and vigorous approach to the problem.

Passow, A. Harry: "The Comprehensive High School and Gifted Youth," *Teachers College Record*, vol. 58 (December, 1956), pp. 144–152. Shows how the well-organized high school, through special curricular arrangements, can meet the needs of gifted learners.

Reynolds, James W.: "There Are Private Junior Colleges Too," *Junior College Journal*, vol. 29 (September, 1958), pp. 1–2. Emphasizes the important role of private junior colleges and how they differ from their public counterparts.

Roland, Leo J.: "The American Junior College," *Social Education*, vol. 22 (November, 1958), pp. 357–360. Traces the development of the junior college and presents statistics concerning its present status.

Saylor, Galen: "Contributions of the American High School to National Life," *High School Journal*, vol. 41 (April, 1958), pp. 303–307. Suggests eight ways in which America has benefited as a result of its secondary school system.

Shaw, Archibald, and John L. Reed: "The Random Falls Idea," *The School Executive*, vol. 75 (March, 1956), pp. 47–86. A case study of a hypothetical, bold new design for American secondary education, with illustrations.

Siggelkow, Richard A.: "Do Modern High Schools Prepare for College?" *National Association of Secondary School Principals Bulletin*, vol. 42 (May, 1958), pp. 131–135. Advances proposals whereby secondary schools can do a better job of preparing youth for college.

chapter 8

Higher education

In 1862, the darkest hour of the Civil War, President Lincoln signed the Morrill Act, which offered land to each state for the support of a college of agriculture and mechanical arts. As Andrew D. White, first president of Cornell University, one of the institutions founded by this act, observed, "In all the annals of republics, there is no more significant utterance of confidence in national destiny out of the midst of national calamity."

A century later, America finds its destiny even more dependent upon the adequacy and vigor of its colleges and universities. Paradoxically, higher education today is less able to meet the heavy challenges of the future than any other level of American education. Colleges and universities face an avalanche of college-bound youth with faculties, facilities, and finances that are greatly inadequate.

America's 1,900 colleges and universities comprise a wide variety of institutions: tiny colleges with less than a hundred students and vast universities with sprawling campuses; tax-supported municipal and state universities with low tuition and quite expensive private schools; colleges that are wealthy and colleges that are poverty-stricken; colleges for men, for women, and for both; schools specializing in technical fields and others offering only general education. In higher education's diversity lies much of its strength.

Foundations

DEVELOPMENT OF HIGHER EDUCATION

European Antecedents. Universities, like cathedrals and parliaments, are a product of the Middle Ages. The world's oldest university dates back to A.D. 841, when the Moslems founded Al Azhar ("The Resplendent") in Cairo, Egypt. In the days of ancient Greece and Rome, the source of much wisdom were men of great knowledge and personal magnetism, such as Plato, at whose feet sat young and old. This personal and informal fellowship in learning was the remote genesis of the modern university, which unfortunately has lost some of the close teacher-student relationship in its colossal campuses, big buildings, and scurrying students.

These early schools, however, were not university organizations in the modern sense of the term. It was the intellectual activity of the twelfth and thirteenth centuries that gave rise to the university type of organization. When the number of students and professors at a church or cathedral school grew so large that they found it necessary to organize themselves into a guild or *universitas* for mutual welfare and protection, then a university may be said to have come into existence.

The oldest university in Europe was Bologna, founded by a guild of students in a city of that name in northern Italy during the twelfth century. The study of law was of prime interest to medieval Italians, and soon Bologna developed a position of leadership in this field. In southern Italy the city of Salerno, a health resort, became famous for its lectures and collection of materials in the field of medicine.

In France, another medieval institution, the University of Paris, developed from a cathedral school. Naturally this school attracted a large number of students of religion. Although theology was the core, other fields, such as the arts, were stressed. Paris was the greatest of the medieval universities.

The old University of Prague, founded in 1348, was attended by students from many nations. All the early universities had a very loose form of organization, a crude type of democracy. When a group became discontented, they moved to another center, where they established a new college.

Thus emigrants from Paris established in the twelfth century the great University of Oxford. Modeled after Paris, Oxford stimulated the development of the college to the point where it overshadowed the university and provided the prototype for the colleges of today. Today Oxford is a federation of twenty or more colleges, such as Exeter, Queen's, and Jesus, each with

its own government, but the degrees are granted by the university.

The contrasts between these early institutions of higher learning and those of today are striking. The medieval university had no libraries, laboratories, or museums, no endowment or buildings of its own; it could not possibly have met the requirements of modern accrediting associations. The old university was *bâtie en hommes*—built of men. It created the university tradition and laid a firm foundation for higher education in America. The late Edgar W. Knight, an authority in the history of education, states that the American college is a native institution only in the sense that it is a European institution transplanted here in the seventeenth century by the early settlers who brought it from England along with their Bibles and their axes.

The European university today differs markedly from the American in that the European student has in a great measure finished his general education by the time he enters the university, that European higher learning is more restricted than in the United States, and that student life is less highly organized than in America.

Early American Colleges. Although the first institution of higher learning in the United States was Harvard College, it is not the oldest in the Americas. The University of San Marcos at Lima, Peru, and the University of Mexico at Mexico City both opened their doors in 1553—eighty-three years before Harvard.

As indicated in the right column of the historical calendar, the first college in continental United States was Harvard, founded in 1636 in Massachusetts. The basic motive for its establishment may be gleaned from this inscription on the west gate on its campus:

After God had carried us safe to New England, and wee had builded our houses, provided necessaries for our livelihood, rear'd convenient places for God's worship, and setled the Civil Government: One of the next things we longed for, and looked after was to advance Learning and per-

National Development		The Development of Higher Education
Discovery and early settlements	**1636**	Harvard University founded 1st
The Colonial period	**1693**	William and Mary College established
The struggle for independence and constitutional government	**1785**	First state university chartered in Georgia
Launching the new nation	**1803**	First federal land granted for state "seminary of learning" in Ohio
Maritime troubles and the War of 1812		
Era of good feeling	**1819**	Dartmouth College decision rendered by U.S. Supreme Court
Jacksonian Democracy	**1837**	Coeducation started at Oberlin College, founded in 1833
	1838	Mount Holyoke College organized as first women's college
Westward migration and expansion	**1839**	First state normal school organized in Massachusetts
Controversy and war between the states	**1862**	Land-grant college act passed by Congress
	1868	Hampton Institute organized as first Negro school of higher education
Aftermath and reconstruction	**1876**	First graduate work begun at Johns Hopkins University
Immigration and industrial growth		
The progressive era	**1902**	First public junior college established at Joliet, Illinois
World War I		
Depression and recovery		
World War II	**1944**	GI Bill for veterans' education passed by Congress
	1947	Reports issued by President's Commission on Education
	1948	First Fulbright scholarships opened for China and Burma
	1952	Reports issued by Commission on Financing Higher Education
The Cold War struggle		
	1957	Educational Policies Commission report, *Higher Education in a Decade of Decision*, published
	1958	Report of the President's Committee on Education Beyond the High School presented

NATIONAL DEVELOPMENT   **THE DEVELOPMENT OF HIGHER EDUCATION**

HISTORICAL CALENDAR

The American institution of higher learning, with its roots firmly in the past, looks to the challenges of the future without departing from its traditional functions of discovering and disseminating knowledge.

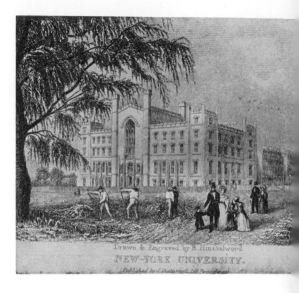

NEW-YORK UNIVERSITY.

petuate it to Posterity; dreading to leave an illiterate Ministry to the Churches when our present Ministers shall lie in the Dust.

According to the Charter of 1650, the purposes of Harvard were as follows: the advancement of all good literature, arts and sciences; the advancement and education of youth in all manner of good literature, arts and sciences; and all other necessary provisions that may conduce to the education of the English and Indian youth of this country in knowledge and godliness.

For many years Harvard was the only voice of higher education in the wilderness of America. Attempts to found a college in Virginia began, before the *Mayflower* sailed to Plymouth, with the grant of land for a university by the Virginia Company, but not until 1693 were the planters able to obtain adequate aid from England for their "place of university." Thus started the College of William and Mary at Williamsburg, Virginia.

In the colonial period of the United States nine colleges were founded. In connection with the last arose the historical Dartmouth College case. The decision of the Supreme Court threw protection around higher education and stimulated the growth of colleges. All nine colonial colleges, with the exception of Benjamin Franklin's Academy, were sectarian. By 1800 there were 25 colleges in the United States but their enrollments were small. Not only did the presi-

dent's house occasionally serve for recitations in these early colleges, but he was often the sole member of the faculty, teaching all subjects. Even in later years the faculties were small.

Name	Location	Year
Harvard	Cambridge	1636
William and Mary	Williamsburg	1693
Yale	New Haven	1701
Princeton	Princeton	1746
Pennsylvania	Philadelphia	1751
Columbia	New York	1754
Brown	Providence	1764
Rutgers	New Brunswick	1766
Dartmouth	Hanover	1769

The history of these institutions of higher learning affords interesting reading. Most of them were supported financially by grants of land or money from legislatures, by donations of money or kind, and by miscellaneous means, such as lotteries.

State support was slow to develop. As late as 1860, only 17 of 264 institutions of higher learning were financed by the state. The first state university to be chartered was in Georgia; the first to be opened was in North Carolina,

The following is a reproduction of an old announcement:

UNIVERSITY OF THE CITY OF NEW-YORK.

The Annual Course of Instruction in the Institution, will commence on Monday, the 3d of October, under the direction of the following Professors.

Rev. JAMES M. MATHEWS, D. D., Chancellor.

DAVID B. DOUGLASS, Professor of Civil Engineering and Architecture.
S. F. B. MORSE, Professor of the Literature of the Arts of Design.
Rev. HENRY P. TAPPAN, Professor of Intellectual and Moral Philosophy and Belles-Lettres.
ROBERT B. PATTON, Professor of Greek Language and Literature.
Rev. JOHN PROUDFIT, Professor of Latin Language and Literature.
CHARLES L. PARMENTIER, Professor of French Language and Literature.
LORENZO L. DA PONTE, Professor of Italian Language and Literature.
MIGUEL CABRERA DE NEVARES, Professor of Spanish Language and Literature.
CHARLES RABADAN, Associate Professor of do.
ISAAC NORDHEIMER, Acting Professor of German Language and Literature.
Rev. GEORGE BUSH, Professor of Hebrew, and Oriental Languages and Literature.
CHARLES W. HACKLEY, Professor of Mathematics.
WILLIAM A. NORTON, Acting Professor of Natural Philosophy and Astronomy.
LEWIS C. BECK, M. D., Professor of Chemistry and Botany.
Hon. B. F. BUTLER, Professor of Law, and Principal of the Law Faculty.*
L. D. GALE, M. D., Professor of Geology and Mineralogy.
ISAAC NORDHEIMER, Professor of Arabic, Syriac, Persian, and Ethiopic.
Rev. CYRUS MASON, Professor of the Evidences of Revealed Religion.

* The other Professors in the Law Faculty will be appointed within a few weeks; and the course of legal instruction will be commenced simultaneously by Mr. Butler and the other Professors early in May, 1837.

SCHEDULE OF THE RECITATIONS, AND OTHER EXERCISES, DURING THE WEEK.—(Prayers in the Chapel at half past nine o'clock A. M.)

HOURS.	MONDAY.	TUESDAY.	WEDNESDAY.	THURSDAY.	FRIDAY.	SAT.
From 10 to 11 A.M.	Latin. Belles-lettres. Natural Philosophy. Architecture and Civil Engineering. * Geology and Mineralogy.	Latin. Belles-lettres. Natural Philosophy. Greek. Architecture and Civil Engineering. Geology & Mineralogy	Latin. Belles-lettres. Natural Philosophy. Chemistry. Architecture and Civil Engineering. Geology & Mineralogy	Latin. Belles-lettres. Natural Philosophy. Chemistry. Architecture and Civil Engineering. Geology & Mineralogy	Latin. Belles-lettres. Natural Philosophy. Chemistry. Architecture and Civil Engineering. Geology & Mineralogy	
From 11 to 12 A.M.	Mathematics. Latin. Greek. Psychology and Moral Philosophy.	Mathematics. Greek. Latin. Psychology and Moral Philosophy.	Mathematics. Greek. Latin. Psychology and Moral Philosophy.	Mathematics. Greek. Latin. Psychology and Moral Philosophy.	Mathematics. Greek. Latin. Psychology and Moral Philosophy.	
From 12 to 1 P.M.	Greek. Mathematics. Logic. Philosophy of Rhetoric and Criticism. Natural Philosophy.	Greek. Mathematics. Logic. Philosophy of Rhetoric and Criticism. Chemistry.	Greek. Mathematics. Logic. Philosophy of Rhetoric and Criticism. Natural Philosophy.	Greek. Mathematics. Logic. Philosophy of Rhetoric and Criticism. Chemistry.	Greek. Mathematics. Logic. Philosophy of Rhetoric and Criticism. Latin.	
From 1 to 2 P.M.	Evidences of Revealed Religion. Hebrew. New Testament as a Classic. Elementary Drawing.	Belles-lettres. Chaldaic and Syriac.	Evidences of Revealed Religion. Hebrew. Elementary Drawing.	Belles-lettres. Chaldaic and Syriac.	Evidences of Revealed Religion. Hebrew. Elementary Drawing.	
From 2 to 3 P.M.	Rabinical Hebrew.				Rabinical Hebrew.	
From 4 to 5 P.M.	Arabic.	Hebrew.	Hebrew.	Hebrew.	Arabic.	
From 7 to 8 P.M.	Persian.		Sanscrit.	Persian.	Sanscrit.	

* The class in Geology will commence in April.
Note.—There are also classes in French, Spanish, Italian and German, taught at such hours as will be found most convenient to the students and professors.

(Vertical note in right margin: Declamation in the Chapel.)

---

and Ohio was the first commonwealth to receive federal land grants to start a "seminary of learning." Nearly sixty years later the passage of the Morrill Act by Congress inaugurated the development of the so-called land-grant colleges for agriculture and mechanical arts. Hampton Institute at Hampton, Virginia, organized in 1868, was the first school of higher education for Negroes. One of its early graduates was Booker T. Washington.

Higher Education for Women. In the biography *Madam Curie* are found, by inference, many interesting reflections on the educational restraint upon women in the latter half of the nineteenth century. When the Sorbonne appointed Mme. Curie to carry on the work of her husband in the Faculty of Science in 1906, it "was the first time that a position in French higher education had been given to a woman." It is significant that in England women were not admitted to degrees at Oxford until 1920.

During the nineteenth century, higher learning in America gradually ceased to be the prerogative of one sex. Most of the women from coast to coast who today confidently attend college classes are perhaps unaware that their sex was once denied entrance to the portals of higher institutions. Coeducation on the college level began as late as 1837 when four women were accepted in a standard course at Oberlin College. Life for women in the early days of higher education and today is a vivid contrast.

Mount Holyoke, the first college for women in America, was established in 1838 by the academy teacher, Mary Lyon, who begged pennies, nickels, and dimes in order to found a "permanent seminary in New England with accommodations, apparatus, etc., somewhat like those for the other sex." Mount Holyoke epitomizes the history of education for women; as a seminary and later as a college, it exemplifies in its evolution every stage of the general advancement.

Today coeducational institutions and women's colleges have gained for women the right and the opportunity to obtain higher learning comparable with that for men. Not only is general education theirs, but also a wide selection among the professional curriculums. Women outnumber men in the teaching profession; in the medical field they comprise a small percentage of the doctors. What a numerical contrast between almost a million women now in attendance at institutions of higher learning and the three "females" who in 1841 were the first American women to earn a regular bachelor of arts degree by the completion of a program of studies identical to that required of men candidates for the same degree! The granting of several thousand advanced degrees annually to women is a far cry from the days when there appeared in *The Atlantic* a caustic article entitled "Should Women Learn the Alphabet?"

Historic Leaders in Higher Education. In the long history of higher education in America there have been numerous dynamic leaders. It was John Harvard who donated his name, library, and money as the initial gifts to Harvard College. It was Charles W. Eliot who fought for the elective system in higher education and sponsored five revolutionary advances during the first years of his administration at Harvard: the elevation and amplification of entrance requirements; the enlargement of the curriculum and the development of the elective system; the recognition of graduate study in the liberal arts; the raising of professional training in law, medicine, and engineering to a postgraduate level; and the fostering of greater maturity in student life. Eliot was one of a half-dozen statesmen who emerged as personal forces in American higher education immediately following the Civil War. Others were Andrew D. White of Cornell, Nicholas Murray Butler of Columbia, James McCosh of Princeton, Noah Porter of Yale, James B. Angell of Michigan, Daniel Coit Gilman of Johns Hopkins, William Rainey Harper at Chicago, Horace Mann at Antioch, Mark Hopkins at Williams, Mary Lyon at Holyoke, and Herman Schneider, father of cooperative education, at the University of Cincinnati. The catalogue of "who was who" and "who is who" in American higher education makes a ponderous tome.

Role

Many people are unaware of the varied roles that institutions of higher education play in man's struggle for a better life. Colleges and universities fulfill many important functions in addition to the education of individual students.

Role of Higher Education in Research. Many of man's great discoveries have emerged from college and university research laboratories. Dr. Selman Waksman won the Nobel Prize for his discovery of streptomycin and other antibiotics after thirty years of research at Rutgers. Professor Herman Schlesinger accidentally discovered a new kind of jet and rocket fuel at the University of Chicago. Dr. Jonas Salk's discovery of a vaccine against polio at the University of Pittsburgh was a monumental advance in medical science.

Much of our knowledge of child growth and development has been yielded through the researches of Dr. Arnold Gesell and Dr. Frances Ilg at the Clinic of Child Development, School of Medicine, at Yale. Cornell University's Crash Injury Research Project has revealed striking new knowledge about highway safety. The pioneering work of Professors John Dewey, Edward Thorndike, George Strayer, and others at Teachers College, Columbia University, has added much to our knowledge of the educative process.

Some of this research is accomplished by great teams of investigators supported by grants of money from government, foundations, or industry. Other important research has emerged from the indefatigable efforts of a dedicated individual scholar working on his own. Some of the discoveries have come from famed men at great universities. Others have resulted from the work of little-known men from almost obscure campuses. Medicine and education, meteorology and agriculture, sociology and physics, astrodynamics and oceanography, nuclear physics, and economics—in short, every field of human inquiry has been illuminated by college and university research. Through research and scholarly inquiry, higher education in America has made a tre-

The modern college recognizes its responsibility for improving the community of which it is a part. Cooperation with municipal, civil, welfare, religious, and fraternal groups in community planning is one approach. In remodeling its campus in industrial Philadelphia, Drexel Institute of Technology, for example, has played a role in urban development, removing blight, improving traffic patterns, and becoming truly a part of the community without being dominated by it.

The present campus is split by industrial, commercial, and depressed residential structures into two sections (A and B).

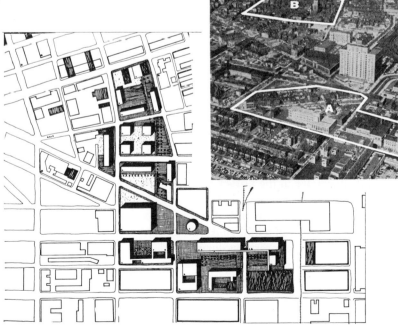

Plans for the future would eliminate this segmentation, utilizing existing structures where possible, adding new ones, and landscaping with green areas.

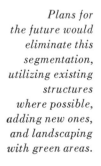

mendous contribution to man's relentless march toward a richer and fuller life.

Role of Higher Education in Public Service. The various public services rendered by American colleges and universities would fill volumes. For example, thousands of New Yorkers catch New York University's predawn television class, "The Sunrise Semester," in their own homes. The University of Nebraska's Teachers College is helping four Nebraska towns to improve community life through their local school systems. In California, San Bernardino Valley Junior College presents a series of weekly radio programs on anthropology, literature, science, and other topics. Nearly one thousand people participate in one hundred organized discussion groups, gathering in homes to listen to the broadcast, to discuss the topic among themselves, and to phone their questions back to the panel of experts at the radio station, who give their replies over the air.

Indeed, many colleges extend their public services around the world. The North Carolina College of Agriculture and Engineering is helping strengthen agricultural research in Peru. The University of Oregon is establishing a new educational system in Nepal. Harvard is helping Latin American countries develop better nutrition programs. The University of Tennessee is providing home economics specialists for India.

Countless other examples of university public services, both at home and abroad, could be cited. Thus many American colleges have come to view the world as their classroom and the general public as their ultimate clientele.

Role of Higher Education in Defense. An important chapter in the history of higher education for women and men in the United States was written during World War II. Approximately one-third of a million American women were in the military services during World War II. An undetermined but very large number were engaged in work closely related to the war, in business, in industry, and in various

volunteer services such as the Red Cross. These experiences have had profound effects upon the position of women as citizens and as students, particularly in higher education. A woman in uniform on a college campus is a long cry from 1837 when coeducation started. The trend toward coeducation has been definitely continued by the war and postwar training programs for women. The GI bills for education have been benefiting women as well as men, on an equal basis.

All the colleges and universities of the land cooperated indirectly and directly in the gigantic struggle to win World War II. Thousands of students left the campuses to fight in all parts of the world, hundreds of colleges loaned the services of their best professors to the United States government, and one-third of all the institutions participated directly in war-service training programs, converting their curriculums to the training of Army, Navy, Marine, and Air Force officers and enlisted men and women. Even the atomic age dates back to a pile of fissionable material on the campus of the University of Chicago. Such procedures as accelerating programs, retooling the minds of faculty members, meeting the needs of more mature and motivated students, stimulating research, and equalizing educational opportunities for students to secure higher education are some of the by-products of college war-training programs which will influence higher education for a long time.

Currently many universities participate in defense programs. More than one hundred institutions of higher education are offering off-duty courses for men and women on military bases in the United States.

Nature

Articulation of Secondary and Higher Education. So wide a gap exists between the completion of high school and the beginning of college that many students who should continue their schooling fail to do so. In answer to the question "Why do so many superior youth not go to college?" the Commission on Financing Higher Education gives two broad reasons: financial and motivational.

Various efforts are being made to bridge the chasm between the high school and college, especially through preventive and corrective guidance. Historically significant was the work of the Commission on the Relation of School and College, sponsored by the Progressive Education Association. But college admission policies and practices still need to be improved markedly, according to various surveys. As a result of his comprehensive study of the achievements of the junior high school and junior college, Leonard V. Koos considered the six-four-four plan as the best for integrating high school and college. The four-year junior college, combining grades 11 through 14, tends to eliminate the barrier that traditionally isolates the twelfth from the thirteenth years.

Guidance and structural reorganization of secondary education must be accompanied by financial aid to deserving and needy students. Many quite able young people do not attend college for financial reasons. This loss of talented manpower is one that the nation can ill afford. In recognition of this problem, many scholarships have been established from both private and public funds. A few states, notably Illinois, New York, Delaware, and California, have enacted legislation guaranteeing financial assistance toward college education for the needy and deserving students. The National Merit Program awards scholarships to a large number of college-bound youth from the joint contributions of a number of large industries. Many industries, such as Westinghouse, and private foundations, such as the Sloan Foundation, provide additional scholarships. Most colleges are also striving to increase their scholarship funds. However, even all of these increases in scholarship monies do not appear adequate for the surge of able young men and women on the threshold of college entrance.

Many able high school students are not fully aware of their potential. Some lack sufficient motivation. More efforts, such as the University of Texas' admission testing program, are needed. Ten per cent of this university's students overcame the uncertainty about college only after their test scores had demonstrated their superior ability. The National Defense Education Act has strengthened the guidance of high school students, encouraging and assisting them in planning for college education. It has also provided increased loan funds for college students.

The School and College Study of Admissions with Advanced Standing, initiated by the Ford Foundation, has emphasized the importance of guidance, selection, reform in admission policies, and increased financial support in attracting more able youth to college. The Advanced Placement Program, whereby talented high school students can complete college level work while still in high school, has shortened the length and reduced the cost of college work for many students. Furthermore, as demonstrated by such institutions as Columbia University's School of General Studies, many mature persons can gain a bachelor's degree without having earned a high school diploma.

Accrediting Agencies. The hiatus between secondary schools and universities is also being reduced by the ceaseless efforts of various accrediting associations. The entire United States is covered by a network of state and regional associations, which have six geographical divisions: New England, Middle States, Southern, North Central, Northwest, and Western. Over one hundred nationwide organizations, such as the National Council for Accreditation of Teacher Education, and the National Commission on Accrediting, certify institutions in all states. Accreditation practices are in a state of flux. Ultimately may come one association that evaluates elements common to all institutions and other accrediting bodies that appraise particular aspects. The numerous state, sectional, and national organizations at work on the problems of accrediting have shifted

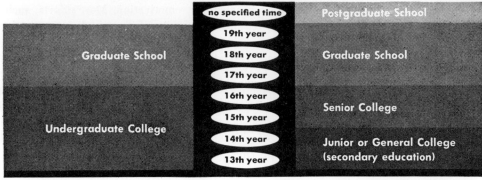

Fig. 8-1. Organization of higher education.

in recent years from quantitative to qualitative standards or to a synthesis of both, with emphasis on the total pattern of the secondary school or the institution of higher learning.

Scope of Higher Education. The period of so-called advanced education has been measured in various ways. Traditionally it includes four years of college or university and from one to three or more years of graduate work. Today the scope of secondary education, as indicated in Chapter 7, includes, at least in theory, the work of grades 7 to 14. Therefore the scope of higher education in this newer sense is delimited to the senior college division—that is, the fifteenth and sixteenth years of schooling—plus the graduate work, as shown in Fig. 8-1.

Until recently it was assumed that graduate work in education was limited to three years of work beyond the bachelor's degree. There is a trend, however, toward additional courses for persons who have completed the doctor's degree. This is true of a few colleges of education and of some professional schools, such as those of medicine and dentistry, which sponsor postdoctoral work. The traditional practice and the modern concept are pictured in the diagram in Fig. 8-1, which applies specifically to persons working for a degree such as Doctor of Philosophy. The degree of Doctor of Medicine requires at least three years of medical school. This period of study is followed by internship.

Public and Private Control. Diversity is the key to freedom in higher education. It permits not only different types of institutions but also diverse sponsorship, which is generally public or private.

Objectives

Why Are You Going to College? An interesting collection of statements regarding the objectives of higher education results from asking students on various campuses the question: "Why are you going to college?" Their answers include:

To continue my education
To carry out a family tradition
To get a degree
To be a better citizen
To render better service to society
To do research or specialize
To earn more money
To explore vocational possibilities
To prepare for a vocation or career
To get semiprofessional education
To complete preprofessional education
To enter a profession
To broaden my outlook
To develop a philosophy of living
To acquire more culture
To get a liberal education
To develop higher ethical standards
To meet people
To get a spouse
To acquire social prestige

√To enjoy college social life
To share in extracurricular life
To escape doing other work
To develop avocational interests

Many other sources of student motivation might be listed.

President Pusey's Purposes. Nathan Pusey, the twenty-fourth president of Harvard University, the national's oldest institution of higher learning, believes that the true business of liberal education is greatness:

It is our task not to produce safe men, in whom our safety can never in any case lie, but to keep alive in young people the courage to dare to seek the truth, to be free, to establish in them a compelling desire to live greatly and magnanimously, and to give them the knowledge and awareness, the faith and the trained facility to get on with the job. Especially the faith, for as someone has said, the whole world now looks to us for a creed to believe and a song to sing.[1]

Thus the Harvard president believes that the purpose of liberal education is not merely to impart knowledge but also to "transform personality by transforming minds."

Suggestions from Statesman Stevenson. Adlai E. Stevenson, a former governor of Illinois and Democratic presidential candidate, said in 1954, at the bicentennial of Columbia University, that the American people, beset with doubts and difficulties, seek direction:

And we look, finally, to the free university, whose function is the search for truth and its communication to succeeding generations. Only as that function is performed steadfastly, continuously, and without interference does a university keep faith with a great humanist tradition of which it is a part. . . . Men may be born free; they are not born wise, and it is the duty of the university to make the free wise. The university is the guardian of our heritage, the teacher of our teachers. It is the dwelling place of the free mind.

[1] "Unconquered Frontier," *Time*, Mar. 1, 1954, pp. 62, 64.

It is symbolic that Columbia University, founded as a *King's* college, accented in its bicentennial the advancement of *free men* through knowledge.

Five Fundamental Purposes. The Educational Policies Commission report, *Higher Education in a Decade of Decision*, notes five basic purposes of higher education in American life:

To provide opportunity for individual development of able people
To transmit the cultural heritage
To add to existing knowledge through research and creative activity
To help translate learning into equipment for living and for social advance
To serve the public interest directly[2]

Obviously these purposes are interrelated and mutually supporting.

Types

President Pusey's predecessor, James Bryant Conant, who left Harvard to become United States High Commissioner for Germany, says of higher education in America, "As regards the numbers and diversity of institutions there is nothing faintly resembling it anywhere in the world." This diversity—the result of higher education's freedom, its restlessness, its competition, its geography, and its tradition—is the genesis of much of the strength and vigor of American colleges and universities. Previous mention has been made of the two major types, public and private. But many institutions of higher learning defy classification, either because they cannot be placed in a general category or because their work is of a multiple nature. The types selected for emphasis here are the following: (1) junior colleges, (2) community or technical colleges, (3) general colleges, (4) liberal arts colleges, (5) municipal colleges and universities, (6) universities, (7) land-grant colleges and univer-

[2] Educational Policies Commission, *Higher Education in a Decade of Decision*, National Education Association, Washington, D.C., 1957, pp. 6–10.

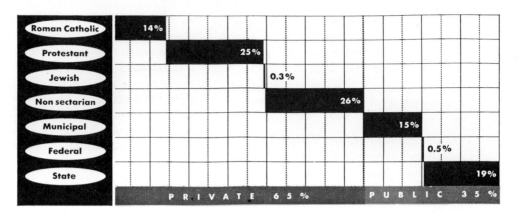

Roman Catholic	14%													
Protestant			25%											
Jewish					0.3%									
Non sectarian							26%							
Municipal										15%				
Federal												0.5%		
State														19%
	P R I V A T E 6 5 %								P U B L I C 3 5 %					

Fig. 8-2. Type of control of colleges and universities.

sities, (8) professional schools, (9) graduate schools, and (10) other institutions of higher learning. Figure 8-2 shows the distribution of United States colleges and universities according to the various types of control.

At the outset it may be helpful to differentiate between the terms "college," "university," and "school," as applied to institutions of postsecondary education, although there are no standard definitions:

In general, the first is used to designate the institution with a four-year general course leading to a B.A. or B.S. degree, unless qualified specifically in the case of a technical institution, as a "teachers college" or "agricultural college." The second ordinarily is applied to institutions having, in addition to an undergraduate nonspecialized college, a general graduate school and special professional schools reaching a graduate level. Not a few institutions lacking these characteristics call themselves universities, and there is no legal restriction upon such use. The term "school" is applied to divisions of a university as the "graduate school," the "school of journalism" and to many special institutions such as "agricultural school," "law school," "normal school," and the like.[3]

Obviously the name of an institution is not a reliable guide to its academic rank or its special function.

[3] L. M. Wilson and I. L. Kandel, *Introduction to the Study of American Education*, Thomas Nelson & Sons, New York, 1934, pp. 234–235.

JUNIOR COLLEGES

It is a moot question whether junior colleges belong to the field of higher secondary education or lower higher education. The independent junior college often forms the upper division of secondary education, whereas the freshman and sophomore years of college may constitute a junior college division in a school of higher education. The junior division of Louisiana State University affords an example of the latter.

Junior colleges, like most institutions of higher learning, may be classified by: sex admitted—men, women, or both; length of course—one to six years; function—terminal or preparatory; size of enrollment; age—date of establishment; method of origin—school elongation or university amputation; and method of control or support—public or private. Today more than five hundred junior colleges enroll about 15 per cent of the total college enrollment. About half of the junior colleges in the United States are privately controlled but these enroll less than one-fourth of the total junior college enrollment.

COMMUNITY AND TECHNICAL COLLEGES

Many colleges do not like the term "junior," with its diminutive and preparatory connotation. This dislike is a sign that these institutions are growing up and assuming a new role, as indicated in a book title like *The New American College*. The Educational Policies Commission suggests the term "community institutes"; however, the term "community college" appears to be more commonly used. The President's Committee on Education Beyond the High School recommends the expansion of junior and community colleges as the next logical step in filling in and rounding out our educational system. However, it warns against creating junior colleges that are too small to be economical or to attract good teachers.

One variety of community college is the technical institute, or institute of applied arts and sciences. Those in New York State are designed "to make preparation for occupational competence the core of education for social living." The technical institutes usually combine general education with specialized training for a single, technical, semiprofessional occupation or for a cluster of allied occupations. Geographically they are local, regional, state, and interstate in the area served. The basic functions of the community college include preparation for advanced study, vocational education, general education, adult education, and community service.

GENERAL COLLEGES

As indicated previously, one objective of higher learning is to provide general education. For the attainment of this goal, courses replete with basic information are given in many colleges during the first year or two. In some instances a specific organization unit called the general college, consisting usually of two years of study, has been established. This type of school does not follow a uniform pattern.

LIBERAL ARTS COLLEGES

The liberal arts program is usually offered by two types of institutions: the liberal arts college and the division of liberal arts of the large university. Their purposes are those of liberal education, preprofessional preparation, and some specialization. When the college is organized on a four-year basis, there is usually a gradual shift in emphasis, with the first two years devoted primarily to general education and the last two years directed toward majors or field of concentration.

Although students in liberal arts programs are permitted some degree of concentration, it is undoubtedly desirable that they dip into each of the three great divisions of the curriculum, viz., the humanities, the natural sciences, and the social sciences, as recommended by H. W. Dodds, former president of Princeton University, who once said, "Never in our history has the need for the liberally educated mind been so grave." The liberal arts college and divisions in private and state universities constitute a bulwark against too early overspecialization.

These particular institutions, catering to men and/or women, have a greater enrollment than any other type of school for higher learning. Nearly all the seven hundred and more liberal arts colleges are privately controlled. Liberal arts colleges enroll slightly more than one-fourth of the total college population. The liberal arts college is the oldest as well as the uniquely American institution of higher education.

MUNICIPAL OR URBAN COLLEGES AND UNIVERSITIES

Another type of higher institution is the locally financed municipal college or university, which, under the control of a municipal or city board of education, offers a standard degree after four or more years of work. This institution represents secularization in the extension of education, because, being supported primarily by city taxes and controlled by public authorities, it is in effect a part of the public school system and a people's university. A board of higher education appointed by the mayor of New York governs the largest city college system in the world, viz., the College of the City of New York, embracing four colleges: City (men, with women admitted in some branches), which was the first tuition-free, city-owned college in the United States; Hunter (women); Brooklyn (coeducational); and Queens (coeducational).

These colleges, few in number but great in influence, arose through a wide variety of circumstances: a normal college became a city college; a bequest was given to the city for educational purposes; a financial foundation started another; the public junior college and normal school were extended upward; a favorable vote of the people authorized the establishment of the school; and existing institutions changed their status to city colleges. The latter was the case with Charleston and Louisville, two municipal institutions that reach back over a hundred years.

The next decade will undoubtedly see many more city colleges established in connection with the present accent on youth and their education.

UNIVERSITIES

Many institutions are universities in name only. The Commission on Financing Higher Education defines universities as "large, complex institutions which offer the usual undergraduate curriculum, graduate studies leading to the degree of Ph.D., and a variety of professional curriculums—medicine, law, agriculture, engineering and others." The university usually includes a liberal arts college. The universities, both public and private, conduct most of the federally sponsored research in higher education.

They render many other services, such as extension work and adult education. They enroll approximately half of all the students in higher education. The hundred-odd universities are about evenly divided according to public or independent support. These two types "supplement and complement each other extraordinarily well."

State Universities. These institutions, which are usually a general responsibility of all the citizens of a state, are under one or more publicly controlled boards of higher education, elected by the people or appointed by state officials. Every state of the Union has its university or university system. The state university, as part of American public education, is regarded as a natural and inevitable culmination of the public school system. Its function is assumed to be that of supplying all the needs of society that fall within the sphere of higher education. As mentioned earlier, many state universities claim that the whole state is their campus. Several extended their activities beyond the boundaries of the commonwealth and some to other countries.

Private Universities. Private universities, and colleges too, are a vital part of the American educational system, drawing most of their support directly from private funds. Although sometimes referred to as independent institutions, they are not entirely independent of the public domain. They are chartered by the state; their programs are affected by state licensing requirements; their finances are subject to certain state regulations; and their accreditation is determined by outside agencies. Their alumni frequently wield heavy influence. The close relationship between the community and the university, whether public or private, tends to keep higher education attuned to the expectations of the public.

LAND-GRANT COLLEGES AND UNIVERSITIES

Origin and Development. A land-grant college or university is an institution of higher education that has been designated by the state legislature as qualified to receive the benefits of either or both of the Morrill funds. The term "land-grant college" originated from the wording of the first Morrill Act, adopted by the Congress of the United States in 1862. This act provided, on the basis of each senator and representative in Congress, for a land grant of

30,000 acres or its equivalent in scrip to the several states for an endowment, the interest from which was to furnish instruction in "agriculture and the mechanic arts, without excluding other scientific and classical studies and including military tactics." This act, sponsored by Justin S. Morrill, Vermont congressman, and signed during the Civil War by Abraham Lincoln, was followed by several related acts.

Number and Types of Institutions. There are 69 land-grant colleges and universities which may be grouped as follows:
24 separate colleges
28 universities specializing in agriculture, engineering, and home economics
17 Negro institutions
Many are state universities, several are agriculture or technical universities and colleges, and a few are junior colleges and teachers colleges.

Functions, Activities, and Influence. A typical land-grant college consists of three divisions: resident instruction; research, especially by the experiment stations; and the extension service. On-campus instruction is effectively supplemented by the two other services. After the land-grant colleges had been in existence some twenty-five years, arrangements were made to establish experimental stations for agricultural research. At present an agricultural experiment station is found in every state that has a land-grant college. The most widely known activity is the extension service, or off-campus teaching, made possible by the Smith-Lever Act in 1914. This work is conducted by well-trained personnel consisting of county agricultural agents, county home demonstration workers, boys' and girls' club workers, and other specialists. In many instances these representatives are partly supported from county funds. The land-grant colleges are directly concerned with the welfare of a large group of the population, viz., the homemakers and the farmers.

The triangular base of research, campus instruction, and extension education makes the land-grant college a potent force in American higher education. The land-grant movement created many new institutions, such as the universities of Illinois, California, and Minnesota, and the agricultural colleges in Michigan, Massachusetts, and Texas. It also led to reorganization in numerous existing institutions. It gave breadth to coeducation. It has been called democracy's college. It represented a liberalizing of the old classical college course, particularly in the emphasis on agriculture and home economics. In line with its own expanded offering, a land-grant college may change its name and shift its emphasis.

All the land-grant colleges and universities require that men students take military training unless excused for reasons of health or age. The Reserve Officers' Training Corps (ROTC), established in 1920 with passage of the National Defense Act, maintains units at all land-grant institutions as well as at many other colleges and universities. Through providing a reserve of competent officer strength in virtually all arms of the service, the land-grant colleges play an important role in the defense program for the United States.

PROFESSIONAL SCHOOLS

Former President of Harvard James B. Conant has stated that "the common denominator among all universities past and present is professional education." An avowed purpose for the establishment of Harvard College in 1636 was the preparation of learned ministers for the church. Since the middle of the eighteenth century, professional education has developed gradually in American colleges and universities. Separate professional schools for the ministry, engineering, medicine, dentistry, pharmacy, teaching, and other professional and technical fields have developed. Some of the land-grant agricultural colleges were set up as special technical and engineering schools combined. Many of the stronger professional schools grow into universities themselves or become incorporated within universities. Some teachers colleges are being transformed into liberal arts colleges. Some of the major institutes of technology are also incorporating liberal education into their curriculums.

About three hundred of the institutions of higher education in America are professional schools. Many of these schools are teachers colleges. These professional schools have been created to meet career needs that are indispensable to the public welfare. New professional schools will arise and old ones will change as social and technological evolution continues.

GRADUATE SCHOOLS

The system of American education reaches its apex in the graduate or advanced professional school. A technical distinction between a college and a university is that the former offers only undergraduate work while the latter offers both undergraduate and graduate courses. Many colleges, however, have a graduate division, whereas many so-called universities have none. In some universities all the graduate work is centered in the graduate school. In others, graduate work is offered in the professional schools. Genuine graduate training was not known in the United States until after the Civil War; in 1876 Johns Hopkins became the first school to organize graduate study. Recent years have brought a significant expansion of graduate work. Because of the need for costly equipment, small classes, and highly trained faculty, graduate schools are the most expensive type of education. The professions are dependent upon specialization and research, and the university of today and tomorrow will continue to give much attention to its graduate program.

Master's Degree. Beyond the baccalaureate is the master's degree which usually requires (1) at least a year of study beyond the bachelor's degree, (2) completion of a certain number of credits or courses totaling approximately thirty semester hours, (3) examinations, both prelim-

inary and final comprehensives, oral and written, and (4) the completion of some research project, either a thesis, or its equivalent, or added course work. Certain schools and departments stipulate additional requirements or permit substitutes. For the master of education, Harvard and the University of Illinois require two years beyond a bachelor's degree. Some institutions offer an intermediate degree between the master's and doctor's.

Intermediate Degree. An increasing number of institutions are offering an intermediate degree or diploma between the master's and doctor's degree. This award usually corresponds to two years of graduate study. It is probable that this type of award will continue to grow in frequency and significance, since public school salary schedules and state certification agencies often recognize this level of education in salary increments and certification requirements.

Doctor of Philosophy. Numerous doctors' degrees, such as doctor of medicine, doctor of dentistry, and doctor of philosophy, are offered in the graduate and advanced professional schools. The degree usually granted for advanced graduate work in education is that of doctor of philosophy. The usual requirements for this degree are two years of residence beyond the master's degree; accumulation of courses and credits amounting approximately to seventy-five or eighty semester hours; written and oral examinations; a dissertation or its equivalent; a reading knowledge of two foreign languages, usually French and German; and other requirements or substitutes, some of which must be met prior to admission to candidacy. Some universities are compressing the time requirements for the Ph.D. degree and adjusting the requirements to the actual uses of advanced study in the everyday work of the professions. This movement has been stimulated by concern over the grossly inadequate number of advanced students seeking this degree. The provision of fellowships for advanced study by the National Defense Education Act is helping to ameliorate this problem.

Doctor of Education. Another degree, doctor of education, is advancing in popularity and significance among educators. The nature of this degree is determined by the character of the institution that confers it. In the main, the Ed.D. differs from the Ph.D. in direction and requirement. Whereas the Ph.D. is primarily a research degree, the Ed.D. is basically a professional award. The former requires foreign languages and accents specialization; the latter demands cognate work and stresses professional competence in teaching or administration. For example, some graduate schools require that the doctor of education candidate show three years of successful teaching experience in the field of professional education.

Postdoctoral Work. Teachers College, Columbia University, and a few other institutions have arranged a program and scholarships for persons who desire to study beyond the Ph.D. or Ed.D. degree. These postdoctoral programs arc incrcasing in popularity in all professions. It has been suggested that all graduate degrees be abolished within ten years after they have been granted, unless the recipient shows tangible evidence of professional growth within that period.

OTHER INSTITUTIONS OF HIGHER LEARNING

Federal Institutions. Another group of institutions consists of federal or semifederal colleges and universities. The United States government has always entertained an interest in higher education, although it has never established a national university. One of the universities already mentioned as being supported by national funds is Howard University, a school primarily for Negro students, located in Washington, D.C. Since many of its students are college graduates, advanced work constitutes a conspicuous phase of the program.

The Military Academy at West Point, New York, established in 1802; the Naval Academy at Annapolis, Maryland, organized in 1845; the Coast Guard Academy at New London, Connecticut, started in 1876; the Air Academy at Colorado Springs, Colorado, launched in 1955; the Merchant Marine Academy, made the nation's fifth permanent service academy in 1956 — these and others are in reality schools of higher learning dedicated to national defense. A national institution to educate leaders for public service of a nonmilitary nature at home and abroad has been suggested repeatedly. Fortunately numerous colleges and universities are now training young men and women for public service. The major objective of these schools is to elevate public service from the slough of political despond to the worthy calling of social and civic statesmanship.

Summer Schools. A product primarily of the twentieth century is the ubiquitous summer session. These schools are attended largely by teachers who are employed in the public and private schools during the balance of the year. Many city schools grant a bonus to teachers for summer attendance, or other incentives in the form of salary increments. Furthermore, there has been a marked increase in summer school attendance by graduate students seeking advanced degrees such as the master's and doctor's.

Other Types. Somewhat related to the summer school is higher education in the form of extension, correspondence, radio, and television courses, which are discussed in the next chapter. The President's Commission on Higher Education included in its report a classification called proprietary schools—those educational institutions authorized to earn a profit. The most common examples are the private technical schools and business colleges. The number of these colleges increased markedly after the passage of the GI bills for veterans' education. A National Committee on Fraudulent Schools and Colleges has been organized to check the growth of spurious institutions of all types.

Cooperation and practices

COOPERATIVE COLLEGES

The term "cooperative colleges" is applied to certain higher educational institutions that offer instruction to students with the cooperation of industrial or commercial concerns. A brochure of Northeastern University, Boston, Massachusetts, entitled *Higher Education on the Cooperative Plan*, contains this definition:

Cooperative education in simplest terms may be defined as a complete and thorough college training complemented and balanced by an extended experience in industry under faculty supervision. It aims to consolidate in a single well-integrated educational program the values of classroom study and industrial-commercial experience. The plan provides for the alternation of pairs of students between school and cooperative work.

This plan originated in the College of Engineering of the University of Cincinnati in 1906. At first the labor unions were opposed to the scheme, but later, owing largely to the friendly attitude of the American Federation of Labor, they recognized that the plan would help rather than injure the cause of labor. Since this initial experiment, many institutions have adopted or adapted the cooperative plan, which now enrolls several thousand students. The aid of local businessmen is essential to the success of these plans. For example, the Peoria (Illinois) Manufacturers and Merchants Association cooperates with Bradley University of that city in its study-work plan, which is a five-year course.

Although the plan is practiced largely by schools and colleges of engineering, cooperative courses may be offered in many fields and may reach several states. For example, Antioch College (Yellow Springs, Ohio), where the first year of the five-year study-work program is spent on the campus, has numerous cooperating employers located in the majority of the states and in the District of Columbia. The University of Cincinnati, which pioneered in this field, now has numerous cooperative firms. Much of the success of the plan depends upon an official who is known as the coordinator and who confers with employers, students, instructors, and others.

Students are usually paid while on the job, and at the end of the full period of cooperative study they are awarded the baccalaureate. In some colleges the cooperative idea is extended to the graduate level. A modification of this plan is that of internships in teaching, as at Northwestern University, Evanston, Illinois. The major objective of these cooperative plans is to project the student into the practical aspect of the workaday world. Another type of work-study plan is employed in the cooperative or semicooperative living centers such as are found at Syracuse University, where economical housing is provided for women students who spend part of each day working in their houses. Many colleges maintain an industries plan for providing work for deserving students.

COOPERATION AMONG INSTITUTIONS OF HIGHER LEARNING

Cooperation with the Federal Government. The federal government cooperates with institutions of higher learning in many projects, such as giving financial aid to the land-grant colleges, providing tuition and subsistence for veterans' education, furnishing funds and personnel for military units, and aiding in research projects like atomic energy. Much of the research on the release of atomic energy and the development of guided missiles has been accomplished by universities in collaboration with the government. The Division of Higher Education in the U.S. Office of Education assists various institutions of higher learning. During and since World War II, many colleges have loaned personnel and facilities to the national government. Many professors serve overseas in federal-aid programs. The

American Council on Education has a Committee on the Relationship of Higher Education to the Federal Government.

State Programs of Cooperation. In several states, coordination has been effected by legislative enactment creating one board to control all the state higher institutions. For example, the board in charge of the State University of New York has general direction over a large cluster of state institutions.

Regional Programs in Higher Education. A regional program within a state is exemplified in southern California where several colleges have established an intercollege graduate program. The most conspicuous example of regionalism in higher educational efforts is found in the South, where several states have banded together to improve educational opportunities and facilities in the related states, through the Southern Regional Education Board.

Cooperative Agreements between Colleges. Although coordination among state-controlled institutions is usually effected by legislative enactment, numerous cooperative agreements are entered into voluntarily by schools of higher learning, especially privately controlled colleges and universities. One of the oldest plans of affiliation has been between a state-supported university (North Dakota) and a church-related institution (Wesley College), whereby students at either institution could take courses at the other. The Midwest Interlibrary Corporation, consisting of several cooperating colleges and libraries, renders wide research service from its center in Chicago. Many universities are joint sponsors of the nonprofit Oak Ridge Institute of Nuclear Studies, with the nation as the campus. The Brookhaven Laboratory on Long Island is a cooperative research laboratory in the physical sciences, shared in its use and support by several eastern colleges. Such joint efforts are supplemented by many experiments in individual institutions.

Cooperative Associations. There are a number of voluntary cooperative associations of American colleges and universities aimed toward the advancement of higher education. These include the Association of American Universities, the American Association of Land-grant Colleges and State Universities, the Association of American Colleges, the American Association of Junior Colleges, the American Council on Education, the American Alumni Council, the Association of Urban Universities, and the National Catholic Welfare Conference. Several associations, such as the Association for Higher Education of the National Education Association, the American Association of University Professors, and the American Association of University Women, enroll individual members who work in higher education.

TRENDS

Unfortunately, many colleges and universities are afflicted with an unwarranted faith in the infallibility of their practices. There is, however, a distinct trend toward an experimental approach in higher education. Under the captions (1) Organization and Administration, (2) Curriculum and Teaching-learning procedures, and (3) Personnel, the epitomes that follow sketch a few of the many interesting and varied experiments and trends in higher education.

Organization and Administration. Under the stimulation of grants from the Fund for the Advancement of Education, several institutions of higher learning are conducting self-surveys. Several state surveys of higher education have been completed recently. Accreditation procedures are being reevaluated and modified, looking toward the reduction in the number of accrediting agencies. Qualitative as well as quantitative standards are being developed. Many colleges have been reorganized internally within the component divisions and externally in a state pattern. With the unprecedented demand for higher education, many institutions are expanding. Several have established off-campus branches or centers. Colleges, returning to the European pattern of administration, are becoming more democratic in control. Faculty salary committees and faculty councils are on the increase.

Following the accent on technical courses during two world wars and the Korean conflict, many colleges are now increasing the required courses in general education. The United States Military Academy, for example, once the citadel of vocational education, in 1959 revised its curriculum as a result of a two-year survey. The new program of studies places greater emphasis upon such fields as social sciences, foreign languages, logic, written and spoken English.

College counseling procedures seek to help the individual student.

Creative approaches to financial help for students are being explored. Scholarship programs and loan funds are being enriched. By 1960, the National Merit Scholarship program alone had awarded over fifteen million dollars to more than three thousand scholarship holders. More opportunity for part-time work and work-study programs is being provided. Deferred tuition payment plans are becoming more common. Some colleges are forming cooperative arrangements with banks and insurance companies to provide college financing on the installment plan.

Laymen, as members of advisory committees and boards of trustees, are participating to a greater degree in forming policies for colleges.

Cooperative endeavor among colleges is becoming much more common. Colleges conduct cooperative research, cooperative fund-raising programs, and cooperative arrangements for

Today's colleges and universities are trying to meet the additional demands of a rapidly changing world . . .

by maintaining close student-faculty relations in an age when increased specialization makes counseling especially important . . .

by accommodating a stream of eager students from other lands . . .

and an increasing number of married students and their families.

*Modern
institutions
of higher
learning are
using
new tools . . .*

*and technological equipment
to enrich instruction.*

screening scholarship candidates through the College Scholarship Service at Princeton, New Jersey.

Regional planning continues to play a conspicuous role in the development of higher education.

The U.S. Office of Education has expanded its services to colleges.

The work of the Commission on Financing Higher Education and the President's Committee on Education Beyond the High School have directed the nation's thinking toward these problems, especially in the private and parochial institutions. The Council for Financial Aid to Education was organized in 1953 as a corporation to coordinate fund-raising efforts of various independent college associations. Non-tax-supported institutions in various states have joined to raise free enterprise money for regular sources of income from large business and industrial enterprises.

Curriculum and Teaching-learning Procedures. The basic curricular conflict in higher education centers around the appropriate balance between general and specialized education or, in other words, between liberal arts and professional studies. A 1959 report of a study by the

*They are answering the call
from government and industry
for new research
while providing students with
valuable experience.*

*They are aiding educators abroad
to develop the know-how to help themselves.
Here, an Afghan teacher uses
visual materials in his classroom
that he learned to use
during a two-month workshop sponsored jointly
by the Afghanistan Ministry of Education
and a team from Columbia University.*

Institute of Higher Education at Teachers College, Columbia University, *The Liberal Arts as Viewed by Faculty Members in Professional Schools*, revealed two aspects of the problem: (1) lack of agreement upon the common core of general education needed by all students, and (2) disinterest or inability of faculties to relate the liberal arts to the specialized needs and interests of students. This, of course, is one of the perennial problems of higher education. The ultimate solution, if it may ever be reached, will lie in a course of studies hammered out by professional and liberal arts faculties cooperatively and in which technical and general studies merge.

Religion, so important in the early colleges, is being reaccented today in higher education. Public as well as independent institutions are seeking to convey to students the significance of religion in human affairs. The American Association of Colleges for Teacher Education received a grant from the Danforth Foundation to conduct a five-year study of the role of religion in teacher-educating institutions. A Commission on Christian Higher Education is working on the problem of making religion a vital force in the curricular and extracurricular life of Protestant and Catholic colleges and universities.

The Committee on Institutional Research of the American Council on Education is seeking to develop a balance between practical research aimed at solutions for immediate and specific problems, and basic research designed to increase human knowledge broadly.

An increasing number of institutions are adding television stations or are participating in television and radio programs. A number have credit courses over the air. The Allied University TV Council assists laboratories for educational ideas in television.

Internship programs are on the increase. The Ford Foundation for the Advancement of Education has provided several internships in teaching.

Countless curricular reforms have been initiated, such as the abolition of course credits, course examinations, compulsory class attendance, and time requirements. Instead, comprehensive examinations are taken when the student is ready for them. Many colleges permit students to omit required courses through passing proficiency examinations.

Several institutions are experimenting with concentrated and intensive study plans, such as dividing the year into five seven-week periods, during each of which only one subject is studied.

Advanced placement programs enable gifted students to pursue college-level courses while still in high school. Early admission programs make it possible for brilliant students to begin college early as a result of shortened high school programs. Some graduate and undergraduate schools are speeding up their degree programs.

Students are encouraged to take interdepartmental majors.

Several colleges are employing professional musicians, artists, dramatists, and other specialists as distinguished professors in order to broaden cultural life and liberal education on the campus.

Scores of new courses have been added: courtship, marriage, and sex education; geopolitical interpretations of current affairs; great issues; communications; musical therapy; languages such as Hebrew, Russian, Urdu, and Hindustani; geography, history, and literature of various areas, such as India and Korea.

Among the newer specialties which are dignified with degrees in the undergraduate or graduate fields are: bachelor of science in editing and publishing, doctor of social work, master in public service, and degrees in nuclear physics and electronics.

Since the arrival of the space age, many universities are supplementing aerodynamics and astronavigation with the new science of astrodynamics.

In order to give selected students a more realistic approach to national affairs, a group of institutions cooperate in providing a Washington seminar in the nation's capital.

Cocurricular or extracurricular activities have been expanded markedly to include such activities as forums, intercultural clubs, mock presidential elections, volunteer fire departments, and an extracurricular course in college teaching.

University presses are furnishing leadership in the publication of scholarly studies.

Research remains one of the most important functions of the universities. A few examples of technological and scientific investigations in higher education are the Atomic Energy Commission's sponsored programs, as the Oak Ridge Institute of Nuclear Studies, atomic-energy education, radioisotope units, cosmic-ray cyclotron, aeronautical research, radio and television centers, statistical centers, cancer and polio research, and investigations of the earth's microorganisms and of the earth's neighbors in outer space.

Personnel in Higher Education. Institutions of higher learning accent personnel relationships in guidance programs and human relations centers.

Intercultural and intergroup relations are being studied from coast to coast and overseas. Many white institutions admit Negroes, and several Negro colleges are open to all.

One striking phenomenon in higher education is the added stress on international and world relationships—a reflection of the position of the United States in world leadership.

Many American universities have arrangements for a year abroad. Overseas summer sessions are numerous.

Fulbright and Smith-Mundt programs have stimulated the exchange of students and professors. With the aid of GI bills, hundreds of United States veterans have studied overseas.

Many college campuses are meccas for students and teachers from other lands.

Scores of international educational conferences are being held.

Special student visas are issued by the United States government to students from other lands.

The New York State Board of Regents has given a provisional charter to the Free University in Exile, a corporation formed to organize an educational institution—undergraduate and graduate—for refugees and exiles from certain communist-dominated countries.

A closer relationship is being developed between the university and the outside world. More professors are working on governmental, industrial, and community projects. This is true in the humanities as well as in the natural and social sciences.

Recent studies have shown that college life is more serious. Students come with greater seriousness of purpose, which is reflected in their higher academic achievements.

Much unpublicized experimentation and many innovations of significance are being conducted in many institutions. There is no end to experimentation in higher education. It is a symptom of the fact that colleges and universities rely not upon dogmatic but upon flexible purposes which can be adjusted to meet new needs.

Future

Higher education is on the threshold of many changes. Some of these impending changes can be seen clearly—others dimly, or not at all. Certainly the most apparent and most pervading changes arise from the vast expansion in college enrollment. As indicated in Fig. 8-3, college enrollments will continue to rise sharply during the 1960s. Prodigious increases in money are essential. This financial problem is basic to the continued vitality of American higher education. Fortunately, this problem is now generally recognized. Voluntary private contributions to higher education now exceed half a billion dollars annually and are increasing. Individual alumni across the country are responding more generously with gifts and bequests to their alma maters. Although exceptionally large alumni gifts are becoming fewer, many more alumni are making smaller contributions. Corporations large and small are also giving increased financial support to colleges

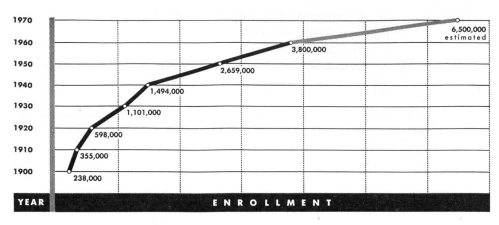

Fig. 8-3. Enrollment in colleges and universities.

and universities, demonstrating industry's increased recognition of its stake in the vitality of higher education. Private foundations are cognizant of the need and are providing substantial monetary support for higher education. Especially noteworthy was the Ford Foundation's 350 million-dollar grant to private institutions of higher learning to increase faculty salaries. But state expenditures for higher education have not kept pace with the need or with other sources of revenue. The federal government, through the National Defense Education Act, provided monies for loans and fellowships. College administrators are becoming more skilled and attentive to the task of fund raising.

However, this increased giving is still inadequate. The Council for Financial Aid to Education estimates that an additional half billion dollars is needed annually. Barring depression or war, this nation will be able to afford what is needed to extend and enrich its system of higher education. There are strong indications that this will be achieved but that economies will be necessary and adjustments difficult in the transition years.

Expanded enrollments also presage a severe shortage of teaching personnel. The Educational Policies Commission believes that five approaches must be undertaken with respect to this problem: faculty salaries must be raised

substantially; strenuous recruitment, drawing upon all available and qualified personnel, must be undertaken; preparation of college teachers must be improved; the most efficient use must be made of the college faculty's abilities; and academic life must be made as attractive and satisfying as possible.

Expanded enrollment brings other problems. It may threaten the rapport between professor and student and impair the quality of individual guidance and attention. Academic quality may suffer under the sheer mass of numbers. One professor, distressed by the long line of students waiting to register at a large university, asked, "What is to become of the genius or two in this crowd?"

Certainly most present colleges and universities will grow larger and many new ones will be established, particularly new junior colleges and community colleges. Four-year colleges and universities will place more emphasis upon selective recruitment, that is, attracting the particularly talented individual. As admission to college becomes increasingly difficult, colleges will select students more rigorously, particularly those institutions that do not wish to grow.

College curriculums will expand to keep pace with the explosive growth of human knowledge. Controversy will continue with regard to the appropriate emphasis for general and specialized education. Those professional schools which are presently narrowly vocational in character will probably give increased attention to liberal education. More responsibility for learning will be placed upon the student, with less emphasis upon formal classroom work. The use of electronic teaching devices, particularly television, films, and tape recordings, will continue to increase.

Colleges and universities will give increased attention to adult education. Refresher courses will become a more common means of helping adult workers keep up to date in their fields. More provision will be made for campus centers, like the American Assembly at Columbia University, to which people may come for conferences with college faculty experts. Industry and government will make increasing use of college faculty members as consultants. The demand for American professors as consultants to other countries will continue. Universities will play an increasingly important role in research with greater emphasis probably upon basic research.

Although all the manifestations of future change are not clear, it is certain that substantial change is both inevitable and desirable. As a distinguished college president points out:

I am convinced that the tremendous and terrifying problems which suddenly face higher education in America are fortunate; they make it mandatory for us to examine what we are doing—to reassess our educational philosophy; to adopt new methods and adapt old ones; to find new resources in teachers, facilities, and financing; and in general to raise hob with the *status quo*. . . . Changes . . . are necessary and important, and they will come. But they are on the plateaus of adventure.[4]

Alfred North Whitehead, the famed English philosopher, prophesied, "In the conditions of modern life, the rule is absolute: the race which does not value trained intelligence is doomed." This, then, appears to be the preeminent challenge confronting higher education in the 1960s.

[4] Samuel B. Gould, "The Challenge," *Educational Record*, vol. 36 (July, 1955), pp. 205–206.

Summary

Although American universities have been influenced by their European antecedents, they differ markedly from foreign institutions of higher learning. The rise of American universities was stimulated by the Dartmouth College decision which protected the charters of private institutions and by the Morrill Acts which offered grants of land to the states for higher education in agricultural and mechanical arts.

American colleges and universities have not only provided general and professional education for millions of young people and adults, but have also made significant contributions to research, national defense, and to the general welfare of our nation and many other lands.

Efforts are being made to bridge the chasm between secondary education and higher education. Advanced placement programs, increased scholarship funds, and other resources have been developed to interest competent young people in higher education.

The objectives of higher education include the self-realization of individuals, the transmission of the cultural heritage, the extension of human knowledge through research, the improvement of living through advanced learning, and public service.

There are many types of institutions of higher learning in America: public and private institutions, junior colleges, community colleges and technical colleges, general colleges and liberal arts colleges, municipal and state colleges and universities, professional and graduate schools, military academies, men's, women's, and coeducational schools, and institutions of all sizes. This great diversity of American colleges has been the source of much of its vitality.

Colleges and universities cooperate with each other and with other agencies in many ways. This has led to much worth-while experimentation and research and has strengthened many aspects of American life.

Enrollments in higher education have multiplied sixteen times since the turn of the century and will increase even more sharply during the present decade. This surge of new students poses difficult problems: "Can enough funds, facilities, and faculties be provided? Can quantity be achieved without loss of qual-ity?" Colleges are being forced to assess their purposes as well as their resources. There is evidence of considerable adaptation under way to meet these new challenges.

Suggested activities

1. Turn to the historical calendar and review the development of higher education in the United States.
2. Evaluate the standards of the sectional accrediting association for the state in which you are located.
3. Consult old newspapers, magazines, and books for interesting side lights on the history of American higher education.
4. Write a brief history on the topic "Land-grant colleges in America."
5. Review the circumstances and effects of the Dartmouth College case.
6. Name 10 outstanding college presidents and their institutions.
7. Identify 30 prominent colleges in the United States.
8. Prepare a list of all the institutions of higher education in your state.
9. Make a list of the various divisions or schools in your state university.
10. Study the program and requirements of a profession other than teaching, such as medicine, dentistry, or law. Compare or contrast that program with the preparation for the teaching profession.
11. Prepare a list of national organizations for teachers in institutions of higher learning.
12. Examine masters' and doctors' theses and comment as to the practicality of the research.
13. Describe clearly a significant college experiment in higher education.

Bibliography

Books

American Colleges and Universities, American Council on Education, Washington, D.C., 1960. This standard reference work gives detailed information about major colleges and universities in addition to several chapters dealing with higher education—its history, philosophy, and status.

Association for Higher Education: *Current Issues in Higher Education*, National Education Association, Washington, D.C., 1960. Presentation of addresses and discussions on wide range of problems in higher education as presented at annual conference of the Association for Higher Education.

Brubacher, John S., and Willis Rudy: *Higher Education in Transition*, Harper & Brothers, New York, 1958. Discusses the changes that are taking place in America's institutions of higher education and the challenges that lie ahead.

Educational Policies Commission: *Higher Education in a Decade of Decision*, National Education Association, Washington, D.C., 1957. Deals with the questions: "What is the role of higher education?" "What should be taught?" "Who will go to college?" "How will higher education be financed?" "How should policy be made?"

Hillway, Tyrus: *The American Two-year College*, Harper & Brothers, New York, 1958. Discussion of the two-year college movement—its history, status, philosophy, administration, programs, problems, and future possibilities.

Hunt, Herold C., and Paul R. Pierce: *The Practice of School Administration*, Houghton Mifflin Company, Boston, 1958, pp. 420–440. Presents the principles and objectives, administration, resources and facilities of higher education in America.

Johnson, B. Lamar (ed.): *The Public Junior College*, University of Chicago Press, Chicago, 1956. Sixteen educators examine the role of public junior colleges in meeting the expanding need for post-high school education and make recommendations concerning their development.

Wilson, Howard E.: *American College Life As Education in World Outlook*, American Council on Education, Washington, D.C., 1956. The author examines the informal forces and influences of college life that affect students' outlook on world affairs.

Wise, W. Max: *They Come for the Best of Reasons*, American Council on Education, Washington, D.C., 1958. Interesting report of a research study showing the characteristics of today's college students that challenges current popular impressions.

Wriston, Henry M.: *Academic Procession*, Columbia University Press, New York, 1959. An enjoyable account of the administration of colleges and universities as seen by a distinguished college president.

Periodicals

Church, Frank: "Role of College Education in a Free Society," *Junior College Journal*, vol. 27 (May, 1957), pp. 497–503. Argues that the battle for freedom must be won in the classroom and emphasizes the importance of liberal education.

Cole, Charles C., Jr.: "Flexible College Curriculums," *NEA Journal*, vol. 48 (April, 1959), pp. 47–48. Argues that college programs of study ought to be more attractive and stimulating intellectually as well as better attuned to individual differences.

Derthick, Lawrence G.: "College on the Threshold of Tomorrow," *College and University*, vol. 32 (Summer, 1957), pp. 457–466. Discusses the great population rise in the United States and the challenges it poses for higher education.

Fleege, U. H.: "Trends in American Higher Education," *Association of American Colleges Bulletin*, vol. 43 (October, 1957), pp. 479–484. Discusses current changes in higher education: readiness for change, flexible programming, more responsibility upon the student, extending the length of the program, and others.

Folsom, Charles A.: "Education Beyond the High School: Second Report of the President's Commission," *Higher Education*, vol. 14 (September, 1957), pp. 7–9. Discusses the needs of higher education: more qualified teachers, financial assistance for students, expansion and diversity of programs.

Gardner, John W.: "Quality in Higher Education," *Junior College Journal*, vol. 28 (May, 1958), pp. 522–526. Argues that both quality and quantity are possible if present diversity and excellence are maintained.

Gould, Samuel B.: "The Dimensions of a College," *School and Society*, vol. 85 (March 2, 1957), pp. 67–70. A college president's philosophy of higher education built upon intellectual adventuresomeness and spiritual dimensions.

Kirk, Grayson: "Higher Education—Not above Criticism," *NEA Journal*, vol. 48 (March, 1959), pp. 18–20. Stresses the importance of critical reexamination of college traditions and suggests some needed changes.

Medsker, Leland L.: "The Junior College Picture," *NEA Journal*, vol. 47 (December, 1958), pp. 628–630. Discusses junior colleges from the public school teacher's point of view, dealing with the different types of junior colleges and their advantages and disadvantages.

Meyer, A. W.: "University Ideal," *Journal of Higher Education*, vol. 28 (March, 1957), pp. 155–159. Challenging article about the realities of college life which impair the search for knowledge.

Partch, C. E.: "Is Your State Closing the Door to Higher Education?" *Phi Delta Kappan*, vol. 39 (November, 1957), pp. 61–64. Analyzes the facilities for higher education on the basis of states and shows alarming inadequacies.

Stokes, Joseph M.: "America's Most Practical Export," *Educational Record*, vol. 28 (July, 1957), pp. 198–203. Cites the problems and limitations of universities in other lands and stresses the need for exporting America's diversity of education.

Taylor, Harold: "Let's Give Our Colleges Back to the Students," *NEA Journal*, vol. 45 (September, 1956), pp. 367–368. Makes a plea for a larger share of participation and better educational opportunities for students in colleges.

———: "Our Expanding Opportunity," *National Parent Teacher*, vol. 52 (May, 1958), pp. 4–7. Sees a privilege in disguise in the tidal wave of college students—the unleashing of educated manpower on a gigantic scale.

Van Nolte, William G.: "The College Faculty Crisis," *School and Society*, vol. 85 (January 5, 1957), pp. 4–7. Shows how the financial crisis affects colleges at the most crucial point —its faculty—and suggests needed reforms.

Wilson, Howard E.: "The College Way of Life," *Teachers College Record*, vol. 58 (March, 1957), pp. 310–315. Discusses changes in the college community—more heterogeneous student body, more "practical minded" faculty, and the changing mores of students.

chapter 9

*Adult
education*

Adult Education in a Democracy. The foundations of adult learning in the United States are imbedded deeply in the philosophy and history of a democratic society. "Freedom to learn" meant to the American pioneers not only an open gate to knowledge wherever their curiosity led them, but also a long pathway on which they could travel all the days of their lives. Coupled with the formal accent on the three R's—reading, 'riting, and 'rithmetic—for school children was the insatiable zeal to pursue informally the three L's—life long learning.

Particularly necessary is continuous education in the United States, since a democracy draws more upon the intelligence and character of its citizens than does any other form of government. In an informed democracy it is difficult for a government to enforce censorship and for demagogues to operate successfully. America needs more, not less, adult learning.

Former United States Commissioner of Education John W. Studebaker once raised the question: "What sort of educational base supports democracy in America?" He answered with the illustration of an inverted pyramid precariously balanced on a small apex of those who have had ample education. Even the adults in the educational apex of the inverted pyramid are constantly in need of re-education.

Many others need basic training in how to read. Through various educational agencies, the number of illiterates has been reduced. But even though statistics show a high degree of literacy in America, a large percentage of the literate do not know how to read in the modern sense. The late Edward L. Thorndike, in *Why We Behave like Illiterates*, said, "The ignorance of people concerning economics and business is on a level with their ignorance concerning physiology and medicine." Medicine has helped elongate life and thus increase the number of adults.

More and More Adults. The expectation of life at birth has increased markedly throughout the world. In many countries the life-expectancy figure exceeds the Biblical threescore and ten years.

The United States is no longer a country of young and middle-aged people. Less than 1 per cent of the population dies every year. Both numerically and proportionately, the adult population of this country is increasing. America, historically and humanly, is growing older.

When today's grandparents were children, the average adult lived fewer than fifty years and many children never knew what it was like to have grandparents. Ethel Sabin Smith points out in her book *The Dynamics of Aging* that today a man may expect to live twenty years longer than his grandfather. As indicated in Fig. 9-1, the span of life has been lengthened. A baby born in 1960 could look forward, as a personification of all babies born that year, to a life expectancy of nearly seventy years. Women in the United States live more than six years longer than the men. Experts predict that the average life span in the United States will be extended to more than ninety years within the next twenty-five years. Body and mind usually do not march side by side toward the

Fig. 9-1. Life expectancy has increased substantially in the United States over the years. The average life of a child born in 1960 is about seventy years as compared with only fifty-one years for a child born in 1920.

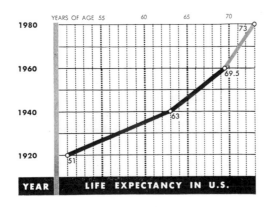

chronological milestones and inevitable tombstones. Gerontologists—those interested in the complex problems of old age—accent the need for research with oldsters as well as youngsters. They corroborate their contentions convincingly with the data in Fig. 9-2.

The number of persons sixty-five and over is increasing by more than one thousand every day. The percentage of the total population over sixty-five years in the United States will soon reach 10 per cent. Americans will have to live longer in order to die!

Why Stop Learning? Can adults learn? This is an old question. The usual answer has been "You can't teach an old dog new tricks." William James and other older psychologists believed that the mind was set like plaster at the age of twenty-five and that the acquisition of new ideas was extremely difficult, if not impossible. Modern experimental psychology has invalidated this dictum of James: "Outside of their own business, the ideas gained by men before they are twenty-five are practically the only ideas they shall have in their lives." The long-sanctioned superstition that adults cannot learn has been dissolved by a series of experiments. Edward L. Thorndike, who through his long years of productive research demonstrated that an adult can perform new tasks, was an outstanding pioneer in experimentation that proved adults can learn. The research of George Soule as reported in *Longer Life* shows that it is a myth that "everything must go down hill" in the latter years of life. Not only can adults learn, but continuous practice in learning helps them to retain their mental powers longer. One grows through living, so that ripeness of life may actually offset the decrease in speed of learning. There is no terminal point in one's education—no mental retirement age. Old persons will continue to learn new things. Adulthood is the period of having learned and of learning. People can learn to learn. The real question is not "Can adults learn?" but "Why stop learning?" As John F. Kennedy has put it, "It is not enough that our schools be great

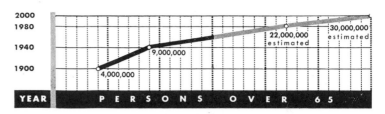

Fig. 9-2. Persons over sixty-five years of age.

centers of learning, they must concern themselves with the uses to which learning is put after graduation. Indeed, care must be taken to see that learning is not left behind after graduation."

Maturity and Achievements. H. A. Overstreet, in *The Mature Mind,* challenged each adult "to mature psychologically as well as physically, to mature along the line of what is unique in him and what he healthily shares with his fellows, and to continue the maturing process throughout his life. This is the *maturity concept.*"[1]

Another writer, Walter B. Pitkin, helped to popularize adult education with his books *Life Begins at Forty* and *Careers after Forty.* In the first he contended that life can become meaningful at the age of forty, and in the second he pointed out that careers were made after forty by persons like the actress Marie Dressler and humorist Will Rogers.

Countless are the examples of advanced learning and remarkable achievement by humans well along in years. Sir William Osler, a British scientist of note, once said, "The effective, moving, vitalizing work of the world is done between the ages of twenty-five and forty." Yet he, who urged that older people be liquidated, or "Oslerized," did his most important work as a great humanitarian and physician after he had reached the age of forty. Many men and women around the world have achieved greatness in their later years. A few Americans who did outstanding work after reaching threescore years and ten are

[1] H. A. Overstreet, *The Mature Mind,* W. W. Norton Company, Inc., New York, 1949, p. 41.

mentioned here. Oliver Wendell Holmes, who said, "If you haven't cut your name on the door by the time you have reached forty you might just as well put up your jackknife," wrote prodigiously and lucidly in his later years. The actress Ethel Barrymore wrote her *Memories* while in her seventies. Helen Keller served as president of the John Milton Society for the Blind when she was in her seventies, at which age she wrote *Teacher, Anne Macy Sullivan* and *The Open Door.* Edith Hamilton at the age of ninety wrote *The Echo of Greece.* "Grandma" Anna Mary Moses did not think of painting until she was seventy-six. John Marin, one of America's greatest artists, was painting in his eighties. Frank Lloyd Wright in his eighties was still designing buildings in organic architecture. Clark Griffith in his eighties and Connie Mack in his nineties were active in baseball management. General Douglas MacArthur in his seventies was democratizing Japan. Cornelius Vanderbilt increased the mileage of railroads from 120 to 10,000 after he reached seventy years. John Robert Gregg represented productivity in youth and age: at nineteen he organized the Gregg system of shorthand and at eighty he was still directing the operations of Gregg College. The Reverend Arthur Judsen Brown wrote a book on his first one hundred years of life! Sister Mary Gregory, the oldest nun in the Franciscan order, was serving as a nurse in her nineties. David O. McKay served as president of the Church of Latter Day Saints while in his eighties. Many persons in political life do not in their closing years return to second childhood, but get their second wind and thus advance to new goals. Former President Herbert Hoover in his eigh-

*In a rapidly changing world,
where the oldest citizen
recalls the horse and buggy
while young people may
soon explore the far reaches
of the universe,
education has a new task.
It must help both youths
and adults to adapt to
new developments and needs.
In this context,
adult education takes on
a vast new scope.*

*Adults attend a political
science seminar
at the Continuing Education Center
at Michigan State University.*

*The Georgia Center for Continuing Education
explores the possibilities of
television as a medium for adult education . . .*

ties was promoting the work of the Federal Commission on Reorganization of the Executive Branch. Many Supreme Court justices and congressmen serve their country in an official capacity after they have passed their three-score years and ten, and even fourscore years. Cicero at the age of sixty-two wrote in *De Senectute,* "Intelligence, and reflection, and judgment reside in old men, and if there had been none of them, no states could exist at all." Many oldsters have lived up to the challenging book titles *How to Stop Killing Yourself, Forget Your Age,* and *Creative Old Age.* Great achievements in all areas of human endeavor testify in defense of maturity. Longfellow posed a pertinent question for adults in "Morituri Salutamus":

> What then? Shall we sit idly down and say
> The night hath come; it is no longer day?

His answer is the challenge of adult education:

> The night hath not yet come; we are not quite
> Cut off from labor by the failing light;
> Something remains for us to do or dare;
> Even the oldest tree some fruit may bear; . . .
> For age is opportunity no less
> Than youth itself, though in another dress,
> And as the evening twilight fades away
> The sky is filled with stars, invisible by day.

In the starlit eventide of life, with head lifted skyward, the adult marches briskly to his task of continued learning. Old age is challenged by new ideas.

History

Early Beginnings. Early America faced the prodigious task of reeducating a generation of

sponsors concerts . . .

people from subjects to free citizens. The form of this reeducation, which might be regarded as the earliest manifestation of adult education, included town meetings, pamphlets, correspondence, books, speeches, plays, and other media.

The nineteenth century witnessed the founding of many institutions which provided facilities for adult education, such as the American Academy of Arts and Sciences, the Smithsonian Institute, the YMCA, Cooper Union, Red Cross, Rotary, Kiwanis, public libraries, women's clubs, PTAs and a host of others.

Several of these early organizations are especially noteworthy because of their particular importance in the adult education movement. The American Lyceum, founded by Josiah Holbrook in Massachusetts in 1831, established lecture-discussion groups in some three thousand towns. Although established "for the mutual improvement of their members and the common benefit of society," the principal purpose of the Lyceum was to advance the public school movement. With this accomplished, the Lyceum rapidly disappeared, but not until after it had established the lecture-discussion as an important medium of adult learning.

The Chautauqua Institution, founded in New York in 1874 for the original purpose of training Sunday school teachers, broadened its program to raise the general cultural level of adults, particularly in rural communities, through local reading circles, correspondence courses, and traveling chautauquas.

The Rise of School-centered Programs. Following the Civil War, public schools and colleges developed educational programs for adults. Waves of immigration established the evening class in public schools as the vehicle for Americanizing the nation's new citizens. State aid for Americanization programs became common after the turn of the century and accelerated the movement.

Colleges and universities began to perceive their mission in adult education. The University of the State of New York, the University of Chicago, and the University of Wisconsin established early prototypes of university extension programs for adults. These programs centered about the day-to-day problems of people—agricultural, economic, political, social, moral. The land-grant colleges, with their na-

and offers demonstrations of folk dancing.

The University of Omaha has more students enrolled in its night courses than in its daytime program.

Many public school systems operate full educational programs for adults in academic, vocational, recreational, and cultural pursuits.

tural disposition toward field service, adapted easily to the movement.

The Smith-Lever Act of 1914 stimulated the establishment of agricultural extension education. County agents, vocational agriculture teachers, and other specialists influenced millions of farm families, not only in farm practices, but in child raising, health, nutrition, and many cultural activities. Malcolm Knowles,

executive director of the Adult Education Association, has concluded that this movement has had a greater impact upon our national culture than any other induced force in history.[2]

Private correspondence schools, notably the International Correspondence Schools, sprang into being, providing education to millions of Americans on a home-study basis.

Schools and teachers of adult education began to form associations. Although these associations were not then concerned exclusively with adult education they nevertheless served to disseminate ideas and practices regarding adult learning.

The Modern Era. Until World War I, adult education had been developed as an adjunct to other programs or institutions. Indeed, the term "adult education" did not come into general use in America until Frederick P. Keppel, president of the Carnegie Corporation, returned in 1924 from an inspection trip of adult education programs in Europe. He had a vision of an organized movement in adult education which eventuated in the founding of the American Association for Adult Education in 1926. This organization, financed in part by the Carnegie Corporation, served as a clearinghouse for ideas and resources, sponsored conferences and publications, and brought integrity and organization to the national movement.

The Department of Adult Education of the National Education Association emerged as an important professional association of adult educators. In 1951 it merged with the American Association of Adult Education to form the Adult Education Association of the NEA.

Meanwhile, the federal government had undertaken several noteworthy adventures in adult education. During the depression years, the Works Progress Administration, the Civilian Conservation Corps and other programs provided emergency funds for worthwhile activities of otherwise unemployed adults

[2] Malcolm S. Knowles, "Adult Education in the United States," *Adult Education,* vol. 5 (Winter, 1955), p. 17.

NATIONAL DEVELOPMENT		THE DEVELOPMENT OF ADULT EDUCATION
The Colonial period Launching the new nation	**1661**	Evening schools reported in New York State
Maritime troubles and the War of 1812 Era of good feeling	**1808**	Prototype of university extension class established at Yale
	1831	American Lyceum established in Massachusetts
Jacksonian Democracy	**1839**	First general state law providing for evening schools enacted in Ohio
Westward migration and expansion		
Controversy and war between the states	**1859**	Cooper Union opened in New York City with public forums
Aftermath and reconstruction	**1874**	Chautauqua Institution founded *Sunday School teachers*
	1883	The Correspondence University founded at Ithaca
Immigration and industrial growth	**1891**	International Correspondence School established at Scranton
	1897	National Congress of Mothers called in Washington, D.C.
The progressive era	**1914**	Smith-Lever Act provided for agricultural extension work
World War I		
	1924	Cleveland, first community organized for adult education program
Normalcy and prosperity	**1925**	Public adult education first recognized by law as an integral part of free public school system
	1926	American Association for Adult Education formed
Depression and recovery	**1933**	TVA and WPA established including provisions for adult education
World War II	**1946**	USAFI established officially as permanent peacetime organization
	1951	American Association for Adult Education and Department of Adult Education joined in Adult Education Association
The Cold War struggle		Fund for Adult Education established by Ford Foundation
	1952	*Adult Leadership* magazine launched by AEA
	1958	Publication of *Handbook of Adult Education in the United States* under the auspices of the Adult Education Association

HISTORICAL CALENDAR

and out-of-school youth. Indeed, one of the most striking examples of community-wide adult education was provided by the Tennessee Valley Authority with the support of the federal government.

Powerful stimulation has been given the adult education movement by the impetus of private foundations. The aid of the Carnegie Corporation has been mentioned. The Kellogg Foundation, the Sloan Foundation, and the Ford Foundation, through its Fund for Adult Education, have been noteworthy in advancing adult education. About half of the states now provide state aid for public adult education and employ specialists in the state department to assist in the development of adult programs.

It is estimated that the number of adults engaged in education programs now exceeds the number of students in public elementary and secondary schools. Thus adult education is being established as the fifth level of our educational system—the natural culmination of pre-elementary, elementary, secondary, and higher education.

Purposes

Scope of Adult Education. In its broadest sense, adult education embraces all informal and formal activities which promote more learning and better living for persons of approximately twenty-one years of age and over. In its narrowest sense, it is institutionalized instruction for mature persons who usually are not full-time students. Most summer school and graduate students in the regular sessions of the colleges and universities are adults.

Beliefs of Adult Education Association. Seeking to build a stronger adult education movement, the Adult Education Association of the United States expresses the following beliefs in the Preamble to its constitution:

In the belief that only a vigorous, informed, and democratically vigilant people can remain free—

In the recognition that among a free people, learning for every citizen must be a process continuing throughout life—

In the understanding that the capacity to perfect skills, to enrich living, and to increase social understanding and effectiveness is ever present in human beings—

In the knowledge that adults through education must seek continuously new and better ways to achieve these ends and ideals—

These general beliefs acquire a higher degree of specificity when they are translated into definite goals for the education of adults.

Bill of Objectives for Those Past Sixty-five. The governors of the various states in the Union asked the Council on State Governments to prepare a bill of objectives for those past sixty-five years of age. Ernest W. Burgess, authority on aging and professor emeritus of the University of Chicago, directed the study, which was presented to the governors' conference in 1955. The set of ten objectives is as follows:

1. Equal opportunity to work
2. Adequate minimum income—sufficient for health and for participation in community life as a self-respecting citizen
3. Home living—the satisfaction of living in a home of their own, or if this is not feasible, in suitable substitute private homes
4. Homelike institutional care
5. Physical and mental health—supported by adequate food and medical care
6. Physical and mental rehabilitation—the right of the handicapped to be restored, if possible, to independent, useful lives
7. Participation in community activities in their own social groups and in groups of all ages
8. Social services—counseling, vocational retraining and social casework
9. Research, professional training—research on aging and the training of workers in the field

10. Freedom, independence, and initiative—increased emphasis on the right of free choice, self-help, and planning of their own futures

This semiofficial bill of rights for the older part of the nation's population gives a broad frame of reference for goals in adult education.

Some Goals of Adult Education. The Division of Adult Education of the National Education Association in 1953 completed a comprehensive study of public school adult education and revealed the following objectives as those reported to be most important by adult educators. These goals are listed in order of importance:

Enrichment of life

Vocational competence and economic efficiency

Awareness of civic responsibilities to the community, the nation, and the world

Extension of educational background

Improvement of understanding of and adjustment to socioeconomic trends

Improvement of physical and mental health[3]

Other goals of adult education would include elimination of illiteracy, Americanization of immigrants, education for parenthood and family life, vocational and avocational guidance, and improved consumership.

Developmental Tasks of Adults. Robert J. Havighurst, chairman of the Committee on Human Development at the University of Chicago, lists for adults those developmental tasks which arise at or about a certain period in the life of the individual, the successful achievement of which leads to his happiness and to success with later tasks:

Tasks of early adulthood
Selecting a mate
Learning to live with a marriage partner
Starting a family
Rearing children

Managing a home
Getting started in an occupation
Taking on civic responsibility
Finding a congenial social group

Tasks of middle age
Achieving adult civic and social responsibilities
Establishing and maintaining an economic standard of living
Assisting teen-age children to become responsible and happy adults
Developing adult leisure-time activities
Relating oneself to one's spouse as a person
Accepting and adjusting to the physiological changes of middle age
Adjusting to aging parents

Tasks of later maturity
Adjusting to decreasing physical strength and health
Adjusting to reduced income
Adjusting to death of a spouse
Establishing an explicit affiliation with one's age group
Meeting social and civic obligations
Establishing satisfactory physical living arrangements[4]

These developmental tasks are being met, at least in part for many adults, through significant life experiences and through a broad-gauge program of numerous activities ranging from passive listening to radio and TV programs to active participation in teaching other adults.

Program

The objectives of adult education are being implemented by multifaceted programs of activities. Geographically, some aspects of the vast programs are found in various parts of the world and in the political areas mentioned in Chapters 1 to 4, viz., national, state, county, and local units respectively. Academically the

[3] Helen Allion and Robert A. Luke, "Public School Adult Education in the United States," *Adult Education*, vol. 3 (February, 1953), p. 71.

[4] Robert J. Havighurst, *Human Development and Education*, Longmans, Green & Co., Inc., New York, 1953, pp. 2, 9–283.

adult learning activities stretch across the organizational levels discussed in Chapters 5 to 8, viz., pre-elementary, elementary, secondary, and higher education. Alphabetically, the programs for adults are unique in that they span the entire list of consonants and vowels from A to Z, as described tersely in the following pages.

Programs for adults from A to Z

A *Americanization.* This type of adult education was designed originally to teach the rudiments of the English language and the elements of the United States Constitution to resident alien adults seeking formal admission to American citizenship. The rigid subject matter of earlier years, in which the letter rather than the spirit of the immigration laws dominated the program, has expanded into a functional Americanization program which includes vocational and avocational guidance, civic awareness, and participation in all aspects of democratic processes. Typical of Americanization classes years ago was a lecture by a salesman of American ideals to a group of bewildered "foreigners"; illustrative of the present program is a folk festival in which the people of all nations are given a chance to re-create the cultural values of their homelands. Under the requirements for citizenship set up by the Immigration and Naturalization Service, a period of two to seven years must elapse from the time an alien takes out the first papers until he receives final citizenship. This period is long enough for interested agencies to provide a broad naturalization program.

The number of aliens granted citizenship papers has risen sharply in recent years. The unsettled world conditions, the arrival of many displaced persons, the overseas friendships established during and since World War II, and the ruling that certain federal-state benefactions, like old-age pensions, be paid only to citizens of the United States are causal factors in the increase.

The influx of many well-educated and cultured newcomers necessitates a revision of the Americanization curriculum with literature

on a higher level of difficulty and with more emphasis on oral English and on American institutions, traditions, and practices. Among the by-products of a modern functional Americanization program are more effective cooperation and better understanding between home and school, and between foreign-born parents and their American-born children.

B *Books.* Many adult education programs center around books. "A true university," wrote Thomas Carlyle, "is a collection of books." Thomas Jefferson once said, "I cannot live without books." Some aspects of adult education, such as Bible classes, are centered around one book. Some noncredit and credit courses in universities are pivoted around several great books of the ages. One of the most significant recent developments in adult education has been the organization of a number of book-based discussion groups, such as the Great Books Program; the World Politics Program of the American Foundation for Political Education; the Study Discussion Program of the Fund for Adult Education; and the American Heritage Discussion Programs of the American Library Association.

Many blind adults read acoustically by means of talking books presented on records or tape, or they get book learning kinesthetically by touching the braille letters with their trained fingers.

Although approximately a thousand new books are published each month in the United States, this nation is not known as a book-reading country. The pressures of American life, plus other factors, such as the availability in the average home of radio and/or television, militate against extensive voluntary reading of books by adults as well as youngsters. An encouraging fact in youth and adult reading is the heavy sale of paper-bound books available in drug stores, newsstands, and bookstores.

C *Chautauquas.* The original Chautauqua Institution was started in the 1870s on the shores of the lake of that name in western New York, as a summer training camp for Sunday school teachers in the Methodist Church. The chautauqua programs of yesteryears with their lectures and money-making schemes helped to keep Americans informed and entertained and saved many a small town from its year-round stagnation. Its place, however, is being taken by the forum, radio, television, lectures, and organized educational efforts such as summer schools.

Churches and Synagogues. Many forums and educational discussions, some of long standing, are conducted variously by religious organizations. An example is church night, which consists of a series of evening programs of interest and help to churchgoers and nonchurchgoers. Church and synagogue are intended to meet the whole need from worship, to education, to play, for the whole family. Joy Elmer Morgan, editor of *Senior Citizens*, states that the church should organize groups to serve senior citizens in their membership and in the surrounding neighborhood. A recent study, *Design for Adult Education in the Church*, led to the formulation of the so-called Indiana Plan whereby many denominations have built in the local church an effective, continuous, adult education program.

Clubs. Foreign visitors to America have often noted the disposition of Americans to form clubs. Alexis de Tocqueville, the distinguished French scholar, for example, wrote that "Americans of all ages, all conditions, and all dispositions constantly form associations . . . associations of a thousand kinds—religious, moral, serious, futile, general or restricted, enormous or diminutive."

Women's clubs were pioneers in adult education and still constitute a vital factor. Bryson says that in spite of ridicule and masculine opposition, women's clubs have been educational institutions of real value. He points out also that the historic function of these clubs has been in some degree fulfilled and that

younger women are being drawn into associations with specific interests, such as the League of Women Voters, the Business and Professional Women's Club, the Junior League, the American Association of University Women, and an endless chain of other societies for women only.

Men eat, talk, and listen at their luncheon and dinner clubs, which are also infinite in number and variety. Numerous evening study and discussion clubs include both men and women. Some of these adult clubs serve specific purposes, such as the garden clubs and investment groups of neighbors or friends who meet periodically to study stocks and other investments. Cultural, financial, social, educational, recreational, political, religious, racial, and professional groups provide intermittent avenues of adult learning.

Some clubs are specifically designed for the older people. The Forty-plus clubs specialize in placing persons over forty who are unemployed American citizens. Senior Citizens of America is a nonprofit organization incorporated under the laws of the District of Columbia to serve persons over forty years. Many Golden Age groups have been formed for those persons over fifty years of age. Some senior groups own or rent clubrooms or clubhouses.

Correspondence. The art of personal letter writing was a real means of adult learning for sender and recipient in the frontier days of America. Unfortunately, modern transportation, telephones, and telegrams have helped to make personal correspondence almost a lost art.

Correspondence schools are, however, a very important institutional means of adult learning. Millions are enrolled. In some sparsely settled western regions of Canada and the United States, children are taught elementary and high school rudiments by correspondence courses. The Benton Harbor (Michigan) Plan seeks to meet individual needs of high school students through public school-administered correspondence courses purchased by the local board of education from nationally known correspondence schools.

Learning by mail is a very old form of adult education. Following the formation of the Society to Encourage Studies at Home in 1873, came the so-called Correspondence University of Ithaca, New York, in 1883. Then came the extension correspondence courses from the Chautauqua Institution and the Extension Division of the University of Chicago under William Rainey Harper. Prior to the establishment of college extension divisions, much pioneering work in selling education to adults was done by the commercial correspondence schools. The International Correspondence Schools of Scranton, Pennsylvania, developed out of an experiment by Thomas A. Foster, editor of the *Mining Herald* of Shenandoah, Pennsylvania, who began in the eighties to print questions and answers dealing with the problems of safety in the mines.

Thousands of different home-study courses are available to the individual who finds it impractical to attend a resident institution of learning. Of the many correspondence schools only a small proportion are admitted to membership in the National Home Study Council, which was organized in 1926 for accrediting correspondence schools. This council, with headquarters in Washington, D.C., is attempting to eliminate racketeering schools and salesmen from the home-study field. The United States government through USAFI offers to enlisted men correspondence courses, and through the Federal Trade Commission has adopted trade practice rules for private home-study schools in order to foster and promote fair competitive conditions. The importance of correspondence work is reflected in the numerous bills that have been introduced into Congress to establish a national system of supervised correspondence courses.

Counseling. John Dewey once said, "Guidance is not external imposition. It is freeing the life processes for its own most adequate fulfillment." This is the role of counseling for adults.

Guidance is the keystone of the adult education program. Much of it is self-guidance, but the high art of counseling is much needed from others by many adults. In her work in the Old Age Counseling Center, which she founded in San Francisco after retiring from the faculty of Stanford University, Miss Lilien J. Martin found best results from personal counseling through a series of planned interviews. These interviews were organized around such questions as "What is the senior citizen's personal background?" "How does he use and how can he organize time?" "How does and how can he budget money?" "What goals does he have and how can plans be made to achieve them?" "How can the senior citizen develop participant roles?"

Group guidance is also necessary at times in helping people to become mature. To be ashamed of one's age is in itself a sign of immaturity. At one of the institutes for the preparation for retirement at Purdue University it was stated that problems of aging, retirement, and adjustment are so broad and complex that every resource in the community must be utilized in their solution. With the aid of the Fund for Adult Education, a helpful manual has been prepared under the caption *Aging in the Modern World: Guidebook for Leaders.* The U.S. Department of Labor has prepared a helpful bulletin entitled *Counseling and Placement Services for Older Workers.* The Society of Friends long ago summed up the basic needs of the aged simply and succinctly: "Somewhere to live, something to do, some one to care."

Curriculum. The heart of formal adult education is the curriculum, which is as broad as life itself and extends from the reading readiness of the kindergarten level in learning English to the rigorous internship of the postdoctoral work in medicine. As to the curriculum of public school adult education, Arthur P. Crabtree, head of the New York State Civic Education Bureau of Adult Education, has been constructively critical. He believes that "give-them-what-they-want" is an inadequate philosophy and that the trivial "smörgasbord offerings" in many public school adult education programs attest to this fact. In his critique *Civic Education Programs for Adults,* published by the National Association of Public School Adult Educators, Crabtree pointed out that adult education has not done its most basic job—that of preparing adults for citizenship in a free democracy.

In *Learning Comes of Age,* published by the Adult Education Association of the United States of America, John Walker Powell recommended that the major concerns and deepest interests of people be a core for the adult curriculum. The five fields he suggested as major constellations are (1) democracy, (2) the family, (3) the job, (4) enrichment of living, and (5) self-understanding.[5] The curriculum of formal adult education is undergoing a gradual metamorphosis from a potpourri of courses determined by popular fancy to a more academically respectable curriculum of rich cultural content.

Discussions. Discussions probably date back to the earliest days of human history. The American Lyceum and Cooper Union have been particularly noteworthy in stimulating discussion as a medium of adult education in America. Free discussion is a *sine qua non* in a democracy. It is an excellent antidote for bias and dogmatism. Discussion helps individuals find deeper meaning and wider perspective in problems by bringing together the ideas and experiences of many people. Discussion helps folks identify people with common problems and helps unite folks into effective group action on such problems. It provides one of the highest levels for human learning.

Exchanges. Related to the interchange of ideas is the exchange of persons. Modern Americans are a mobile people and one can always learn from travelers. Especially fruitful has been the exchange of persons program promoted by the

[5] John Walker Powell, *Learning Comes of Age,* Association Press, New York, 1956, pp. 21–22.

United States and other governments of the world. In 1958 an exchange of persons program was initiated between Russia and the United States. It is a platitude to say that the best way to send an idea abroad is to wrap it up in a person. Obviously people speaking to people make the world smaller.

Entertainment. Some adult education ventures have been criticized because they fail to progress much beyond the level of sheer entertainment. This is not to imply that adult learning cannot be both fruitful and pleasant, nor to suggest that recreation is an improper objective. Certainly, adult education should help people find greater joy through knowledge. However, adult programs that aim exclusively at entertainment fall far short of the mark. Fortunately, most adult education programs, both public and private, are attuned to quite serious purposes and progress far beyond the level of mere fun.

Family. Family life education is one of the oldest forms of adult learning. Children learn from their parents and also teach them a thing or two. Parental education is child- and parent-centered. The Jewish people have a fine tradition and long-established practice of family life education which helps to militate against juvenile and adult delinquency. Many adult education programs include classes for young people long before they marry and have children. Some local centers have special lectures for expectant mothers (and fathers). Among the many national organizations promoting family life education are the National Council of Parent Education, the National Congress of Parents and Teachers, the American Home Economics Association, and the Department of Agriculture. Many churches also conduct programs for adults emphasizing family life and education.

Groups. American society is composed of many groups other than families. These comprise people of the same race, religion, political affiliation, ethnic origin, type of employment, or any other common interest. Sometimes these associations find themselves in sharp conflict. For example, when labor-management relations deteriorate, costly strikes frequently result. In recent years much study has been directed toward the interaction of individuals within organizations and to the relationships between groups. A new field of knowledge known as group dynamics has emerged. The improvement of intergroup relations is being sought through adult education programs. The National Council of Christians and Jews, the Anti-defamation League of B'nai B'rith, the Research Center for Group Dynamics at the University of Michigan, and the National Training Laboratory for Group Dynamics are some of the organizations interested in this important objective.

Health. As one grows older, ill health becomes a greater problem. While chronic disorders are disabling to the aged particularly, half of the chronically ill are less than forty-five years of age. An alarmingly high rate of young men, supposedly in the prime of life, had to be rejected from military service during World War II because of poor physical or mental health. Highway fatalities have risen sharply. Nearly half of the hospital beds in the United States are occupied by the mentally ill. Yet according to one authority, greater progress has been made by medical science in the past fifty years than in the previous five thousand. Obviously there is a great gap between medical knowledge and individual health practices. Many diseases are partially or completely controllable. Most accidents are preventable. Much mental illness could be avoided. Herein lies a challenge for the education of adults as well as of children and youth.

Many adult education programs include courses in mental hygiene, driver training, safety education, personal hygiene, child care, home care of the sick, first aid, life-saving, nutrition, and others. Lecture and discussion series led by physicians and dealing with per-

sonal and public health problems are becoming more widespread in adult education programs. Increased attention is being given to geriatrics, the division of medicine concerned with the aged. Because of the sharp increase of aged persons in our population, their problems are regarded by some as our number one health problem.

Many national agencies, such as insurance companies, the National Safety Council, the Red Cross, the U.S. Public Health Service, are lending valuable assistance and support. The accent on health in adult education is not only lengthening life but also is making the body a healthier organism at a given age. The goal is to add life to years, not just years to life.

Hobbies. Sir William Osler, the distinguished British surgeon, once observed that "no man is really safe or happy without a hobby. . . . Anything will do as long as he straddles a hobby and rides it hard." Many public school adult education programs give considerable attention to the pursuit of such hobbies as gardening, hi-fi, photography, reading, golf, boating, dramatics, swimming, dancing, bridge, music, painting, and other crafts. Many aspects of home maintenance, now regarded as hobbies by many folks, are included in adult education programs. Scarcely any hobby has escaped the do-it-yourself craze. There are self-teaching materials in almost anything from apiculture to zoology.

Our machine age has brought the adult worker leisure hours undreamed of a generation ago. Labor-saving devices in the home permit housewives to spend more time on hobbies and recreational pursuits. Lengthened life span has increased the proportion of retired persons who find a renewed interest in life through hobbies. Social security, pension funds, and life insurance annuities provide oldsters with more money to invest in leisure-time pursuits. Many adults return to hobbies which they neglected since youth. Many develop new avocations as they forsake their vocations. Interest in hobbies is a most important means of sustaining a sense of achievement and an interest in life, not only for retired persons, but for other adults and youth as well. Furthermore, more creative use of leisure time has resulted in a cultural renaissance that is manifest in such things as the spread of folk crafts, little theaters, music groups, literary clubs, hi-fi, and others.

Informal. While it is estimated that more than one-fourth of the nation is engaged in formal learning, much of adult education is characterized by informality. The breakfast club, the coffee break, the informal luncheon meeting, the afternoon tea, the casual conversations at dinner, the after-dinner club meetings—all can contribute to the enlightenment of peoples.

Individual. Much adult education must be tailor-made to fit the individual. Unfortunately, when one grows older, his clothes may not fit him too well; so too, many programs do not fit the needs and interests of adults. The drop-outs from formal adult classes can often be traced to the failure to harmonize the presentation with the individual students. Much of adult learning, such as quietly reading a book in one's home, will continue to be a one-person program.

International. One of the books in the series of World Perspectives raises the following question in its title: *Can People Learn to Learn How to Know Each Other?* The author, Brock Chisholm, answers with this challenge: "Let us try to put ourselves in the place and conditions of living of various people, attempting to feel with them some of their preoccupations and to see world problems from their point of view. We may start anywhere, spin a globe, point a finger, and imagine."[6] In this shrinking world, most adult education programs recognize the extreme and urgent importance of international activities. Brotherhood Week and many programs on individual countries or special areas,

such as the Middle East, are integral parts of international adult learning and understanding. The International Geophysical Year demonstrated the merits of nations learning together.

Journeys. Adult education programs include journeys. Benjamin Franklin, himself an overseas visitor, once said, "Traveling is one way of lengthening life." Benjamin Disraeli added, "Travel teaches toleration." Travel teaches many people many things. As the Twentieth Century Fund studies have pointed out, more Americans go more places more often than do the people of any other land. It is estimated that the typical American travels more than five thousand miles a year. Many travel much more.

An adult can travel abroad by reading an atlas while seated in his rocking chair at home. He can similarly take journeys into outer space. One can explore in his own community many places unvisited before. The 50 states provide free travel information. The national parks and historic sites are rendezvous for many oldsters in quest of more knowledge. International tours are very popular with many retired persons who have the time and money for sightseeing. Seminars abroad are becoming increasingly popular, not only for college students, but for adults as well. Approximately twelve thousand American students and teachers study and work abroad annually.

Knowledge. The real quest in adult education is for knowledge. As a former vice-president of the Adult Education Association emphasized:

The fact remains that adult education is *education*, just as surely so as is the education of youth, and one day we will see it for what it is: a natural and necessary continuation of that process which begins with the child in the kindergarten and continues as long as he lives.[7]

The continuation of man's quest for knowledge throughout life becomes even more im-

[6] Brock Chisholm, *Can People Learn to Learn How to Know Each Other?* Harper & Brothers, New York, 1958, p. 5.

[7] Arthur P. Crabtree, "What Adult Education Is— And Is Not," *The New York Times Magazine*, May 27, 1956, p. 62.

perative in an age of technological revolution such as the present, when knowledge becomes outdated so rapidly. Because of the accelerated pace of human discovery, books in science and other fields become obsolete almost as soon as they are printed. No longer can one assume the constancy of knowledge acquired years ago in high school or college. It is said that 90 per cent of the prescriptions written by physicians today could not have been filled twenty-five years ago. Imagine the difficulty of the pharmacist in keeping his professional knowledge up to date! Whole new fields of human knowledge, scarcely known a generation ago, have burst upon us—astronautics, oceanography, areology, atomic physics, geriatrics, and group dynamics, to mention a few.

Adult education programs are placing increased emphasis upon keeping the learner's knowledge up to date. Sound concepts of adult education regard this extension and modernization of knowledge as the central aim of adult education. Adults are responding as never before to the intellectual challenges. It is quite apparent that man's thirst for knowledge is never quenched.

Libraries. As early as 1732 the versatile Benjamin Franklin, through his famous Junto Club, started the first subscription library in the world. The city of Boston initiated the public library movement. A Frenchman, wishing to start an international exchange of books, persuaded the city of Paris to present the city of Boston with 50 volumes. Consequently a Boston committee was named to "consider and report what acknowledgment and return should be made to the city of Paris for its gift of books, and to provide a place for the same." This committee, which was acquainted with the publicly used, privately supported libraries, contributed to library ideology by giving public support to the public library. A few years later the city of Boston was granted legal authority by the Massachusetts Legislature to tax itself for this purpose. This started the free public library move-

ment in the United States, which at the turn of the twentieth century was accelerated by the numerous gifts from Andrew Carnegie. Now every state in the Union legalizes public libraries and every city of any size supports one. The federal government aids in the development of rural libraries.

A marked contrast exists between the old museum of books and the modern public library. It is the difference between taking a container to the pump several rods away and bringing a public water system into one's own home and having water available from the tap. The chains that once shackled the books to the reading desks have been broken. Whereas many librarians used to hoard books, they now wish to show how many are off the shelves in actual use. An active reading public eliminates the librarian's dust cloth. The open-shelf system, while costly in losses, is the open sesame to the wonderland of books. Furthermore, where the library was once a repository for books only, it is now an instruction and information center with files replete with clippings, pictorial aids, phonograph records, and many other multisensory aids; with reference, committee, lecture, radio, and television rooms; and with other facilities, not the least of which is the telephone, which enables a person to use the public library without leaving his home.

Despite good libraries, the United States is not a book-reading nation. Not many adults make constant companions of books, as did the clerk of Oxenford thus described by Chaucer:

> For Him was lever have at his beddes heed
> Twenty bokes, clad in blak or reed,
> Of aristotle and his philosophye,
> Then robes riche, or fithele, or gay sautrye.

The bookmobiles, therefore, constitute a great advance in educational engineering. The library truck and its trained attendant carry a rich cargo to remote parts of the United States. Not only are adults the recipients of these books, but children are given the opportunity to develop good reading habits and tastes which will carry over into maturity.

The Library Service Division in the U.S. Office of Education lists as one objective that of "furthering library participation in the adult education movement." The American Library Association, which held its first meeting in 1876, has been a tremendous force in adult learning, particularly through its Commission on the Library and Adult Education.

The public library movement finds its highest fulfillment in the Library of Congress in Washington. It was established in 1800 by an act providing for a library for the two houses, at an initial cost of 5,000 dollars. Housed in the Capitol, it was burned by the British and revived by Thomas Jefferson with his own books as a nucleus. In 1886 Congress decided to dedicate the library to the services of all the people, and a new building was commenced.

Of all the institutions in the United States that have a part in the American dream, the late James Truslow Adams said, "The one which best exemplifies the dream is the greatest library in this land of libraries, the Library of Congress. . . . Founded and built by the people, it is for the people."[8] This national institution of public learning is a prototype for other adult educational agencies.

Literacy. In the most exhaustive survey ever made on the subject, UNESCO's publication *World Illiteracy at Mid-century*, contains the sad statistic that 44 per cent of the world's adult population (those over fifteen years of age) cannot read and write. Although the Soviet Union is conducting a Down with Illiteracy campaign, the survey estimates that between 5 and 10 per cent of the adult population cannot read and write. The United States has an adult illiterate group of between 3 and 4 per cent.

For many years part of the adult education program in the United States has been directed toward reducing illiteracy. Literacy education

[8] James Truslow Adams, *The Epic of America*, Little, Brown & Company, Boston, 1932, pp. 414–415.

aims to provide classes for adults unable to read and write English with sufficient facility to be able to read a newspaper with understanding and to write an intelligible letter. In World War II, the armed forces conducted very successful programs of literacy training. After rejecting more than 200,000 men of draft age because of illiteracy alone, the armed services eventually inducted twice that number who had never reached the fourth-grade standard of literacy. A large percentage of them was brought up to or beyond that level over a period of two or three months.

Ambrose Caliver, chief of the adult education section of the U.S. Office of Education, recently stated that illiteracy in the United States is increasing rather than decreasing. The United States should seek to equal the record of such countries as Denmark, where illiteracy is only 0.1 per cent. May the time come when American checks and legal documents will not bear the wording, "If you cannot write your name, place a cross and have it witnessed by two persons."

Mental Health. Almost one-half of the adults in hospitals are afflicted with poor mental health. Unfortunately, much mental illness stems from the harmful belief that aging itself is a disease rather than a natural maturing process. For a long time it was widely held that senility was the product of physical deterioration of the aging brain. Recent research indicates that psychological factors, such as a fear of growing old and frustrations in later years, accelerate senility. Many old persons, while showing their age, are nevertheless in very good health, physically and mentally. Psychotherapy can help overcome some of the frustrations of aging. Books such as the Overstreets' *The Mature Mind* and Norman Vincent Peale's *Stay Alive All Your Life* accent the positive factors in aging. As Robert Browning wrote:

Grow old along with me!
The best is yet to be,
The last of life, for which the first was made . . .

Movies. Motion pictures constitute one of the mass media of communications used in adult education. The movies are usually designed for large audiences and lack the face-to-face contacts of individuals in panel discussions. Although television has subtracted from motion-picture attendance, there are millions of Americans who weekly see and hear movies in a theater. Many millions view pictures via television sets. A great many excellent 16 mm films, prepared expressly for educational rather than entertainment purposes, are in wide use in adult education programs. The need for screening pictures and previewing them is very essential in adult work. Follow-up discussion and implementation add meaning to movies for adults. Color has greatly enhanced the value of many motion pictures.

Linked with motion pictures are other audio-visual aids such as filmstrips. Illustrative of these are the current events strips produced by the *New York Times.* These are accompanied by a helpful printed guide giving the background for each picture filmed.

Newspapers. Another form of mass communication is the newspaper—daily and weekly. It helps to enliven discussion of current events and the study of special fields and areas. Unfortunately, the editorials, which should be the cream of the newspaper, are usually neglected for watered-down versions of minor happenings in the community, state, nation, or world. The decrease in the number of newspapers, the increase in their price, and the decreased use of newspapers in favor of radio and television make this media less significant than formerly in adult education. However, people still grab newspapers while they pick up magazines at leisure. Almost all adult centers subscribe to one or more newspapers. This mass media also reaches the front porch of most American homes.

Organizations. The Adult Education Association classifies organizations active in this field

into five general categories.[9] First, many *voluntary associations*, such as the National Congress of Parents and Teachers, YMCA, the National Council of Churches, the National Safety Council, and Rotary, operate educational programs for adults through local units. Second, various *educational associations*, such as the Adult Education Association, the National Association of Adult Educators, the American Association of Junior Colleges, the American Library Association, the National University Extension Association, and many others, are concerned with the advancement of adult education. Third, *associations in related professions*, such as the American Management Association, American Society of Newspaper Editors, the National Association of Manufacturers, the American Medical Association, are concerned with the education of adults in their specialized fields. Although their primary task is not adult education and although they may not provide any institutional program, they usually conduct activities designed to influence public understanding in their realm of interests. Fourth, *specialized interest groups*, groups interested in specific areas, such as public health, education of the aging, vocational education, civil liberties, arts and crafts, international affairs, and others, conduct programs aimed toward the advancement of knowledge according to their interest. Illustrations of this type might include the American Social Hygiene Association, the American Civil Liberties Union, the American Home Economics Association, the League of Women Voters, the American Vocational Association, and scores of others. The fifth and last group includes *federal organizations and workers*. There is a rapidly growing number of specialists, field agents, and teachers in such organizations as the Civil Defense Commission, the Department of Agriculture, the U.S. Office of Education, the Atomic Energy Commission. These workers have common interests with workers in other groups mentioned

9 "An Overview and History of the Field," *Adult Education*, vol. 7 (Summer, 1957), pp. 219–230.

previously and often regard themselves as professional adult educators.

Periodicals. Magazines and other periodicals are used widely in adult education, both informal and formal. Adults subscribe to or purchase at newsstands in large numbers nationally known monthly and weekly publications, such as *Time, Newsweek, Fortune, Farm Journal, National Geographic, U.S. News and World Report,* and many others, including various women's magazines. Many adult centers also subscribe to a number of periodic publications to help adults keep up to date. In the doctors' offices, and the public libraries the well-thumbed weekly and monthly magazines attest to the constant use of these tools in the education of adults. (At the close of this and other chapters in this volume are listed several periodicals pertinent to the contents of the chapter.)

Quizzes. Most adult programs include in their plans periodic quizzes and questionnaires to ascertain "How are we doing?" Formal adult courses offered by colleges and universities obviously include periodic examinations. Standard tests to determine the intelligence quotient are not widely used in adult learning for fear that slowness in writing responses and vocabulary difficulties may discourage oldsters. They, however, have a function to serve in some adult work. Many adult education programs, with their emphasis on vocational guidance and rehabilitation, make use of interest and aptitude tests.

Radio. Another mass means of communications in adult learning is the radio. Related to it are the recordings, including hi-fi players. Most homes in the United States have one or more radios and many adult centers use them too. In addition to being passive listeners, oldsters often put on radio programs as active participants. One of the favorite programs on radio is the newscast, which helps oldsters to keep up to date on current happenings.

Recreation. Education and recreation are inextricably linked in adult programs. Physical exercises, reducing classes, outdoor camping, hiking expeditions, and the like are for the more vigorous. One of the favorite programs at adult centers is square dancing. For those less active there are such pastimes as chess, checkers, dominoes, and cards.

Reading. Reading is one of the most universal media of adult education. It provides ready access to knowledge for everyone. Reference has already been made to the importance of libraries in adult education. Newspaper subscriptions flourish. The Book-of-the-Month Club, the Literary Guild, and other book clubs have helped to extend the scope and raise the level of adult reading. Extremely helpful, especially for leaders, are such books as William Gray and Bernice Rogers' *Maturity in Reading,* Paul Leedy's *Reading Improvement for Adults,* and the National Society for the Study of Education Yearbook, *Adult Reading.*

Retirement. One of the most neglected and newest emphases in adult education is preparation for retirement and postretirement living, including appropriate housing for the aged.

Preparation for retirement is as important as any form of readiness work. Parents prepare the baby for childhood, the child for adolescence, and the youth for adulthood. Why not prepare for retirement? During their early forties people should start planning for the day when they will be separated from active full-time employment. Phased or tapering retirement is increasing. Too often the cessation of regular employment comes as a severe shock. Too many people die, at least mentally, when they reach the compulsory retirement age. Frustrations fill the following years. One must face the facts of aging and take stock periodically. A good practice is to figure the remaining years of life on an actuarial basis and make a written plan of proposed activities for creative retirement, including all of one's needs. The planning for these days and years includes various inventories—financial, medical, social, and personal. In planned programs one can, in the words of Clarence B. Randall, retired president of Inland Steel Company, "recapture control of one's life."

Helpful publications include *Looking Forward to the Later Years,* published by the U.S. Public Health Service and National Institute of Public Health, and *The Pre-retirement Manual,* issued by Senior Citizens. It is obvious that one who retires today or tomorrow must plan for a longer life than did his grandparents or parents. The gold watch presented at retirement can symbolize many golden years ahead.

Schools. Irving Lorge, who has done much research on the learning of adults, has stated, "Since the population is growing older, formal schooling must either last for a longer span of life or it must be supplemented." This is true for the undereducated as well as the educated citizens.

The three main types of schools engaged in furnishing adults with learning opportunities are (1) parochial, (2) private, and (3) public schools.

Parochial schools offer adult work in various forms. Many accent religious activities. Groups in churches and synagogues have done much in welcoming and educating strangers from other lands. One of the favorite forms of adult religious education is the so-called Sunday school.

For many years private correspondence schools have enrolled more new students annually than have entered the freshman classes of all universities and colleges. The merits of home study, including its economy, have been pointed out by the National Home Study Council.

Ambrose Caliver, chief of the adult education section of the U.S. Office of Education, has indicated that public schools should offer elementary and secondary school subjects on an accelerated basis: "The public school is the one agency best equipped to meet these demands; it belongs to the people, is located in the community, has the facilities and staff; and its financial support is accepted as a public responsibility." Homer Kempfer, director of the National Home Study Council, has added that "public-school adult education has been the fastest growing part of public education since World War II." A very helpful publication as a guide for administrators and teachers is *Public School Adult Education,* issued by the National Association of Public School Educators.

One institutionalized source of enlightenment is the so-called night school. The evening classes of universities, commonly offered under extension divisions, are opportunity schools for thousands of adults who, equipped with brief cases, inquiring minds, and pointed questions, nightly go willingly to school in order to learn and to earn undergraduate or graduate credit. In addition, numerous public and private night schools, usually held in school buildings, have become centers of community light and life. The work offered is academic on the elementary or secondary level, or recreational and cultural. Educational trips to museums and other cultural centers are popular. Consumer education, commercial courses, homemaking, and parental education are some of the practical phases of adult learning. In many cities expenses are defrayed by means of local school taxes, state contributions for part of instructors' salaries, and enrollment fees. In some cities more adults are enrolled in their opportunity schools than there are children in daytime attendance. The Denver, Colorado, opportunity school teaches thousands of adults and youth each year. Many so-called night schools are becoming opportunity schools for adults, with evening sessions, Sunday afternoon forums, and day meetings. The New York City school system, through its department of adult education, offers day courses for adults who cannot attend in the evening. The San Diego public school system offers a full-time day program of adult education in addition to night classes. In most cities informal noncredit courses are proving very popular.

Unfortunately, adult classes as conducted at

present are not drawing a proportionate share of older people. Yet many oldsters, through adult study classes, have gained a new surge of courage and a new joy in living. Older people can be buoyed up so that they talk of their recent accomplishments and current interests rather than of their remote past and alleged or actual physical infirmities. Many grandfathers and grandmothers have learned to ride a hobbyhorse youthfully by taking courses at night in schools attended in the daytime by their grandchildren.

Television. In Chapter 15, reference is made to television as equipment in modern education. Here the accent is on TV as a means of mass learning for adults, and on ETV as a tool designed for educating adults in the classroom and in the home.

It is estimated that television has an audience of 50 million Americans. In one week Americans may invest a billion clock hours in TV programs. Unfortunately, entertainment and commercials exceed the emphasis on educational programs.

However, Richard D. Heffner, program director of the Metropolitan Educational Television Association, recently wrote: "Indeed, it would seem that television is destined to have an even more fundamental impact on the traditional American educational structure than upon our patterns of entertainment."[10]

In 1952 the Federal Communications Commission set aside a limited number of nonprofit educational television stations. This helped to initiate the ETV movement, which is steadily growing, with the aid of such organizations as the Ford Foundation's Fund for Adult Education and the U.S. Office of Education. Through educational television, millions of older people are making up for what they have missed in earlier education, what they have neglected, what they have forgotten, and learning what they want for present and future use. As the

[10] Richard D. Heffner, "TV as Teacher: Of Adults, Too." *The New York Times Magazine*, August 17, 1958, p. 19.

electronic blackboard of the future, through such means as direct telecasts, closed-circuit programs, kinescopes, and other avenues, ETV is becoming one of the great hopes of tomorrow's adults.

Universities. As indicated in Chapter 8, the colleges and universities have long participated in programs of adult education. Examples of their programs are briefly mentioned here.

Alumni colleges are among the newer developments. Several colleges, among them Dartmouth, Wilson, Hope, and Barnard, hold alumni or alumnae college sessions which seek to refresh the minds of their graduates. This refresher college, which usually consists of a series of lectures and tours immediately following or preceding commencement or homecoming, is increasing in popularity among graduates, especially women. The American Association of University Women, the American Alumni Council, and countless other groups are interested in stimulating the minds of alumni through various phases of adult learning.

College courses of countless types are slanted toward adults. The University of California launched a series of evening lectures by space scientists in several California cities. The University of Wisconsin has offered several jiffy courses for short periods. The University of Chicago has added courses in the administration of adult education programs. The University of Colorado has offered work in a neglected subject, viz., common sense. For years the University of Illinois and other land-grant universities have provided annual winter short courses in agriculture. Boston University admits to the evening division without charge those persons over sixty-five years.

Extension courses and services are offered by most colleges, the latter being stressed by the land-grant colleges in agriculture and home economics. The Association of University Evening Colleges and the Center for Liberal Education for Adults have published a study of the evening colleges under the catchy caption *Ivory*

Towers in Market Places. Many institutions offering extension courses are affiliated with the National University Extension Association or the Teachers College Extension Association.

Research in gerontology is under way in numerous universities. For example, the federal government has given Albert Einstein College of Medicine of Yeshiva University a substantial grant for research on the medical and biological aspects of aging. The Kellogg Foundation has given grants for centers for continuing education to several universities. One of these centers of opportunity is located at Michigan State University, East Lansing, Michigan.

Vocations. Vocational education is one of the major fields of adult education in both public and private programs. Indeed, industry spends more money annually in the training of adult workers than is spent in the public elementary and secondary schools of the nation. For example, commercial airlines maintain schools for the training of pilots, mechanics, and stewardesses. Hospitals have training programs for nurses. Most industries operate extensive training programs for their salesmen. Even top executives go to school. General Electric sends its top managers to a three-month in-service training program at its Institute for Management Development and Research at Ossining, New York. Many companies send their executives to management-development training sessions sponsored by the American Management Association. The armed forces, of course, maintain a far-flung educational system for the training of officers and enlisted men. Countless other examples could be cited. Small wonder, then, that the number of adults currently participating in some form of adult education now exceeds the number of students in public elementary and secondary schools.

As automation becomes more widespread, old vocational skills become obsolete. Since many men seek two jobs, they often want training in a second occupation. With nearly a third of the adult women employed, the demand for vocational education for women is great. Thus many adults seek new vocational skills as a means of occupational advancement. Many adult education programs in public schools and colleges try to meet these needs. Vocational education courses meeting the Smith-Hughes requirements are offered in many vocational evening schools.

Worker Education. Related to the stress on vocational education for adults is labor education. Workers' education in its broad sense applies to everyone. In its unfortunate restricted meaning, it tends toward class difference in meeting the practical, educational, and cultural needs of a special group of adults, viz., industrial workers.

Its early growth in America consisted in the establishment of mechanics' institutes and evening classes which were largely brought about by workers themselves through trade unions and other agencies. A. J. Muste and others have been instrumental in developing labor colleges, which first came into existence about 1900. The International Ladies Garment Workers Union in 1916 started the first educational department among the American trade unions, to which have been added recreational and social activities. The Cafeteria Employees Union in New York City, through its educational director, has developed a well-rounded educational program for its members. In 1921 the Workers' Educational Bureau of America was established by members of trade unions and teachers to serve as a clearinghouse and as a guide in the development of the activities.

The organized labor movement wields a powerful influence in improving the working and living conditions of the older generation. Many unions have sponsored surveys of their retiring and retired members to ascertain their needs and wants. The United Auto Workers have used geriatrics experts to work out programs for their members. The Inter-university Labor Education Committee has published reports such as *Labor Education*. The publication of the Twentieth Century Fund under the title *Economic Needs of Older People* suggests better provision for senior citizens in the United States. One of the recent developments is the establishment of a National Institute of Labor Education to assist workers, through education, to develop their maximum effectiveness as individual human beings, as laborers and as citizens.

X—The Unknowns. In adult education programs are still many X's, or unknowns. The past has revealed certain facts about aging but much is left to be learned. The psychological factors in adult education are only partially known. Many types of programs are being tried but much remains to be known and done in developing a national, coordinated program.

Yardsticks. The curriculum in adult education has grown like Topsy and needs serious and prolonged evaluation. Wider use needs to be made of such yardsticks as *Measures for Evaluating Educational Programs for the Foreign Born,* and *Check Lists for Public School Adult Education Programs,* prepared by the U.S. Office of Education.

Zones. The various geographical areas in which adult education programs are carried out are: international, national, state, regional, and local. Procedures used in implementing programs in these areas are described in the following sections under Practices.

Practices

Supplemental to the programs already described, brief descriptions are here provided of some current illustrative practices in adult education, as found in the four geographical areas: (1) international, (2) national, (3) state, (4) local. These practices include governmental and nongovernmental activities.

International Procedures. The International Gerontological Congress is held annually in various countries of the world to discuss prob-

lems and to seek solutions for the aging, including their education and reeducation.

The program of the United States Operations Missions is basically adult education.

The United States National Commission for UNESCO maintains an active panel on adult education. Since nearly half the human race is still illiterate, one of the most significant movements in adult education is the fundamental education movement launched by UNESCO.

The World Confederation of Organizations of the Teaching Profession studies the role of adult education, particularly as related to the profession of teaching oldsters.

One of the greatest boons to cooperative adult education was the International Geophysical Year in which over sixty nations of the world participated. It has stimulated many people to take a lively interest in science and the interdependence of people.

National. Through direct, speeded-up classroom teaching and through developing reading materials suited to the interest and abilities of the men in service, the Department of Defense is waging a continuous war against illiteracy.

The off-duty study programs of the Department of Defense include such procedures as stimulating the use of libraries and counseling in the selection of correspondence courses from the United States Armed Forces Institute.

The Internal Revenue Service helps adults through publications, conferences, and telephone calls to prepare their income-tax returns.

Federal and state governments through their old-age relief, pensions, or insurance are helping to finance senescence so that fewer old people need to work. Thus they have more leisure for study and hobbies.

With the aid of federal funds, rural adult learning is stimulated through bookmobiles and agricultural and home extension services personalized by the county agent.

Through direct instruction in its classrooms, the federal government provides thousands of adults on its payrolls with opportunities to learn in government schools, such as the part-time graduate school of the Department of Agriculture, and orientation workshops for those going into overseas services.

Programs of informal and formal education are being carried forward aggressively in federal territories, dependencies, and Indian reservations.

Classrooms, libraries, and teachers help provide correctional education in prisons and reformatories. According to a survey conducted by the Bureau of Prisons, the typical inmate of a federal prison reads from five to ten times as many books a year, preferably nonfiction, as does the average citizen.

The federal government helps states and communities to rehabilitate the physically handicapped.

The United States Employment Service provides counseling services, career materials, and placement procedures, especially for older persons.

Through their organizational procedures, dozens of national nongovernmental organizations promote adult learning.

The National Commission for Adult Literacy, a nongovernmental agency, has been established by the Adult Education Association of the United States.

The American Legion issued thousands of booklets, written simply, with language keyed to a basic 1000-word vocabulary, and with readability tested through reader surveys.

The American Library Association and other groups have published books for adult beginners, geared to the reading ability and interests of older learners. The Association also spearheads many campaigns such as Library Week.

The American Medical Association, colleges of medicine, and other organizations and institutions are stimulating and evaluating work in gerontology. National conferences on aging are held periodically.

The National Recreation Association is providing interesting programs for elders in the proprietary nursing homes in the country.

Specialists with technical know-how in adult and post-high school education have been added to the staffs of organizations such as the National Education Association.

The Center for the Study of Liberal Education for Adults works with member institutions of the Association of Evening Colleges in experimental liberal arts discussion groups.

Personalized adult reeducation is furnished by Alcoholics Anonymous through the rehabilitation of alcoholics.

The American Council on Education, through its Commission on the Implications of Armed Services Educational Programs, made descriptive and evaluative studies of adult education as reported in *The Armed Services and Adult Education*.

The Bureau of Immigration and Naturalization of the United States government sends to public schools the names of new arrivals and of applicants for citizenship. These lists have been helpful in recruiting adults for Americanization classes.

The Displaced Persons Commission has developed functional programs for refugees who come here to begin a new life.

The third Sunday in May has been designated by Congress as I Am an American Day. On this day ceremonies are held for those foreign-born persons who become citizens through naturalization, and also for those native-born who come of age.

State. Several commonwealths have established commissions on aging which help to set goals and programs and to implement them with appropriate procedures.

Many states are giving legal recognition and financial support to adult education as an integral part of the public school system.

Several state departments of education have appointed full-time or part-time directors of adult education to help improve programs and practices in the area.

A sampling of some state practices in adult education are mentioned by states:

Georgia. The Kellogg Foundation and the State of Georgia recently erected the most complete building thus far designed exclusively for adult education. Here are flexible facilities for counseling, conferences, institutes, seminars, and short courses.

Illinois. The state legislature created the Gerontological Committee at the University of Illinois to study the economic problems of older workers, to develop research programs, and to issue informational pamphlets.

Massachusetts. Massachusetts has passed a law to restrain employers from discriminating against older workers in hiring and firing.

New York. Through the work of the Joint Legislative Committee on Problems of the Aging, state aid is made available on a 50-50 matching basis for cities to establish day centers and Golden Age clubs for the aged.

Wisconsin. The state created an Interdepartmental Committee on Aging Population which makes a biennial report on progress of programs for the aged in Wisconsin.

Many interesting and helpful programs and practices are described in *The States and Their Older Citizens*, published by the Council of the State Governments.

Local. Hundreds of communities have adult education councils. One of the oldest is the Denver Council, which publishes a monthly periodical.

Many school buildings have become civic and community centers. For example, the Bakersfield, California, elementary schools serve the adult population of the community.

Hundreds of cities have adult clubs. Cleveland, Ohio, has organized a Senior Council of blue-chip executives.

Many industries conduct their own educational programs for their employees. In large corporations, the cost of these programs sometimes exceeds the budgets of large universities.

Labor unions operate several local adult centers. In Detroit, Michigan, unions have drop-in centers where workers can use hobby facilities, see and hear television, and attend social programs.

In some cities a pool of older experienced clerical and office workers is made available for business places. Chicago, Illinois, has a private agency, Senior Achievement, Inc., which hires older workers for others.

Television courses for credit are offered in many communities. In Chicago, Illinois, many adults take junior college courses via television at home. The University of Detroit offers a full college curriculum with credit via television.

Countless courses, credit and noncredit, are offered by local adult education councils, Bloomington, Illinois, has one on lip reading and another on auto driving.

These are a few of the practices, indicating that adult education is flourishing at the grass roots.

Future

Adult education has been born of specific needs—education for Americanization, education for vocation, education for national defense, and education for social needs. In one form or another, adult education has met most of these needs well.

However, it is probable that in the future adult education will go beyond meeting the overt day-to-day needs of people. It will become more attuned to the long range social, economic, and cultural forces of society. In other words, adult education of the future will not be so preoccupied with the practical that liberal education is lost.

It is evident that the spectacular expansion of adult education will continue. Man's increased leisure, longer life, and changing needs accentuate his thirst for continued learning.

The poet W. H. Auden speaks informally of his art to advanced students and interested adults at Columbia University.

The explosive rate of growth of new knowledge and the accelerating obsolescence of old knowledge will intensify the need for continuing education throughout life. There will be larger enrollments, broader curriculums, and more programs. Adult education will continue to be manifest in a large variety of programs and sponsors. Indeed, this diversity is one of the great strengths of adult education in meeting such a large variety of needs and clientele. Churches, industries, and other organizations are already manifesting vigorous effort in planning adult programs.

The number of public school systems offering adult education programs will undoubtedly increase, stimulated in part by the American Association of School Administrators' resolution in 1959 that "a comprehensive and diversified educational program for adults should be an integral part of every public school system."

Institutions of higher education will continue to reach for new formats for adult education. The continuing education centers will increase and flourish. The community college will play an increasingly important role and will make adult education more widely available geographically. Research will continue to broaden our knowledge of adults and how they learn. This will lead to newer and better methods of teaching, including case studies, role playing, audio-visual aids, brain-storming, and other informal methods rather than the traditional methodology. Adult education faculties will become better trained, more highly skilled, and more professional.

Undoubtedly adult education will become the *fifth* level of education. Then the other four areas—pre-elementary, elementary, secondary, and higher—may be free of teaching those things needed only in adult life. There will be less need for younger learners to cold storage knowledge for adulthood.

Summary

A baby born in 1960 will live the oft-quoted Biblical quota of threescore and ten years. With the increase in the length of life, in the number of older people, in the amount of leisure time, adult education is a must for the United States. A dynamic democracy supplements the three R's with the three L's—life-long learning.

Informal adult education is as old as history. The wigwams of the American Indians were centers of culture before the twentieth century pitched its chautauqua tents. Formal learning for senior citizens has been greatly accelerated and expanded. Adult education has become a mighty mass movement, pivoting around personal preferences.

One of the goals of continuous learning is to keep America democratic and free. The Council of State Governments has prepared a set of propulsive purposes for adult education. Developmental tasks in early, middle, and later life call for clear purposes and planned programs.

The objectives are being implemented by a multifaceted program through the four levels of education—pre-elementary, elementary, secondary, and higher. The learning activities spread their initial letters across the entire alphabet.

Varied and venturesome practices are found in the many countries around the world, in this nation in the 50 states, and in thousands of local communities where adult education thrives at the grass roots.

Adult education may become the fifth level of learning. Then the other four areas can be freed of the necessity for containing subjects and courses needed only in adult life. With medicine increasing the length of life, and automation adding to the amount of leisure time, tomorrow's adult will have more time, through added education, to create desirable changes in the world itself and within himself. He will enjoy his maturity and seniority. He will help "the sunset paint the sky before it goes," and will "see beyond the sunset to the sunrise."

Suggested activities

1. Review the development of education for adults as found in the historical calendar in this chapter.
2. List great men who made contributions to civilization after reaching sixty years of age.
3. Discuss the role of the public school in the education of adults.
4. Describe programs for vocational education and rehabilitation for adults.
5. List some informal means of adult education.
6. List all agencies in your community which are directly or indirectly connected with adult education.
7. Write a brief history of some phase of adult education, such as the labor colleges, the chautauquas, religious activities, and others.
8. Describe the program of adult education in a foreign country.

9. Make a case study of some adult who is enrolled in a night school.
10. Report on one of the scientific investigations of the learning ability of adults.
11. Report some implications for education re-

sulting from the fact that America as a nation is growing older.

12. List desirable qualifications for a teacher of adults. Do you possess these qualifications?

Bibliography

Books

Clark, Harold F., and Harold S. Sloan: *Classrooms in the Factories*, New York University Press, New York, 1959, chap. 9. Describes the tremendous scope and interesting nature of adult education programs conducted by industry.

Clift, David H. (ed.) : *Adult Reading*, University of Chicago Press, Chicago, 1956. Experts report on the state of adult reading—the reader himself, how well, what, and why he reads.

Dyer, John D.: *Ivory Towers in the Market Place*, The Bobbs-Merrill Company, Inc., Indianapolis, 1956. Examines the nature of the evening college, its practices, problems, and role in American society.

Gratton, C. Hartley: *In Quest of Knowledge*, Association Press, New York, 1955. A popularly written history of man's efforts to continue his learning through adulthood, with a look at the future of adult education.

Kempfer, Homer: *Adult Education*, McGraw-Hill Book Company, Inc., New York, 1955. Discusses program development and evaluation, organization and administration of adult education.

Olds, Edward B.: *Financing Adult Education*, U.S. Office of Education, Government Printing Office, Washington, D.C., n.d. Scholarly report on costs and sources of revenue for adult education programs.

Powell, John W.: *Learning Comes of Age*, Association Press, New York, 1956. A description of adult education programs in libraries, public schools, voluntary groups, and other institutions.

Sheats, Paul H., Clarence D. Jayne, and Ralph B.

Spence: *Adult Education: The Community Approach*, The Dryden Press, Inc., New York, 1953. Describes the role of community agencies in adult education.

Periodicals

Crabtree, Arthur P.: "What Adult Education Is—And Is Not," *The New York Times Magazine*, May 27, 1956, pp. 20f. Adult education is not a hodgepodge of activities to occupy the idle, but should be education in its best sense.

Erdman, Loula G.: "Night College for the Wide Open Spaces," *NEA Journal*, vol. 44 (September, 1955), pp. 337–338. Describes an adult evening school, the variety of its students and their thirst for knowledge.

Henriksen, G. C.: "You Have a Job in Adult Education," *The School Executive*, vol. 76 (July, 1957), pp. 64–67. Suggests the mission of the public school in the adult education field and how to make programs popular.

Holmbraker, Harry R., Jr., and L. C. Reynolds: "The Public Adult School," *NEA Journal*, vol 48 (May, 1959), pp. 45–46. Argues that adult education is a public concern and thus the logical prerogative of the public school system which also becomes its beneficiary.

Knowles, Malcolm S.: "Adult Education in the United States," *Adult Education*, vol. 5 (Winter, 1955), pp. 67–75. Presents brief history of adult education, national and local adult education organizations, new methods and knowledge, scope and quantity of adult education.

———: "Charting the Course of Adult Education in America's Future," *Adult Leadership*, vol. 6 (October, 1957), pp. 99–102. Discusses the various functions of adult education, its current status and trends, and probable future course.

———: "What Should You Know about Adult Education?" *The School Executive*, vol. 77 (August, 1958), pp. 19–21. Expresses the need for adult education and how to plan programs to meet the needs of adults.

Luke, Robert A.: "The Cost of Adult Under-education," *NEA Journal*, vol. 45 (October, 1956), pp. 428–429. Shows the economic liability of undereducated adults and the need for expansion of adult education to reach more people.

Radcliffe, Charles H., and John B. Holden: "Adults in the Public Schools," *School Life*, vol. 40 (April, 1958), pp. 7–10. Describes the extent and nature of adult education in the United States.

Strub, Grace F.: "Adult Education Facilities," *The School Executive*, vol. 77 (November, 1957), pp. 43–53. Portrays the kind of school buildings and facilities needed to house a good program of adult education.

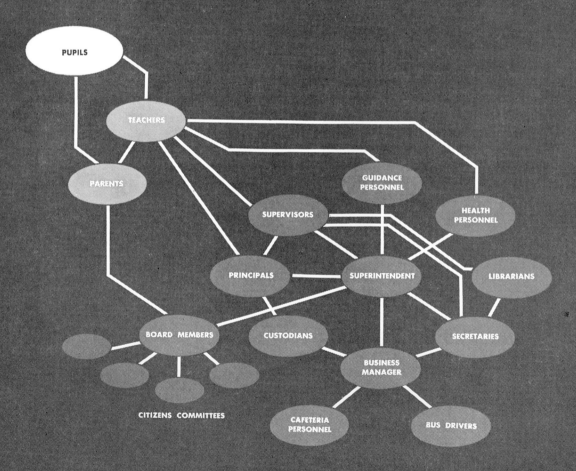

PART THREE

PUPILS

TEACHERS

PARENTS

GUIDANCE
PERSONNEL

SUPERVISORS

HEALTH
PERSONNEL

PRINCIPALS

SUPERINTENDENT

LIBRARIANS

BOARD MEMBERS

CUSTODIANS

SECRETARIES

BUSINESS
MANAGER

CITIZENS COMMITTEES

CAFETERIA
PERSONNEL

BUS DRIVERS

Personnel
in education

The administrative structure of American education and the various academic levels are avenues through which constantly flow the influence of the educational personnel. The human factor is paramount. Numerically, one in four persons in the United States is actively engaged in education as learner or teacher.

As indicated in the facing figure, the child is the focus surrounded by the major persons that influence him—teachers, parents, principals, and other school personnel. The school exists primarily for the pupil. The child grows and develops in at least four dimensions: physical, mental, social, and spiritual. Many children are atypical—they deviate from the norm sufficiently to warrant special consideration and treatment. Modern society treasures the child, be he gifted, normal, or atypical (Chapter 10).

Among the persons who exert an abiding influence upon the child is the teacher. The pupil and the teacher are joint partners in learning and teaching. The teacher is not an automaton but a human worker, who should be well educated and professionally alert. Teaching is becoming more of a profession. Standards for selection, as well as preservice and in-service education, are being elevated. Teacher welfare provisions are being improved. The great shortage of well-qualified teachers constitutes a threat to the welfare of the nation (Chapter 11).

The classroom teacher, however, is but one of the numerous persons engaged in education in the United States. Special teachers, administrative and supervisory officers, educational personnel from other professions, and other nonteachers contribute to the education of the well-rounded pupil. The opportunities to serve in educational work are numerous and varied. Persons not interested in direct classroom teaching can find many opportunities for other significant service. No economy is so shortsighted as that which dictates the employment of unqualified personnel in education, where human values are paramount (Chapter 12).

chapter **10**

Pupils

A story is told of Colonel Francis Parker, the pioneering educator who came to Quincy, Massachusetts, as superintendent of schools. When asked by many of his teachers to explain his theory about the place of the individual in education, Parker called a faculty meeting. When the teachers were assembled, Parker entered with a little girl at his side whom he seated at the front of the room. He then gave the shortest and most insightful address in the annals of education: "My fellow teachers, you have asked me to tell you why we are making changes in our schools." Placing his hand on the little girl's shoulder he said, "Here is your answer." He then left them wondering and thinking.

Parents, teachers, and administrators sometimes become so preoccupied with the *means* of education—buildings, books, budgets, buses—that they lose sight of the *ends* of education—pupils. To teach a child is to understand and respect him. Thus attention to children and youth becomes the heart of a teacher's work.

In recent years the behavioral sciences have yielded new knowledge of the growth and development of children and youth. This understanding points the way toward better adaptation of the school to the unique needs of the pupil and toward more effective teaching.

Although certain patterns of mental, physical, emotional, and social growth are fairly common, each child is a unique organism. Public education in a democratic society is responsible for nurturing the full development of each of these organisms to the maximum of his potential, regardless of how great or modest that potential may be. American education is founded on the belief that mass education does not deny respect and care for the individual, that quantity and quality in education can coexist. To meet this challenge demands attention to the normal or average child as well as concern for the exceptional child—the mentally, physically, emotionally, or socially atypical child.

Foundations

Since his earliest recorded history, man has been engaged in the study of children and youth. The story of educational progress is, in large measure, the story of deeper understanding of the learner. The lifeblood of a democratic society is a dynamic educational system, free to all, and attuned to the needs, interests, and abilities of all.

The American people have given expression to society's responsibility to children in a number of ways. One of the most statesmanlike pronouncements is the Pledge to Children adopted by the Midcentury White House Conference on Children and Youth (see page 227):

Aware that these promises to you cannot be fully met in a world at war, we ask you to join us in a firm dedication to the building of a world society based on freedom, justice and mutual respect.

SO MAY YOU grow in joy, in faith in God and in man, and in those qualities of vision and of the spirit that will sustain us all and give us new hope for the future.

The Individual Pupil. Joy Elmer Morgan, one-time editor of the *NEA Journal*, has expressed thus the importance of the child:

Let us set the child in our midst as our greatest wealth and our most challenging responsibility. Let us exalt him above industry, above business, above politics, above all the petty and selfish things that weaken and destroy a people. Let us know that the race moves forward through its children, and by the grace of Almighty God, setting our faces toward the morning, dedicate ourselves anew to the service and the welfare of childhood.

As every parent thinks and lives in terms of his child, so too the teacher thinks first of the child and second of the subject matter. The White House Conference on Children in a Democracy stated, "The supreme educational and social importance of individual traits should be recognized throughout the educational system."

The Educational Policies Commission considers the supreme importance of the individual as the basic moral value in American life:

The inherent worth of every human being is basic in the teaching of Christianity and of many other great religions. . . . This doctrine sharply challenges every form of oppression. It implies that each human being should have every possible opportunity to achieve by his own efforts a feeling of security and competence in dealing with the problems arising in daily life. . . . In educational terms, this value requires a school system which, by making freely available the common heritage of human association and human culture, opens to every child the opportunity to grow to his full physical, intellectual, moral, and spiritual stature. . . . By exploring and acknowledging the capacities of each child, education seeks to develop all of his creative powers, to encourage him to feel that he can do things of value, that he belongs, and that he is wanted. . . .

It assigns no superior moral status, but rather a more definite moral responsibility, to the strong and the able. It endeavors to arouse in each individual a profound sense of self-respect and personal integrity.[1]

Understanding a Child. All children must be studied longitudinally over accumulating years and horizontally through all areas of their living. Good teachers study their pupils as well as their lessons; they learn about pupils while teaching them. Among the experimental methods used in child study are: questionnaires and direct questioning, systematic observation, standardized tests, ratings, projective techniques, parallel groups, laboratory techniques, case histories, and parental interviews.

A pupil, like any human being, is a biological organism, consisting of skin, bones, muscles, nerves, glands, organs of special sense, a digestive system, and a circulatory system, working interdependently. Integration in its restricted sense exists within the pupil rather than between bits of subject matter. An inte-

[1] Educational Policies Commission, *Moral and Spiritual Values in the Public Schools*, National Education Association, Washington, D.C., 1951, pp. 18–19.

What are forward-looking schools doing to emphasize individual development and personality and to realize the potentialities of every youth?

They test pupils to discover interests, needs, and abilities . . .

and provide special correctional activities for handicapped children.

Whenever possible, they encourage atypical children, like this blind boy, to continue in the regular classroom . . .

grat*ing* child who adapts himself at all levels of learning and life is the goal rather than an integrat*ed* mass. To this end the teacher should be familiar with the developmental patterns at various levels as revealed in numerous current texts on child growth. Furthermore, the teacher ought to understand lifelong human growth and development.

Child growth and development

Basic Principles. The *increased* understanding of children is fundamental to the task of teaching children. Complete understanding is never reached but increased understanding is achieved through study of the expanding body of knowledge concerning child growth and development. Certain generalizations can be made from this knowledge:

1. Children's behavior is influenced by many complex and often obscure causes. Behavior is based upon past experiences, shaped by present circumstances, and influenced by hopes and plans for the future.

2. Learning is a natural process, although the capacity for learning varies widely among individuals. When a child fails to learn it is because some impediment has arisen to obstruct learning.

and for those too severely handicapped, special bedside instruction is provided.

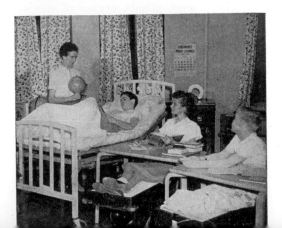

Good schools help youngsters
learn through experiment . . .

exploring vocational fields . . .

using a variety
of instructional media . . .

and encouraging self-expression through
drama, dance, music, writing, and the arts.

3. Each child is unique. He not only differs from others but is in a constant process of change himself. Individual differences increase as children grow older.
4. All children have some potential for growth and development. None are so hopeless as to merit rejection.
5. The entire human organism is involved in learning and development. Mental development cannot be considered in isolation from the learner's physical, social, and emotional well-being.
6. Child growth is continuous but not constant. Various developmental stages are discernible among children, but growth varies among children. Learning tasks must be attuned to the individual learner's readiness and stage of development.
7. Children are influenced greatly by the values of the groups to which they belong. To understand a child is to understand his family and his comrades.

The teacher's skill in understanding children can be extended greatly through systematic observation and study. Successful teaching is hardly possible without deep understanding of children.

A long-time observer of the child, Dr. Arnold L. Gesell, formerly of the Yale University Clinic of Child Development, studied youngsters for forty years. His research indicates that "there is a basic ground plan of growth peculiar to the species, and always a variation of the ground plan distinctive for the individual."

Developmental Periods. Although the divisions are not clear-cut, it is helpful to think of human life as comprising several developmental stages:
1. The *prenatal period* extends from conception to birth, a period of about nine months. Physical health in later life is influenced by this period.
2. *Infancy* is the period from birth until approximately two years of age. This is a

period of great physical growth and an extremely formative period of life.
3. *Childhood* includes the years from age two to puberty. Intellectual development is quite rapid during this period.
4. *Adolescence* extends from puberty, which begins from eleven to thirteen—somewhat later for boys than girls—until maturity is reached at about age twenty-one. This is a period of rapid physical growth and a period of difficult adjustment from childhood to adulthood.
5. *Early adulthood* may be regarded as the years from the early twenties to about age forty-five, the period when most people are most productive and independent.
6. *Middle adulthood* includes the period from the mid-forties until retirement, often about age sixty-five. This is a period of transition from the full vigor of maturity to the slackened pace of later years.
7. *Later adulthood* is the period in life after retirement. As the human life span is extended and better health achieved, this period of life takes on new significance and is no longer regarded as borrowed time.

Most normal individuals pass through these major stages.

Phases of Growth. A pupil, typical or atypical, has not one but several ages. He may have simultaneously a chronological age, which is his actual span of life in years; a mental age, which is his ability to perform certain intellectual tasks; an educational age, which usually denotes his academic level of achievement; a physical age, which ranks him among his colleagues in such matters as stature and weight; an emotional age, which may be revealed in his affective behavior; a social age, which depends greatly upon his experiences with people; a vocational age, which may provide much of the drive for completing his studies; and an avocational age, which in an activity like stamp collecting may place a sixth grader high above a college student. Unevenness may exist in these various ages within a pupil, especially if there is poorly synchronized growth among the different systems of the body. Through cumulative continuous growth the individual pupil becomes a well-balanced person in all areas of living.

An excellent description of all-round growth and development is furnished by that great textbook of life, the Bible, in this account of the early life of the Great Teacher: "And Jesus increased in wisdom and stature, and in favor with God and man" (Luke 2:52). He increased in wisdom (mentally), in stature (physically), in favor with God (spiritually), and man (socially). The teacher and parent should promote this four-dimensional growth for every child.

Mental Development. One of the most important facets of human growth from the standpoint of the school is mental development. The growing mind is an integral part of the growing organism. Healthy mental development is dependent upon wholesome physical, emotional, and social development. This important point was not recognized by early theories of psychology and is still missed by many critics who fail to appreciate the importance of the school's attention to the total development of the child. Pleas for exclusive concentration by the school on the mental development of the child—without regard for his physical, social and emotional well-being—are not in accord with modern knowledge of psychology. A hungry or frightened child can not learn effectively. Before learning can take place, it is often necessary for the school to help the child establish a sense of security and belonging, a feeling of personal importance.

The comparison of the human mind with clay has often been used. This analogy is most faulty because it suggests that the mind—like clay—can be made over by strong external pressures. However, the mind is molded largely from within through the forces of growth. Since growth may be influenced by external forces applied to the environment, intelligent concepts of shaping mental development must begin with the idea of stimulating wholesome growth through environmental influences.

Intelligence may be defined as the *capacity* for learning. It must be emphasized that intelligence is an important factor, but not the only factor affecting the learner's progress in school. It was generally believed that this mental capacity, or intelligence, was determined largely by heredity and that it remained fairly constant throughout life. However, a number of recent investigations suggest that it is possible under certain conditions to accelerate the rate of mental growth. For example, gains up to three points in the intelligence quotient have been registered in cases where students have had the benefit of nursery education or where mentally retarded children have received special class instruction. This and other evidence suggest that the child's intelligence is somewhat dynamic and not entirely a fixed characteristic. Apparently mental development is influenced by the child's environment somewhat more than was once believed.

Intelligence is commonly measured by the IQ, or intelligence quotient. This is the quotient obtained when mental age is divided by chronological age. Thus a six-year-old child with a mental age of nine would have an IQ of 150. (The decimal point which would normally appear between the 1 and 5 is dropped.)

The child's academic achievement in school is commonly measured by standardized tests which express results in terms of normal achievement for students of a certain age. This measure is sometimes referred to as educational age. By comparing the learner's educational age with his mental age, it is possible to determine whether or not his achievement is commensurate with his capacity.

Physical Growth. Rapid growth takes place during the prenatal period. The human organism develops from a single cell to a complex system capable of many activities in a short span of nine months. Birth, therefore, is not really the beginning of life and growth but rather an important change in the environment of the human organism.

After birth the infant grows very rapidly in height and weight. However, this rate of growth is vastly slower than that during the prenatal period and the rate actually slows down progressively from birth to maturity. Legs grow more rapidly than the trunk and head during infancy. The brain also grows quite rapidly. Muscles grow fast during infancy, and many complex physical skills, such as walking and talking, are acquired during this period.

Gradually the rate of physical growth in children decelerates until about nine to thirteen years of age when another spurt of growth continues for two or three years. For the first decade of life boys and girls grow at about the same rate. But puberty overtakes girls earlier than boys with the result that girls from eleven to fifteen are heavier and taller than most boys of the same age. At fifteen or sixteen, girls' rate of growth slows markedly while boys continue to grow until about age twenty. After twenty most people continue to grow in weight but not in height.

During surges of growth, children need greater energy to sustain the growth itself. During these periods they find it more difficult to study and to withstand strain. This is often a difficult period for their parents and teachers, as well as for the children. Anything which disturbs a child or youth may interrupt his growth. Maladjustment at school, anxiety, disease, emotional disturbances, and other factors may retard normal growth. When a child fails to grow or loses weight, something is interfering with his normal well-being and is cause for alarm. On the other hand, spurts of growth occur at slightly different times for different children. If this is not understood, undue alarm may result from normal periods of slow growth.

Tallness and shortness are partly hereditary. Environment and nutrition also have an effect upon growth. Studies seem to indicate that each generation is slightly taller and healthier than preceding generations. There are still many aspects of human physical growth which are not understood.

For example, it is known that physical growth is related to intellectual and emotional growth but the exact nature of these relationships is not fully understood. In many ways, the school seeks to insure wholesome physical growth. Throughout the school program, instruction is offered on health and safety. Physical education is also an important part of the school curriculum. The school lunch program was initiated to improve the nutrition of school children. Most schools provide periodic physical and dental examinations for school children and youth. Nurses, psychologists, dental hygienists, and other health specialists are becoming more commonplace on public school staffs.

Social and Emotional Development. Children mature socially and emotionally as well as physically and mentally. Social and emotional maturity are related to other facets of development. For example, children of advanced mental maturity tend to be more advanced socially and are larger and stronger physically as well. However, this is a general rule to which there are many exceptions.

One of the first tasks of social development is the adjustment of the child in his transition from home to school. This means extending his social attachments from his immediate family to his peers. This is an enormous adjustment for children to make and some accomplish it only with extreme difficulty. Nursery schools and kindergartens help to ease the burden. This transformation from home to school involves also the adjustment from the small, simple group of the home to the large complex groups of the school. Not only is the new group foreign but it is also much larger than was customary at home.

As the child becomes a member of a large and more complex group, he becomes more aware of and responsive to others. The rugged individualist gives way to the social conformer.

He learns to be more sensitive to the feelings of others, more cooperative in groups. He forms strong attachments to peer groups and participates more effectively in team sports, gangs, clubs, and other cooperative activities.

As the child reaches puberty he acquires greater understanding and acceptance of himself. He develops more confident relations with both peers and adults. While he still needs guidance and support from family, he is becoming less dependent upon parents. However, puberty presents a special social problem since girls mature more rapidly than boys during this period. Children of the same age but different sex, in the same classes in school, have quite different attitudes toward the opposite sex. Girls at this age are quite interested in boys who—alas!—are likely to hold girls in disdain. Fortunately this condition does not continue for long.

As adolescence is reached, boy-girl relationships become more mature. But rapid sexual maturation poses difficult new problems. Relationships with the opposite sex are one of the most difficult problems of teen-agers. Adolescence is a turbulent period of development. At one moment a parent or teacher is insisting that "you are now old enough to. . ."; and the next moment the child is reminded that "you can't do that yet, you're much too young." Physical growth is rapid—sometimes too rapid from the standpoint of poise and grace. The adolescent yearns for the independence of adulthood but, at the same time, is perhaps frightened by the prospect of it. Adolescence is characterized by a strong need to conform to the mores of peers. Habits of dress, talk, and other manifestations are powerfully influenced by the gang, often to the consternation of parents. Adolescence is indeed a period of great turbulence and stress. If parents and teachers find difficulty understanding adolescents during this period, it is not unusual, because in all probability teen-agers don't understand themselves!

The social development of children and youth can be strengthened immeasurably by the school. Fine schools do not leave social maturation to chance. Opportunity is given children within the school program to develop wholesome understanding and relationships with others. Life adjustment programs, in spite of the severe criticism which they have suffered in recent years, have made a significant contribution toward the wholesome social and emotional development of youth.

The key person in the school environment is the teacher. More than any other adult in the school environment, the teacher is in intimate contact with the child. Thus the teacher is in better position to observe symptoms of social or emotional difficulties. If the teacher is sympathetic and understanding, if he can establish good rapport with students, they will often turn to him for counsel. This day-to-day, informal counseling of students by understanding teachers is one of the great but less well-known contributions of education to the growth and development of wholesome children and youth.

One of the great bastions of American melting-pot society has been the role of the public school in socializing millions of young people of diverse backgrounds. By learning and playing together in the public schools in their formative years, they have developed mutual respect and understanding that withstand the strains of later years.

Moral Development. Ethical, moral, and spiritual development are important dimensions of human growth. But herein lies one of the great dilemmas of American education. nonsecular schools While recognizing the importance of moral and spiritual values on the one hand, American society has also insisted quite properly upon the separation of church and state. Thus it has been considered inappropriate, indeed unconstitutional, for public schools to offer religious instruction on school premises, even on a voluntary attendance basis. Many parents, concerned about the importance of providing religious instruction, have chosen to send their children to private sectarian schools, a right upheld by the courts. However, in the minds of many, this is not the end of the dilemma. For, it is argued, when large numbers of children are separated in school attendance on a religious basis, the socialization of children of diverse backgrounds and beliefs, mentioned earlier in this chapter, is weakened.

The Educational Policies Commission, in a pronouncement on this dilemma, reached a number of important agreements:

1. The American people, regardless of religion, are agreed upon certain basic values and standards of behavior.
2. These moral and spiritual values should be stated as aims of the school.
3. All of the school's resources should be used to teach moral and spiritual values, but without sectarian indoctrination.
4. The public schools should guard religious freedom and tolerance and be friendly toward all religions.
5. The home is the greatest single factor in forming character.
6. But powerful community forces may work against the schools and the home in developing higher moral and spiritual conduct.[2]

Actually, there is no complete solution that is acceptable to all in this dilemma. Inevitably, the public schools are caught in the center of opposing charges. Some will complain that they are godless while others will insist that they must remain that way. In any event, it can be agreed that it is important for public schools to inculcate high moral and ethical standards of conduct in young people and, at the same time, to avoid sectarian indoctrination.

Exceptional children

As mentioned earlier, children are subject to wide individual differences in their physical, mental, social, and emotional development. Children who differ so widely from the normal or average as to require substantial modifica-

tions in their educational environment are regarded as exceptional or atypical children. The aspect of education related to meeting the needs of exceptional children is usually referred to as special education.

It is helpful to consider exceptional children in four basic categories: mentally, physically, socially, and emotionally atypical. In their mental development, children range all the way from young geniuses to youngsters that are entirely uneducable. Children are often classified according to their mental ability into several groups: the gifted or talented, the normal or average, and the mentally retarded. Physically atypical children may be further categorized into four basic classes: the visually handicapped, the crippled or orthopedically handicapped, the aurally handicapped, and the orally handicapped. Socially and emotionally distressed children also present special educational problems.

Some children are mildly handicapped, requiring only minor modifications in the regular classroom environment. Others are substantially handicapped, requiring special classes or special schools. Others are so severely handicapped that they cannot attend school at all. Some youngsters suffer from multiple handicaps. Unfortunately, many school districts are unable to meet fully the needs of handicapped children.

Dr. Howard Rusk, a physician at New York University's Bellevue Medical Center and an eminent authority on the rehabilitation of the handicapped, has emphasized two fundamental principles concerning the education of exceptional children.[3] First, he insists that public education is the inalienable right of every child, the handicapped child not excepted. He warns against the easy shirking of this responsibility by rationalizing that "this child doesn't belong in this school." He points out that the handicapped child's ability to accommodate to the school environment frequently exceeds the

[2] Adapted from Educational Policies Commission, *Moral and Spiritual Values in the Public Schools*, National Education Association, Washington, D.C., 1951.

[3] Howard A. Rusk, "Square Pegs in Round Holes," *NEA Journal*, vol. 47 (December, 1958), p. 608.

school's willingness to make adaptations. Second, Dr. Rusk insists that handicapped children are essentially like normal children. That is, they are children first and handicapped children second.

Any plans for the education of handicapped children must be based on recognition of both their basic needs as children and their special needs as handicapped children. Frequently, the special needs of these children are such that they can be met best with those services we term "special education."

Sound educational principles dictate that these special-education services should be applied only when they are demanded by the needs of the child. The regular classroom is the best educational environment for any child to meet his basic needs.[4]

The processes of learning and development are not easy for children. They are even more difficult for the handicapped child. The teaching of exceptional children demands even greater ingenuity, patience, and resourcefulness than teaching the normal child. All too often parents, teachers, and classmates aggravate the handicapped child's adjustment through overt deference and sympathy to him. It is rather difficult to steer a wise course between coddling and rejecting the atypical child. The atypical child needs to experience security, joy, opportunity, and satisfaction of accomplishment just as any normal child. More and better ways must be found to meet the special needs of the atypical child, in the regular school classroom as much as possible, but in special classes or schools when necessary.

The International Council for Exceptional Children was established in 1922:

1. To unite those interested in the educational problems of the special child
2. To emphasize the education of the special child rather than his identification or classification
3. To establish professional standards for teachers in the field of special education

[4] *Ibid.*, p. 608.

Mentally gifted

Concern for the mentally gifted child is by no means new. Nearly a century ago Thomas Huxley wrote that "the most important object of all educational schemes is to catch these exceptional people and turn them to account for the good of society." Eminent educational psychologists, such as Lewis Terman, Robert Havighurst, Paul Witty, and others have been concerned with the education of gifted children for decades. But the recent explosion of technological advancement has focused new attention dramatically upon the shortage of top manpower and has precipitated one of the most vigorous academic talent hunts known to man. The great intensification of interest in finding and developing top intellectual talent is one of the most significant and widespread developments of the current decade.

Good teachers and good schools have always sought ways of identifying and encouraging able students. On the other hand, many teachers have found it easy to become preoccupied with helping slow learners and assumed that the bright students would take care of themselves. With little effort, either on the part of the teacher or the learner, these students usually did meet academic standards geared to the average ability of the group. However, in too many instances they were not challenged to the full measure of their ability. Too often they became indifferent. Conant's study of American high schools, cited in Chapter 7, points out this lack in many high schools.

Who Are the Gifted? There is no universally accepted definition of the mentally gifted—sometimes referred to also as talented or superior. For example, one writer defines the term to include the upper 2 per cent of the school age population; another's definition would include the upper 25 per cent of all children. Perhaps the most common concept of the academically gifted child would include those with IQs exceeding 125 or 130. These learners can be identified by standardized intelligence tests, marks, and teachers' judgments. The term "giftedness" can be applied, of course, to a variety of talents. A child may be gifted in reading but not in art.

The old stereotype of the shy, stooped, little, unhealthy genius is not supported by the evidence. Research studies indicate that, although there are many individual variations, the intellectually gifted person is usually superior in other ways as well. Physically they are taller, stronger, and healthier than average. Socially, they are more confident and better poised. They are likely to seek association with older children rather than children of their own age. Gifted children come from all races and from all strata of society.

What are good schools doing to encourage the gifted?

Here are examples from the arts . . .

the sciences . . .

Intellectually, the gifted child of course learns more easily and rapidly. He possesses superior ability in reasoning and generalizing. He can deal with the abstract ideas more easily than other children. He has a more positive attitude toward school. He tends to be more creative and inquisitive. The gifted child has a higher vocabulary level and a longer interest span. He is more capable of independent study and usually has more varied interests. He is likely to be more interestd in non-fiction than in fiction and outgrows children's literature earlier.

Providing for the Gifted. Many proposals have been advanced for caring for the gifted in school. Most procedures can be classified into three basic patterns: grouping, acceleration, and enrichment.

Grouping according to academic ability was once widely practiced but then fell into disrepute on the grounds that it fostered an educational elite, encouraged undesirable feelings of superiority or inferiority among students in the upper and lower groups, denied future leaders an opportunity to associate with their future followers, and was undemocratic. In some cases superior students are grouped in separate classes. In some city school systems, special high schools have been established for the gifted. The trend at present, which seems to be consistent with the recommendations of experts, is toward grouping superior children together for part, but only part, of the day in the same school with other children. Since most children are not equally gifted in all areas, some schools have developed flexible groupings. Thus a child may be in an advanced science group, an average art group, and a lower group in physical education. A student may move up or down in this group at any time. In this way inflexible cleavages between able and less able students are not fixed; and each student is in a group of relatively equal ability for each subject. Primary teachers, of course, have practiced this type of grouping for many years. Grouping makes it possible

and the humanities.
This special social studies class for bright students at
Baldwin High School, New York, is exploring
Spinoza and the soul.

for the teacher to work with a narrower range of ability.

Acceleration is an arrangement in which the gifted child advances through school more rapidly than others. This may be accomplished by early admission to kindergarten and first grade, by going through an ungraded school in less time than others, by skipping grades, by completing high school work early and undertaking college-level work in high school, or by advanced placement in college. One argument favoring acceleration is that it permits students to complete college and undertake careers and marriage earlier in life. Since the early twenties are the most productive and creative years for many people, it is argued that entry into a career should come as early as possible. The usual argument against acceleration is that an accelerated student's social and emotional maturity may not be commensurate with that of his older classmates. The

Early Admissions Program, sponsored by the Fund for the Advancement of Education, in an experiment in admitting bright students to college early, has achieved encouraging results.

Enrichment is an arrangement whereby the gifted student is neither segregated nor accelerated but rather is given enriched and extended work beyond that expected of average students. This arrangement is less disruptive of the school organization. Also it means that the gifted child receives a greater total education than is possible under an accelerated program, since his years of schooling are not cut short. In an enriched program, gifted students may go either farther or deeper than the remainder of the class. It may mean extra work in the same area in which the class is working, such as research or creative writing beyond that expected of others. Or it may involve working at a level in advance of the rest of the class, such as studying elementary algebra in a junior high school general mathematics class.

Many claims and counter-claims are made for each of these patterns. Such evidence as already exists indicates that all three patterns show considerable promise and that superior youngsters are able to profit from any of the arrangements. There is little evidence to support the alleged disadvantages that were thought to apply. However, more experimentation and research are needed before full or final answers to the education of the gifted can be yielded. It is important that a plan or combination of plans best suited to the individual school, its students, and its faculty be undertaken. It is important also that the gifted child be provided with sufficient testing and guidance so that his abilities and interests are clearly understood and developed. Harry Passow, Director of the Talented Youth Project at Teachers College, Columbia University, has identified several crucial aspects of the problem of educating the talented:

1. Educational imperatives for gifted children must be clarified.
2. Modifications of curriculum, instruction, and organization are required to provide differentiation in learning experiences for gifted students.
3. The attitudes and values of society are important influences on the flourishing of talent and the vigor with which it is nurtured.
4. Since the teacher has the greatest influence in creating a rich learning environment, the success of programs for the gifted will depend on bringing together mature, insightful teachers and able students under circumstances which breed exciting learning experiences.[5]

Much interesting experimentation in meeting the educational needs of the gifted is under way. Many different approaches are being tried. Many high schools offer special seminars or advanced honors courses for bright students. Gifted high school students in Decorah, Iowa, for example, can study analytic geometry and calculus. In Dade County, Florida, able high school students undertake advanced science study by working with scientists in the community.

One of the oldest and most successful elementary programs for gifted children has been developing at the Hunter College campus school. From kindergarten through the upper grades, gifted children have opportunity to go far beyond the usual educational experiences for their grade. Among other things, these gifted elementary school pupils learn typing, French, and German. They write original music and dramatic offerings, which they present at school assemblies. It is not unusual to find young scholars at work with compasses, slide rules, adding machines, and protractors. Special interest clubs in chess, photography, and dramatics help them learn worthwhile leisuretime activities.

Several national scholarship programs, such as those sponsored by the Fund for the Advancement of Education, the Science Clubs of America, and the National Merit Scholarship Program, are helping to identify talented youth

[5] A. Harry Passow, "We Must Multiply Our Efforts," *NEA Journal*, vol. 47 (October, 1958), p. 70.

and provide them with financial assistance in higher education. The National Scholarship Service for Negro Students is helping talented but underprivileged Negro students, particularly from the South, find high-quality college education that might not otherwise be available to them.

Meanwhile, fundamental research on education for the gifted is being advanced by such projects as the Talented Youth Project at Teachers College, Columbia University, and the National Education Association's Academically Talented Pupil Project. Recently the National Council for the Gifted was established to bring together scholars interested in this work and to stimulate and coordinate further research. From these efforts may come eventually much better insight into how American common schools can help our most gifted young citizens make the fullest possible contribution toward man's search for a richer life.

Mentally retarded

Equality of opportunity to learn in a democracy demands adequate attention to the "slow learner." This term includes the entire range of mental subnormality in pupils. Among the characteristics of the mentally slow are these:

Physical. They closely resemble normal children of corresponding chronological ages.

Mental. Their mental age and IQ suggest the limitations of the retarded child's abilities of association, comparison, comprehension, generalization, and symbolization as compared with the normal child.

Social. The mentally retarded pupil has less ability to learn from experience, to take in all the elements in a complex situation, to foresee the consequences, and to form judgments than has the normal child. He is less capable of making adequate social adjustments.

Emotional. Retarded children's needs, desires, and emotions are greatly intensified, resulting in more crying, laughter, fighting, talking, and physical activity than the average child.

Some of the characteristics may be detected through age-grade progress reports, close observation by the teacher, and case studies. Any rule-of-thumb judgment must not be final. The American Association on Mental Deficiency recommends a mental examination for all backward children. Both physical and mental examinations should be given in most cases to be sure that the apparent mental retardation is not in reality the manifestation of some physical disability such as poor hearing.

Mentally retarded children are commonly classified into three groups: the educable, the trainable, and the custodial. While the lines of demarcation between these groups are not absolute, the educable are generally regarded as those with IQs between 50 and 75, approximately 2 per cent of all children. The trainable are those few children with IQs under 50 but capable of some learning. Custodial children, extremely few in number, are practically incapable of any learning. The term "slow learner" is sometimes used loosely to apply to all children of less than average mental ability.

Educable children may be included in regular classrooms in some cases or in special classes in other cases, depending upon the severity of their retardation or upon the availability of special classes, or opportunity classes, as they are sometimes called. In either case, different standards of achievement must be applied to educable children. Materials and content must be within the range of the educable child's capacity if they are to be meaningful to him. Materials should be closely related to the child's environment and experience. Assignments should be within his range of ability. He ought to be encouraged to contribute whatever he can to the work of the class, regardless of how modest his contribution may be. It is important that he achieve some feeling of success even if only in the most simple tasks. As much as possible, extra help should be given him. Since slow learners have particular difficulty with verbalization and abstractions, television and other visual aids are particularly helpful. This means also that the slow learner should be shown rather than told how to do things. Since much of his learning is by habit, the mentally retarded child needs considerable repetition to reinforce desirable habits.

Trainable pupils are those who are unable to profit from regular classroom experience, but who will not need to spend their lives in institutions. With appropriate instruction, trainable pupils are often capable of learning to take care of themselves, to make a reasonably adequate social adjustment, and to learn simple occupational skills. Many, however, are not able to become occupationally self-sufficient. Some trainable children are enrolled in special ungraded classrooms in public school systems. Others are provided for in residential schools for the mentally deficient. These residential schools have an advantage over day schools in that they can work with the whole child over the whole day and for the entire year. There is considerable disagreement over whether trainable children should be the responsibility of the public school or of special institutions. On the one hand, there is the desire to give them every opportunity to live in an environment as nearly like that of a normal child as possible, a desire that underlies the entire philosophy of all special education. On the other hand, severely retarded children often pose a real danger to other children or create a distraction severe enough to hinder the educational well-being of the rest of the school.

Custodial children are so limited in intelligence that they require custody in a mental institution or close supervision and care at home. Education is out of the question for these children.

One of the most moving paragraphs in all of the literature on handicapped children is this passage from the hand of Pearl Buck, well known as an author and adventurer but less well known as the wise and understanding mother of a mentally handicapped child:

I found that my child could learn to read simple sentences, that she was able, with much effort, to write her name, and that she was able to sing simple songs. I think she might have been able to proceed further but one day, when I took her little hand to guide it in writing a word, I noticed that it was wet with perspiration. I realized then that the child was under intense strain, submitting to something she did not in the least understand, with an angelic wish to please me. She was not really learning anything.[6]

Many mentally retarded youngsters are further handicapped in life by parents who are unwilling to accept their child's mental handicap. Frequently parents are ashamed and perhaps even nourish feelings of guilt because of their children's shortcomings. They may try to isolate the child from association with others to hide their shame. Or they may threaten the child in exhorting him to achievement of which he is hopelessly incapable. When this happens, emotional disturbances are compounded with mental retardation. Unfortunately, some teachers are not as sympathetic and understanding of mentally retarded youngsters as they should be. Like all handicapped children, they must be accepted for what they are and helped to achieve up to their level of ability, however modest it may be. The National Association for Retarded Children was founded to help achieve this end.

Physically handicapped

Visually Handicapped. The alert teacher is always on the lookout for any physical disadvantage which the pupils in her classroom may manifest, especially defective vision. Among the symptoms are these: frequent mistakes with words or figures; inability to study without eye discomfort; complaint of headaches; peculiar head positions, as in the case of cross-eye or strabismus; bodily tension; squinting or frowning; stumbling or falling; losing place on the printed page; ability to see objects at a

[6] Pearl S. Buck, "The Child Who Never Grew," *Reader's Digest*, vol. 57 (September, 1950), pp. 18–25.

distance more clearly than those at close range; inability to see objects at a distance, such as words on a blackboard; inability to distinguish colors; redness and swelling of the lids; congestion of the vessels of the eyeball; discharge of tears or pus from the eye; the wearing of glasses; and inability to pass a satisfactory test with an eye chart.

The typical screening test for locating those pupils who should be sent to an ophthalmologist for thorough eye examination is the Snellen letter chart or the symbol E Chart, the latter being used with young and foreign children who cannot read. For identifying some eye troubles the Betts or Eames test is helpful. A skilled oculist can detect and help correct muscular impairment and many other afflictions.

Teachers and other nonmedical examiners perform a genuine service in locating by observation and preliminary examination cases that require special attention. But the teacher, administrator, and parent must remember that in no case should a test made by an examiner other than a specialist be considered final. Any symptoms of defects discovered by the teacher should be reported for further examination, diagnosis, and remedial treatment by an expert. Many schools employ the services of an eye specialist who makes examinations or to whom suspicious cases are referred for decision. If these services are not available, the school should advise the parents to obtain the necessary assistance.

Medical treatment obviously is the first provision. The educational treatment of blind and partially seeing pupils varies according to the degree of visual acuity. The degrees are the blind, the partially seeing, and those with eye difficulties that can be corrected readily with glasses. The last group is not usually considered visually handicapped.

For the blind the braille system of raised dots is employed to supplement the auditory sense. These magic dots constitute braille, worked out by Louis Braille, a twenty-year-old blind teacher in the Paris Institution for the Young Blind. This opened the way for the enlightenment and expression of such brilliant minds as that of Helen Keller and hundreds of others, through silent unassisted reading.

Perhaps not more than one-fourth of the blind people in the United States make any practical use of books in braille, since reading by touch is a slow and fatiguing method. For these persons a great boon is the talking book, of which several hundred volumes are circulated annually. The talking book consists of voice transcriptions of written material recorded on large phonograph discs, each of which will play many pages.

The organized education of the blind in the United States has reached the point where every state now makes provision for them. Most blind children are educated in special state-operated schools. Some are educated in private schools for the blind. The residential schools for the blind enroll a number of pupils in the low-vision group as well as totally blind children. A few city school systems operate their own schools for the blind. Experts in special education believe that the blind, like other atypical children, should be educated in classes in local public schools wherever possible. This reduces the social and psychological adjustments imposed by living away from home.

Several hundred sight-saving classes are established in the United States, but the program is still far from adequate. A sight-saving class is one for pupils whose eyes do not permit them to do the work of the regular grades, either because their sight will be further impaired by such study or because their vision is too low to assure their progress in school by the usual methods and equipment.

Visiting teachers often supplement the regular classroom work. Interdistrict arrangements make special schooling available for youngsters in small districts, but the majority of partially seeing pupils depend largely on the regular teacher in the usual classroom. Sight-saving instruction has been increased to include pre-elementary children and the parents of children with sight handicaps.

Partially sighted pupils are those with vision of 20-70 or less after correction. Some systems maintain special classes for them. However, many partially sighted youngsters, whose visual defects are not too severe, can be educated in regular classrooms. It is important for the teacher to be aware of such handicaps and make appropriate adjustments in classroom organization and procedure. For example, the partially sighted student should be located so that his desk receives adequate light. He should be located near the front of the room so that he can see the teacher and chalkboard as easily as possible. He should not face into the light. Highly reflective surfaces should be covered or repainted. Rest periods should be provided and the schedule planned so that there are not long periods of work requiring close visual tasks. These guides are important, not just for the partially sighted, but for the protection and conservation of the vision of all children.

Other special adjustments for the partially sighted child are also desirable. His reading assignments should be less rigorous than those for children with normal vision. He should be encouraged to avoid rough play that might further damage his eyes. An able student might be seated near him to read material that he can not see. Frequently he can be permitted to make oral reports rather than written reports. The tape recorder permits him to communicate by speaking rather than writing. His use of a typewriter will also help to conserve his eyesight. Typewriters with large type are now widely available. So are large type books. Magnifiers for reading may be useful. Soft, dark lead pencils that make wide lines will reduce his eyestrain. The classroom teacher should check with eye specialists when possible to be sure that the use of the above procedures are in the individual child's best interests, since conditions vary. The visually handicapped child needs help in minimizing his defect and in gaining a feeling of security and respect without self-pity.

Orthopedic. Whatever the defect, all crippled children should be enumerated through the official agencies operating under the laws of the local, state, and federal governments. The classroom teacher can bring cases to the attention of the local school nurse or physician. County and state health authorities cooperate in helping those who are afflicted physically. The state and federal rehabilitation services and some phases of the social security program are also available for the older persons, many of whom are placed in gainful occupations through cooperative efforts on the part of the schools and all concerned. Many organizations, such as luncheon clubs, seek to locate and help children who are crippled or otherwise handicapped.

The major causes are orthopedic poliomyelitis or infantile paralysis, spastic paralysis, brain injury, rheumatic fever, tuberculosis, and other congenital or acquired deformities. The major scourge has been polio. But with the advent of the Salk polio vaccine, this once dread disease appears headed for virtual extinction. Medical advances have reduced also the crippling effects of tuberculosis of the bone, epilepsy, and other disorders. This would suggest that the number of crippled children might be reduced. However, medical science is also saving more malformed and defective babies at birth. Moreover, highway and other accidents are increasing the number of crippled children. Presently, cerebral palsy accounts for a great number of physically disabled children.

Transportation of crippled pupils to and from school is provided free in many school systems. In a one-teacher school, a crippled pupil may be transported by the teacher, parents, or other adults. In some instances, rural children are boarded in nearby cities where special classes are maintained. Recent programs of state aid are recognizing the need for paying transportation and boarding costs of all children who need these services. States also reimburse local school systems over and above the cost of educating a normal child, if special instruction is given.

At school the crippled pupil is helped to forget his handicap. As much as possible he should be placed in an environment as nearly like that of a normal child as his condition permits. Active membership in clubs and organizations is encouraged. Under the direction of a doctor, nurse, or physiotherapist, the paralytic pupil may take exercises or receive treatment under a health-giving lamp or in the heated swimming pool.

Most school systems do not have a separate classroom for crippled pupils. Several schools, however, may cooperate to provide a special room for them. In cases where the child's disability does not permit attendance at school, instruction is often provided at the hospital or at his home. Many states provide special reimbursement for homebound instruction. In some school systems instruction of homebound youth is accomplished through television. Sometimes two-way radio-telephone is provided so that the bedridden student and his class can communicate with each other.

Among the major problems in educating crippled children are transportation, since the children must be carried to and from the school; type of equipment, since many pupils need special desks, cots, and other furniture; curriculum, which may differ from the typical one, since the cripple's vocational area is limited and he often needs activities of a special nature; follow-up work, which is usually neglected; and costs, since the instruction of crippled children calls for large per-pupil expenditures. The extra cost, however, is a profitable investment that reaps dividends for the crippled child as he becomes a self-confident, economically self-sufficient member of society. In some cases no provision is made for the education of crippled children. Great is the tragedy of bedridden, isolated crippled children who do not have a chance to learn.

Deaf and Hard-of-hearing. The acoustically handicapped are grouped into two major classes, distinguished by the type of instruction needed. They are the deaf and the hard-of-hearing. The ratio of the hard-of-hearing to the deaf is 100 to 1. Naturally there are graduations in hearing loss. Deaf children require education in special classes. Hard-of-hearing pupils, if their hearing loss is not too great, can be educated in the regular classroom if adequate accommodation is made for them.

Since defective hearing is less detectable than faulty eyesight, identification of the former is neglected more frequently than the latter. The National Education Association calls the teacher's attention to the following as possible symptoms of loss of hearing: failure to respond to calling of a name, cocking of the head to one side, failure to follow directions, looking in a direction other than the source of sound, watching others and following their movements, frequent requests for repetition of a word or phrase, faulty pronunciation of common words, speaking in an unusual voice, inattention, restlessness, aggressiveness, apathy, earache, discharge from the ear, and persistent mouth breathing. The easiest and surest way of identifying pupils with impaired hearing in one or both ears is through the use of the audiometer. Four to five hundred children may be examined in a day in groups up to forty by means of the audiometer, which consists of a portable phonograph with several attached phones. Tests with audiometers and other approved scientific devices should be made periodically.

Progressive deafness comes on so gradually and so insidiously that it frequently escapes notice until it is too severe to be corrected. Since nearly all instances of deafness in adults are traceable to the first ten years of life or the so-called delicate age, periodic checks and adequate medical care for young children are all-important. Chief among the numerous causes of deafness are diseases and accidents. Among the former are running ears; enlarged and diseased tonsils and adenoids; bad teeth and malnutrition, which make it easy to contract diseases; severe colds, infections, and diseases, some of which are accompanied by dangerous inflammation of the middle ear. Among the accidental causes are automobile collisions, especially those producing a fractured skull; hard blows on the ears; and things placed in the ear. One of the simplest causes of hearing impairment is hardened impacted wax in the ears. A complicating cause may be the Rh factor in the red blood cells.

After detection of hearing impairment, the next step is to induce the pupil and his parents to take advantage of corrective physical treatment.

The education or reeducation of deaf and hard-of-hearing children is conducted in private and public institutions, the latter including local schools and state residential institutions. More modern procedures involve the communication of ideas by means of speech and lip reading as well as by the sense of vibration through tactile experience. Those skilled in lip or speech reading add to what they hear that which they see in the movement of the speaker's lips and facial expression, and thus they are able to hold effective conversation.

Children with residual hearing are usually given auricular training by means of mechanical aids, such as the radio ear, an instrument that magnifies the human voice so that the pupils can hear the words of the teacher. Every desk is equipped with a headphone and a rheostat so that each pupil can adjust the intensity to his own need. In addition, there are the individual mechanical hearing aids.

Many children with various degrees of hearing loss are enrolled in regular classes. Some receive supplementary instruction by special teachers trained in the education of the hard-of-hearing. This may include instruction in lip reading or instruction in the use of electronic hearing devices. The regular teacher should maintain close contact with the special teacher so that their joint efforts can be reinforced. If the child is undergoing medical treatment, it is important for the teacher to encourage full cooperation with the physician.

It is especially important for the teacher to understand the background of the hard-of-hearing child. Frequently, but not always, the hard-of-hearing child is retarded educationally because of the handicap of his hearing. Retardation is likely to be most severe in those subject fields in which sound and verbal communication are most involved—language, spelling, reading.

Hard-of-hearing children frequently make use of lip reading. Since this requires strenuous concentration, the class schedule should be arranged so that there are not long periods of verbal communication. Lip readers will need to have adequate rest. They should be seated so that they have a clear view of the teacher's face and the faces of classmates. Seating an able student nearby as a helper is often desirable. Exaggerated facial movements and loud speaking often confuse the lip reader.

The teacher will often need to help the hard-of-hearing child's parents understand the problems related to poor hearing and to acquire means of adjusting to them. It is especially important to recognize that the hard-of-hearing child is socially disadvantaged. Since he has trouble participating in games and other social activities, he may become withdrawn or prone to bickering when he can't understand the rules. Above all, he needs to acquire confidence in his ability to live with normal people in a world of sound. To achieve this, he must acquire confidence through success in the classroom.

Handicapped in Speech. Speech defect has been defined as any acoustic variation from an accepted speech standard so extreme as to be conspicuous in the speaker, confusing to the listener, or unpleasant to either or both. Among these defects are stammering and stuttering, lisping, lalling, cluttering, nasality, thick speech, baby talk, hoarseness, foreign accent, and defects caused by organic difficulties.

Undesirable personality traits may accompany poor speech. An enfeeblement of the general health or extreme nervous excitement may aggravate the condition of a confirmed stammerer. Because of speech defects a child may not display his normal ability and may thus be rated falsely as low in mentality. Hence teachers should seek to identify pupils with speech difficulties and to understand the major causes of the trouble. The chief causal factors are anatomical handicaps, mental shortcomings, educational backwardness, lack of motivation, diseases, injuries, and environmental handicaps. Examples of these disabilities respectively are cleft palate, low IQ, defective learning, lack of interest, cerebral palsy, broken nose, and foreign accent.

The classroom teacher through her daily contacts with the pupils is the usual avenue for locating speech defectives. Many a teacher with a trained alert ear and a knowledge of the symptoms of major speech irregularities detects pupils who need help. Some schools employ speech correctionists who make periodic surveys of all children and undertake speech correction treatment with those having speech difficulties.

A very common but fallacious observation is that a child will outgrow a speech defect. Lisping tends to cure itself, but other defects are more deep-seated and complex in origin. These require the attention of the specialists. Fortunately, it is true that no group of physically handicapped children can be helped more completely than those having speech defects. According to many case studies, pupils of anti-social habits have improved their personalities as a result of corrective treatment in speech. To effect such changes, the pupil must be more than a passive participant in the process; he must have the will to improve, plus courage, patience, and perseverance. Listening to his own voice recorded on a phonographic disc or tape aids the pupil in perfecting his pronunciation. The mirror technique for seeing speech is also helpful.

Since the general health affects the voice, physical examinations and health-building activities play important roles. Ability to relax mentally and physically is a great aid to fluent speech. Role playing and drama work give impetus to speech correction. Habits of independence and self-confidence are also assets. The voice quality of handicapped and normal children may be made more pleasing and effective by their activities in creative speech classes and choral speaking. Attention by the teacher to her own speech will help decidely to improve the imitated utterances of the pupils.

A neglected means for overcoming hesitancy in speech is the development of a copious vocabulary. A person poverty-stricken in words frequently is halting in speech. To this end all teachers should seek to develop in themselves and in their pupils an extensive vocabulary. A dictionary for each pupil is an investment in speech education and communication.

The human values of speech reeducation cannot be overemphasized. People are prone to make allowances for the blind, the deaf, and the crippled in limb, but not for those crippled in speech. A child may actually be punished for reciting. Even though he knows his lesson, a stammering pupil is often a source of merriment to his comrades, a torment to himself, and an object of sympathy to his teacher.

Other Physically Handicapped. This group includes a wide variety of lowered-vitality children who because of weakened conditions are not able to keep pace physically with normal children in their daily school life. Among these are the malnourished, the undervitalized, and those suffering from cardiac, tubercular, and other defects. Children differ widely in energy and physical strength. The malnourished child is usually identified by the teacher, nurse, or doctor through observation and the daily health inspection. Although some children are naturally small, underweight is due often to infection, faulty food habits, or incorrect diet. The child may not be receiving a sufficient quantity of food; therefore he is undernourished and does not do effective schoolwork. On the other hand, a child may be receiving the proper quantity of food but not the right quality. He may be having an unbalanced diet with overemphasis upon carbohydrates and insufficient emphasis upon other elements, such as iodine, protein, fats, minerals, and water. All these are needed to maintain body balance.

The teacher should refer to doctors suspected cases of heart trouble, anemia, and tuberculosis. The most common signs of heart weakness are shortness of breath, cold extremities, and blue lips. Anemic pupils are often identified by absence of healthy color in face and lips. If a child tires readily, sleeps in class, has a persistent cough, and fails to participate in the normal activities, the teacher should refer him to a doctor for tuberculin and X-ray examinations. Periodic physical examinations often reveal incipient tuberculosis.

The undervitalized pupil should be given a school day and program commensurate with his physical ability. A half-pint of milk once or twice daily during school hours is sometimes provided. Many school boards have provisions for supplying needy children with food, cod-liver oil, and other essentials. The school lunch program provides many children with a hot, well-balanced meal during the school day. Ample rest periods during the school day are needed for all small children and most handicapped children.

Several other less pronounced types of physical difficulties exist. Many pupils have posture defects and minor foot trouble. Some children receive an unfortunate start in their school careers because of excessive underweight or overweight due to glandular disturbances or improper diet. Nine out of ten American school children have one or more decayed teeth, or teeth in the process of decay.

Education and health are intimately tied together. The education of a child may be facilitated through the correction of a physical defect like muscular imbalance of the eyes; likewise, the health of a child may be improved through health education, as in the case of preventing diseases. Nationwide programs, such as those prepared by the American Association for Health, Physical Education, and Recreation, by the American Medical Association, by the American Public Health Association, by the American Organization for Rehabilitation through Training, and the U.S. Office of Education, will help markedly to prevent and correct physical handicaps among children and adults.

All school children should have annual physical and dental examinations so that disorders may be identified and corrected early. Unfortunately, many school health examinations are too superficial to detect maladies, particularly in their incipient stages.

Emotionally maladjusted

It is often difficult to discover those children and adults who are mentally and emotionally unadjusted. Their number is legion; hence their early identification is extremely desirable. Since many symptoms and causes can be traced to early childhood, every teacher is challenged to be a mental hygienist, alerted to danger signals.

The parents, and even his own peers, have often discovered the mentally maladjusted child before he reaches school. The observing teacher may see symptoms and find causes through personal interviews or case histories, and in the daily life of the child. The family physician and pediatrician-psychiatrist can lend a discerning eye and ear in early identification. School psychologists and trained personnel in community clinics can help locate behavioral cases.

The first task is the preservation of mental health, one of the basic goals of the school. The chief therapeutic resource, after the child starts school, is the classroom teacher.

Often the school contributes to poor mental health through obsolete methods of teaching, rigid standards for grade promotions with the consequent numbers of failures, and inflexible curriculums. The curriculum should help build security in the minds and hearts of children. Socially useful work is one way to meet the need for self-respect, which is related to personal security. Mental hygiene should be an operational principle of the total school program, including cocurricular activities.

Individual therapy in the treatment of psychotic and neurotic children and adults calls for specialized services of the psychiatrist and the physician. The number of mentally ill patients in the United States exceeds the number of patients suffering from any other type of illness. Almost half of all hospital beds in the United States are used for this group.

The National Mental Health Act, passed by Congress in 1946, has helped states, counties, and cities through subsidizing psychiatric services and establishing a National Institute for Mental Health.

Socially handicapped

Every child is at times socially atypical. Some pupils are oversocial, seeking constantly to be in a crowd; some are nonsocial, striving to avoid people; and others are antisocial, working against human beings and social institutions. These deviates may be termed "socially handicapped."

The socially handicapped are found in every grade from the nursery school through the university and in adult life. Problem behavior has been defined as "that which is objectionable to others or which makes the individual himself unhappy." Behavior problems range all the way from temporary minor infractions of social etiquette to severe problems of delinquency, such as theft, adultery, or murder.

As with pupils who are physically and mentally handicapped, the classroom teacher who is alert, sympathetic, and understanding can identify many cases of maladjustment. Behavior problem children are not merely disciplinary cases for the teacher to handle. Many have physical disabilities. Some should be institutional charges. All, however, are not severe cases. Some youngsters are merely petulant, plaintive, or overassertive. Often the home conditions are responsible: there is a high correlation between broken homes and child delinquency. Incorrigibility often has been asso-

ciated with low intelligence, but studies show that delinquent minors in criminal institutions do not differ markedly in intelligence from typical minors on the street, although they are lower in the amount of educational achievement.

Teachers usually are impressed with behavior difficulties that interrupt the work of the class or the smooth functioning of the school, but are not so concerned with social traits that are symptomatic of serious maladjustments of life in general. Various investigations reveal that teachers label as most serious such behavior problems as untruthfulness, bullying and cruelty, cheating, talking to other pupils in class, impertinence, and truancy. On the other hand, mental hygienists note as highly undesirable such traits as depression and unhappiness, unsocial attitudes, withdrawal, suggestibility, resentfulness, fearfulness, overcritical attitude, suspiciousness, and restlessness. The latter traits are the most serious for the general adjustment of pupils to life. Children behave as they do because of the conditions existing at the time. Hence behavior is a symptom of underlying maladjustment and not a disease. Furthermore, delinquency is no longer regarded as the result of a single factor; it is explained in terms of the effects from many unfavorable factors in multiple causation.

Classroom teachers need to know more about the significance of certain traits, to have experience in the observation of behavior so that they may recognize undesirable traits, to have training in the treatment of specific problems, and to know where to go for technical help in difficult cases. A reliable way of studying a child intensively is the case-study method, which gathers systematically all types of information from all possible sources and then coordinates these many items in such a manner that the caseworker or teacher sees the child as a real, living individual reacting to many stimuli in a surveyed environment. The autobiographical letter containing a straightforward self-portrait is a valuable tool. Clinics are the best means of identifying behavior-problem children and starting them on the right road to better adjustments.

One of the main provisions for the socially handicapped is a constructive attitude on the part of all. Genuine help and prevention are directed toward deep-seated causes. A threefold program consists of drying up sources of infection in the community (preventive), helping the child in trouble (remedial), and producing continuously wholesome living (developmental).

The specific treatment varies with the problem to such a marked degree that no single rule can be offered. Physical and mental examinations are very desirable for pupils who are extreme disciplinary problems. Psychiatric services are often quite helpful. Group therapy is an effective means of helping children break down antisocial attitudes. All too often such services are not available in public schools in sufficient scope to care for the needs.

Some cities make definite provision for the segregation in special schools of those students who are socially maladjusted. New York City recently created a number of schools to care for potentially antisocial children. The Montefiore and Moseley schools in Chicago are other examples.

J. Edgar Hoover, Director of the Federal Bureau of Investigation believes that children are driven into crime because of deep-laid faults of society—poverty, degeneracy, and neglectful parents. Consequently it is difficult for many youths to make successful social adjustments if they remain in poor home environments. This has led to the establishment of parental or residential schools. In addition to supplying home needs, such as lodging and boarding, these schools seek to educate potential delinquents and to give them the security and affection that they failed to find in their own homes. Perhaps the most wondrous example of this type of institution is Boys Town, founded by the late Father Flanagan. This haven for homeless and underprivileged boys has enjoyed remarkable success. Today residential schools for the socially maladjusted are

found throughout the United States. Unfortunately, in most cases the administration of such organizations is separated from that of the public schools. Furthermore the traditional idea persists that the residents are offenders who must be punished and that the institution is correctional rather than reeducative and redirective in social living. Fortunately the objectives and procedures of many of these institutions are being altered. Incarceration gives way to education; the negative is replaced by a positive force. The return of the individual to the community as a fairly well-adjusted person, capable of entering into normal life, is the recognized objective of all these schools. Today many states are removing a large number of delinquent girls and boys from residential schools, allowing them to attend a regular day school, and paying for their board, room, clothing, and other essentials in foster homes, where they return to a more normal form of living.

Other exceptional children

To the many types of exceptional pupils already mentioned may be added an endless array of pupils with special problems, such as those living on federal reservations, those in rural or sparsely settled areas, those in congested city neighborhoods, the overly ambitious pupils, the lazy, the irregular in attendance, the homebound, the timid and passive, the overprivileged, the allergic, the diabetic, the adopted, the foster, the orphaned, the left-handed, those from minority groups, from low-income families, from migrant families, and the refugees. Transportation, housing, and schooling have been provided here in recent years for many children fleeing from other shores. Unlike the totalitarian, so-called *ism* countries, which aim to regiment children and their thinking, through its schools America seeks to cultivate a profound respect for individual*ism* in society. A democracy believes that every child, youth, or adult—normal or handicapped—is important.

PLEDGE TO CHILDREN

(Midcentury White House Conference on Children and Youth)

TO YOU, our children, who hold within you our most cherished hopes, we the members of the Midcentury White House Conference on Children and Youth, relying on your full response, make this pledge:

From your earliest infancy we give you our love, so that you may grow with trust in yourself and in others.

We will recognize your worth as a person and we will help you to strengthen your sense of belonging.

We will respect your right to be yourself and at the same time help you to understand the rights of others, so that you may experience cooperative living.

We will help you to develop initiative and imagination, so that you may have the opportunity freely to create.

We will encourage your curiosity and your pride in workmanship, so that you may have the satisfaction that comes from achievement.

We will provide the conditions for wholesome play that will add to your learning, to your social experience, and to your happiness.

We will illustrate by precept and example the value of integrity and the importance of moral courage.

We will encourage you always to seek the truth.

We will provide you with all opportunities possible to develop your own faith in God.

We will open the way for you to enjoy the arts and to use them for deepening your understanding of life.

We will rid ourselves of prejudice and discrimination, so that together we may achieve a truly democratic society.

We will work to lift the standard of living and to improve our economic practices, so that you may have the material basis for a full life.

We will provide you with rewarding educational opportunities, so that you may develop your talents and contribute to a better world.

We will protect you against exploitation and undue hazards and help you grow in health and strength.

We will work to conserve and improve family life and, as needed, to provide foster care according to your inherent rights.

We will intensify our search for new knowledge in order to guide you more effectively as you develop your potentialities.

As you grow from child to youth to adult, establishing a family life of your own and accepting larger social responsibilities, we will work with you to improve conditions for all children and youth.

Summary

Pupils are the end of education and therefore the most important objects of the teacher's study. The individual child is of surpassing worth in our society. Thus schools must seek to understand each child and to stimulate his development up to his full capacity.

Each child is unique. His behavior is influenced by varied and sometimes obscure causes. Children vary widely in their ability to learn but virtually all children are capable of some learning. A child's development is dependent upon his total organism—mental, physical, social, and emotional. A teacher must understand and be concerned about all of these aspects of growth. Although general patterns of growth are discernible, children will vary widely in the rate and extent of growth.

Children and youth who differ so widely from normal as to require substantial modifications in their educational environment are regarded as exceptional or atypical children. They may be mentally atypical—either gifted or retarded; physically atypical—crippled, blind or partially sighted, deaf or hard of hearing, handicapped in speech; or emotionally or socially maladjusted. The atypical child should be educated in a school environment like that of normal children if at all possible, since sharp departures from his normal world confront him with additional adjustments. However, his malady may be so great that it is not feasible to educate him in the regular classroom. Special classes may be provided in the local school system. In extreme cases, it may be necessary to remove him from the home and community to a residential school.

Atypical children must learn to accept their abnormality, to gain confidence in themselves, to achieve up to the level of their abilities, and adjust as well as possible to the world. They must be neither rejected nor coddled. As Emerson put it, "The secret of education lies in respecting the pupil." Parents, teachers, and other children frequently have difficulty understanding and accepting atypical children, which adds to their difficulty. There is the danger of expecting too much of them on the one hand and, on the other, of capitulating to them. With sympathetic understanding and appropriate adjustments in their learning environment, many atypical children are capable of making amazing accommodations, growing up to be reasonably happy and useful citizens in spite of their handicaps.

Vigorous attention is being given to gifted learners so as to challenge them up to the full measure of their abilities. This consists usually of enriching their program, accelerating their progress through school, or grouping them for instructional purposes with other gifted children. Much experimentation and research is presently being undertaken in this field of special education.

Through local, state, national, and international agencies, such as city councils, the state departments of education, the U.S. Office of Education, the International Council for Exceptional Children, and the Personnel and Guidance Association, better services can be developed for socially maladjusted as well as other pupils.

Suggested activities

1. Explain what is meant by a pupil-centered school. Evaluate this concept.
2. Describe the normal physical, mental, spiritual, and social development of typical pupils in the elementary school, secondary school, and college.
3. Give a brief life sketch of some distinguished physically handicapped person, such as Helen Keller or Franklin Delano Roosevelt.
4. Explain the provisions your state laws contain relative to the care and education of handicapped children.

5. Prepare a list of local organizations that cooperate with the schools in educating exceptional children.
6. List specific contributions that the medical profession makes to the welfare of handicapped children.
7. List the ways in which the mentally gifted child might be helped most effectively in the regular classroom.
8. List the ways in which the mentally retarded child might be helped most effectively in the regular classroom.
9. Study carefully one exceptional pupil, keeping a careful record of all pertinent data; also study one normal child.
10. List specific ways of helping a bright or a slow learner in school.
11. Explain how the teacher helps to discover the latent interests of children.
12. Describe what is meant by the mental health of the school pupil.
13. Describe the particular problems presented by pupils who come from homes of the foreign-born or migrant parents.
14. Make a list of guides that are helpful to the classroom teacher in gaining better understanding of all atypical children and their proper adjustment to the regular classroom.

Bibliography

Books

Abraham, Willard: *Common Sense about Gifted Children*, Harper & Brothers, New York, 1958. Comprehensive treatment of the education of the gifted, how to identify them, their relations with parents, teachers, and others.

Cruickshank, William (ed.): *Psychology of Exceptional Children and Youth*. Prentice-Hall, Inc., Englewood Cliffs, N.J., 1955. A number of experts deal with the psychological adjustment of children with impaired hearing, speech, vision, mentality.

Featherstone, W. B.: *Teaching the Slow Learner*, Bureau of Publications, Teachers College, Columbia University, New York, 1955. Suggests specific methods and materials for teaching the slow learner in elementary and high school classes.

Frandsen, Arden N.: *How Children Learn*, McGraw-Hill Book Company, Inc., New York, 1957, chap. 12. An excellent chapter dealing with the nature of intelligence, means of measuring it, and its relation to school achievement.

Haskew, Laurence D.: *This Is Teaching*, Scott, Foresman and Company, Chicago, 1956, chap. 3. Case material is used to help the reader understand children as they are seen in school.

Jersild, Arthur T.: *The Psychology of Adolescence*, The Macmillan Company, New York, 1957. A standard textbook dealing with the growth and development of the adolescent, emphasizing the importance of helping him discover and accept himself.

Nicola, Ethel, and Diane Witte: *The Rabbit with the High I.Q.*, Bureau of Publications, Teachers College, Columbia University, New York, 1956. A charmingly illustrated parable in light verse dealing with the trials of the bright rabbit in school, highlighting the problems and opportunities in teaching the gifted.

Olson, Willard C.: *Child Development*, D. C. Heath and Company, Boston, 1959. Provides a comprehensive introduction to the major concepts of child development and describes the characteristics of periods of growth.

Prescott, Daniel A.: *The Child in the Educative Process*, McGraw-Hill Book Company, Inc., New York, 1957, part II. Deals with the bases for understanding children, interpreting behavior, observing development, and gathering information.

Shaffer, Laurence F., and Edward J. Shoben, Jr.: *The Psychology of Adjustment*, Houghton Mifflin Company, Boston, 1956. A basic introductory textbook on the psychology of human personality, drawing upon recent research.

White, Verna: *Studying the Individual Pupil*, Harper & Brothers, New York, 1958. Shows how teachers in the normal classroom can study children as a means of improving their teaching and counseling.

Witty, Paul (ed): *The Gifted Child*, D. C. Heath and Company, Boston, 1960. Presents practical suggestions from a group of outstanding authorities for handling problems of gifted children.

Periodicals

Benson, Robert M.: "The Hard of Hearing," *NEA Journal*, vol. 47 (December, 1958), pp. 612–613. Practical suggestions for meeting the needs of the hard-of-hearing child in the regular classroom.

Bryan, J. Ned, and Charles E. Bish: "Boys and Girls with Special Abilities," *NEA Journal*, vol. 47 (October, 1958), pp. 469–481. A series of articles on meeting the needs of gifted high school students, approached from different subject areas.

Fischer, John H.: "Function of Today's School," *The Nation's Schools*, vol. 63 (January, 1959), pp. 46–49. A discussion of the school's responsibility for the education of pupils of varying abilities and a look at some of the issues related to special education.

Galisdorfer, Lorraine: "The Partially Seeing," *NEA Journal*, vol. 47 (December, 1958), pp. 614–615. Practical suggestions for meeting the needs of the partially sighted youngster in the regular classroom.

Gallagher, James J.: "Rejecting Parents?" *Exceptional Children*, vol. 22 (April, 1956), pp. 273–276. Deals with the crucial problem of helping parents accept and adjust to the problems of their atypical children.

Glick, Selma J.: "Spotting Potential Delinquents in the School," *Exceptional Children*, vol. 20 (May, 1954), pp. 342–346. Practical suggestions for the teacher on symptoms of delinquency and the importance of early discovery and help.

Goldberg, I. Ignacy, and William M. Cruickshank: "The Trainable but Noneducable: Whose Responsibility?" *NEA Journal*, vol. 47 (December, 1958), pp. 622–623. Two opposing points of view regarding whether or not the trainable child is the responsibility of the public school.

Goldberg, Miriam: "Recent Research on the Talented," *Teachers College Record*, vol. 60 (December, 1958), pp. 150–163. A scholarly roundup of findings of recent research on gifted learners, their characteristics, motivations, attitudes, and the advantages and disadvantages of different types of programs for them.

Mahoney, Agnes: "The Slow Learner," *NEA Journal*, vol. 47 (December, 1958), pp. 618–621. An excellent article with suggestions for meeting the needs of the slow learner in the regular classroom.

Morse, Arthur D.: "They're Breaking the Lockstep in Our Schools," *National Parent Teacher*, vol. 51 (October, 1956), pp. 7–10. Report of Ford Foundation-sponsored experimentation with accelerated programs for the gifted student.

Mullen, Frances A.: "The Crippled," *NEA Journal*, vol. 47 (December, 1958), pp. 616–618. Excellent suggestions for meeting the needs of the crippled child in the regular classroom.

Passow, Harry, and others: "The Gifted in Our Schools," *NEA Journal*, vol. 47 (September, 1958), pp. 67–77. A series of articles illustrating actual programs for meeting the needs of academically talented children.

Redl, Fritz, and Stanley Jacobson: "The Emotionally Disturbed," *NEA Journal*, vol. 47 (December, 1958), pp. 609–611. A guide to understanding the problems of the emotionally disturbed child and how the regular classroom teacher can help.

Rusk, Howard A.: "Square Pegs in Round Holes," *NEA Journal*, vol. 47 (December, 1958), p. 608. A brief but excellent statement of the philosophy and psychology of special education.

Witty, Paul: "Pied Piper?" *NEA Journal*, vol. 47 (December, 1958), pp. 638–639. An interesting discussion of the effect of television on the mental, emotional, and social development of children.

chapter 11

Teachers

Old teacher institutes
Teacher training - Normal school

Teacher Education

Teaching is a profession of paramount importance. With almost one-fourth of the nation enrolled in educational programs, teaching is by far the largest of the professions, numbering nearly a million and a half men and women in the United States. Because of rapidly increasing enrollments and the extension of educational programs and services, the number of educators is constantly expanding. Teachers work in five major areas of learning considered in Part 2, viz., pre-elementary, elementary, secondary, higher, and adult education. Certainly no other occupation affects the lives of so many people so directly and so significantly. Teachers are important qualitatively as well as quantitatively. Richard M. Nixon has observed that "the teaching profession, underpaid and sometimes unappreciated, is one of the noblest in a free society as our own." Teaching bears the major responsibility for the preservation of civilization, the transmission and improvement of culture, the strengthening of ideals and values, and the perfection of free, democratic government.

Thus the quality of an educational system depends in very large measure upon the excellence of its faculty. Consequently the recruitment, education, certification, selection, and in-service development of teacher personnel become a paramount concern to society and are matters that are subject to careful scrutiny and widespread debate.

Shortage of Teachers. Despite the tributes to teachers, there is a critical shortage of well-qualified professional workers in educational institutions. In its research bulletin *The Postwar Struggle to Provide Competent Teachers*,[1] the National Education Association enumerates some of the causes for the shortage of manpower in the profession. Starting with 1945, during the four years of total war effort, the flow of students into teacher-education pro-

[1] National Education Association, Research Division, "The Postwar Struggle to Provide Competent Teachers," *Research Bulletin*, vol. 35 (October, 1957), pp. 99–123.

grams fell to a small fraction of the need. The Korean conflict also invaded upon the availability of manpower for teaching. The technological advance in this country is double-barreled in that it not only calls for a high level of preparation for many students who need more teachers, but also creates a competitive demand for persons who might go into teaching. The changed pattern of early motherhood has a compound effect on the schools: it removes many young women from possible positions in teaching, and it adds to the number of children soon to enter school. Furthermore secondary school enrollments have increased rapidly. The growth of college population has increased the demand for teachers in higher education. Another factor is the great increase in the demand for teachers of adults.

A nationwide survey by the U.S. Office of Education indicates that more than half of the young people starting teaching plan to leave in five years. This tends to make teaching a procession rather than a profession. Certainly an end to the struggle to provide competent teachers is not in sight. Good teachers are always in short supply.

Opportunities Unlimited. The shortage of teachers has created unlimited opportunities for young and older persons to enter upon this great professional work. A former president of a university and President of the United States, Dwight D. Eisenhower, said, "The education of young Americans is our first line of defense and a broad highway to greater opportunity." The challenging positions at all the levels are described in Chapters 5 to 9 of this volume, viz., pre-elementary, elementary, secondary, and college and adult education. As noted in the previous chapter, careers abound for teachers in special education—education of the gifted, the mentally retarded, and the physically handicapped. In the chapter that follows are described almost one hundred areas of educational service other than straight full-time classroom teaching.

The NEA identifies five specific types of needs for new teachers: to replace those who quit, to serve the larger enrollments, to relieve overcrowding and half-day sessions, to add necessary services, and to replace the unprepared.

As to the latter group, during World War II it became general practice to issue emergency certificates to almost anyone who would accept a teaching position. The accent now is away from the subminimum or minimum requirements and toward a high-standards approach for teaching. This is defined as enforcement of professionally accepted standards in selective recruitment and retention of students, pre-service education, orientation for new teachers, in-service growth, and teacher welfare services. The critical challenge today is for good recruits to do their best in teaching. To invest one's life in others is currently and historically important.

Foundations

MAJOR STAGES OF DEVELOPMENT

Teaching has undergone three not too well-marked stages of development which have been epitomized by the terms (1) teacher *training*, (2) teacher *preparation*, and (3) teacher *education*.

Teacher Training. Most of the earliest teachers were not even trained: they taught, or rather kept, school by rule of thumb or with a heavy hand, without any specific practice or pedagogy. Gradually the need for definite training became articulate through the words and deeds of such men as the Reverend Samuel R. Hall, who in 1823 established a private academy at Concord, Vermont, for the preparation of teachers; and Horace Mann, Edmund Dwight, and the Reverend Cyrus Pierce—all real pioneers. Pierce became the first principal of the first state-supported normal school in the United States, located at Lexington, Massachusetts, where on July 3, 1839, three young ladies commenced training. Entrance examinations were required at the new normal school in Lexington.

The enlightenment that came from this fire kindled in Massachusetts spread gradually to

NATIONAL DEVELOPMENT		THE DEVELOPMENT OF THE TEACHING PROFESSION
Era of good feeling	1823	First private normal school started in Vermont
Jacksonian Democracy	1839	First state normal school established in Massachusetts
Westward migration and expansion	1845	First state teachers associations organized in New York and Rhode Island
Controversy and war between the states	1857	National Teachers Association formed, later became the National Education Association
Aftermath and reconstruction	1887	Teachers College, Columbia University, established
Immigration and industrial growth	1893	Normal school at Albany, New York, made Albany State Teachers College and empowered to grant degrees
	1896	First state-wide teacher retirement system adopted in New Jersey
The progressive era	1909	First state teacher tenure law passed in New Jersey
World War I	1916	American Federation of Teachers organized as an affiliate of the American Federation of Labor
	1917	American Association of Teachers Colleges formed
Normalcy and prosperity	1930	National Survey of Teacher Education authorized by Congress
Depression and recovery	1938	National Organization of Future Teachers of America organized
World War II	1946	National Commission on Teacher Education and Professional Standards launched by the NEA
		British-American exchange of teachers inaugurated
		World Organization of the Teaching Profession started
The Cold War struggle	1948	Three teacher education groups merged into American Association of Colleges for Teacher Education
	1953	First meeting held by World Confederation of Organizations of the Teaching Profession, formerly WOTP
	1954	National Council for Accreditation of Teacher Education made operative
	1957	National Organization of Future Teachers of America replaced on college level by Student National Educational Association
	1959	Ford Foundation announced grant of 9 million dollars to strengthen teacher education

HISTORICAL CALENDAR

and down the Mississippi Valley and to the Pacific Coast. City school systems followed the lead of the states. In 1848 the city of Philadelphia, which as early as 1818 had been given the legal right to train teachers, established the first city normal school.

Teacher Preparation. Many of the early students at normal schools attended only one term. Gradually it became apparent to educational leaders that teachers had to be *prepared* over a period of years rather than *trained* in a term of eleven weeks or a summer session or two. The quality as well as the quantity of instruction had to be altered. Instead of equipping the prospective teachers with a bag of tricks, it was necessary to prepare them for teaching and living with children.

For this purpose an institution with a higher rank than a two-year normal training school was needed. The name of Illinois State Normal *University*, established in 1857, is symbolical of this upward reach in teacher preparation.

The interest of higher education in the preparation of teachers was evidenced in the creation of education departments in colleges and universities. The first part-time chair devoted to professional training was established at the University of Iowa in 1873, and the first permanent chair at the University of Michigan in 1879. An institution that has markedly affected teacher education in America and abroad is Teachers College, established at Columbia University in 1887 by Nicholas Murray Butler, then professor of philosophy. A few years later the state normal school at Albany was given power to grant degrees. Toward the end of the century Colonel Francis Parker accepted the principalship of Chicago Institute which later became the School of Education, now the Department of Education, at the University of Chicago.

Teacher Education. Teacher preparation stresses vocational training, whereas teacher education is professional education at its best. William Heard Kilpatrick stated that one *trains* circus performers, buffoons, and animals, but one *educates* teachers. A modicum of training

is necessary, but the real outcome desired is teacher education, which is broader, longer, and deeper than teacher training. It affects all areas of living, it requires many years of learning, and it has its roots in a vital philosophy of daily living with children.

The current emphasis on teacher education has no definite starting point; it was latent in the minds of the early educators. With the beginning of this century the name National *Education* Association came into use as the official title of the national organization of teachers.

A three-year survey, authorized by Congress and conducted under the leadership of E. S. Evenden of Teachers College, Columbia University, was designated National Survey of Teacher Education. The special committee organized by the American Council on Education in 1938 was entitled Commission on Teacher Education. The names and content of courses for teachers and current titles of professional periodicals, such as *Teacher Education, Journal of Teacher Education,* and *Teacher Education Journal,* indicate this shift in emphasis from training to education. Book titles too, such as *Teacher Education for a Free People,* accent the prevailing concept of education. The latter may be divided into two major phases: (1) preservice and (2) in-service education.

Preservice

Preservice education includes such factors as the recruitment and selection of students for the teaching profession, the in-college education of these candidates, their certification upon meeting the necessary standards, and their placement in teaching positions.

RECRUITMENT AND SELECTION OF STUDENTS

Recruitment. The best timber for teaching is not driftwood. The best is carefully selected and tested human resources.

Many outstanding members of professions other than teaching selected their life work early in their teens. While a large number of persons will continue to drift into teaching, the future will undoubtedly witness for many young persons an early professional orientation and commitment to teaching, reaching down into the junior high and high school years.

Secondary school recruitment techniques are numerous and varied. Some high schools offer psychology as an elective subject or a pre-teaching course in American education or have education units in subjects regularly offered, such as social institutions. Some high schools permit students to observe teaching and/or get direct experience in assisting elementary school instructors in the actual classroom. One of the most influential organizations for en-listing secondary school students for teaching is the Future Teachers of America, a voluntary cocurricular organization launched in 1938. The FTA clubs are exploratory, prevocational, and character forming. The National Commis-sion of Teacher Education and Professional Standards, through the National Education As-sociation, which initiated the movement, has prepared a *Manual for FTA Clubs in High Schools.*

On the college level the future teacher groups are organized as chapters of the Student NEA. Local chapters and state student education as-sociations are integral parts of the Student NEA on the national level.

A publication of the Educational Policies Commission *Manpower and Education* urges better use of our manpower talents, including minority groups and retired personnel. Among the books helpful in the recruitment of teach-ers are Richard Wynn's *Careers in Education,* Louise Sharp's *Why Teach?,* and a great many *NEA* pamphlets. Many programs of the press, radio, and television are directed toward teach-er recruitment. In connection with Teaching Career Month, the National Education Asso-ciation prepared a pamphlet addressed to parents, and indirectly to students, entitled *Ten Practical Reasons Why Teaching Would Be a Wonderful Career for Your Child:*

Jobs will be plentiful for many years to come.
He can earn a good living.
He'll have plenty of chances for advancement.
He'll have time to improve his status.

He can work overseas if he likes.
He can be a specialist.
He'll share a retirement plan.
Scholarships can help pay his college costs.
He'll have job security.
He'll be happy in his work.

Various other national organizations, such as Delta Kappa Gamma, Phi Delta Kappa, and state groups, such as chambers of commerce, have launched programs for attracting people into teaching. Several state departments of education have a full-time specialist delegated to the work of enlisting teachers. Many states have scholarships and loans for those going into teaching. The federal government provides scholarships in certain professional fields, such as science and the teaching of the mentally re-tarded. The National Defense Education Act provides fellowships for persons preparing for college teaching.

The recruitment programs are directed not merely to young students but to mature grad-uates with liberal arts degrees, to married women, to retired military personnel, and others.

Selection. T. M. Stinnett, executive secretary of the National Commission on Teacher Educa-tion and Professional Standards, has stated, "It is the belief of the Commission that indis-criminate recruiting is unsound and harmful. The emphasis should be upon *selective* recruit-ment." The best human resources available must be attracted into the teaching profession through an upgrading of students and teach-ers.

A marked trend is toward continuous selec-tion and elimination, which extends even into the period of in-service education. Medicine, law, and other professions have long been on a selective basis whereby the students must meet certain requirements before being ad-mitted to professional education.

The selection of students for the teaching profession is made usually on several of the following bases: the scholastic record of the applicant, participation in extracurricular ac-tivities, recommendation from the high school principal, physical and psychological examinations, quality of voice, use of English, personal interviews, personality ratings, and scores in a series of entrance examinations and aptitude tests. Little confidence can be placed in any single aspect or measuring instrument. However, the data revealed by all of the above facilitates more confident selection. Thus a cumulative record covering the whole previous life of the candidate is also valuable.

Selection is difficult because the evidence regarding characteristics of teachers and success in teaching is not too conclusive. For example, it is known that some minimum level of intelligence is needed, but just how important superior intelligence may be to success in teaching is not known. Much is written about the need for sound personality, yet there is little measured data on personality and success in teaching. Studies of the relationship between interests and motivations and success in teaching have not been too rewarding. One of the difficulties arises from disagreement over what constitutes "success in teaching," a term that virtually defies definition, agreement, or measurement.

TYPES OF TEACHER-EDUCATING INSTITUTIONS

The main institutions for educating teachers are (1) normal schools, (2) teachers colleges, (3) departments of education, and (4) schools or colleges of education.

Normal Schools. The first normal schools were established in order to prepare teachers for the elementary schools. Students were admitted on the basis of their elementary school records. The curriculum was usually a year in length and contained very little of what is now considered professional education. Today it may be a state, county, municipal, or high school normal school—all of which are part of the public educational system. A few private normal schools prepare teachers for such fields as primary and physical education. Although there are still a few normal schools in the United States, they are gradually disappearing in name and function. Historically, the normal schools were important institutions.

Teachers College. This institution, which is fast losing the name teachers college, is usually a degree-granting institution. Several interesting histories have been written of public teachers colleges. Among the outstanding private schools is Teachers College, Columbia University, whose program in education is now almost entirely at the graduate level. The largest private institution of this type with a wholly independent organization is George Peabody College for Teachers at Nashville, Tennessee. Nearly all states of the Union once established teachers colleges or state colleges with teacher education as one of their functions. Some of these now grant the master's degree, and a few award the doctor's degree. Whereas the old normal school trained teachers for elementary service only, the teachers college spread its offerings to include the education of secondary and special teachers. Some educate teachers for colleges and universities.

A significant transformation is taking place in the teachers colleges. Many have broadened their curriculums to include general or liberal education. Many are enrolling students preparing for fields other than teaching. Some states have changed the names, as well as the purposes, of state teachers colleges to state colleges. This is part of the trend toward more general education for all of the professions.

Departments of Education. The liberal arts college and many of the newer state colleges usually include a division known as the education and/or psychology department. The requirement in terms of hours of education and psychology is about the same as the minimum in teachers colleges. Student teaching usually is coupled with this program. In some universities, work in education is organized as a department. In some universities, teacher education is a function of a department within a larger division, such as social sciences or liberal arts.

Schools or Colleges of Education. Professional work in education at state and private universities is usually centralized in a separate entity, the school or college of education. It may accept students at the beginning of the freshman year, at the end of a period of general education in the sophomore or junior year, or for graduate work. An illustration of the evolution of schools of education is shown in the history of the University of Michigan, one of the first American universities to offer education courses. Its first permanent chair in this field, established in 1879, was called The Science and Art of Teaching; in 1921 it gave way to a School of Education, coordinate with the other professional schools. Most teachers today are prepared in private and public liberal arts colleges and universities.

IN-COLLEGE EDUCATION FOR TEACHING

Major Curricular Beliefs. The National Council for Accreditation of Teacher Education, under the leadership of W. Earl Armstrong, director of the Council has prepared a working statement entitled "The Teacher Education Curriculum." It contains the following major beliefs regarding in-college preparation for teachers: "The curriculum for teacher education should be attractive to capable students who seek a good basic education for themselves and adequate preparation for a professional career."

The statement also includes the following major convictions:

All teachers should be well-educated persons.

The curriculum should produce an area of subject-matter concentration for each teacher.

Teachers should have specific preparation for their specific responsibilities.

The curriculum should include a well-organized program of professional work, including laboratory experiences.

These beliefs are usually implemented through curricular programs in at least three areas.

The teacher is an interpreter of the general culture; hence his preparation must include general education. He teaches some specialized subject or generalized field; hence he needs subject-matter or field preparation. He teaches learning pupils; hence he takes professional work in education and psychology, including student teaching. These three areas—general education, specialization, and professional education—are considered briefly here.

General Education. Fundamentally, general education includes the social sciences, the natural and physical sciences, and the humanities. The title of a recent book, written by Charles R. Wilson, indicates the importance of such general education for teachers. The title is *A Teacher Is a Person*. The teacher works in a broad profession and not a narrow trade. He is responsible for the general education of young Americans—the workers and citizens of tomorrow. Therefore, teachers are expected to have a rich cultural background.

Specialized Education in Subjects, Fields, or Levels. As indicated in the beliefs previously listed, prospective teachers should complement a broad cultural and general education with specialization in terms of the subjects, fields, or levels in which they expect to teach. For the elementary school, the preparation is usually in terms of grade levels and the subjects and fields. For teachers in the smaller secondary schools the preparation is in subjects and fields. For teachers in the smaller high schools, it is recommended that preparation be in terms of fields rather than specialized narrow subjects and that at least two fields be selected for possible work. In addition to specialization in academic work, there must be concentration in child study and the methodology of learning and teaching, usually termed "professional education."

Professional Education. Usually, the requirements in specific professional education are stated in terms of semester hours. A minimum in most states is 15 semester hours for certification; however, most teacher-education institutions go beyond the legal minimum. A sample program of a teachers college that requires 24 semester hours in education and psychology for secondary school teaching shown on the following page.

Courses	Hours
Educational psychology	3
American public education	3
Methods of teaching	4
Introduction to philosophy of education	3
Student teaching and special methods	8
Electives in education and psychology	3
Total hours in education and psychology	24

The quality of an educational system depends heavily upon the excellence of its teachers. The teaching profession needs increased numbers of highly competent, well-educated persons. What comprises the preparation of a teacher at a modern teacher-education institution?

In some colleges this professional work is concentrated in the last year or two, but in the majority it is spread over the upper three years.

Directed observations, case studies of pupils, and pre-student-teaching activities form essential phases of professional education because they include actual experience with children. As has been repeatedly stated, the verb "to teach" has two accusatives—the pupil and the subject. Some knowledge of pupils can be acquired through observation, junior-year participation, and direct student teaching in the senior year.

One of the most important aspects of pre-service education is experience as a student teacher. "Student" or "cadet" or "practice teaching," as it is variously termed, gradually inducts the prospective teacher into full responsibility of the teaching-learning activities under the skillful guidance of a supervising or helping teacher. This may well be the summation of all the student's work and the climax to a long period of steady initiation, including directed and undirected observation in schools and limited duties in the classroom, including so-called junior participation prior to the senior year.

Nearly all teacher-education institutions provide facilities for students to experience actual teaching, either in the campus laboratory school or in off-campus schools. The laboratory school and student teaching, both on- and off-campus, will play increasingly dynamic roles. The national organization in this field is the Association for Student Teaching, organized in 1920.

3

5

1

2

4

6

1   *This future home economics teacher is a junior at Montclair State College, New Jersey. Her program includes many courses in her subject field, such as clothing and textiles.*

2   *She takes professional education courses, like this one in educational psychology, to equip her with a basic understanding of the methods of teaching.*

3   *At a seminar on marriage and family relations, she acquires some basic insights that will help her prepare her students for better family living.*

4   *Student teaching is an important aspect of professional preparation. Under the helpful eye of an experienced classroom teacher, she assumes genuine teaching responsibilities in the college's demonstration high school.*

5 & 6   *Since a teacher must be a well-rounded individual, her program permits study of many electives, like chemistry and English literature.*

Teacher Aides. Some school systems, notably Bay City, Michigan, have experimented with teacher aides, who, like nurses' aides, assist the professional worker in several duties. The superintendent of the Bay City public schools stated, "Good aides have an interest in children, and under proper guidance can be very helpful in creating the kind of classroom atmosphere which encourages wholesome personality development." The need for more on-the-job experience for young prospective teachers and for more stenographic and clerical assistance for regular teachers is obvious in most school systems.

Internships. A higher level of experience for future teachers is provided through internships comparable to those in medicine. In addition to the fact that it very vitally integrates the theoretical and practical aspects of the student's education, internship has many other significant values. It gives the beginning teacher a chance to spend the first year in a superior school under conditions conducive to growth, it provides guidance and supervision at the time when most needed, it makes possible a gradual transition from student to teacher, and it serves as a period of testing and probation. These values and others are derived from internship plans now conducted jointly by many institutions of teacher education and cooperating schools. These internships are often found in curricular patterns such as the five-year programs.

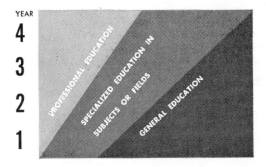

Fig. 11-1. Four years of parallel study in all fields of study.

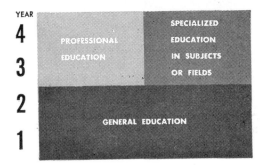

Fig. 11-2. Two years of general education followed by two years of study in professional and subject fields.

Fig. 11-3. Four years of study in general education and subject fields followed by fifth year of study in professional education.

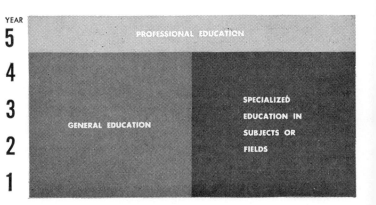

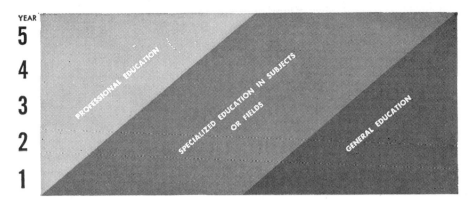

Fig. 11-4. Five years of parallel study in all fields.

Curricular Patterns in Teacher Education. The three areas—general or liberal education, specialization in terms of subjects or fields in which the student expects to teach, and the professional work, including student teaching —are organized in various patterns. Three of the prevailing curricular types are tersely illustrated here.

Four years of undergraduate work are divided into the three areas which are spread over the four years in various proportions, depending upon the philosophy and practices of the institution, as shown in Fig. 11-1. This pattern is found in several single-purpose, teacher-educating institutions.

Two two-year programs are used in which the professional work is offered in only the last two years, and general education primarily in the first two, as indicated in Fig. 11-2. This pattern is found in some colleges of education which admit students in the third year. Some junior colleges furnish the basis for the first two years of such a program.

Five-year programs are increasing in frequency. As the Commission on Teacher Education and Professional Standards has pointed out, "The period is rapidly approaching when a minimum of five years of college preparation will be regarded as essential for fully qualified elementary and secondary school teachers." Indeed, many teacher-education institutions are offering five-, six-, and seven-year programs, the latter usually culminating in the

doctor's degree. Opinion is sharply divided over the proper pattern of five-year programs. Some believe that five-year programs ought to be established along the pattern suggested in Fig. 11-3. In this arrangement, the first four years are devoted exclusively to general education and specialized education in subjects or fields. The fifth year is devoted exclusively to professional education, with much of the work consisting of student teaching, internships, or other forms of supervised field experiences. This pattern has the advantage of assimilating easily those students from other fields of study who have not decided upon teaching until the end of their four-year programs. However, many educators, while favoring five-year preparation programs, view with alarm the complete separation of professional work from the other two areas of study. They favor a pattern which provides for concurrent pursuit of general, specialized, and professional work throughout all four years, as shown in Fig. 11-4.

Actually this disagreement is part of a larger quarrel over the proper balance among these three areas—general, special, and professional education—in the total preparation program. This issue is discussed at greater length in Chapter 17.

CERTIFICATION OF TEACHERS

The National Commission on Teacher Education and Professional Standards issues periodically a manual of certification requirements in the United States. The organization has prepared a helpful brochure the title of which poses the question: *"What Does a Teaching Certificate Mean?"* The Commission answers that the license to teach means the chances are greater that the child will have capable, trained, dedicated teachers. It means that fine, intelligent boys and girls will seek and find long, happy careers in teaching. It means that teachers can hold their heads high as professional men and women—preserving a great tradition of learning and public service.

The certificate of a teacher serves to give status; to protect its holder against unfair competition with unqualified teachers; to control the granting of licenses; to provide a means for the improvement of instruction; to yield information on which a continuous inventory of teachers and their qualifications may be based; and to authorize the payment of salaries.

A license, certificate, or permit to teach in the elementary and secondary schools is required in all states. Most of them request a statement that the applicant for a teaching position is in good health. In general, standards for and procedures in certifying teachers ought to be improved. The late Edgar W. Knight stated that "any real reform is likely to be delayed in the education and certification of teachers until we have had an end of adding-machine and clerical bookkeeping devices both in teacher-education institutions and the state agencies that license teachers." Fortunately, there is a marked trend toward more simplification and less specificity in certification requirements.

Among the better current practices are the following:

Reduction in the policing power of the piece of paper

Elimination of substandard or emergency certificates

Four years of approved teacher preparation with a bachelor's degree as a minimum and with a fifth year as soon as possible

A minimum of fifteen semester hours of professional work including student teaching

A probationary period of not less than three years under professional guidance

Discontinuance of permanent or life certificates

Centralization of general certification in a state agency

Reciprocity between states in certifying qualified teachers

Greater accent on qualitative competencies and professional growth

Increasing responsibility for teacher-educating institutions through an approved program approach to accreditation and certification.

PLACEMENT OF TEACHERS

The educated and dedicated teacher, properly certified or able to meet legal requirements, is ready for work. Will he or she receive a position? The answer depends upon several contingencies, not the least of which is the candidate's ability.

Placement Agencies. Positions in education and psychology are usually obtained through (1) noncommercial agencies or (2) commercial or private placement bureaus.

Teacher-educating institutions maintain the most important noncommercial agencies for placing their graduates and alumni. The services are gratuitous, although a small fee may be charged to cover incidentals of registration. A member of the faculty is in charge and serves as a liaison officer between the employer and future employee. New York University was the first to establish a placement agency for retired faculty members. The National Institutional Placement Association is seeking to promote greater economy and efficiency in the placement of teachers by educational institutions. Other noncommercial bureaus are maintained by state departments of education, state education associations, and state employment services.

Commercial agencies, several of which are banded together in the National Association of

Teachers' Agencies, are those private bureaus which locate positions for teachers at a fixed percentage of their first year's salary. Fees vary with the nature of the service rendered. A registration fee may be required in addition to a percentage charge.

Teacher supply-and-demand studies are made periodically. At present the information available for estimating the demand is limited and spasmodic; furthermore, little is being done toward controlling the supply of teachers. Of course, not all persons who prepare for teaching either desire or secure employment. The outstanding reasons for failures in placement are as follows:

Lack of extracurricular experiences
Low grades in teaching subjects
Low grades in practice teaching
Narrow specialization
Physical defects
Poor preparation
Preparation in overcrowded fields
Religious and racial discrimination
Untidiness in dress
Unpleasant personality

Many of these obstacles to placement can be surmounted through programs of selective admission and retention, limited enrollment, and guidance. Although affected by cycles of unemployment, the teaching profession has increased steadily. Including teachers in private elementary and secondary schools and instructional staff members in all institutions of higher education, the teaching profession in the United States numbers approximately a million and a half. For the immediate future, at least, the demand for teachers will outrun the supply in many fields and in most school systems.

Appointment to Position. The appointment of teachers—a power that should be carefully exercised—is usually made upon the basis of credentials, record in college, participation in extracurricular activities, personality, personal interview, and experience. Then, too, there is a growing reliance upon examinations. The American Council on Education, through its National Committee on Teacher Examinations and with the aid of a grant from the Carnegie Foundation, launched a nationwide series of tests as part of a program to find an objective basis for testing candidates for teaching positions.

The best practice in employing teachers is to have the board of education appoint persons recommended by the superintendent. Where there is no school executive, as in the thousands of one-teacher schools, the appointment is made by the board or by the county superintendent of schools. A teacher seeking a position in a village or city school system should apply directly to the superintendent of schools, but not unless there is a vacancy. After the candidate has obtained a position, he continues his growth through planned orientation and other phases of in-service education, a requirement that many other professions do not have.

In-service

The teacher never arrives at the ultimate in his own education. Throughout his career he is in pursuit of fuller knowledge—general education, specialized education in his subject field, and professional education. This continuing education is frequently referred to as in-service education. This stimulation toward fuller knowledge, unsurpassed in any other occupation, represents one of the great satisfactions and attractions of teaching. It is known that many folks with vigorous intellectual curiosity are attracted to teaching because of its incitement to constant inquiry. As the American author Gamaliel Bradford so aptly put it, "Many earnest persons . . . declare they first began to learn when they began to teach, and that in the education of others they discovered the secret of their own."

The National Society for the Study of Education, which devoted one of its yearbooks to in-service education, stated that this continuing education of teachers include all activities engaged in by professional personnel during their service and designed to contribute to improvement on the job. The following purposes for in-service education are given:

To promote the continuous improvement of the total professional staff of the school system

To eliminate the deficiencies in the background preparation of teachers and other professional workers

To give much needed help to teachers who are new in the particular school and to those who are entering a new responsibility or a new field of work in the profession[2]

ORIENTATION FOR NEW TEACHERS

Beginning Teachers. Various national surveys concerning beginning teachers have been made. Two of these are the survey made by the U.S. Office of Education and reported in *The Beginning Teacher* and the survey conducted by the Research Division of the National Education Association and published in the *Research Bulletin* under the title, "First Year Teachers." These studies reveal the great need for help felt by teachers during their first teaching assignments. An unfortunate by-product of this need for guidance and help is revealed in the Office survey which stated, "In general the proportion of teachers with a really strong commitment to a continuous teaching career appears to be quite small." The NEA study showed that "the typical beginning teacher gets more help from fellow classroom teachers than from anyone else." The beginning teacher can get much help from books, such as *Your First Year of Teaching* written by Marion M. Lamb, and various brochures, such as *Off to a Good Start: Teacher Orientation*, prepared by the American Association of School Administrators.

Orientation Meetings. The American Association of School Administrators has enumerated some of the values to be derived by new teachers from orientation meetings held each year prior to the opening of school:

1. A feeling of security and a better professional outlook
2. An overview of the educational program of the school system
3. An opportunity to meet the superintendent, the supervisory staff, and other colleagues
4. An opportunity to meet coworkers on an informal basis at the coffee, lunch, and party periods
5. Knowledge of the many services offered teachers through the library and the instructional aids department
6. Information on the help to be expected from the consultant teaching staff
7. Information about the curriculum productions prepared by teachers to help fellow teachers
8. Acquaintance with basic subject matter and expectancies for each particular grade assignment
9. Information about the opportunities for professional growth[3]

One of the means for further growth is supervision.

SUPERVISION OF TEACHING AND LEARNING

Preservice education must be supplemented by much in-service learning through supervision. In contradistinction to preteaching, the in-service growth is more a result of doing than of listening. The essential bases for effective in-service teacher education are a continuing zeal for learning, a broad outlook on the role of the school in modern society, an understanding of learning procedures, the improvement of teaching skill, an appreciation of the role of administration, and, finally, the scientific use of evaluation procedures.

At first, supervision was limited to matters directly associated with classroom teaching, but now it is extended to the entire field of learn-

[2] National Society for the Study of Education, *In-service Education*, University of Chicago Press, Chicago, 1957, p. 13.

[3] American Association of School Administrators, *Staff Relations in School Administration*, National Education Association, Washington, D.C., 1955, p. 119.

ing and teaching. This guidance is provided by the superintendent of schools, the principal, the department head, the supervisor, or the teachers themselves. There is a marked trend on the part of supervisors to encourage self-direction for teachers. Many supervisors have come to regard their role as that of helper or stimulator rather than that of inspector or director.

In some of the schools, the title "supervisor" is being displaced by "helping teacher." The helping teacher cannot assume the entire responsibility for the improvement of instruction; all professionally minded teachers are very desirous of self-guidance and development. To this end the supervisor is not content with a laissez-faire policy, but, with complete faith in their ability to advance, she stimulates the teachers to progress. She visits their classrooms less and less as they grow in self-supervision. Just as the modern instructor seeks to teach through pupil effort, so the modern supervisor strives to improve instruction through teacher effort. The endeavors of teachers to reduce pupil failures are likewise being matched by genuine attempts of administrators to decrease the number of teacher failures.

OTHER MEANS OF STIMULATING TEACHER GROWTH

The main entrance to the New Jersey State Teachers College at Newark carries this quotation: "Who dares to teach must never cease to learn." No person should decide to teach unless he is resolved to *learn*, for the real teacher is a part-time student all his life in a continuation school from which he does not graduate. Like Chaucer's scholar in *The Canterbury Tales*, "gladly would he learn, and gladly teach."

Learning to teach and teaching to learn are the goals of the artist-teacher. The more one teaches, the more educated he becomes. As Tennyson wrote:

Yet all experience is an arch where-thro'
Gleams that untravell'd world, whose margin fades
Forever and forever when I move.

A teacher must move forward if his pupils are to develop. Teaching as a profession will advance as long as the individual teachers continue to progress.

Teaching provides a challenge to continued growth. Yet too many teachers are bound by self-satisfaction and callous complacency—they do not stretch forward in the pursuit of perfection. On the other hand, many of them work too hard, endangering their health. They neglect recreation, possibly because they do not know how to relax or to enjoy wholesome avocations or helpful hobbies. Some teachers need a change of environment or rest. The granting of periodic fellowships to teachers has been recommended. These scholarships would allow the outstanding teacher a year on salary for travel, further study, or rest. It has been suggested that schools employ a sabbatical stagger plan whereby teachers who have been in service for a period of six years or more be given a year's or half year's leave of absence with pay, while substitutes are employed at reduced salaries.

One of the new media for in-service teacher education is television. For example, North Carolina teachers have used a series of TV programs "Methods for Modern Teachers." Many media multiply opportunities for growth in the teaching profession.

Among the types of in-service educational growth are these: consultative service in school, demonstration and school visits, exchange teaching, extension and home study, fall planning conferences, institutes, panel method of discussion, professional and cultural reading, professional organizations and meetings, research investigations and surveys, radio and television, sabbatical leave, salary increments and scholarships, summer study, teachers' meetings, travel, workshops and clinics.

Pamphlets and books describe these various

types, as, for example, Harold Spear's *Curriculum Planning through In-service Programs*, which presents a double-barrelled approach to improve the learning of pupils and the teaching of professional workers.

Teaching profession

TEACHER WELFARE

Teachers as a professional group and as individuals naturally are concerned about their own welfare as well as that of the children. Among the welfare factors in which teachers are usually interested are (1) salaries, (2) fringe benefits, (3) tenure, and (4) retirement.

Salaries. Annual wages have increased steadily over a long stretch of time, but teachers still earn less, on the average, than do skilled tradesmen. Costs of living have mounted appreciably, and the educational qualifications for teachers have risen, necessitating a greater investment in preparation. The National Education Association has prepared the following principles of salary scheduling:

1. Minimum salaries should be high enough to attract well-educated, promising young people into teaching.
2. Maximum salaries should be high enough to retain highly competent and professionally ambitious men and women in classroom teaching.
3. Equity of treatment to classroom teachers of like qualifications and experience is essential.
4. Annual increments should provide an orderly progress to the maximum salary.
5. The salary schedule should offer professional stimulation through incentives in recognition of professional qualifications.
6. Salary schedules should be adjusted periodically, with due consideration for trends in earnings in other professions and for changes in the cost of living.
7. Salaries of professional school personnel other than classroom teachers should be scheduled in accordance with the principles that apply to classroom teachers, with suitable recognition of responsibilities and preparation for leadership.
8. There should be professional participation by classroom teachers in the development and administration of salary policies.

A former president of the University of Chicago, Robert M. Hutchins, has said that society cannot get good schools without good teachers, and that by paying them like coolies, society shows no respect for the teaching profession.

Minimum salaries vary widely from one school district to another and from state to state. The fact that teachers' salaries in some states are very low has given rise to agitation for minimum-salary laws—a floor under wages. For the 1959–1960 school year, the National Education Association has recommended a minimum of 6,000 dollars. If starting salaries were established at that level, many more young men and women of outstanding ability would undoubtedly be attracted to lifelong careers in teaching.

School systems usually adopt a salary schedule. This is a plan for the payment of school employees formally accepted by the school committee or board of education. To a large degree it automatically determines the initial salary, the amount and number of yearly increments, and the maximum salary received by the various employees with specified qualifications. Among the factors determining the place of teachers on the regular salary schedule are amount of professional education, number of years of service, ratings on an efficiency scale, and position held. A salary schedule obviates the perennial question of the teacher: "How much money will I get next year?"

Fringe Benefits. Another question, borrowed from labor and industry, is "What are the fringe benefits in teaching?" In private enterprise these marginal benefit packages are often large. In teaching there are some secondary rewards monetarily, but they are small and not universal. One of the real gains sought by labor unions is a guaranteed annual wage. Most teachers have such security although it is usually for only nine or ten months. Arrangements for vacations and holidays are usually quite generous for teachers, who, however, often argue that this is vacation without pay. Sick and maternity leaves are found in most school systems. In addition, sabbatical leaves with and without pay are granted by many educational institutions, especially for further study or teacher enrichment. Some local districts pay teachers for summer school attendance.

Most states, as indicated later, have retirement systems for educators. Insurance programs—health, accident, and life—are often secured reasonably by groups of teachers. Credit unions have been established by many teachers' associations for their members.

Most educational institutions provide faculty rest rooms, smoking rooms, lounges, and recreation areas. Even the common coffee break is permitted in many schools to give teachers a recess period.

Social security benefits are available to many educators as employees of nonprofit organizations and of federal, state, and local governments and as persons self-employed through lectures, writings, and consultative assignments.

Teachers, like any federal taxpayers, under a ruling made by the United States Treasury in 1958, can deduct the cost of education for job advancement through summer school work and late afternoon and evening classes. Retired teachers, like others, can exempt part of their income from federal taxes. Other monetary extras will increase in number and size for teachers.

III *Teacher Tenure.* Fundamentally, tenure laws are enacted to serve the learner and the public, protecting them from teachers intimidated by fear of dismissal because of beliefs or teachings. Prior to passage of such laws, many teachers were dismissed arbitrarily because of their political, religious, or other beliefs. Thus tenure helps to protect the academic freedom of the learner and the teacher. However, these laws should not be drawn so tightly as to discourage the dismissal of incompetent, immoral, or unprofessional teachers. The National Education Association has framed certain basic principles that should guide tenure legislation and policy. Provisions vary among the states, resulting in annual contracts, permissive contracts for more than a year, continuing contracts, or permanent tenure.

IV *Teacher Retirement.* Another moot question among teachers and other professional people is "When do you expect to retire?" or "What do you expect to do when you retire?"

As indicated in Chapter 9, "Adult education," in bygone years retirement was associated with physical or mental infirmities. Retirement provisions for aged and disabled employees originated as private or local enterprises on a charity basis. Today a different idea prevails: there is a growing sense of social and public responsibility for old-age protection. A newer trend is phased retirement, whereby a teacher moves from full-time teaching, through successive stages of part-time work, to ultimate full-time retirement. Readiness for retirement is important.

Responsibility for the retirement of teachers began in cities and local districts. Establishment of these systems reached the peak about 1915. Since that time many local plans have become inoperative or have been absorbed by state-wide retirement or pension systems. New Jersey was the first state to enact provisions for a state-wide retirement system for teachers in 1896. The majority of states and dependencies have since followed suit. The retirement systems are supplemented by many varied and interesting forms of teacher welfare evolved by individual states and cities. In 1927, the Council of the California Teachers Association, Southern Section, authorized the establishment of a home for retired teachers who could not finance themselves. A few associations and cities have similar arrangements. Many public and private school and college teachers benefit from the retirement provisions of the Social Security Act. Many teachers retired from one institution get employment from another school or college. A National Association of Retired Teachers, an affiliate of the NEA, has been organized.

PROFESSIONAL ETHICS FOR TEACHERS

A profession can rise no higher than the code of ethics it adopts and uses daily in living. Among the groups with whom teachers come in contact in their work are the board of education, administrators, supervisors, teachers, non-teaching staff, pupils, parents, and the community. Teachers are frequently confronted with ethical problems: "Should one accept gifts from his students?" "Should one discuss another teacher's weaknesses with a parent?" "Should one support a school policy that he doesn't believe in?" "Should one resign to accept a better position two weeks before the opening of school?" As guides to the ethical behavior of teachers, codes of ethics have been evolved by state associations and the National Education Association. The latter is reproduced in the Appendix of this book.

PROFESSIONAL ORGANIZATIONS

The Educational Policies Commission has published a report, *The Teacher and Professional Organizations,* which describes the role of professional organizations as means of continuing growth.

Educational organizations may be classified by primary objective, such as the promotion of childhood education (Association for Childhood Education); by major function, such as the accrediting of schools (National Council for Accreditation of Teacher Education); by the significance of leaders in education (Horace Mann League or John Dewey Society); by academic level of institutions, such as elementary teachers (Los Angeles Elemen-

tary Teachers Club or National Society of College Teachers of Education); by religious affiliation (National Catholic Education Association or Association of Hebrew Teachers Colleges in America); by labor affiliation (American Federation of Teachers); and by scope, such as geographical areas (Memphis Education Association, or Illinois Education Association, or National Education Association). Because of their simplicity, the geographical classifications, (1) local, (2) state, (3) national, and (4) international, are utilized here as a framework for outlining the professional educational associations.

Local Organizations. Teachers are not organized in some communities, but nearly all public and private school teachers do belong "to a whole or a part of a whole." This banding together serves many purposes. The Department of Classroom Teachers of the NEA states that it is the peculiar function of local teachers' organizations to provide teachers with an opportunity to understand the problems of their respective communities and to acquaint the public in each community with the needs of its teachers and its schools. In the local education association is found the growing edge of the organized teaching profession.

Marked variation are found in types of groupings. Some organizations restrict membership to instructors in a certain field; others are open to all members of an educational staff of a particular school. No one type seems to predominate, although a single organization to include all teachers is growing in favor. Cities with more than one association often have a council, composed of representatives of each group, to look after common interests. Recent years have brought increased interest in and debate about the affiliation of local teachers' organizations with labor groups. This issue is presented later in Chapter 17. Suffice it here to state that teachers are becoming more sensitized to the problems of labor and that enrollments in teachers' unions have increased markedly in recent years.

State Organizations. Local units may be organized as parts of some larger whole, such as the county or state associations. Many of these are determined by fields, as social studies; by grade levels, as elementary teachers; or by function of personnel, as city superintendents. The main core of organized professional activity within the state, however, is the state-wide, all-inclusive society, which is usually known as the state education association or state teachers' association. The usual purpose of these organizations, as indicated in their state journals and as reflected in their activities, is to perform on a state-wide basis what the local groups seek to do. There is a major emphasis on professional improvement of the members, the advancement of teacher and pupil welfare, service to the schools and communities in the state, particularly through legislation, and active cooperation with the associations of other states and national associations.

Many state associations or state departments of education have set up long-term planning commissions which seek to view education within the state with a telescopic vision rather than with a microscopic dissection of minute current problems. This movement is one of the bright spots on the educational horizon, especially since it is being matched by long-term planning on a national scale.

National Organizations—General. The *Educational Directory,* prepared periodically by the U.S. Office of Education, lists numerous educational organizations whose names begin with the word "National" or "American." All these and many others are nationwide in scope. Although most of them represent some special field, they are permeated with large elements of common interest. In recent years many national agencies have made critical analyses of particular aspects of American public education. The *Directory of Deliberative National Committees* lists over 250 such groups which prepare reports on various school problems. The American Council on Education, composed of representatives from various national associations and educational institutions, is a significant coordinating body. This council, organized in 1918, has sponsored such important projects as the Commission on Teacher Education and the American Youth Commission.

Another grouping is the Associated Organizations in Teacher Education, including the American Association of Colleges for Teacher Education. The accreditation function for institutions that prepare teachers is performed by the National Council for Accreditation of Teacher Education. The National Council on Teacher Retirement was launched with the help of the National Education Association.

National Education Association. This national, all-inclusive educative organization is also the largest teachers' association in the world. It was organized in 1857 when 43 educators gathered in Philadelphia and formed the National Teachers Association. The name was changed to the National Education Association in 1907, when it was incorporated under a special act of Congress. By 1960 membership in the NEA had reached 700,000. Its membership goal is expressed in the ideal: "one hundred per cent enrollment in local, state, and national associations, with every teacher at work on the problems of the profession."

In brief its purposes are these: "The National Education Association is dedicated to the upbuilding of democratic civilization and is supported by the loyal cooperation of the leaders of the United States to advance the interests of the teaching profession, promote the welfare of children, and foster the education of all the people." It renders two kinds of services. First come those services that reach the members directly, such as the *NEA Journal,* issued nine times a year, and other publications, as well as conventions of the association, its departments, and allied organizations. These help to promote personal growth and educational research and to build up the common mind of the profession. The second type of service is indirect. Like the values which

the citizen receives from his taxes, these benefits are often overlooked. An important function of the association is to develop high public
understanding of education and desire for
good schools. It aims to elevate the character
and advance the interests of the teaching profession and to promote the cause of education
in the United States. It is not, however, an
agency of the federal government.

The National Education Association, as an
all-inclusive voluntary organization of teachers
and administrators in pre-elementary, elementary, secondary, higher, and adult education,
is a democratic institution. Its policies are determined by the representative assembly coming from all over the United States each summer in connection with the annual convention.
This body consists of delegates elected by state
and local organizations of teachers. The administration of the affairs of the association is
handled by this representative assembly, a
board of trustees, an executive committee, and
a board of directors. The professional and clerical staff, working under the direction of the
executive secretary, are housed in the association's own building at 1201 Sixteenth Street,
N.W., Washington, D.C. This comprehensive
association has 30 departments. The following
list prepared by the NEA omits the organizational names (association, conference, council,
department), and gives only the field of professional activity:

Administrative women in education
Adult education
Art education
Audio-visual instruction
Business education
Classroom teachers
Deans of women
Educational research
Educational secretaries
Elementary school principals
Exceptional children
Health, physical education, and recreation
Higher education
Home economics
Industrial arts
Journalism directors in secondary schools
Kindergarten-primary education
Mathematics teachers
Music education
Retired teachers
Rural education
School adminstrators
School public relations
Science teachers
Secondary school principals
Social studies
Speech education
Supervision and curriculum development
Teacher education
Vocational education

The NEA has served the profession through
national commissions in the following areas:
legislation, educational policies, the defense of
democracy, safety education, and teacher education and professional standards. It is allied
with other organizations, such as the National
Congress of Parents and Teachers, and it cooperates with many agencies, such as the
American Council on Education and the Council on Cooperation in Teacher Education. It is
not connected with labor unions. The story of
this important national organization is told in
NEA: The First One Hundred Years, written by Edgar B. Wesley for the centennial
celebration in 1957.

B American Federation of Teachers. This national organization is affiliated with the American Federation of Labor but is relatively autonomous with respect to its program and
policy. The AFT contends that education has
traditionally had its greatest support from organized labor and that affiliation with the AFL-
CIO offers the best hope for correcting the social, economic, and political injustices from
which education allegedly suffers. The federation has two main objectives:

1. To consolidate the teachers of the country
   into a strong group which would be able
   to protect its own interests.
2. To raise the standard of the teaching class
   by a direct attack on the conditions which,

according to the belief of the Federation, prevent teaching from reaching its desired status. Among these conditions are lack of academic freedom and civil liberty, the absence of self-determination of policy and of democratic control.

The story of the American Federation of Teachers is told in a publication by its Commission on Educational Reconstruction titled *Organizing the Teaching Profession*. The official organ of the AFT is the monthly journal *The American Teacher*. The federation maintains the following standing committees: academic freedom, democratic human relations, pensions and retirement, protection of teachers' rights, state federations, taxation and school finance, vocational education, working conditions, adult and workers' education, child care, and educational trends and policies.

The federation has launched a drive to unionize college professors. Administrators are not permitted membership in the AFT on the grounds that they represent management rather than labor in the classic cleavage between employer and employee. Most of the AFT locals and AFT membership are found in city school systems. Although the federation does not release data regarding its membership, it is estimated that less than 60,000 of the nation's teachers belonged to the AFT in 1960.

National Catholic Educational Association. Another rapidly growing organization of teachers is the National Catholic Educational Association. The teachers in Catholic schools and colleges wield a great influence, not merely on the academic study of students but also on their religious life. The National Catholic Educational Association in its annual meeting in 1955 reaffirmed its conviction that there should be no deviation from the policy of insistence "upon the necessity of adequately prepared teachers at every level of Catholic education."

One of their accents has been the improvement of curriculums in the Catholic institutions. Working through the College and University Department of the Association, and with a grant from the Fund for the Advancement of Education, sister formation conferences on curriculum have been held. The *Sister Formation Bulletin* and publications of the National Catholic Welfare Conference, which has headquarters in Washington, D.C., carry much information and inspiration for teachers in Catholic institutions. One of the major book publishing companies has recently launched a program of publishing several textbooks known as the Catholic Series in Education, the first of which is *Education for American Democracy*, by Edward J. Power of the University of Detroit.

International Organizations. Many organizations listed in the *Educational Directory* contain in their titles the words "World" or "International"; only a few can be mentioned here. The International Council for Exceptional Children holds annual sessions. The National Education Association has an active Committee on International Relations. The World Federation of Education Associations was a pioneering organization in the field of world-wide general education. Many countries were represented in the World Organization of the Teaching Profession, which was organized in Glasgow, Scotland, in 1947 and reorganized as the World Confederation of Organizations of the Teaching Profession in 1953 at Oxford, England. This organization has been recognized by the United Nations as an official consultative body. As previously indicated, the United States has a National Commission for UNESCO—United Nations Educational, Scientific, and Cultural Organization—and is actively working with the United Nations in world-wide education. W. G. Carr states that WCOTP is to UNESCO as the NEA is to the U.S. Office of Education.

Founded in Heidelberg in 1918, the New Education Fellowship, with the main purpose of making education a "force for improving the world order," is another world-wide organization. Still another is the International Association of Professors and Lecturers, constituted in Brussels in 1947.

Organizations and the Advancement of Education. According to Mark A. May of the Institute of Human Relations at Yale University, "It is an open secret that in the hierarchy of respectability of professions in American society, the teaching profession ranks rather low." Through continuous and all-inclusive membership in strong, active organizations—local, state, national, and international—teachers can achieve the ethical, economic, and professional respectability toward which they are striving. Although the main purpose may sometimes be tinged with the secondary motives of personal and professional profit and protection, nevertheless teachers' organizations at their best serve as honorable means toward the primary end of providing better educational opportunities for children through improving the standards of teaching personnel.

Teaching personnel

Most school positions are for teachers. The major types of teaching personnel described here are (1) classroom teachers, (2) special classroom teachers, (3) teachers in federal jurisdictions and foreign countries, and (4) teachers of teachers. Other persons engaged in educational work are treated in Chapter 12.

CLASSROOM TEACHERS

The largest number of teaching opportunities are in regular classroom-teaching positions. Although there are numerous private and parochial schools, the public school system affords the largest number of these teaching positions. Classroom teachers are found in nearly all the institutions mentioned in Chapters 1 to 4, viz., national, state, county, and local systems. They work in all the academic levels considered in Chapters 5 to 9, viz., pre-elementary, elementary, secondary, higher institutions and adult education.

The special teachers are those who deal with: (1) particular types of pupils, as the exceptional; (2) special methods or materials, as audio-visual education; (3) specialized subjects or fields, as vocational education; and (4) special institutions, as hospital schools.

Teachers of Special Pupils. Chapter 10 centers around the two major types of pupils, viz., the normal and the atypical. The former, because of their natural resourcefulness, ability, and ambition, may succeed in school and life despite their teachers, but the disadvantaged pupils may be further handicapped in a marked degree because their teachers are inefficient or not specially educated for their particular tasks. The atypical pupils, especially those severely handicapped, need teachers expert in the special areas appertaining to the major types of exceptional pupils described in Chapter 10. The laws of most states stipulate that teachers of exceptional children must have specialized preparation and certificates.

Many educational institutions offer this special preparation. A number of residential schools prepare teachers of exceptional children, particularly teachers of the mentally handicapped.

In addition to special preparation, the teacher of handicapped children should have patience, a sympathetic and thorough understanding of the principles and facts of physical growth, buoyant optimism, and a healthy social philosophy. Several thousand more teachers are needed for a large number of handicapped pupils in public schools. In view of the specialized preparation, the exacting nature of the task, and the special state aid for such children, the salaries of these special instructors are usually higher than those of the regular classroom teacher. The monetary rewards, however, are insignificant in comparison to the heart-felt thanks of those who profit most—the pupils, many of whom have ears but hear not, eyes but see not, tongues but talk not, and feet but walk not.

B *Teachers with Special Methods or Materials.* Among those who devote full or part time to instructional procedures or materials of a special nature are those engaged in audio-visual or multisensory education. Schools of the air, made possible by radio, facsimile broadcasting, and television will need many experienced teachers. Many schools have set up departments with directors of audio-visual education and curriculum materials. The directors and others engaged in this special work ought to understand thoroughly the curriculum and child growth in order to coordinate their efforts with those of the regular classroom teachers.

C *Teachers of Special Subjects or Fields.* Nearly every teacher works at least part of the time in a special subject or field. Each general subject or field offers many specific phases; for example, several different kinds of English are taught. There is always plenty of room at the top for persons who possess the uncommon blend of artistic sense and teaching skill. A shortage of superlatively good teachers exists in almost every area of learning.

Three fields that are increasing their number of workers are science, mathematics, and foreign language, which received special impetus as a result of the National Defense Education Act in 1958.

A *Teachers in Special Schools.* Thousands of teachers are employed in special schools, such as church and Bible schools, technical schools, correctional institutions, experimental centers, and hospital schools. The last are briefly described here.

Some hospital schools are in private institutions, whereas others are in municipal or state hospitals. The services rendered in this type of teaching are threefold: therapeutic, vocational, and general educational. It seems reasonable to expect that states will give increased financial and moral support to this type of teaching and that many positions will have to be filled in the years to come.

TEACHERS IN FEDERAL JURISDICTIONS AND FOREIGN COUNTRIES

Many teachers are employed or supervised by the federal government. Aside from the instructors in the nationwide federally aided programs of emergency and vocational education, many persons teach in the federal reservations, in the territories, dependencies, and special areas in and outside the United States. In some of the dependencies, only natives or resident white people are employed as teachers.

Exchange Teachers. Many opportunities to teach away from home are provided by exchange teaching. Exchanges in teaching personnel are made between cities and between countries, usually for one-year periods. The purposes of these temporary transfers are to trade educational and social ideas; to dissolve provincialism; to foster better feeling between sections of the United States and between various countries; to understand better the countries of the world; and to promote a broader outlook on the part of students, faculties, and communities. Teaching experience is usually a prerequisite for appointment as an exchange teacher. Information on reciprocity in teaching positions is available from the International Division of the U.S. Office of Education in Washington, D.C., and from the Institute of International Education in New York.

TEACHERS OF TEACHERS

Thousands of persons are engaged in teaching teachers, in public, parochial, and private schools, normal schools, teachers colleges, and departments and schools of education in colleges and universities. Among the positions are those held by associate teachers or supervisors of cadets in teacher-education institutions or in affiliated schools, and by members of the various departments in colleges and universities, especially in the education and psychology departments. Opportunities for this work are thus available on all academic levels, from preservice education of prospective teachers for the nursery schools to the in-service education of faculty members in graduate schools. Usually, the minimum academic requirement is a master's degree, with some courses in education and psychology and practical experience in public schools. Increasingly, actual school experience is required of supervising teachers and regular collegiate staff members in order that they may be familiar with the needs of prospective teachers in these schools. The supply of new, capable supervisors of student teachers is very limited. The supreme challenge in teacher education lies in the unsurpassed opportunities to multiply oneself, since an instructor of prospective or regular teachers potentially reaches thousands of pupils. A teacher of teachers is also an indirect teacher of pupils.

Shall I teach?

Obviously the choice of any vocation depends upon a number of related questions, which are discussed briefly.

How Important Is the Vocation to Society? People like to feel that they are engaged in work that is socially useful. Throughout its entirety, this book has stressed the preeminent importance of teaching in our society. No other profession is of greater consequence in advancing man in his march toward a finer life and a higher civilization.

What Interests and Abilities Must One Have? Many researchers are seeking the answer to this question. Many studies have been made of the relation between interests and ability and success in teaching. The scientific evidence is not too conclusive but there are hunches galore. In general one should have an attractive personality. This means a sense of humor; a respect, love, and sensitivity for people—especially children; emotional stability; an abundance of optimism, trust, and confidence; strong moral values. One must have certain intellectual qualities. These include superior intelligence, intellectual curiosity, respect for truth, thirst for knowledge, and intellectual honesty. Physical attributes help. These include good physical and mental health, good appearance, pleasing voice, physical vigor, and good health habits. As one eminent teacher put it, "What a teacher is, as a human being, is as important as what he knows or can learn."

What Are the Opportunities for Employment? Education offers a tremendous variety of positions in almost unlimited specialties, working with people at every age level. Geographically, educators are to be found in virtually every city and hamlet in this country and throughout the world. One can be sure that teachers are employed in almost any location where one might like to live. For the immediate future, at least, the demand will outrun the supply for most positions in education so that able persons will have little difficulty in finding employment.

What about the Availability of Teacher Education? Because of the great number of teachers needed, teacher-education institutions are more widely available than any other field of professional study. Virtually every major university offers a program of teacher education. In several other professions, the supply of potential students far exceeds the demand, so that many candidates must be eliminated. This is not true in education. Since many teacher-education institutions are publicly supported, tuition fees are low. Many students are able to afford professional preparation for teaching who could not afford a college education in preparation for other professions.

What Is the Status of Teachers in Society? It is difficult to answer this question categorically. The evidence is conflicting and the situation is changing. While our people have written and talked about the great importance of teachers, teachers have often received shabby treatment. At times they have been subject to low salaries, restrictions in their private lives, loyalty oaths, and unfair criticisms. Most teachers are associated with the lower middle socioeconomic level. Many parents would not urge their children, particularly their sons, to become teachers. Radio, television, and movies usually portray teachers as stodgy or eccentric. Teaching has not been generally regarded as a high-status profession.

On the other hand, it appears that significant progress has been made and continues to be made in elevating the status of teachers. Salaries, while still inadequate, are improving. Restrictions upon the freedom of teachers are less common. Anti-intellectualism is receding and a new respect for teaching and teachers seems to be emerging. Spectacular technological developments, such as guided missiles and earth satellites, have demonstrated the importance of knowledge and have generated new respect for teachers.

What Are the Economic Rewards of Teaching? The inadequacy of teachers' salaries is well known. This is particularly true for male teachers. Many other occupations, demanding less responsibility, preparation, and skill, offer the male worker higher wages. But for women, salaries in teaching rank somewhat above average among the occupations that attract college women. The economic position of teachers is improving gradually. Minimum salaries for teachers are guaranteed by law in most states. Most salary schedules provide annual increments for teachers up to a certain maximum. Moreover, the employment of the teacher is steady, unaffected by recessions, weather, or other conditions. Many teachers capitalize upon the long summer vacation by taking summer jobs.

Many teachers enjoy sick-leave benefits, retirement funds subsidized by public funds, and other fringe benefits.

What Are the Other Job Satisfactions of Teaching? American school buildings, books, libraries, laboratories, and other teaching facilities are the envy of the world. Although there are exceptions, most teachers find their classrooms and teaching tools clean, attractive and well kept. Their colleagues, for the most part, are intelligent well-educated people. Living with children is sometimes aggravating but also high adventure. No other occupation offers the intellectual stimulation and opportunity for one's own continued learning as does teaching. The environment of teaching is clean, healthful, and free of physical danger. Long vacations offer opportunity for travel, relaxation, advanced study, or part-time jobs. Knowledge of and experience with children provides priceless preparation for parenthood. Although the work of the teacher is under close public scrutiny and often subject to criticism, this is infinitely more challenging and satisfying than occupying a position in which one's work is ignored.

Teaching yields its highest satisfactions in imperishable intangibles—rewards that money cannot buy. These rewards are in the realm of ideas and ideals, visions and values. These rewards are manifest in many ways—a very young gentleman in the first grade announces to his teacher that he loves her; a third-grade boy insists that his loose tooth must be pulled by his teacher; a former student wins a college scholarship; one's patience and trust transforms a misbehaving freshman into a future Congressional Medal of Honor winner; one's hospital room is submerged with get-well cards and wonderful young visitors. The examples are infinite; their frequency, abundant; and their scope, universal. William Douglas found the intangible income of the American teacher in faraway lands:

The greatest heritage that America has in the East comes from our teachers and missionaries. Through our educational emissaries the people of Asia came to know the warm and understanding heart of America. . . . We must emulate the

Few professions offer to the young man or woman of fine mind and warm heart a greater opportunity for service than teaching. The teacher is constantly in the midst of an adventure in knowledge in the company of vibrant young citizens and professional colleagues.

teacher and missionary, identify ourselves with the aspirations of the parents, and help them by kindness and understanding to achieve a fuller life.[4]

Our Ambassador from the Philippines, Carlos Romulo, discovered the psychic pay of the American schoolteacher in his country:

On August 23, 1901, The United States Army transport *Thomas* docked at Manila with some six hundred American schoolteachers aboard. . . . These young schoolteachers had the qualities we like to consider peculiarly American. . . . They scattered through the provinces, into our little barrios and throughout our towns and cities. They boarded in modest Filipino homes. They came to know our people well, and they came to love our children. And our people, young and old, came to know and love these schoolteachers from far away. For they were young men and women fulfilling a great and unselfish mission. . . . The American schoolteachers joined with us in creat-

[4] William O. Douglas, *Strange Lands and Friendly People*, Harper & Brothers, New York, 1951, pp. 325–326.

3 *At his desk in the department office, he uses his free time for coffee and a look at the rest of the day's work.*

2 *He pauses to discuss a classroom problem with two male colleagues and a young student teacher assigned to his class by her college.*

1 *Here a Baldwin High School, New York, social studies teacher begins the day with a special history class for bright students who are exploring the realm of social and philosophical thought.*

*5   As football coach, he shows
the proper way of faking a hand-off.*

ing the literacy, the knowledge, the self-confidence, and the devotion to democracy on which it was possible for us to establish our Republic.[5]

Certainly few, if any, other occupations are of greater consequence or offer larger reward to young men and women of keen minds, diligent hands, and warm hearts.

Summary

Teaching, the largest of all professions, can also be the grandest for many. Teachers work in all areas of learning, described in Part 2, from pre-elementary through graduate and adult education. Despite the increase in salaries, there is a critical shortage of good teachers in the United States today.

The historical calendar in this chapter chronicles some of the events in the development of teaching. Historically, the major periods are: training, preparation, and education.

The best human resources must be recruited for the teaching profession. The education of teachers is conducted in various types of institutions of higher learning. Most are educated

[5] From an address by Carlos P. Romulo at Teachers College, Columbia University, November 21, 1955.

*4   Once a week he attends
an in-service course on school-community
communications with other teachers.*

*6   After school, he asks his
neighbors to sign a
nominating petition for a
candidate of the political party in
which he serves as county committeeman.*

*7   At home, he concludes
his daily pursuit of knowledge in the company of
three very young foreign language scholars.*

in private and public liberal arts institutions. The three major areas usually included in the teacher's preparation are: general education, specialized education in subjects or fields, and professional education, of which the keystone is student teaching. Properly certified and placed, the beginning teacher starts his work.

No graduate of a teacher-education curriculum is a finished product. The teacher learns continuously on the job, especially through supervision and self-supervision. Educational organizations of myriad types stimulate teacher growth.

Many types of teaching positions in various fields are available including teaching teachers.

No profession demands so much, for so many, for so long, and with so little as teaching. Yet it has its innumerable rewards, both tangible and intangible. Tangible things include sufficient salary, brand-new buildings, and teaching tools.

Teaching brings rich rewards in imperishable intangibles. The real rewards are the timeless verities of the unseen. They are in the realm of ideas and ideals. The mighty militarists have tried to make a new and better world and have failed, and the partisan politicians have not succeeded either. Teachers dedicated to the joint ideals of selfless service and sacred sacrifice can help make a better world for this generation and for those yet unborn.

The continuing challenge to the teacher who is dedicated to tomorrow is found in the pearls of the poet James Russell Lowell:

> Be noble, and that nobleness that lies
> In other men, sleeping but never dead,
> Shall rise in majesty to meet thine own.

Suggested activities

1. Study the historical calendar for an overview of the development of teacher education.
2. Explain the purpose and program of the Future Teachers of America or the Student NEA.
3. Write a letter of application for a teaching position.
4. Examine the certification requirements for teaching in your state.
5. Describe some organized means for in-service education of teachers.
6. Make an annotated list of the best professional magazines available in your teaching field or area.
7. Prepare a history of the National Education Association or some other professional organization.
8. Make a list of educational organizations in your state.
9. Study the laws of your state which deal with tenure, salaries, and retirement.
10. Describe the best elementary or secondary school teacher you know.
11. Investigate the opportunities and rewards in teaching overseas.
12. Investigate the types of positions available for teachers of teachers.
13. Make a critical self-evaluation to determine whether you should enter or remain in the teaching profession.
14. Study an NEA report of teacher supply and demand and make a report on those types of fields that are most undercrowded and most overcrowded.
15. Prepare a report on the topic "The Basic Changes Needed in the Legal and Administrative Structure of Public Education To Further the Professionalization of Education."

Bibliography

Books

Association for Supervision and Curriculum Development: *Learning and the Teacher*, National Education Association, Washington, D.C., 1959. Discusses the effects of the teacher's attitudes and behavior on his interpersonal relations with students.

Chamberlain, Leo M., and Leslie W. Kindred: *The Teacher and School Organization*, Prentice-Hall, Inc., Englewood Cliffs, N.J., 1959, chaps. 5, 6, 8. Discusses teacher preparation, securing a position, and teacher welfare and security.

College Teaching as a Career, American Council on Education, Washington, D.C., 1958. Describes the opportunities in college teaching, preparation needed, conditions of work, and personal messages from some distinguished college teachers.

Eastmond, Jefferson N.: *The Teacher and School Administration*, Houghton Mifflin Company, Boston, 1959, chaps. 16–19. Discusses the in-service concerns of teachers, professional growth, salaries, economic status, turnover, tenure, and retirement.

Employment Outlook in Teaching, U.S. Department of Labor, Washington, D.C., 1960. This annual report reviews the current employment outlook, salaries, and other vocational information for teachers.

Huggett, Albert J., and T. M. Stinnett: *Professional Problems of Teachers*, The Macmillan Company, New York, 1956, part II. Professional personnel policies and working conditions are discussed in detail in these chapters.

Lieberman, Myron: *Education as a Profession*, Prentice-Hall, Inc., Englewood Cliffs, N.J., 1956, chaps. 8, 12, 14, 15. A scholarly and provocative discussion of the circumstances impeding the professionalization of teaching; characteristics, economic status, and occupational status of teachers.

Moustakas, Clark E.: *The Alive and Growing Teacher*, Philosophical Library, Inc., New York, 1959. Emphasizes the importance of knowing and accepting oneself in teaching, presenting a helpful picture of how the teacher thinks, acts, and grows.

Sharp, D. Louise: *Why Teach?* Henry Holt and Company, Inc., New York, 1957. A fascinating collection of essays by important people regarding the importance and the joys of teaching.

Stinnett, T. M.: *The Teacher and Professional Organizations*, National Education Association, Washington, D.C., 1956, sec. III, units 2–4. Excellent and thorough treatment of local, state, and national teachers associations.

Wesley, Edgar B.: *N.E.A.: The First Hundred Years*, Harper & Brothers, New York, 1957. An interesting history of the NEA describing its contribution to the development of teaching and education and a description of its present status.

Wilson, Charles H.: *A Teacher Is a Person*, Henry Holt and Company, Inc., New York, 1956. An experienced teacher's popular account of his experiences and perceptions of the teacher in American society.

Wynn, D. Richard: *Careers in Education*, McGraw-Hill Book Company, Inc., New York, 1960. Written for persons considering a career in education, providing information about employment opportunities, salaries, and other conditions of work.

Periodicals

Armstrong, W. Earl: "The Teacher Education Curriculum," *Journal of Teacher Education*, vol. 8 (September, 1957), pp. 230–243. An authoritative statement of the criteria of excellence in teacher-education programs.

Barnes, David H., and Sam M. Lambert: "The Guy in the Shiny Pants," *Phi Delta Kappan*, vol. 39 (June, 1958), pp. 398–401. A popularized account of a research study of men teachers—their economic and social position and how they feel about teaching.

Barzun, Jacques: "Oldest Profession in the World," *Educational Digest*, vol. 22 (March, 1957), pp. 6–8. Interesting account of teaching as a profession.

Chandler, B. J.: "What It Takes to Professionalize Teaching," *The School Executive*, vol. 77 (December, 1957), pp. 48–49. A hardheaded look at some unprofessional aspects of the profession and what needs to be done about them.

Davis, Hazel: "The Case for Professional Salaries," *NEA Journal*, vol. 47 (October, 1958), pp. 484–485. Relates the salary problem to national economic trends and salaries in other occupations and looks into the desirable level of teachers' salaries.

Haskew, Laurence D., and others: "Teacher Education," *NEA Journal*, vol. 48 (April, 1959), pp. 15–31. Excellent series of articles explaining America's design for teacher education; how it compares with European models; arguments for and against general, specialized, and professional education; and certification practices and problems.

Krastin, Alexandra: "Don't Tell Me Teaching's a Soft Job," *Saturday Evening Post*, vol. 226 (May 8, 1954), pp. 22–23. Description of the frustrations of teaching, with a resolution to continue in this important work.

Leonard, George B., Jr.: "What Is a Teacher?" *Look*, vol. 20 (February 21, 1956), pp. 29–39. An interesting picture story of the teacher at work with a discussion of some of the problems and issues affecting teachers.

Maul, Ray C.: "College Teaching: Challenge and Opportunity," *Phi Delta Kappan*, vol. 38 (February, 1957), pp. 175–180. Surveys the need for college teachers and describes the career opportunities in this field.

McLaughlin, W. J.: "Wear the Mantle Proudly," *NEA Journal*, vol. 48 (April, 1959), pp. 35–38. Tells the true story of a busy and rewarding life of a great teacher who is also an active citizen and a zealous worker in his professional association.

National Education Association: "The Postwar Struggle to Provide Competent Teachers," *Research Bulletin*, vol. 35 (October, 1957), pp. 99–127. Research report analyzes the effect of population trends, competition of other occupations, and other factors affecting the supply of teachers.

Star, Jack: "Comeback of the Male Teacher," *Look*, vol. 23 (February 17, 1959), pp. 84–89. Pictorializes the increasing number of men entering teaching—the reasons for and the results of this trend.

Stinnett, T. M.: "Standards Are Still Going UP!" *NEA Journal*, vol. 44 (December, 1955), pp. 541–542. Argues that the best way to increase supply of teachers is to raise standards and reports progress in this effort.

Stocker, Joseph: "Teachers in California: 'He Who Can, Must'," *The Reporter*, vol. 16 (February 21, 1957), pp. 22–25. Story of how one of the best state teachers associations is rapidly professionalizing teaching.

Wynn, Richard: "Teachers Are Entitled to Job Satisfaction," *The Nation's Schools*, vol. 55 (May, 1955), pp. 43–45. Describes working conditions necessary for happiness in teaching.

chapter 12

Other personnel

Varied Opportunities in Education. For many positions of significance, classroom teaching is a prerequisite, but many persons in educational work are not directly engaged in actual teaching. No one can overestimate the importance of teachers, but neither should he ignore or forget the million and more other educational workers in the United States. Unfortunately, the emphasis in recruitment of personnel has been unbalanced, limited to the customary and established positions for classroom teachers; the wide range of educational activities in which careers have been established or are now emerging has not been revealed. This has tended to inhibit social progress and to drive away from educational service many talented persons.

Several hundred different positions are now found in education. Approximately fifty types of educational work are mentioned briefly in this chapter. Teaching personnel, especially classroom teachers, are described in Chapter 11. The pages that follow are concerned primarily with those persons engaged in educational work other than full-time classroom teaching, as listed in the five divisions indicated in the outline.

Part-time and semiteachers

Thousands of educational workers do not devote a full school year or their entire time to teaching. Those who are not administrators may be grouped in four categories, viz., (1) part-time teachers, (2) off-campus workers, (3) personnel workers, and (4) other specialists. Various persons within these groups are described briefly.

PART-TIME TEACHERS

Substitute Teachers. Work opportunities for many persons, particularly married women, are afforded by part-time instruction in the form of substitute teaching. Occasional teachers should be carefully chosen according to

Orientation
Part-time and semiteachers
Administrators and supervisors
Personnel from other professions
Other nonteaching personnel
Nonpaid personnel
Summary

definite standards. The fact that an unemployed person who taught twenty years ago needs a few dollars should not be the sole basis for selection. The candidate for substitute teaching is usually required to fill out and file with the superintendent of schools an application blank giving data as to education, ability, past experience, and certification. The applicant is also subject to an oral interview before being placed on the eligibility list. Adequate preparation is essential, since a poor substitute in one day may undo a week's work of the regular teacher.

Other Part-time Teachers. Others who give a portion of their time to instruction include those special teachers employed for only a part of a day or week on a regular schedule. For example, a special music teacher may work a few hours daily; in college, a specialist from the business world may teach an economics class or an expert surgeon may serve part time as a special lecturer in certain aspects of surgery. Teaching provides part-time employment for many persons. With the great increase in pupils and the resultant shortage of teachers, many married women are entering or returning to full-time or part-time educational service.

OFF-CAMPUS WORKERS

Extension Workers. Many college and university instructors devote part of their time to extension teaching. One important type of off-campus activity in which they may become involved is the Cooperative Extension Service, which involves the federal government through the Department of Agriculture, the federal government and the states through their land-grant colleges, the counties through their governing boards, and the local communities through their cooperating organizations and committees. All workers must be approved by the state and federal officials. This approval makes them employees of the agricultural college, which acts for the state, and of the Department of Agriculture. Several members of

the federal Extension Service devote themselves to extension administration, research studies, and teaching; an additional number are engaged in visual instruction and editorial activities. Foremost in the Cooperative Extension Service are the resident agents in the counties and their assistants, -viz., the county agent, as he is usually called; the home demonstration agent; and the boys' and girls' club agents or counselors. The National Association of County Agricultural Agents has recommended that county agents pursue systematic graduate study as a part of their activities. It is significant that the Advisory Committee on Education stated, "Everywhere in the Extension Service the work is considered as teaching."

Other Off-school-ground Workers. Many other educational workers spend much of their time away from the school grounds. For example, the coordinators in the federally aided vocational plan are constantly making contacts with employers and workers. Some of the personnel workers mentioned later spend much of their time in home, fields, and factories. Outdoor education, including camping, is one of the newer career challenges.

PERSONNEL WORKERS

This chapter and the preceding two deal with the personnel of American school systems, including pupils, teachers, and other workers. Obviously many employees are especially delegated to tasks that deal almost entirely with the human or personal agents in education. This very important group, segregated here as personnel workers, includes (1) visiting teachers, (2) attendance officials, (3) guidance personnel, (4) placement officials, (5) deans of boys and men, (6) deans of girls and women, and (7) recreational leaders. These are singled out from a larger number for special emphasis in the succeeding pages.

Visiting Teachers or Counselors. A challenging form of service with dual duties is performed by a visiting teacher or counselor, who acts as educator and social worker. Since she works with the two groups of adults who have the greatest influence on the child, viz., parents and teachers, the visitor with her dual contacts is able to study the child as a product of both home and school. As a member of the teaching staff, she works closely with the school, and, as a social worker, she cooperates with existing social agencies. In many instances the visiting teacher is the home teacher or counselor. She is the representative of the classroom teacher in dealing with the pupil who must for physical or other reasons remain at home. As a social worker, she knows the organized social agencies upon which she can call for assistance in the material needs of the underprivileged pupil and his family. The visiting teacher also calls in the homes of well-adjusted, successful pupils.

The role of the visiting or home teacher requires insight, skill, conversational ability, a high degree of personal fitness, and the two-fold basic training and experience of a teacher and a social caseworker. Through a well-qualified visiting teacher the school looks *out* as well as *in* and stresses preventive as well as remedial procedures for normal and problem pupils. Visiting teacher work has its hardships, like any profession. The hours are irregular, including calls in the evening and often on Saturday and Sunday. Furthermore, tackling one serious problem after another brings a certain discouragement, and the constant handling of children's difficulties means a drain on the emotions. Despite these hardships, visiting teachers all over the United States are engaged in this new educational profession.

Attendance Personnel. Among the employees of the school district are full-time or part-time census enumerators and attendance officials. Sometimes these two functionaries are combined in the same person, who may also be engaged in teaching. Although the trend is toward the establishment of a continuous school census, the enumeration of pupils of school age usually is a periodic task, especially in the small cities. The National League to Promote School Attendance is working toward a broader acceptance of the ideal of attendance work as an integral and continuing part of the total educational program.

The enforcement of attendance is a continuous obligation assigned to full-time workers in the large school administrative units. These personnel workers are relatively recent in certain areas, for only since 1918 have all the 50 states had compulsory attendance laws. In the early days these employees were called truant officers. Current practice favors a title such as attendance worker, since it emphasizes the positive philosophy of improving the attendance of all pupils rather than the negative and often temporary remedy whereby a burly policeman caught a truant and dragged him back to school. The old practice aimed at making the pupil conform to the school laws, whereas the modern objective implies the willingness of school authorities to adjust the program to the pupil's peculiar needs, interests, and abilities. Home and school cooperation is sought.

Whereas an officer's badge and knowledge of school laws were formerly the prerequisites for an attendance worker, now the qualifications demand an understanding of child welfare problems and social casework. A national organization of attendance officers as well as state and local agencies are trying to raise the present level of school attendance service so that it will attract competent personnel. The attendance supervisor should be a well-balanced, dynamic person, broadly experienced and adequately trained.

Guidance Personnel. Marked improvement in school attendance results from the adoption of guidance programs. Many persons are employed in this work which has been defined previously as "seeing through John and then helping John to see himself through." It involves studying an individual; learning his capacities, needs, and interests; guiding his efforts; and then seeing him through until he obtains a position and succeeds in it. Guidance ought to be systematic and functional so that students will not make important educational decisions, vocational choices, and life adjustments on mere guesses, false assumptions, or meager information. It is desirable for the counselor to have had experience as a classroom teacher.

The American Psychological Association has recognized three different levels at which counselors function. The first level they call part-time counselors. This group consists of persons who are carrying on some counseling in connection with their other duties in schools, industries, churches, or social agencies. The second level they designate psychological counselors. These positions require the equivalent of two years of graduate training and would probably carry some sort of master's degree label. The third level they call counselor-psychologists. Positions in this area call for a longer period of graduate work leading to a doctor's degree. Workers at all levels are direly needed today.

One type of specialized counseling is vocational counseling, which has been defined as the process of assisting the individual to choose an occupation, prepare for it, enter it, progress in it, and retire from it. The work of the vocational counselor is outlined by the National Vocational Guidance Association, which lists the following specialized activities: study of the individual through interviews, school records, questionnaires, examination and tests, and employment records; study of the occupations, through surveys and compilations of literature; interviews with groups and individuals; employment certification and placement; follow-up services; and related activities, such as club work. The increasing national concern for adequate pupil guidance is revealed in the fact that Congress in 1958 appropriated federal funds for improving the work in this important field.

Placement Officials. Junior placement or employment for youth is becoming an increasing responsibility of the schools. In many cities the junior consultation service for out-of-school youth is also sponsored by the public schools. All placement workers have certain basic duties, whether they perform them in a school, social service agency, or state employment service. The duties include analyzing jobs, registering applicants, interviewing them, classifying registrants, receiving employers' orders, selecting and referring applicants to prospective employers, verifying placement, following up the employees, doing field work to contact employers, keeping records, preparing reports and statistical data, and continuously evaluating.

The placement worker's stock in trade is information about the world of work. Furthermore, he has to establish numerous contacts with school staff members, parents, school psychologists, employers, and community agencies. He must have as varied an occupational experience as possible, with prolonged training and education in the same disciplines as are required of other professional personnel who are dealing with human beings in their individual and social adjustment. This task is being increasingly recognized as a career that requires professional standards, certification, and supervised internship.

Many public and private agencies cooperate with the schools in solving the problems of youth placement. Some junior placement services are affiliated with state and federal employment bureaus.

Deans of Boys and Men. Many counselors for male students are called deans of boys in the high schools and deans of men in the colleges. In the secondary school some titles are dean of boys, vice-principal, assistant principal, administrative assistant, boys' adviser, boys' counselor, director of guidance, coordinator, class adviser, and guidance teacher.

The outstanding qualifications for deans in secondary schools are: special training in guidance; a knowledge of adolescent physiology and psychology; a liking for and sympathetic understanding of teen-age boys, their problems and possibilities; the ability to aid in the solution of individual problems; the art of inspiring confidence and respect; and plenty of patience. Usually a master's degree is required. Among the responsibilities are attendance problems, vocational guidance, curriculum development, discipline, food and clothing for needy students, interviews with parents and prospective employers, supervision of leisure-time activities, and individual counseling.

Deans of men are found in most colleges and universities. Paramount among their many duties is that of counseling. The National Association of Student Personnel Administrators is one of the many professional organizations.

Deans of Girls and Women. The guidance of pupils is usually assigned to a person of their own sex. Obviously the administrative and supervisory responsibilities of the position vary with the size and type of school. The qualifications for deans of girls and women are similar to those for the deans of boys and men. The former have a national association which is a department of the National Education Association. This National Association of Women's Deans and Counselors holds annual meetings.

Recreational Leaders. The inextricable relationship of recreation and education is evidenced in the similarity of their objectives. In many communities, school authorities have incorporated play and leisure-time activities into the program at preschool, inschool and postschool levels. The practice of providing for community recreation as part of a broad educational program is growing. Many communities have recreation in conjunction with school services. Although most communities do not supply the recreational-educational workers, the joint programs are steadily increasing.

The persons selected for the recreational leadership in school or community or joint programs should be carefully chosen for their personal and professional qualifications. Many directors are college graduates who have

specialized in teaching and in group activities. Courses for developing leaders cover a broad range of subjects and activities, since recreation, which was once limited to play or sports, now includes all activities involving the free use of leisure time. The most popular are swimming, picnicking, softball, and skating.

Among the many specialists engaged in semi-teaching in American education the following are mentioned here: (1) curriculum personnel and (2) research workers.

Curriculum Personnel. Several state departments, institutions of higher learning, and many city school systems employ persons especially trained in curriculum procedures. Such a worker is usually designated as director of the curriculum bureau, assistant superintendent in charge of the curriculum, curriculum supervisor, or director of surveys. The effort to adjust curriculums to the pupils and to societal needs, as indicated in Chapter 13, is a challenging task.

Research Workers. Early school administrators were guided primarily by guess, intuition, and practical experience earned by dint of trial and error. Today local, state, and federal educational divisions ferret out pressing problems and subject them to research.

A broad program of research operates as a steadying force in locating superior practices, in justifying expansion of programs, in facilitating scientific evaluations, in improving the quality of the program, in advancing the teaching profession, and in furnishing a common method of approach for all members of the staff. The classroom teacher may be a research worker. There are indeed many types of studies and experimentation that classroom teachers can and should make.

Usually the formal research of a school system is conducted or summarized by an administrator or a semiteaching worker known as the director of research. Such directors are usually located in large school systems that employ also one or more full-time workers, clerks and statisticians. Many of the latter are members of such national associations as the American Educational Research Association and the American Statistical Association. Directors of research are among the best-trained workers in the educational system; several possess doctor's degrees. Many are women.

Despite the rather limited number of positions available at present as directors of research in various schools, opportunities in this field are multiplying. Furthermore, assistants are required in the various bureaus of research already established to conduct needed studies. Then, too, most state departments of education and many state educational associations employ a director of research and assistants. Many persons have been engaged in research conducted through the cooperative efforts of the U.S. Office of Education and various universities. In addition to the agencies already mentioned, educational foundations require annually a large number of skilled, well-trained persons who have the technical precision and professional background for educational research.

Audio-visual Coordinators. A growing field of service in schools and colleges is that of audio-visual education with its multisensory aids—slides, filmstrips, motion pictures, charts, radio, television, and allied materials and equipment. The coordinator of audio-visual education must be a specialist in the instructional materials of the curriculum, must see equipment and materials as tools—means for the achievement of the ends of education—and must understand learning.

Radio and Television Specialists. The technical fields of radio and television are lifted out here for special accent as these two mass-communication media are also teaching tools with a promising future. Many radio stations on and off the campuses have full-time or part-time educational program directors and producers. Thousands of classrooms are equipped with radios.

Educational television specialists are increasing rapidly in number. The allotment of certain channels to educational TV by the Federal Communications Commission has stimulated the teaching uses of TV. Dr. Harold E. Wigren, educational television consultant for the National Education Association, states that television should be a part of an "integrated teaching package" to do a specific job for the typical teacher and to utilize superior teachers more effectively by bringing them in contact with large groups of students. Educational institutions are using television in public relations programs (televising meetings of the board of education), in-service programs for teacher education, inschool classroom instruction, teaching for homebound pupils, readiness programs for the pre-elementary school child, help for out-of-school youth, instruction for adult education, credit telecourses for students, and closed-circuit programming. Instructional television for inschool and incollege uses will demand many specialists.

The National Defense Education Act provides about five million dollars a year to help schools and colleges make wider and more effective use of these new media of mass communication. Several states have appropriated money for the development of educational television, as have several private agencies, notably the Ford Foundation.

Administrators and supervisors

Thousands of positions of an administrative or supervisory nature are available in American education, particularly for persons with experience, leadership, and initiative. Contrary to general belief, these positions do not exclude women. Many county superintendencies are held by women; grade school principalships and supervisory work are shared by women and men. However, few city superintendencies or high school principalships are held by women. One of the recommendations of various manpower studies is that more effective use be made of outstanding women in administrative positions.

Among the persons engaged in an executive capacity are (1) superintendents, (2) principals, (3) supervisors of instruction, (4) department heads and deans, (5) presidents, and (6) other administrators, including business and building officials.

SUPERINTENDENTS OF SCHOOLS

According to the main geographical divisions, the superintendents of schools are (1) local, and (2) county, and (3) state, whereas the chief school superintendent for the United States is known as the Commissioner of Education. American education also employs many assistant superintendents, in both public and private education. The Committee for the Advancement of School Administration has recommended that a person have two years of education beyond his bachelor's degree before he be admitted to membership in the American Association of School Administrators. At least one state requires a doctor's degree as a prerequisite for being elected local superintendent of schools in the larger cities.

Local Superintendents. The multiple duties of the city superintendent of schools are listed in Chapter 4. His main function is to serve as the chief administrative officer of the board of education. He is usually called the city superintendent of schools, but in some instances he is designated the community high school principal or the supervising principal. Technically a local superintendent is the professional leader who works directly with the board of education as its chief educational officer. His is the best-paid position in the public schools and also the most difficult. But the local superintendent finds many rewards other than monetary. Although a village may engage as superintendent a person just graduated from college, most accredited schools, especially in cities, require the superintendent to have graduate work plus experience either in the classroom or as a principal or assistant superintendent. In addition to these professional qualifications the highest personal attributes are expected in the local superintendent of schools.

County Superintendents. Nearly all of the 3,000 counties in the United States have a chief educational officer, usually designated as the county superintendent of schools. The duties and qualifications of these superintendents are enumerated in Chapter 3. The legal eligibility requirements in most states are low. Unfortunately most counties in the United States, instead of appointing their superintendents or commissioners from the best candidates available, elect them on a partisan ticket. A man or woman (many women are county superintendents in the United States) of demonstrated ability may lose an election because of wrong political affiliations. The situation is improving, however, and today in many states the county board of education or a similar body selects the superintendent from a list of thoroughly qualified persons. Low standards, popular election, and small salaries deter many promising candidates from an office which should call for educational statesmanship rather than political strategy.

State Superintendents. The usual tasks of the chief state educational officer are mentioned in Chapter 2. As in the case of the county superintendents, political affiliation is often a determining factor in the selection of a state superintendent or commissioner of education.

Many states have no minimum professional qualifications for the chief state school officer, and only a few states make any requirement as to graduate preparation. The opportunities for securing state superintendencies obviously are restricted by the number of states and dependencies, but unfortunately the vicissitudes of the office occasion frequent turnovers.

Assistant Superintendents. Since good administration involves both the centralization of authority and the delegation of responsibility, a large system employs not only an executive but also a staff of assistants. The increasing demands laid upon the chief educational officers have led to the development of many well-paid positions for assistant superintendents in charge of educational supervision, business management, and buildings and grounds. Many persons in the business side of education are known as business managers, secretaries, or clerks of the board.

To assistant county superintendents are usually delegated special activities, such as supervision or clerical work. Likewise the assistant state superintendents, directly under the chief official, head a special form of work in the state department of education. In many instances, local, county, and state assistants bear the brunt of the work. Assistant superintendencies are excellent training grounds for other educational positions; in and by themselves they also constitute an enviable opportunity for continuity in selfless service for others.

PRINCIPALS OF SCHOOLS

The unit of education that means the most to children, parents, and community is the individual school of which the principal is the head. Principals comprise by far the most numerous group of administrators. These positions range all the way from teaching principals in small schools to principals of immense schools. There are elementary school principals, high school principals, and evening school principals. In some cases, particularly when they have charge of both elementary and secondary education, they are known as supervising principals. Many large districts employ assistant principals. A master's degree and successful teaching experience are usually required.

The principalship is a position of large responsibility. The principal is the person to whom teachers are directly accountable.

Ideally, the principal should be responsible for the total educational program in his school, as well as a member of the administrative team in the cooperative development of system-wide program and policy. Many educators regard it as the most strategic position in our entire educational system. There is a trend toward increased professionalization of the principalship. The National Education Association includes in its organization the National Association of Secondary School Principals and the Department of Elementary School Principals.

SUPERVISORS OF INSTRUCTION

Many educators are engaged in instructional supervision, a work that has been broadened to involve the entire field of teaching and learning, deepened to reach down into a functional philosophy of education, and elevated to higher altitudes through the better attitudes of teachers toward supervision. Six major functions of this work, according to an analysis of duties performed by supervisors, include study of the pupil, in-service education of teachers, conduct of curriculum investigations, preparation and installation of courses of study, selection of textbooks and preparation of materials of instruction, and conduct of the public relations program. Most of these duties call for teaching experience and special preparation. The typical supervisory positions are those in elementary schools, secondary schools, and other educational institutions. Many counties and all state departments of education also employ supervisors. Supervision on all educational levels helps to implement the objectives of education through improving both teaching and learning.

DEPARTMENT HEADS AND COLLEGE DEANS

Heads of Departments. The large secondary schools and the colleges have semiadministrative officials known as heads or chairmen of departments. To them are delegated details of administration and supervision within their fields of instruction. Department heads in high schools were known as early as 1858 when Malden, Massachusetts, established commercial and Latin departments. At the present time some high schools with only a few hundred students designate heads for the larger departments, usually English, social science, and commerce. These persons are appointed frequently on the basis of seniority or desire to increase salaries, rather than on professional qualifications. In the secondary school the department head should hold a master's degree, whereas in colleges and universities he is usually expected to have a doctor's degree. His main task in all educational institutions is to improve instruction through aiding members of his department and cooperating with others on the staff.

College Deans. The liaison officer between departments and between them and the president of the institution of higher learning is usually the dean. Some universities have several: a dean of instruction, an administrative dean, and deans of women and men. These officers must possess at least a master's degree, several years of teaching experience, and administrative ability. In very few institutions is the position of dean a highly centralized administrative office. The dean's office almost universally combines teaching with administrative duties. With the recent rapid development of graduate work many colleges and universities have added a graduate division under the direction of a graduate dean or a chairman, who has a doctor's degree.

PRESIDENTS OF EDUCATIONAL INSTITUTIONS

Almost one thousand nine hundred presidents direct the colleges and universities of the United States. Many of them have charge of private or parochial institutions, but a large number are directly engaged in public education, particularly the presidents of community junior colleges, state teachers colleges and universities, and land-grant colleges.

Presidents of Junior Colleges. The executive officer of the community or junior college, especially if it is linked with the high school, is usually known as the principal or superintendent. His duties are similar to those of a local superintendent of schools, although technically he is president of the institution.

Presidents of Colleges and Universities. Among the coveted and well-paid positions in American education are college and university presidencies, several of which are held by women. A presidency is not, however, a bed of roses devoid of thorns. Says one president in a caustic vein, "A college president is so harassed by the time-consuming minutiae of administration and finance that he cannot be an educator." William A. Neilson, former president of Smith College, once urged a "Be-kind-to-college-presidents Week." The administrator of higher education has a difficult task but also unexcelled opportunities for educational leadership and for a permanent influence upon many phases of American life. The late Nicholas Murray Butler, in his autobiography, reveals the multiplicity of activities—social, economic, political, and educational—in which he engaged for over fifty years during his presidency of Columbia University. Busy years await anyone who ascends to the leadership of an American institution of higher learning.

OTHER ADMINISTRATIVE OFFICES

Long and varied is the list of administrative officers in schools, colleges, universities, and other educational organizations. Two of the many officials engaged in administrative or supervisory activities are (1) business and (2) building officials.

Business Officials in Educational Institutions. Since education is a big business involving an annual expenditure of several billion dollars and an invested capital of many billions more, obviously schools and colleges must be run on a businesslike basis. The business official in the

*The school business manager is
an important person in larger districts
where the superintendent must be relieved
of some of the difficult
administrative functions.*

*His major responsibilities are
plant operation and maintenance,
purchasing and accounting,
supervision of nonacademic personnel,
and transportation.
He works with school architects . . .*

small school is usually the superintendent, who works with the board of education in solving the financial problems of the district. In the large schools a business manager, an assistant superintendent in charge of business, or a board secretary or clerk carries the major financial responsibilities.

financial

The ideal business manager has a practical background and teaching experience—a sharp business outlook and an educational point of view. There is a dearth of well-educated persons with teaching and business experience plus personal assets to qualify them for the office of assistant superintendent of schools in charge of business. A similar lack of well-educated business officers is evident in colleges and universities. Nationwide organizations are seeking to improve business personnel and procedures in schools and colleges.

2 *Building and Grounds Superintendents.* The business aspects of education embrace the care and maintenance of buildings and grounds. Usually in the large city systems and in the colleges, both public and private, a separate administrative officer, such as the superintendent of buildings and grounds, is in charge. His duties are to supervise repairs, make inventories, direct the maintenance and operation of the plant, improve the grounds, and assist in the planning of new structures. Practical experience, as a building contractor or in the building trades, aids in the successful execution of these duties. As considered in Chapter 15, the erection, operation, and maintenance of educational buildings call for a well-trained personnel.

Personnel from other professions

Obviously most educational workers are teachers and administrators, but doctors and lawyers may also perform school duties. Among the other professional workers mentioned in the succeeding pages are (1) librarians, (2) health personnel, (3) business and building personnel, (4) lawyers, and (5) other professional or semiprofessional workers such as sociologists and social workers.

LIBRARIANS

The library is indeed an indispensable educational and social institution in a democracy. The role of libraries and books is treated further in Chapter 15; attention is here directed to librarians.

The fields of employment for librarians are in (1) schools and colleges, (2) public libraries, (3) combined school and public libraries, and (4) others.

School and College Librarians. Broad culture, enthusiasm, approachability, tact, poise, and

supervises custodial employees . . .

understanding are indispensable traits for school librarians, who are slowly being recognized as important members of the faculty.

Many institutions in the United States now provide thorough library education. Today a school librarian should have a college education and at least one year of library school training. In several states she must also possess a teacher's certificate or special state certificate.

Unfortunately elementary school libraries are the last to be recognized for their importance in lifelong learning. Most elementary schools today are sorely in need of libraries and librarians. Many junior high school and high school libraries are unorganized and inadequately staffed. College libraries, too, offer many opportunities for employment in this educational service.

2 *Public Librarians.* The status of the public library as an educational institution has long been established in America. Rather recently the federal government granted funds for improving libraries in a third of the United States —rural territory—which was without any kind of library service. Additional library personnel and equipment, especially for bookmobile services for rural areas, are urgently needed.

If the successful librarian could be described in general terms, scholarship, professionalism, social consciousness, imagination, sense of humor, and acceptable personality would be requisites. The librarian is no longer a mere

and the switchboard operator.

painters and other maintenance people . . .

cafeteria personnel . . .

the secretarial and clerical staff . . .

not a mere keeper of books but a scholarly administrator who uses scientific methods in making library materials available. This challenge to work in public libraries will be met by thousands of young people who yearn to live with people and recorded communications.

3 Combined School and Public Librarians. Some persons work in public libraries controlled by boards of education. The Educational Policies Commission envisioned the ultimate unification of all public educational activities, in communities or areas of appropriate size, under the leadership of a public education authority.

4 Other Librarians. Many public and private agencies other than schools, colleges, and cities employ librarians. Among these are: foundations, research associations, private firms, educational associations, settlement houses, hotels, hospitals, and other agencies that promote reading and research.

HEALTH PERSONNEL

The school health program is composed in whole or in part of the following services: health instruction, health examinations, medical attention, communicable disease control, promotion of mental health, provision of healthful environment and regimen, and health supervision of teachers and employees. To perform these services well, a large and varied personnel is needed, including the (1) physician, (2) dentist, (3) nurse, (4) health educator, and (5) psychiatrist and psychologist.

School Physicians and Dentists. Ever since the city of Boston, faced with an epidemic of dreaded diphtheria, initiated in 1894 a program of school health inspection, the physician has assumed an important role in education. School dentists, too, have a real role in the health program of the school.

The health of the pupils is not the responsibility of the school physician alone; all doctors may promote this cause through participation in campaigns for immunization against contagious diseases and in their daily duties as family physician. In their private practice the physicians, especially the pediatricians and psychiatric workers, have numerous heavy educational responsibilities devolving upon them.

The school physician or dentist, whether a full-time or part-time employee of the board of education or the city, has educational obligations, such as emphasizing to the pupils and parents the importance of proper care of the body. He should have a thorough understanding of the school health program. Inspections by the school dentist or doctor do not take the place of a careful and thorough examination by the family dentist or physician. Furthermore, medical care is not a public school function.

2 School Nurses. The school nurses usually devote part of their time to the preparation of instructional materials, to giving individual health instruction and examinations, and to interpreting the results of the examinations to parent, child, and teacher. Success in this field requires certain natural qualifications, such as a genuine liking for children. In addition to natural accomplishments the school nurses must have high professional and educational qualifications. It is significant that the field of nursing, which was formerly almost 100 per cent for women, is now being entered by a number of men.

3 Health Educators. A position that is increasing in number and significance is that of health educator or coordinator. Many state departments, county boards, and local school systems employ personnel experienced in health and education to work with nonschool children, pupils, parents, teachers, nurses, doctors, and dentists. The professional preparation usually required is training and experience in health and teaching, with the technical degree of Master of Public Health. Some are Doctors of Public Health.

In addition, larger school districts typically employ other specialized personnel, both professional and non professional:

librarians . . .

*the school nurse
and other
health workers . . .*

*test experts
and other guidance functionaries . . .*

and bus drivers.

School Psychiatrists and Psychologists. A broad health program includes mental and emotional as well as physical health. Many schools and colleges are employing psychiatrists and psychologists in an effort to treat causes rather than symptoms of unusual pupil behavior, and to prevent mental illness and maladjustments. Only in the large school systems is a full-time psychiatrist or psychologist needed; part-time psychiatric services are obtained from hospitals, universities, foundations, or other agencies, such as clinics.

Clinical psychologists are increasingly in demand. Groups such as the Association of Consulting Psychologists and the Division of School Psychologists of the American Psychological Association have helped to establish and elevate standards for clinical psychologists and for their training programs. The National Committee for Mental Hygiene has also made recommendations. Students contemplating careers in clinical psychology will find helpful these published recommendations. Obviously, since these specialists are to work with school pupils, they should have teaching experience.

BUSINESS AND BUILDING PERSONNEL

In addition to the business manager and the building and grounds superintendent previously mentioned as administrators, schools and colleges employ other members of the business and building professions on a part-time or full-time basis. Those who belong to groups considered as professional are (1) accountants and auditors, (2) architects, and (3) engineers.

School Accountants and Auditors. Thousands of accountants are employed in educational work periodically or full time. They should be trained not only in accountancy but also in education. The accountants need to know something about the educational program of the school so that they may make interpolations and comments of an educational nature. There is a dire need for educational auditors—men and women seasoned by experience as school administrators, who are just as thoroughly grounded in accountancy as a certified public accountant. Schools of business and education should assume aggressive joint leadership in preparing these experts. Improvement of current accountancy practices can be hastened by the appointment of more educational auditors in the state departments of education. The U.S. Office of Education has recommended a new, uniform classification for receipts and expenditures. With the increased tendency toward uniform accounting systems in schools and colleges, and for compulsory audits of educational and extracurricular funds, the demand for school accountants and auditors will rise to new levels.

School Architects. Large city systems and some state departments employ full-time school architects. Some architectural firms specialize in school buildings, and others have a department of school architecture. The definite relationship of buildings to the curriculum makes school architecture extremely important. The school architect must have a thorough knowledge of modern education so that the building he designs will facilitate the education of the pupils. (See Chapter 15.)

School Engineers. Most school buildings are in charge of engineer-custodians. In the small systems the persons who direct the maintenance, operation, and care of school plant and properties are often called janitors. In the large systems, engineers are assigned to definite tasks in terms of their specialties, such as mechanical or electrical work, usually after having passed civil service examinations.

SCHOOL LAWYERS

Law is the basis for all school transactions; hence the significance of the legal profession in education. Among those engaged in school law work are (1) lawyers and (2) other legal advisers.

Lawyers. Most positions in this service, full-time or part-time, are available only to persons who hold a bachelor of laws (LL.B) degree and membership in the bar. The Association of American Law Schools and the Council on Legal Education of the American Bar Association maintain certain standards for approving law schools. The typical law curriculum has had marked leanings toward the needs of private practice and has not given much emphasis to the needs of the schools. Only a limited number of law schools and teacher-educating institutions offer courses in school law. There is some demand in large school systems for well-qualified lawyers who have taught and have specialized in school law.

Other Legal Advisers. Many state departments have legal advisers who may or may not hold legal degrees although they have studied both school and general law. Their business is to help interpret the school laws. Occasionally lawyers who specialize in certain phases of law are called upon for school service. Some universities teach school law. The National Organization for the Promotion of Legal Education, organized in 1956, has helped to stimulate research in law affecting education.

OTHER PROFESSIONAL OR SEMIPROFESSIONAL GROUPS

Among the many other professions or semi-professions having representatives engaged in educational work are (1) school sociologists, (2) social workers, and (3) educational consultants.

School Sociologists. At present the nation's schools employ few sociologists. Courses in sociology, particularly in the secondary schools, would be far more functional if a sociologist were engaged to make actual community contact through social surveys and other means. The school has too long tried to insulate itself against direct community service. Administrators have been likely to think in terms of education but not of society. A crying need exists, therefore, for educational sociologists who seek the improvement of society as a whole rather than merely that of the schools. In addition to excellent personal qualifications, the educational sociologist should possess at least a master's degree.

Social Workers. Social responsibility is the keynote of twentieth-century legislation. In its publication *Social Services and the Schools,* the Educational Policies Commission states that "the schools, in particular, are obligated not only to see and provide for their educational responsibilities to the community but also to cooperate in providing welfare services that are closely related to education." Many writers have shown the need for this cooperation as they picture the migrant who teaches his children to pick fruit or cotton as long and as fast as their aching backs will permit, with never any thought of school. The task of social workers is economic and educational as well as social.

The social worker of today, in contrast with the lady bountiful of yesterday is a trained member of a profession, usually holding one or more college degrees. Employees in some public agencies must have civil service status. Among the many forms of individual and group social services are child welfare, family welfare, community organization, institutional work, parole, probation, psychiatric social work, public assistance, unemployment relief, social group work, social research, visiting teacher, and the teacher of social service. Organizations such as the National Association of School Social Workers and the Russell Sage Foundation are seeking to make social service an attractive career. The schools need not only specially trained teachers, nurses, and counselors but also social workers who have the desire and ability to interpret democracy in terms of human betterment, as did Jane Addams, Julia Lathrop, and Florence Kelly.

Workers in Religious Education. Dr. Paul Tellich, a noted theologian, has stated that one of the lost dimensions in religion is "depth." To recapture this lost depth for oldsters and to lay a firm foundation for youngsters, many men and women are needed in the field of religious education.

The parochial schools and denominational colleges have a clear-cut obligation to teach religion. Many instructors are needed for this purpose. Usually the requirements for collegiate positions are graduation from a theological seminary and practical experience in preaching, or teaching, or religious educational work. The seminaries of the land are expanding and need many professors, especially in the rapidly growing area of directors of religious education, a field open to men and women.

Educational Consultants. Many school systems and universities employ various educational consultants or specialists to serve on a part-time basis. Most of them come from colleges and universities or private firms that specialize in advisory services. They usually work with a board or committee in the local community, the state, or nation, on short-term or long-range educational problems. They seek to analyze systematically the educational problems, to design alternate solutions in the form of programs, to supplement plans, and to evaluate the procedures employed.

Other nonteaching personnel

The vast array of nonteaching workers not definitely ranked as a professional group include the following: (1) school clerks and secretaries, (2) cafeteria and lunchroom workers, (3) building service personnel, (4) those engaged in school transportation, (5) school publications and sales personnel, and (6) others employed in education. Each of these groups is described briefly.

SCHOOL CLERKS AND SECRETARIES

Countless opportunities for educational work are available in the field of clerical and office service. Positions include typists, stenographers, secretaries, bookkeepers, and similar employees. These persons can and do perform many tasks of an educational nature, thus releasing administrators and teachers for purely professional duties.

An important school business official, especially in the East, is the school board secretary. Secretaries should be provided for every administrator, especially the county superintendent, in the number needed to relieve him and his professional assistants from clerical duties. Many attendance clerks are needed in public schools. Obviously secretaries, as well as all school employees, should be appointed upon strict professional bases rather than because of political influence or nepotism.

Opportunities are numerous in the school offices for young people and married women who do not care for classroom teaching but who like the school atmosphere. It is not to be inferred that clerical help is of inferior quality; in fact, some of the best secretaries are those who have academic degrees and who have had some teaching experience. In order to secure and maintain a stable, efficient, and loyal group of office workers, it is necessary to have careful selection and training of new clerks, an adequate salary schedule, and justly planned provisions for tenure, working hours, leaves of absence, and retirement. The National Association of Educational Secretaries is developing a service program that seeks to make the secretarial position in the school system a professional position requiring specialized training and experience.

CAFETERIA AND LUNCHROOM WORKERS

Ever since the depression days following World War I, when the federal government started the school lunch program, the demand has been steadily increasing for competent food service personnel. Too often tired teachers try to direct school lunch programs as an extra duty. The school cafeteria and lunchroom are powerful factors in the educative process of growing physically and socially. Their functional relationship to the health program is evidenced in that a trained dietitian or home economics worker, often paid in part from federal funds, is usually a member of the cafeteria staff. Too much care cannot be exercised in the selection of a manager for the cafeteria or lunchroom.

As cleanliness is essential to health, all the workers in the cafeteria must be immaculately clean. Periodic inspections and examinations should be made by the city health officers, the school nurse, or the cafeteria committee. The lunchroom can be a real asset to the school if it emphasizes the educational rather than the financial, and if it seeks to train children in health habits, in food standards, in business sense, in self-control, and in social niceties. These are some of the goals of the American School Food Service Association.

During early colonial days most teachers performed the housekeeping duties in the schools, a practice that still exists in many rural communities. Today the large schools employ numerous caretakers and assistants with specific titles and definite responsibilities, such as engineer, fireman, cleaner, carpenter, mower, electrician, and playground caretaker. In most systems, however, these duties devolve upon one person, who in the past has usually been called the janitor. The more acceptable nomenclature today is school custodian (man) and school maid (woman). Whatever the term, the modern school requires from its custodian less manual labor but more knowledge and skill than were formerly required.

Custodians must be trained in the installation and care of delicately adjusted equipment and various machinery. The pioneer work of the late George F. Womrath of Minneapolis and others in providing this practical training is being expanded by colleges, universities, state departments, and other agencies. Eventually preservice and in-service training will be required of all custodians. Some systems have a civil service examination for the purpose of selecting desirable custodians. Among the great hindrances to the improvement of school maintenance and operation personnel are too-frequent political interference in their appointment, insecurity of tenure, no retirement allowance, low pay, and inadequate recognition. Occasionally a custodian gets recognition as indicated in the following story taken from a bulletin of the U.S. Office of Education:

Set in the wall of the main corridor of a public school in a small city of Iowa is a bronze tablet bearing, in low relief, the heroic likeness of a man and the inscription—"He gave thirty-two years of faithful service to the youth of this community." From the dedicatory program we learn that the tablet was placed "by its hundreds of donors with the belief that all those who shall frequent these halls in the years to come will be inspired, as we who present it were inspired, by him."

This superior personage, so memorialized, was not a member of the board of education; he was not a superintendent; not a principal; nor an exceptional teacher, but the school janitor or custodian.

The janitor or custodian is usually one of the many forgotten men and women who daily serve the youth in school.

Transportation has developed into a major educational enterprise, particularly in states that have adopted larger units of school administration. Several states are now paying part of the costs of conveying pupils, and many local districts have added the school bus driver to their payroll. In some instances the school bus driver is accompanied by an assistant who flags the bus over unprotected railroad crossings and other hazards. The large systems employ various mechanics in their garages and repair shops. School transportation has developed to such significance that specific qualifications and training have been set for those engaged in this all-important work of bringing pupils in safety to the teachers.

EDUCATIONAL EDITORS, PUBLISHERS, AND SALES PERSONNEL

Thousands of persons who render educational services are employed in the publication of textbooks, in the manufacture of educational supplies and equipment, and in sales work. Contrary to general belief, those who enter the publishing and editorial field do not lose their educational status.

Educational Editors and Publishers. One aspect of textbook publication is editorial work. In addition to the editors, numerous persons are employed as directors of educational research service with publishers of textbooks. The work of field consultant for a textbook company is largely professional and includes such activities as lecturing or making informal talks to groups, training of teachers in service, and conferences with various kinds of committees and individuals. Opportunities for women, especially teachers, are multiplying in the textbook field. A challenging task for all educators, especially for classroom teachers, is that of writing articles and books for publication. The preparation of children's books is now an enormous enterprise that employs a great many educators.

Sales Personnel. Many persons are engaged in selling schoolbooks, supplies, and educational equipment. Undoubtedly the best textbooks, educational supplies, and school equipment in the world are made in America. These are available as teaching tools for American schools, but unfortunately the best is not generally used. Restricted budgets and the apathy of the general public account in part for this situation. Then, too, many classroom and laboratory teachers are not acquainted with the wide variety and high quality of modern educational materials. Promotional and sales personnel, traveling from schools to colleges, from educational exhibits to state and national conventions, serve as so-called educational missionaries and spread the news of improvements. The best preparation for this salesmanship is teaching and business experience.

OTHERS EMPLOYED IN EDUCATION

Workers in Nonschool Organizations. Many educational, recreational, and professional organizations employ thousands of trained workers. For example, UNESCO, Red Cross, YMCA, the National Congress of Parents and Teachers, the Boy Scouts and Girl Scouts of America, the 4-H clubs of America, educational fraternities, sororities, foundations, state and national educational associations, and countless other groups, some of which are enumerated in Chapter 14, draw heavily upon the teaching profession for their personnel. Most industrial corporations maintain extensive educational programs for their employees and sometimes for their families. The Arabian American Oil Company, for example, maintains a complete school system for Americans in Arabia. The Armed Forces also operate a vast educational program hiring many professional educators both at home and abroad.

Challenging Career Services in Education. The largest groups in the employed personnel of the typical city school system have been mentioned, viz., teachers, custodians, and clerks. Among the many others not yet listed are day laborers, laundresses, electricians, plumbers, telephone operators, and messengers. Some of these have detailed, pigeonhole jobs, but most of them perform tasks that permit initiative and growth.

The improvement of many nonteaching positions requires more than higher standards of recruitment. These positions, especially for clerks and stenographers, must become career services if they are to enlist adequately trained personnel. The term "career" used here means a life work in an honorable occupation which one normally takes up in youth with the expectation of advancement and pursues with happiness and profit until retirement. School service in both public and private institutions should be so organized and conducted as to encourage continuous challenging careers.

Though the role of some employees in education may appear insignificant, each professional or nonprofessional worker, from the chief executive officer of the educational institution down to the lowest paid day laborer, can make a direct and significant contribution to American education.

Nonpaid personnel

This chapter on other personnel concludes with a discussion of the role of the unpaid persons who labor for education. The three main groups are members of boards of education, lay committees in education, and parents.

Members of Boards of Education. In Chapter 4, "Local School Districts," there is an extended discussion of the important role of members of school boards or boards of education, the latter being the preferred terminology, as "education" is broader than "schooling." With the consolidation of schools, the number of board members has decreased, but their importance has not waned. They are the elected representatives of the people, and, except for expenses incurred in the line of duty, they do not receive any compensation. They are the lay leaders in learning and their decisions directly affect millions of pupils.

Many men and women serve also on other boards of education of various types, such as county and state-wide boards of education. Examples of the latter are the state retirement board, the state certification board, the state board of education having general jurisdiction over public elementary and secondary schools, and the group selected or appointed to work with the presidents of colleges and universities, both public and private. These men and women serve unselfishly the cause of education, and they donate millions of clock hours and dollars to their tasks. Just as teachers have local, county, and state and national organiza-

tions, so do the board members. Jointly, they spearhead lay leadership in learning.

Lay Advisory Committees on Education. Lay advisory committees in education are not new. In the early days the schools were close to the community and the entire community, as a committee of the whole, acted in an advisory capacity in the improvement of education. Gradually the community assigned duties to the board of education. The pendulum is swinging back partly and now the local board often appoints an advisory committee of citizens to help with school policies. These lay groups, selected by the board of education and/or community groups, bring the citizens back into educational partnership with the board, the superintendent of schools, and the teachers. This total team marshals lay leadership on the side of better education. They are often short-term committees assigned a specific project such as a building program, or long-span groups delegated a continuing constructive challenge.

Many states have advisory lay boards, such as a commission on higher education or a school problems advisory committee. The National Citizens Commission for the Public Schools, formed in 1949, reorganized into the National Council for Better Schools, stimulated the formation of lay groups to study education and to make recommendations to the boards recognized in law. Lay advisory groups have grown from a handful in 1945 to nearly fifteen thousand in 1960. It must be borne in mind that these groups are not superboards, and that the official agencies have the legal authority for making final decisions affecting education.

In its brochure *Lay Advisory Committees,* the American Association of School Administrators stated that readiness for an advisory committee is just as important as reading readiness for a first-grade pupil. The administrator and board must sincerely want the advice of lay citizens and believe their fact finding, group thinking, joint interpreting, and constructive planning will be of genuine worth to education.

Parents as ~~Educational Personnel~~. One of the current criticisms of education is that the parents have abdicated from their rights and responsibilities, and have assigned too much to teachers. Education is too important to be left entirely to paid professional personnel. The perennial partnership of parent and teacher must be promoted. Each needs the other, and the pupil needs them both.

Parents can assist teachers in various ways. The parents are the child's first tutors and as such can ready him for school; then they can supplement and support the work of the teacher. No teacher seeks to supplant the parent.

The local, county, state, and national groups most concerned with volunteer leadership for parents are the parent-teacher associations. On the country-wide level the main organization is known as the National Congress of Parents and Teachers with its headquarters in Chicago. This is the largest organization in the world, with more than eleven million members, and is still growing like a mighty oak tree.

A descriptive brochure, *A Teacher's Guide to the P.T.A.* is published by the National Congress of Parents and Teachers. It states that the national, state, and local associations are governed by four basic policies. In brief, these policies affirm that the organization (1) shall be educational, and shall develop its program through conferences, committees, and projects; (2) shall be noncommercial, nonsectarian, and nonpartisan; (3) shall work to improve the schools without seeking to direct their administration or control their policies; and (4) shall cooperate with other organizations and agencies having common interests. Parents and teachers can promote a paying partnership that brings rich rewards for children.

basic policies of national, state, and local associations

million men and women are employed in educational positions other than straight classroom teaching, in which another million and more work. Careers challenge the talents of nonteachers in a hundred and more types of positions. Hence recruitment for education should not be limited to classroom teachers. The best human resources need to be enlisted for all types of educational work.

Among the semiteaching personnel are part-time teachers, such as substitutes; off-campus leaders, such as extension workers; personnel people, such as guidance and placement officials; and other specialists, including curriculum and research directors.

Many positions in the higher salaried group are of an administrative and supervisory nature. These positions are found in all levels from pre-elementary through adult learning. Administrators should be the servants and not the masters of education.

From professions other than teaching come many educational workers, such as librarians, doctors, dentists, nurses, accountants, architects, lawyers, social workers, religious education directors, and consultants.

Among the other nonteachers employed in education are clerks, secretaries, food-service personnel, custodians, bus drivers, authors, publishers, salesmen, and day laborers. Many institutions employ a director of nonacademic employees.

Education is too important to be left to those who receive direct compensation. Among the unpaid persons who labor for learners are three major groups: members of boards of education; lay committees in education; and last, but not least, parents. The perennial partnership of parents and teachers must be promoted. The interested parents, the child's first tutors, supplement the work of the talented teacher. No teacher supplants the pupil's parents. Lay participation must be marshaled with professional leadership in a spirit of teamwork for the welfare of the learner and society.

Summary

Personnel management is extremely important in education, which has a huge task force engaged in human engineering. More than a

Suggested activities

1. Compare the salaries, other financial rewards, and opportunities for personal and professional growth in several different positions in education.
2. Enumerate some of the obstacles faced by substitute teachers.
3. Investigate the nature of extension work.
4. Investigate the opportunities for training as a school librarian.
5. Find out what qualifications your state requires for city, county, and state superintendents of schools.
6. List some of the advantages and disadvantages in being a school principal, supervisor, or head of a department.
7. Study the types of positions available in higher education.
8. Describe the ideal qualifications for a college president.
9. List the duties of a school or college business manager.
10. Investigate the positions in health work offered in the schools and colleges.
11. Evaluate the role of the school architect.
12. Tell why accountants and auditors are needed in education.
13. Explain some of the functions of a school psychologist.
14. Describe the role publishing firms play in education.
15. Describe the ideal qualifications for a school custodian.
16. Discuss the importance of transportation services in education.
17. Prepare a list of national professional organizations of educational personnel other than teachers.
18. Explain the type of educational work other than teaching that might interest you.

Bibliography

Books

American Association of School Administrators: *Staff Relations in School Administration*, National Education Association, Washington, D.C., 1955, chap. 3. The human relationships aspect of effective teamwork among personnel in school systems is discussed.

———: *The Superintendent as Instructional Leader*, National Education Association, Washington, D.C., 1957, chaps. 6, 7. Discusses the interrelationships of school personnel with the community and how to improve these relationships.

Campbell, Roald, and others: *Introduction to Educational Administration*, Allyn and Bacon, Inc., Englewood Cliffs, N.J., 1958, chap. 13. Describes the positions, qualifications, and conditions of employment in educational administration and supervision.

Chandler, B. J., and Paul V. Petty: *Personnel Management in School Administration*, World Book Company, Yonkers, N.Y., 1955, chap. 17. Describes various nonprofessional positions in education, particularly from the point of view of administration.

Gordon, Ira J.: *The Teacher as a Guidance Worker*, Harper & Brothers, New York, 1956, part 3. Examines the guidance role of the teacher as a group worker, individual counselor, and action researcher.

Hahn, Milton E., and Malcolm S. MacLean: *Counseling Psychology*, McGraw-Hill Book Company, Inc., New York, 1955, chap. 1. Presents a history of counseling in education and discusses the function of the guidance specialist.

Linn, Henry H.: *School Business Administration*, The Ronald Press Company, New York, 1956, chaps. 15, 16. Discusses the business aspects of school operation with attention to the variety of personnel needed for this function.

National Society for the Study of Education: *In-service Education,* University of Chicago Press, Chicago, 1957, chap. 8. Examines the role of the educational consultant in promoting improvement in educational practice.

Peters, Herman J., and Gail F. Farwell: *Guidance: A Developmental Approach,* Rand McNally & Company, Chicago, 1960, chaps. 1, 2, 9, 10. Presents a point of view of classroom-centered guidance and relates this important function to the total environment of the child.

Tompkins, Ellsworth, and Mabel C. Rice: *Clerical and Custodial Staff in Public Secondary Schools,* Government Printing Office, Washington, D.C., 1955. Describes the clerical and custodial personnel employed in school systems, their functions and qualifications.

Yeager, William A.: *Administration of the Noninstructional Personnel and Services,* Harper & Brothers, New York, 1959. Discusses the administration of business, plant, attendance, health, food, and transportation personnel and services.

Periodicals

Allen, James E.: "Good Guidance and Enough of It," *Personnel and Guidance,* vol. 36 (May, 1958), p. 639. Clarifies the objectives of the guidance function with ways of accomplishing them.

Averill, Hugh M.: "Program Planning for School Dental Health Services," *Teachers College Record,* vol. 59 (January, 1958), pp. 201–210. Discusses the role of the health coordinator, health councils, school dentists, dental hygienists, and school nurse.

Barnhardt, Richard E., and Robert J. Baldaud: "The Role of the School Psychologist," *The Nation's Schools,* vol. 61 (April, 1958), pp. 49–51. Describes the function of the school psychologist in diagnosing and caring for students' adjustment problems.

Clark, David L.: "The Modern Way," *The School Executive,* vol. 76 (October, 1956), pp. 74–75. Case studies of the organization of two school systems reveals the different kinds of noninstructional personnel and their duties.

Fowlkes, Johy G.: "Training and Selection of School Administrators," *The Nation's Schools,* vol. 61 (May, 1958), pp. 52–53. Describes and endorses a proposal for improving the selection and preparation of school administrators.

Heisner, H. Fred: "Ten Point Program for Guidance," *The School Executive,* vol. 78 (May, 1959), pp. 66–67. Establishes ten principles upon which a strong, workable guidance program can be developed in schools.

Hirning, L. Louis: "Functions of a School Psychiatrist," *Teachers College Record,* vol. 59 (January, 1958), pp. 211–224. Describes the work of the school psychiatrist and his relations with pupils, teachers, parents, and physicians.

Houk, A. E.: "Selecting and Training School Bus Drivers," *The Nation's Schools,* vol. 60 (September, 1957), pp. 81–82. Discusses the qualifications needed by good school bus drivers and how they can be trained for their work.

Linton, Thomas A.: "Selection and Qualifications of School Business Managers," *School Business Affairs,* vol. 24 (February, 1958), pp. 3–4. Presents the qualifications necessary for the school business manager and how he should be selected and trained.

Martin, M. S.: "Your School Custodian Has Rights Too," *The School Executive,* vol. 76 (September, 1956), pp. 68–69. Discusses the rights of an important but often overlooked employee, the school custodian.

Mumford, L. Quincy: "The Teacher Librarian," *NEA Journal,* vol. 45 (April, 1956), p. 209. Describes the important teamwork that should exist between the teacher and the school librarian.

Osborne, Maurice M.: "The School Doctor: Link between Medical Care and School Environment," *Teachers College Record,* vol. 59 (January, 1958), pp. 196–200. Clarifies the job of the school physician—his relationship to the school, the home, and the family physician.

Romans, Robert: "Eight Planks of the Elementary Principalship," *The School Executive,* vol. 77 (September, 1957), pp. 72–73. Presents eight prerequisites for the job of the elementary school principal.

Tipple, Dorothy C.: "The Changing Role of the School Nurse," *Teachers College Record,* vol. 59 (January, 1958), pp. 191–195. Describes the new tasks, such as health education, that have accrued to the school nurse and how she is discharging them.

Wrenn, C. Gilbert: "Guidance—an Overview," *NEA Journal,* vol. 48 (January, 1959), pp. 16–18. Discusses the close relationship between the guidance worker and the classroom teacher and effective ways of working together.

PART FOUR

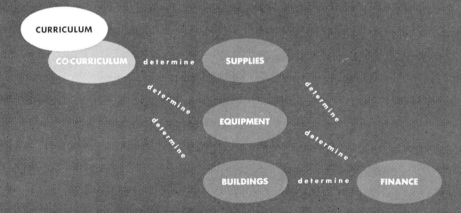

Provisions
for educational
materials
and environment

The pupils and teachers need plans, tools, and a place in which to live creatively. The program, facilities, and environment markedly affect teaching, learning, and living.

The design for education is found in the curriculum, which consists of all the experiences that pupils have under the guidance of the schools. It is life material used in building soul structure. The modern curriculum is developed cooperatively by administrators, teachers, pupils, and laymen. Most schools are engaged in the continuous task of curriculum revision (Chapter 13).

Related to the curriculum as a dynamic part of pupils' education are the extracurricular or cocurricular activities of the school. The cocurricular programs have accumulated great importance at all levels of American education. They help the youth of America to conserve and develop a democratic way of living (Chapter 14).

In order to work effectively, the teacher and pupils need supplies and tools. They must also have a place to use these tools. The school grounds and buildings constitute the workshop or laboratory of American education. The modern school building is intimately fitted to human needs—physical, educational, psychological, and aesthetic. The students and teachers breathe into the architect's creation the breath of wholesome life. The building is not merely located in the community; the school is a part of the community. Modern schoolhouses are needed in many communities (Chapter 15).

The curricular and the cocurricular activities, the supplies and the equipment, and the grounds and buildings are made available through public expenditures for education. Equalization of educational opportunity and burden is the golden rule of educational finance—"Thou shalt educate thy neighbor's children as thine own. . . ." Expenditures for education are not a cost—they represent a long-term investment for which the public should be willing and able to pay (Chapter 16).

chapter 13

Curriculum

Orientation
Foundations
Objectives
Principles
Procedures
Organization
Practices
Summary

In this modern scientific age when soaring satellites and mighty missiles are being shot into outer space, many caustic criticisms are being launched against the inner heart of education—the curriculum. Current criticism of American education orbits around the curriculum, which, in a broad sense, consists of all the experiences the pupil has under the direction of the school or college. In a narrow sense, the curriculum consists of the subjects taught in school and university. Idealistically, the curriculum is used in building soul structure.

A few of the many current complaints against the curriculum are tersely enumerated. The elementary school neglects the three R's. The high school has a watered-down curriculum that does not challenge the gifted, but perpetuates mediocrity. In college and university, with unselected or semiselected students, the extracurricular tail wags the academic dog. Even in adult education the cafeteria curriculum gives smorgasbord-seeking students what they want rather than what they need in today's interdependent world.

Obviously the curriculum must be content-centered. Academic excellence and not merely social adjustment is the top priority in education. The real school is a *labor*atory—a place for hard work with a necessary minimum of recreation. Intellectual exercises precede but do not preclude social experiences. Homework must be retrieved from the wastebasket of educational history. It is desirable for a high school student to know how to drive a car safely, but first he must know how to read well. From the horse-and-buggy-years till these days of accent on outer space, the inner mind of man has historically been the main concern of the curriculum at all levels.

Foundations

Since there is a return to some of the values of the past, it is pertinent to review briefly the historical development of the curriculum. It is difficult to chart the changes in curriculum with a high degree of specificity. Many modifications had their genesis in the slow and imperceptible changes in philosophy, psychology, and research.

In the early days of American education the curriculum was very simple in pattern although its content was heavy—too substantial for many. The pre-elementary program did not exist. The elementary school stressed four R's —reading, 'riting, 'rithmetic, and religion. In the high school the emphasis was on college preparation, whereas in the college there were no electives. The curriculums for adults were unknown.

Today offers a marked contrast. Some of the curricular changes that have taken place are mentioned in Part 2, Chapters 5 to 9, where historical overviews are presented for pre-elementary, elementary, secondary, higher, and adult education. Others are briefly mentioned here.

Various Committees. Important factors in the historical development of curriculums have been and still are the efforts of various national groups. The *Report of the Committee of Ten*, published in 1893, was a significant document in the history of American education. Associated in this work with Charles W. Eliot, then president of Harvard University, were such eminent leaders as William T. Harris, James B. Angell, and Henry Churchill King. Their report marked the beginning of the emancipation of secondary schools from the domination of college entrance requirements, which were interpreted largely in terms of mathematics and language requirements; it included the findings of nine national conferences made up of leading educators in as many subject-matter fields.

The *Report of the Committee of Fifteen*, published in 1895, was another pioneer document in the fields which it covered, viz., the training of teachers, the correlation of studies in elementary education, and the organization of city school systems. This committee included in its membership William T. Harris, William H. Maxwell, and Andrew S. Draper.

A Committee of Nine on The Articulation of the High Schools and Colleges, which, like the two preceding committees, was named by the National Education Association, recommended in 1911 that the completion of practically any broad, well-planned high school curriculum should be accepted as preparation for college.

A year later this committee also recommended that a Commission on the Reorganization of Secondary Education be appointed with 12 subcommittees to study the reorganization of high school subjects. Among those who served on this commission and its subcommittees were: Thomas H. Briggs, Alexander Inglis, Henry Turner Bailey, James F. Hosic, Philander P. Claxton, and William H. Kilpatrick. This commission formulated in 1918 the Cardinal Principles of Secondary Education, previously mentioned.

Individual Contributions to the Curriculum. In addition to the individuals already mentioned in this chapter, countless others contributed to the development of the modern curriculum of today. The publication by G. Stanley Hall of his *Adolescence* in 1907 had a marked, if indirect, effect on the curriculum for high school youth. In his pioneering work, Arnold L. Gesell, formerly of the Yale University Clinic for Child Development, studied youngsters and how they learn for more than forty years. His observations affected the curriculum for pre-elementary and elementary children. The individual who greatly changed college curriculums has been mentioned, Charles W. Eliot, a former president of Harvard, who worked for the elective system which is now being critically scrutinized. Edward L. Thorndike, through his productive research at Columbia University, demonstrated that adults can learn and this affected the programs for adults. Countless others in yesteryears and recent years influenced curriculum builders.

Role of Organizations in Curriculum Reform.
In addition to the aforementioned committees and individuals, various professional organizations have helped to give some direction to curriculum builders. Among other national societies that have stimulated curriculum reform are the National Society for the Study of Education (through its yearbooks), the Progressive Education Association (through its Eight-year Study), the Commission on Life Adjustment (through its efforts to meet the imperative needs of youth), and the American Council on Education (through its various commissions, such as the American Youth Commission and the Commission on Implications of Armed Services Educational Programs). The U.S. Office of Education has also been active in promoting curriculum work.

The organizations with membership from specific academic areas or levels have left their imprint on the curriculums of their respective fields. Some of them are The National Association for Nursery Education, The National Association of Elementary School Principals, the National Association of Secondary-school Principals, The Association for Land Grant Colleges and Universities, The American Association of Colleges for Teacher Education, and the Adult Education Association.

A dynamic influence in curriculum development, through establishing goals and policies, has been the National Education Association. Its Educational Policies Commission, in collaboration with the American Association of School Administrators, has published several monumental works affecting curriculum development. Various departments of this association have issued and will continue to disseminate publications in the field of curriculum.

In its centennial report, the National Education Association listed among others the following developments in curriculums from 1857 to 1957:

Changes from the faculty psychology of learning with emphasis upon memorization and mental discipline to an organismic, dynamic psychology with emphasis upon the powerful forces of purpose, meaning, goal-seeking, differentiation, and integration of the learning process.

Changes from reliance on tradition and subjective judgment as a basis for educational procedures to concern for scientific research and the application of scientific method and findings.

Changes in patterns of participation in curriculum building. Now teacher participation, teacher-pupil planning, and lay participation in curriculum building are widely used.

Changes in methods and materials that have grown out of the idea that how one learns is as important as what one learns. Among these modifications are the new relationships in teacher-pupil planning, the direct firsthand experiences, and the evolution of the unit method of teaching.

Historical Evolution of Teaching-Learning Units. One of many changes in the organization of curriculum materials, especially for the elementary and secondary schools, is illustrated in the historical evolution of the so-called unit method.

The forerunner of the unit method was probably Johann Freidrich Herbart (1776–1841). The five Herbartian steps were preparation, presentation, comparison, generalization, and application. A center of the Herbartian movement in the United States was Illinois State Normal University at Normal, Illinois, where Charles De Garmo, the brothers Charles and Frank McMurray, and other great teachers, several of whom studied in Germany, helped spread Herbart's ideas and started the Herbartian Society, now the National Society for the Study of Education. The Herbartian method was especially well adapted to the logically organized materials of instruction.

Current emphasis on the unit method of instruction was stimulated by Professor Henry C. Morrison of the University of Chicago. Through his classroom instruction and his writings, Professor Morrison's interpretation of the unit became widely accepted throughout the United States and abroad. The five Herbartian steps have their modern counterpart in the Morrisonian operative technique of exploration, presentation, assimilation, organization, and recitation. This is coupled with the mastery formula which is to pretest, teach, test the result, adapt procedure, teach and test again to the point of actual learning. Others have modified and interpreted the Morrisonian method in the light of their objectives of education.

Objectives

Since the curriculum is a direct outgrowth of the aims and purposes of education, attention is here centered upon some definitions and the major goals of education.

WHAT IS EDUCATION?

This common but difficult question may be attacked from both the negative and the positive sides.

What Education Is Not. Education is not a mere preparation for life—getting ready to do things, rather than doing them. Education is not synonymous with schooling; it begins with the parents before the child's birth, whereas schooling usually starts about the fifth year of life. Education is not simply the acquisition of knowledge or the accumulation of grades, credits, and degrees. Education is not book learning; much wisdom comes from activities other than reading a textbook. Education is not something apart from life; it is not restricted to a cloistered atmosphere. Education is not a summation of discrete parts; it is a whole that is greater than its components.

What Education Is. On the positive side education has been defined literally and figuratively. Here are some of the old and new concepts:

A good education consists in giving to the body and to the soul all the beauty and all the perfection of which they are capable.—Plato

What sculpture is to a block of marble, education is to the soul.—Addison

'Tis education forms the common mind;
Just as the twig is bent the tree's inclined.—Pope

Education is the instruction of the intellect in the laws of Nature, under which name I include not merely things and their forces, but men and their ways; and the fashioning of the affections and of the will into an earnest and loving desire to move in harmony with these laws.—Thomas Henry Huxley

Education has for its object the formation of character.—Herbert Spencer

Education includes everything that exerts a formative influence, and causes a young person to be, at a given point, what he is.—Mark Hopkins

Education alone can conduct us to that enjoyment which is, at once, best in quality and infinite in quantity.—Horace Mann

Knowledge does not comprise all which is contained in the large term of education. The feelings are to be disciplined, the passions are to be restrained; true and worthy motives are to be inspired; a profound religious feeling is to be instilled, and pure morality inculcated under all circumstances. All this is comprised in education. —Noah Webster

Education is a social process; our schools and colleges neither operate in empty space nor serve identical communities.—James Bryant Conant

Education is that reconstruction or reorganization of experience which adds to the meaning of experience, and which increases ability to direct the course of subsequent experience.—John Dewey

The popular concept today is that of Dewey, viz., that education is growth resulting from experiences. This education may be good, bad, or indifferent, although common usage refers to socially desirable development. If education is conceived in terms of growth, then it is as difficult to educate children as it is to grow plants. The teacher as a gardener of human growth seeks to provide conditions conducive to development through learning. Basically education is a lifelong learning process involving all-round development accompanied by adjustments within oneself to things, circumstances, and people. Intrinsic self-adjustment and extrinsic social adjustment are both concomitants of healthy growth. Educators must be concerned with the direction in which such development should be kept moving, and the ultimate goals toward which it should be directed. In the final analysis, the objectives of education are determined by the very nature of man himself.

The depth, length, breadth, and height of education are revealed more pointedly in its objectives, aims, or purposes than in terse definitions. These objectives when implemented by a functioning curriculum become a program of social action.

OBJECTIVES DEFINED BY INDIVIDUALS

Just as education is a process of growth, so too the objectives of education slowly evolve. Every statement of purposes develops from the judgment or scale of values held by some person or group. Educational leaders and professional groups have listed the objectives in various ways. A few illustrative statements by individuals and groups are included here.

Herbert Spencer's Classification of Objectives.
Herbert Spencer, who has never been accorded his just place in the field of education, as early as 1861 revealed his social insight through his published classification of human activities as a basis for grouping educational objectives. His five major areas of human conduct were as follows:

1. Self-preservation
2. Securing the necessities of life
3. Rearing and discipline of offspring
4. Maintenance of proper social and political relations
5. Activities which make up the leisure part of life, devoted to the gratification of tastes and feelings

This list helped to popularize the practice of classifying human activities.

James Bryant Conant's Objectives for Public Education. To his own question: "Why should one be taxed to provide schools for other people's children?" Harvard's former president James Bryant Conant gives these answers:

1. Education for citizenship
2. Education for the good life
3. Vocational education, of which professional education is a special case

The threefold division of education, Conant states, may serve as a rough guide to a layman seeking to penetrate the tangle of verbosities that surrounds many academic discussions.

Robert J. Havighurst's Developmental Tasks.
Robert J. Havighurst, chairman of the Committee on Human Development at the University of Chicago, defines this term as follows:

A developmental task is a task which arises at or about a certain period in the life of the individual, successful achievement of which leads to his happiness and to success with later tasks, while failure leads to unhappiness in the individual, disapproval by the society, and difficulty with later tasks. The prototype of the developmental task is the purely biological formation of organs in the embryo.[1]

He lists sequential activities for the various periods in life. These are presented in the sections of the book devoted to the appropriate age or maturation levels. These developmental tasks need to be met with graduated curricular materials and significant life experiences.

OBJECTIVES PREPARED
BY PROFESSIONAL GROUPS

Collective professional opinion as to what constitutes the goals of education has been crystallized periodically in statements prepared in connection with local, state, regional, and national programs, such as those described later in this chapter. Illustrative group statements

[1] Robert J. Havighurst, *Human Development and Education*, Longmans, Green & Co., Inc., New York, 1953, p. 2.

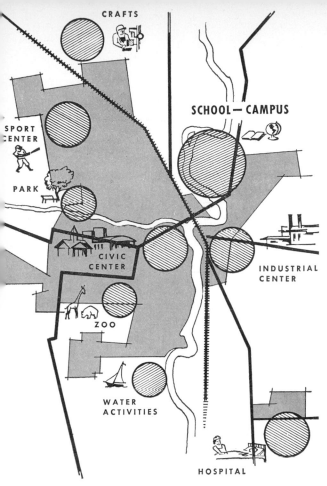

CRAFTS

SPORT CENTER

PARK

SCHOOL — CAMPUS

CIVIC CENTER

INDUSTRIAL CENTER

ZOO

WATER ACTIVITIES

HOSPITAL

*The ideal school curriculum is
as broad as life itself.
Education reaches more and more
into the community,*

as suggested here
by the "Random Falls Idea,"
in which most of the community is seen
as a vital part of
the total educative process.

on the purposes of education are the North Central Association objectives and the Life Adjustment Principles, as formulated respectively by a regional and a national committee. The latter are in Chapter 7. Here are summarized general objectives or the purposes of education in American democracy, prepared by the Educational Policies Commission.

Purposes of Education in American Democracy. These are both general and specific. Some of them undoubtedly possess the important quality of universality and eternal validity. The commission identified four aspects of educational purpose, centering around (1) the person himself, (2) his relationship to others in home and community, (3) the creation and use of material wealth, and (4) sociocivic activities. The first area calls for a description of the educated *person;* the second, for a description of the educated *member of the family and community group;* the third, of the educated *producer or consumer;* the fourth, of the educated *citizen.* The four great groups of objectives are stated as those of: (1) self-realization, (2) human relationship, (3) economic efficiency, (4) civic responsibility. Each of these, related to the others in a whole, is capable of further subdivision. A summary of each major objective is presented in *Policies for Education in American Democracy.*[2] As pointed out by the Educational Policies Commission, the applications of values vary from place to place and from hour to hour; hence it is impossible in a dynamic, changing world to develop detailed purposes that are universally applicable and perpetually enduring. Therefore both the philosophic fundamentals of education and the curriculums must be subject to constant revision if they are to be meaningful to the people and effective in schools, colleges, and life. Furthermore, realistic objectives should stimulate goal-directed activity and develop into desirable outcomes. Too often objectives exist merely for historical purposes and are as ineffective as New Year's resolutions.

Principles

A common practice in the initiation of programs for curriculum development is to prepare a list of basic principles or guiding assumptions. This initial attack provides a unified point of view and a basis for consistency of action among the educational workers as they develop curriculums.

[2] Educational Policies Commission, *Policies for Education in American Democracy*, National Education Association, Washington, D.C., 1946, pp. 185–252.

*But the curriculum
nevertheless
places heavy emphasis
upon the mastery
of fundamental
skills . . .*

The Curriculum Is Broad and Comprehensive.
As defined previously, the curriculum consists
of the "organized experiences of an individual
under the guidance of the school." Some authorities go to the extreme in stating that the
curriculum consists of all the experiences a
person has, irrespective of what, when, and
where. Obviously there must be some limitation. Generally, however, the term "curriculum" is interpreted broadly.

The curriculum is not simply a series of
printed pages written in some central office
for the information and guidance of the teachers in the classroom. Such published materials
are often extremely helpful to the teachers in
their work, but the curriculum itself is not what
is written but what is done. Today's program
for youth accents the kind of experiences he
ought to have rather than the names of the
subjects he should take. These experiences
are facilitated and directed through the development of curricular materials. The activities
and materials are as broad as life itself. The
curriculum is life material used in building
body, mind, and soul structure.

such as mathematics . . .

*The Curriculum Has Its Roots in a Philosophy
of Education.* A broad, well-grounded curriculum reaches down into the bedrock of the
school's educational principles. Since educational philosophy is primarily concerned with
a criticism of experience, it is obvious that
its formulation follows prolonged study. As
William James once stated, philosophy is a
particularly obstinate effort to think closely.
A deep, sustaining philosophy is more likely
to result from the leisure meditation of the
Indian oriental who spends hours in contem-
plative thought than from the mile-a-minute
dash of the occidental who does much of his
thinking while he talks. There is imminent
danger that teachers will seek to "Simonize"
their curriculums by applying hastily a thin,
top coat of diluted educational philosophy. A

language . . .

frame of reference cannot be formulated in one teachers' meeting—it is evolved from life through <u>continual reflection.</u> Furthermore, caution must be expressed against the current practice of parroting the trite phrases of educational theorists instead of building a strong philosophy upon the inner convictions and firsthand knowledges of those who work daily with pupils and who have digested the thoughts of yesterday's and today's scholars.

*science,
both
in
the
classroom
and
in the field (or stream)* . . .

Curriculum Building Is a Democratic, Cooperative Enterprise. In local, state-wide, or national programs, <u>cooperative effort is essential in curriculum work.</u> One postulate of democracy is that persons enjoy those things in the building of which they have shared. This is doubly true in regard to the curriculum of the school. The course of study is not a dictator's manifesto or an executive fiat. <u>The modern curriculum is based upon the democratic tradition that the purposes and programs of education should be developed cooperatively through interactive processes of living.</u> Furthermore, <u>participation is not limited to teachers and administrators. Pupils, parents, interested patrons, and specialists,</u> as active

and homemaking . . .

with time for independent study.

agents in the educative process, can contribute to the broadened offerings of the community school. Therefore, of extreme importance in curriculum building are group dynamics—the productive processes of collective actions and interactions in furthering school and society.

The Administrative Organization Should Be Simple and Flexible. An individual teacher, zealous for curricular reform, need not wait for complex administrative machinery to be installed locally or for a slow-moving state-wide program to be launched. The organization for curriculum production, especially in the typical school, may be very simple, with equipment and personnel added as needed and as funds become available. The committee system can be employed with a wide degree of fluidity and a high degree of effectiveness.

The Housing of the School Should Conform to the Curricular Needs. A principle hard to apply in many schools is that of adjusting the building to the educational program rather than that of developing a curriculum that will conform to the brick and mortar limitations imposed by existing structures. Many school buildings are obstacles to educational progress. A typical illustration is a high school erected before the course in auto mechanics was introduced so that today it is impossible to bring an automobile into or near the building. The housing as well as the educational supplies and equipment should function in the service of educational goals.

The Curriculum Must Provide for Individual Differences. A basic principle is that the curriculum should recognize the pupil as an individual who has a right to his characteristic type of personality development under such guidance as is needed. Figuratively, some puny pupils are required to struggle with a 20-pound load when all they can carry is 10 pounds, whereas mentally husky individuals who can shoulder 50 pounds with ease are permitted to play with ounces. The former practice re-

sults in retardation, and the latter produces lazy workmen. A difficulty with the old order of curriculums was that the child was divided: the teacher demanded one thing and the pupil's nature and interest dictated another loyalty. Individual differences must be considered if the pupil is to develop his personality quotient, to use his own leisure time wisely, to select a suitable vocation for himself, and to be a dynamic part of a larger whole. Meeting these individual requirements does not necessitate a contest between individual and societal needs, and between specifics and generalities. Education has general principles applicable to the whole of its citizenry, but it must be individualized even in social application.

The Creative Must Be Encouraged. Since education tends to become too wooden and mechanical, much emphasis today is placed upon developing creativeness in the pupil and teacher. The school, which often stifled genius, now encourages deviations from a fixed pattern. Gone is the day when all pupils in an art class drew a flower in identical patterns and with the same color. Creative self-expression is the antithesis of moronic imitation. Intrinsic interests rather than extraneous assignments goad pupils to action. *Memoriter* learning except in basic essentials is being dethroned. Skills are taught through functional use in meaningful situations. Curriculums are built out of knowledge about the individual pupil. The modern curriculum functions best for teachers under an eclectic procedure which necessitates that teachers think creatively and ingeniously of many learning-teaching possibilities.

Guidance Is Inextricably Linked with the Curriculum. A student or teacher cannot isolate a guidance program from the curriculum; their synthesis is inevitable. A desirable practice is to map out in advance a tentative curriculum for all four years of the student's proposed stay in the high school. This tends to make the student feel that each course is a part of a larger plan for rounding out his education. This long-term curricular outlook is also being provided for college students in an increasing number of institutions. Guidance is not a disparate service to be performed only by specialists. The classroom instructor, through the curriculum, makes many adaptations to allow the pupil a maximum of self-direction. The course of study is in itself a mere guide for the teacher. Modern school administration is designed to provide curricular help for both students and teachers through person-to-person guidance and individual therapy as well as group advisement.

The Curriculum Should Be Life-centered. Although the individual pupil must be recognized, the modern school is not restricted to a child-centered curriculum. Neither should the curriculum be adult-centered. The focal point is life itself. A life-centered curriculum recognizes the past of the race plus the present and future life of the learner and society. To be life-centered the modern curriculum must function twenty-four hours a day.

Evaluation Is Essential for Pupil and Curriculum. Evaluation in its broad scope is replacing tests. Many instruments of diagnosis and reliable measures of pupil growth are employed rather than mere pencil-and-paper tests and lesson reciting, which often consists of repeating to the teacher stereotyped phrases and clauses. The atomistic character of appraisal revealed itself in yesteryear in the extreme emphasis upon subjects rather than upon pupils, upon what they wrote rather than what they did.

Evaluation of curricular materials is also inevitable. Sometimes this is made voluntary; often, however, circumstances such as a financial stringency force a reappraisal of a school's offerings. Accretions in course offerings do not necessarily mean improvement; elimination is unavoidable in curricular reform. This involves a related principle expressed many years ago by Herbert Spencer in the query: "What knowledge is of most worth?" A pupil receives his formal education in a relatively short span; hence evaluation must result in the elimination as well as the addition of curricular materials.

Constant Curriculum Revision Is Imperative. It is the law of growth that things must change; hence constant curricular modifications are inevitable. Teachers are likely to work feverishly on curriculum reform for a few years and then write an indelible finis to materials committed to permanent print. The curriculum at its best is an evolving series of experiences; hence it does not need to be copyrighted for twenty-eight years or registered in the U.S. Patent Office. Constant revisions, which should be made in such a manner as to avoid educational chaos, will lead to intellectual emancipation for the schools and will enable educators to meet the challenges of contemporary life. A changeless curriculum postulates a static society, and, vice versa, an unchanging society demands no curricular innovations. The American Association of School Administrators, in recognition of the importance of change, chose as the theme for its 1960 convention: "Creating and coping with change through education." Education must recover what is valuable in the residue of the past, but it must also break away from the authority of outworn tradition. A curriculum devised for an age of ground travel via horse and buggy or Model-T Ford must be renovized, at least in part, to fit the challenge of flight in a supersonic space age.

Procedures

Intertwined with the principles just enumerated are the procedures or techniques in curriculum development. Several major approaches and steps are listed, and then a few detailed techniques are described.

APPROACHES TO CURRICULUM WORK

Three major methods of *organization* of staff for curriculum improvement are: centralized, decentralized, and coordinated approaches. The last, a partnership program of administrators, teachers, and parents, is widely used.

Usually the approaches to curriculum *activity* are: the cooperative development of basic principles that underlie the evolution of curriculums; a study of the characteristics and needs of pupils, adults, and society; or the immediate direct attack upon subject matter and content, as through a production committee for mathematics. These approaches are often combined, or each is lifted up for periodic emphasis as curriculum building progresses.

MAJOR STEPS IN CURRICULUM ACTIVITY

Curricular procedures are influenced so markedly by the community school and personnel engaged in the work that it is impossible to set up a uniform series of sequential steps. Some of the major procedures follow:

Initiating teachers
Inviting cooperation and support
Organizing personnel
Formulating statement of principles
Selecting work procedures
Educating teachers in techniques of revision
Consulting outside specialists

Surveying
Studying needs, interests, and abilities
Surveying legal prescriptions
Making historical surveys
Getting parental opinion
Investigating community resources
Making detailed job analyses

Developing
Formulating general curricular aims
Collecting materials and studies
Selecting and organizing content
Suggesting teaching-learning procedures

Correlating work in various areas and levels
Determining time allotments
Establishing standards of achievement
Organizing experimental groups
Selecting textbooks and library materials
Recommending supplies and equipment
Educating in the use of reorganized curriculum

Evaluating
Checking content for duplication or omission
Editing material
Preparing materials for evaluating growth
Appraising results of curricular work
Providing for continuous development
Interpreting the program continuously
Evaluating the curriculum continuously

A few of the detailed techniques employed by curriculum workers will be described briefly.

SPECIFIC TECHNIQUES IN BUILDING CURRICULUMS

Organization of Personnel. Curriculum work is best promoted under a simple but effective coordination of workers. One notes the wide use of an educational council or committee which works closely with the curriculum department in the development of materials.

Survey of Legal Prescriptions. No group engaged in curriculum work can afford to ignore the mandates of the lawgivers. To the courses of study the lawmakers have added many requirements, from the general order in the first grade that basic instruction must be in the English language to the federal stipulation that land-grant colleges must teach military science. The most frequent legal accretions to the curriculum concern the teaching of United States history, civics, safety education, and the evil effects of narcotics and alcohol, plus the obligatory observance of special days.

Investigation and Use of Community Resources. The community school as an agency for achieving social ideals seeks to draw upon curriculum resources in the local setting as well as in larger spheres. Periodic inventories of the community resources made by pupils, teachers, and others will help to locate potential sources of curriculum enrichment and of work experiences for pupils.

Activity or Job Analysis. In this technique the surveyor makes a detailed study of the various duties entailed in a particular job, such as office secretaryship. After the minute tasks have been located and defined, the school can better prepare a student for this position by giving him much specific information and many direct experiences. One of the chief proponents of these analytical procedures has been W. W. Charters, who has applied this technique to teaching. The curriculum at Stephens College, Columbia, Missouri, has been built primarily upon an analysis of activities performed by women.

Research and Experimentation in Curriculum Development. With the twentieth century began that emphasis in education which is called the scientific movement, although from the days of Benjamin Franklin a small group of educators have been interested in objectivity and the scientific spirit. Gradually educators in larger numbers turned to experimentation and research instead of to opinion, tradition, and the paste-pot-and-scissors method in the making of courses of study.

Some research, however, does not merit the name, since it is mere busy work. Not only is much research of inferior quality, but significant findings obtained scientifically have been interpreted and applied in an unscientific manner. Teachers must become educated consumers as well as indefatigable producers of research. Among the genuine research investigations that have had a marked influence on the curriculum are controlled studies of how human beings learn, as Gesell's investigations of the early years of childhood; experimentation with learning in animals, particularly white rats and monkeys, as Kofka's work with the insight in monkeys; research to find the most needed subject matter, as Hocking's early study

DETERMINANTS OF CURRICULUM

Fig. 13-1. Determinants of the curriculum. (Courtesy of Ivol Spofford, Virgil Herrick, and Paul R. Pierce.)

of place geography; investigations of maturation and grade placement, as the work of the Committee of Seven in Arithmetic; construction of intelligence tests, as the new revision of the Binet test; the development of various types of achievement tests, as the well-known Stanford achievement tests for elementary schools; and the perfecting of the newer types of evaluation, as the measures prepared by Tyler and his associates. Pioneers who gave much thought and effort to research in building curriculums are E. L. Thorndike, W. W. Charters, and Charles Judd. Today research and experimentation have numerous implications for the classroom teachers as well as for the builder of a more scientifically prepared mental diet for the pupils.

Illustrative Diagram. Some of the techniques and principles in curriculum development are illustrated by the equilateral triangle. The three factors to be given paramount consideration are indicated by the sides of the triangle:

1. A factor basic to the modern curriculum is the philosophy of life and education possessed by those who are making the curriculum. Here the question of values, under-

standings, and procedures essential to the democratic society arises.

2. There are the needs of society. Social changes are occurring rapidly and new issues are constantly emerging. Among the areas of social change are population movement, technological development, and home living. The curriculum must take into account the need for dealing with such developments.

3. But in a democratic society the interests and needs of the individual pupils are as important as the needs of society. Changes in psychological principles, enunciation of new laws of learning, and data from pupils' physical, mental, and emotional development profoundly affect the building of an educational program.

The relationship of the three factors is shown in the diagram, in which the philosophy of life and education of those responsible for the educational program forms the base line of the chart, the needs of the pupils and the needs of society the sides, and the apex the outcomes for the pupils.[3] The outcomes for the pupils are affected by the way in which curricular materials are organized.

Organization

The organization of learning experiences in the curriculum is very important because it affects the effectiveness of teaching and learning. Through the cumulative impact of many organized individual learning experiences, human behavior is gradually modified. In his chapter on "Curriculum Organization" in a yearbook of the National Society for the Study of Education, Ralph W. Tyler, formerly with the University of Chicago, wrote:

Without organization, learning experiences will be perceived by many learners as isolated, chaotic, and haphazard. . . . No matter how effective an individual learning experience may be, if it is not

[3] Adapted from Paul R. Pierce, "The Curriculum Council of the Chicago Public Schools," *Chicago Schools Journal*, March–April, 1949, p. 177.

followed up with related ones, it is not likely that significant changes will take place.[4]

So much of the pupil's life outside the educational institutions is unorganized that he must have some systematization in school.

In general theory, some learnings are organized like a stair with successive steps, as in moving from short division to long division. Some are like a gradual upward-moving escalator which takes the pupil smoothly to a higher level, as in reading. Some are like a pole vault where one returns to the starting point to try for successive higher jumps, as in experiments in physics. Some are like a series of concentric circles where the learner moves from the starting point to wider areas of knowledge, as in map reading. Some are organized on the basis of an upward spiral which starts from the beginning and moves outward and upward simultaneously, as in philosophy. Some are organized in straight-line verticals as between the seventh- and eighth-grade levels in the same subject, as arithmetic. Some are also systematized horizontally, as correlating lines between two subjects, such as arithmetic and science in the seventh grade. Whatever the subject, most learning experiences must be organized.

TYPES OF CURRICULUM ORGANIZATION

Curricular patterns range from the traditional type to extreme experimentation. Five of the curricular patterns with alternate designations are (1) subject or traditional, (2) correlated or fused, (3) broad fields or areas, (4) core or common learnings, and (5) experience or functional curriculums. These types, which are not mutually exclusive and have numerous variations, are described as follows.[5]

[4] Ralph W. Tyler, *The Integration of Educational Experiences*, National Society for the Study of Education, University of Chicago Press, Chicago, 1958, p. 106.

[5] Adapted from L. Thomas Hopkins, *Integration: Its Meaning and Application*, Appleton-Century-Crofts, Inc., New York, 1937, pp. 197–275, Good, *op. cit.*, pp. 113–114, and American Association of School Administrators, *American School Curriculum*, National Education Association, Washington, D.C., 1953, pp. 57–70.

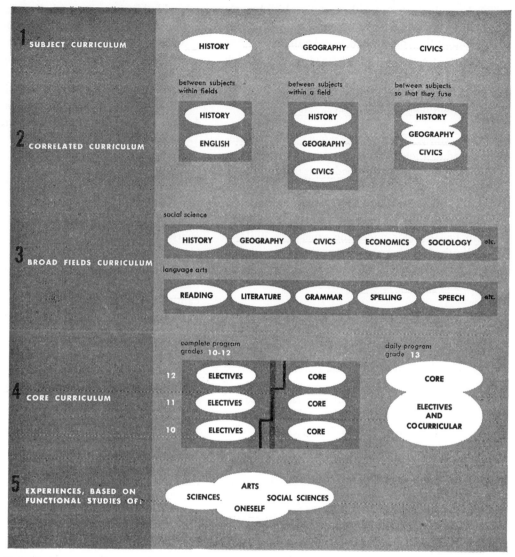

Fig. 13.2. Major types of curriculums.

Subject Curriculum. This is characterized by a large number of subjects taught independently of each other. Most of the time of the pupil is spent in learning from books and other written and printed materials in various subjects in which the accumulated wisdom of experts in that field has been recorded. The emphasis is upon the learning of subject matter selected long before the children appear in the classroom.

In such a curriculum, history, geography, and civics usually are isolated subjects (see Fig. 13-2).

Correlated Curriculum. Here the underlying ideas are those described for the subject curriculum. The starting point is subject-matter-set-out-to-be-learned. The correlated curriculum can be carried out in numerous ways which can be conveniently arranged on a scale. At the bottom would be located the casual and incidental efforts to make relationships between or among subjects. At the top of the scale would be located those conscious and definitely planned efforts to see that relationships among subjects were made and carried out effectively. Among the correlations may be those between subjects within a field, as social science, or between subjects within two or more fields, as English and history. Subjects may be fused so that boundaries disappear.

3 *The Broad Fields Curriculum.* This is composed of a few fields rather than a large number of small subjects. In broad fields under the subject philosophy the learning area is restricted, although definitely broader than what would be expected as a summation of various subjects. In broad fields under the experience philosophy the learning area is greatly increased. Examples of these broad fields or areas are social science and the language arts.

4 *The Core Curriculum.* This includes subjects or a common body of experiences required of everyone but with variability of content and activities to meet the varying needs of individuals. The term "core" is used to cover a wide range of types of curriculum practice. Part of the work in the senior high may be a basic core running through grades 10, 11, and 12 with variable time allotments. A certain portion of each day may be devoted to the core, or common learnings.

5 *The Experience Curriculum.* This is a series of purposeful experiences growing out of pupil interests and moving toward an ever more adequate understanding of and intelligent participation in the surrounding culture and group life. The experience curriculum has its beginnings in the situations which confront children in their immediate living.

One comprehensive example is the directly functional curriculum suggested by Lester Dix. He proposes for the general divisions of his functional curriculum the following:

1. The study of oneself—embracing the functions of guidance, of health development and emotional adjustment, of the provision of basic necessities, of play, recreation, club,

and hobby interests, and all social activities
2. The study of the social environment—the evolution, functions, and structures of cultures, particularly American society
3. The study of the national environment—the relationship of man and nature; his sciences of control, adaptation, and utilization
4. The study of the arts—the evolution, material, skills, and attitudes of the arts of human expression, communication, and imagination[6]

These areas are overlapping fields. The directly functional type is a variety of experience curriculum. Two kinds of curricular organization currently stressed in many schools are the core curriculum previously described and the organization of subject matter and activities in teaching-learning units. Because of the significant role of units in current curriculums, this organization of materials and activities is described further.

UNITARY PROCEDURES IN TEACHING AND LEARNING

Definition. A teaching-learning unit is a teacher-pupil designed series of significant experiences so related as to function in the all-round development of an integrating person in a dynamic world. This concept stresses the fact that the unit embraces both learning and teaching, involves both pupil and teacher activity, calls for planning, includes significant experiences, aims at many-sided development through a totality of learnings, and seeks to develop not an integrated but an integrating person who can adjust to ever-changing situations in a kaleidoscopic world. Furthermore, unit procedures are not designed exclusively for children but are used extensively and effectively for any learner—be he child, youth, or adult.

Organization of a Unit. The elements included in a teaching-learning-living unit vary with the

[6] Lester Dix, *A Charter for Progressive Education,* Bureau of Publications, Teachers College, Columbia University, New York, 1939, p. 57.

pupils, teacher, supervisor, school, and community, but the following list covers most factors in its organization:

1. A meaningful title
2. Objectives—teacher and pupil
3. Grade placement—academic level
4. Approximate time elements
5. Orientation—setting the stage
6. Initiation of unit—pretest
7. Guidance of pupils—unit guide sheets
8. Organization of materials
9. Proposed teaching-learning procedures
10. Suggested activities—initiating, developing, and culminating
11. Suggested materials and equipment
12. Adaptations—provisions for flexibility
13. Bibliography—pupil and teacher
14. Evaluation—actual outcomes
15. Report and historical record
16. Provision for continuous revision

The format or mechanical make-up of the unit should give consideration to such elements as initial page, table of contents, numbering of pages, title headings, binding, and other physical features.

The eclectic method of teaching and learning employs many techniques and curricular patterns, including the teaching-learning unit just described. The unit does not have any rigidly fixed content but is flexible to meet times, places, and circumstances. A realistic unit of work is a designed program of teaching, learning, and living.

Practices

Through the combined efforts of local, county, state, regional, and national agencies the curriculum is becoming functional and elastic. In no area of education has so much improvement been effected in the last decade as in curriculum.

Some General Curricular Trends. Specific trends in pre-elementary, elementary, secondary, higher, and adult education are found in the concluding portions of Chapters 5 to 9, re-

spectively. Among the trends discernible today in the development of curriculums are the following general practices:

1. The concept of the curriculum is broadened to embrace all the experiences which pupils have under the guidance of the school.
2. Teachers study the philosophy that undergirds society, education in general, and the local school system.
3. Curriculum workers apply the best developments of the psychology of learning and physical growth, particularly maturation.
4. The course builders give much consideration to sequential developmental tasks in meeting the life needs of pupils and students.
5. The functional concept calls for a correlated curriculum and an integrating child.
6. The four walls of the classroom are extended through utilization of the community resources.
7. The program of studies is being reorganized on the bases of great central concepts, understandings, themes, fields or units, but with protection for pupils against the neglect of necessary skills, informations, and attitudes.
8. Measurement through pencil-and-paper tests is being supplemented by a many-sided program of qualitative evaluation.
9. Some of the deadwood and soft spots in the curriculum are being eliminated and validated; solid content is being substituted.
10. The program of continuous curriculum revision is cooperative with pupils, teachers, administrators, and laymen participating.
11. The individual creative talents of pupils and teachers are being unleashed.
12. Specific remedial programs are based upon careful individual diagnosis.
13. There is a reduction in electives and an increase in required subjects.
14. Some cocurricular activities are being incorporated in the school program.
15. A wide variety of materials and equipment,

including multisensory aids and instructional materials centers, reinforce the content of the curriculum.

16. School buildings are being designed to meet the requirements of a flexible program.

17. Schools are developing curricular guides containing rich sources of raw materials and curriculum laboratories for materials.

18. A functional program of curricular services is being developed to meet fundamental human needs—mental, physical, social, and emotional.

Specific Curricular Trends. Many definite curricular trends in the various academic areas are found under the section Practices at the conclusion of each of the chapters in Part 2 of this volume as follows:

Pre-elementary education, Chapter 5
Elementary education, Chapter 6
Secondary education, Chapter 7
Higher education, Chapter 8
Adult education, Chapter 9

In conclusion, the most specific and yet universal trend in all these levels of teaching and learning is that of effective evaluation. At no time has education in the United States from bottom to top received such critical and careful scrutinizing as today. Schools have become conversation pieces. Educators, parents, and pupils should be grateful to the Russian sputniks for launching in this country a period of arduous appraisal of education in general, and of the curriculums in particular. The future demands a critical and continuous evaluation of both current offerings and future deletions and accretions in order that present assets may be consolidated, weaknesses may be eliminated, and dynamic mental growth may be challenging to the pupils of today and tomorrow. In this space age the curriculum problem is great, but the need for democratic academic education is greater, and the opportunity is the greatest in the history of curriculum building in American education.

Summary

Idealistically the curriculum is life stuff used in building mental maturity and soul structure. Educationally it is the sum total of the experiences the pupil has under the direction of the school. Academically it is the schedule of subjects and fields taught. Currently the curriculum is the center of attacks on schools and colleges. Academic excellence is emerging as the top priority in education at all levels.

The colonial school was a center of learning. Franklin's academy (a word borrowed from the French word "académie") accented the training of the mind. Early college curriculums were not diluted with a plethora of electives. Commissions, organizations, and individual pioneers contributed to the historical development of the modern curriculum.

Education can be defined by what it is not and what it really is. Too often educational objectives are mere New Year's resolutions of intent. The current emphasis is on outcomes—what comes out of the teaching-learning-living program broadly called the curriculum. The nation as a whole, as well as each individual school system, must do some tough thinking about the goals of modern education.

The chapter describes several basic principles to be employed in building curriculums. A basic principle is that a curriculum designed for an age of ground travel via horse and buggy or Model-T Ford must be renovized, at least in part, to fit the functions of flight in a supersonic space age.

Intertwined with principles are the techniques of curriculum building. The staff must be organized for continuous curriculum work through the major steps of: initiating, surveying, developing, and evaluating materials.

So much of the pupil's life outside of the educational institutions is unorganized that he must have some systematization in instruction in school. The more common types of curricular organization are: subjects, correlation, broad fields, core, and experience curriculums, with teaching-learning-living units which are widely used.

Through the combined efforts of local, county, state, and national agencies, the curriculum is becoming more fundamental and functional. School buildings are being designed as facilitating devices for implementing effective functioning of the curriculum. The most specific and universal trend at all levels of learning is a nationwide scrutiny of the curriculum. The opportunities for improvement are the greatest in the history of curriculum building in the United States.

Suggested activities

1. Study definitions of education. Write in one paragraph your definition.
2. Analyze critically several sets of objectives of education.
3. Make a list of principles that underlie curriculum development.
4. What is meant by developmental tasks?
5. What are some of the current criticisms of the curriculum?
6. Draw a diagram of organization of school personnel engaged in curriculum work in some school system.
7. Examine courses of study in your major field of interest.
8. Investigate the legal prescriptions set up by your state legislature for the curriculum in elementary and high schools.
9. Study the resources in your community with a view to discovering teaching-learning materials.
10. Gather a few illustrations of scientific findings established by research and applicable to a school curriculum.
11. Sketch the life of a pioneer in curriculum like E. L. Thorndike.
12. Discuss the function of educational measurement and evaluation.
13. Describe ways of organizing curricular materials, such as core curriculum.
14. Study several teaching-learning units.
15. Describe a state program of curriculum building.
16. Report on the curricular recommendations of a national group.
17. Should there be a nationwide set of goals for the school curriculums?

Bibliography

Books

Association for Supervision and Curriculum Development: *Curriculum Materials for Creative Thinking, Living, and Teaching*, National Education Association, Washington, D.C., 1957. Describes the selection and use of instructional materials and their relationship to the curriculum.

———: *Learning and the Teacher*, National Education Association, Washington, D.C., 1959. Using realistic classroom situations as illustrations, the influence of the teacher's personality and behavior upon learning is revealed.

———: *What Shall the High Schools Teach?* National Education Association, Washington, D.C., 1956. Discusses the issues and problems of curriculum development in secondary education with suggestions for improvement.

Bereday, George Z. F., and Joseph A. Lauwerys: *The Secondary School Curriculum*, 1958 Yearbook of Education, World Book Company, Yonkers, N.Y., 1958. Considers the ways in which secondary school curriculums are organized and their content in different cultures and national settings.

Elsbree, Willard S., and Harold J. McNally: *Elementary School Administration and Supervision*, American Book Company, New York, 1959, chap. 6. Discusses the issues, various designs, and types of organization of the elementary school curriculum.

Frandsen, Arden N.: *How Children Learn*, McGraw-Hill Book Company, Inc., New York, 1957, chaps. 1, 14. Discusses the aims of the elementary school curriculum and how learning can be evaluated.

Krug, Edward A., and others: *Administering Curriculum Planning*, Harper & Brothers, New York, 1956, chaps. 3–6. Discusses the role of the teacher, students, central office, board of education, and public in curriculum planning.

McNally, Harold J., and A. Harry Passow and Associates: *Improving the Quality of Public School Programs*, Teachers College, Columbia University, New York, 1960. Presents guiding principles of curriculum development with specific examples of practices drawn from actual school situations in a variety of communities.

Morphet, Edgar L., Roe L. Johns, and Theodore L. Reller: *Educational Administration: Concepts, Practices, and Issues*, Prentice-Hall, Inc., Englewood Cliffs, N.J., 1959, chap. 14. Discusses factors affecting the educational program, the methods of improving it, and some related problems and issues.

National Society for the Study of Education: *The Integration of Educational Experiences*, University of Chicago Press, Chicago, 1958, chaps. 4, 6. Discusses educational objectives and shows how a variety of educative experiences can be woven effectively into the curriculum.

Power, Edward J.: *Education for American Democracy*, McGraw-Hill Book Company, Inc., New York, 1958, chap. 14. Discusses liberal and general education and their proper emphasis in the school program.

Smith, B. O., William O. Stanley, and J. Harlan Shores: *Fundamentals of Curriculum Development*, World Book Company, Yonkers, N.Y., 1957, chaps. 10–14. Discusses subject, activity, and core curriculums—their characteristics, strengths, and weaknesses.

Stratemeyer, Florence B., and others: *Developing a Curriculum for Modern Living*, Bureau of Publications, Teachers College, Columbia University, New York, 1957, part III. Treats the selection of curriculum content, guiding of learners, providing for individual differences, evaluating learning, and capitalizing upon community resources.

Periodicals

Alberty, Harold: "A Sound Core Program," *NEA Journal*, vol. 45 (January, 1956), pp. 20–21. Discusses some of the principal characteristics of the core curriculum and clears up some common misconceptions of it.

Caswell, Hollis L.: "Great Challenges for Education," *Teachers College Record*, vol. 59 (November, 1957), pp. 69–75. Establishes four fundamental requirements for the kind of education needed in today's world.

Hanna, Paul R.: "Design for a National Curriculum," *The Nation's Schools*, vol. 62 (September, 1958), pp. 43–45. An unusual proposal for a carefully prepared national curriculum for use in all schools.

Herrick, Theral: "Curriculum Problems: Some Basic Issues," *Teachers College Record*, vol. 60 (February, 1959), pp. 242–244. Presents 10 basic issues which underlie curriculum theory and practice.

Shoemaker, Francis, and Arno Bellack: "Curriculums for Youth," *Teachers College Record*, vol. 56 (April, 1955), pp. 371–376. Sets forth basic ideas underlying secondary education and faces the dilemma of caring for all children while also challenging the gifted.

Stanley, Julian C.: "ABC's of Test Construction," *NEA Journal*, vol. 47 (April, 1958), pp. 224–231. Establishes basic considerations important to the teacher in constructing tests.

Walsh, J. Hartt: "Education in 2000 A.D.," *The Nation's Schools*, vol. 57 (April, 1956), pp. 47–51. A fascinating prediction of what schools will be like at the end of the century —teaching methods, curriculums, and buildings.

chapter 14

*Cocurricular
activities*

*See copy of curriculum
guide.*

*insist on school
insurance.*

The various *extra*curricular activities of the school are becoming less and less *anti*curricular and more and more *co*curricular. Formerly the curriculum was so rigid, formal, academic, and teacher-dominated that any informal, semiacademic, and pupil-initiated undertaking was labeled as extracurricular. The latter included all those pupil enterprises that were not a part of regular classroom subjects. These activities were usually under the direction of the school but were conducted at the close of the school day. Their phenomenal growth was due largely to the dullness and monotony of the regular curriculum. Fortunately, the term "extracurricular" is disappearing.

In many schools the old extracurricular activities are assuming a prominence and function almost parallel with the curricular undertakings. These activities should grow out of the curriculum and enrich it. They are so closely related to the curriculum that they are properly called cocurricular. They may also be called extracurricular, extraclass, collateral, semicurricular, incurricular, allied, or nonclass. In general, they should not be anti-intellectual but procurricular. These activities must not exist by or for themselves—they must contribute to the whole program of the school. This relationship makes it desirable that the active sponsors of the organizations be regular staff members of the school.

Cocurricular enterprises have accumulated importance on all levels of American education, in both public and private institutions. In the pre-elementary and elementary school, these activities are so closely allied to the curricular program that there is often little distinction between the two. At the secondary level, particularly in the junior and senior high schools, many cocurricular meetings are scheduled during the school day but are not arranged as classes. In the junior and senior colleges the student activities revert to being almost extracurricular. Usually graduate students in universities are so busily concerned with study, research, and other problems that they neglect nonacademic activities, ofttimes to the detriment of their physical, social, and mental health. Many universities treat their nonathletic extracurricular activities too lightly.

In her interesting autobiography, *A Peculiar Treasure,* Edna Ferber devotes more space to the extracurricular or cocurricular aspects of her school life at Ryan High School of Appleton, Wisconsin, than to the curricular side of her formal education there. The permeating influence of character-building activities in schools is generally acknowledged. The most classic tribute is the oft-quoted phrase of the Duke of Wellington that the battle of Waterloo was won on the playing fields of Eton. A former university president James Bryant Conant predicts, "It may be that the ideological struggle with Communism in the next fifty years will be won on the playing fields of the public high schools of the United States."

Foundations

Extracurricular activities are as old as schooling. From the early Greeks came the modern Olympic games. The classic cup race between British and American sailing yachts is more than one hundred years old. In 1869 Rutgers beat Princeton in the first American intercollegiate game of football. At Yale University, where the *Yale Daily News,* "the oldest college daily," was started, the first college annual appeared in 1806. Many older colleges organized debating societies during the first year the institution started. High school graduation exercises are only a few years younger than the institutions themselves. As early as 1917 the famous Seven Cardinal Principles of Education listed "preparation for the worthy use of leisure time" as a basic goal of education. E. K. Fretwell, a pioneer in promoting knowledge of and practice in extracurricular activities, published his book, *Extracurricular Activities in Secondary Schools* in 1931.

It is difficult to trace the exact genesis date of many of the extracurricular activities in schools and colleges of yesteryears in the United States. In *Allied Activities in the Secondary School* are listed three stages of historical development:

1. Activities were disregarded, ignored, or tolerated.
2. Activities were opposed—first condemned and then prohibited.
3. Approved activities are encouraged under proper supervision.[1]

Currently much encouragement is given to extraclass activities.

The arrival of the air age inaugurated the formation of many aviation clubs in the country. The orbiting in outer space of the Russian and American satellites stimulated the formation of science, mathematics, and satellite clubs. The current accent on foreign languages in elementary, secondary, and higher education has encouraged the formation of language clubs.

The extreme fiscal importance of cocurricular activities in recent years is attested to by the publication in 1957 of *A Manual of Accounting Principles and Procedures for Student Activity Funds* by the Association of School Business Officials. Congress and President Eisenhower recognized the significance of guid-

[1] Louis R. Kilzer, Harold H. Stephenson, and H. O. Nordberg, *Allied Activities in the Secondary School,* Harper & Brothers, New York, 1956, pp. 3–4.

ance as an instrument of national policy by appropriating funds in 1958 for the improvement of guidance programs in schools and colleges.

Current programs for erecting school and college buildings often include quarters for the student center or the student unions.

In addition to the fiscal and physical recognition of the role of student activities, a philosophy has developed that supports these cocurricular programs. The fundamental philosophy undergirding modern cocurricular activities has been expressed thus by the National Association of Secondary-school Principals: "All youth need to be able to use their leisure time well and to budget it wisely, balancing activities that yield satisfaction to the individual with those that are socially useful." The modern trend is toward a balanced program, conducted in harmony with fundamental principles of education.

Genuine cocurricular activities grow out of the curriculum and return to it. These activities must not exist by or for themselves: they must contribute meaningfully to the whole program of the school. What, then, are the principles of sound cocurricular activities?

Principles

Cocurricular activities are being reevaluated in terms of a balanced program which gives the top priority to the academic accents of the school or college. The two programs—the academic and the extraclass—can coexist but the

They enrich the curriculum and contribute to the total school program.

*They train for democratic living.
These student council members are the popularly
elected representatives in student
government who assume responsibility for
the general welfare of others.*

*Sound cocurricular activities help develop
individual personality and self-realization.*

intellectual pursuits should come first. Genuine cocurricular activities grow out of the curriculum and return to it. All cocurricular activities should reinforce the curriculum and the latter should permeate the former. They feed, and are fed by, the academic pursuits. Brain power is the highest criterion for manpower in educational institutions. The academic dog should not be wagged by the extracurricular tail. First things must come first in American education. Hence to insure the priority of education, these extraclass activities must be supervised, and by members of the educational staff. One of the perennial questions to use in evaluation is: "What are the educational goals of the extraclass organization or activity?"

Educating for Democratic Living. A cardinal tenet governing the school program is that America must educate for a progressing democracy. Cocurricular activities can help the school youth of America to conserve and develop the cultural pattern of a democratic way of living. Educational leaders have urged greater opportunity for pupil participation in the government of the schools, so that by the time the students have reached the senior year in high school they are able to take over a major part of the responsibility for their own education and for their life together within the institution. The validity of the democratic faith is demonstrated daily in numerous cocurricular activities.

Promoting Good Citizenship. The school promotes good citizenship within its walls and out in life. The cocurricular activities provide excellent opportunities for pupils to study citizenship and "to put their creed into deed." Students may acquire civic intelligence and loyal citizenship through having membership in a democratic group, drawing up a constitution and bylaws for the organization, becoming eligible for holding school offices through the fil-

They develop skills for hobbies and other recreational pursuits.

ing of petitions, registering for elections, voting intelligently in an election, taking the oath of office, demanding integrity and efficiency in officeholders, and submitting to a rigorous daily examination of conduct as citizens in the school and in society. These activities help to bridge the gap between the formal knowledge of the structure of government as gleaned from books and the informal but functional daily practice of citizenship in the complex arena of life.

Of specific interest in this connection, especially to out-of-school youth and those of college age, is the growth of Citizenship Recognition Day, which is designed to receive annually into citizenship with suitable ceremonies all those young men and women who have reached voting age.

3. *Developing Leadership.* The principle that school activities should develop leadership is compatible with promoting good citizenship and democratic living. As former congressman T. V. Smith has pointed out, each person should lead his fellows where his knowledge justifies and follow where his ignorance compels. Both leading and following are essential in conserving human resources. Cocurricular activities are potential producers of leadership qualities in students. Unfortunately some sponsors inhibit rather than inspire leadership. This is true of the athletic coach who gathered the boys around him before the game and said, "Now, boys, the purpose of this game is to develop character and leadership; now go in there and do just what I tell you to do." The old practice whereby the coach appoints the captain is replaced by the democratic election of the captain by the team. The debate coach who writes the speeches for his team does not stimulate independent thinking thereby. By and large the sponsors and students sense the leadership training possibilities in cocurricular activities,

for they know that the future leaders of the nation are now in the classroom and on the playgrounds.

4. *Promoting Social Living.* Although cocurricular activities seek to develop the individual, their larger emphasis is upon group living. The fraternal rather than the differential marks these organizations, which provide many opportunities for teachers and pupils to meet as friends, to foster the sharing mood, and to cultivate the art of companioning. These groups stress the fact that the school is society and that social life is a part of the racial heritage.

5. *Utilizing Effective Motivation.* The individual as a dynamic organism living in a social environment releases his energies and talents un-

They build health and physical well-being.

der personal and social motivation. The co-curricular acts are psychologically sound and are in greater consonance with human nature than are many curricular activities. The former are builded upon inner urges and intrinsic drives of pupils. They are concerned in a large degree with the release of potential energy under internal and environmental stimuli. They epitomize learning by doing. The cocurricular program, through such means as eligibility lists for athletes and membership in honor societies, may motivate lagging students to improve their curricular work. Many situations outside the classroom unlock powers of genius and unleash the highest development of human personalities.

6. Using Leisure Time Wisely. As work time decreases, leisure time increases. Unfortunately many leisure activities of youths and adults are merely time-killing amusements. Too often recreation wrecks rather than builds. As the late Dean Inge wrote, "Our minds are dyed the color of our leisure thoughts, and the inner man makes the outer." Therefore, as John Dewey stated, "A new conception of the uses of leisure has to be created; boys and girls need to be instructed so that they can discriminate between the enjoyments that enrich and enlarge their lives and those which degrade and dissipate." The quality of life and one's success in it are often determined by the degree of intelligence with which one uses his leisure time. Youth cannot solve this problem alone; the cocurricular program of the school should help him to develop the ability and inclination to spend his spare time wisely. Clubs, especially those of a recreational and hobby nature, make distinctive contributions to the present and possible future needs of the pupils. The school's educational-recreational program is a positive means for promoting the worthy use of leisure time, through what Thomas Briggs called teaching pupils to do better those desirable activities that they will do anyway. Many lifelong avocational interests that pay generous social annuities are started in the school's cocurricu-

lar program. The carry-over power of school activities can be raised even higher through better and wider selection of activities and individual mastery of the skills involved.

7. Exploring Vocational Possibilities. Vocational as well as vacational possibilities are explored in a broad program of school activities. Often a student's abilities are inventoried and developed during the presentation of a class play, the production of a school annual, the editing of a school paper, or the business managership of a school event. Therefore every school should have a club or organization to meet the needs, interests, and abilities of each pupil. Then the cocurricular program can supplement the curricular offerings by promoting vocational interests and special aptitudes.

8. Building Sound Character. The cocurricular activities are not designed with the negative purpose of killing time but with the positive intent of building sterling character. If a youth has warped ideals, low standards of conduct, or improper attitudes, the school program of activities seeks to modify them. This is not accomplished through sermonizing, for character is caught rather than taught. Through the impact of group mores, ideals of sportsmanship, and a perennial program of character-in-action, the organizations of the school strive ceaselessly to elevate individual as well as group standards. To this end the sponsors must themselves seek to raise their personality quotient and to lead lives that are positively above reproach and impeccably honest. The sacred principles of careful custodianship and honest stewardship of funds must be maintained by sponsors and students alike. Time-honored civic and moral values must be stressed if the varied and extensive program is to justify the time and money expended upon it.

Program

The numerous organizations and the complex interrelation of the various cocurricular activities make it difficult to group them, since many may be classified properly under several headings. The following eight classifications are arbitrarily established here for the purposes of organized arrangement: guidance activities, student participation in government, journalistic activities, musical organizations and activities, speech activities, school clubs, athletic activities, auxiliary organizations and activities.

These various undertakings, which might have several subdivisions, are described tersely in the pages which follow.

GUIDANCE ACTIVITIES

Although all cocurricular activities contribute to personal, social, educational, avocational, vocational, or other phases of life guidance, some organizations are directly characterized by their guidance function. Chief among these are (1) the class organizations, and (2) the home rooms.

Class Organizations. An old and prevalent cocurricular activity is that of class or grade organizations. These groupings may be found all the way from the kindergarten through higher education. The classes usually elect a president, vice-president, secretary, treasurer, representatives to the student council and other organizations, and a class sponsor or sponsors from the faculty. Preferably all classes, except the incoming freshman class, choose their officers and sponsors in the spring before the close of the school year. This permits more careful planning, more mature selection of plays to be given in the fall, and enables other organizations dependent upon class elections, such as the student council, to function early in the fall.

The main function of the class organization, particularly in the freshman year, is that of orientation and guidance. This orientation may well begin before the freshmen arrive on the grounds. A spring visitation day when the whole school plays host to the visiting eighth graders is a growing practice. In many institu-

tions of higher learning a freshman week is an effective phase of a larger program of adjustment. Special assemblies for freshmen and the utilization of class meetings are common methods of orientation. The guidance function is particularly effective again in the senior year when in class meetings and home-room organizations particular emphasis is given to the student's adjustment to his future college or out-of-school activities. Although this aspect of guidance is stressed usually in the later years of the student's schooling, it should be a part of a pyramidal program which has its broad base laid early in his school career.

Home Room. The class organization is affected by the existence of a home-room program. Most elementary pupils are assigned to a room which is their home during the school day. This plan is continued in the secondary school and helps to bridge the gap between grades. Under the guidance of an older person, the teacher, the pupil finds in his school home the common bonds of understanding and allied interests that characterize family life.

This coordinating center serves many purposes, such as helping the pupil feel at home, developing desirable pupil-teacher relationships, guiding the pupil, building desirable ideals and habits of citizenship, and expediting the handling of administrative routine. Thus the home room is not merely an administrative arrangement; it is a learning environment rich in opportunities for cultivating citizenship and democracy through well-organized procedures. The group and personal contacts stimulate friendships and make the student feel that he has a place even in a large high school. The Detroit house plan, employed in a modified form in Evanston (Illinois) Township High School, is an example of this individualized administration, which encourages students to share in the task of ruling themselves and to develop poise and assurance.

Membership of the room is arranged on any one of several bases such as by alphabet, by intelligence or ability ratings, by horizontal sectioning (as by grades), by vertical arrangement cutting across all years, by first-period class, by chronological age, by sex, by previous school, by major interest, or by curriculum. Each school should select the organizational pattern that best fits its peculiar needs.

Guidance is the predominating activity of the home room. Therefore the teacher in charge must be genuinely interested in pupils and their welfare. Some sponsors visit the homes of their counselees in order to learn more about them and their background. Through arrangements made by parent-teacher organizations a home-room father or mother often cooperates with pupils and teachers.

In order to be educationally effective, the home room needs a well-balanced program of activities planned by a special room committee or all-school committee on programs and activities. An important feature is the daily meeting arranged as a part of the regular school schedule. Appropriate programs are often exchanged between rooms or presented in assembly. All school members should participate in some home-room activity—this is the essence of democratic participation in home life. The home room may well be the starting point in the organization of the cocurricular activities. Representatives from it serve on the student council. Delegates from other organizations and clubs may send representatives to the meetings.

STUDENT PARTICIPATION IN DEMOCRATIC GOVERNMENT

The decades of the 1950s and the 1960s in American education will undoubtedly be known for the emphasis upon democracy. The American Council on Education, the Educational Policies Commission, the Citizenship Project with headquarters at Columbia University, the U.S. Office of Education, the National Association of Student Councils, the American Legion, and many state and local organizations have directed attention to the current problem of making democracy work, es-

pecially in education. As John Dewey once said, "Democratic ends demand democratic methods for realization." A cocurricular group that fosters the practice of democratic procedures is the student or school council. Also designed to help students share in some or all phases of self-government are school service organizations, such as the safety and citizens' clubs; boards of control; student-faculty committees; home rooms; interclub and interfraternity organizations; and informal student-faculty-community partnerships. The student council is the most prevailing type of formal organization. It is discussed here under the headings What the Student Council Is Not, and What the Student Council Is.

What the Student Council Is Not. The statements which follow are intended to correct a few misconceptions:

1. The student council is not a substitute for school administrators. The public pays the school executives to manage the school, thus centering responsibility in trained educational leaders.

2. It is not a supreme court. It is not a substitute for the board of education, which is the highest legally established authority for the conduct of the affairs of the school district.

3. It is not a robot of the administration or faculty. The council president and secretary are not just radio or TV announcers doing commercials, often in the preordained words of the principal.

4. It is not a secret society. Its business is not conducted behind closed doors.

5. It is not a spy system. It is not instituted as a snooper council to ferret out violations of school regulations.

6. The council is not a group of do-nothings. Seldom do the members refuse to work at challenging tasks.

7. It is not merely extracurricular—it is cocurricular and often curricular. It is not apart from but a part of the educational program.

8. The organization is not confined to secondary schools and colleges. Many elementary schools have superior pupil-participation programs.

9. The student council is not a spasmodic organization that is here this year and gone the next. It provides a long-term program for improving the school.

What the Student Council Is. On the affirmative side, the student council is all-important:

1. As a body of school citizens, it is dedicated to cooperative living in a democratic society. The school council promotes a community way of living through providing an apprenticeship in the practical processes of genuine democracy.

2. It is a training ground. The development of continuous constructive citizenship among its members and the student body is its chief challenge.

3. The student council is a parliamentary body. A concomitant learning experience in student council work is the opportunity for the members to practice parliamentary procedure. They draw up their constitution, bylaws, rules and regulations and abide thereby. It is a formal forum for freedom.

4. It is an organization for building school morale at all times. A vigorous council is a dynamo which daily generates energy, enthusiasm, and loyalty to the faculty and school.

5. The council is a challenge to a high sense of honor and honesty. Its task is to make the ethical health of the entire student body so wholesome that cheating and stealing will be condemned.

6. It is a stimulant to scholarship. The members should be intelligent representatives of the school community.

7. It is supposed to stimulate and regulate cocurricular activities. In many schools all organizations are chartered by the council.

8. The student council is designed to develop satisfactory leadership in school and society. Although followers are needed to cooperate with leaders, student council membership provides opportunity for leadership.

9. One goal of student council activities is to develop intelligent voters. Voting in student council elections should be such an interesting and stimulating experience that the student looks forward to the time when he can vote as a citizen of his community, state, and nation.

10. Finally, the student council through its numerous activities is a personalized instrument for unifying the school. The story is told of a piccolo player who stopped in the midst of a selection because he felt he was not making a contribution. The orchestra leader, whose ears detected the inactivity, stopped the entire orchestra to remind the piccolo player that his efforts counted. So too a student council seeks to make each person in school feel that he has a part to play in the harmonious symphony of the socialized school in a democratic society.

JOURNALISTIC ACTIVITIES

The benefits of journalistic activities in schools are manifold to the pupil. Here is his environment clarified and interpreted for him. While he writes and reads his school paper, he is informed of his world; guided personally, vocationally, and educationally; and influenced toward such desirable attitudes and habits as tolerance, sound thinking, and school spirit. These are the objectives toward which journalistic efforts are directed in elementary, secondary, and collegiate institutions. The major types of student publications are (1) newspapers, (2) annuals, (3) handbooks, and (4) magazines and other publications.

School Newspaper. The most common form of student publication is the newspaper. These papers may be daily, biweekly, weekly, bimonthly, or monthly. Many elementary school papers are mimeographed, whereas in the larger high schools and colleges the papers are printed. Often in elementary and small secondary schools the pupils and teachers cooperate with the local newspaper in producing a school page.

At least half of the secondary schools have some form of news organ. Paralleling the growth in scholastic journalism has been the increase in state, regional, and national press associations for schools, among these being the National and the Columbia Scholastic Press Associations. Annually the Educational Press Association publishes a helpful yearbook. The cumulative efforts of these associations, the courses in school journalism, and the enriched training of the sponsors of publications have all contributed to making the school newspaper today an important agent in the transmission of ideas and school spirit. Furthermore, through this medium many young people first learn the privileges and responsibilities involved in the freedom of the press in a democracy. Significantly, the principals of the schools usually rank the newspaper as the most important extracurricular activity.

School Annual. The yearbook, which may be traced as far back as the collegiate booklet, *Profiles of Part of the Class Graduated at Yale College, September, 1806,* is usually an expensive publication. In many quarters justification for its costly existence is seriously questioned. Numerous schools now print a less expensive brochure dedicated especially to the senior class; others have their annuals mimeographed or typewritten. Many benefits that might accrue to the students from creating an annual are sacrificed when the make-up of the book is planned solely by the sponsor and executed by paid commercial talent. The yearbook, once the only publication in most schools, is now being subordinated to the school newspaper, although its archival function will always give it a place in the program.

Handbook. A publication of growing popularity is the freshman or institutional handbook. This manual is a far more effective aid in freshman orientation than the old-fashioned hazing. Inexpensive handbooks packed with useful information and published in concise and attractive form are welcomed by newcomers to the complex life of the modern high school or college, whether they be new students, teachers, or board members. These small books also provide an inexpensive vehicle for interpreting the schools to the parents and general public.

Magazines and Other Publications. The current emphasis upon unleashing creative efforts and developing literary interests of pupils has focused attention upon school magazines and similar avenues for expression. The number of magazines submitted to the National Scholastic Press Association is steadily increasing. These periodicals, issued in duplicated or printed format, constitute outlets not only for literary creativeness and insight, but also for expression through drawings, cartoons, and photographs. An interesting cooperative public relations medium is a carefully designed and cleverly edited student-faculty magazine, which presents, chiefly through photographs, a story of the students and faculty members at home, at school, and in their cocurricular activities. Several schools and colleges issue alumni bulletins.

Several school organizations issue their own publications. For example, the Future Farmers of America may prepare its local program for the year in a printed form. The student council often publishes a bulletin in connection with its activities. School publications of all types and the numerous allied journalistic clubs, such as the Quill and Scroll, are vitalizing agencies in the education of the consumer and the producer—the reader and the writer.

Unfortunately in the United States reading and writing are fading as neglected arts do. The modern mass media of communication, such as television and radio, militate against the writing and reading of letters, periodicals, and books. The printed work is not ephemeral —it lasts after the TV program stops. Journalism in grades, high school, and college can help promote perennial print.

4 MUSICAL ORGANIZATIONS AND ACTIVITIES

Music is the center of many curricular and cocurricular activities, which are classified here as (1) vocal and (2) instrumental. Singing is often combined with acting, as in operettas, and with instrumental accompaniment, as in a cantata. The music groups are naturally interested in both performing and listening. A separate music appreciation club may be organized for nonperformers who are unable or unwilling to produce music but who, as consumers, are desirous of raising their level of music appreciation. "Music for everyone and everyone for music" is fast becoming a school realization.

Vocal Organizations and Activities. The chief vocal organizations, either curricular or cocurricular, are glee clubs boys', girls', or mixed. Their chief objectives are recreation, entertainment, and appreciation. Their origin may be traced to the old singing schools. Today a typical secondary school or college has several glee clubs, such as a first, second, and freshman group for either or both sexes. The *a cappella* choirs and madrigal singers are increasing in popularity. The operetta, allowing opportunity for solos, duets, quartets, and other combinations, is a pleasing musical entertainment, especially in the elementary and junior high schools.

Instrumental Organizations and Activities. The instrumental groups most frequently formed in secondary schools are bands and orchestras. Smaller groupings, such as string ensembles, present chamber music, whereas harmonica and other instrumental clubs meet the music hobby interests. The various musical organizations may contribute jointly to a public pro-

gram or festival, the latter usually being given outdoors. In some cities skilled musicians from the various schools are selected for an all-city glee club, orchestra, or band. Many states stage an annual program of high school talent.

5 SPEECH ACTIVITIES

The drama is one of the oldest mediums of organized human speech, extending from the Greek plays down through the French and Elizabethan plays to the present period of drama, which includes legitimate, motion-picture, and television acting. The greatest forensic activity in American life was during the revolutionary period when oratory flourished. Today the emphasis is upon informal techniques, such as panel discussions and forums.

Dramatic Activities. Generally school dramatics are handled either in regular classes or through cocurricular activities. The major productions or one-act plays may be promoted by a local drama club or a chapter of National Thespians, or by the junior or senior class. Usually the work is divided among various committees for costuming, lighting, scenery, and advertising. The drama coach may encourage the more backward students to self-expression through acting; he may even contribute to the legitimate stage through the development of latent histrionic talent in his pupils. Many by-products accrue from drama whether it be a farce, melodrama, comedy, tragedy, or sociodrama. Among these concomitants are the extensive reading of many plays and the acquiring of clear enunciation. In fine, the school drama helps students to see, to read, to hear, to act, to construct, and to write their own plays.

Forensic Activities. Chief among the forensic activities are declamations, orations, debates, poetry reading, extempore speaking, choral reading, telecasting, radio speaking, role playing, docu-drama, panel discussions, and forums. Several speech activities, for example, decision or nondecision debates, are conducted on an interschool basis. Writing original speeches appeals especially to students who possess creative literary talents and who hope thereby to inform, impress, or persuade the audience to thought or action. Debates constitute the chief activity in the field of public speaking and are the most criticized. Properly conducted, however, debates may help pupils to think logically, to organize materials carefully, to cultivate mental alertness, to analyze an argument critically, to promote reliance upon facts and research rather than prejudice, and to develop a lifelong interest in socioeconomic and governmental problems. Debate and discussion are the breath of democracy. Poetry reading, extempore speeches, choral reading, broadcasting, forums, junior town meetings, classrooms organized as national congresses, model United Nations assemblies, and panel discussions are among the popular forms of speech activities, all of which can contribute markedly to wholesome character development. The major objective in contests in speech and other competitions should be not to win a decision or to secure a prize but to pace each other on the road to excellence.

6 SCHOOL CLUBS

Most cocurricular activities may be classified as clubs. Nowhere in the school life is more freedom and variety displayed than in the names of the clubs. Their vast variety testifies to the individualistic interests of youth as well as to its gregariousness. The launching of the space age led to the formation of many science and satellite clubs.

Louis Adamic has said, "People without a firm sense of 'belonging' cannot properly develop, cannot play their full parts in the American scene." Through a wide variety of organizations, the school seeks to interest each student in at least one meaningful cocurricular activity in which the desideratum is not mere membership but active and voluntary participation on the part of the boy or girl. Unless there is some

surveillance the clubs are likely to grow up like mushrooms and then die; hence all charters should be granted by the student council or a similar organization and adequate sponsorship provided. Any club that fails to function or to live up to the tradition of the school should be warned and then disbanded if no improvement results. Emerson once said, "We send our children to the master but the boys educate them." School clubs, an outlet for the urge to gregariousness, should have definite educational and recreational values.

7 PLAY AND ATHLETIC ACTIVITIES

Children love to play. The recess period with its opportunities for games is often cherished more than the regular three R's. Play is an international activity and a trip around the world reveals many identical elements in games children play at school and at home.

Often the extracurricular activities of schools and colleges that receive the major share of financial support and the largest amount of publicity are of an athletic nature. A well-balanced physical education program in secondary schools and colleges includes athletics, in addition to the regular programs for guidance and instruction in health and physical activities. Athletics include two major phases: (1) intramural sports and (2) interscholastic. These are not disparate elements but parts of a larger whole.

Intramural Sports. The term "intramural," derived from the Latin words meaning "within the walls," refers to the activities conducted within the walls of a particular school. The intramural sports program may also include several schools within a city.

Intramurals, as distinguished from interscholastic sports, encourage participation by local boys and girls with a minimum of the competitive spirit. Based upon the theory of athletics for all, the intramural program seeks to maintain many sports for the sake of all students rather than for the sake of a few athletic teams. It is directed toward developing lasting recreational interests and sport skills in people who must live in a highly industrialized civilization.

Many intramural sports have been transferred from the open lot or street to the school grounds; many of them carry over during the vacation periods. Initiative is maintained through a system of student managers. The units of competition vary: in one school it may be by classes and in another on the basis of physical aptitude tests. In addition to the activities listed later under Interscholastic Athletics, the following are among the favorite intramural sports: swimming, hockey, touch and flag football, softball, badminton, ping-pong, volleyball, shuffleboard, horseshoes, archery, hiking, camping, and various winter sports. Today intramural programs, sports days, and physical activity clubs enlist many students under the direction of well-trained instructors and coaches.

Interscholastic Athletics. This is the most maligned part of the entire cocurricular program in schools and colleges, particularly the latter. The Educational Policies Commission commences its publication *School Athletics* with several positive affirmations, including these: "We believe in athletics as an important part of the school physical education program. We believe that the experience of playing athletic games should be a part of the education of all children and youth who attend schools in the United States."[2] Carping critics find fault with huge football stadiums, large gate receipts, larger expenditures, postseason games, salaried athletes, athletic scholarships, lax scholastic requirements for athletes, long practice sessions, game schedules that take athletes away from their studies, and high-salaried and over-zealous coaches whose tenure depends upon the production of winning teams. Despite these accusations, interscholastic athletics con-

[2] Educational Policies Commission, *School Athletics*, National Education Association, Washington, D.C., 1954, p. 3.

tinue to grow. Conscientious efforts are being made to eliminate or reduce the evils in the system, including "athlete's head."

Many schools have developed a system of major and minor sports. The former usually include football, basketball, track, and baseball; the latter embrace tennis, swimming, wrestling, golf, fencing, and boxing.

Naturally, many changes occur in athletic competition through progressive modifications of the rules. Many small high schools have turned to six-man football teams. Modifications are constantly being made for the benefit of either the players or the spectators or both groups. Because of rigorous training received in high school, many modern youth break records athletically in college and professional competition, such as running a mile in less than four minutes. In a land of free enterprise such as the United States, athletic competition has a tremendous appeal to youth.

AUXILIARY ORGANIZATIONS AND ACTIVITIES

Ancillary to the curricular or extracurricular programs are the following: (1) assemblies and programs, (2) commencements, (3) parliamentary procedures, (4) social, and (5) miscellaneous activities.

Assemblies and Programs. In the early days the assembly was a period of devotional exercises, perhaps an outgrowth of the college chapel. These morning exercises are found even in the small rural school where a few minutes each day are devoted to announcements and other activities.

The purposes of the assembly, which Fretwell calls "the town meeting of the school," are numerous, but conspicuous among its modern uses are the following: orientation into school life, cultivation of school spirit, unification of the entire school, dissemination of general information, inspirational help, spiritual aid, opportunity for pupils and faculty to appear before an audience, all-school special convocations, installation of student council, and cultivation of effective listening and courteous audience habits.

The programs are planned by an assembly committee and usually given once a week. Something is lost in the school or college where assemblies or convocations are held only once or twice a year. The growing practice of increased student and audience participation in assemblies is a wholesome trend. These convocations may be held outdoors.

Many programs are presented by students and faculty sponsors for community organizations like the parent-teacher association, noonday luncheon clubs, and women's clubs. These performances help to interpret the school to the community; therefore the participants and the type of program should be carefully chosen. Usually a large number of pupil performers increases not only the benefits to the participants but also the number of interested spectators.

Commencement. The old-style graduation program has been replaced by the modern vitalized commencement, often held outdoors. Even the old-fashioned mottoes, banners, and streamers have given way to a simpler and more effective decoration. The present commencement means more than the mere handing out of diplomas to graduates after they have listened to a long-winded orator. It means a pupil-planned program in which the activities are a culmination of the year's work. Elaborate graduation exercises for eighth graders have been superseded by promotion exercises designed to shift the emphasis from graduation to continuation. These modern programs center attention on the students and help to enlist community interest in the school and the results of its work. Important parts of the older graduation programs, as class history, will, poem, and prophecy, are scheduled on class night during commencement week. Senior vesper services in the high schools and the baccalaureate services in the colleges and universities sound an essential spiritual note in the commencement week activities. Each year the National Education As-

sociation publishes a very useful *Commencement Manual*, which contains numerous suggestions for improving commencement programs.

Parliamentary Procedures. Most cocurricular organizations employ parliamentary procedures in the conduct of their meetings. As the name indicates, parliamentary law and practice have been derived from the traditions and rules for transacting business in the British Parliament. Later the terminology was applied to the routine procedures of any deliberative assemblage. In the United States which, as a young nation, has not had the time or inclination to develop respect for moldy traditions, a unique system of written and unwritten laws has evolved for the conduct of legislative assemblies and organized bodies. Responsible for the plan most widely used in the United States is General Henry M. Roberts of the U.S. Army. His *Rules of Order* is usually the final dictum regarding actions taken or to be taken by deliberate bodies. Many organizations select a member as parliamentarian whose chief function is to rule on questions relating to the proper conduct of meetings.

The functioning knowledge of these procedures gives grace, poise, and dignity to the presiding officer and helps to ensure the rights of the members. In a dynamic democracy these rules for the conduct of meetings protect the rights of the minority and restrain the majority from undue privileges. Parliamentary law, as a code of group conduct at meetings, is designed as a facilitating tool and should not be used as an end in itself so that it obstructs rather than abets efficiency.

Social Activities. An individual must learn to live not only with himself but also with others. Nearly all cocurricular activities encourage companionship between the individual and his associates and provide social functions that rub down the rough spots. These may be parties, teas, banquets, or dances. They help the student to feel at home in a social environment and give him a lifelong appreciation for the little niceties, the social techniques, and pleasurable amenities so necessary in a human world. School parties, properly supervised, promote simple pleasures and platonic relationships between boys and girls, and counteract in a measure the present undue emphasis upon commercialized amusements.

Unfortunately, for some students the socializing process is carried to excess through too many social affairs. Furthermore, the school environment alone does not ensure fraternizing on the part of the participants. Overstreet, in his *Guide to Civilized Loafing*, caustically pictures the couples who attend a dance in perfect isolation from every other couple. A modern social dance is often a most unsocial phenomenon. Under reasonable guidance, periodic school-sponsored social affairs can be associational activities for social therapy and character development.

E School Lunch Program. The marked increase in the number of pupils transported to school and of mothers employed outside the home has magnified the importance of the noon hour in school. (Some pupils eat breakfast at school.) Most schools today have a lunch program. At its best the lunch period involves not only the serving of food, but also definite physical, social, emotional, and educational values. It becomes a broad curricular and cocurricular activity.

The financial support of school lunch programs has traveled the long road from the national emergency aid of the 1930s, through the federal surplus program of the 1940s, to the local, state, and federal subsidized aid of the second half of this century.

F Camping and Outdoor Education. Ranking high in character-building potentialities are camping and other forms of outdoor learning, teaching, and living. Historically it was only yesterday that most of the education for the original Americans—the Indians—took place in the freedom and reality of God's great out-

of-doors. Today, too much education is limited to windowed walls, firm floors, and ceilinged classrooms.

Various educational organizations have long recognized the value of outdoor education, especially camping. Charitable associations sponsor camps for the underprivileged and private ones often cater to the well-to-do, but millions of youth do not enjoy continuous out-of-door living. Hence many school systems seek to provide outdoor education and camping as curricular and cocurricular activities. Of increasing popularity are the various types of outdoor camps—the permanent, the summer, the week-end, the overnight, and the travel camp or youth hostel. The camp is becoming one of the school's best laboratories.

Miscellaneous Activities. Many auxiliary organizations are found in schools and colleges. Of a military nature are military training camps, schools, and special units, as the Reserve Officers' Training Corps (ROTC). Among the organizations meeting the religious needs of students are the Young Men's Christian Association, which was formed in 1844, the Young Women's Christian Association, the Hi-Y, and the Girl Reserves. Secret societies, as a rule, are not permitted in public elementary and high schools, though numerous in most colleges and universities.

Growing in favor are the school-sponsored educational trips. These afford students the opportunity to visit local, county, state, and national sites. A favorite destination for senior classes is Washington, D.C. The National Capital School Visitors Council, a daughter organization of the Bureau of University Travel, has been organized to assist groups visiting the nation's capital.

Among the hundreds of other cocurricular activities found in American educational institutions are alumni organizations, student speakers' service bureau, correspondence and personnel exchange with students in foreign countries, visitation of other schools by students, community fund drives, and social service work, particularly at Thanksgiving and Christmas. The organization and administration of these activities constitute a major task in American education.

Administration

The remaining phases of cocurricular activities to be considered here are (1) development of the local program, (2) sponsorship, (3) participation, (4) financing, and (5) cooperation with state and national organizations.

DEVELOPMENT OF THE LOCAL PROGRAM

Many teachers and administrators who formerly tolerated extracurricular activities as necessary evils are now aggressively promoting the program that pays increasing dividends on society's investment.

Initiating the Activities. Most cocurricular programs have their genesis in the home rooms and in class organizations from which come the student council representatives. All proposed organizations should be evaluated carefully before they are started. Furthermore, they should be begun on a modest scale. For example, if a school does not have home rooms, such a system is best introduced gradually, preferably after a close study and visitation of other schools by both teachers and pupils. The plan can then be presented by student leaders. Unless there is a demand for it, an organization should not be launched. The formulation of objectives for the entire cocurricular program may well constitute an important element in its organization and administration. Furthermore, the program must be consonant with the peculiar needs of the community.

Administering the Program. Since the principal of the school is responsible to the board of education, he should have the right of veto power over any and all actions of extracurricular groups. Of course, he will seldom exercise this direct control, and then with discretion. Greater diplomacy on the part of principals, superintendents, teachers, and boards of education will prevent many a school strike.

Scheduling the Activities. Ellsworth Tompkins of the U.S. Office of Education found that school organization for extraclass activities generally follows one of these three patterns:

1. The *activity period*, which is intended to provide for most extraclass activities *within* the daily time schedule
2. The *core program*, which consolidates much of the extraclass activities with the class activities
3. The *before-school and after-school activities program*, which provides for most of the extraclass activities *outside* the regular school session

A growing practice is to schedule the cocurricular activities in the daily program. This increases the participation of pupils, especially of those who, because of bus transportation or early home-going, cannot remain after school. A special portion of the day is allotted in the regular schedule, usually a set time, as the first or last hour in the morning, or a floating period. If there have been seven regular periods, an eighth period is added during which all organizations meet. Such arrangements reduce the sponsor's afterschool work and obviate parental criticism that pupils spend most of their afterschool hours at school.

The scheduling of the activities as a whole is not sufficient; the programs for each organization must also be carefully planned. A complicated problem is that of avoiding conflicts between groups, particularly in a high school where the gymnasium and auditorium are combined. Wherever possible, it is very desirable to make school activities a part of a community calendar.

Evaluating the Activities. The activities must constantly be evaluated. Ofttimes a club starts with much gusto and then disintegrates. An annual report, plus periodic checkups by a student-faculty committee, will aid in determining whether the charter should be regranted the next year. If a group is guilty of misconduct of a serious nature, a warning may be issued and the charter revoked if the abuse continues. Every organization should seek a worth-while project for its year's work. A stepping-up program, like that of the Scouts with their tenderfoot, second-class, and first-class stages, aids in evaluating individual and group progress. It has been found in field work that those institutions with strong, balanced, graduated extracurricular programs make outstanding contributions in promoting an active, intelligent loyalty to democratic ideals.

SPONSORSHIP OF COCURRICULAR ACTIVITIES

Qualifications of Advisers. The success of many an extraclass organization may be traced to the sponsor. Although the latter does not assume the dominant role that he does in the classroom as a teacher, nevertheless he can exert a real influence. Some general qualifications for sponsors are sympathy with boys and girls, their temptations and problems; ability to win the confidence of both youth and parents; capacity to lead and to follow; willingness to be identified wholeheartedly with the organization and to put in extra hours of work in its interest; high standards of personal conduct and morals; sense of humor; alertness to what is going on outside as well as inside school; and good sense of values in the expenditure of time, money, and talents. Besides these general requirements, the directors of certain groups need specialized training, for example, the sponsors of journalistic, athletic, and music events. There is no set pattern for sponsors. On the whole they must possess the quality of "teaching as though they taught not," while bearing constantly in mind the purposes for which the activity is designed.

Selection of Advisers. How shall the sponsors be chosen? Usually the procedure involves selection by the principal, election by the pupils, or a combination or compromise. For example, pupils may choose a sponsor from a recommended list. Often the advisers for activities that call for technical training are appointed to that task when employed by the board of education and superintendent of schools. Both sponsors and pupils should be happy and congenial in their cocurricular relations.

Training of Advisers. The typical secondary school teacher is called upon to supervise at least one extraclass activity. A good preparation for this assignment or choice is to have participated in this activity in high school and college and to have taken a course in extra-instructional duties, such as those offered in many colleges and universities. These courses are designed to give prospective or experienced teachers a knowledge of the entire cocurricular program and an opportunity to assist in sponsoring a specific group. Furthermore, many books and periodicals aid the sponsors of school activities. A popular periodical is *School Activities.* A magazine helpful to both students and sponsors of student councils and chapters of the National Honor Society is *Student Life,* issued under the aegis of the National Association of Secondary-school Principals. Many secondary and college teachers secure positions because of special qualifications for sponsorships of extracurricular activities.

Coordination of Efforts. In recent years, particularly in large schools, concentrated efforts have been made to coordinate the entire extracurricular program. To this end a director supervises all the activities or a committee of sponsors may meet periodically to plan the coordination of efforts. An example of the recognition given to extraclass life in general education is the extracurriculum division at Stephens College, Columbia, Missouri, one of the coordinate educational divisions of the college. It is administered by a director, who, with the aid of teachers, advisers, and residence-hall counselors, encourages students to utilize out-of-class life as a means of attaining individual objectives.

3 PARTICIPATION IN ACTIVITIES

A Stimulation of Participation. A goal in extra-class work is that of universality—all pupils in the school participating in at least one cocurricular activity. This necessitates promotion and stimulation, preferably by the student body. Many schools and colleges now require a certain number of extracurricular units toward graduation. Most activities, except those overemphasizing interscholastic competition, are based upon the slogan, "The more the merrier."

B Restriction of Participation. A corollary is the principle that participation must be restricted. These are two parts of the same basic idea that cocurricular activities must be regulated in order to avert the danger that the pendulum for some pupils will swing to the extreme of nonparticipation and for others to that of overparticipation. In the latter case the cocurricular becomes anticurricular. Two methods of curtailing the ambitions of the overzealous or talented individual are a point system and a program of majors and minors. The former assigns to each activity a specified number of points and stipulates the maximum permitted each student. The latter divides activities or offices into majors and minors, each student being restricted to a specified number. Sometimes an effective control is a sliding scale whereby the aggregate number of points or majors that a student may carry is determined by his scholastic and health records and his years in school. A system of checks and balances tends to distribute more evenly the opportunities for both participation and leadership. Any method of encouraging, limiting, or redirecting participation necessitates an accurate record of the membership and officers of the various organizations.

C Participation in Contests. Many school people are contest minded—they accept numerous invitations to compete for prizes and honors.

Several boards of education have been forced to pass rulings against the abuse of contests; many state educational organizations are aligned against competition. Some state-wide high school activities associations decide which contests shall be held. The Contest Committee of the National Association of Secondary-school Principals periodically issues lists of approved national school contests in which the educational values outweigh the direct or implied commercial or propaganda aspects. The tendency is to replace highly competitive events by festivals, play days, nondecision debates, and other forms of talent matching which are not dominated by the slogan "Anything to win."

4 FINANCING THE ACTIVITIES

A Budgeting. Too often, extracurricular organizations go into the red because of poor initial planning of finances. Each group ought to prepare a budget consisting of its proposed program of activities, estimated expenditures, and proposed receipts. Furthermore, a central committee should draw up one consolidated budget for all the school activities. Aside from its function as a control, the budget has a definite educational value if the students participate in planning and executing it.

B Sources of Receipts. Among the usual sources of revenue for the cocurricular program are the following: student fees, funds from the board of education, sales, donations, and gate receipts. A common procedure is an activity fee whereby each student pays a fixed amount that covers all activities. An allotment board composed of students and teachers allocates the funds.

C Expenditures. All expenditures for extracurricular activities must be carefully accounted for. Usually both receipts and expenditures are administered through a central treasurer who may be a clerk in the principal's office or an instructor in the commerce department. He is usually assisted by student treasurers who work under his immediate surveillance.

Auditing and Protection. All extracurricular accounts should be carefully checked. This includes the preaudit of bills before they are paid, the monthly audit, and the annual audit. The audits should be of two types: the administrative check usually made by students, faculty, or a fiscal officer within the employ of the school; and the independent examination of accounts conducted by a person not connected with the school system. Some states require that all extracurricular school funds be audited by a bonded person employed by the school district. Everything should be done to ensure protection of both money and persons who handle it, particularly since many schools use public funds to finance part of the cocurricular activities. A very helpful bulletin for improving the financing of these activities is *A Manual of Accounting Principles and Procedures for Student Activity Funds* published by the Association of School Business Officials.

5 COOPERATION WITH STATE AND NATIONAL ORGANIZATIONS

State Organizations. Many local cocurricular groups are chapters of state organizations or are banded informally in state groupings. Interscholastic high school athletic groups are often affiliated in a state high school athletic association, which divides the state into districts. Some states have a high school activities association that encompasses a large number of varied cocurricular undertakings. The principals, sponsors, and students meet in conferences and conventions. A noticeable trend is the development of a formal state-wide organization with a competent executive staff to direct and coordinate all interscholastic activities.

National and International Organizations. A well-balanced program of cocurricular activities includes not only independent organizations developed locally, but also affiliations with such state, national, and international organizations as are demanded and approved. Examples respectively are: State Chapter of Future Teachers of America, National Registry of Student Rocketeers through the Rocket Research Institute, and United Nations Clubs. Many local and state associations are affiliated with national and international organizations. Among the projects of the American Youth Commission of the American Council on Education was that of gathering information about national agencies that serve youth. Many are primarily membership organizations. Numerous national meetings are held for youth interested in religion, as the YMCA, the YWCA, and the Catholic Youth Organization.

America does not have a youth movement— it has many movements, since its youth belongs to many organizations and has many allegiances in and out of school.

Summary

The *extra*curricular activities are becoming less *anti*curricular and more cocurricular. These programs coexist with the curriculum but the latter comes first. Genuine educational activities grow out of the curriculum and return to it to enrich it. These allied activities have accumulated much importance on all levels of American education, in both public and private institutions. It has been said that the battle of Waterloo was won on the playing fields of Eton, and that the war with communism may be won on the activity fields of high schools and colleges in the United States.

Extracurricular activities are as old as schooling. During the three stages of their historical evolution, these allied activities were: (1) disregarded, ignored, or tolerated; (2) condemned and prohibited; and (3) encouraged under proper supervision. Automobile, air, space, and international travel have stimulated the current formation of clubs accenting "hotrods," aviation, science and mathematics, and foreign languages, respectively. Modern educational buildings include quarters for student activities. The current trend is toward a well-balanced program of activities in harmony with fundamental principles of education.

Among the propulsive principles for the program are these. The top priority in educational institutions should be the intellectual interests. The academic dog should not be wagged by the extracurricular tail. The validity of the democratic faith in America is demonstrated daily in cocurricular activities that promote cooperative living. These pupil-centered programs promote constructive citizenship through creed and deed. Here youth learns leadership and followership. Since school is society, the social life of youth cultivates the art of companioning.

The cocurricular activities epitomize learning by doing. The quality of life is often dyed the color of one's leisure thoughts and pursuits. A broad program explores vocational as well as avocational and vacational avenues. The cocurricular activities are not designed to kill time but to build sterling character.

The cocurricular program is prolific with activities and organizations. The following eight classifications are tersely described in this chapter: guidance, student government, journalism, music activities, speech, clubs, athletics, and auxiliary organizations. A broad program is balanced, and buttressed by the curriculum.

All organizations should be evaluated before and after they start. The principal should have veto power over the local program. The activities are usually scheduled as (1) a period during the school day, (2) a core within the curriculum, or (3) a period before or after school. The activities must be subjected to serious scrutiny and surveillance. The sponsor plays a different role in out-of-class work where he teaches as though he taught not, for character is caught, not taught. Hence, sponsors must be carefully selected and trained. The efforts of the numerous faculty advisers must be coordinated. Students should be stimulated to participate but they ought also be restricted if they are overzealous extracurricularly. The main purpose of participating in contests is to pace each other on the road to excellence.

Fiscally, cocurricular activities should be on a sound budgetary basis, with receipts exceeding expenditures and with auditing a must. It is best to have a director of extracurricular activities in the larger schools.

Many local programs are affiliated with state, national, and international organizations. The United States does not have a youth movement—it has many movements calling for many allegiances.

Just as radioactive by-products can be a nasty liability of nuclear fission or a technical tool for medicine, industry, and research, so, too, cocurricular activities can endanger the curriculum or, if properly controlled, enhance learning and living.

Suggested activities

1. What cocurricular activity do you like most? Why?
2. Develop principles that you think should govern cocurricular activities.
3. Define the qualities required of student leaders.
4. Investigate why many class and home-room organizations are ineffective.
5. List the main criticisms against student councils. Enumerate some of their accomplishments.
6. Collect samples of school publications and evaluate them.
7. Enumerate musical organizations in the elementary or high school in your home town.

8. List typical speech activities students engage in outside of classwork.
9. Enumerate all the clubs found in your high school or college. Evaluate them.
10. Describe a good intramural physical education program in a high school.
11. List in two parallel columns the advantages and disadvantages of interscholastic competition in high school athletics.
12. Prepare an assembly program for some high school club.
13. Describe a new type of vitalized high school commencement.
14. Evaluate one or more social affairs held in high schools and colleges.
15. Describe a military organization found in high schools or colleges.
16. Diagram a plan for coordinating the extracurricular activities of a school.
17. List the desirable qualities of a sponsor for a specific extracurricular activity.
18. How are activity programs financed in high school? In college?
19. Name some national and international organizations for youth.

Bibliography

Books

Adams, Georgia S., and Theodore L. Torgeson: *Measurement and Evaluation*, The Dryden Press, Inc., New York, 1956, chap. 26. Describes the use of evaluation procedures to assess individual and group participation in educational experiences.

French, Will, J. Dan Hull, and B. L. Dodds: *American High School Administration*, Rinehart & Company, Inc., New York, 1957, chap. 11. Deals with the proper function and place of student activities in the high school; guiding principles are established.

Kilzer, Louis R., and others: *Allied Activities in the Secondary School*, Harper & Brothers, New York, 1956, chap. 7. Discussion of student participation in school government; proper organization and operation is described.

Miller, Franklin A., and others: *Planning Student Activities*, Prentice-Hall, Inc., Englewood Cliffs, N.J., 1956, chap. 11. Describes outdoor education—the values to be derived and appropriate planning and operation of programs of this sort.

National Society for the Study of Education: *The Integration of Educational Experiences*, University of Chicago Press, Chicago, 1958, chap. 7. Deals with extraclass experiences of students and the means by which they can be related meaningfully to the total school program.

Power, Edward J.: *Education for American Democracy*, McGraw-Hill Book Company, Inc., New York, 1958, chap. 10. Discusses the relationship between cocurricular activities and the guidance program.

Schorling, Ralph, and Howard T. Batchelder: *Student Teaching in Secondary Schools*, McGraw-Hill Book Company, Inc., New York, 1957, chap. 6. Discusses the extraclass duties of the student teacher and prepares him to meet this responsibility.

Tompkins, Ellsworth: *Extraclass Activities for All Pupils*, Government Printing Office, Washington, D.C., 1954. Treats the organization, administration, and evaluation of extraclass activities in secondary schools.

Williamson, E. G., W. L. Layton, and M. L. Snoke: *A Study of Participation in College Activities*, University of Minnesota Press, Minneapolis, 1954, chap. 7. An interesting study of how college students participate in cocurricular activities and the values derived.

Periodicals

Bateman, E. Allen: "How to Coordinate School Lunch with Total Curriculum," *The Nation's Schools*, vol. 62 (September, 1958), pp. 72–76. Views the school lunch program as an opportunity for learning and a part of the school's total curriculum.

Eblen, Viola: "A Guided Program of Student Clubs," *The Nation's Schools*, vol. 60 (November, 1957), pp. 60–61. Describes a well-planned program of club activities in which 90 per cent of the students pursue varied interests and learn to work together.

Evans, Dina R.: "The Creative Approach to Dramatics," *NEA Journal*, vol. 44 (December, 1955), pp. 550–552. Describes an interesting approach to dramatics in which the emphasis is upon the development of participants rather than upon the finished product.

Fritts, Chantrey A., Jr.: "A Junior High School Weekly Goes to Press," *NEA Journal*, vol. 45 (January, 1956), pp. 30–31. Describes how junior high school students maintain their own newspaper and the values they derive from it.

Glascow, William M.: "ROTC—Readying Our Teenagers for Citizenship," *The School Executive*, vol. 76 (July, 1957), pp. 46–47. Describes the Reserve Officers Training Corps and its contribution to the high school cocurricular program.

McLean, Robert C.: "The Extra Curriculum: Some Steps toward Integration," *National Association of Secondary-school Principals Bulletin*, vol. 40 (October, 1956), pp. 135–138. Discusses an approach toward bringing unity into the secondary school's cocurricular program.

Miller, Franklin A.: "Co-curriculum Activities— Tolerated, Accepted or Promoted by School Administrators?" *NEA Journal*, vol. 43 (October, 1954), pp. 408–409. Report of an interesting study of cocurricular activities in American high schools—the most valuable ones, the problems, and the common ways of organizing them.

Myers, Donald A.: "'Extra' Costs of High School," *The Nation's Schools*, vol. 63 (January, 1959), pp. 66–67. A survey reveals the surprising amount of cost in participating in high school cocurricular activities and suggests a solution to this hidden tuition.

Scott, Paul A.: "Co-curriculum Activities of Study Halls," *Bulletin of the National Association of Secondary-school Principals*, vol. 40 (October, 1956), pp. 139–141. Develops the relationship between the study hall and the extracurricular program in high schools.

White, William L.: "400,000 Boys Are Members of the Club," *The Reader's Digest*, vol. 70 (February, 1956), pp. 71–77. A popularized account of high school club programs and the values which boys derive from them.

chapter 15

Educational supplies, equipment, sites, and buildings

No farmer would send his hired help to work in the fields without providing suitable supplies, tools, and equipment. Many school board members, however, ask their teachers "to make bricks without straw"—to teach without the necessary learning materials. Paradoxically, in the United States, which leads the world in the publication and manufacture of educational materials, thousands of pupils are empty-handed or poorly stocked with supplies and equipment. The National Defense Education Act of 1958 provided federal funds for equipment in a few selected areas—mathematics, science, and foreign languages.

The educational supplies and equipment should meet certain curricular criteria. They should harmonize with the philosophy of education, conform to curricular content, fit the facts, and utilize the best research in teaching and learning. Many educational materials in machine-making America fail to meet these criteria.

Much school equipment is archaic. Although many teachers drive to school in this year's model of automobile, they use constantly in the classroom much equipment and many supplies of Model T vintage. The quality of school supplies is as important as the quantity. For example, an inferior grade of penmanship paper may be a decided handicap to neatness in handwriting. Restricted budgets and the apathy of the general public account in part for the failure to provide the best. Then, too, many classroom and laboratory teachers are unfamiliar with the wide variety and quality of modern educational materials. Even after being supplied with the latest tools of learning, teachers and pupils often do not use them effectively. For a proper learning-teaching environment, supplies and tools are essential; they are, however, merely physical means for facilitating the educational process. All aids to teaching may prove sterile unless they are applied intelligently.

As to definition, a supply item is usually distinguished from a piece of equipment in that the former has a shorter service life than the latter. An illustration of the first is school chalk, which is used up in a short period of time; an example of equipment is a school desk, which may last for several years. Textbooks are technically considered as equipment, whereas workbooks may be either equipment or supply items. Supplies and equipment may also be classified on the basis of whether they are primarily instructional or building items. Educational supplies and equipment are exemplified respectively in chalk and books, whereas two building items are illustrated by sweeping compound and drinking fountains.

Building supplies and equipment are given special emphasis in the last part of this chapter. Here the educational materials are grouped as (1) schoolbooks, and (2) other instructional supplies and equipment.

Books

HISTORICAL DEVELOPMENT

The Role of Print in Education. "What is the greatest invention in human history?" To this question there are many answers but for education there is only one: "The greatest invention is printing." The first press in the territory now included in the United States was set up at Harvard College, Cambridge, Massachusetts, by Stephen Daye in 1639. In the three hundred and more years that have elapsed since that time the relationship between the printing press and institutions of learning has been vital. The publishing of educational books and other materials today constitutes a big business.

Early American Textbooks. The change in schoolbooks forms a fascinating chapter in the history of printing and American education. The hornbook, a paddle-shaped contrivance which hung from the pupil's neck, usually contained the Lord's Prayer and the alphabet. *The New England Primer,* an example of the small, moralistic textbook used in the colonial

days, is said to have taught millions to read and not one to sin. *McGuffey's Readers* emphasized the Bible and morals by means of interesting stories. America's textbook best seller—over one hundred million copies—was the *Elementary Spelling Book,* the "blueback" speller of Noah Webster, in whose honor a memorial stamp was issued in 1958 to commemorate the 200th anniversary of the birth of this pioneer lexicographer. In his speller one finds a list such as the following "words of seven syllables having the accent on the fifth":

im ma te ri al' i ty
in com pat i bil' i ty
im per cep ti bil' i ty
ir re sist i bil' i ty
in com bus ti bil' i ty

Another speller bore the ambitious title *New England's Perfect Schoolmaster.* The titles of books reveal marked changes between yesteryear and now.

Memory was a cardinal virtue in early American education. For the schoolmaster there was a book entitled *Mnemonics Applied to the Acquisition of Knowledge* whose authors, Pike and Pike, challenged any six men to learn as much as the Messrs. Pike could in any given length of time. There was Grimshaw's huge volume devoted to "tables and explanation necessary to be learned by heart by every pupil studying arithmetic." Often the textbooks, which contained valuable materials in small-type footnotes, failed to challenge the interest of the reader.

In the development of modern schoolbooks the four main influences were child psychology, textbook publication as a specialized industry, the improvement in printing and binding, and research by authors and publishers.

The Textbook in Modern Education. Over a century ago Emerson, in his memorable address, "The American Scholar," distinguished clearly between the use and the abuse of books. Although books contain the inheritance of past thinking and as such are invaluable to the scholar, they should not be a substitute for his own thinking. On the other hand, some things can be learned better and more economically from books than from other sources. The American Textbook Publishers Institute has produced a motion picture with the tenable title "Textbooks: The Second Most Important Influence." Next to teachers is the tool of textbooks.

Procedures in Selecting Textbooks. In contrast to the old practice, whereby one person, usually the administrator, selected the textbooks used by the teachers and pupils, is the more democratic procedure by which an appointed or elected committee of teachers recommends the texts. In this way teacher and pupil interests, needs, and likes are known and given consideration. Obviously the educational interests and needs of pupils must have priority in the writing, publishing, and selecting of textbooks.

The two general techniques in evaluating textbooks prior to their adoption are subjective judgment and objective appraisal. Usually both are employed. The one is a casual examination of the book or books, often preceded by a sales talk by a representative of a book company or the receipt of a letter or descriptive folder. The other technique is a painstaking scrutiny by means of a check list, score card, or guide for textbook analysis. Some of these are intended for all books in general, whereas others are for a specific field or an area, as first-grade reading. Guides for textbook analysis usually contain the following major items: authorship, date of publication, suitability of content, organization, vocabulary burden, readability, methods of teaching and learning, teaching aids, pupil helps, mechanical make-up or format, and miscellaneous details, such as illustrations and physical attractiveness. Content, format, and suitability are the big three.

The content of American textbooks has been criticized as being too radical or too conservative. Certain groups have launched periodic attacks on textbooks, especially those in social science. They claim that, although few can be classified as subversive, many of the books tend to instill in the reader's mind a discontent with American democracy and the workings of private enterprise. Certain members of the Congress of the United States have questioned the content of textbooks as "un-American." In answer to the question, "In your opinion, how satisfactorily do school textbooks help pupils to attain the American ideal of 'equal opportunity for all'?" a professor in the teaching of social studies expressed the following opinion: "No book that attempts to deal with any vital issue or problem in a vital way can be published at the present time without balanced sentences in which one pressure group is played off against another, or without the usual dodges of a so-called judicious character." Several book surveys stress the need for using objectivity and coming to grips with basic issues. The fault lies often in the courses of study for which the textbooks are prepared. Discretion must of course be used in selection of materials for schoolbooks, but there is too much timidity in the writing and publishing of materials not only on American democracy but on many controversial issues. Some textbooks in American history are published in two editions, one to be used north of Mason and Dixon's line and the other south of it. Frequently books have to be written for particular states because of legislation that prohibits the inclusion of certain materials. Schools should furnish enough books on a particular subject to present different points of view, particularly for older pupils. The texts should be chosen not only for content but also for eye appeal.

The format or mechanical construction of the book is a very important factor. The physical appearance is affected by size of page and book, binding, cover, paper, illustrations, type, spacing, and margins. Many schoolbooks have been too "textbooky." Today better paper, types, colored illustrations, and binding materials, plus stronger binding processes, make textbooks attractive, appealing, and durable. The modern textbook is an invitation to learning, silently saying, "Look, and read me." Most of the changes in format that have been effected through the joint efforts of teachers, administrators, librarians, authors, and publishers are improvements. A few of the modern tendencies, such as freakish page make-up that presents broken lines of varying lengths and placements, present difficulties, especially to young readers. The American Institute of Graphic Arts, through leading book designers and printers, has launched a nationwide campaign for better-looking books—books that please the eye as well as the mind. Several awards are issued annually, including the Newberry medal to the author of the outstanding book for children, and the Caldecott award to the illustrator of the most distinguished picture book for children.

Adoption of Textbooks. Textbooks, supplementary readers, and workbooks usually are adopted by (1) local authority, (2) the county superintendent or county board of education, or (3) a state textbook commission.

The most usual procedure in the choice of basal textbooks is that of local selection upon the recommendations of teachers. This permits adaptability to conditions such as the length of the school year and the nature of the community. A major handicap in this method is that students moving from one district to another, even within the same county, do not find uniform textbooks.

Many times the selection of textbooks is made by either the county superintendent or the county board of education. The county superintendent is frequently assisted by a committee of teachers in the adoption of textbooks.

Another method is that of state-wide adoption, usually by a state schoolbook commission. Approximately half the states have statutes requiring uniform textbooks. The largest single purchaser of textbooks in the United States is Texas, which buys books for all elementary school children in the state.

Purchase and Distribution of Textbooks. After the textbooks have been selected and adopted, they are purchased and distributed for use. The distribution of books to pupils is usually accomplished through three major purchasing procedures: (1) pupil purchase, (2) school ownership, and (3) other methods.

The common practice whereby pupils purchase their own books may be argued pro and con. It stimulates a learner to begin the acquisition of his own library and relieves school board finances. On the other hand it retards the introduction of up-to-date textbooks. The basic objection to this procedure is that it is not fully in accord with the democratic concept of supplying free education and free instructional materials. To furnish free instruction but to require the purchase of educational tools is an anomaly.

Frequently a caste system prevails in American education, since the pupils who live on one side of the railroad tracks are able to purchase textbooks while those on the other side are denied equal opportunity to learn because their parents cannot afford to buy adequate learning material. The supplying of free textbooks by the board of education is far more common on the elementary than on the secondary level. There are many pertinent obstacles, especially that of defraying the cost. The pupil purchase of basal textbooks remains one of the hidden costs of so-called free education.

The rental of textbooks has been called a child of the depression. The books, purchased by the board of education or other agencies, are rented to the pupils on a per capita or per subject basis. The fee system is similar to the rental plan: the school or pupil may purchase the basal text for a course such as high school English, and then upon payment of a fee the pupil is supplied with the classics and other required supplementary materials. There are numerous other deviations and combinations of systems. No matter what procedure is used in supplying children with textbooks and materials, it is necessary to keep these tools up to date and to increase in most schools the amount of money thus expended.

Their Role in Education. The library ought to be the heart of the school, with arteries running into each room, and capillaries to each pupil. The plan of extensive reading requires much supplementary material. Therefore administrators and teachers should be familiar with the library and competent to guide pupils in its use.

Elementary and secondary schools and libraries should have a close and cooperative relationship. In some large cities and in many small districts the school library is operated as a branch of the city or county system and draws freely on the larger collection of books. Rolling libraries and bookmobiles are increasing in number and in services to rural areas. Tennessee is one of several states where the county circulating library system has proved very successful. Several school districts cooperate in the establishment of a central library system whereby the books obtained are made available by a well-planned system of circulation. Federal funds for rural library service have stimulated the use of more books in small communities by pupils and adults.

On the college level the library is the keystone of the academic arch. J. Donald Adams of the *New York Times* once wrote, "Of every college and university it may be said that the library is the most vital, the most essential organ of that institution's body." The English scholar George Dawson regarded the library as a "solemn chamber in which a man may take counsel with all who have been wise, and great, and good, and glorious among the men that have gone before him."

Evaluation of School Library. In measuring the adequacy of libraries, a publication of the

Cooperative Study of Secondary School Standards states that a satisfactory book collection for a library should have a fairly high rating in number of titles, balanced distribution, appropriateness for secondary school purposes, and recency of publication.

A rough index of balance is the number of volumes in the various areas of one of the major library classification systems, viz., the Dewey Decimal System, whereby nonfiction books are arranged according to numbers and decimals. The major classifications in this system are as follows:

000	General works	500	Natural science
100	Philosophy	600	Useful arts
200	Religion and mythology	700	Fine arts
300	Sociology	800	Literature
400	Language	900	History

Subdivisions of these major classes are used. Fiction books are listed alphabetically by author. Modern education requires a well-balanced library in every building as a central opportunity for extended reading experience. Furthermore, in a pupil-centered library the emphasis is on the reader rather than the book.

Equipment for the Library. Among the items of equipment other than books are suitable lights, clock, lounging chairs, reading tables and chairs, charging desk for librarian, cabinet and stand for card catalogue, magazine rack, vertical files, bulletin boards, newspaper holders, display racks, dictionary stand, book truck, an atlas case, a display case, and a regulation executive's desk for the librarian. These articles should come from dependable firms, harmonize with the other school furnishings, and reduce eyestrain.

Other materials

Space does not permit a detailed list of all the supply and equipment items other than books that are found in a modern school. The two types singled out for emphasis are (1)

ancillary reading materials, and (2) multi-sensory aids to learning.

ANCILLARY READING MATERIALS

The Dictionary. An important book, which should receive special attention in all educational institutions, is the dictionary. A large dictionary placed on a bookshelf or desk in the front or rear of the room is not adequate. Each pupil ought to have an attractive dictionary gauged to his level and at hand for steady use. This may be supplemented by larger lexicons available for the group. Extensive reading and frequent reference to a dictionary help to develop a copious vocabulary and fine discrimination in meanings.

The Workbook. Recent years have witnessed a growing demand for workbooks and kindred materials. Valuable as workbooks may be, an intelligent teacher will not rely implicitly upon anything mechanical; she will vary the mediums of work as well as the methodology.

Newspapers. Students are interested in newspapers. Today thousands of classrooms contain newspapers. Many teachers employ the news, magazine, financial, and sport sections as means of general knowledge enrichment; they depend upon the book review, magazine, theater, movie, art, music, radio, television, science, travel, and hobby sections for cultural guidance and enrichment. Yale's famous professor of English William Lyon Phelps once said the newspaper is one of the greatest aids to vitality Americans have. The emphasis on newspaper reading in schools has been primarily for keeping up with current events. The habit of reading current news is, of course, a first step, and the human-interest story is probably a natural starting point. The ultimate aim is to develop an intelligently critical attitude.

Magazines. Allied with the use of newspapers is that of magazines and periodicals. Many schools subscribe to publications such as *Our Times, Reader's Digest, My Weekly Reader,* and *Scholastic.* The current emphasis on candid photography and pictorial sections in popular magazines brought about the introduction of these aids into the school. It is obvious that the school must give attention to the selection and use of periodicals.

Tests. The National Defense Education Act has stimulated renewed interest in tests. Alarmed by the large number of able young people who drop out of high school and who turn their backs on college, Congress in 1958 decided to encourage a search for talent among young people through testing and counseling in schools. It provided money for the states to develop their own means of testing students in both public and private schools.

Many good standardized tests are available for schools. There are achievement tests for measuring academic progress, useful in evaluating both learning and teaching and in diagnosing problems. Intelligence tests measure the learner's mental capacity. Interest tests and aptitude tests help the student to arrive at a vocational choice more confidently. Obviously the choice of a test will depend upon the purpose for which it is used.

Probably the most comprehensive school testing program is the system of Regents Examinations required for students throughout New York State. It has been criticized on the grounds that it encourages teachers to teach for the test rather than for the real needs of students. Someone has said, "Let me write your tests and I will have written your curriculum." Certainly the test maker has a heavy responsibility, particularly when many people are disposed to attach more confidence in test results than their makers would claim for them.

MULTISENSORY AIDS IN LEARNING

Multisensory aids, usually limited to audio-visual, include many facets of learning. Utilizing the five senses of seeing, hearing, smelling, tasting, and feeling, the multisensory materials run the gamut of the alphabet from the touch-and-see ABC block in the nursery to the smell-and-taste of zymurgy in the college chemistry laboratory. In the "cone of experience," Edgar Dale lists the various types of audio-visual aids, as well as their relative position in a scale, from the apex of verbal symbols to the broad base of direct, purposeful experiences: (1) verbal symbols, (2) visual symbols, (3) recordings, radio, still pictures, (4) motion pictures, (5) television, (6) exhibits, (7) field trips, (8) demonstrations, (9) dramatized experiences, (10) contrived experiences, (11) direct, purposeful experiences.[1] Obviously these divisions overlap and include many specific mediums such as globes, maps, slides, films, tape recorders, radio and television, plus books previously mentioned.

Globes. This is a global age literally and figuratively. Supersonic jet planes make any part of today's world no farther away than tomorrow morning. The manufactured globe is a simple but significant symbol of this shrinking world of which the classroom is a part. As a teaching tool it possesses great versatility, especially with attachments showing man-made moons and God-created constellations.

Many different types of globes are available: the small, individual size and the large, classroom globe; the mapped surface and the plain spheres, on which lines can be drawn with chalk or crayon; the political and the physical; and those made of various materials such as paper maché, metal, plastic, and rubber which can be inflated. Globes can embellish the classroom and enrich the curriculum.

Maps. The United States is a land with millions of maps. In addition to the maps on globes, many others are available as teaching tools. These visual aids include a mite map made of a first-grade classroom; a sketch of each

[1] Edgar Dale, *Audio-visual Methods in Teaching,* The Dryden Press, Inc., New York, 1954, p. 43.

school building; a master plan of the entire campus, with its long-term projections for the future; the community map; the county plot plan; the state survey; the national resources locations; and the world-wide maps. The International Geophysical Year has italicized the important role of maps. From the small, inexpensive, pupil-made plan to the large, expensive, manufactured wall maps, extends an endless variety of realistic resources available to the teacher in many fields of learning.

Slides. Maps are also available on slides for projection purposes. Countless other slides, manufactured and pupil-teacher-made, enhance learning by tailor-making pictures to fit the discussion or unit. Many grade and high school and college students have access to colored slides available for group sharing.

Films. Of the motion picture, George F. Zook, when president of the American Council on Education, said, "It is the most revolutionary instrument introduced in education since the printing press." Sound and silent, black-and-white and colored motion pictures, carefully selected and previewed, enhance learning. A significant development is the textbook-movie-filmstrip package in which a motion picture is correlated with a textbook and its showing is followed by a tailor-made filmstrip to capitalize on pertinent, meaningful discussion and evaluation.

Tape Recorders. A comparatively new teaching-learning instrument is the recorder with its versatile and timely tapes. Teaching tapes are available for learners of all ages. The pupils can make their own recordings. Learning English or a foreign language is facilitated with this time-saving teaching tool.

Radio. News commentator H. V. Kaltenborn, speaking of the radio as the "fifth estate," said that the radio, wrongly exploited, is capable of creating confusion, discontent, ignorance, incompatibility, intemperance, and moral and social disintegration; but just as easily it may concentrate on public enlightenment, intellectual stimulus, social awareness, diplomatic cooperation, greater understanding, and economic advancement. The Federal Communications Commission allocated numerous channels for noncommercial, educational FM (frequency modulation) service, with its static-free, high-fidelity bands. Increasing in use is the audio-correspondence course, the lesson material for which is broadcast. Through the addition of the so-called fourth R (radio), many rural schools are losing their one-teacher status. Many large schools have installed central sound systems.

Television. One of the most dramatic—and controversial—instructional tools to appear on the educational scene is television. Although still in its early stages of development as an educational medium, its use is spreading widely. It has been stimulated by grants of money from the Ford Fund for the Advancement of Education and from the federal government under the provisions of the National Defense Education Act of 1958.

Educational television takes many forms. For example, the Philadelphia schools offer daily curricular programs as well as special weekly programs designed to supplement and enrich regular classroom work. The Oklahoma City, Pittsburgh, Hagerstown, Milwaukee, St. Louis, and other city school systems are experimenting with television in school classrooms. A New York commercial channel, in cooperation with the Metropolitan Educational Television Association, an organization chartered by the New York State Board of Regents has been presenting a series of daytime educational programs telecast into hundreds of school classrooms throughout the state.

Colleges too have found television a promising tool. The Chicago City College offers college courses for credit via open-circuit television. The University of Detroit offers a full college curriculum with credit through tele-

vision. Millions of adults across the nation receive hundreds of educational television programs from scores of educational TV stations as well as via commercial channels.

It is still too early to be sure of the values and limitations of television as an instructional tool. Extravagant claims and unrestrained reservations are exchanged. This controversy is explored in greater detail in Chapter 17. A survey by the National Citizens Council for Better Schools reports the following sample of opinions across the country:

ETV, at first resisted in the education field because of unfavorable impressions of commercial television, is gradually earning the respect of educators.

ETV programs which have the widest acceptance in schools are those which answer a real need for materials, expert techniques and demonstrations, and personalities not otherwise available to classrooms.

Students retain with accuracy ideas and information received through TV.

Teachers in whose classrooms TV is used benefit by watching methods and techniques employed by other expert teachers.

TV films offer small schools a chance to enrich their curriculums by offering work in science, languages, and other fields which could not ordinarily be provided.

Lower ability groups seem to learn more effectively through television.

Students can get a close-up view of science demonstrations and experiments.

Diagrams and other visual materials can be presented faster and more effectively.

TV allows direct teaching for homebound children.

TV provides interesting opportunities for the in-service training of teachers.

TV provides an effective medium for adult education, bringing education to people who cannot attend classes.

Some shortcomings are also evident:

Two-way communication between pupil and teacher is often sacrificed.

Close teacher-student rapport is lost.

The TV teacher can't judge how well he is being understood.

The installation of TV equipment is quite expensive.[2]

In any event, television offers a fascinating new tool that is certain to have a profound effect upon instructional methods and learning. Television receivers have already become commonplace classroom commodities in many schools.

MISCELLANEOUS SUPPLIES AND EQUIPMENT

Current school budgets and catalogues reveal an endless array of educational supplies and school equipment, from a small piece of chalk to a microscope and up to a large, expensive grand piano or bus. All special types of rooms, such as household arts, industrial arts, fine arts, laboratories, cafeterias, gymnasiums, and auditoriums contain special supplies and equipment.

SELECTION, PURCHASE, AND USE
OF MATERIALS

Many principles and procedures are involved in the selection, purchase, and management of materials. Supplies and equipment should be selected in terms of the educational program of the school. Therefore teachers should be consulted as to the need.

Ethics in Handling School Supplies and Equipment. To improve the selection of school supplies and equipment and to maintain a high professional standard of conduct, a code of ethics has been developed by the Associated Exhibitors of the National Education Associa-

[2] "What Will TV Contribute to Education?" *Better Schools*, vol. 3 (January, 1957), p. 7.

tion. This code should be supplemented by a nationwide code for schoolteachers and administrators relative to the handling of textbooks, supplies, and equipment. For example, some administrators, teachers, and professors have a penchant for collecting free textbooks by asking publishers for samples, under the pretext of possible adoptions. Another unethical procedure often followed by teachers is that of duplicating or mimeographing portions from textbooks. Parts of a copyrighted book should not be duplicated unless the permission of the publisher has been obtained. The present standard of ethics in the selection, sale, and use of textbooks and school materials is a challenge to the teaching profession and to those engaged in the schoolbook and supply business to improve current practices.

Use of Supplies and Equipment. Despite this age of automation, schools do not use enough machines in making their work more scientific and accurate. Administrators and teachers should take advantage of technically accurate and professionally useful devices like the audiometer, which is the best-known way of testing the hearing of pupils; the lightmeter, which is an accurate measure of the foot-candles of light in any part of a room; and the electric test-scoring machines. The mechanical media stretch alphabetically from an abacus for arithmetic instruction to a zither for music teaching.

An increasing trend in planning new and renovizing old buildings is to provide a materials and equipment center. Here are found facilities for making teaching-learning supplies and equipment for classroom use. These materials centers are equipped with such items as hammers and saws, lettering outfits, cardboard for posters, paint and brushes, metal supplies, and dozens of other production items for making learning more meaningful in the classrooms.

Curriculum libraries and materials centers are becoming more common, particularly in larger districts. In these centers sample textbooks in all fields from many publishers are kept in one place for all to use. Other instructional materials, such as films, tapes, tests, manuals, and many others, are kept in one central location to be more easily available for all.

Most modern classrooms are equipped with steel file cases. The teacher should know how to file personnel records and other materials for present and future use. Records and reports are becoming more numerous as activity increases in the field of child and teacher accounting. The classroom furniture—desk, files, and cupboards—should be arranged economically, for many useless steps can be eliminated through an alert analysis of arrangements within the room.

Consumer education in the purchase and use of educational supplies and equipment is on the increase. Information in regard to analyses of products is available from federal agencies, like the U.S. Bureau of Standards, and from organizations, like the National School Supply Association. Much additional literature and corroborating research are needed in connection with the manufacture, purchase, and use of school supplies and equipment. In order to make teaching-learning aids more readily accessible to teachers, many schools have established special rooms as instructional service centers. Students and teachers need instruction in the wise and economical use of school materials. Unfortunately, many pupils willfully destroy property and some unwittingly damage materials through improper use, as in the careless handling of a textbook or of playground apparatus. Vandalism is on the increase in schools.

Sites

Influence on Learners and Teachers. The abiding influence of environment in the life of a child is appropriately expressed in the following lines from Walt Whitman:

There was a child went forth every day,
And the first object he look'd upon, that object he became,
And that object became part of him for the day or a certain part of the day,
Or for many years or stretching cycle of years.

School sites and the buildings and equipment thereon are a material part of the daily scenes of the child. The building should be intimately fitted to the grounds but formed and fashioned to human needs—practical, psychological, and aesthetic. The structure ought to be planned as a unified collection of functional relationships, erected in such close sympathy with its surroundings and so fittingly furnished that its beauty charms the students, who breathe into the architect's creation the breath of life.

School Building Needs. One of the most critical problems in American education, both public and private on all educational levels, is that of providing adequate and satisfactory sites and buildings. Various factors have contributed to the current acute shortage of physical facilities: earlier marriages, larger families, resultant enrollment increases, mobility of population, reorganization of school districts, extension of the educational program, school construction backlog, and financial problems. The situation is acute, and the crisis may continue to worsen. School-housing shortages may seriously impair the quantity and quality of learning. One lesson educational history teaches is the dire necessity of long-span master plans for sites, buildings, and equipment.

LONG-TERM MASTER PLANS FOR FACILITIES

The selection and development of sites and the planning and erection of educational buildings are a long-span proposition. Since a new structure usually involves bonded indebtedness, it is necessary to project the estimated cost ten to twenty or more years in the future. This is not unwarranted, since the building may be used for fifty years or more. A school erected in the

1960s will probably be in use in the twenty-first century. Hence, extensive long-range plans for sites and buildings must be developed far in advance of actual needs. This long-period plan is not a hard and fast predetermined schedule, for it must allow for variables and extraneous factors which cannot always be predicted precisely in advance. Innumerable advantages accrue from looking far into the future for this implies that the cost of educational facilities is a continuing appropriation, a fixed charge for the future. Era-long planning is a deliberate attempt to substitute intelligent forecasts for the opportunism of a laissez-faire philosophy. Continuous long-term planning entails the techniques of adjusting master-plan forecasts annually or periodically.

Each individual building is part of the ultimate master program, which should embrace three essential and integrated phases, viz., (1) the educational plan (2) the expenditure program, and (3) the financing plan.

Educational Plan. School buildings and sites are merely facilitating mediums for the instructional process. Functional planning demands that the educational aims of the school be translated into an actual workable program for the architect and that his drawings and specifications then be checked with it.

Expenditure Program. Costs fluctuate with the price of materials and labor. Building costs will probably continue to rise generally. Some critics have complained that too much money is spent in school construction. This issue is discussed at length in Chapter 17. Certainly some money has been wasted. On the other hand, false economy is often practiced. Inexpensive materials of poor durability or necessitating high maintenance costs have often been used.

Financing Plan. The erection of new school buildings or the rehabilitation of old structures is usually financed by the community through the pay-as-you-build plan or some means of borrowing. Because the former method calls for payment out of the current school budget, it is used sparingly and only in large cities. The second plan calls for either long-term or short-term bonds or loans. It is recommended that bonds should not extend over a period longer than twenty years. Usually the erection of a building is preceded by a school election that authorizes the board of education to bond the district.

A marked trend is that of paying some of the

Fig. 15-1. Cost of educational buildings constructed annually. ("Educational Buildings in 1958," tenth annual survey, American School and University, 1959.)

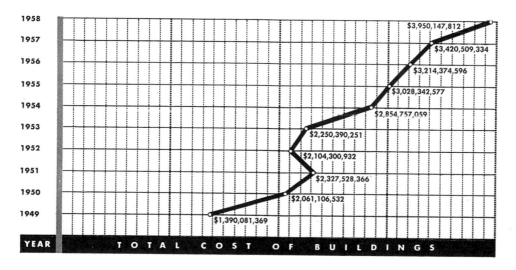

YEAR	TOTAL COST OF BUILDINGS
1958	$3,950,147,812
1957	$3,420,509,334
1956	$3,214,374,596
1955	$3,028,342,577
1954	$2,854,757,059
1953	$2,250,390,251
1952	$2,104,300,932
1951	$2,327,528,366
1950	$2,061,106,532
1949	$1,390,081,369

building costs from the state treasury as part of the minimum foundation program. Typical state grants are: stimulation aids, flat grants, emergency aids, continuing grants, equalization grants, loan funds, and money from state building authorities or commissions.

Several bills in Congress have included the provision of federal funds for the planning and/or construction of local school buildings. Congress did allocate funds for the nationwide survey of school facilities and for the construction of school buildings in federally affected areas. The federal government has also allocated funds for equipment for buildings.

Private agencies and individuals are also interested in financing school and college buildings. Many buildings are the gifts of groups and individuals. The Ford Foundation in 1958 allocated several million dollars for the establishment of the Educational Facilities Laboratories, an independent, nonprofit organization concerned with research and experimentation in school and college facilities. Over forty years ago the National School Supply and Equipment Association was organized with the twin goals of helping industry and rendering services to educational institutions.

SITE SELECTION AND USE

Selection of Site. The school site—its size, dimensions, character of the ground, location of the building, and space for play and sports—is of fundamental importance, since it conditions not only the development of an adequate recreation program but also possible additions to the existing school plant. In the early days plots of ground unfavorable for other purposes were chosen for schoolhouses. Conditions were so deplorable that Horace Mann, in a supplement to his first annual report in 1838, pleaded for the improvement of school sites and buildings. Much advance has been effected in the last hundred years.

The National Council on Schoolhouse Construction has stated:

School site selection is a technical problem involving the cooperative efforts of school officials, the architect, recreational consultants, urban planners, and legal consultants. . . . School sites should be selected well in advance of actual needs.[3]

Obviously, programs for site selection and development should be made prior to or concurrently with plans and specifications for buildings.

Development of the Site. The school site, which is as important to the complete educational program as classrooms, must be planned to serve its many uses effectively. Among the factors in site selection and development are its location, nature of the soil, size and shape, location and orientation of the building, outdoor activity spaces, service areas and facilities, and planted areas.

Size of Sites. Most school sites are too small. Even in rural or suburban communities where farm land can be purchased rather inexpensively, many elementary schools have a fenced-in area so small as to prohibit a game of baseball. The grounds around many secondary schools are hopelessly inadequate, especially in parking facilities. Furthermore, the modern program of health and physical education requires several additional acres. The National Council of Schoolhouse Construction makes these recommendations for minimum site areas: for elementary schools, 5 acres, plus an additional acre for every 100 pupils of ultimate enrollment; for junior high schools, 20 acres, plus an additional acre for every 100 pupils; and for senior high schools, 30 acres, plus an additional acre for every 100 students of peak enrollment. Thus a senior high school of 1,000 pupils would have a site of 40 acres.

Landscaping and School Gardens. Much importance must be placed upon the aesthetic influ-

---

[3] Research and Publications Committee, *Guide for Planning School Plants*, National Council on Schoolhouse Construction, 1958, p. 17.

ence of the school site. The beautification and upkeep of school grounds and buildings may depend upon a standing committee from the board of education, a teacher-pupil committee, or a special group from the parent-teacher association. Appropriate landscaping helps to soften the building and hide some of the ugliness of foundations. Daily contact with a beautiful school framed in a natural setting is uplifting and beneficial to all. The wonders of nature upon the school premises, as trees, shrubs, grass, and flowers silently unfold their splendors, may initiate a program for beautifying the entire community.

Community Playgrounds. The school's program for leisure should be integrated with the community's needs. The facilities in and out of school must be available to persons with an eye not only to future generations but also to the adult life of the community.

A neglected phase of school and community life is the summer program. Too many schools are closed for two, three, or four long months, the very time when they might be directing play activities. Articulation of all community efforts in the development of a twelve-month program of education and recreation includes a flexible, unregimented vacation plan for children.

Site Equipment. The procurement and maintenance of school and community playgrounds are so important that most states have provided for them in their laws. The immediate vicinity of a school building is often used for a kindergarten playground and for apparatus for small children. Older children also need play space and equipment. They look forward to the recess period because they can go out to play. The major criteria for selecting equipment should be benefits to and interests of pupils, initial cost and upkeep, and safety. In this era of cycling, simple stands for parking bicycles should be provided on school property.

On the secondary school and collegiate level, parking facilities for cars are often needed. The athletic fields and areas for intramural sports should be well supplied with suitable equipment and storage spaces. Bleachers are an important part of the grounds equipment where a stadium is not provided with seats. In addition to the regular athletic program of the schools, playground work and recreation in general have spread out into many new situations. Increasing are the demands for outdoor education and for water and winter sports facilities at or near educational buildings.

Buildings

Major Steps in a School Building Project. On the selected sites are erected school and college buildings which usually follow three major phases of development:

1. The program of educational and community requirements, the first phase of a school building project, is a compilation of all data pertinent to the proposed school and should be so complete that the entire building may be envisaged. This program has as its base the philosophy under which the school operates. The curriculum and the general methods of instruction that will be followed are discussed at length. . . . This analysis, with its layouts and educational building standards, when once approved by the board of education, become the guide for the building architect, and the engineer. . . .

2. The second phase is the development by the architect of his complete working drawings and final specifications for materials and workmanship. . . . These represent a high degree of professional skill which the architect and his staff bring to many aspects of their work. The planning has ended, and contracts for construction may now be entered into, provided the bids conform to the budget allotment.

3. The third major stage is the completion of the buildings according to plans and specifications. If the planners have done their work well, the building should serve the community for many decades.[4]

Obviously the educational buildings erected are of various types.

[4] N. L. Engelhardt, N. L. Engelhardt, Jr., and Stanton Leggett, *School Planning and Building Handbook,* F. W. Dodge Corporation, New York, 1956, pp. 5–6.

Types of Construction. In addition to classifications as to style of architecture, buildings are also grouped in terms of the degree of fire safety—A, B, C, D, and E. Type A buildings represent the greatest protection in materials of construction, since the gross structure and interior are of fire-resistive materials. The insurance term "fire-resistive," which is preferred to "fireproof," means that the parts of the building so labeled are made of nonburning or fire-resisting materials such as steel, stone, brick, tile, and metal lath. Structural types B, C, D, and E make increasing use of more inflammable materials, the last being constructed

A   auditorium
Ad   administration
B   boiler building
C   cafeteria
CR   classroom buildings
F   future classrooms
G   gymnasium
H   homemaking classes
I   industrial arts
L   library
M   music
O   offices, health, guidance
S   science labs

A good school plant has an adequate, well-located site, with room for expansion. This is Middleville Road High School built on a campus plan in Northport, New York.

*A good school plant is designed for beauty
as well as function, as illustrated by the Mattie L. Jones
Elementary School, Tyler, Texas.*

*What are the characteristics of
well-planned, well-designed,
well-equipped school buildings?*

*A good school plant is the result of
sound, careful, comprehensive planning
by school administrators, staff, students,
citizens, board of education,
educational consultant, and architect.
The Baldwin High School, New York,
(below) is such a plant.
This 3-million-dollar structure
was designed after many hours spent in assessing
the needs of the community and its youth.
Typifying this planning team are
a member of the local citizens committee
for better schools, a teacher, a principal,
students, and the superintendent.*

A good school has adequate lighting.

chiefly of wood. The records of the National
Fire Protection Association reveal an average
of seven or eight school fires a day, very few of
which originate in Type A buildings.

One development in architecture is dimen-
sional coordination of building materials and
equipment, popularly known as modular or
unit construction. Four inches were determined
as the optimum size for the standard module.
Products are so designed that their dimensions,
plus the required joint, fit the 4-inch dimension
(or multiples thereof) in the modular grid.
When all building materials and equipment are
designed in 4-inch multiples, large savings in
construction may be expected.

Types of construction materials defy classification. Technical mediums are extremely
varied, including directional glass blocks,
pressed wood, colored plastics, hard and
spongy rubber, and many metallurgical miracles. Factory-fabricated materials are used in
increasing quantities. Many schools employ

structural materials and architectural designs indigenous to the particular region.

Educational buildings are also classified on the basis of temporary and permanent structures. Among the temporary types is the so-called portable building, usually found in large cities or in areas of rapid growth in school population. Today thousands of pupils are housed in these temporary or war-surplus structures rather than in permanent fire-resistive buildings.

Schools are also grouped according to their condition. Some are brand-new, some are rehabilitated or modernized, and many are merely old structures in need of rehabilitation or elimination.

As to shape, school buildings are usually erected in the form of the letters T, I, U, N, B, E, H, X, or O, or combinations or modifications thereof. Each shape possesses distinctive advantages and limitations. Buildings may have three degrees of enclosure: the closed, the semiopen with porch or patio effect, and the enclosed but unroofed play space.

The height varies from a one-story structure, the prevalent type, to skyscraper schools in large cities, as, for example, the 15-floor Lindsey Hopkins Vocational School in Miami, Florida. In California the one-floor type has become increasingly prevalent, owing in part to the safety factor in times of earthquakes. Among the many interesting and functional school buildings today are the homemaking cottages.

The building of superior schoolhouses is of course a highly technical task requiring the cooperative efforts of school superintendents, school consultants, engineers, building architects, landscape architects, health specialists, contractors, lawyers, and experts in air conditioning, lighting, and sanitation.

Characteristics of a Good School Building. Buildings can have a personality. The essential qualities of a good school structure include: (1) educational adequacy, (2) safety, (3) healthfulness, (4) efficiency, (5) econ-

A good school plant is designed and equipped to meet the needs of youth, educators, and citizens who will use it.

Furniture and equipment should be scaled to the size of the user, be movable to permit flexibility, and meet the special requirements of all youth.

Large spaces like cafeterias, gymnasiums, and auditoriums may be combined into multipurpose rooms, with flexible furniture which can convert it to the particular function easily and quickly. This room is in the Taylor Avenue Junior High School, Greenlawn, New York.

A school commons is a central area where students, staff, and citizens can meet and relax between classes or activities.

The best in modern instructional materials and equipment are found in a quality school plant.

omy, (6) expansibility and contractibility, (7) flexibility, (8) durability, (9) utility, and (10) beauty.

Many new school buildings are of highly creative design, with effective use of light and color, presenting an environment quite conducive to wholesome living and learning. The architect must be allowed the reasonable luxury of artistic creativeness if school buildings are to be satisfyingly beautiful and functionally useful.

Equipment for Buildings. Some of the criteria for good buildings also apply to the equipment installed in it. The criteria of healthfulness, for example, can be applied to many types of equipment. The two singled out here for accent are lighting and seating.

Gradually organizations like the National Society for the Prevention of Blindness, the Illuminating Engineering Society, and the American Institute of Architects are making the public conscience of eye health. Many classrooms lack adequate and appropriate lighting, either natural or artificial. "Better light for better sight" means basically the admission of abundant natural light through careful, efficient window planning and through the controlled use of artificial lighting when needed. The two basic factors affecting good visual environment are: light intensity, the amount of light falling on a given surface measured in foot-candles; and brightness, the amount of light emitted by or reflected from a surface measured in foot-lamberts (foot-candles times the amount of light reflected from the object).

Seating requirements in educational buildings differ greatly. A kindergarten chair obviously is designed so that it varies greatly from a tablet arm chair for a left-handed college student.

The key element in equipment flexibility is seating. . . . While seats should be movable and desirably of a design which permits their being safely stacked when the floor area is to be cleared, this flexibility should not be achieved at the expense of good postural design, stability, or safety

343

factors. Among the foremost requirements for seating is that of providing correct working heights.[5]

Modern movable classroom seating is a sharp contrast from the screwed-down double desks of yesteryears. Buildings and equipment wage a perpetual battle against the elements of water, wind, sun, and extremes of temperature. A school-painting renaissance is needed in many communities. Paint, usually regarded as a mere protection, is an integral part of a structure. The use of bright color, an essential phase of Egyptian architecture, has been revived. Many large school systems have specially trained maintenance men for carrying on needed renovations. Teachers and pupils, through cooperation with the administration and the custodial force, can make decided contributions to effective and economical operation and maintenance of the school equipment, plant, and grounds, as well as to their beautification.

Evaluation of School Buildings, Sites, and Equipment. Two general criteria in the evaluation of school facilities are these: "How effectively do they promote the instructional process?" and "How do they protect the health of the pupils and teachers?" In many school districts an independent survey of buildings is made to determine strengths and weaknesses. A score card or check list is usually employed in evaluating physical facilities. An example is the *Citizens Workbook for Evaluating School Buildings*, prepared by Jack L. Landes and Merle R. Sumption.

A very important test in evaluating a school building is the utilization of the plant. The percentage of utilization is calculated by taking the number of periods when each room might be utilized and then checking that number against the number of periods when it is actually in use.

Evaluation of a public school building should

[5] Merle R. Sumption and Jack L. Landes, *Planning Functional School Buildings*, Harper & Brothers, New York, 1957, p. 211.

also include utilization by the community. The building is not an island. The school is not merely located in a community; it is an integral part of it. In the forty-ninth state, Alaska, schools have long been centers of economic, social, and recreational life for the people, young and old. School plants ought to be designed not merely for youth but for all learners.

The first three words of the Constitution of the United States, "We, the people," express the thought of cooperation. This ideal should permeate the planning, erection, and use of educational buildings in the community, state, and nation.

In conclusion, the story is retold of the visitor to a stone quarry. He asked the first stonecutter he met, "What are you doing?" The laborer replied, "I'm earning twenty dollars a day not including overtime." The visitor asked a second workman, "What are you doing?" This workman, keeping his eyes fastened down on his work, stated, "I am cutting a stone." The question was asked of a third stonecutter. Looking up with shoulders back and a gleam in his eye, the workman replied, "I am building a school. This stone on which I am working is to be a part of a beautiful school." The first man thought primarily of salary; the second saw only stone; but the third had a vision—he saw himself, working down in a dusty stone quarry, as a partner in the team that was building a beautiful school for a better civilization. Vision makes material meaningful in education.

Summary

Although human resources rank first in American education, appropriate physical properties must be provided. Supplies, equipment, sites, and buildings affect markedly the work of the teacher and learner. In 1958 the Congress of the United States recognized the realistic role of teaching tools and their use by granting federal funds for equipment for science, mathematics, foreign languages, guidance, and evaluation. Material matters are, however, mere means for facilitating and improving the teaching-learning process. All academic aids may prove sterile unless used intelligently.

The greatest educational invention is printing. From the early part of the seventeenth century when the first press started printing at Harvard College, the preparation of books and educational materials has grown into a big business. In the development of modern textbooks the four main influences were: psychology of learning, textbook publication as a specialty, improvements in printing and binding, and rigorous research by authors and publishers. Next in importance to the talents of teachers is the tool of textbooks. Therefore, of extreme importance is the selection, adoption, purchase, and use of these books.

The library should be the heart of the school with arteries running into each room and capillaries to each pupil. The school or college librarian must like pupils and love books, and seek to bring the two together. The federal project for rural libraries has stimulated book services for youth and adults.

Ancillary reading materials include: dictionaries, workbooks, newspapers, magazines, and tests. Television has become one of the most dramatic and promising instructional mediums to burst upon the educational scene. Other audio-visual aids include globes, maps, slides, films, tape recorders, and radio.

Miscellaneous mechanical media in education stretch alphabetically from an abacus to a zither. They vary in size from a thumbtack to a school bus. An increasing trend is to provide a materials and equipment center for the study, construction, and use of teaching tools. The selection, purchase, and use of educational supplies and materials should be on a high educational and ethical plane.

The ground, buildings, and equipment for schools and colleges decidedly affect learning-teaching possibilities. The school sites of yesteryears were often selected on the shortsighted basis that they were not usable for other purposes. Modern plans for sites and buildings are long-term, embracing the three integrated phases of educational, spending, and financing plans. Advance in the selection of sites has been accelerated in recent years. The number of acres for modern schools and colleges has greatly increased. The daily picture of a beautiful school framed in a natural setting is uplifting to pupils, parents, and public.

After the site and architect have been carefully selected, the next major step is to erect an educational structure that will protect pupils, implement the curriculum, and assist the teachers. The current shortages in school buildings are due to such factors as: earlier marriages, larger families, enrollment increases, mobility of population, reorganization of districts, extensions of educational programs, construction backlog, and problems of finance.

Each individual educational building should be a part of a long-term master program. Educational buildings may be classified on such bases as: style of architecture, shape of building, degree of safety, life of plant, and purpose of the program.

Among the important items of furnishing for schools and colleges are a good lighting system and satisfactory seating. Modern schools provide play space and also parking facilities. The planning and use of schools and colleges in the community, state, and nation are permeated by the philosophy of cooperation expressed in the first three words of the Constitution of the United States, "We, the people."

Suggested activities

1. Indicate the role of material in education in the United States.
2. Write a short history of schoolbooks.
3. Contrast an old schoolbook with a modern one in the same field.
4. Contrast some titles of schoolbooks published prior to 1900 and of recent books.
5. How are textbooks adopted in your district or county?

6. Examine or prepare a score card for evaluating a textbook in your major field.
7. Prepare a list of the books given the Newberry or the Caldecott Award.
8. Investigate the methods by which textbooks are furnished to pupils in the schools of your community.
9. Explain the statement: "The library is the heart of the school."
10. Investigate thoroughly the Dewey Decimal System for classifying books.
11. List the advantages and disadvantages in the use of a workbook.
12. Make a scrapbook from the contents of one issue of a daily newspaper, showing how the clippings might be used in various school subjects or areas.
13. Examine two standardized tests in your major field of interest.
14. Investigate equipment used in audio-visual education.
15. List some radio and television programs that have an educational emphasis.
16. Suggest how teachers can promote effective use of supplies and equipment.
17. List the steps necessary in securing a new school building.
18. Examine a score card for evaluating school buildings.

Bibliography

Books

American Association of School Administrators: *The Superintendent As Instructional Leader*, National Education Association, Washington, D.C., 1957, chap. 8. A discussion of the advantages of an adequate school building and facilities from the superintendent's point of view.

Englehardt, N. L., N. L. Englehardt, Jr., and Stanton Leggett: *School Planning and Building Handbook*, F. W. Dodge Corporation, New York, 1956, chap. 1. A guide to the entire process of planning and building school plants.

Herrick, John H., Ralph D. McLeary, Wilfred F. Clapp, and Walter F. Bogner: *From School Program to School Plant*, Henry Holt and Company, Inc., New York, 1956, chap. 13. Discusses the important features needed in school classrooms.

Hunt, Herold C., and Ralph R. Pierce: *The Practice of School Administration*, Houghton Mifflin Company, Boston, 1958, chap. 19. Discussion of the processes of planning, financing, building, equipping, and maintaining the school building.

MacConnell, James D.: *Planning for School Buildings*, Prentice-Hall, Inc., Englewood Cliffs, N.J., 1957, chap. 5. Explains how educators, lay people, and technicians work together to translate the school program into an adequate school plant design.

McQuade, Walter (ed.): *Schoolhouse*, Simon and Schuster, Inc., New York, 1958. An exciting book with many sketches and pictures showing how good school buildings result from the best thinking of many people working together.

Miller, Van, and Willard B. Spaulding: *The Public Administration of American Schools*, World Book Company, Yonkers, N.Y., 1958, chap. 14. Describes the planning of school buildings and discusses new trends in school plants.

Morphet, Edgar L., Roe L. Johns, and Theodore L. Reller: *Educational Administration: Concepts, Practices, and Issues*, Prentice-Hall, Inc., Englewood Cliffs, N.J., 1959, chaps. 18–19. Deals with the selection and use of instructional materials, planning and utilization of the school plant, and related issues.

Perkins, Lawrence B.: *Work Place for Learning*, Reinhold Publishing Corporation, New York, 1957. A well-illustrated book showing the relationship of attractive buildings to the student's learning experiences.

Scott, Harry A., and Richard B. Westkaemper:

From Program to Facilities in Physical Education, Harper & Brothers, New York, 1958, chap. 11. Describes physical education and recreation facilities needed in outdoor areas.

Sumption, Merle R., and Jack L. Landes: *Planning Functional School Buildings*, Harper & Brothers, New York, 1957. A guide for citizens studying their school program in relation to planning school buildings.

Periodicals

Anderson, Harry D.: "Three High Schools under One Roof," *The Nation's Schools*, vol. 63 (January, 1959), pp. 59–63. Interesting description of a new trend in school construction—housing three small high school settings in one large plant.

Brainerd, David S.: "Selection of Equipment in Elementary Schools," *American School and University*, vol. 27 (1955–56) pp. 181–184. Presents basic criteria for the selection of equipment for elementary schools.

Brubaker, Charles W., and Lawrence B. Perkins: "Space for Individual Learning," *The School Executive*, vol. 78 (February, 1959), pp. 43–58. Two outstanding school architects sketch a bold new design for space to stimulate learning—a bold look into the future.

Casey, Leo M.: "Selection of Equipment in High Schools," *American School and University*, vol. 27 (1955–56), pp. 253–256. Suggests criteria to be considered in equipping a high school building.

Caudill, William: "A School for Tomorrow," *The School Executive*, vol. 76 (February, 1957), pp. 53–68. An outstanding school architectural firm takes a bold and imaginative look at the future in school building, a real trip to tomorrow in education.

Cocking, Walter D.: "Getting Quality School Buildings," *The School Executive*, vol. 77 (June, 1958), p. 7. Defines good buildings in terms of materials and processes, craftsmanship, design, and adequacy of facilities.

Hutchins, Clayton D., and Elmer C. Deering: "Financing Public School Buildings," *School Life*, vol. 41 (March, 1959), pp. 9–11. Cites statistics on amount of local, state, and federal funds used for school construction, and other methods of financing buildings.

Mroch, Raymond: "Museums Are for Learning," *NEA Journal*, vol. 48 (January, 1959), pp. 64–65. Discusses the wealth of learning opportunities inherent in museums and how they can be used by teachers.

Pharis, William L., Jr.: "Focus for 1958—Expanded Use of Audio-Visual Aids," *Educational Business*, vol. 78 (November, 1958), pp. 43–47. A roundup of uses, practices, and ideas in audio-visual education programs.

Purcell, Carl: "Camera in the Classroom," *NEA Journal*, vol. 48 (February, 1959), pp. 26–27. Explains the usefulness of the camera as an instructional tool with practical suggestions for its use by teachers.

Smith, Eberle M., and others: "New Directions in School Design," *The School Executive*, vol. 78 (June, 1959), pp. 64–69. Describes and illustrates with pictures some bold and creative school building designs.

chapter 16

Educational finance

backbone of education

Education Is Big Business. In many communities the largest industry is education. Often at least half of the local tax dollar goes to the public schools. Many states spend more money on education than on any other function of government. Nationally, over twenty billion dollars is spent annually on education—public and private, elementary, secondary, and higher. While the federal government dedicates only about 4 per cent of its income to education, it has manifested an increasing fiscal concern about schools and colleges under the permissive "general welfare" clause of the Constitution. An example is the recent four-year grant from 1958 to 1962 of nearly a billion dollars for new defense education—loans to students and to organizations for guidance, science, mathematics, and foreign language equipment and instruction. The Northwest Ordinance clearly postulated: "Religion, morality, and knowledge being necessary to good government and the happiness of mankind, schools and the means of education shall be forever encouraged."

Finance is the supporting backbone of education. The rolling dollars are the cart wheels that move education forward. These dollars support the curriculum (Chapter 13), they assist cocurricular activities (Chapter 14), they finance educational buildings, school supplies, transportation, and equipment (Chapter 15), and, most important of all, they provide the salaries for the human resources mentioned in Chapters 11 and 12, "Teachers" and "Other Personnel," respectively.

While education is big business, it is a common fallacy to liken the fiscal management of schools directly to that of private business. They are not directly comparable. Education is an investment that pays tangible and intangible dividends in the development of human life. The stockholders, the public, and the products (the pupils), reap the daily dividends in lifelong learning and living.

Foundations

Chance, charity, churches, courts, chattel, commodities, credit, and cash were common sources of fiscal support in the early days of American education.

Lotteries and similar games of chance were legitimate means of raising money for schools and colleges in colonial America. These indirect and painless ways of obtaining funds took the place of direct taxation. Then too, much education was financed through charity. Direct gifts by individuals and groups to semipublic or charity schools enabled many poor children to obtain some pauper schooling. Churches through their denominational schools have always financed the education of many children. Barter, the exchange of commodities and services, has been frequent even in the present century. One commodity was wood. In lieu of money a parent furnished the equivalent in wood to keep the schoolroom warm in winter. The teacher often boarded around, receiving his board and room in exchange for part of his services. The practice of barter was revived during the depression of the 1930s when many school employees received gasoline coupons, grocery purchase orders, and IOUs in return for part or all of their services. Many novel methods have been resorted to in the long effort to finance schools through the use of credit.

The best means of support, viz., cold cash, was gradually made available for the operation of schools. Tuition was charged at an early date. A unique form of cash support was provided in the rate tax, which assessed pupils on a per capita basis to cover the costs of schooling above the funds provided locally.

Taxation for school support was at first on a permissive basis. The little word "or" in early legislation proved a mighty obstacle in the development of mandatory public support. It was not until about 1825 that direct taxation of all property for the support of schools was generally recognized.

The Battle for Publicly Supported Education. Cubberley uses the term "battle" to describe the efforts to win public funds for education. It was indeed a prolonged war in which the major victories may be recorded as follows:

1. Permission to communities to organize a school district and to levy a local tax for schools on the property of those consenting
2. Local taxation extended to all property, regardless of consent
3. The organization of school districts made easy, and mandatory on proper petition
4. Small state aid to all organized school districts to help support a school
5. Compulsory local taxation to supplement the state aid
6. Permissive, and later compulsory, township or county taxation to supplement the district taxation
7. Larger and larger state support, and assumption of public education as a state function
8. Extension of the taxation idea to include high schools as well as elementary schools[1]

The present era is marked by three additional struggles in financing schools:

1. Extension of the taxation idea to include pre-elementary education, college education, and education for out-of-school youth and adults
2. Equalization of educational opportunity and burden through state and national equalization funds
3. Procurement of sufficient funds to meet the critical shortages in school and college buildings and in teaching personnel

The extension of public education from the pre-elementary age through adult life has been considered previously; the equalization principle is presented later as one of the basic tenets in modern educational finance; and the battle for more fiscal support is discussed in Chapter 17. Today public educational finance includes such local educational provisions for the pub-

[1] E. P. Cubberley and Walter C. Eells, *An Introduction to the Study of Education*, Houghton Mifflin Company, Boston, 1933, p. 478.

	1633	The Dutch in New York established a town school and levied a school tax
	1643	Earliest record found of rate bills or tuition fees for support of Massachusetts schools
Discovery and early settlements	**1693**	Massachusetts gave towns the legal power to levy school taxes
The Colonial period The struggle for independence and constitutional government	**1785**	Ordinance of 1785 set aside land in the Northwest Territory for schools, beginning federal aid for education
Launching the new nation Maritime troubles and the War of 1812	**1795**	First permanent public school fund established in Pennsylvania
	1819	Dartmouth College decision established inviolability of college charters and stimulated growth of private colleges
Era of good feeling	**1821**	First free public high school was organized in Boston
Jacksonian Democracy Westward migration and expansion	**1834**	Free elementary education was first adopted by by state of Pennsylvania
Controversy and war between the states Aftermath and reconstruction	**1872**	Taxation for secondary schools was upheld in Kalamazoo case
Immigration and industrial growth The progressive era	**1902**	First publicly supported junior college was established at Joliet
World War I	**1917**	Smith-Hughes Act provided federal funds on matching basis for vocational education
Normalcy and prosperity	**1923**	Equalization principle in school finance first enunciated clearly by Strayer and Haig
Depression and recovery	**1931**	National Advisory Committee on Education recommended federal aid for education
World War II	**1944**	Congress enacted GI Bill with federal subsidies for veterans' education
	1946	Membership in and funds for UNESCO approved by Congress
The Cold War struggle	**1947**	National School Lunch Act passed by Congress providing federal funds on permanent basis
	1952	Reports issued by Commission on Financing Higher Education
	1955	Ford Foundation contributed 2½ million dollars for college teachers' salaries
	1958	National Education Defense Act enacted

NATIONAL DEVELOPMENT **THE DEVELOPMENT OF EDUCATIONAL FINANCE**

HISTORICAL CALENDAR

School finance has purpose only to the extent that it helps future citizens become better educated. It has justification to the extent that society values richer, fuller lives for its future citizens.

lic as are supported solely by local funds; community and state financing of pre-elementary, elementary, secondary, and, in certain sections, higher and adult education; state financing of the educational institutions, especially schools of higher learning and residential schools for handicapped children; state and federal support of certain joint efforts, as the land-grant colleges; federal financing of several projects, as veterans' education; and local, state, and federal support of certain special fields, as Smith-Hughes vocational education. In addition millions of dollars are spent annually for the support of private and parochial educational institutions and of numerous foundations.

Principles

Thirteen related principles basic to the financing of American public education are presented here. These principles are neither automatic nor all-inclusive.

Public School Finance Must Be Related to Public Finance. Public school finance is only a part of the larger whole, viz., public finance. The fact that public school finance is a part of public finance is illustrated in the distribution of the tax dollar in any community. The implications of this fact are far reaching. Since the school is only one of the many enterprises supported by the public taxation, schoolmen may well approach their own isolated interests from the broad view of *public* rather than *school* financing. Other general activities, such as those of fire and police departments, aim at goals similar to those of education—they seek to protect the individual, his property, and his right. Education, in the long run, serves as a form of insurance for which the public ought to be both willing and able to pay.

Schoolteachers, and administrators must see the financing of schools in relationship to the problem of support for all public functions, just as public officials must see the correlation of school and public finance. This first tenet, therefore, may be termed the principle of economic interdependence. It calls for economic and social vision.

School Finance Should Be the Servant of Education and Society. Finance should function as the servant, not as the master, of education and society. The child is more important than the dollar. In many school systems, however, money is the dictator, and education is the slave. The opposite condition is likewise unfortunate for lavish spending brings financial disaster to the school district and the allied tax-

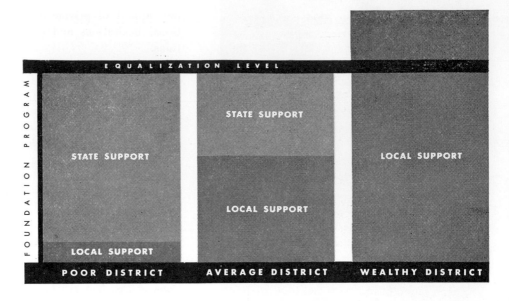

Fig. 16-1. State and local support of education. In poor districts, local effort to support schools produces only a small fraction of the cost of a state-guaranteed minimum or foundation program. State support is provided in an amount necessary to meet the equalization level or foundation program. In average districts, the amounts of state and local support are more nearly equal. In wealthy districts, little or no state support is needed, since local wealth is sufficient to reach and often surpass the equalization level.

ing units. School finance helps to give a child the best education possible within practical limits.

Educational finance serves not only schools but also society. It is a social as well as economic factor. The social motive, thus far subordinated, now bids fair to assume a larger control in public education. Educational finance is indeed the servant of society as well as the handmaiden of education. Money spent for education is an investment for the defense of the American faith in democracy.

Public Education Should Be Fiscally Free for All Pupils. Basic to the financing of public education is the democratic concept of free education. How long education should be provided at

public expense is a debatable question. Practices vary markedly between states, but there is general agreement that children should be educated through high school at public expense. Some authorities would extend tuition-free schooling through the junior college years. This does not mean that everything is free. Many costs are hidden. There is disagreement as to the number of elements that should be provided without cost to pupils. For example, in the education of rural high school pupils, some states furnish only tuition, whereas others include free transportation, textbooks, or board of pupils in lieu of transportation. Many states have set up what is called a defensible minimum program to be furnished tuition-free to all pupils. Along with the American bill of rights, including guarantees for freedom of speech, of religion, of the press, and of assembly, is the dictum that American public education shall be free to all pupils. The emancipation proclamation in school finance precludes dependence upon charity, fees, and tuition. Free public education is the American's birthright.

The State Should Be Primarily Responsible for Public Education. The Tenth Amendment to

[handwritten margin notes: best education possible within financial limits]

[handwritten margin note: Strengthen democracy]

the Constitution of the United States made education the primary responsibility of the individual states (see Chapter 2). Hence the support of public education became mainly a matter of state concern. Today every state makes some contribution from its revenues for the support of public schools through many types of funds, some of which are described later. An inconsistency exists, however, between the legal intention to provide state support and the many cases of neglect and inadequacy. For the nation as a whole, state governments supply only about 40 per cent of the cost of schools. Furthermore, the method of distributing such aid is an important factor. Despite arguments for federal support of public education, the fact remains that the individual states will have to give more assistance to schools, particularly through the application of the next principle.

Educational Opportunity and Burden Should Be Equalized. Strayer and Haig in 1923 were the first to give a clear-cut picture of the equalization principle. Their analysis interpreted this principle as the complete equalization of the burden of a satisfactory minimum educational program below which no locality could be allowed to go, but above which any locality would be allowed to rise by means of local support. In contradistinction to the payment-for-effort or matching principle, the operation of the equalization plan tends to shift to more able communities some of the undue burden carried by the less wealthy localities (see Fig. 16-1). Most states today have a state-local partnership foundation program in which the commonwealth bestows more on those schools which have less in fiscal resources. Local school districts should receive enough state aid to relieve the local property tax and thus provide enough local tax leeway to adapt to peculiar local needs. On the other hand, complete financing through state aid preempts local responsibility for finance and undermines local initiative. For this reason also, most experts on school finance want boards of education to be fiscally independent, that is, free from fiscal

dependence upon other units of local government.

In brief, the equalization principle means that governmental agencies collect educational funds where the money is and spend the money where the pupils are. Every man's property and income must be taxed to educate every man's child. Even though a man chooses to send his own children to a parochial or private school, he is not exempt from contributing his support to the education of all children. The golden rule in education finance is "Thou shalt educate thy neighbor's children as thine own."

Initially this idea of equalization was applied to small areas, as the county and state. Now the old slogan "The wealth of the state must educate the children of the state," is being supplemented with the clause "and the wealth of the United States must be used to equalize the education of all the children in the nation." Furthermore, the phrase "all the children in the nation" implies that more adequate educational opportunities and greater financial support be provided for exceptional or atypical children, since their learning opportunities, as in the case of the blind, are below par, and the costs of their instruction are above average. American public education will not be genuinely democratic until there is nationwide application of the principle that opportunity and burden shall be equalized for all learners.

Lighthouse Schools Can Indicate Better Practices through Their Richer Resources. Related to the promotion of equalization of opportunity and burden is the principle of adaptability. According to this rule, the state tries to keep schools wholesome and vigorous by preserving local initiative and utilizing other devices. Its early application consisted of a program of fiscal rewards to a community for supporting its schools. This reward-for-effort device is being modified because in practice it gave most help to the rich district. The modern interpretation of this principle makes it possible for wealthy districts to use their wealth in going far beyond the foundation or equalization level guaranteed to all schools. These better-financed schools, or lighthouse schools as they are sometimes called, help point the way to future progress for all schools.

Efficiency Must Be Practiced in Educational Finance. The efficiency principle is aimed at promoting expertness in school management. Despite the fact that most school people are conscientious, they may at times be inefficient. A cardinal principle of public school finance is that efficiency shall always be promoted.

Education Should Be Economically Administered. Every school system must practice economy at all times. Groups as well as individuals should heed the advice of Ralph Waldo Emerson "to make money spend well." The term "economy" is often misunderstood, since there are false and true economies. Educators and laymen must distinguish between retrenchment and economy. Retrenchment is merely a reduction in expenditures. Genuine economy is effected through intelligent spending and vigilant administration. Benjamin Franklin wrote, "Human felicity is produced not so much by great pieces of good fortune that seldom happen, as by little advantages that occur each day."

Increased Responsibilities Must Mean Increased Costs. Those who are prone to cut the educational budget with one hand and to give the school increased responsibilities with the other should realize that the two acts are incompatible. Among the major causes for rise in school expeditures are (1) decline in purchasing value of the dollar, (2) increase in enrollments, (3) increase in the size of the educational tasks, especially in the relatively expensive junior college years, and (4) higher standards of educating, akin to the higher standards of living in vogue today. The first causal factor is primarily monetary. The last three are educational in nature and account for a large share of the enlarged costs. The extension and enrichment of educational services call for expansion in school revenue.

Fiscal Management of Schools Cannot Be Identical with That of Private Business. A common fallacy is to liken the fiscal management of public schools to that of private business. Although both strive after economy and efficiency, they differ decidedly. In the first place, the former is a public matter, and the latter is mainly private. Then too, one is education and the other is business. Furthermore, although money is invested in both public education and private business, the major objective of the latter is quarterly cash dividends, whereas the former seeks long-time returns in character, personality, skills, and the changes wrought in the child through growth and development. A business, although employing many people, is run for the special benefit of a few stockholders; public education is conducted cooperatively for the benefit of all members of society. Of course, the public schools can profit much from observing private business even though they are dissimilar in philosophy and function.

Personnel in Fiscal Management Should Be Well Trained and Honest. Both business and school officials advocate that those engaged in fiscal management be well trained. The persons handling school finances should have specific training for their jobs. The school treasurer, the superintendent, the business manager, or whoever is in direct charge of school finances should be versed in the theory and practice of business accounting. They should also be professionally trained educators. Increasingly, superintendents of schools and other staff members are taking courses in school finance and business management.

The personnel should be not only efficient but also impeccably honest. As a precautionary and custodial measure, all persons who handle school money should be bonded. The staff is usually trustworthy, but unfortunately the schools are tempting objects for despoilation by greedy politicians and racketeers.

Expenditures for Public Education Should Be Recorded and Reported. A person may be care-

[handwritten top margin: public wants to know where money goes]

less about recording his personal receipts and expenditures, but he cannot be so with public money, which must be accounted for meticulously and honestly. The receipt of money and its expenditure should be registered promptly and accurately. Records ought to be kept in a fire-resistive vault and subjected to scientific scrutiny through periodic audits.

✳ Not only must school money be accounted for, but its receipts and expenditure should be reported to the board of education, the teachers, the taxpayer, and the public. The old cry was "taxation without representation," but the new complaint is "taxation without explanation." Fiscal reports are improved by numerous explanations and attractive illustrations. The concept of stewardship, also termed the "fiduciary" or "prudential principle," calls for a perennial procession of publicity. The German philosopher Kant makes publicity the test of fair dealing: "All actions relating to the rights of other men are wrong if the maxims from which they follow are inconsistent with publicity." A periodic channel for publicity is provided through the nationwide annual American Education Week. One objective of such organizations as the National Congress of Parents and Teachers and the National Citizens' Commission for Better Schools is to interpret and improve education continuously through grass-roots programs.

Fiscal Planning Is Necessary for Education. Educational welfare necessitates fiscal planning. Many administrators build their curriculums carefully but estimate their finances hurriedly. Many school boards spend months going over blueprints for buildings but devote a half-hour to the fiscal framework for the education of children. *[handwritten right margin: Delay in budget but benefit in student in best way]*

✳ Education is a long-term investment by the public, which reaps dividends in the enriched lives of its citizens. A long-term fiscal program is essential, since schooling extends forward not backward; the education of a child calls for a long-period plan, not only because he requires eight to fifteen years of schooling, but also because the entire cost is often borne by one school district. Long-period planning for education is an attempt to substitute intelligent forecasts for the opportunism of a laissez-faire philosophy. Effective long-range forecasting must rest upon improvement in the short-term fiscal plan; that is, the annual school budget.

Budgeting

The budget is an important instrument in education. Through it, many of the basic principles of public school finance, if not all, are applied. *[handwritten: principles of finance applied to these]*

Fig. 16-2. Evolution of the school budget.

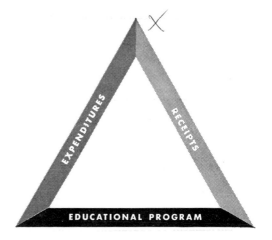

EARLY FORM   TRADITIONAL TYPE   MODERN BUDGET FOR SCHOOLS

Evolution of the Modern School Budget. Years ago the school budget consisted of one major item, viz., expenditures. One director probably met another in the country store and asked, "How much money shall we spend for the school next year? We spent 1,200 dollars last year." So the budget became 1,200 dollars, which indicated the limit on expenditures. Later, school officials, imitating the business world, drew up a budget not only of estimated expenditures but also of probable receipts, with the latter presumably greater than expenditures.

The modern school budget, as indicated in Fig. 16-2, (page 355), differs visibly and functionally from a commercial or a traditional budget in that the first is represented by an equilateral triangle. In this balanced triangle, the educational program is the base which represents the working plan of the school, the qualifications of the teachers, and other educational specifications including supplies, textbooks, and program of supervision. The estimated expenditures necessary to conduct this educational program form the spending plan. The proposed receipts to pay for putting the plan into operation constitute the financing plan. The school budget, then, is a detailed professional forecast, consisting of both (1) estimated expenditures and (2) receipts, based in turn upon (3) the proposed educational program.

Function of the School Budget. Despite its numerous shortcomings the public school budget serves many practical purposes. The budget is important because it:

1. Is a servant of education
2. Gives an overview of the entire school system
3. Aids in analysis of new and old school activities
4. Develops cooperation within the school
5. Stimulates confidence among the taxpayers
6. Estimates the receipts
7. Determines the tax levy
8. Authorizes expenditures
9. Aids in economical administration
10. Improves accounting procedures
11. Aids in extracurricular activities
12. Projects the school into the future

The entire period of time covered by the budget is designated as the fiscal year, which usually extends from July 1 through June 30. An increasing number of schools, however, prepare long-term as well as annual budgets.

PROGRESS OF THE ANNUAL SCHOOL BUDGET

Budgeting in public education may be divided into four major steps: (1) preparation, (2) presentation and adoption, (3) administration, and (4) appraisal.

Preparation of the Budget. Budget building is a continuous job. The starting point is the development of an educational program that helps to make the school budget a professional document rather than a statistical report. This educational emphasis in school accounting is made possible through the cooperation of all staff members and the board of education. The preparation of the educational specifications is inextricably linked with the development of the spending and financing plans for the budget.

Presentation and Adoption. After the budget has been prepared in tentative form, it is usually presented to the board of education and to other legal and extralegal groups. Fiscal publicity plays an important part in the broader program of public relations. Various techniques aid in interpreting the budget to the boards of education, the school personnel, and the general public. After the budget has been presented with interpolations, it is legally ratified by the proper body or bodies, such as the board of education and the city council, or by the people in some states.

3 *Administration of the Budget.* After the estimated figures have been transferred to the school accounting books as initial entries, the budget is ready to be administered. It functions not as a dictator but as a definite guide for the economical and efficient conduct of the schools.

4 *Appraisal of Budgets and Budgetary Procedures.* One means of appraising budgets and budgetary procedures is the school audit. Then there is also the objective appraisal of the format and content of the document itself. The annual document can best be appraised in relation to a long-term budget of two or more years. In the final analysis, the role of budgeting in public education must be evaluated in terms of the service it renders to the learner and society.

what service did it render

Expenditures

The school budget, as previously mentioned, consists of three parts, viz., the educational plan, the expenditures program, and the financing plan. The educational plan is treated throughout this volume and particularly in Chapter 13. The remainder of this unit is devoted to the two other programs, viz., those for expenditures and receipts.

CLASSIFICATION OF SCHOOL EXPENDITURES

Research in school finance has been handicapped because school systems have used many different types of school financial accounting forms, making the compilation and comparison of financial data most difficult. To remedy this condition, the U.S. Office of Education has recently prepared a standard accounting classification form for schools. The major headings and subheadings are as follows: administration, instruction, attendance and health, pupil transportation, operation of plant, maintenance of plant, fixed charges, food services, community services, capital outlay, debt service, outgoing transfers.

Where the School Dollar Goes. The school tax dollar does not go into hiding; it is seen in circulation. But teachers and administrators are frequently asked, "Where does the school dollar go?" "How is the money spent?" The classroom teacher as an agent in the public relations program should be fortified with facts so as to give an intelligent answer to such inquiries. Obviously the dollar is not spent in the same way in every school system. Two extremely variable items listed are debt service and capital outlay.

debt service, capital outlay & others.

For the entire United States, the percentage distribution of the school dollar for current expenditures is revealed in Fig. 16-3.

Annual Cost per Pupil in Average Daily Attendance. The percentage distribution of the school dollar is not the only way of calculating school costs. Another method is that of figuring the cost per capita for an area as large as the United States or as small as a local school district. The basis in determining these unit costs is usually the average daily attendance (a.d.a.), the number enrolled in school, or the total population of the United States.

unit costs based on attendance

Annual Cost per Pupil Enrolled and per Capita of Population. The cost of education in the public elementary and secondary schools can be calculated also on the basis of the number of pupils enrolled. This total unit cost is less than the cost per pupil in average daily attendance. Another unit, less reliable than per pupil average daily attendance, is the cost per person in the United States. Figs. 16-4 and 16-5 reveal the per capita cost and the cost per pupil enrolled. The tabulations show interesting trends in public school expenditures both per pupil enrolled and per capita of population. As the nation develops a program of lifelong learning for all individuals, the cost per capita of population will be increasingly indicative of the cost of public education per consumer.

unit costs based on pupil enrollment cheaper

$ cost per person

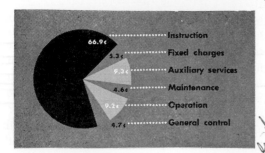

Fig. 16-3. Where the school's current-expense dollar goes.

Daily Costs per Pupil Enrolled. Costs for education may also be calculated on the basis of the daily rather than the annual expenditures indicated thus far. In a typical school the costs for current expenditures average approxi-

Fig. 16-4. Cost of education per capita of population.

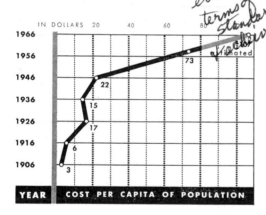

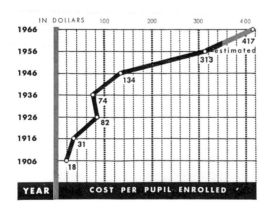

Fig. 16-5. Cost of education per pupil enrolled.

mately a dollar and a half a day for each pupil enrolled. The cost-per-day unit for calculating school expenditures is advantageous, since it is small, easily handled, and readily understood by the man in the street.

These data on school expenditures, either for a state or for the nation as a whole, refer only to the direct expenditures for public schools. The complete cost of education in America embraces expenditures by a large number of private and parochial schools, by institutions of higher learning, by libraries, by children for school supplies, and by parents who pay indirect costs such as the loss of possible earnings by older students.

The total expenditures are inadequate measures of either the cost or the worth of education. Increasingly the public is learning to evaluate this service not in terms of dollar aggregates but by means of standards and results achieved. The quality and quantity of educational returns must be considered as well as the nature and amount of expenditures. Furthermore, expenditures are made possible only through the receipt of adequate revenue.

Receipts

CLASSIFICATION OF SCHOOL RECEIPTS

Less uniformity is found in classifying school receipts than in classifying expenditures. Receipts are usually grouped by (1) taxing or political unit, (2) method of production, (3) accounting classification, and/or (4) specific funds. Each of these methods is briefly described here.

Taxing or Political Unit. A convenient way to group estimated or actual school receipts is according to the taxing unit that provides the revenue. These main political units are local, township, county (parish), state, and federal. Patently these geographical categories overlap somewhat. For example, property taxes may come from more than one political unit.

Method of Production. The more common forms of financing public education are listed alphabetically here: endowments, gas tax, grants, income tax, inheritance tax, interest, personal-property tax, real-estate tax, rentals, sales tax, subventions, tuition. It is difficult to determine the exact methods by which all school revenue is obtained.

Accounting Classifications. The U.S. Office of Education recommends the following major accounting classifications for school receipts:

Revenue receipts ~~Where to obtain revenue~~
Revenue from local sources
Taxation and appropriation
Tuition from patrons
Transportation fees
Other revenue from local sources
Revenue from intermediate sources
Revenue from state sources
Revenue from federal sources

Nonrevenue receipts
Sale of bonds
Loans
Sale of school property and insurance adjustments
Income transfer accounts

Specific Funds. It has been suggested that legal stipulations separating school money into special distinct funds be abolished. Many of these regulations, however, have long histories that fortify them against change. Rigidity in accounting is exemplified in Illinois, where school money must be separated into educational and building funds. Numerous special school funds have been created by state legislatures.

State and National Uniformity Recommended. Many other systems of revenue classification are employed. The most common practice is that of listing receipts by local, state, and federal sources. As in the case of expenditures, a combination of systems is recommended, with due regard to state laws and national uniformity, as advocated by the U.S. Office of Education.

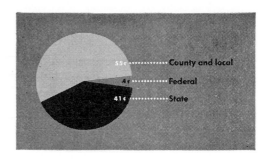

Fig. 16-6. Where the school's dollar comes from.

SOURCES OF SCHOOL REVENUE

Where the School Dollar Comes from. People are usually more interested in the answers to the question, "Where does the school dollar go?" than in those to the query, "Where does the school dollar come from?" The latter, however, is more important, for it goes to the root of the American economic system. Since school finance is a segment of public finance, the teacher and administrator are drawn into broad problems of public financing when they seek the deep sources of the dollar that the school receives. As in expenditures, there is little uniformity in receipts throughout the United States.

Decrease in Revenue from Local Sources. In continental United States the county contributes a small part of school revenue. The consolidation of schools and the enlargement of the taxing unit to embrace entire counties cause county and local sources to coalesce. The proportion of school revenue derived from local districts in the United States as a whole has decreased markedly in the past two decades from 80 to less than 60 per cent, including county support. Figure 16-6 reveals the sources of school revenue according to political units.

Although all school revenues are derived from federal, state, county, township, and local units, the types of receipts and the methods of financing public education vary widely. Two main sources, viz., taxation and nonrevenue receipts, are presented here elliptically and briefly. A third source, apportionments, is treated later under Distribution of School Funds.

Taxation. Edwin A. Seligman, a noted economist, defines a tax as "a compulsory contribution from the person to the government to defray the expense incurred in the common interest of all without reference to special benefits conferred." In other words, through taxes people contribute to the cost of different services and common social purposes. Since most of the support for American public education comes from taxation in its myriad forms, laymen, teachers, and administrators desire a good tax system, which is not too dependent upon a single tax, such as that on property. The general property tax is becoming increasingly unsatisfactory because of the difficulty in assessing all kinds and classes of property at the same rate. Many European nations have to a large degree abandoned this method, but in America some modified plan of taxing property for schools will exist for a long time.

A tax bill is rarely welcome. The first school-tax notice may seem to a new homeowner like a request from the school: "Let us place your name on our wailing list." But the late Justice Oliver Wendell Holmes, who willed his estate to his country, said, "I like to pay taxes. It is buying civilization." Certainly when the American citizen pays his taxes for public education he is helping to buy civilization.

Among the numerous plans for making the property tax less painful are classification of property; equalization of assessments; more economical, efficient, and honest administration in assessing, levying, and collecting taxes; and the inclusion of the property tax as a part

of a broader tax base. It is the abuse rather than the use of the property tax that constitutes a menace to the schools. As Emerson wrote in his essay "Compensation," "If you tax too high, the revenue will yield nothing."

A promising revenue is the income tax, on which England depends in a far greater degree than America. Linked intimately with the problems of broadening the tax base for school support are the issues of increasing efficiency through the consolidation of small weak units and of reducing costs through carefully planned economies. Archaic taxing systems are not the only cause of trouble, for even where tax systems have been revised, revenues are often inadequate. Some of the difficulty lies not so much in the failure of taxation as in increased expenditures. Many schools may well give less emphasis to raising more funds to spend and may well devote more thought to spending money more efficiently.

Nonrevenue Receipts. As previously defined, nonrevenue receipts do not constitute a genuine source of income, since they incur an obligation that must be met at some future date. These receipts include mainly the revenue either from selling property and bonds or from obtaining loans. Since property is not frequently sold by the school district, attention is directed here to the common practice of borrowing money.

The prevalent ways of financing schools when cash is not available are (1) long-term and (2) short-term obligations, and (3) refinancing. Illustrative of the first are the straight-term bond, which is used for a stated number of years, to be repaid or refunded at the date of maturity; the sinking-fund bond, which is made for a definite period of years, to be paid from a fund which is collected and invested during the term of the bond; and the serial bond, which is paid in installments during the period of the total bond issue. Among the numerous types of temporary school finance are short-term bonds, loans, tax-anticipation warrants, scrip, and other forms of paper money. Refinancing or refunding involves the legal procedure of reestablishing an old debt as a fresh obligation, perhaps at a lower rate of interest. Often this merely postpones the evil day of accounting for past debts.

Many schools have erred in borrowing too much money. Practices such as erecting school buildings beyond the ability of the community to pay within a reasonable length of time, funding debts for annual expenditures, legislating state-wide tax limitations that are inadequate, collecting only a meager portion of the tax levy, and creating sinking funds that disappear are costly procedures that work the greatest hardships upon the generation now in school, for later as adults they will have to pay the costs of their own schooling.

DISTRIBUTION OF SCHOOL REVENUE

The development of a sound system of raising money for public and private schools is a major problem. A sequential task of prime import is the distribution of the money thus obtained. School money may be collected by reliable

Fig. 16-7. Guaranteed minimum expenditure level.

methods but distributed through unsatisfactory channels.

As the word "distribution" indicates, school funds are allocated to the states, counties, or local districts by a higher organization. The federal government allots its Smith-Hughes fund to the states, and the latter give it to the local districts. In West Virginia, the state treasury apportions certain school funds to the county units.

Bases for Distribution of Funds. The bases upon which school monies are distributed are very important. Among the criteria for the apportionment of funds for education are the number of children of school age who reside in the district or county as revealed by the school census; the number of children enrolled in the schools; the number of children in average daily attendance (a.d.a.); the "weighted" pupil with special consideration given to the rural or atypical pupil; the number of teachers employed; the number of instruction units (usually one teacher for each stated number of pupils); the partial or complete support of a state-prescribed minimum educational program; and other forms of flat grants and equalization programs. Combinations of these

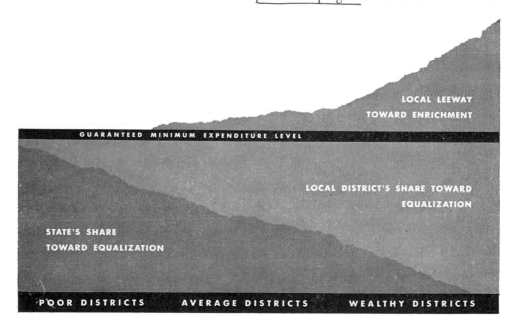

apportionment methods are employed in several states.

State Equalization Fund. As the term connotes, an equalization fund is intended to equalize educational opportunity and burden. Too often the type and amount of a child's schooling are the result of chance or geography. The child who through the felicity of circumstances lives in a school district that can tax a railroad line or a uranium company enjoys enhanced opportunities for an all-round education. The accidental meanderings of a river several hundred years ago often determine the boundaries that demarcate superior and inferior educational opportunities. Unfortunately, even when the highest permissible tax rate has been applied to the areas of low valuation, the funds secured are insufficient to run the schools in many districts throughout the United States. Even if a model tax plan were put into effect, the poorer districts and states would still be unable to support their schools adequately.

Figure 16-7 illustrates a typical state equalization program. The state provides most of the revenue for the education of children in impoverished districts, guaranteeing that children shall not be denied a minimum educational opportunity because of the accident of their birth in a poor community. Less state aid is provided in districts of average wealth. Wealthy districts often receive no state aid or, at most, little state aid. The justification of providing state aid to districts of average or better ability is that they are given financial leeway and incentive to use local funds to enrich or extend their educational programs beyond the minimum level. The guaranteed minimum expenditure level is regarded as a floor, below which no district may go, rather than as a uniform level for all, or as a ceiling.

The amount of state aid varies widely—from 85 per cent to 5 per cent. Approximately three-fourths of the states distribute all or part of their state school funds upon an equalization plan. The funds for these equalization plans have been derived from state-wide sources.

Every state needs a program, built upon research and individually patterned, which provides for local initiative and state equalization. This forms the groundwork upon which a federal equalization program may be based.

Federal Equalization Fund. Education is not primarily a personal benefaction, such as the sidewalk leading to one's home. Nor is it merely a community benefit, like a street light. Rather it is a boon to all. In many ways it is comparable to a city street which is also a state highway and a national route. Both the building and the maintenance of that local-state-national highway are the obligation of all people, not just of those who happen to live near or travel that route. Likewise in the building and maintenance of schools, the local, state, and national interests are merging.

Yet the very schools designed for promoting common local, state, and national welfare may fail in their task. As an illustration, witness the inability of the depressed economic areas and groups to provide proper education for their children from generation to generation. Some school districts have 60 times more wealth per child than others. Any federal funds that are or may be made available for public education should be so distributed as to guarantee equity and to correct the present glaring inequalities in the use of school funds for children of the different races. According to many fiscal experts, no sound program of local or state taxation can be devised and established which will support in every community a school system that meets minimum acceptable standards. Time can never efface the inequalities in natural resources that exist between states. Therefore, unless the federal government participates in the financial support of the schools and the related services in the less able areas, several million children in the United States and the outlying territories and possessions will continue to be denied the educational opportunities that should be regarded as their birthright. Most recommendations and recent proposals for federal aid stipulate positively that such grants shall not entail federal control over education. They also specify that the money shall be apportioned to the states, except that for cooperative educational research, which shall be administered by the U.S. Office of Education.

Several decades ago Rutherford B. Hayes, then President of the United States, sent to Congress a message in which he said, "No more fundamental responsibility rests upon Congress than that of devising appropriate measures of financial aid to education, supplemental to local action in the states and territories and in the District of Columbia." This challenge has not yet been adequately met. Federal aid to public education is one of the moral musts of America. Federal aid should be provided only to those needy public school districts that are unable to reach a satisfactory minimum level after making a genuine effort. This issue is discussed in detail in Chapter 17.

Other finance

As previously stated, American public education is broader than schooling. Accordingly, public school finance is not exactly synonymous with public educational finance. The former is usually restricted to public elementary and secondary schools, whereas the latter embraces expenditures and receipts for all educational institutions and undertakings supported in part or whole by public taxation. This distinction, however, is hard to follow since in some places these areas overlap or fuse. One of the remaining forms of American public education not yet treated from the fiscal viewpoint in this volume is that of publicly supported higher education. *To be discussed*

PUBLICLY SUPPORTED HIGHER EDUCATION

Public elementary and secondary schools receive more tax dollars than do public institutions of higher learning. The operating or current educational expenditures for *all* institutions of higher education are 2.1 billion dollars

a year. According to the Twentieth Century Fund study, this is about 1.8 billion short of what should be spent to meet our needs fully. Capital outlay for college buildings and equipment is about 600 million dollars annually, less than half the estimated need of 1.4 billion dollars.[2]

The President's Commission on Higher Education grouped the sources of income available for the financing of current educational expenditures under four main headings: (1) philanthropy or private sources, (2) student fees, (3) public sources or government appropriations, and (4) miscellaneous, including receipts from sales and services of organized institutional activities. Obviously, publicly controlled institutions of higher learning receive less from philanthropy, less from student fees, and more from public sources than do the private colleges and universities.

The state is the chief provider of income both for teacher-educating institutions and for other public higher education. The next source of income is institutional, such as tuition, fees, and sales. The state leads in the support of teacher education and other higher education: the local districts rank first in the support of elementary and secondary education. The branch of higher learning receiving the largest share of county assistance is the gradually disappearing county normal school, whereas the junior college and the municipal university are the usual recipients of local tax support on the

[2] Twentieth Century Fund, *U.S.A. in New Dimensions*, The Macmillan Company, New York 1957, p. 55

Fig. 16-8. State expenditures for education in Wisconsin.

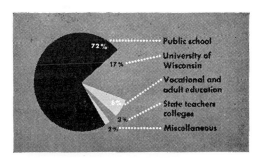

higher level. Local, state, and federal support of public higher education will undoubtedly increase as a result of larger enrollments, the prolongation of secondary education, and the development of various phases of public adult education.

In its forward look, the President's Commission on Higher Education recommended the following three types of federal aid to higher education: (1) for current educational expenditures by publicly controlled institutions, (2) for capital outlay by publicly controlled colleges and universities, and (3) for a national program of scholarships to be administered by the states in accordance with general standards established by the federal government.

OTHER PUBLICLY SUPPORTED EDUCATION

Federal Projects. Other publicly supported educational projects of nationwide and world-wide significance are the various national surveys authorized by Congress and the promotion of democratic educational systems in such countries as Germany, Austria, and Japan. Congressional grants have financed such outstanding surveys as those of secondary education, teacher education, school finance, higher education, and Negro education. Through such agencies as the Department of State and the Department of Defense, many educational experts

Fig. 16-9. Expenditures for elementary and secondary education.

from the United States have served as consultants in occupied areas, and many teachers, students, and other educational personnel from foreign countries have visited and studied in the United States.

In addition the federal government has continued and expanded its regular activities to assist education. The most significant project has been the federal fiscal support of the GI bills, which have aided directly and indirectly many institutions of secondary and higher education. (See Chapter 1 for further details on federal financing of public education.)

State Support. In the state of Wisconsin, for example, public educational finance embraces the agencies shown in Fig. 16-8 which expend the indicated number of pennies and mills of each dollar received.

This list of educational institutions and functions reveals that public school expenditures constitute but one aspect of state disbursements for education. Every commonwealth provides funds from its treasury for one or more special projects in connection with the public schools, or as separate undertakings, such as the library (see Chapter 2).

Local Support. Local and intermediate school units, such as the county, township, and city school districts, sponsor many educational projects. The county pays most of the bills for the office of the county superintendent of schools, the county normal schools, county li-

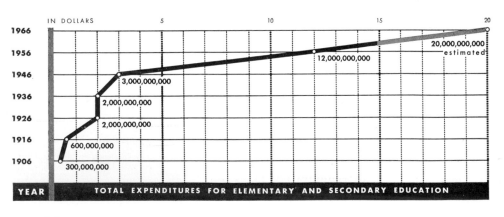

braries, agricultural agents, and certain club activities like the 4-H (see Chapter 3).

Local and intermediate school units promote types of public education in addition to schooling for children. Among these activities are recreation and other phases of adult education, library and museum facilities, and special projects predicated on local needs, interests, and fiscal abilities (see Chapter 4).

PRIVATELY FINANCED EDUCATION

In the early years of the United States, most education was privately financed. As state systems of public education became established and as the principle of separation of church and state emerged, most elementary and secondary education became publicly supported. However, the right of parents to send their children to private schools has been upheld by the Supreme Court. Thus private schools have become an accepted and important part of our educational system. About one-sixth of the elementary school population and one-eighth of the secondary school students attend private schools. One-seventh of the total cost of educating elementary and secondary students is paid from private funds; the other six-sevenths come from public monies. Approximately half of the college students attend private colleges, but approximately one-third of the total cost of higher education is borne privately. Most of the cost of adult education is paid from private funds.

The majority of private schools and colleges are sectarian, receiving financial support from churches, donations, and student fees. Some private schools are nonsectarian, receiving their financial support largely from tuition and benefactions. In most colleges, a student's tuition pays less than half the actual cost of his education. Industries and private foundations are contributing substantially to the support of colleges and universities. Nevertheless, one must view with alarm the financial plight of institutions of higher education, particularly

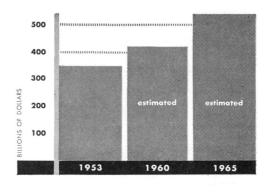

Fig. 16-10. Growth of gross national product, the market value of all the goods and services turned out by the nation's economy.

those financed privately. This problem is discussed at length in Chapter 8.

Financial effort

Various estimates have been made of the increase in costs of all elementary and secondary education that will be necessary in the decade from 1956 to 1966. It appears that the minimum increase in expenditures (merely that needed to maintain present quality and scope but for increased numbers) will be about 6 billion dollars in 1966, an increase of 50 per cent over 1956. However, when estimates of cost include improvement of quality (through the elimination of overcrowded classrooms and substandard teachers, reduction of drop-outs, strengthening of teachers' salaries and other improvements) an 8 billion dollar increase in 1966 appears more appropriate. This would be an increase of about 67 per cent over 1956 school expenditures.

In 1959, the President's Science Advisory Committee, after a study of America's educational needs and resources, recommended that the nation should double its expenditures for education as a minimum effort.

It appears that the gross national product will increase somewhere between 40 and 55 per cent during the same decade. For the past quarter-century, the United States has spent

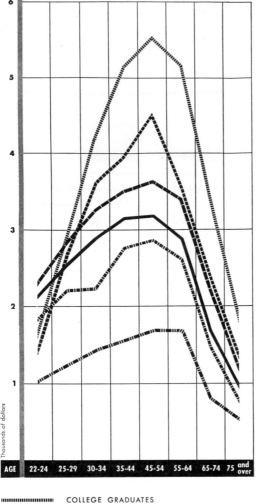

Fig. 16-11. Median income level for males by education level and age groups.(U.S. Bureau of the Census.)

about 3½ per cent of this national product for education. As national income has increased, it has resulted in an increase in dollars spent for education. But the dollar increase has not been enough to keep pace with skyrocketing enrollments. In other words, the nation has been spending a proportionately smaller per

cent of its national income *per pupil*. The Rockefeller Report on Education concludes that it will take nearly 5 per cent of our national income during this decade to keep pace with the growing student population and to make simultaneous advances in school quality.[3] Since Russia, England, and many other nations spend between 5 and 10 per cent of their national income for education, this would not appear to be an unreasonable expectation in the United States, the cradle of free public education.

However, as the Rockefeller Report points out, it will be difficult to channel enough of this increased prosperity to schools without major changes in the pattern of school finance:

In the past, Americans have preferred to accomplish the financing of public education, like the financing of most nondefense public facilities and services, at the state and local level. But state and local tax systems are in some respects archaic and it is very difficult to keep the revenues from this source growing in step with the economy or with the growing demand for governmental services which an expanding economy creates. This is due partly to the excessive dependence of state and local revenues—particularly the latter—upon the real property tax, which is notably laggard in its response to rising income.[4]

The problem of federal aid to education is discussed at length in Chapter 17.

The American people must come to realize that adequate financing of education is not really a levy upon their pocketbooks but rather an investment in their most priceless resource, young people. It is an investment that pays liberal dividends. As numerous studies have shown, when the level of education is increased, the level of personal and private income is increased far beyond the added costs of education. Thus education improves the people's economic well-being far out of proportion to

[3] From *The Pursuit of Excellence: Education and the Future of America*, © 1958 by Rockefeller Brothers Fund, Inc., p. 34. Reprinted by permission of Doubleday & Company, Inc.

[4] *Op. cit.*, p. 35.

education used in defense of at nation .

its original cost. Those countries with the highest standards of living are inevitably the countries with the best educational programs. It is increasingly apparent that sound education is also quite fundamental to our national survival. A nation cannot maintain a sound defense posture in this era of international tension without large numbers of intelligent, well-trained persons in many critical areas of human endeavor.

The people of the United States spend 122 per cent more for gambling than they do for education; 37 per cent more for alcohol and tobacco; 33 per cent more for vacation travel; 22 per cent more for beauty preparations and services; 11 per cent more for recreation. A nation whose real per capita income, after all taxes, has risen over 60 per cent in the last twenty years can hardly be incapable of providing better schools. Clearly the effort that the United States makes to educate its people is not equal to its ability or its needs. As Walter Lippmann warned:

We must measure our educational effort as we do our military effort. That is to say, we must measure it not by what it would be easy and convenient to do, but by what it is necessary to do in order that the nation may survive and flourish. We have learned that we are quite rich enough to defend ourselves, whatever the cost. We must now learn that we are quite rich enough to educate ourselves as we need to be educated.[5]

Trends

Among the many discernible directions are these:

1. The increase in school population, the rising standards in education, and the decreased purchasing power of the dollar and the continued rise in national income obviously call for an increase in expenditures for public and private education.

2. A current trend is to continue present forms of federal aid to education, including school lunch, aid to federally affected areas, and the possible further extension of federal aid to general education.

3. In recent years the tendency has been to increase the proportion of funds supplied to local districts from state sources.

4. Aid for special services, such as the education of exceptional children, tends to increase.

5. Due to the shortage of classrooms, many

[5] Walter Lippmann, "The Shortage in Education," *The Atlantic Monthly*, vol. 193 (May, 1954), p. 38.

Fig. 16-12. Comparison of costs of education with other expenditures.

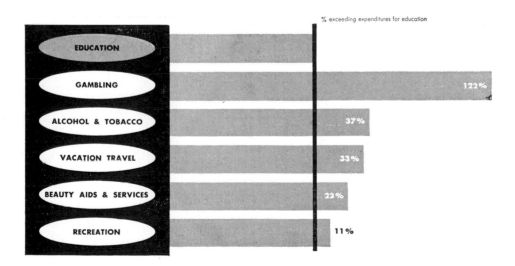

% exceeding expenditures for education

EDUCATION

GAMBLING — 122%

ALCOHOL & TOBACCO — 37%

VACATION TRAVEL — 33%

BEAUTY AIDS & SERVICES — 22%

RECREATION — 11%

states have established school bonding authorities or revolving funds for aiding districts which have reached the limit of their bonding power.

6. The inflation spiral is causing hardships for current and capital expenditures for school districts.

7. In view of the consolidation movement and the resultant increase in transportation of pupils, larger sums of money tend to be allocated for transportation.

8. Teachers' salaries will continue their upward trend.

9. The new accounting system, developed through the U.S. Office of Education, will improve school accounting throughout the nation. Machine accounting is on the increase.

10. Although public hearings on the school budget are not well attended, this safety valve continues to serve a useful function.

11. Fiscal publicity, as an aspect of public relations, is receiving increasing attention.

12. Assessment of property, including real and personal, is being reevaluated with a view to correcting inequities and securing more funds for education.

13. The perennial search continues for new sources of funds for schools.

14. Industry and philanthropic foundations, such as the Ford Foundation, are increasing scholarships and direct aid, especially to higher education. Some corporations grant scholarships to students, plus another amount to the college for part of the students' per capita costs.

15. Educational expenditures continue to be a long-term investment in democracy for which the public ought to be willing and able to pay.

Summary

Education in early America was supported largely private funds. As education became universal and compulsory, it came to be more public in its support and control. However, private elementary and secondary schools and colleges continue to exist and are an important part of our educational system. About one-ninth of the cost of elementary and secondary education and two-thirds of the cost of higher education is borne privately.

The budget is an important instrument for the planning and control of school expenditures and receipts. The budget consists of three basic parts: the educational plan, the expenditure plan, and the financial plan. In public school districts, about 70 per cent of school funds is spent for instruction; operation and auxiliary services account for about 9 per cent each; fixed charges, maintenance, and general control account for 5 per cent each. About 55 per cent of public school revenues comes from county and local funds, 41 per cent from state funds, and 4 per cent from federal funds. However, the proportion of state support for education varies widely among the states. Most states allocate aid to the districts on the basis of need, providing larger sums for poor districts and smaller amounts for wealthier districts. This is known as equalization aid, since it guarantees a minimum foundation of expenditures for each district regardless of its wealth and at the same time provides financial leeway and incentive for local districts to exceed the foundation level.

The costs of public education have increased sharply for a number of reasons: increased school enrollments, longer attendance at schools, increased scope and quality of education, and rising costs. Further increases in school expenditures are inevitable. About $3\frac{1}{2}$ per cent of the total national income is spent for education. This should be increased to 5 per cent in the years ahead to achieve both higher quality and quantity. It is reasonable to believe that our prospering economy can easily afford this kind of support for education. However, this is not likely to eventuate unless the pattern of school revenue is revised to capitalize upon the more abundant yield of federal taxes.

Suggested activities

1. Prepare a report on the topic "The High Cost of Poor Education."
2. Trace the historical development of fiscal support for schools in the United States.
3. Trace the history of federal grants to education.
4. Study the history of school support in your state.
5. Defend or criticize the proposition: "Collect the money where it is and spend it where the pupils are."
6. Examine a school budget and evaluate its format and content.
7. Analyze an annual financial report of a school district.
8. Attend a public hearing on a school budget.
9. Find out how much it costs per year for current expenses to educate a pupil in the public schools of your state.
10. Find out the costs per student for current expenses in the institution that you are now attending.
11. Draw a large circle to represent a dollar. Divide it into segments to show where the school dollar goes in your district or state.
12. Draw a large circle to represent a dollar. Divide it into segments to show where the school dollar comes from in your district or state.
13. Make a list of the safeguards provided by law to protect against the fraudulent or unwise use of school money in your state.
14. Learn how your state institutions of higher learning are supported.
15. How are parochial and private schools and colleges supported?
16. Should private industry contribute more money for education? Why?
17. Prepare a report on the topic "The Relationship between Standard of Living and the Quality of Education."

Bibliography

Books

American Association of School Administrators: *School District Reorganization*, National Education Association, Washington, D.C., 1958, chap. 9. Shows how state-aid plans can influence the reorganization of school districts.

Burke, Arvid: *Financing Public Education in the United States*, Harper & Brothers, New York, 1957. Provides a background for policy and practice in public school finance, stressing expenditure problems.

Can Our Schools Get By with Less? National Education Association, Washington, D.C., 1958. Essentially a critical rebuttal to Freeman's *School Needs in the Decade Ahead*, presenting the case for higher school expenditures.

Chamber of Commerce of the United States: *Education—An Investment in People*, Washington, D.C., n.d. Graphical presentation of the relationship between education and the economic well-being of nations, states, and cities.

Citizens Speak Out on School Costs, National Education Association, Committee on Tax Education and School Finance, Washington, D.C., 1959. Summarizes well the issues inherent in school finance, drawing upon statements from outstanding citizens and commissions that have studied the problem.

Does Better Education Cost More?, National Education Association, Committee on Tax Education and School Finance, Washington, D.C., 1959. Cites numerous investigations of the relationship between educational costs and quality; concludes that good education must cost more.

Financing Public Education in the Decade Ahead, National Citizens Commission for the Public Schools, New York, 1954. An excellent forecast of the financial needs of education through 1965 with helpful statistics.

Freeman, Roger A.: *School Needs in the Decade*

Ahead, Institute for Social Science Research, Washington, D.C., 1958. A controversial book that presents the case against higher expenditure for schools, claiming that they are growing too fast and becoming too expensive.

Hunt, Herold C., and Paul R. Pierce: *The Practice of School Administration*, Houghton Mifflin Company, Boston, 1958, chap. 20. Discussion of fiscal planning, budgeting, sources of revenue, management of receipts, and distribution of funds.

Morphet, Edgar L., Roe L. Johns, and Theodore L. Reller: *Educational Administration: Concepts, Practices, and Issues*, Prentice-Hall, Inc., Englewood Cliffs, N.J., 1959, chaps. 20–22. Discusses school business administration and school finance with particular attention given to the major issues involved.

National Policy and the Financing of Public Schools, National Education Association, Committee on Tax Education and School Finance, Washington, D.C., 1959. Discusses local, state, and federal revenues in relation to the proper financing of expanded educational needs.

Public Understanding and Support for Education, American Council on Education, Washington, D.C., 1958. A brief statement of imperative propositions relating to education that need public understanding and support.

Periodicals

Bemis, Maynard: "Men and Money," *Phi Delta Kappan*, vol. 40 (March, 1959), pp. 240–242. Shows how the state and local sources of school revenue have been dried up by the expansion of federal tax levies.

Dale, Edwin L., Jr.: "Are We Americans Going Soft?" *The New York Times Magazine*, (December 1, 1957), pp. 21f. Demonstrates America's willingness to spend for material comforts but reluctance to support education; the unwholesomeness of this for the nation.

Engleman, Finis E.: "The White House Conference and School Finance," *NEA Journal*, vol. 44 (October, 1955), pp. 397–398. Discusses the financial needs of education and the ability of our economy to support it at a higher level.

Johns, R. L.: "Where's the Money Coming from?" *NEA Journal*, vol. 46 (November, 1957), pp. 525–527. Analyzes federal, state, and local tax structures and their shortcomings with respect to educational finance.

Lippmann, Walter: "The Shortage in Education," *The Atlantic Monthly*, vol. 193 (May, 1954), pp. 35–38. Argues that education is as vital to national survival as is military defense and shows that educational effort is not equal to the needs or ability of the nation.

McCloskey, Gordon: "What Is the Value of Education?" *NEA Journal*, vol. 47 (February, 1958), pp. 115–117. A collection of statements from outstanding Americans about the value of education to individuals and to the nation.

Meyers, Anges E.: "The Nation's Future Will Be Won or Lost in the Classroom," *The School Executive*, vol. 77 (June, 1958), pp. 47–50. Powerful testimony is presented to a congressional committee on the urgent need for federal support for education.

National Education Association: "Can America Afford Better Schools?" *NEA Journal*, vol. 48 (February, 1959), insert. Presents in simplified graphical form the problems underlying the financing of education.

Norton, John K.: "Current Proposals for Federal Promotion and Support of Education in the States," *Teachers College Record*, vol. 59 (April, 1958), pp. 367–378. An analysis of the National Defense Education Act, its strengths and shortcomings, and other proposals for federal support.

Russell, James E.: "The High Price of Poor Education," *NEA Journal*, vol. 47 (February, 1958), pp. 111–112. Argues that the cost of correcting the consequences of poor education is more expensive in the long run.

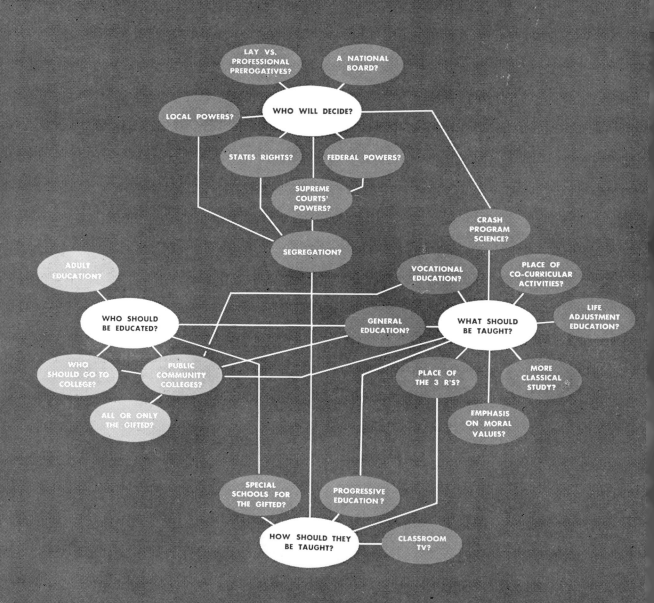

PART FIVE

LAY VS. PROFESSIONAL PREROGATIVES?

A NATIONAL BOARD?

LOCAL POWERS?

WHO WILL DECIDE?

STATES RIGHTS?

FEDERAL POWERS?

SUPREME COURTS' POWERS?

SEGREGATION?

CRASH PROGRAM SCIENCE?

ADULT EDUCATION?

VOCATIONAL EDUCATION?

PLACE OF CO-CURRICULAR ACTIVITIES?

WHO SHOULD BE EDUCATED?

GENERAL EDUCATION?

WHAT SHOULD BE TAUGHT?

LIFE ADJUSTMENT EDUCATION?

WHO SHOULD GO TO COLLEGE?

PUBLIC COMMUNITY COLLEGES?

PLACE OF THE 3 R'S?

MORE CLASSICAL STUDY?

ALL OR ONLY THE GIFTED?

EMPHASIS ON MORAL VALUES?

SPECIAL SCHOOLS FOR THE GIFTED?

PROGRESSIVE EDUCATION?

HOW SHOULD THEY BE TAUGHT?

CLASSROOM TV?

Interpretation of
education

The concluding chapter deals with some of the issues and trends in American education. They are organized under the four major topics used in this volume: (1) organization and administration, (2) areas of public education, (3) personnel, and (4) provisions for educational materials and environment. The issues presented are challenges to thoughtful study. A discussion of them, either in the classroom or elsewhere, invokes that fundamental principle of civil liberties which Voltaire expressed succinctly in the words: "I disapprove of what you say, but I will defend to the death your right to say it."

The nature of current criticisms of education is also explored in relation to the larger context of forces and controversies at work in society at large.

This part serves as a review or overview of the 16 aspects of education discussed in preceding chapters. This synthesis helps to bind the significant components into a dynamic whole—American education.

chapter 17

Issues in
American
education

The story is told of a pilot forced to parachute from his disabled plane during the war. Immediately upon his return to his air base, he hastened to the parachute building to express his gratitude to the noncom there for the perfect care of the parachute which had saved his life. The noncom replied somewhat philosophically, "You know, Lieutenant, in this work we never get any complaints!"

Certainly educators do not enjoy such freedom from complaint. Few if any institutions in American life are subject to such careful scrutiny and intensive criticism as the public school. Although the criticism of education is as old as the schools themselves, it seems clear that criticism has been increasing in both scope and intensity. For example, a look at *The Education Index* shows that the number of articles in the professional literature relating to criticisms of American education has increased remarkably.

Old issues continue to be the source of wide controversy while new issues constantly arise. Some of the criticisms strike at the very heart of public education, even questioning whether universal public education should continue to exist. Others focus upon fringe issues.

This chapter deals with a number of the more crucial contemporary issues in education. Some are stated briefly, others are analyzed in detail. Many of the issues are interrelated, depending for their solution upon the resolution of prior questions. Because of the limitations of space, complete treatment cannot be given to all issues. In most instances, both sides of the issue are presented. In the discussions which follow, it is possible that the biases of the writers are evident. So be it. However, it is not intended that these discussions shall eventuate in a final, arbitrary solution to any of the problems. If attention is drawn to the most fundamental issues confronting education and the reader is helped to consider these problems more rationally, the purpose of the chapter will have been achieved.

THE PHENOMENA OF CRITICISM

Before undertaking an analysis of contemporary issues of education, it is important that certain phenomena regarding criticism of education be understood.

Responsible, constructive criticism is desirable. Discussion is the best antidote for dogmatism and complacency. As Macaulay, the great English historian, observed, "Men are never so likely to settle a question rightly, as when they discuss it freely." Criticism, if honest and rational, causes open-minded people to reexamine assumptions, gather and evaluate evidence, consider alternatives, and view problems anew. Through these processes of rational inquiry, educational practices and policies are often reassessed and improved. For example, some years ago Rudolf Flesch wrote a best seller entitled *Why Johnny Can't Read.* It forced educators to gather evidence concerning Johnny's reading ability and the effectiveness of modern teaching methods in reading. Old research was reviewed and new research undertaken on this important question. Objective study of the research evidence did not support Flesch's allegations. However, the important point is that a fundamental educational question was raised and subjected to widespread reexamination. Certainly there is more widespread knowledge today, among both teachers and parents, regarding the teaching of reading as a result of Flesch's book. More recently, criticism of the school's neglect of the gifted child has resulted in adaptations of the school program to provide more adequately for talented children and youth.

In recognition of the value of honest and responsible criticism, good schools make provision for the encouragement of discussion through PTA meetings, open meetings of the board of education, budget hearings, advisory committees, teachers' councils, student councils, administrative cabinets, and a variety of other arrangements. Schools that fail to encourage responsible criticism are implying that their policies cannot stand public inspection or that their own judgment is infallible.

The schools are the center of intense public interest. People can become most aroused over those institutions that affect their children. A proposal to admit Negroes to a white church may generate little public interest, while a proposal to integrate the public schools may turn a community upside down. Quite understandably, people have an intense interest in the educational well-being of their children.

Moreover, education is big business. It represents by far the largest local expenditure in most communities. The price is high and it is increasing. The public is not inclined to pay the freight willingly unless it has an opportunity to examine the needs and resources carefully. On the other hand, it is pretty clear that most people are eager to provide the best that they can afford for their children when the need is made clear.

Because education is subject to close local control, the public is more responsive to educational problems than to many others. If a citizen is displeased with the route of a new highway, he must usually visit the state capitol to be heard. In all probability, his complaint will not reach the people with the real power of decision-making in this instance. On the other hand, if he is concerned over his child's schooling, he can walk down the block and be assured of a hearing by the local school board. If he considers his income tax too high, there is little that he can do about it immediately and directly. But if he believes his school tax is too high, he can vote down the school budget within a few months.

While educators may be distressed and distracted at times by the public's vigorous exercise of its interest in education, they have real satisfaction in knowing that they are working in an enterprise that commands such public concern.

The schools are a convenient scapegoat. When Russia preceded the United States in placing a satellite in outer space, many people were sure that the sole fault lay with our schools. When the number of cases of juvenile delinquency rise, there are those who are certain that the fault is with the schools. If young people appear irreligious, it is concluded that the schools must be godless. Folks like to seek simple answers for complex problems. As pointed out later, schools often mirror the values and the shortcomings of society. In reality, weaknesses ascribed to the schools often have much deeper roots in the weaknesses of the home, the church, and the entire society.

Everyone thinks he is expert on educational matters. Most folks wouldn't think of criticizing a surgeon's handling of an operation or a lawyer's conduct of a case. Indeed, most folks wouldn't even dare criticize a TV repairman's approach to an inoperative TV set. Yet most people have no hesitancy in advising a teacher about reading instruction or telling the superintendent what's wrong with textbooks. Since everyone has gone through school himself, he regards himself as a qualified expert on education. The teacher has less professional autonomy, less privacy in his practice, and less insulation from public criticism than any other professional worker, with the possible exception of the minister.

Almost every criticism of education has some basis in fact somewhere. Much of the criticism of education is of the "I know a child who can't read" variety. Certainly there are individual instances to support almost any criticism that is made. There are some children who, for one reason or another, haven't learned to read. There are high schools that, for one reason or another, teach no chemistry. There are schools with soft curriculums. There are teachers who are poorly educated. Thus the problem becomes one of recognizing and admitting weaknesses where they exist without employing drastic remedies that would repudiate the good and the true.

Critics are usually more vocal than supporters. Critics have a way of making known their complaints. But people who are satisfied with the schools seldom go out of their way to make known their satisfaction. The critic is much more visible and vocal than the supporter. Thus educators are often the victims of a distorted image of public opinion.

These observations have been made, not to minimize the importance of honest criticism or to apologize for the conditions under which it is manifest, but rather to encourage intelligent understanding of criticism and enlightened discussion of issues confronting American education.

THE NATURE OF THE ISSUES

Fundamentally, there are four classic issues in American education: "Who shall be educated?" "What shall be taught?" "How shall it be taught?" "Who will decide?" These issues have been debated in one form or another since the early days of the Republic and such debates will probably continue. Although different controversies erupt from time to time, many of them are ramifications of these basic issues. For example, during the near hysteria over subversive influence in American life in the early 1950s, much controversy was generated over the censoring of textbooks. Although nearly all could agree that subversive textbooks were undesirable, the real issue was: "Who will decide what textbooks are subversive?" Teachers insisted that this was a professional prerogative and that their academic freedom was at stake. Some laymen insisted that they must exercise this function if the nation was to be saved from subversive influence in the schools.

Issues in American education differ in nature. Some, like the segregation issue, are contested largely in the realm of legal opinion even though they involve morality as well. Others, like the question of whether academic standards are being eroded, are subject to scientific investigation. Others, such as the place of athletics in the school program, are largely philosophic in nature.

Since the early days of the republic,
several basic issues have been paramount
on the educational scene.
As long as men are free to debate and decide,
Americans will continue discussing
and evaluating these issues.
They may be stated in simple form:

Superior students only?

Who shall be educated?

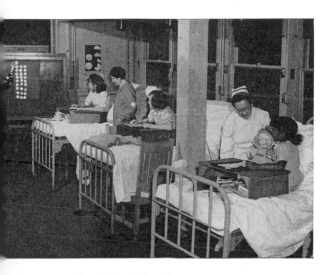

Atypical children?

Adults?

How shall they be taught?

For example, what is the proper place of educational television?

Does the use of television in education threaten close student-teacher relations?

THE NATURE OF THE CRITICS

Critics range all the way from competent, sober, thoughtful, constructive persons to carping, incompetent, irrational, and sometimes vicious propagandists. Many are sincerely interested in improving schools. Others clearly

wish to destroy or, at best, to severely circumscribe public education. Most of the more vocal critics appear to be professional educators and professional writers. Both of these groups include people who support and criticize education.

THE EXTENT AND EFFECT OF CRITICISM

In general, it appears that the more destructive critics have not had very much impact upon public opinion. A study by the NEA[1] revealed that the vast majority of teachers across the country reported that there had been little or no destructive criticism of public education in their communities. They reported little evidence that local critics were incited by the national critics. A number of polls have been conducted to measure public opinion concerning education. In general, these studies have shown that about a third of the people are very well satisfied with their schools; about half are fairly well satisfied; and about a sixth are dissatisfied or have no opinion.[2]

Various opinions with respect to the major issues in education are reviewed in the following sections which are organized around the chapter headings of this book.

Organization and administration

NATIONAL PROGRAM

Should the federal government participate in the financial support of education? Although the federal government has provided financial support for education ever since the Northwest Ordinance of 1785, the issue continues to be widely debated. Most of this support has been for special purposes, designed to encourage some limited aspect of education, such as school

[1] *State of the Nation in Regard to Attacks on the Schools and Problems of Concern to Teachers,* National Education Association, Washington, D.C., 1955, pp. 2–3.
[2] *Public Opinion Polls on American Education,* National Education Association, Washington, D.C., 1958, pp. 1–12.

lunches, vocational education, or research. Argument continues to rage over the desirability of both special- and general-purpose support.

Those who oppose federal support argue that undesirable control has resulted in many instances, such as in the case of the Smith-Hughes Act. The Hoover Commission on the Organization of the Executive Branch of the Government concluded that:

Grants-in-aid programs have removed large areas of discretionary power from the hands of state officials and have transferred a measurable degree of policy-making to the national government.

Some folks are concerned about the increasing concentration of power in the hands of the national government and see federal financial support for education as another step in that direction.

The advocates of federal financial support for education, although opposed to this type of control of education, do not believe that control must be feared. Governor Williams of Michigan, for example, points out that "our Federal government is not our enemy . . . it is not a foreign government . . . it is our government, as much our instrument to achieve the needs of the people as is a local city council, a local school board or a State legislature." Citing the Morrill Acts and the GI bill as examples, Williams concludes that "the Federal government has given direct help to schools and students in the past without the dire results which those who oppose Federal aid predict will be forthcoming."

The opponents of federal support argue that it is unnecessary. They contend that the states and local communities, if they were to put their tax structures in order and make reasonable effort, could afford to pay for the schools that they need. They cite the warning of the Joint Conference of Representatives of the United States Congress and the Governors' Conference: "Our states must cease relying

is its continued growth justified by the reduction in accident rates by those who have taken it?

upon the federal government to do things for them and their citizens which they can do for themselves as well as, or better than, the federal government." They view with alarm the increases in federal taxes and in the national debt and conclude that the government cannot afford this added financial burden.

However, advocates of federal support for education argue that some states cannot provide adequate education even if they spend all of their state income for schools. In many cases, the states with the most children and the least money are spending the highest percentage of their income for schools, thereby making great effort. Some states have six times as

What shall be taught?

Is driver education, for example, a fad and frill or . . .

much wealth per child as others. Thus, some children are destined to inferior education by the accident of the location of their birth. This is held to be unfair because the wealth of the nation is the product of the cooperation of the whole population.

Advocates of federal support point out also that the federal government, with its vast and increasing taxing machinery, collects four out of every five tax dollars but pays only 3 per cent of the cost of education; moreover, federal taxation is drying up the sources of state and local taxes. As Frank Bane, director of the Council of State Governments, puts it, the federal tax collector fishes for revenue with a net, the state collector uses a hook and line, and the local tax collector uses a bent pin. Thus,

What is the proper relation between public education and religion?

The American tradition of separation of church and state discourages the use of public money in private schools. It prevents, also, sectarian instruction in the public schools.

Many citizens, desiring religious instruction and services for their children, send them to privately supported schools.

the schools cannot benefit appreciably from our rapidly expanding national prosperity as long as they are so largely dependent upon the local property tax.

It is pointed out also that the federal government provides financial support for many other enterprises of less consequence, such as highways, farm production, slum clearance, and many others. (Apparently no one argues that the states can meet these needs better or that federal control results.) In many cases, federal support for these purposes is on a matching basis. This provides an additional handicap for schools. State governments, when pressed for economy, are hesitant to reduce expenditures for highways since cutting a dollar of state money here means the loss of a matching dollar from the federal government. However, the elimination of a dollar from state funds for education is accompanied by no such penalty. Since our national security and our economic prosperity are so dependent upon the vitality of our educational system, education would appear to merit more adequate federal support.

Federal support for education inevitably involves religious considerations. Some insist that public monies must not be allocated to private schools. Others contend that federal money should follow the child, regardless of whether he is enrolled in a public or private school. Attempts have been made to dodge this

However, public schools nevertheless deal with morality and values in many facets of the curriculum.

issue at the federal level by proposing that money should be distributed to schools by the states in the same way that state monies are now distributed. This would place the responsibility for this issue at the state level.

The segregation issue has also impeded federal support for education. Amendments have been added to bills to prevent the distribution of money to segregated school systems. This has been done in the name of forcing compliance with the Supreme Court decision on segregation. But this has invariably contributed to the defeat of the bill by alienating the support of Southern legislators. Many people feel that the segregation issue is a judicial matter and should not be confused with the legislative function of enacting federal financial support.

Controversy arises also with respect to the apportionment of funds among the states. Some argue that federal support should be in the form of equalization, providing substantially more money per child to those states with the least per-pupil wealth. This would tend to equalize educational opportunity among the states in the same way that state equalization aid equalizes opportunity among districts within the state. This is thought desirable by many because of the very uneven ability of the states to support schools. However, this arrangement is not likely to find sanction from the wealthier states.

In looking toward the future, it seems clear that the federal government will continue to increase its share of the financial support for education. The participants in the White House Conference on Education, by a ratio of more than two to one, favored increased federal support in financing public education. According to recent public opinion polls, the general public favors this policy by an even larger margin of about three to one. [Roper concluded that] the orators who declaim against too much Federal aid to education are in for a shock—the public does not agree with them. . . . The answers are startling. They reveal that the public is strong for more and more Federal aid—not just for school buildings but . . . for

whatever is needed to keep us abreast in our race for knowledge.[3]

This federal participation in school finance will come to be regarded not as aid in the form of a handout but rather as a necessary and desirable means of bringing our rapidly expanding national prosperity to bear upon the vitality of our schools through the increased taxing capacity of the federal government. This is the reason that the term "federal support" rather than "federal aid" has been used throughout this discussion.

Shall the United States Supreme Court have authority over the states in matters of educational policy? As noted in Chapter 1, the United States Supreme Court is interested in educational policy or practice only when it conflicts with the United States Constitution. In 1954 the Court ruled that the segregation by race of students in public schools was a violation of the Fourteenth Amendment which guarantees "equal protection" to all. The court held that separate school facilities could not be equal and ordered the states to integrate public schools with "deliberate speed."

This decision has precipitated one of the most violent and crucial controversies in the history of American education. On moral grounds, it is argued that racial discrimination in schools—whether in the South or elsewhere—is in sharp conflict with the basic democratic doctrine of the equality of mankind; that it weakens democracy and the United States in the cold war struggle. It is argued also that the expense of maintaining a dual school system is an economic luxury that the states cannot afford. Many other arguments have also been advanced.

Advocates of segregation, on the other hand, have contended that separate Negro schools are often equal to the white schools in quality; that the integration of schools strikes at the heart of one of the South's deepest customs; that attempts to integrate schools may result in violence; that the quality of education will

[3] Elmo Roper, "Trend Seems to Favor U.S. Aid to Education," *Washington Sunday Star*, May 12, 1957.

suffer by mixing white and Negro students; and that many years will be needed to achieve integration if it can be achieved at all.

Legally, the debate over segregation centers around the collision of state and federal powers. Education is a legal function of the states. Nevertheless, the United States Supreme Court stands as the watchdog of the Constitution, circumscribing practices in any field that violate the Constitution. While there are some who argue that the court's decision is "an illegal encroachment upon our sovereign powers," most constitutional lawyers agree that there can be no legal authority superior to the Constitution and no judicial jurisdiction higher than the United States Supreme Court.

Many years have passed since the Court's historic and controversial decision. What progress has been made? Some would say that progress, particularly in the Deep South, has been much too slow. Others would argue that progress has been too fast. Despite widespread publicity given to a few cases, there has been little violence in most areas where desegregation has been put into effect. Since the issue strikes so hard at one of the South's oldest customs and since it is laden with so much emotion, it is quite clear that it will be many years before it can be fully implemented. Unfortunately, in many communities leadership is being provided in this struggle not by moderate, fair-minded persons of good will but by radical rabble-rousers. Unfortunately, race relations have suffered and both sides have become more entrenched rather than more conciliatory in their positions. Obviously this is one of the bitterest and most fundamental issues ever to confront American education. However, it is by no means the first time that America has been so sharply divided. It must be hoped that eventually this problem will be solved in the American tradition of respect for law, recognition of the brotherhood of mankind, and protection of equal rights under the law. Perhaps it can be hoped that adults may someday come to face this problem with the open-minded acceptance of one's fellow man that is so typical of children.

Should there be a minimum, basic program of education for the nation as a whole? Just as several states have prepared a foundation program for the schools within their boundaries, so too the United States as a unit should set up minimum standards to be met by all schools of the nation. The Educational Policies Commission has outlined the kind and amount of schooling that would increase the positive economic effects of education. This program calls for lifting the poorest schools to a minimum of efficiency.

Should there be a national board of education comparable to a local board of education? That is, should there be a national board of education which should determine nationwide policies and evaluate practices in education?

At present, no such national board really functions for all education. It has been argued that a competent commission, selecting the United States Commissioner of Education as its own executive without reference to party politics, would follow the American tradition of acknowledging the function of education in American democracy and would separate its leadership and administration from other governmental functions. There are some educational organizations which have officially recommended the establishment of the U.S. Office of Education as an independent, adequately financed agency, directed by a national board of education appointed by the President.

STATE SYSTEMS

What is the nature of the state's responsibility for providing universal free public education? This question, and, of course, many related questions, have been brought into sharp focus as a result of the United States Supreme Court's decision on segregation in the public schools. Several Southern states have amended their constitutions or enacted legislation which provides for the closing of public schools to evade compliance with the Court's decision.

The courts are not disposed to tolerate this kind of maneuvering. As Justice Frankfurter once observed, the Bill of Rights "nullifies sophisticated as well as simple-minded modes of discrimination."

Shall the individual states, rather than the federal government, be primarily responsible for public education? That the states are in their own areas the legitimate units of educational control seems to be manifest for several reasons. The debates of the constitutional conventions in the various states reveal that a great majority of the delegates felt that it was the duty of a state to establish and maintain a system of public education for the purpose of educating its citizens. The states are the generally accepted legislative units for public education, whereas the contained areas—district, town, city, township, community, and county—are the units to which much administration has been delegated. State responsibility for education is firmly established in the constitutions of the states, reinforced by court decisions, and buttressed by long tradition.

Shall the states, rather than the local communities, be primarily responsible for the ultimate control of public education? Controversy frequently arises over the proper balance of authority between state and local government. The major problem confronting the American people is not to decide a priori at which level of government the major responsibility shall be fixed, but to study educational needs and determine which level of government—local, county, state, or national—can best carry on particular functions.

Shall the state assume greater responsibility in the support of public education? Shall the state, as a central agency, increase its appropriations for public education? The trend, as evidenced by statistics, is toward decreasing the amount of local support and increasing state support.

Shall the state superintendent of public instruction be elected rather than appointed? Shall he run for office or shall the office seek him? The trend is toward appointing state superintendents. The choice may be made by the governor or preferably by the state board of education. Just as the popular election of city school superintendents has become obsolete, so too the election of county and state superintendents is giving way to appointment.

COUNTY AND INTERMEDIATE UNITS

What shall be the role and nature of the intermediate unit? Three-fourths of the states have intermediate units—intermediate in the sense that they function between the local and state levels. In most of these states, the intermediate district is coterminous with the county. Yet it is clear that the county is not always the logical boundary for intermediate districts. In sparsely populated areas, several counties should be combined to form an intermediate unit large enough to function effectively. In more populous areas, the county should be subdivided into several intermediate units. Yet, because of the long tradition of the county in American government, it is often most difficult to alter its structure in relation to school organization.

The county unit began as an arm of state government, a downward extension of state control. Yet it is apparent that the proper role of this unit lies in leadership and service rather than control. While some states have made progress in this direction, the historic role of administrative control is difficult to modify in many instances.

How can school districts that are large enough to be educationally adequate and economically efficient be established through reorganization without losing local control and interest? It is known that a great many school districts are too small in both population and wealth to offer an educational program that is adequate at a cost that is reasonable. This results in both marginal educational opportunity for some children and an exhorbitant cost to the taxpayer. Consolidation of small districts tends to overcome these difficulties but it does so, particularly in rural areas, at the cost of removing some degree of local control and interest in schools. This problem is particularly noteworthy in county unit plans where control and initiative for education have been removed entirely from local communities and placed at the county level. Simply stated, the choice is between being big enough to be efficient or small enough to retain control locally.

Should provision for school district reorganization be permissive or mandatory? Although the state has the legal power to reorganize districts at its pleasure, many states are hesitant to exercise this power arbitrarily, feeling that this is an unwarranted invasion of local control and initiative. Yet progress is often painfully slow under permissive arrangements. Meanwhile, a generation of students may suffer from the handicap of an inadequate program. Stated simply, the choice is between speed through mandatory legislation and dilatory action with the preservation of local initiative.

Should the county superintendent of schools be appointed by a county board of education rather than elected by the people? He ought to be given every opportunity to be a professional educator rather than a professional politician. Unfortunately, the states that do not have appointive county educational officers are very slow to accept this preferable method of obtaining educational leadership in the county.

LOCAL DISTRICTS

Should the local school district be separate and independent of other branches of local government? Political scientists have generally argued against the creation of special boards elected at separate elections and separate taxing authorities. This argument holds that there will be less duplication of services, less overburdening of taxes, and less division of responsibility and accountability. Proponents of this point of view would favor boards of education appointed by and responsible to the mayor, school budgets approved by the town council, and integration of the school district's taxing authority with that of the municipality. This results in a dependent board of education merged into municipal government. This pattern of organization is fairly common among city school districts.

Most educators, on the other hand, take the position that education is too vital a concern to be equated with highways, agriculture, and law enforcement. Because of its unique nature and singular importance, it is felt that it justifies a separate organization independent from general government and unencumbered by partisan politics.

The weight of opinion seems to be with the latter position, which is reflected in practice in the great majority of school districts. However, there appears to be little disposition on the part of dependent, politically oriented school districts to modify their structure.

What are the proper prerogatives of lay and professional persons in controlling education? Much confusion arises over the proper division of control of education by lay versus professional persons at the local level, as well as at the state and national level. Are lay committees competent to censor textbooks, to select principals, to participate in curriculum planning, to evaluate teaching methods, to plan school buildings?

At the state and national levels there are many instances of groups organized to bring about change in education, often *without involving educators* in any fundamental way. Certification requirements for teachers are established by *lay* boards, a practice virtually without precedent in other professions. At the national level, the President in 1957 appointed a group of advisers, completely void of educators, to write a bill for emergency federal aid for school building construction (which turned out to be a disastrous venture).

To what extent is it desirable—either for education or for the profession—for professional autonomy to be diluted in these ways? To what extent would other professions tolerate, much less encourage, this abdication of professional prerogatives to lay persons?

Should the superintendent be the sole execu-

*tive, reporting directly to the board of educa-
tion and accountable for the entire educational
program?* Or should there be a business manager, usually a layman, coordinate with the
superintendent and responsible for the business affairs of the district? The principle of
unity of command appears to be thoroughly
established and accepted in virtually all but
educational organizations. The notion of two
coordinate bosses is as wrong in education as
it must be in all human endeavor. Yet examples
of dual control continue to exist in many educational organizations, particularly in city
school systems.

Areas of public education

PRE-ELEMENTARY EDUCATION

*Shall public education be limited to school-
ing in certain areas, as elementary and secondary levels, or shall it be broadened and
lengthened to embrace lifelong learning?*

Specifically, shall early education be incorporated as part of the public school system?
It is difficult to answer the question as to when
American public education should begin. Very
few public schools offer both a nursery school
and a kindergarten. Many persons oppose early
education for all children at public expense
because of the additional taxes involved. Despite this objection, the American people are
gradually accepting the theory that at least kindergartens may be included as part of the
public school system. The American Federation of Labor, the National Congress of Parents
and Teachers, the American Association of
University Women, and other civic and professional organizations have lent their support to
the movement for nursery schools and kindergartens. The fact that nearly one-third of the
married women are employed away from home
has stimulated the demand for early education
for their young children. Most states have
taken a generous attitude toward kindergarten
support, but, by and large, few states and local

communities have furnished nursery education.

ELEMENTARY EDUCATION

*Has students' achievements in the three R's
deteriorated?* Some critics contend that progressive education has neglected the three
R's. Many of the critics treat this issue as if it
were a matter of opinion rather than a matter of
fact. Consider the evidence typically advanced
by the critics. One asserts that *in his opinion*
"the literacy of public school graduates deteriorated during the inter-war period." A
magazine alleges, without citing a single study,
that tests showed that the quality of American
education has deteriorated in the past half-
century. Another refers to an unspecified number of unidentified people who *believe* that
education is poorer today. One author reaches
the same conclusion based upon *his recollec-
tion* of school achievement a generation ago as
compared with that of today. A typical lament
for the better old days is this one:

When we were boys, boys had to do a little work
in school. They were not coaxed; they were hammered, and you had to learn. In these more fortunate times, elementary education has become in
many places a sort of vaudeville show. The child
must be kept amused and learns what he pleases.
Many sage teachers scorn the old-fashioned rudiments and it seems to be regarded as between mis-
fortune and a crime for a child to learn to read.

Does this sound like a contemporary complaint? Actually it is from an editorial in the
New York Sun in 1902! As Will Rogers said,
"Things ain't as good as they used to be and
probably never was."

Actually, what are the facts? The director
of the Research Division of the NEA compared recent students' scores with those of
students several decades ago on the same tests.
The gist of his conclusion is that students today
do as well or better in the fundamentals; that
they make progress more efficiently; that they
make better use of knowledge; and that they

study in many new fields, such as intercultural relations, which were not included in the curriculum a generation ago.[4]

Professor Arthur Gates of Teachers College, Columbia University, author of a standardized reading test that has been widely used in elementary schools for many years, recently restandardized his tests. Norms had to be moved upward substantially because, in a period of twenty-five years, elementary school pupils had improved significantly in reading achievement.[5]

Similarly, the California Test Bureau, in reviewing test scores of a quarter of a million students over a ten-year period, found that their achievement in reading, mathematics, and language usage had improved by 12 per cent over a period of only ten years.[6]

The College Entrance Examination Board, which conducts college entrance tests all over the nation, finds no decline in the quality of college freshmen of today as compared with that of a generation ago. It considers this especially noteworthy in view of the increased percent of college-age youth now going to college.[7]

Many other similar studies could be cited. In virtually every instance they reveal an advance in achievement by today's students in almost every area of learning. And this is despite the fact that today's scholar is younger per grade.

In spite of the charges of the critics, the vast majority of the American public do not believe that education was better in the good old days than it is today.[8]

Should promotion and reporting practices be based upon rigid standards of achievement? Should students' achievement be evaluated in relation to rigid academic standards applied to all students, regardless of their ability? Should pupils, regardless of ability, be held back until they have met the fixed standards for that grade? Certain critics have contended that reporting practices have become meaningless when pupils' progress is evaluated in terms of their own potential rather than in comparison with arbitrary grade standards for all children. They contend also that automatic promotion of students reduces incentive by eliminating competition and removing the threat of retardation. They see in this a general deterioration of intellectual discipline. For example, one writer compares American and Russian practice in this regard (a fashionable approach in these days):

A disturbing paradox in comparative education is revealed by Russia's triumph with the Sputniks. How is it that the Communists who decry competition, emphasize it so strongly in their schools while we, claiming to believe in free enterprise, have gone so far to eliminate the competitive spirit from the classrooms? . . . In the Soviet schools there is no promotion until the pupil has passed examinations specifically designed to weed out the unfit. . . . By contrast, . . . in many of our public schools annual promotion is now all but automatic, with no relation to individual effort. . . . Intellectual competition is viewed with mistrust and anything more than perfunctory discipline is frowned upon as frustrating.[9]

However, another writer supplies the answer to the question in the same issue of the same journal:

The highly demanding (Russian) curriculum fails to carry along with it a good part of the student body. Some serious observers of the Soviet scene suggest that the washed-out middle school students serve as a source of disaffection, swell the numbers of juvenile delinquents who are re-

[4] Frank W. Hubbard, "Volleyed and Thundered," *NEA Journal*, vol. 43 (October, 1954), pp. 397–400.

[5] Hollis S. Caswell, "The Attack on American Schools," from the *Annual Report to the Trustees*, 1957–58, Bureau of Publications, Teachers College, Columbia University, New York, 1958, p. 5.

[6] *A Comparison of Pupil Achievement Before and After 1945*, Bulletin of the California Test Bureau, Los Angeles.

[7] "The Truth about Our Public Schools," *Changing Times*, vol. 8 (June, 1954), pp. 7–11.

[8] Henry T. Boss, "Questionnaire Results Analyzed," *Phi Delta Kappan*, vol. 37 (November, 1955), pp. 66–68.

[9] Felix Morley, "The State of the Nation," *Nation's Business*, vol. 46 (January, 1958), p. 21.

luctant to join the labor force on the low level to which their record in education has condemned them.[10]

Most studies have shown that most repeaters do not do better work during their second year in the same grade. In many cases retardation is accompanied by loss of interest and self-confidence and undesirable social and emotional manifestations. Actually the number of schools practicing 100 per cent promotion is as small as the number of schools practicing a rigid standard of promotion. Thus the trend is away from rigid promotion practices to a more flexible multiple-standard policy.[11]

Stephen Corey has advanced perhaps the most defensible position with regard to promotion and reporting policy:

Assuming that whatever children learn in school is significant to them, the standards a particular youngster is expected to reach should be (1) high, and (2) attainable, and (3) should not preclude achieving high standards in respect to other desirable school activities. All children should measure up to school standards that are, for each of them, high enough to assure effort and genuine learning. There is, of course, no point in setting tasks for any child that he cannot achieve. This leads to an academic dream world that no one wants. It would be foolhardy, too, to establish standards for academic achievement altogether apart from reasonable standards in physical or emotional health or any other important school learning.[12]

Thus many schools are abandoning organization of pupils by grades, particularly in the early elementary period, seeking better ways of flexible grouping of learners according to their ability and achievement. In all probability, the future will see continued experimental

practice in this direction. The trend toward grouping, evaluating, and promoting children according to their individual abilities will increase in the years ahead, the critics notwithstanding.

Shall the elementary school be reorganized? The trend continues toward a rearrangement of the eight elementary grades. At the lower end there is a dipping down into pre-elementary education. The upper grades are gradually being recast into some type of secondary unit, such as the junior high school. Unfortunately many so-called junior high schools are too dominated by the philosophy and program of elementary education.

SECONDARY EDUCATION

Although many of the issues and trends in the elementary field apply also to secondary education, the latter has certain unique problems. Also some issues in secondary education arise again in higher education.

Who should attend secondary schools? This question is raised in various forms and is the most basic question raised with regard to secondary education. Traditionally the practice has been to provide secondary education for all American youth. As noted in Chapter 7, the proportion of high school youth has risen steadily until today nearly nine out of ten young people of high school age are enrolled. Yet the proposals of many of the critics would strike at the heart of this tradition of universal secondary education. One writer, for example, describes his interview with a famous critic of secondary education—one who has advocated a tough, single-track high school program that would weed out unmercifully those who are not intellectually superior. When asked what is to become of these less able students, the critic shrugged his shoulders, smiled, and said, "Let them dig ditches."[13] Thus the enforcement of rigid academic standards, the ruthless elimi-

10 *Nation's Business*, vol. 46 (January, 1958), p. 93.
11 National Education Association, "Ten Criticisms of Public Education," *Research Bulletin*, vol. 35 (December, 1957), p. 152.
12 Stephen M. Corey, "Are Our School Standards High Enough?" *Spotlight on Education*, Alumni Fellowship Fund Committee, Bureau of Publications, Teachers College, Columbia University, 1958, p. 1.

13 Robert L. Shayon, "Report from the Grass-roots," *The Saturday Review*, vol. 41 (September 13, 1958), p. 15.

nation of the intellectually less gifted, the creation of tough high schools would deny secondary education to a large number of youth.

This would represent the reversal of one of America's most basic and most fruitful traditions in secondary education. It is a revolutionary proposal that must be examined most carefully. It assumes that it is either not possible or desirable to educate all American youth up to the maximum of their ability through the secondary level.

As the Rockefeller Brothers Fund has pointed out, there need be no forced choice between *quality* and *quantity* of education. Our society has the ability and the obligation to educate everyone up to the level of his ability without sacrificing excellence in education.

Should separate high schools be established for the most able students? Many people advocate the creation of separate, high-quality secondary schools for the most gifted students. Admiral Hyman G. Rickover, creator of the atomic submarine, for example, has recommended the creation of a private "council of scholars" that would establish high national uniform standards for high schools. High schools accepting these standards would receive an official accreditation that would be denied to other high schools with less rigorous academic programs geared to the needs and abilities of less talented youth.[14]

James Bryant Conant, the noted educator, on the other hand, after a first-hand study of American high schools, disagrees with those who demand radical changes in our high schools. Conant urges that the comprehensive high school, serving all American youth, if it is large enough, is meeting the needs of both quality and quantity. However, he recommends that within the comprehensive high school, diversified grouping of students by ability be arranged so that the talented may be adequately challenged.[15]

[14] "Rickover Offers New School Plan," *The New York Times*, November 23, 1957, p. 1.

[15] James Bryant Conant, "Diversified Studies for Diversified Students," *National Parent-Teacher*, vol. 53 (October, 1958), pp. 4–6.

Most professional educators would hope to find within the comprehensive high school the modifications necessary to meet the needs of superior, average, and below average students. They would see, in the abandonment of this traditional melting pot agency, the loss of one of democracy's most liberating forces.

Is Russian secondary education better? The thesis has been advanced in recent years that Russia, by denying secondary education to students of inferior ability, has achieved a higher quality of high school education. Therefore this policy is advocated as the panacea for the alleged weaknesses of American secondary education. Many competent observers of the Russian educational scene have warned of the Soviet's total commitment to education— their race for knowledge as a means of national advancement—and the seriousness of this challenge to America.[16] However, it is also quite clear that comparisons of the Soviet or other European educational systems with our own are most hazardous. Only about 13 per cent of Russian youth of high school age attend secondary schools. In America nearly 90 per cent attend. Obviously, it is grossly unfair to attempt to compare the achievement of this small per cent of highly gifted students in Russia with the achievement of all American high school students. It would be much more appropriate to compare the achievement of all Russian high school students with the achievement of American National Honor Society students only. At the college level, comparisons should be made between all Russian or European college students with American Phi Beta Kappa students only. A comparison on this basis would not only be more fair but would also reflect much more favorably upon Ameri-

[16] See particularly Lawrence G. Derthick, "The Russian Race for Knowledge," *School Life*, vol. 40 (June, 1958), pp. 3–4; Andrew R. MacAndrew, "Are Soviet Schools Better than Ours?" *The Reporter*, vol. 18 (February 20, 1958), pp. 10–16; Herold C. Hunt, "An American Educator Views Soviet Education," *National Parent-Teacher*, vol. 53 (December, 1958), pp. 4–6; William H. E. Johnson, "Recent American Interest in Soviet Education," *Teachers College Record*, vol. 59 (May, 1958), pp. 474–480.

can education. As several observers have pointed out, the aims of Russian and European educational systems are so different from ours as to make comparisons unreal.

Oddly, many of the critics fail to mention other quite significant aspects of Soviet education, viz., that Russian teachers are very well paid, chosen on a highly selective basis, held in high esteem, and available in sufficient numbers; that classes are of reasonable size; that plenty of money is available; and that Russia spends a much higher proportion of her national income on education than does the United States.

It would seem most ironic if America were to alter her educational system in the direction of European education at the very time when European countries are moving in the direction of American education—free and universal for all! Every new nation established since World War II has created its educational system more closely in the image of the American than the European tradition. American educators are in wide demand as consultants to foreign governments seeking to reconstruct their educational systems. How wrong it would be for America to abandon its educational traditions at the very time when they are so eagerly emulated by so many other lands!

Do schools fail to challenge talented youth? Many critics argue that the presence of soft courses in the curriculum has distracted the gifted learner who should be pursuing more rigorous training. However, James Bryant Conant, in his study of 107 public high schools, discovered that most of the academically talented boys were studying mathematics and science, taking five solid subjects, and otherwise pursuing intellectually challenging work, despite the presence of life adjustment or other soft courses. On the other hand, Conant found that many high school girls, quite capable of high intellectual achievement, were not taking advanced courses in mathematics and science but were surpassing academically talented boys in their pursuit of advanced study of foreign languages.

Several critics, notably Arthur Bestor, have cited figures showing that the *per cent* of high school students studying mathematics, science, and languages has declined over the past fifty years.[17] However, as a number of educators have been careful to point out,[18] this decline in the per cent of students studying such courses is the result of the substantial change in high school population. In 1900, only very able, college-bound youth attended high schools, for the most part. Admittedly, a large per cent of this type of student did pursue tough academic curriculums. However, with the explosive increase in high school enrollments that included young people across the whole spectrum of ability, many non-college preparatory courses had to be introduced to meet the needs of these less gifted and less ambitious students. This has resulted in a reduction in the percentage of high school youth studying mathematics, science, and languages. However, if one considers all youth of high school age today and fifty years ago, the *percentage* of this figure who are studying mathematics, science, and physics has increased substantially. Obviously, the latter comparison is much more appropriate.

However, this is not to imply that high schools have reached the ultimate in challenging better students. There is no room for complacency. It must be admitted that many schools have failed to challenge academically gifted students to the utmost of their ability. As was noted in Chapter 7, many high schools are undertaking practices that seek to meet this need more fully.

Are many American high schools too small? Several critics, notably Arthur Bestor, have decried the fact that about a quarter of the high schools offer neither physics nor chemis-

[17] Arthur Bestor, "What Went Wrong with U.S. Schools?" *U.S. News and World Reports*, vol. 44 (January 24, 1958), pp. 68–77.
[18] Walter Eells, "Let's Talk Facts," *The School Executive*, vol. 76 (March, 1957), pp. 41–46; Harold C. Hand, "A Scholar's Devil Theory," *The High School Journal*, vol. 41 (April, 1958), pp. 270–278.

curriculum to satisfy community needs

try.[19] However, Bestor fails to point out that, almost without exception, these are the very small high schools that enroll less than 6 per cent of all high school students. While the figures cited may be substantially correct, the inference that is drawn is quite wrong. Bestor concludes that this has resulted from some sort of conspiracy by professional educators to deny youth training in mathematics and science. Actually, as a number of educators have pointed out,[20] it is simply a reflection of the inadequacies of the small high school, a problem that educators themselves have emphasized for many years. This problem has been discussed more fully in Chapter 3. However, the magnitude of the problem can be seen from the following simple set of data. The National Commission on School District Reorganization concluded that a satisfactory school district should have at least 1,200 pupils between the ages of six and eighteen.[21] Conant, in his study of American secondary education, concluded that a high school should have a graduating class of at least 100 students if it is to be large enough to provide a quality program.[22] Yet, according to a recent study, only 1 district in 10 has more than 1,200 pupils.[23] The median high school in the United States enrolls less than 200 students in the entire high school. Obviously these small high schools, while they serve a relatively small percentage of American youth, present a real obstacle in the improvement of high school education. Limited in both students and in finances, their programs are badly restricted. Truly it is impossible for them to offer well-balanced, comprehensive programs that meet

Small schools restricted.

the needs of all youth. This is indeed one of the urgent problems confronting American education. While it has been widely recognized by professional educators like Conant, it has been strangely ignored by some of the less rational critics like Bestor.

Are guidance services adequate for secondary youth? There are certainly a number of fine high schools that offer excellent guidance services to their students. However, it seems clear that guidance facilities are not adequate in most American high schools. Reference has already been made to the tremendous variety of employment opportunities available to American youth. The task of selecting a vocation, one of the most important choices in life, is usually accomplished at a most primitive level. This represents a tremendous wastage of manpower. Through lack of guidance, many youth are unaware of their interests and talents. Even if aware of them, they often lack help in capitalizing upon them for employment purposes. The task of finding an appropriate college and gaining entry is one which often requires expert guidance. Many young people with ability fail to attend college because of lack of motivation, encouragement, or money. Expert guidance could often provide these needs. Guidance is important also with respect to the social and emotional development of the student. Many small schools provide no specific guidance services. Even in larger high schools, guidance services are often notoriously inadequate. The National Defense Education Act, by providing subsidies for the extension and improvement of guidance, has improved this important facet of education.

Is the junior college secondary or higher education? As noted in Chapter 7, the appropriate place of the junior college is not yet universally accepted. The dynamic and most acceptable view, in the opinion of many, is that the junior college rises upward from the democratized secondary school level. It is believed that the junior college is closer in purpose and character to the secondary school than to the university.

[19] Arthur Bestor, "We Are Less Well Educated than 50 Years Ago," *U.S. News and World Reports*, vol. 41 (November 30, 1956), pp. 68–72.

[20] See Walter Eells, "Let's Talk Facts," *The School Executive*, vol. 76 (March, 1957), pp. 41–46.

[21] National Commission of School District Reorganization, *Your School District*, National Education Association, Washington, D.C., 1948, p. 87.

[22] James B. Conant, "Some Problems of the American High School," *Phi Delta Kappan*, vol. 40 (November, 1958), p. 55.

[23] Bureau of the Census, *Governments in the United States, 1957 Census of Governments*, vol. 1, no. 1, U.S. Department of Commerce, 1957, p. 1.

Shall higher education place more emphasis upon classical study? Shall higher education be dominated by the conservatists' emphasis upon the classics rather than by a progressive reliance upon an experimentalist theory of knowledge?

The outstanding exponent of classical knowledge is Robert M. Hutchins, who has deplored an "anti-intellectualism which denies, in effect, that man is a rational animal." Hutchins derides "the concept of the educational system as a gigantic play-pen in which the young are to amuse themselves. . . ." He advocates instead discussion of the great books of the greatest writers.[24] Diametrically opposed to this classical point of view is the progressive philosophy of experimentalism as stated by the late John Dewey and interpreted by William Heard Kilpatrick. The progressives emphasized the importance of relating education to the real problems and experiences of life. This controversy continues to rage, not only in higher education but in secondary education as well. The conflict between the conservatives or idealism—as their philosophy of education is sometimes called—and the moderns or progressives—as they are sometimes called—is natural, necessary, and desirable in the development of our educational philosophy.

Who should go to college? Should college and university doors be open to all who wish to enter? This question is closely related to the preceding issues.

The Commission on Financing Higher Education devoted an entire volume to this problem—*Who Should Go to College?* Byron S. Hollinshead, writing for the Commission, outlined three chief points of view:

1. Let us continue to enlarge the number who go to college, say its exponents, and let us expand the facilities in higher education by doubling them during the next ten years.
2. The opposite position . . . is that higher education should provide the facilities necessary to meet the needs of those who present themselves at the colleges, providing the students can meet the entrance requirements and providing the colleges can finance their programs from student fees and other income.
3. There is a third position which is somewhat of a compromise. Proponents of this position would agree that a higher percentage of students should go to college, but they would say that the percentage of young people with ability to do creditable four-year college work is closer to 25 per cent than to 32 per cent and that the percentage of those who would benefit from two years of college training is closer to 35 per cent than to 50 per cent.[25]

These three major positions may be modified by details and by variations or combinations.

Is the admission of students to college made on democratic bases? Telltale data and observations on this issue have been accumulated in numerous studies. Among the questionable practices followed by some colleges and universities in admission procedures are these: admitting veterans on the basis of General Educational Development (GED) Tests and denying the privilege to other mature persons; giving preference to applicants from the state in which the institution is located; legislating against those who are foreign visitors because they are not citizens of the United States; setting up rigid subject-matter patterns for entrance; demanding extremely high tuition charges; favoring children of alumni; and discriminating against students on the basis of race and/or religion. Much progress has been made in recent years, however, in opening higher educational opportunities to all qualified persons, without discrimination as to race or religion. College admission is not on a democratic basis as long as students who could benefit therefrom are denied the privilege because

[24] Robert M. Hutchins, *The Conflict in Education in a Democratic Society,* Harper & Brothers, New York, 1953, p. 98.

[25] Byron S. Hollinshead, *Who Should Go to College?* Columbia University Press, New York, 1952, pp. 39–40.

of economic difficulties. To aid these deserving students many types of scholarships have been established or proposed, including the National Science Foundation, state, and national fellowships.

How shall the rising costs of college be met? Chapter 8 explored the critical problem of rising costs of higher education and the impact that this has had upon private institutions in particular. On the one hand, it has been proposed that the rising costs be borne through increased tuition. Yet many are concerned by the fact that this will place even heavier hardships upon economically underprivileged youth. Virgil Hancher, president of the State University of Iowa, has warned that this practice will threaten the "dual mandate of quality and quantity education." Otherwise, the nation risks the danger of rearing an educationally elite society rather than an open society. It has been proposed by some that the solution lies in making loans more widely available to poorer students. However, President Hancher believes that the increased burden should be borne in larger measure, not by the student, but by increased public support through taxes and private giving.

Probably the most substantial contribution to this increased cost will come from college teachers who, by working at shamefully low pay, contribute an amount more than double the grand total of alumni gifts, corporate gifts, and endowment income.

American society must help institutions of higher education continue to provide education both in quality and quantity. There is no single, simple solution to this problem.

ADULT EDUCATION

When should public education end? Specifically, shall adult education be made a legitimate part of public education? Since subjects requiring maturity can be learned only by the experienced, the education of adults is extremely important. Adult learning is not merely remedial, to correct mislearning or to substitute for education missed previously; it is a sequential and essential stage in lifelong learning. It is difficult to establish terminal facilities for education at public expense. For persons physically or mentally handicapped, free education should never cease. There is a growing conviction also that adult education, along with the education of out-of-school youth, should be a legitimate charge against public funds. In the years to come, adult learning will continue to assume a conspicuous and effective role.

How shall adult education be financed, when funds are insufficient for the preceding phases of learning? Studies reveal that public adult education does not cost much (approximately 2 per cent of the day school expenditures) since it is largely part-time. In most cases regular taxes, plus small fees, furnish most of the receipts. But as adult education grows in scope, in enriched services, and in numbers involved, much more money will be needed. Support for adult education will have to come from public and private funds. The main source for the former obviously is taxes. The latter includes many resources: personal fees, private donations, parochial funds, and contributions from industry and labor. Adult education must clarify its purposes, organize its program, and launch an aggressive battle for ample budgets.

Personnel in public education

PUPILS

Shall special classes be organized for exceptional pupils? Many people believe that exceptional or atypical pupils—the gifted, the mentally, physically, socially, or emotionally handicapped—should be educated in separate classes or schools. This position is based upon the beliefs that they can be better educated separately and that the regular classroom is less disrupted by reason of their absence.

On the other hand, it is argued that exceptional pupils need association with typical children and the normal school environment if they are to be able to adjust to the world in later life.

The trend appears to be in the direction of accommodating as many of them as possible in the regular school environment, with certain necessary modifications. However, separate schools and classes should be provided for those whose deviation is severe enough to prohibit their profiting from the regular classroom.

The grouping of pupils and the methodology of instruction depend in a practical school situation upon the specific needs of an exceptional child, the preparation of teachers, and the available facilities and finances.

What is the proper approach to school discipline? Several generations ago the hickory stick and dunce cap were standard accessories in every classroom. Corporal punishment and other forms of harsh discipline were commonly administered. Several critics of modern educational practices have contended that laxity in discipline has resulted. However, the following excerpt from the annual report of the New York Superintendent of Schools *in 1856* is quite interesting:

No observing man can have failed to note at any and all hours of the day that there are multitudes of boys wandering about and congregating on corners of the streets, idle in their habits, dissolute in their conduct, profane and obscene in conversation and gross and vulgar in their manners. Decency is shocked at what is seen and heard, individual remonstration or kind advice is treated with contempt or insult. If a female passes one of the group, she is shocked by what she sees and hears; if our children pass, they may be assaulted and whatever they have in their possession wrested from them.

Perhaps three conclusions can be reached. First, the old harsh methods of discipline were certainly no panacea; second, juvenile delinquency is not a phenomenon of contemporary times; and third, the school is limited in its ability to raise standards of pupil behavior by the influence of the home.

Clearly, the best discipline results from students who are purposefully engaged in worthwhile learning with a teacher who merits rather than commands their respect. Discipline which is imposed by threats and force not only destroys rapport between teacher and learner but also establishes little basis for continued self-discipline beyond the classroom. Perhaps the larger challenge lies in intelligent study and correction of the forces that create disciplinary problems rather than punishment for the symptoms of maladjusted personality. In spite of the publicity given to the small minority of badly behaved pupils, there is little if any reason to believe that today's student is less well behaved generally than youngsters of any period of history.

TEACHERS

To what extent will television replace the classroom teacher? Wide difference of opinion exists concerning the need for and desirability of replacing the classroom teacher, in part at least, by television. The Fund for the Advancement of Education, for example, reviewed the teacher supply-and-demand picture in 1955 and concluded that it was not possible for the United States to supply enough teachers to meet the demand created by present teacher-student ratios. It suggested that class size would have to be increased, either through the use of teacher aides, television, or some other modification of practice.[26] Extravagant claims have been made in both lay and professional journals about the savings that television will effect in our schools. Alexander Stoddard, former Los Angeles superintendent of schools, now with the Ford fund, for example, predicts that the nationwide use of classroom television could save 100,000 teaching positions and half a billion dollars annually in salaries. The use of teacher aides has been advanced also as the panacea for the teacher shortage.

However, the assumption that schoolteachers

[26] *Teachers for Tomorrow,* Fund for the Advancement of Education, New York, 1955, pp. 40–42.

are destined to be in short supply needs reexamination. Careful studies by the NEA predict that teacher supply and demand may be in fairly good balance by the middle 1960s. If this is so, then the replacement of teachers by television would have to be considered on its desirability rather than on its necessity. The real issue with respect to educational television would seem to be whether or not it is capable of improving the quality of education rather than its inevitability in solving the teacher shortage.

As noted in earlier chapters, there is evidence that television is no less effective an instructor than the classroom teacher, if one considers academic achievement only. *Look* magazine once carried a delightful picture story of a teacher at work. One interesting episode concerned an alert teacher who had spotted a youngster crossing the street in an unsafe manner and the thoughtful way in which the teacher counseled the child on this dangerous practice. It is impossible to conceive of a television receiver serving this kind of function.

While few people would deny that television has a valuable contribution to make toward the enrichment of instruction, there are many thoughtful persons who are most cautious of the prediction that television could and should replace large numbers of teachers. Earl Kelley, a professor at Wayne State University, states his reservations as follows:

The machine has almost "got" us already. The standardization of human beings through manufactured products, canned music, uniform recreation and entertainment, need not be elaborated. The teaching-learning process is a human affair, between unique teacher and unique learner. Individualism depends upon this unique interaction. Without it, we will promote uniformity and lose our individuality. The human relationship between teacher and learner is one of the few last bastions for individualism. The television screen can become the final triumph of the machine over man.[27]

[27] Earl C. Kelley, "The Menace of Mass Media in Education," *Current Issues in Higher Education*, National Education Association, Association for Higher Education, Washington, D.C., 1957, p. 120.

It would appear that the teacher should regard television as a useful and fascinating tool and make of it the most effective use possible. On the other hand, the time has not yet come, if indeed it ever will, when large numbers of teachers ought to be displaced by television unless we envision a kind of education quite different in purpose from the education that we have known in the past.

Does the teaching profession have too much or too little autonomy? A few of the less responsible critics of education attribute its faults to the organized teaching profession which they see as an all-powerful (and sometimes sinister) educational lobby that controls educational policy and practice. Some have referred to the teaching profession as "the super-professional racket." They usually see the teacher as the innocent and helpless victim of the school administrator and the professor of education, whom they like to call "educationist" (a perfectly respectable designation, according to Webster).

Some of these critics seem to feel that all would be right in American education if control of educational policy could be wrested from the professional educators. John Keats, for example, in *Schools without Scholars* pleads for the formation of "citizens grand juries" to make investigations of schools and see that the resulting recommendations are followed.

Actually the teacher has less professional autonomy and independence of practice than any other professional. Education, for example, is the only profession in which certification requirements are set by nonprofessionals. No other profession finds itself so publicly scrutinized and roundly criticized as does teaching. This is true, and properly so, because with few exceptions the teacher is almost the only professional who practices his work publicly and is paid by public funds.

Actually the control of educational policy at both the state and local levels is controlled by lay boards of education. These boards of education are probably more responsive to the people than any other boards of control in American life. As has been noted so often throughout this book, the schools of America have been closely controlled by the people and responsive to the will of the people, perhaps more than any other institution in American life. What other American institution is so overrun with citizens' advisory groups, school-community councils, parent-teacher study groups, and other forms of cooperative planning?

Actually, a far better case could be made on the other side of the argument, viz., that the professional autonomy and authority of the teacher have been severely invaded. In all of the states, the state board of licensure for physicians, dentists, and attorneys is composed predominantly of professional practitioners. In only five states is this true for teachers. In some states, textbooks—the professional's tools—are selected by lay boards. In many school systems the determination of subjects to be taught is handled by the lay board of education. There is considerable reason for believing that education, notwithstanding the critics, is characterized by the strong control which the lay public exercises over professional practice—even to the extent of dangerous invasions of the professional's prerogatives.[28]

Thus it would seem most reasonable that much of the blame for the alleged shortcoming of education should rest with the public which exercises so much control over education. As Hollis Caswell, president of Teachers College, Columbia University, points out:

In America, schools are to a great extent a reflection of the hopes, aspirations, and beliefs of people in the communities which support them. With our system of local control, an educational program cannot deviate far from community standards. It must be recognized also that in many communities intellectual competence in the academic fields of study is not highly prized. Consequently, the climate of opinion often is not one to encourage the young to seek recognition through intellectual excellence. As soon as America begins to prize intellectual achievement more

highly, we may rest assured that its cultivation will find heavier emphasis in our schools.[29]

To what extent are teachers disloyal? A decade ago many loose charges were made about the number of disloyal teachers in America. Fortunately this issue has become subject to much more rational consideration in recent years. Rarely does one now hear irresponsible and unsubstantiated charges about large numbers of disloyal teachers. There is no evidence to suggest that teachers are disloyal to any greater extent than the population in general.

Should loyalty oaths be required of teachers? When concern arises over the loyalty of teachers, the loyalty oath is often advanced as a means of protecting society against disloyalty in faculties. Since concern over disloyal teachers has subsided in recent years, teacher loyalty oaths have been proposed less frequently. The arguments in support of loyalty oaths are that teachers should be eager to affirm their loyalty; that oaths are stimulating and satisfying; that they have a good effect upon the public; that they are taken by many public officers; and that they may provide a legal basis for dismissal, since it is presumably easier to prove violation of an oath than it is to prove disloyalty.

On the other hand, it is argued that such oaths are ineffective (since Communists take them anyway); that they are sometimes dangerously worded, threatening the academic freedom of loyal teachers; that some people object to the implication; that people of certain religious faiths cannot take any type of oath; and that they lead the public to a false sense of security.

Should Communists be permitted to teach? Some people take the position that a teacher's qualification for employment should be determined solely on the basis of his professional competence regardless of his political beliefs. Most people, however, believe that Communists should not be employed as teachers. Member-

[28] For an excellent discussion of this point, see Myron Lieberman, *Education as a Profession*, Prentice-Hall, Inc., Englewood Cliffs, N.J., 1956, chap. 4.

[29] Hollis L. Caswell, "The Attack on American Schools," *Annual Report, 1957–58*, Bureau of Publications, Teachers College, Columbia University, New York, 1958, p. 9.

ship in the Communist party appears to require the surrender of intellectual integrity and the adherence to doctrines that are inimical to the principles of American education. The National Education Association, for example, supports the belief that membership in the Communist party inevitably renders an individual unfit to discharge the duties of a teacher in this country.

Should teachers be dismissed for invoking the Fifth Amendment? During the rash of investigations of teacher loyalty during the early 1950s, a number of teachers were summoned to testify before congressional committees and other investigative agencies. In some cases teachers invoked the Fifth Amendment, which liberates a witness from the obligation of testifying against himself. Arguments raged over whether a teacher who invoked this privilege (designed to protect the innocent as well as the guilty) should be continued in employment.

The board of trustees of one large state university took this position:

The duty is imposed upon all called to testify; that they must testify truthfully and honestly, except those who would incriminate themselves by so doing. Their refusal is not mitigated by opposition to the interrogaters or their methods.

The faculty of another large university took this position:

(We) defend the right of teachers to use the Fifth Amendment on the ground that it cannot be made a condition of membership in the teaching profession that a person surrender rights which are guaranteed by the law of the land.

Both educators and lay people differ widely in their opinions with respect to this issue.

Should teachers be entitled to academic freedom? Academic freedom is fundamentally a protection of *freedom of learning* rather than a privilege of the teacher. In principle, most people would probably support the academic freedom of teachers. But in practice, many people would impose severe restrictions. The history of these restrictions would fill a volume. At one time or another, teachers have been chastised

for teaching classes about evolution, the Reformation, the United Nations, *The Merchant of Venice*, the germ theory of disease, communism, the New Deal, sex education, Russia, the Whiskey Rebellion, and scores of other topics. In fact, the editor of one periodical dealing with education advanced the ridiculous notion that no controversial issue should be dealt with in the classroom. It would be a tragic day in American education if the exploration of controversy were denied as an educational pursuit. Indeed, it is difficult to conceive of what might remain in the curriculum if all controversy were removed. The process of free rational inquiry into controversy has always been regarded as the foundation of our liberties. Many teachers' associations and boards of education have attempted to establish reasonable policies regarding the treatment of controversial issues in the classroom and the protection of the teacher's academic freedom.

Is teacher education in need of reform? This issue, although an ancient one, has generated renewed interest and discussion in recent years. The contenders are often professors of education (who see little need for fundamental change) and college and university personnel from other fields (who argue for fundamental changes). In some cases, the lines of controversy are drawn between the teachers colleges and the liberal arts colleges. Some of the conflict may grow out of a fear of encroachment of the liberal arts professor's domain by the professor of education.

The basic issues may be stated as follows: "Is too much emphasis now given to professional education or 'methods courses'?" "Do teachers receive too little training in general education and in their subject fields?" "Are education courses poorly taught?" "Should professional education work be postponed until the fifth year and undertaken largely in the field?"

The first two issues are related, of course. The critics argue that because education students must take so many education courses, they have too little time left for general education and study in their subject fields. Actually these issues are manifestations of the old conflict over general versus vocational education.

The position of the professional educator, as established in Chapter 11, is that teacher-education programs should include a proper balance of (1) general or liberal education, (2) education in subject fields, and (3) professional education or education courses, as they are frequently called. This position is made specific in the classic recommendation of the Commission on Teacher Education which recommended that at least three-eighths of the undergraduate work of teachers should be in general education and one-eighth to one-sixth in professional education.[30] This would leave nearly one-half of the program for advanced study in subject fields.

Now what is the actual situation? According to the critics, professional course work in teachers colleges is described as "two-thirds," "very heavily loaded," and "about twice that required by liberal arts colleges." However, careful study of actual requirements for high school teachers in 114 teachers colleges, liberal arts colleges, and private and public universities reveals that about 16 to 21 per cent of the course work is devoted to professional courses and about a third of this is taken up in practice teaching.[31] The study points out also that the proportion of professional work is decreasing rather than increasing, as the critics assert. This is very close to the one-sixth recommended by the Commission on Teacher Education, cited previously. Laurence Haskew, dean of the University of Texas College of Education, reports that for secondary teachers, requirements for both general education and subject-matter education are equal or higher than for noneducation students in universities offering professional work for teachers. Haskew believes that this is true also in teachers colleges and teacher-

education programs in other colleges.[32] Thus it would appear that the criticisms of teacher-preparation programs—as being overloaded with work in professional education at the expense of general education and work in subject fields—is not supported by the facts. It seems clear that it would be unwise to eliminate or even to reduce the proportion of the program devoted to professional education. It is difficult to support the position that the teacher needs no knowledge of the history of education, philosophy of education, child growth and development, psychology of learning, methods of teaching, curriculum theory and practice, guidance, and other understandings basic to good teaching.

It is difficult to appraise the issue of whether or not teacher-education courses are poorly taught. There is no objective evidence to support or deny this charge. The critics offer only their opinion or the unsubstantiated testimony of unidentified students who allegedly do not like education courses. Undoubtedly, education courses (as well as courses in other fields) are poorly taught in some institutions. Schools of education have no monopoly on poor or good teaching. Even if the teaching were poor, relief should be sought in improving the faculty and the curriculum rather than throwing out preparation that is vital to the work of the student.

Another controversy arises over the *location* of professional education in the teacher-preparation program. Should professional education be undertaken parallel with general education and subject-field education throughout the four- or five-year program? Or should the first four years be devoted entirely to general and subject-field education with the last year devoted to professional education—to be gained largely through work in the field? The latter position has been endorsed by the Fund for the Advancement of Education and supported in practice by experimental programs of this type,

[30] Commission on Teacher Education, *The Improvement of Teacher Education*, The American Council on Education, Washington, D.C., 1946, p. 114.

[31] Morris L. Cogan, "Professional Requirements in Programs for the Preparation of High School Teachers," *The Journal of Teacher Education*, vol. 9 (September, 1958), p. 274.

[32] Laurence D. Haskew, "The Real Story in Teacher Education," *The Journal of Teacher Education*, vol. 9 (June, 1958), p. 124.

notably at the University of Arkansas. Paul Woodring, in *New Directions in Teacher Education*, written for the Fund for the Advancement of Education, hails this approach (despite its dismal progress so far) as the best hope for the improvement of teacher education.

However, many authorities believe that there is much to commend the practice of including parallel study in general education, subject fields, and professional education throughout all four or five years, rather than organizing these areas in layers. Karl Bigelow, for example, presents this argument:

When a young person conceives an ambition to become a teacher it is psychologically unsound to refuse him all opportunity to find out what teaching is like, to watch and work with children, to check on the validity of his vocational impulse, to begin to see what he is learning everywhere may in due time be brought to bear on the performance of his teaching task. We no more *learn* than we *grow* in layers. We are persons, not things, and the foundations metaphor is dangerous.[33]

This issue, like so many, hinges upon one's conception of the goals of American education. If the main purpose of education is restricted to the teaching of subject matter and development of the mind without regard to the growth of the entire human organism, then the teacher may need training only in general education and his subject field. If, however, one views education in a broader concept—including mental, social, emotional, and physical growth of the individual in relation to his environment —then one must accept the need for professional education. Until this basic issue is resolved, controversy over teacher education will continue.

Fortunately, there is considerable hope that this controversy is being reduced so far as professors of education and professors in other fields are concerned. (It is not likely that the professional critics—the writers and others who earn their livelihood by exploiting controversies—will join in this search for agreement.) A historic conference, the Bowling Green Conference, under the sponsorship of the NEA Commission on Teacher Education and Standards, was held in 1958. It brought together the professors of education and professors in other fields interested in teacher education. The conference reached significant agreement on many of the issues discussed above.

Should teachers' organizations be affiliated with labor or be independent of such affiliation? Considerable rivalry exists between the National Education Association, an unaffiliated teacher's organization, and the American Federation of Teachers, which is affiliated with the AFL-CIO. The major arguments against affiliation are that teachers should remain independent from any segment of society; that affiliation with labor denies the professional status of teaching; and that labor-affiliated associations become more interested in teacher welfare than in the general welfare. The arguments in favor of affiliation with labor are: labor has historically befriended the cause of public education; the power of affiliation with labor is needed by teachers; organizations that admit administrators to membership become dominated by them; and labor-affiliated organizations have achieved greater teacher welfare benefits.

This issue is one which is not likely to be resolved and perhaps should not be resolved. It is probable that the NEA and the AFT are each better because of the presence of the other and that American education and the well-being of teachers are better because of the presence of both. However, it seems clear and probably desirable that the majority of teachers will continue to prefer membership in an organization that is independent from all specialized groups.

Should teachers' salaries be based upon merit? A great deal of controversy exists over the basis upon which teachers' pay should be determined. Teachers and their organizations have usually supported salary differentials based upon preparation and experience. Most salary schedules are designed in this way. How-

[33] Karl Bigelow, "How Should America's Teachers Be Educated?" *Teachers College Record*, vol. 56 (October, 1954), p. 24.

ever, may lay people argue that salaries should be based upon the teachers' competence.

The arguments in support of merit salary plans are as follows:

1. Merit rating provides incentive for better work.
2. Merit salary plans make very high salaries available for teachers who really deserve them.
3. Business and industry have made successful use of merit pay plans.
4. Present methods of determining salary differentials are not justifiable.
5. Merit-rating plans stimulate critical evaluation of teaching methods, purposes, and philosophy.
6. Merit-rating plans will encourage more top-ability people to enter teaching.

The arguments against merit rating are usually stated as follows:

1. Merit salary plans may become a gimmick for retarding salary increases for teachers in general.
2. Merit salary plans consume a lot of the time of administrators and impair administrator-teacher relationships.
3. Merit salary plans encourage competition rather than cooperation among teachers.
4. Merit salary plans can be used as a weapon by unscrupulous administrators and boards of education.
5. Merit salary plans undermine the morale of teachers.
6. Teaching is an art and cannot be subject to objective measurement.

Although the principle of rewarding service on the basis of merit is accepted as *desirable*, the means of achieving the principle are held by many to be *unfeasible* with present methods. However, much experimentation and discussion are being applied to this problem. Many different schemes of merit-salary scheduling are being tried, some with apparent success. It is important that both teachers and lay persons approach this problem with open minds, and that experimentation be continued. Search should be continued for better ways of identi-

fying outstanding teachers so that they can achieve the higher salaries which they deserve. If this problem could be solved, it would do much to raise the upper limits of teachers' salaries and thereby attract more top-quality people to the profession.

OTHER PERSONNEL

On what basis should nonprofessional personnel be selected? Practice for the selection of noninstructional personnel varies among school systems. In some city school systems, noninstructional personnel, such as custodians, secretaries, clerks, and others, are selected through civil service. In many school systems operating under dual control, selection of noninstructional personnel is made by the business manager or secretary of the board. Since this person is not usually a professional educator, the selection of these noninstructional personnel may not be well done. This is particularly true in cities where the board of education is politically appointed or elected. Political forces become operative in such instances and secretaries, clerks, custodians, and others are often selected on the basis of party affiliations or influence. The operation of the spoils system in the selection of school personnel, either professional or nonprofessional, is most unfortunate. Ideally, noninstructional personnel should be selected and recommended to the board of education for appointment by the superintendent in the same manner in which instructional personnel are selected. Likewise, they should be responsible to the professional administrative staff of the school.

Provisions for educational materials

CURRICULUM

How can the curriculum keep pace with the rapid increase in human knowledge? Human knowledge has been increasing throughout the history of mankind. However, it is presently increasing at a fantastically accelerated rate.

Whole new fields of knowledge, such as ocean-ography, aerology, astronautics—virtually un-heard of a decade ago—have now been thrust upon us. Knowledge in old fields has burst forth dramatically as, for example, nuclear physics, polar geography, Boolian algebra. Moreover, as William Carr, executive secretary of the NEA, points out, many pressure groups urge the schools to broaden their curriculums to include instruction in areas of special inter-est to these groups. However, the school day and school year have increased very little. The result is that school curriculums are in danger of severe overloading. Another result is that tensions and controversy are generated in the scramble by special-interest groups for inclu-sion of their interests in the curriculum.

Fundamentally, this issue is a manifestation of the broader question: "What shall be taught?" which has plagued man from the earliest days of education, from the nursery school to the graduate school.

Shall progressive or traditional methods of teaching be used? As noted in Chapter 6, the term "progressive education" is one that prac-tically defies definition in terms acceptable to both its protagonists and its antagonists. Har-old Taylor, former president of Sarah Law-rence College, states that the difference between progressive and conservative education is that the former is more concerned with what is learned while the latter is more concerned with what is taught. The progressive considers the school an instrument of social transition; the conservative considers it a form of social pres-ervation.

The critics of progressive education argue that the curriculum has been diluted with a lot of intellectually barren activity; that it has failed to train the mind; that it has removed competition as an incentive; that it has aban-doned rigid standards of achievement; that subject matter has been lost; that the funda-mentals have not been properly taught; and that discipline has been neglected.

The proponents of progressive education—or modern education, as they sometimes prefer to call it—claim that it has made learning meaningful by relating it to life; that achieve-ment should be assessed in terms of personal capacities; that schools must be concerned with the total development of the learner; that self-discipline is more important than dis-cipline imposed externally; that learning has become more interesting; and that better re-sults have been achieved in general.

There are several compelling arguments in support of the modern teaching method. First, it is supported by a psychology of learning and its application to teaching that have emerged from fifty years of research. Or, stated nega-tively, many of the premises advanced by ad-vocates of traditional methods have been dis-credited by the rejection of the older psycho-logical theories of learning.[34] Second, where scientific comparisons have been made be-tween the achievement of students in progres-sive schools and the achievement of students in traditional schools, the advantages—almost without exception—have been with the former.[35]

Actually, progressive methods have by no means taken over American education, as the critics assume. According to a survey by the NEA, 9 out of 10 teachers employ both pro-gressive and traditional methods in about equal proportions.[36]

The real challenge appears to be the fur-ther improvement of teaching without discard-ing new methods in favor of old. Indeed, there is quite a task involved in helping more teach-ers to be trained in effective use of new meth-ods. It is imperative also that research be con-tinued to discover still better methods of teach-ing. But changes in teaching methods should result from well-founded research evidence rather than from unsupported or ill-informed opinion of lay critics.

[34] See William C. Trow, "The Problem of Transfer—Then and Now," *Phi Delta Kappan*, vol. 40 (Novem-ber, 1958), pp. 68–71.
[35] National Education Association, "Ten Criticisms of Public Education," *Research Bulletin*, vol. 35 (De-cember, 1957), pp. 139–140.
[36] *Ibid.*, p. 139.

In criticizing progressive methods, the critics often imply that instruction in public schools compares unfavorably with that in private schools. The implication is that private schools, having retained more conventional methods of teaching, have obtained better results than the public schools, which have resorted to progressive teaching practices. This type of comparison is hazardous because many nonsectarian private schools have made much wider use of progressive methods than have the public schools. Moreover, the quality of both private and public schools varies widely. Some are exceedingly good, others very poor. Evidence on the comparative quality of public versus private school graduates is rather skimpy. However, a survey reported by *Changing Times* revealed that although Harvard receives only 50 per cent of its students from public high schools, 71 per cent of its Phi Beta Kappa members are from public high schools; Yale receives 45 per cent of its students from public high schools but 57 per cent of its Phi Beta Kappa members are from public high schools; Colgate receives 60 per cent of its students from public high schools but 86 per cent of its Phi Beta Kappa members are from public schools.[37] On the basis of quite limited evidence, there is reason to believe that public schools in general do not compare unfavorably with private schools and may indeed surpass them as a general rule. However, many individual exceptions must, of course, be recognized.

What is the place of vocational education in the curriculum? Actually, this issue is part of a larger one, viz., "What is the relative importance of liberal or general education versus practical or specialized education?" This issue arises at both the secondary and higher education levels.

Vocational education has, of course, a long and distinguished tradition in the American schools. Vocational education at the secondary level has been strengthened by a number of forces. The Smith-Hughes Act and other forms

of federal subsidy have helped to entrench it. Parents, particularly during depression years, have insisted that the public schools must provide their children with a salable vocational skill. Educators, faced with increasing numbers of high school students who were unable to profit from the academic curriculum, saw in the vocational curriculum an opportunity for nonacademic youth. Thus vocational education has been a powerful factor in attracting and holding a large number of youth in high school.

Many critics of vocational education at the secondary level now raise a number of fundamental questions. First, is a youth able to make a confident and firm vocational choice while still in his early teens? Most studies of career choices indicate that most people don't make a final career decision until they reach their middle twenties. Is it reasonable then for teenagers to be committed to a specific line of vocational training so early in life? Second, attention is called to the almost unlimited variety of vocational choices. The *Dictionary of Occupational Titles* lists over twenty-two thousand occupations and the number is rising. This leads some to the conclusion that it is becoming ever more futile to pretend that the public schools can begin to train for such an endless variety of jobs. Moreover, many of these jobs face rapid obsolescence in this accelerated age of automation. For example, hundreds of aircraft mechanics, skilled in dealing with internal combustion engines, have been trained in the vocational courses of some city high schools. However, with the advent of jet propulsion, solid fuels, and nuclear-powered aircraft, it is apparent that these persons will soon be vocationally obsolete unless they are retrained. The equipment needed to train aircraft mechanics for the newer forms of propulsion is not only enormously expensive but also quickly obsolete. Industry itself seems to prefer that the high schools provide young people with sound general education and leave vocational training to the industries themselves.

Perhaps Harvard's President Pusey has expressed a most reasonable position with

[37] "The Truth about Our Public Schools," *Changing Times*, vol. 8 (June, 1954), pp. 7–11.

respect to liberal and vocational or professional education:

Today it should be transparently clear to all that our first need is less for specialists than for diffused wisdom and reliability in society. This means that specialized technical knowledge and the broad understanding and moral purpose historically associated with liberal education can no longer be kept separate. Nor can liberal education be ignored or held to be of slight importance. The demand for the professionally trained—engineers, doctors, teachers, administrators—does not slacken. But . . . search is being made for more people who, beyond the minimum professional requirements, can be counted upon also to bring to their tasks imagination, human understanding, a sense of adventure, integrity, devotion, and an awareness of where their activity fits into larger wholes.

Thus one of our primary needs is to join liberal and professional education, or at least see to it that the latter is deeply penetrated by the former. Both kinds of education are needed by society and in public life.[38]

The tradition of vocational education at both the secondary and higher education levels is old and well established. It is doubtful that it will be dislodged in the near future. Perhaps it must be adapted, particularly at the high school level, more toward an *exploratory* experience, helping youth to adventure in the world of skilled labor and to appreciate the dignity of manual labor, rather than striving for highly skilled vocational accomplishment. It may be that the appropriate location for vocational training in depth is in post-high school trade schools, colleges, and adult education programs. But even here, there is an unmistakable trend for vocational or professional education to be accompanied by liberal or general education.

What is the place of life adjustment education in the curriculum? Life adjustment education, as its name implies, is an attempt to help

students, particularly those of modest abilities, "to do better those desirable things (in everyday life) that they will do anyway," viz., drive automobiles, become good homemakers, care for children, budget money wisely, consume goods intelligently, invest wisely, and so on. This type of education has been severely criticized. Many extreme examples, such as making fudge and social dancing have been singled out for particular ridicule. It is charged that this soft education is not respectable academically; that it attracts able learners who ought to be pursuing more rigorous courses; that it represents expensive fads and frills that schools could well do without; that it has transformed the school from an educational institution to a gigantic recreational gymnasium and welfare service agency.

The supporters of life adjustment education, on the other hand, maintain that it helps to prepare all American youth for more useful and satisfying lives as citizens and homemakers; that it does not detract from the school academically since it is aimed largely for the sizeable proportion of students who do not plan to continue in college. It is argued that this type of education has been a powerful force in retaining a large number of students who would have dropped out of school otherwise, since it provides for them the practical education which they seek in meeting real life problems. It is argued that life adjustment education has not watered down the college preparatory or academic curriculums in most high schools. It is contended that life adjustment education is born of the problem of universal education and is most fundamental if schools are to serve all youth—even those of modest abilities and aspirations—adequately.

Is a "crash program" needed in the physical sciences? The dramatic appearance of the Russian satellites in space precipitated an almost hysterical reappraisal of American education. In the minds of many, it presaged the need for an almost frantic crash program in the physical sciences. Proposals were advanced for spirited recruitment of science and mathematics teach-

[38] Nathan M. Pusey, "The Exploding World of Knowledge," *Fortune*, vol. 52 (September, 1955), pp. 96–97.

ers at highly subsidized salaries, the use of federal monies for scholarships in mathematics and science, rigorous upgrading of high school and college courses in the sciences, and a variety of other proposals. To a large degree, the National Defense Education Act of 1958 was born of this spirit of urgency over the sciences.

Certainly, it is essential that instruction in mathematics, science, and language be strengthened at all levels—elementary, secondary, and higher. It is encouraging to see the bold and vigorous effort under way in this direction. However, as many persons have warned, it is important also that no area of the curriculum be advanced out of proportion to others. Indeed, it is impractical to think that science instruction can be improved immeasurably without strengthening instruction in the fundamental skills needed for success in any field. The noted writer Max Lerner has posed the issue even more simply:

When we are told that there is a shortage of technicians in American life, a shortage of engineers, I say, of course there is, but there is also a shortage of good doctors, good psychologists, good psychiatrists, good social workers, and good teachers, and there is, I am sad to say, a shortage of good political leaders. In short, we are long on shortages in these United States. Our problem is to think in terms of what we want our society to be and to shape our young people with that in mind.[39]

Lerner appears to have put his finger on the real dilemma which underlies so many of these issues in American education: "What do we want our society to be?" Closely related to this is the fundamental question: "What are the purposes of American education?" If our most urgent purpose is to surpass Russia in the exploration of outer space, then we should indeed direct all of our educational energies in that direction. If, however, we must continue to be interested in the social, moral, economic,

and political problems of our times, then education must be improved toward these ends also.

If we are interested in providing the best quality of education for the most able students only, then we should indeed enforce rigid academic standards, weed out the incompetent ruthlessly, insist upon courses of hard academic content, and so on. But if we believe that the education of all citizens is important in democracy and that all have a useful contribution to make, then we shall continue to develop educational programs, at least through the secondary level, that seek to meet the needs and interests of all.

If we are interested only in the mental development of young people, if we care not about their morality, their social and emotional growth and development, then we must indeed reject progressive education and concentrate upon vigorous mental growth. If, however, we accept the purpose of developing the learner in the fullest manifestation of his personality and character as well as his mind, then the concept of progressive education holds considerable merit.

COCURRICULUM

How much emphasis should be placed upon cocurricular activities, particularly athletics? This is an issue apparently of more concern to the professional educator than to the lay public. Most citizens seem to enjoy the spectacle of interscholastic athletics, elaborate bands, fancy yearbooks, professional-looking school newspapers, and many other manifestations of cocurricular activities. Local newspapers cover in detail the performance of the high school football team while important curriculum changes may go virtually unnoticed in the press. Class schedules are often interrupted for cocurricular functions. Expensive stadia and other equipment are provided, even though they may be used less than a dozen times a year. Such uneconomical use of any other expensive school facilities would surely bring

[39] Max Lerner, "American Civilization: Goals and Values," *NEA Journal*, vol. 47 (October, 1958), p. 458.

the most vigorous protests. Extra pay scales must be established to take care of the coach or band director, often to the consternation of other teachers working on important but less spectacular enterprises. Time and money are spent to help a few students excel at rugged team sports, in which few can participate in later life. Adult recreational pursuits, like golf, tennis, badminton, may be unknown to the physical education program. Professionalism, particularly at the college level, often creeps in and students learn to wink at practices that could not be condoned elsewhere in the educational program.

Certainly it must be granted that competitive athletics have a long and noble heritage in the American educational tradition. There is much to be said for the character-building value of sport. Surely school plays, newspapers, and yearbooks have some contribution to make to the development of American youth. The question becomes one of their *relative* importance and balance. How much time should appropriately be given to training half a hundred girls to twirl batons? How much character is being built when the coach of a leading college team asks publicly, "How can you be proud of a losing team?" How much per pupil should be spent on the school library when 400 dollars is spent to equip a football player? How much time should be taken from the regular schedule for students to sell advertising for the yearbook or newspaper? When Little Rock's Central High School was closed because of the integration controversy, the public did not become substantially aroused by this action until it was learned that the football schedule had been canceled. Public opinion forced persons in high office to arrange for the football schedule to be played—even if the high school remained closed!

How can the hidden costs of school attendance be reduced? Several studies have been made of the costs of student participation in cocurricular activities, particularly at the secondary level. It is not unusual for these costs to reach several hundred dollars a year. These hidden costs, as they are sometimes referred to, include purchase of textbooks in some states; subscriptions to the school newspaper and yearbook; admission to football and basketball games; admission to class plays, class dances, musicals, operettas; expenses of senior class trips; class rings; commencement invitations; gym clothes; cap and gown rental; contributions to fund drives in the school; and many others. Many substantial incidental expenses are also involved: new gowns for dances, travel to athletic contests away from home, private parties and picnics held in conjunction with school affairs, purchase of musical instruments, and a variety of others.

Many students are unable to participate in some of these activities because of the cost. If these activities have educational value for all, what justification can there be for denying them to some students in a *free* public school system? If they do not have educational value for all, what justification can there be for including them in the school program? Some high schools are examining this problem critically and moving toward the reduction of extraneous cocurricular activities and the inclusion of worth-while activities in the regular program at public expense.

EDUCATIONAL SUPPLIES AND BUILDINGS

Do school buildings cost too much? One of the nation's popular magazines has published and republished at intervals an article alleging that many new school buildings are fabulously expensive "palaces," often the most expensive buildings in town.[40] It cites the provision for swimming pools, air-conditioning, bowling alleys as examples of waste in schools that the writer "knows of." It is certainly true that in some instances school districts have spent money unwisely and wastefully in the construction of schools. It is true also that some wealthy districts have insisted upon facilities, such as

[40] Holman Harvey, "Do School Pupils Need Costly Palaces?" *Reader's Digest*, vol. 71 (September, 1957), pp. 34–47.

swimming pools, that would appear to be beyond the means of many less financially able districts. However, the assertion that new school buildings in general are lavishly expensive cannot be supported. Actually, school building costs have increased much less rapidly over the past two decades than have the costs of other types of construction. According to one set of estimates, school building construction costs over the past twenty years have increased 150 per cent; all buildings—210 per cent; general construction—275 per cent; medium-priced brick residences—225 per cent; medium-priced frame residences—228 per cent; highway construction—200 per cent.[41]

Many schools have been able to exercise economies through the elimination of cupolas, decorative columns, gables, and other nonfunctional paraphernalia that used to characterize school buildings of an earlier period. Ceilings have been lowered and corridor space reduced. The use of a smaller variety of standard-size materials has also helped reduce costs. Most schools are being planned for more flexible use of space, which also helps to reduce cost.

Actually few types of construction are subject to such close scrutiny as are school buildings. School-plant planning is usually undertaken by the board of education with the advisement of the faculty and citizens' committees in many communities. Since the approval of capital outlay expenditures by schools requires the vote of the people in most communities, schools are obliged to interpret proposed construction to the people who must ultimately approve it. In most cities, further review by a municipal board of some sort is usually provided. In virtually all states, final approval by state school building specialists is also required. Therefore, it would seem much more difficult to waste money for school construction than for other types of construction.

Perhaps even more critical than waste in

school plant construction is the problem of false economy in some school building. As one writer points out:

Throughout the nation, parents have been duped by a strong anti-tax, anti-public-education group who have deceptively, but effectively, been attacking badly needed new schools and modern educational facilities—from auditoriums to audio-visual aids—as "frills" that are "squandering" the taxpayer's money on "elaborate educational castles."[42]

In many communities, school building has been delayed through charges that proposed buildings are too elaborate and expensive. Building plans are then revised, facilities eliminated, and more modest construction finally undertaken several years later. But because of intervening increases in costs, the final product has cost more than if it had been undertaken earlier as planned originally! South Carolina undertook a frantic program some years ago to build economy schools with small classrooms which, it is now found, has damaged the educational program badly. In many instances, low-cost materials were used without consideration of the ultimate saving possible in using more expensive materials that would require less maintenance. In many communities, poor quality temporary buildings have apparently become quite permanent. School building must be viewed in terms of its ultimate rather than its initial cost. Too many communities have become penny-wise and pound-foolish.

Actually, the *real* problem in school construction is how can we replace as rapidly as possible the large number of overage, inefficient, and sometimes dangerous buildings now in use? In many communities children attend school in buildings that are dimly lit, overcrowded, unattractive firetraps. School sites are often too small to provide adequate play space and parking area. Although estimates vary widely, it seems that the nation would need to provide nearly 100,000 new classrooms annually to meet the need for in-

[41] "Those Fairy Tales about 'Palaces'," *NEA Journal,* vol. 47 (October, 1958), p. 486.

[42] Martin L. Gross, "Bargain-basement Education Is No Bargain," *Coronet,* vol. 44 (October, 1958), p. 84.

creased enrollments and to replace obsolete buildings. The real issue, in the minds of many educators, is: "How can money be found to meet this urgent need at a time when nearly one-fourth of local school bond elections are being lost?" Tinkering with minor economies and asserting that schools are luxuriously expensive fails to solve the problem and often aggravates it. This problem, like so many other educational problems, is basically a problem in school finance and public understanding.

Shall each state establish a uniform system of textbooks through state-wide adoption? In all states of the Union, school textbooks are adopted in compliance with statutory regulations. At least one state legislature wanted to require an anticommunist certificate from the publisher of each textbook used in the state. About half the states require the use of uniform textbooks either for the state as a whole or within schools of specified grades, whereas the reminder permit choice by the local board of education. Most authorities recommend that the responsibility be delegated to the local boards, but, as usual, practice limps far behind theory. Today the teachers are consulted in the selection of textbooks much more than formerly. Objective evaluations are helpful. Impartial groups, like the National Conference of Christians and Jews, have published helpful studies—for example, *Prejudice in Textbooks.*

Shall textbooks be supplied to pupils at public or at personal expense? Thousands of indigent children are allowed the free use of textbooks. Elementary and secondary schools should furnish all pupils with the basal textbooks at public expense. To provide free instruction and then to require the purchase or rental of learning tools is an anomaly in American democratic education.

Should the censorship of textbooks and other materials be undertaken by lay persons and groups? Many self-appointed groups have sought to censor textbooks and library books in public schools to weed out the works of allegedly subversive writers. This is an extremely dangerous practice because it strikes at the heart of the teacher's competence and the learner's right to free access to ideas. The spirit of American democracy is founded upon and dependent upon free competition of ideas for public acceptance. Unfortunately, there is no universal acceptance of what is subversive. Books that are acceptable to one group would be quite unacceptable to another. Some folks find subversion even in such institutions as the United Nations, the TVA, social security. One group even though it found subversion in the Girl Scouts! Obviously, unless all the people of a community or state can agree that some person or group has omnipotent powers in detecting subversion, the decision in selecting books is best left in the hands of the professional staff. Teachers should guard zealously against invasions of this professional prerogative by lay persons, however well intended it may appear.

FINANCE

Does money make a difference in the quality of education? Perhaps the most basic question to raise with respect to school finance is whether or not the amount of money spent has any effect upon the quality of education. The answer to this question would seem self-evident to most people, viz., that in education, as in most facets of human life, one gets just what one pays for. Actually, there should be little controversy with regard to this issue because the evidence is very clear. Yet critics raise this issue. Some say that it is possible to increase the quality of education without raising the cost. Indeed, one writer takes the ridiculous position that a decline in quality would probably accompany an increase in expenditures!

The American educational deterioration, now painfully focused by Russia's scientific achievement, is thus in no major respect due to any lack of funds. Some of the decline in standards, on the contrary, is probably a result of too lavish, or at least too careless, expenditure. It follows that the problem will not be solved, *and could even be in-*

*Is this citizen carrying
too great a financial burden for
school support through his
local property tax?*

How shall education be financed?

*Should the federal government offer
general financial support for education
as it now does for certain special programs
like school lunches?*

Who shall decide these issues?

*In a democracy, these decisions
rest ultimately with the
people, often through their
elected representatives.*

*Citizens of New Delhi, New York,
attend a meeting on
improving local schools . . .*

*while other Americans from all walks
of life assemble at the White House
Conference on Education to
advise the President
on school needs and policy.*

What is the proper
role of education in the world today?

*A major challenge lies in applying the power
of education and understanding to help underprivileged
people of the world to help themselves.*

tensified, by merely pouring more money into public education. (Italics added.) [43]

The writer presents no evidence, just his surmise, that the road to better education lies in cutting the costs. It would be most fortunate if such were the case. However, there is overwhelming objective evidence to the contrary. Much as we might like it otherwise, high-quality education and low expenditures just do not coexist. Ther are no bargains in education.

Fortunately, there is considerable research to illuminate this issue. Research studies on this problem have been conducted all over the country for a period of half a century. One group of researchers, after summarizing all of the studies of the relationship between cost and quality in education, reached this conclusion:

As schools have increased their expenditures, it is perfectly clear that what they have bought with additional money is *betterment*. . . . The preponderant evidence of the credible studies emphasizes again and again the close relation between cost and quality in education. This relation has been

investigated by so many different research men, over such a long period of time, and under such differing circumstances with such uniform results, that one is forced, in a scientific spirit of skepticism, to question the methods or purposes of any investigation that seems to run counter to the main stream of evidence.[44]

The evidence indicates that money is the most important single factor, accounting for more than half of the variation in quality from one school to another. However, it must not be assumed that cost is the only factor accounting for educational quality.

Should more money be spent for schools? In Chapter 16, the position was taken that the cost of education is not really a financial bur-

[43] Felix Morley, "The State of the Nation," *Nation's Business*, vol. 46 (January, 1958), p. 22.

[44] Associated Public School Systems, *Does Money Make a Difference?* Institute of Administrative Research, Bureau of Publications, Teachers College, Columbia University, New York, 1958, p. 7. See also *Does Better Education Cost More?* National Education Association, Committee on Tax Education and School Finance, Washington, D.C., 1959.

den but rather an *investment* in our most precious resource—people. As the United States Chamber of Commerce proves in its publication *Education—An Investment in People*, as the education of people improves, so does their production, income, consumption of goods, participation in civic and national affairs. This is true whether people are viewed as individuals, communities, states, or nations. The relationship between education and economic prosperity is direct and demonstrable. Moreover, the economic return of money invested in education is far greater in the long run than the original cost. Therefore, school

education is investment in future [handwritten marginal note]

Students at a teachers college in Cambodia, supported jointly by the United States and Cambodia, learn finger-painting techniques.

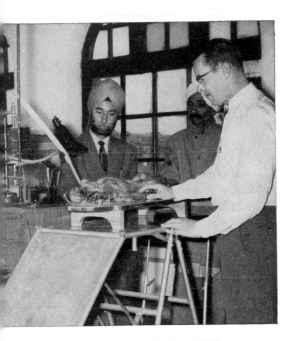

Through help from the International Cooperation Administration of the United States, the Malaria Institute of India has helped that nation learn how to control the scourge of this disease.

This electrical substation and iron and steel plant in Burnpur, India, is part of the Damodar Valley Development Project, sponsored by the United Nations.

costs should be viewed as a most fruitful capital investment. Thus the question of financing education becomes one of how much can we possibly invest as fruitfully as possible rather than how can the costs be cut as much as possible.[45]

45 For further evidence, see John K. Norton, "Education Pays Compound Interest," *NEA Journal*, vol. 47 (November, 1958), pp. 557–559; Educational Policies Commission, *Education and Economic Well-being in American Democracy*, National Education Association, Washington, D.C., 1951, chap. 2.

It is becoming increasingly clear that the nation must view education as fundamental to national security. It is evident that, like it or not, we are engaged with Russia in a race for knowledge. Education must be seen as a powerful weapon in the struggle for peace and national liberty.

As Mrs. Agnes E. Meyer, one of the nation's most competent lay authorities on education, pointed out in her testimony before the House Education and Labor Committee:

There is nothing wrong with our public education system that money cannot cure. Why is this true? It is true because adequate funds would make it possible to have small classes in well-equipped buildings. If we could pay our teachers a wage commensurate with their responsibilities, more and better educated men and women would enter the profession. . . . Despite all the criticism of our schools, we have enough educational leadership in every state of this country to create a first-class public school system, if only the American people can be aroused to pay the price.

And pay the price we must, for today the development of every ounce of talent we possess is not merely a matter of justice and equality of opportunity, it is a life and death issue. All well-informed Americans know that we are losing the cold war for lack of trained personnel. Our inherent defense strength rests upon the quality of our manpower and brain power.[46]

Nelson A. Rockefeller has warned that "we cannot maintain our way of life for ourselves and our children's children without the utmost vigilance and the willingness to accept whatever sacrifices must be necessary to make aggression in all forms an unattractive course for Soviet imperialism."

Clearly the continued prosperity of the nation justifies increased expenditures for education. Today, net corporation profits *after taxes* are more than four times higher than they were two decades ago despite the fact that taxes have increased tenfold. Per capita income *after taxes* has almost doubled within the past two decades. In view of this, it is difficult to conclude that either corporate or personal taxes are confiscatory as some people would charge. A nation that spends more for advertising that it does for education can hardly claim that its schools cost too much. Harold F. Clark, an economist who has devoted his career to a study of education in relation to the economy, concludes that "the American people can support their schools adequately if they want to do so. We not only need but can afford a great expansion in the amount spent on education."[47] However, as was pointed out earlier in this chapter, education will not share the nation's abundant economic prosperity unless part of the yield from federal tax resources is made available for schools.

The ultimate issue

A number of the more important and lively contemporary issues in American education have been discussed in this chapter. Many of the critics are sincerely and constructively interested in the improvement of education. Unhappily, some of the critics are insincere and fundamentally opposed to improving the quality of education for all children and youth. Responsible and enlightened discussion of the issues in education must be encouraged, for this is the means by which progress in education—as in all of man's endeavor—is forged.

The high level of public interest in education is one of the most heartening and wholesome aspects of the current educational scene. Public interest and understanding are quite essential to progress in education. Good schools tend to be found where and when the public is vigorously concerned and interested in them. Indeed, a dramatic surge in educational progress, just since the appearance of the first sputnik, is already evident. Educators are challenged to nurture this interest and direct it toward constructive ends.

[46] Agnes E. Meyer, "Federal Support and National Survival," *Phi Delta Kappan*, vol. 39 (June, 1958), pp. 382–383.

[47] Harold F. Clark, "Education and the American Economy in 1960," *NEA Journal*, vol. 44 (May, 1955), pp. 293–294.

Students from other lands participate in a geography project at the University of Nebraska.

It seems clear that with education rests mankind's best hope for security, prosperity, and freedom.

an educated
people
moves
FREEDOM
—*forward*

Educators must not become so preoccupied in answering criticisms that they fail to direct attention and energy to the really fateful concerns. The real question is not whether schools are better today than they were fifty years ago but rather *whether they are as good as they ought to be*.

Society must come to realize that many of the shortcomings that are attributed to schools are really the deeper failures of society itself manifest in the schools. A popular magazine of wide circulation a few years ago sought to deal with the so-called crisis in education. The remainder of the issue was devoted to:

12 pages on plays and movies (some of questionable taste)
11 pages on auto designs and ads
5 pages on beer, wine, and liquor ads
4 pages on cigarette and cigar ads
3 pages on cosmetic and deodorant ads

3 pages on dresses (of the 80- to 250-dollar variety)
3 pages on horse racing

Thus it would appear that the crisis in education is in reality a crisis in American values. How can a nation that illustrates "men of distinction" in its liquor ads be astonished if young people are attracted to alcoholic beverages? How can a nation that insists upon loyalty oaths for its teachers complain that schools do not encourage creative and independent thinking in children? How can the owner of a car with twin fins and all the other gadgetry complain about fads and frills in schools? How can the parent, who pays an extra 200 dollars for power steering, howl so loudly when his school taxes go up by 25 dollars? How can a community that pays its custodians more than its teachers complain about the quality of teaching? The Oregon

Educational Policies Commission has identified the *ultimate* issue in contemporary education:

Since our public schools are so decidedly 'of the people,' it is—if not erroneous—certainly a superficial view to believe that the present crisis is essentially a school crisis or even an educational crisis. *The crisis today is a total cultural one implicating the basic values of our free society*. It involves business, science, art, government, the press. It involves all citizens in this country and the groups to which they belong. That so much attention is being given to the public schools in the midst of this crisis is an indication of *where*

many of the ctizens are placing their hopes for solving at least some of our most trying social problems.[48]

Clearly the schools reflect the turbulence of society itself. The issues in education will not be settled until the conflicts in American society are resolved. It is clear that the school is the arena in which many of these problems must be solved. It is the destiny of the teacher, then, to share largely in this noble and exciting adventure.

[48] Oregon Educational Policies Commission, *The Public Schools and Our Times*, Oregon Education Association, Portland, 1958, pp. 5–6.

Suggested activities

1. Prepare a report on the topic "How to Distinguish between Responsible, Constructive Criticism and Irresponsible, Destructive Criticism in Education."
2. Prepare a historical calendar of criticisms of education.
3. List a few issues in education which you consider most critical and conduct an opinion poll with respect to them.
4. Would you have preferred to attend a separate high school that enrolled only gifted students? Explain the reasons for your position.
5. Prepare a paper on the topic "The Professional Autonomy of the Teacher in Comparison with Other Professions."
6. Analyze the teacher-education program in your institution in terms of the amount of work required in general education, professional education, and subject-matter education. Make recommendations and reasons for changes, if any.

7. Prepare a statement of your position with respect to independent versus labor-affiliated teacher organizations.
8. Prepare a statement of your position with respect to teachers' salaries based upon merit.
9. In view of your experience as a student, write a paper in support of either progressive or traditional teaching methods.
10. Prepare a report on the topic "The Appropriate Place of Vocational Training in American Education."
11. Make a detailed estimate of the hidden costs of your own high school education.
12. Make a study of how Americans spend their personal income and their national income. Determine whether, in your opinion, too much or too little is spent on education in comparison with the other expenditures.
13. Prepare a statement of your reaction to The Ultimate Issue section of this chapter.

Bibliography

Books

American Association of School Administrators: *Educational Administration in a Changing Community*, 37th Yearbook, National Education Association, Washington, D.C., 1959, chap. 1. Discusses the trends and issues in education made more complex by an ever-expanding community.

Brown, Nicholas (ed.): *The Study of Religion in the Public Schools: An Appraisal*, American

Council on Education, Washington, D.C., 1958. Report of a conference with participants from the major faiths expressing attitudes and practices on this problem.

Educational Policies Commission: *The Contemporary Challenge to American Education,* National Education Association, Washington, D.C., 1958. Reviews the purposes and achievements of education, examines current needs, and suggests means of improving education.

Ehlers, Henry: *Crucial Issues in Education,* Henry Holt and Company, Inc., New York, 1959. A well-balanced anthology of the most outstanding and best-written statements concerning controversial issues in education.

Elsbree, Willard S., and E. Edmund Reutter, Jr.: *Staff Personnel in the Public Schools,* Prentice-Hall, Inc., Englewood Cliffs, N.J., 1954, chap. 12. Discusses academic freedom, loyalty oaths and other threats, communist teachers, and the legal facets of the problem.

Keats, John: *Schools Without Scholars,* Houghton Mifflin Company, Boston, 1958. Charges that the schools are anti-intellectual because of the domination of professional educators and urges reforms.

Lieberman, Myron: *Education As a Profession,* Prentice-Hall, Inc., Englewood Cliffs, N.J., 1956, chaps. 4, 7, 9–11. A scholarly and provocative treatment of the authority of teachers, their education, their associations, and other aspects of the profession.

Rickover, Hyman G.: *Education and Freedom,* E. P. Dutton & Co., Inc., New York, 1959. The father of the atomic submarine and critic of education has put together many of his lectures criticizing education.

Rockefeller Brothers Fund: *The Pursuit of Excellence: Education and the Future of America,* Doubleday & Company, Inc., New York, 1958. A panel of very distinguished Americans looks at educational issues and makes recommendations for improving schools, largely through better financing.

Scott, C. Winfield, Clyde M. Hill, and Howard N. Burns: *The Great Debate,* Prentice-Hall, Inc., N.J., 1959. Excellent collection of statements by both critics and defenders of education ranging over nearly all the issues.

Traxler, Arthur E. (ed.): *Vital Issues in Educa-*
tion, American Council on Education, Washington, D.C., 1957. Report of a conference with addresses and discussions relating to current issues in American education.

What Should Our Schools Accomplish? National Citizens Council for Better Schools, New York, 1955. Pamphlet for lay persons reviews the background of American education and analyzes the controversies.

Periodicals

Bereday, George Z. F.: "Selective Education Versus Education for All," *Teachers College Record,* vol. 58 (January, 1957), pp. 198–206. An expert on European education cautions against following the European tradition of educating only the intellectually elite.

Bestor, Arthur E.: "We Are Less Educated than 50 Years Ago," *U.S. News and World Reports,* vol. 41 (November 30, 1956), pp. 68–72. A critic argues that schools are poorer today because less science is offered, the curriculum is watered down, teachers are poorly educated, and anti-intellectualism prevails in the schools.

Bestor, Arthur E., and Karl Bigelow: "How Should America's Teachers Be Educated?" *Teachers College Record,* vol. 56 (October, 1954), pp. 16–24. A critic and defender debate teacher education.

Carr, William G.: "Not in Our Stars but in Ourselves," *NEA Journal,* vol. 47 (October, 1958), pp. 490–495. The executive secretary of the NEA suggests how teachers should deal with criticisms to bring about better understanding.

Commager, Henry S.: "Victims of Success," *The Saturday Review,* vol. 41 (May 3, 1958), pp. 12–16. A famed historian contends that many of the controversies are straw men and presents the real issues.

Conant, James B., and others: "The American High School," *Phi Delta Kappan,* vol. 40 (November, 1958), pp. 50–87. A series of articles by critics and defenders of secondary education.

Corey, Arthur: "The Real Attack Is on Education for All the People," *The Nation's Schools,* vol. 62 (July, 1958), pp. 38–40. Shows that proposals to apply rigorous standards to all in the public schools would deny education to many.

Cornell, Francis G.: "Federal Aid Is a Religious Issue," *The School Executive*, vol. 72 (June, 1953), pp. 47–49. Examines the religious stumbling block of whether federal monies should go to private schools.

Davies, Hazel, and others: "Merit Salary Schedules for Teachers," *Journal of Teacher Education*, vol. 8 (June, 1957), pp. 127–197. Series of articles dealing with merit rating plans as they exist in schools and industry with a presentation of the issues.

Derthick, Lawrence G.: "Seven Musts for Better Schools," *Parents Magazine*, vol. 34 (January, 1959), pp. 35 and 82–83. U.S. Commissioner of Education discusses seven imperative needs of American education.

Eells, Walter: "Let's Talk Facts," *The School Executive*, vol. 76 (March, 1957), pp. 41–46. Rebuttal to the assertion that high school students are less well educated today.

Eisenhower, Milton S.: "How to Get Better Schooling," *U.S. News and World Reports*, vol. 44 (February 21, 1958), pp. 66–75. President of Johns Hopkins University suggests ways in which American high schools and colleges could do a better job.

Freehill, Maurice F.: "Some Facts for Parents about How We Learn," *NEA Journal*, vol. 47 (May, 1958), pp. 324–327. Shows how concepts of the psychology of learning support modern teaching methods.

Fuller, Edgar: "Criteria for Congressional Action," *The Nation's Schools*, vol. 56 (November, 1955), pp. 53–56. Shows how the federal government has discriminated against schools by preempting tax sources for other purposes.

Gross, Martin L.: "Bargain-basement Education Is No Bargain," *Coronet*, vol. 44 (October, 1958), pp. 83–89. Refutes the charge that school buildings are too lavish, emphasizes the need for good schools, and warns against false economies.

Gustavson, R. G.: "Maintaining Balance between Science and Humanities," *NEA Journal*, vol. 47 (February, 1958), pp. 88–90. Surveys the importance of both science and the humanities and argues against crash programs.

Hand, Harold C.: "A Scholar's Devil Theory," *The High School Journal*, vol. 41 (April, 1958), pp. 270–286. A rejoinder to Bestor on the issues of soft curriculums and failure to challenge gifted students.

Harmon, John E.: "Business and Education: A Growing Partnership," *Phi Delta Kappan*, vol. 39 (June, 1958), pp. 380–381; 415–420. United States Chamber of Commerce spokesman argues against federal support and makes alternative proposals.

Harvey, Holman: "Do School Pupils Need Costly Palaces?" *Reader's Digest*, vol. 71 (September, 1957), pp. 37–47. Asserts that money has been spent too lavishly on school buildings.

Haskew, Laurence D., and others: "A Symposium on Teacher Education," *Phi Delta Kappan*, vol. 40 (December, 1958), pp. 115–129. An examination of the criticisms of teacher education and reports of progress toward reducing this conflict.

Hechinger, Fred M.: "Five Basic Problems of Education," *The New York Times Magazine*, January 25, 1959, pp. 11f. A distinguished educational writer weighs the difficulties confronting education and analyzes the solutions that have been proposed.

Hollinshead, Byron S.: "Is European Education Better?" *The Educational Record*, vol. 39 (April, 1958), pp. 89–96. Points up the shortages in American education but concludes that the answer does not lie in imitating European schools.

Keats, John, and Herbert L. Brown, Jr.: "Are the Public Schools Doing Their Job?" *Saturday Evening Post*, vol. 230 (September 21, 1957), pp. 38. This debate between a critic and defender amounts to quality comparisons between public and private schools.

Levenson, William B.: "Can TV Shorten the Teacher Shortage?" *The Nation's Schools*, vol. 59 (April, 1957), pp. 71–72. Concludes that television can enrich teaching but not replace the teacher.

Lynd, Albert, and Roma Gans: "Are the Schools Neglecting the Fundamentals?" *Teachers College Record*, vol. 56 (October, 1954), pp. 38–47. Debate on the issue of how well the schools are doing with the fundamental skills.

MacAndrew, Andrew R.: "Are Soviet Schools Better than Ours?" *The Reporter*, vol. 18 (February, 1958), pp. 10–15. Discussion of the strengths and weaknesses of Soviet education with implications for the debate over the quality of schools in the United States.

McCaskill, J. L.: "We Need Federal Support *Not* Federal Aid," *Phi Delta Kappan*, vol 40 (March, 1959), pp. 234–239. Clarifies the distinction between federal aid and federal support and establishes the compelling need for the latter.

McGrath, Earl J.: "Sputnik and American Education," *Teachers College Record*, vol. 59 (April, 1958), pp. 379–395. Former United States Commissioner reviews the controversies, particularly in higher education, aroused by Russia's prior entry into outer space.

McLeod, John W.: "Cheap Schools Cost the Most," *Parents Magazine*, vol. 33 (October, 1958), pp. 64–65. Shows the false economy that results when short-sighted savings are imposed on original costs.

Miller, Arthur S.: "The Strategy of Southern Resistance," *The Reporter*, vol. 19 (October 2, 1958), pp. 18–20. Describes the strategy of Southern states in resisting the Supreme Court decision on segregation.

Morphet, Edgar L.: "Who Should Control Education?" *NEA Journal*, vol. 47 (December, 1958), pp. 640–641. Expresses concern over invasion of professional prerogatives by lay people.

Moynihan, Daniel P.: "A Second Look at the School Panic," *The Reporter*, vol. 20 (June 11, 1959), pp. 14–19. Examines post-Sputnik pressures upon schools, with special attention to the implications of the National Defense Education Act.

National Education Association: "Ten Criticisms of Public Education," *Research Bulletin*, vol. 35 (December, 1957), pp. 133–174. Scholarly application of research findings to 10 major issues in education.

Norton, John K.: "Education Pays Compound Interest," *NEA Journal*, vol. 47 (November, 1958), pp. 557–559. Shows how money spent for education pays dividends in economic prosperity.

Orton, Dan A., and others: "Are We Less or Better Educated than 50 Years Ago?" *U.S. News and World Reports*, vol. 42 (June 21, 1957), pp. 114–121. Seventeen educators file rejoinders to Bestor's assertion that education is poorer today.

Pusey, Nathan M.: "The Exploding World of Education," *Fortune*, vol. 52 (September, 1955), pp. 96–97. President of Harvard discusses the financial problems of education in relation to industry and economy.

Renfield, Richard: "The Soviets Are Criticizing their Schools," *NEA Journal*, vol. 48 (March, 1959), 22–25. Describes how some of the features of Soviet education most envied by some of the critics of American education are bitterly assailed by the Russians themselves.

Ruttenberg, Stanley H.: "Citizen Participation Is a Dominant Force in Education," *Phi Delta Kappan*, vol. 39 (June, 1958), pp. 378–379. AFL–CIO spokesman presents organized labor's position with respect to federal support for education.

Shane, Harold G.: "We Can Be Proud of the Facts," *The Nation's Schools*, vol. 60 (September, 1957), pp. 44–47. Criticisms of soft curriculums, decline of quality, evasion of certain subjects, and others are refuted.

Shayon, Robert L.: "Report from the Grass Roots," *The Saturday Review*, vol. 41 (September 13, 1958), pp. 15–17. After visiting American schools widely, the author concludes that the so-called failure of education is really the failure of society.

————: "Let the Debate Be Honest," *NEA Journal*, vol. 48 (February, 1959), pp. 16–18. Criticizes the biases, lack of evidence, and superficial generalizations that the critics of public education often utilize.

"The Truth about Our Schools," *Changing Times*, vol. 8 (June, 1954), pp. 7–11. An objective presentation of facts about the accomplishment of our schools, concluding that they are better than is realized.

Trow. William C.: "The Problem of Transfer—Then and Now," *Phi Delta Kappan*, vol. 40 (November, 1958), pp. 68–71. Shows how many of the critics' attacks on methods of teaching rest on discredited theories of learning.

Van Dusen, Henry P., and John K. Norton: "What Should Be the Relation between Religion and Public Education?" *Teachers College Record,* vol. 56 (October, 1954), pp. 1–15. A noted theologian and school administrator exchange views on the proper relation between religion and the schools.

Woodring, Paul: "The Decline of Educational Philosophy," *Phi Delta Kappan,* vol. 40 (October, 1958), pp. 6–10. A plea for a more knowledgeable view of philosophical values among teachers so that issues can be appraised with more meaning.

"Wrong Emphasis," *The Nation's Schools,* vol. 62 (July, 1958), pp. 25–26. Cautions against the wrong emphasis and sweeping claims for educational television.

Appendix

Code of ethics of the National Education Association

The primary obligation of the teaching profession is to guide children, youth, and adults in the pursuit of knowledge and skills, to prepare them in the ways of democracy, and to help them to become happy, useful, self-supporting citizens. The ultimate strength of the nation lies in the social responsibility, economic competence, and moral strength of the individual American.

In fulfilling the obligations of this first principle the teacher will—

1. Deal justly and impartially with students regardless of their physical, mental, emotional, political, economic, social, racial, or religious characteristics.
2. Recognize the differences among students and seek to meet their individual needs.
3. Encourage students to formulate and work for high individual goals in the development of their physical, intellectual, creative, and spiritual endowments.
4. Aid students to develop an understanding and appreciation not only of the opportunities and benefits of American democracy but also of their obligations to it.
5. Respect the right of every student to have confidential information about himself withheld except when its release is to authorized agencies or is required by law.
6. Accept no remuneration for tutoring except in accordance with approved policies of the governing board.

Second principle

The members of the teaching profession share with parents the task of shaping each student's purposes and acts toward socially acceptable ends. The effectiveness of many methods of teaching is dependent upon cooperative relationships with the home.

In fulfilling the obligations of this second principle the teacher will—

1. Respect the basic responsibility of parents for their children.

2. Seek to establish friendly and cooperative relationships with the home.
3. Help to increase the student's confidence in his own home and avoid disparaging remarks which might undermine that confidence.
4. Provide parents with information that will serve the best interests of their children, and be discreet with information received from parents.
5. Keep parents informed about the progress of their children as interpreted in terms of the purposes of the school.

Third principle

The teaching profession occupies a position of public trust involving not only the individual teacher's personal conduct, but also the interaction of the school and the community. Education is most effective when these many relationships operate in a friendly, co-operative, and constructive manner.

In fulfilling the obligations of this third principle the teacher will—
1. Adhere to any reasonable pattern of behavior accepted by the community for professional persons.
2. Perform the duties of citizenship, and participate in community activities with due consideration for his obligations to his students, his family, and himself.
3. Discuss controversial issues from an objective point of view, thereby keeping his class free from partisan opinions.
4. Recognize that the public schools belong to the people of the community, encourage lay participation in shaping the purposes of the school, and strive to keep the public informed of the educational program which is being provided.
5. Respect the community in which he is employed and be loyal to the school system, community, state, and nation.
6. Work to improve education in the community and to strengthen the community's moral, spiritual, and intellectual life.

Fourth principle

The members of the teaching profession have inescapable obligations with respect to employment. These obligations are nearly always shared employer-employee responsibilities based upon mutual respect and good faith.

In fulfilling the obligations of this fourth principle the teacher will—
1. Conduct professional business through the proper channels.
2. Refrain from discussing confidential and official information with unauthorized persons.
3. Apply for employment on the basis of competence only, and avoid asking for a specific position known to be filled by another teacher.
4. Seek employment in a professional manner, avoiding such practices as the indiscriminate distribution of applications.
5. Refuse to accept a position when the vacancy has been created through unprofessional activity or pending controversy over professional policy or the application of unjust personnel practices and procedures.
6. Adhere to the conditions of a contract until service thereunder has been performed, the contract has been terminated by mutual consent, or the contract has otherwise been legally terminated.
7. Give and expect due notice before a change of position is to be made.
8. Be fair in all recommendations that are given concerning the work of other teachers.
9. Accept no compensation from producers of instructional supplies when one's recommendations affect the local purchase or use of such teaching aids.
10. Engage in no gainful employment, outside of his contract, where the employment affects adversely his professional status or impairs his standing with students, associates, and the community.

11. Cooperate in the development of school policies and assume one's professional obligations thereby incurred.
12. Accept one's obligation to the employing board for maintaining a professional level of service.

Fifth principle

The teaching profession is distinguished from many other occupations by the uniqueness and quality of the professional relationships among all teachers. Community support and respect are influenced by the standards of teachers and their attitudes toward teaching and other teachers.

In fulfilling the obligations of this fifth principle the teacher will—

1. Deal with other members of the profession in the same manner as he himself wishes to be treated.
2. Stand by other teachers who have acted on his behalf and at his request.
3. Speak constructively of other teachers, but report honestly to responsible persons in matters involving the welfare of students, the school system, and the profession.
4. Maintain active membership in professional organizations and, thru participation, strive to attain the objectives that justify such organized groups.
5. Seek to make professional growth continuous by such procedures as study, research, travel, conferences, and attendance at professional meetings.
6. Make the teaching profession so attractive in ideals and practices that sincere and able young people will want to enter it.

Glossary[1]

ACCREDITATION: the type of recognition held by an educational institution that has met accepted standards applied to it by a competent agency or official association.

ACTION RESEARCH: a type of on-the-job study or problem solving used by teachers, supervisors, and administrators to improve the quality of their decisions and actions.

ACTIVITY CURRICULUM: a curriculum design in which the interests and purposes of children determine the educative program. Selection and planning of activities are undertaken cooperatively by teacher and pupils.

ADMINISTRATION: the sum of the techniques and procedures employed in operating the educational organization in accordance with established policies.

ADMINISTRATIVE UNIT: synonymous with SCHOOL DISTRICT.

ADULT EDUCATION: purposeful effort toward the self-development of adults conducted by public or private agencies, such as adult schools, extension centers, settlements, churches, clubs, and chautauqua associations.

APPRENTICESHIP: the period during which a young person works under the direction of an experienced, well-qualified adult to acquire increased skill and knowledge for competent performance.

ARTICULATION: the relationship existing among the different elements of the educational program—among the different curricular offerings; between the school's program and out-of-school educational activities; and among the successive levels of the educational system.

ATTENDANCE AREA: an administrative unit, or subdivision of a unit, consisting of the territory from which children may legally attend a given school building.

ATYPICAL PUPIL: a loose term used in referring to a pupil who differs in a marked degree from others of a given class or category, either physically, mentally, socially, or emotionally.

AUDIO-VISUAL MATERIAL: any device by means of which the learning process may be encouraged or carried on through the sense of hearing and/or the sense of sight.

[1] Many of the definitions are drawn from or adapted from Carter V. Good (ed.), *Dictionary of Education*, McGraw-Hill Book Company, Inc., New York, 1959.

BUDGET: a detailed professional forecast consisting of both estimated expenditures and receipts based upon the proposed educational program.

CERTIFICATION: the act, on the part of a state department of education, of granting official authorization to a person to accept employment in keeping with the provisions of the credential.

COCURRICULAR ACTIVITIES: school-sponsored pupil activities that require administrative provision and organizational involvements somewhat different from the more typical classroom instruction, often called "extracurricular."

COLLEGE: an institution of higher education usually offering only a curriculum in the liberal arts and sciences and empowered to confer degrees; or a major division of a university. The term is sometimes used in a general sense in referring to any institution of higher education.

COMMON LEARNINGS: the knowledges, abilities, skills, attitudes, and appreciations that a school regards as essential for all children and youths.

COMMUNITY COLLEGE: an educational institution, usually controlled and supported locally, that offers instruction for persons beyond normal secondary school age, in a program geared particularly to the needs and interests of the local area.

COMMUNITY SCHOOL: a school that is intimately connected with the life of the community and that tries to provide for the educational needs of all in the locality. It utilizes neighborhood resources in improving the educational program and sometimes serves as a center for many civic and cultural activities.

CONSOLIDATION: the abandonment of one or more attendance units, bringing the pupils into a larger attendance unit. Sometimes used to denote the merger of school districts.

COORDINATION: the process of integrating elements of the educational program, various curricular offerings, or student services.

CORE CURRICULUM: a curriculum design in which one subject or group of subjects becomes a center or core to which all the other subjects are subordinated.

CORRELATION: the process of bringing together the elements of two or more different subject-matter fields that bear on the same large problem or area of human experience.

COURSE OF STUDY: a guide, usually prepared by a school or school system, that serves as an aid to teaching a given subject or area of study for a certain grade or other instructional group.

CURRICULUM: in its broadest sense, the organized experiences that a student has under the guidance of a school; in a more precise sense, a systematic group of courses or sequence of subjects required for graduation or certification in a major field of study.

CUSTODIAL PUPIL: one so limited in mental, social, physical, or emotional development as to require institutional care or constant supervision at home.

DECENTRALIZATION: the process of shifting autonomy, authority, or responsibility from a central source to smaller local units, such as from the state to local school districts or from a central office to individual schools.

DESEGREGATION: the process of bringing nonwhite and white children into the same schools. The term INTEGRATION is also used in this sense.

DEVELOPMENTAL TASK: a task that arises at or about a certain time in the life of an individual, successful achievement of which leads to his happiness and success with later tasks.

EDUCABLE CHILD: a child of borderline or moderately severe mental retardation who is capable of achieving only a very limited degree of proficiency in basic learnings and who must usually be instructed in a special class.

EDUCATION: the aggregate of all the processes by which people are subjected to the influence of a selected and controlled environment (especially that of the school) so that they may attain social competence and optimum individual development.

EDUCATIONAL OPPORTUNITY: the extent of availability of learning experiences for an individual or for a society.

ELEMENTARY EDUCATION: the division of an educational program that is concerned primarily with general education beginning in childhood and ending approximately with early adolescence, typically including grades 1 to

8 or grades 1 to 6 where 6-6 or 6-3-3 plans are in use.

EMOTION: response to a stimulus resulting in physiological changes with a high degree of feeling.

EMOTIONALLY HANDICAPPED: a condition in which an individual's emotional reactions are inappropriate or inadequate, often interfering with harmonious interpersonal relationships or adjustment to demands exerted by environment.

EQUALIZATION: the act of equalizing or making more nearly equal the support of public education among the subordinate units within a central governmental unit.

EQUIPMENT: articles such as furniture, machinery, and books that are used without being consumed.

ETHICS: the science of human conduct; concerned with judgments of obligation and of values.

EVALUATION: the process of ascertaining or judging the value or amount of something by careful appraisal.

EXCEPTIONAL PUPIL: used synonymously with ATYPICAL PUPIL.

EXCHANGE TEACHER: a teacher brought into an educational institution from another school, usually for a year, to replace one who has likewise left his regular position temporarily to teach in another school, often in another country.

EXPERIENCE: the process or the result of a human being's interacting with a physical and cultural environment, doing certain things and having his knowledge, attitudes, and skills conditioned in consequence.

FAMILY LIFE EDUCATION: a special program or course of instruction that is designed to prepare youths or adults for successful marriage, parenthood, and family living.

GENERAL EDUCATION: those phases of learning that should be the common experience of all individuals in a society.

GIFTED PUPIL: one of superior intellectual ability or unusually talented otherwise.

GROUP DYNAMICS: a branch of social psychology concerned with the interaction and psychological relationships of members of a group, particularly with relation to the development of common perceptions through the sharing of emotions and experience.

GUIDANCE: a form of systematic assistance to pupils or others to help them to assess their abilities and liabilities and to use that information effectively in daily living.

HIGHER EDUCATION: instruction offered to persons of considerable intellectual maturity, including all education above the level of the secondary school as offered in colleges, universities, graduate schools, professional schools, technical institutes, teachers colleges, etc.

HOLDING POWER: the ability of the school to hold pupils in school until graduation.

INDIVIDUAL DIFFERENCES: the variations among individuals with respect to characteristics that distinguish one individual from another.

IN-SERVICE EDUCATION: efforts of administrative and supervisory officials to promote the professional growth and development of educational workers through such means as curriculum study, supervisory assistance, and workshops.

INSTRUCTION: synonymous with TEACHING.

INTEGRATION: (1) the process or practice of combining different school subjects and presenting them as aspects of one unifying project or activity; (2) the participation of nonwhite and white students in the same school organization or activities.

INTELLIGENCE: the ability to make successful and rapid adaptation to new situations and to learn from experience.

INTERMEDIATE UNIT: (1) a division of the elementary school comprising grades 4, 5, and 6; (2) a level of school organization between the state and the local district, often but not necessarily coterminus with the county.

ISSUE: a point of contention or disagreement.

JUNIOR COLLEGE: a post-high school educational institution offering usually a two-year program either of a terminal nature or as preparation for further training in college or university.

JUNIOR HIGH SCHOOL: usually a school that enrolls pupils in grades 7, 8, and 9; less commonly, grades 7 and 8 or 8 and 9. It may be a separate entity of the lower part of a junior senior high school.

KINDERGARTEN: an educational unit devoted to the development of small children, usually from four to six years of age, through organized play activities with opportunity for the development of self-expression and readiness for formal learning, and for experience in group living.

LABORATORY SCHOOL: a school that is under the control of, or closely associated with, a teacher-preparation institution, whose facilities may be used for demonstration, experimentation, and practice teaching.

LAND-GRANT COLLEGE: an institution of higher learning established under the first Morrill Act, which granted public lands to the states for the establishment of colleges that would "promote the liberal and practical education of the industrial classes in the several pursuits and professions of life."

LEARNING: change in response or behavior caused partly or wholly by experience; more commonly, the acquisition of knowledge and skills.

LIBERAL ARTS COLLEGE: an institution of higher learning with a four-year curriculum emphasizing broad, general education rather than technical or vocational training.

LIFE-ADJUSTMENT EDUCATION: learning designed to equip youths to live democratically with satisfaction to themselves and profit to society as homemakers, workers, and citizens; having special but not exclusive importance for pupils uninterested in academic or college preparatory curriculums.

MATERIALS OF INSTRUCTION: any device, method, or experience used for teaching purposes, including textbooks, supplementary reading materials, audio-visual materials.

MATURATION: changes in the characteristics of an individual resulting from intrinsic development.

MENTALLY HANDICAPPED: one having mental powers that lack maturity or are deficient in such measure as to be a hindrance to normal achievement.

MERIT RATING: an evaluation of the effectiveness of a teacher or other educator based upon a scale of criteria and frequently used for determining salary differentials.

MOTIVATION: the disposition of the learner toward certain behavior; or the processes by which the teacher arouses, sustains, and regulates the learner's behavior, applying incentives and arousing interest for the purpose of causing the learner to perform in a desired way.

NONTEACHING PERSONNEL: employees of an educational institution who have no duties pertaining directly to instruction.

NURSERY EDUCATION: provision for the physical, motor, health, nutritional, intellectual, aesthetic, emotional, and social development of the very young child.

OBJECTIVE: the aim or purpose of a course of action or of a belief.

ORGANIZATION: the process or result of arranging elements into a functional or logical whole.

ORTHOPEDIC PUPIL: one crippled or otherwise affected by disease or malformation of the bones, joints, or muscles.

PAROCHIAL SCHOOL: an educational institution conducted and controlled by a religious or church group, usually without tax support.

PERSONALITY: the total psychological and social reactions of an individual; the synthesis of his subjective, emotional, and mental life, his behavior, and his reactions to his environment.

PHILOSOPHY OF EDUCATION: a careful, critical, and systematic endeavor to see education as a whole and as an integral part of man's culture.

PHYSICALLY HANDICAPPED PUPIL: one having a physical defect of such seriousness as to interfere with or render more difficult normal progress in the school program.

POLICY: a judgment, derived from some system of values and some assessment of situational factors, operating as a general plan for guiding decisions.

PRE-ELEMENTARY EDUCATION: relates to the period of development from birth to entrance at age six or seven to first grade or year of elementary education; includes infancy and early childhood training in the home as well as nursery and kindergarten education.

PRIMARY UNIT: a division of elementary education, usually comprising grades 1 to 3, devoted primarily to instruction in fundamental skills and the development of social attitudes necessary for democratic living.

PRINCIPAL: the administrative head and professional leader of a school division or unit, such as a high school, junior high school, or elementary school.

PRINCIPLE: a statement of policy by which individual decisions and cases are judged in a consistent and critical manner; a generalization drawn from data that have been systematized and interpreted.

PRIVATE EDUCATION: instruction other than that provided by an agency of government as for example by churches, trade unions, charitable organizations, or nonpublic enterprises.

PROFESSION: an occupation usually involving relatively long and specialized preparation on the level of higher education, governed by its own code of ethics, and demanding a high level of discretion and individual judgment.

PROFESSIONAL EDUCATION: the total formal preparation for teaching that a person has completed in a teacher-education institution, usually including the aggregate of his experience in positions involving educational activities.

PROFESSIONAL SCHOOL: an institution of higher learning or a division of a university that educates persons for the practice of a profession.

PROGRAM OF STUDIES: a number of courses organized into learning units for the purpose of attaining specified educational objectives.

PROGRESSIVE EDUCATION: an educational movement emphasizing democracy, the importance of purposeful and creative activity, the real life needs of students, and closer relationship between school and community.

PROJECT: a unit of activity having educational value and aimed at some definite goal of understanding, usually involving the investigation and solution of problems and the use of physical materials, planned and carried to completion in a "real life" manner.

REORGANIZATION: a change either in the internal organization of a school or in the geographical area included in an attendance area or administrative unit.

RESEARCH: careful, critical, disciplined inquiry directed toward the clarification or resolution of a problem.

SCHOOL DISTRICT: all the schools operated by a given board of education or central administrative authority.

SCHOOL SYSTEM: synonomous with SCHOOL DISTRICT.

SECONDARY EDUCATION: a period of learning planned especially for young people of ages approximately twelve to seventeen, in which the emphasis tends to shift from mastery of basic tools of learning to the use and extension of these tools in exploring thought and living, acquiring deeper information and higher intellectual skills; may be either terminal or preparatory in nature.

SEGREGATION: the separation of individuals having certain characteristics from others; frequently used with reference to the practice of educating Negroes in separate schools from white students.

SEX EDUCATION: learning concerned with the processes and problems of reproduction; designed usually to provide the learner with an understanding and control of his sex impulses and behavior.

SOCIALLY HANDICAPPED: a term applied to those with personality disturbances severe enough to interfere seriously with their interpersonal relations.

SPECIAL EDUCATION: the instruction of pupils who deviate so far physically, mentally, emotionally, or socially from so-called normal pupils that the standard curriculum and school environment are not suitable for their needs.

STUDENT TEACHING: a part of the preservice program of teacher-education institutions in which the student is given opportunity to observe, participate, and actually teach under the direction of a skilled educator.

SUBJECT-FIELD EDUCATION: that part of the teacher-education program in which the student is provided instruction in the subjects that he plans to teach.

SUPERINTENDENT: the chief executive and advisory officer charged with the direction of education in a school system.

SURVEY: an investigation or study of a school system or problem to discover current practices, trends, and/or norms; sometimes includes making recommendations.

TEACHER EDUCATION: the program of activities and experiences developed by an institution responsible for the preparation and growth of persons planning for or engaged in the work of the educational profession.

TEACHING: broadly, the act of providing activities, materials, and guidance that facilitate learning in either formal or informal situations.

TEACHING UNIT: the plan developed with respect to an individual classroom by a teacher to guide the instruction of a unit of work to be carried out by a particular group of learners.

TENURE: a system of school employment in which the educator, having served a probationary period, retains his position indefinitely unless dismissed for legally specified reasons through clearly established procedures.

TERMINAL EDUCATION: a level of education not usually followed by a higher level of instruction.

TRAINABLE PUPIL: one incapable of achieving significant proficiency in academic skills but who may be trained to attain a limited degree of social acceptance, ability to care for himself, and perhaps some measure of self-sufficiency.

UNIT OF LEARNING: a series of organized ideas and activities planned to provide worth-while experiences for an individual or group and expected to result in a desired outcome.

UNIVERSITY: an institution of higher education which has a liberal arts college, offers a program of graduate study, usually has two or more professional schools, and is empowered to confer degrees in various fields of study. (In actual usage, there is some confusion between the terms "college" and "university." Some institutions that are in reality colleges are chartered as universities and vice versa.)

VOCATIONAL EDUCATION: a program of learning organized to prepare the student for entrance into a particular occupation; includes such divisions as trade and industrial education, technical education, agricultural education, distributive education, and home economics education.

YOUTH: a term applying to an individual or to young people collectively within the age span of sixteen to twenty-five years.

Index